GREAT ISSUES OF
INTERNATIONAL POLITICS

SECOND EDITION

GREAT ISSUES OF

The International System and National Policy

INTERNATIONAL POLITICS

edited
by
Morton A. Kaplan *The University of Chicago*

Aldine Publishing Company   *Chicago*

About the Editor

Morton A. Kaplan, Professor of Political Science and Director of the
Ford Workshop Programs in International Relations at the University
of Chicago, is a leading expert on modern international relations and
political systems theory. Among his writings are *Systems and Process
in International Politics* and *The Political Foundations of International
Law* (with Nicholas de B. Katzenbach). The latter was chosen by the
American Political Science Association and the American Society of
International Law as the most significant book on international law of
the postwar period. He is also author of *Macropolitics* (Aldine, 1969).
Professor Kaplan's writings have been translated into many European and Asian languages, and he has lectured throughout Europe and
the Middle and Far East.

First edition published 1970
Aldine Publishing Company
529 South Wabash Avenue
Chicago, Illinois 60605

ISBN 0-202-24139-4 cloth
      0-202-24140-8 paper
Library of Congress Catalog Number 73-84931

Printed in the United States of America

Contents

v

Contributors

Eqbal Ahmad is a Fellow at the Adlai Stevenson Institute on International Affairs.

G. A. Arbatov is the Director of the Institute of the USA in the Soviet Union.

Dennis L. Bark is a National Fellow at the Hoover Institute on War, Revolution, and Peace.

Donald Brennan is Director of Strategic Studies at the Hudson Institute.

McGeorge Bundy, president of Ford Foundation, was formerly dean of Harvard University and an assistant to Presidents Kennedy and Johnson on national security policy.

R. M. Burrell, Lecturer in Contemporary Middle East History, School of Oriental and African Studies, London University.

W. E. Butler, Reader in Comparative Law, University College, London.

Frank Church is a U.S. Senator from Idaho and a member of the Senate Foreign Relations Committee.

Ian Clark is a member of the Research School for Pacific Studies, The Australian National University.

François Duchêne is the Director of the International Institute of Strategic Studies, London.

Richard Falk is Milbank Professor of International Law, Princeton University.

J. William Fulbright is a U.S. Senator from Arkansas and chairman of the Senate Foreign Relations Committee.

Stanley Hoffmann is a professor of government, Harvard University.

Robert E. Hunter is a Fellow of the Overseas Development Council, Washington, D.C.

Robert Maynard Hutchins is the Director of the Center for the Study of Democratic Institutions.

Morton A. Kaplan is professor of political science, The University of Chicago.

William R. Kintner is director of the Foreign Policy Research Institute and professor of political science, University of Pennsylvania.

Edward A. Kolodziej is the chairman of the Department of Political Science at the University of Illinois, Urbana.

Melvin R. Laird is former Secretary of Defense and Assistant to the President for Domestic Affairs.

George McGovern is a U.S. Senator from North Dakota.

Walter Millis was a well known journalist and author and also served as a staff member at the Center for the Study of Democratic Institutions.

R. Judson Mitchell is an assistant professor of political science, Louisiana State University in New Orleans.

Jonathan D. Pollack is in the department of political science at the University of Michigan.

Uri Ra'anan is a professor of political science, M.I.T.

Earl C. Ravenal is a Fellow at the Woodrow Wilson Center, Smithsonian Institute, Washington, D.C.

Edwin Reischauer, University Professor, Harvard University and a former Ambassador to Japan.

Herbert Scoville, Jr. is a Fellow at the Carnegie Endowment for International Peace.

Simon Serfaty is a professor at Johns Hopkins University at Bologna, Italy.

Albert Wohlstetter is University Professor, The University of Chicago, and a former member of the RAND Corporation and consultant to the Department of Defense.

Seymour C. Yuter is a well-known patent lawyer and a writer on international law.

Preface

T here are a number of good textbooks in the areas of international politics and foreign policy. Unfortunately, these textbooks usually fail to make the subject matter of international politics and foreign policy relevant to policy questions or understandable to students.

The demands by students for relevance can be misleading if they result merely in the study of current controversies. And unless the academic aspect of international politics can be brought to life for the student, he will simply memorize a dull subject or engage in bull sessions outside of the classroom. The chapters in this book are meant to bridge the gap between theory and practice. For the most part, they do so in styles that are lively and entertaining and without any impairment—indeed with a heightening—of academic relevance.

We regard the great issues of international relations as those most intimately connected with questions of national security. Others would disagree. Some might feel that the great issues include those related to building a world of law, to restoring equality among nations, and to improving the level of morality as made manifest in state behavior. Two of the essays included in Part One of the book will express this point of view. However, they are included as an atiphonal chorus to the basic assumption that underlies the selection of essays. Although the sentiments expressed are good, the articles do not respond—as so many of the other essays in this book will make clear—to the real problems confronting statesmen in our age. Preoccupation with such questions would lead us to ignore the good for the best; the attainable for the unattainable. They would divert our attention from those actions that statesmen can, but often do not, take to improve the prospects for peace, law, and order in the contemporary world. They divert our attention from and interfere with both our understanding of the quarrels that divide political bodies in the contemporary world and important areas of potential cooperation, such as arms control agreements, the dampening of crises, and the termination of military conflicts.

National security is a broad term that includes more than physical survival. It has reference to the political, economic, social, and moral factors that help to define and identify particular political entities. States do not act in a vacuum in pursuing national security or other values. What they can accomplish depends in part on the character of the international system and the distribution of capabilities within it. It depends upon the state of international law. It is related to the viability of the nation state as an instrumentality of action and to the potentiality of the nation for finding allies abroad. For this reason, radical changes in the characteristics and political purposes of other states may affect national security. Therefore, problems of development and internal war may play an important part in determining whether or not allies are available for foreign policy aims.

In determining its national security policy, a state must orient its policies to the macrofeatures of the international system. It must also take into account the policies and motivations of potential hostile states, the effects of its policies upon potential allies, the consequences of its intervention or nonintervention in problems of development or internal war in other states, the relationships of its economic to its political and military instrumentalities, and the consequences of its style of diplomacy, including cooperation or risk-taking potentialities that may be related either to the personalities or to the philosophies of its decision-makers.

A special role in these considerations is played by that great traditional instrument of foreign policy, military force. In a system of order that is still decentralized, force or the threat of force is not far removed from the immediate perceptions of decision-makers in determining policy. This remains true despite the almost paradoxical impotence of major states in dealing with minor states and with problems of internal war.

In the most general sense, these problems are perennial. Questions concerning the character of the international system, alliance patterns, motivation of states, matters of political style, the arms race, and so forth, apply not merely from year to year but from century to century. These problems could be treated analytically and synoptically and they are so treated in systematic texts on foreign policy or international politics. However, in this form, discussion becomes abstract. The elements of accident, irrationality, perception, and interpretation lose most of their content. The world of foreign policy is reduced to the ghostly relationships of generalizations. This provides genuine advantages, but it also entails real costs. Most students lack the experience required to interpret the generalizations. And they often lack the persistence and desire required to apply them.

Often, more particular discussions excite the interests of students in ways that analytical texts cannot. They permit the students to identify with the issues and to understand their concrete importance. If the material seems more relevant, the student can then extract from the particularities of the case those elements related to generalization. The guerrilla wars in Malaya and Vietnam, for instance, are issues with beginnings and hopefully with ends. They are instances of the larger issue of intervention, and any one instance, even if limited in the amount of evidence it provides, permits the student and teacher to raise the relevant issues about intervention. President Nixon's style of diplomacy in many respects is peculiar to him. On the other hand, it raises the perennial issues of the use of bluff, the manifestation of power, and tough bargaining techniques as contrasted with more cooperative attitudes and unilateral concessions. Every arms race has individual and particular characteristics. What is true of one may not be true of another. Yet whatever conclusion one reaches with respect to a specific issue of a particular arms race, the instance can be used to begin the exploration of more general issues of arms races. This is particularly true if case materials are used in conjunction with a more synoptic and analytical text.

Introduction

Our selections are designed as a starting point for class discussion and for student investigation. They provide a foundation the student can build on, particularly if used with an analytical text. All our readings involve great issues of foreign policy and of international relations. An issue which, when viewed from one perspective—that of the state —is an issue of foreign policy, becomes an issue of international relations when viewed from the perspective of the macrosystem.

Those issues of foreign policy related to the macroframework of international order and those related to the ultimate element of force are usually separated for purposes of convenience. For this reason, our readings are divided into three parts: Great Issues of World Order, Great Issues of Foreign Policy, and Great Issues of Military Policy. Part One—Great Issues of World Order—is designed to raise questions about the character of the international system within which foreign policy is pursued. Is it a realm of anarchy or does it provide a framework for world order? How do different kinds of international systems constrain the use of force? To what extent are legal norms enforceable and what kinds of norms can be enforced in the contemporary international system? What is the role of international organization and what is its relationship to the nation state? What is the potential for regional organization? What difference does it make for world or regional order if the nation state remains a hardy institution? Is nationalism genuinely relevant in the contemporary world?

In Part Two—Great Issues of Foreign Policy—we move to a second set of questions. The chapters in this part raise questions about the types of foreign policies that can be implemented by the United States in a bipolar or a developing multipower system and the constraints put on these policies by domestic opinion, the opposition of the Soviet Union, problems of development, and the rise of new major powers. What types of foreign policy are available to democracies in bipolar systems? How do these change as bipolarity is transformed? Is it possible for the modern democratic state to ignore the popularity of its external policies? What is the challenge of Communism in a bipolar system? In a developing multipower world? How do the Russian Communists perceive what they regard as the crisis of imperialism? How is the competition between Russia and the United States influenced by the end of colonialism and development crises in the third world? How do major changes in the roles of developing great powers—specifically, Japan and China—affect the competition between Russia and the United States? How is this competition affected by specific conflicts such as the Israeli-Arab conflict? What is the effect on the international system of the style of leadership of the President of the United States?

Part Three—Great Issues of Military Policy—looks at that great ultimate resource of states in systems without an effective overall sovereign organization: force. In such systems, the use or threat of force is clearly present in the maintenance of order. Yet if we are to survive in a nuclear age, the use of force must be moderated and reconciled with a viable international order. Part Three, therefore, deals with the problems of arms races, of deterrence theory, and of budgetary conflicts between military and domestic goals. What are the prospects for SALT-type agreements? What changes do they make in the arms race? How do they feed back into the play of foreign policy?

The fact that the selections in this reader focus on the adversary issues of international relations is not intended to slight the importance of issues dealing with population growth, economic and political development, or the control of technology. However, unless the "gut" issues can be controlled in ways permitting the growth of a more durable international order, then the other issues that pit man against nature or the developed nations against the underdeveloped—a subject touched upon in several of the essays in Part Two of the book—are unlikely to be resolved in a manner consistent with reasonable values. Only if the student understands these "gut" issues is he genuinely equipped to understand world politics. In a world in which the peasant of India and the city-dweller in the United States are neighbors, a failure to solve these issues will transform our national institutions, subvert our deepest democratic values, and destroy our hopes for the future.

GREAT ISSUES OF INTERNATIONAL POLITICS

Part One
Great Issues of World Order

Introduction

The great issues of world order involve those features of the international system that drive us toward war, allow us to maintain the peace, enable us to find allies to defend our national interests, and permit us to regulate areas of dispute by means other than military force. The League of Nations was established in the aftermath of World War I on the basis of the Wilsonian principle that the old power politics—which were presumed to be responsible for the system of alliances and war—had to be abolished. When the French asked for guarantees against a restored Germany, the English spoke of the obligations under the League to invoke the principles of collective security. It is now a matter of ancient history that the League did not work. When Mussolini moved into Ethiopia, the Japanese into China, and the Fascist powers interfered in Spain during the Spanish civil war, that organization was impotent to stop them. And, the alliances that in earlier periods had on occasion served to inhibit the resort to force, or to dampen the dangers resulting from such resort, had been effectively dissolved by the Wilsonian myths.

During the Second World War, the United States determined to avoid the mistakes of the Wilsonian heritage. It was the prime mover in founding the United Nations upon the conception that the major victorious powers would serve the new organization as policemen to maintain the peace. The American idealists who played such an important role in the organization of the United Nations overlooked the fact that the Second World War had turned the United States and the Soviet Union into Superpowers, while diminishing the power of the other victorious nations and keeping

3

the defeated Axis powers in thrall. Thus, each of these two states—with such widely different political and ideological systems and with so little experience of cooperation between them—faced the other as its greatest potential threat. It is small wonder that this system also broke down.

The student may object: But didn't the United Nations work in Korea? Formally, yes, it did work. But in that period, "working" meant that the United States became the dominant power in the UN as well as the main organizer of the war in Korea. It was largely an American war under cover of a United Nations flag. The political mechanism that produced the American response had little or nothing to do with the United Nations. The bipolar nature of the international system emphasized the role of the United States. Communist expansion in Korea was viewed as a threat to the national interests of the United States because the U.S. was the only power that had the capability for taking counteraction. This is precisely what is changing as we move toward a multipower world.

The great issues in Part One, therefore, relate to the nature of world order. What are the characteristics of this order? How are these characteristics changing as we move from a bipolar to a multipower system? To what extent will force remain a necessary instrument as these changes occur? To what extent can statesmen guide changes in the structure of the system? To what extent can statesmen take systemic questions into account at the potential expense of immediate national interests? How do system characteristics affect the ability of statesmen to organize support for values they wish to implement in the international order? To what extent will the further proliferation of nuclear weapons affect these questions?

The foregoing questions are among those to which the authors of the essays in Part One address themselves. They attempt to formulate these questions more fully and, on occasion, they offer answers. The answers to these questions in large part will determine which values will be implemented in the world we build.

I

WORLD LAW

Robert Hutchins and Walter Millis take what is often perjoratively termed the "utopian" approach to questions of world organization. I am not unsympathetic to their goals, but it will be obvious that I regard their proferred answers as largely irrelevant to the contemporary world. As the student observes the world around him—the terrorism in Northern Ireland, guerrilla warfare in the Middle East, the bloody suppression of the Biafra revolt, the splitting apart of Pakistan, the inability to establish a Latin American common market, the decline of supranational hopes in Europe—can he believe that we are ready to establish a world government or even a world police force? Considering the problems of the British troops in Northern Ireland, where the language is the same and the cultures surely more similar than most, can we really believe that sufficient world consensus exists to accept the dictates of some international body or police force concerning those problems that might otherwise move us to force? The question is not whether the goal is desirable in the abstract but whether it is practicable in the concrete. Do proferred solutions of the Millis and Hutchins type respond to the problems that we really face in the world today and that will determine whether we remain at peace or blow ourselves up?

No response to these two articles is contained within the present chapter. However, the entirety of chapter II may be considered a response to the "utopian" position. Although the authors included in chapter II differ among themselves, their common style of analysis excludes the solutions accepted by Walter Millis and Robert Hutchins. They are more concerned with what can be done practically to limit and to constrain the use of force and the resort to intervention in the affairs of other states than to devise more stringent, but impracticable, instruments of international government.

Let me hasten to add that a concern with reality does not exclude major changes in interntional politics. I believe that the idea of human freedom remains the most revolutionary idea the world has ever known. However, efforts to transform the world contrary to the interests that uphold the present order are doomed to failure. The principle of ju jitsu depends on using the force of an opponent to overthrow him. This book attempts to outline the actual "forces" extant in the international environment and the meliorative efforts that can be made within their confines. An attempt to show how these forces could be employed to change the world would take us beyond the limited confines of this book into a much more ambitious venture that would be more controversial and more difficult to defend in detail. Moreover, it would divert us from investigating the actual state of affairs—the foundation without which the student cannot hope to transform the world.

1.

Constitutional Foundations for World Order

ROBERT MAYNARD HUTCHINS

THE *New York Times,* in its editorial on the second anniversary of the bomb, said that the ultimate protection against it can only be the abolition of war itself. The Times suggested that the final success of efforts to abolish war could be realized only in an ultimate world government.

I do not understand the use of the "ultimate" in this connection. We have now arrived at the ultimate stage in history. We cannot do something intermediate now and ultimately do something ultimate. What is ultimately required of us is required of us now. If what is ultimately required of us is the abolition of war through a world government, then we had better set about trying to get war abolished through world government now. . . .

It will be said, of course, that if nations will not collaborate in an alliance or debating society or propaganda forum like the United Nations, they cannot be expected to come together or to stay together in a world state. The American states could not or would not collaborate under the Articles of Confederation before 1787, but they did come together, and, with the exception of one period they stayed together under the Constitution.

It may be admitted that there were ties which united them which do not unite nations today. Moreover, they were remote from the rest of the world. Both their enemies and their friends were too preoccupied to bother them. They had the safety valve of a new country and western lands. On the other hand, we should not forget that many differences deeply divided the American states, so much so that, three months before the Constitutional Convention, Madison wrote that he "trembled for the issue."

Reprinted with permission from *Foundations for World Order,* pp. 97–114, Social Science Foundation, University of Denver.

Mr. Hooker has lately shown in the magazine *Common Cause* how serious the divisions among the states in the confederation were. Virginia had twelve times as many people as Delaware. Georgia claimed a hundred times as many square miles as Rhode Island. There were so many Germans in Pennsylvania that Franklin feared they might make German the language of the state. It was impossible to get along in some sections of New York without knowing Dutch. The trip from Boston to New York, which now takes less than an hour, took four days to a week along the finest road, or longer than it takes now to go around the world.

Gouverneur Morris thought that a federal tax was impossible because of the extent of the country; and one member of the Convention asked, "How can it be supposed that this vast country, including the western territory, will, one hundred and fifty years hence, remain one nation?"

When Washington took charge of the armies surrounding Boston, he wrote that the New Englanders were an exceedingly dirty and nasty people. On the other hand, Ephraim Paine of Vermont complained that the southern members of Congress regarded themselves as a superior order of animals. Tariffs were levied by New York, Pennsylvania, and Maryland on the goods of other states; and New Jersey taxed the New York lighthouse on Sandy Hook. New York, New Hampshire, and Massachusetts quarreled about Vermont, and Pennsylvanians battled Virginians on the Upper Ohio. It is no wonder that when the Constitution was completed by the Convention, the principle attack upon it was that it was utopian, a visionary project, an indigestible panacea.

And it barely was accepted. In the conventions in the critical states it just squeaked through. In Massachusetts it carried by twenty-nine votes, in Virginia by ten; and in New York by only three.

What we are talking about is the relation between world community and world law. Reinhold Niebuhr, whom I greatly admire, takes the view that we cannot discuss world government because we have no world community to support it. The discussion of world government, he thinks, may even retard the development of world community and hence retard world government....

But I am afraid that Mr. Niebuhr exaggerates the state of perfection which world community must achieve before world government can be considered....

Those who oppose discussion of world government on the ground that a world community must precede a world government seem to me to overlook the interaction between the two. This is what the Greeks had in mind when they said that law was an educational force and that the city educates the man. The Constitution of the United States has educated the people of this country to believe in and support the Constitution of the United States. We are so used to thinking of law as repressive and constitutions as the embodiment of pre-existing agreement that we neglect the tremendous force which any constitution and any system of law exerts in behalf of its own acceptance and perpetuation. Anybody who has studied the relation between the political institutions of a state and its educational system, for example, must agree with Aristotle that politics is the architectonic science. One of the reasons Aristotle gives for this conclusion is that politics determines what is studied in the state.

The way to promote world community is to have world government. But since we, as private citizens, cannot establish a world government, the next best thing we can do to promote world community is to talk about world government. World discussion of world government, far from disrupting the world, may have some chance of uniting it; for the consideration of what is necessary to unite the world, the discussion of a common problem of overwhelming importance, should lead to a growing sense of community among all peoples.

An important reason for talking about world government is that nobody knows what it is. Should a world government aim at limited measures designed to maintain what is called security, or is security itself dependent on the pursuit of broader purposes? Should a world state be federal or unitary, or should it, perhaps, contain the best features of each? What should be the relation of the world government to the citizens of extant states? What taxing powers shall the world state have, and what order of military forces, if any? This list of questions can be prolonged indefinitely, and there are countless possible answers to each of them. Yet people go around saying world government is wonderful or world government is impossible. It may be that many forms of world government would be something less than wonderful; and it may be that some form of world government is possible. The only way to find out whether any form of world government is possible and practicable in our time is to work at it and talk about it. . . .

Tinkering with the United Nations will not help us, if we agree with the *New York Times* that our only hope is in the ultimate abolition of war through an ultimate world government. An entirely different constitutional foundation is required. A new set of commitments must be made. Commitments to an alliance can be transformed into allegiance to a government only by a change of heart which is embodied in a fundamental constitutional reform. . . .

If peace through intimidation and peace through purchase are failing and in the nature of things are bound to fail, we might try peace through justice. Justice means giving every man his due; it means not doing to others what you are unwilling to have them do to you. Justice is suggested to us by a well-known American document which states that all men are created equal. Justice is the cement which holds a political organization together.

If we will grant that what we want is peace, and that justice is the only way to peace, then we may begin dimly to perceive both the outlines of a policy for the present and the constitutional foundations of a future world order. We are required to abandon a policy of power and purchase and pursue a policy of justice at home and abroad.

In order to pursue this policy we have to make certain moral and intellectual commitments, commitments that threaten to take us, in fact, into the realm of metaphysics. We have to admit that men are different from the other animals and that their moral, rational, and spiritual qualities are the qualities that make them men. These characteristics prevent us from dealing with men as we are free to deal with other animals. Human dignity forbids us to apply force to men, except by law. It forbids us to regard other men as means to our ends, for every man is an end in himself. The prospects of a human community result from our common humanity.

To give every man his due, therefore, is to treat every man as a man, black or white, British or Russian, rich or poor, ignorant or educated. And we may remember, as John Stuart Mill pointed out long ago, that we cannot expect the slave to show the virtues of the free man unless we first make him free. To say that certain men cannot be treated as men means simply that they have never had a chance to be men, and they must be given that chance.

To give every man his due is to give him the Rights of Man. This means that he must be free from want as long as he is willing to work. It means that he must be free from the fear of tyranny, oppression, and exploitation. It means that his claims to life, liberty, and the dignity of the human person are inalienable. It means that the necessities of life must be common property of the human race, and that the management of the necessities of life by individual owners is a trusteeship which such owners hold subject always to the common good. It means that a world government must be a democracy, because only democracy gives every man his due.

It will be said that a world government which is founded on justice goes further than world government has to go and that we should limit ourselves to those objects as to which there can be no debate, the principal one of which is security. It will be said that nobody wants war and that all that a world government should do is to try to prevent war. This it can do by securing a monopoly of arms. Why talk about justice, the rights of man, and the law of nature when all we want is peace?

The answer is that men will fight until they get their rights. The minimum structural requirements of world government are plain enough. A world government, so as to preserve the cultural values that now exist in the states and regions of the world, must be a government which acts directly on the individual, wherever he may be; for otherwise it is merely a league of sovereign, and hence ultimately warlike, states. But these are minimum structural requirements. There are minimum moral and spiritual requirements, too; and these may be summed up in the single word justice. The advancement of man in spiritual excellence and physical welfare is the common goal of mankind. Universal peace is the prerequisite for the pursuit of that goal. Justice in turn is the prerequisite of peace. Peace and justice stand or fall together. Men will fight until they get their rights. . . .

2.

Order and Change in a Warless World

WALTER MILLIS

TO IMAGINE a warless world is to imagine a special kind of world order—
a system of "law and order" which must nevertheless allow for the disorder,
conflict, and change essential to the development of human institutions.
An idea must be formed of how such change, which throughout history
has been so often and so deeply associated with war, can come about with
a minimum of physical violence.

That change through conflict will continue to come about, regardless, is
scarcely arguable. The complicated struggles among individuals, groups,
classes, communities, or nations for wealth, position, and power is inherent
in human nature. No system of world law and order can eliminate these
power struggles; it would be primarily a means of regulating or structuring
them.

The relative "justice" of such regulation is highly important from the
standpoint of support for the system, but it seems essentially secondary—a
by-product, as it were—to the "order" which the system would impose.
There have, of course, been highly unjust orders which have survived over
long periods and others comparatively just which have suffered early collapse. The essential of any order, just or unjust, is that it force the competitive struggles among those subject to it into other than lethal or violent
channels.

In any system of law and order one finds three elements, which are the
mechanisms through which it achieves its purpose: (1) a sovereign "mo-

Reprinted by permission from *Saturday Review*, September 15, 1962, pp. 18–31.

nopoly" of legal force to forbid resort to violence; (2) a system of general rules (law) defining in generalized terms the rights, duties, and, therefore, the power positions of all involved; (3) a judicial system to apply the general rules in specific conflicts and to provide in its decisions a generally accepted alternative to trial by combat or violence.

No system of this kind, of course, is ever perfectly successful. An irreducible minimum of violent crime, usually a certain amount of rioting and group violence, remains under the most developed systems of law and order. Nor has any such system ever completely inhibited change; even the most static and somnolent of social orders has never been "frozen" into a coma. It is true that a developed system of law and order has the effect, at any given time, of defining—crystallizing—the power relations of the individuals, groups, and classes subject to it, and that this crystallized legal structure of power may survive after the actual power relationships in the community have changed. But when the actual power structure tends to get out of line with the legal definition, it is, sooner or later, the legal definition which is altered, not the newly emerging structure of power.

When the discrepancy between the fact and the form grows too great, such changes may be violent, reflected in great wars on the international stage or bloody revolutions within. But war and violent revolution are by no means the only or the necessary means of adjusting the system of law and order to changes in the underlying power structure. The modern world has recorded immense adjustments of this kind largely, if not wholly, effected by nonviolent means.

Nor is it true that these can occur only in those systems which, as in the Western democracies, include formal provision for popular participation in institutional change. Toynbee, in the opening article in this series, cites the abdication of the Tokugawa Shogunate in Japan—at the time anything but a democratic society—and the accompanying political and social revolution, all accomplished with very little violence. Since the death of Stalin, if not before, considerable shifts have plainly been occurring in the power structure both of the Soviet Union itself and among the constituent states of the Communist empire. But the Communist system of law and order (which is no less a system of law and order because it seems to us an unjust one) has accommodated itself to these changes in general without war or revolution. The one violent revolution of importance—that in Hungary— was suppressed by the Soviet police power, thus leaving Communist law and order outwardly intact. But the ruthlessness with which "order" was reimposed in Hungary does not mean that the system is perpetually unchangeable. The Hungarian revolt will still make its contribution toward those changes—hopefully nonviolent, but changes in any event—which shifts in the underlying Communist power structure are certain to bring about.

Even the existing international order, "anarchic" as it is commonly assumed to be, has since 1945 adjusted itself to very great changes in the basic power relations of peoples, states, classes, and groups with, on the whole, a rather surprising minimum of war or other violence. Discussions of a new world order usually overlook the fact that we already possess a more highly developed system of international law and order than ever before in history. It is a system not yet reduced to statutory form or fully embodied in treaty undertakings; and its institutional expressions, such as the U.N., are still quite rudimentary. It is a system, nevertheless. It is incapable, certainly, of "freezing" the political and social institutions of mankind into any perpetual mold; yet it is currently proving itself adequate to insure that for most peoples, most of the time, the infinitely complex struggle for power is carried on by essentially nonviolent means.

Perhaps two-thirds of the population of the globe live today under no more than four or five great, stabilized, and mutually more or less invulnerable centers of power, of law and of order: the United States, the Western European democracies, the Soviet Union, China, and perhaps India. They appear rather effectively to have excluded violence and bloodshed from their domestic affairs as instruments of practical politics. Each has effectively developed the essentials of rule by law: a police force quite capable of forbidding anything more than merely casual resort to violence; a system of general rules to govern the internal power struggles, and at least some kind of adjudicatory and regulatory system to apply the rules and to offer an alternative to trial by violence which, however imperfect or unjust, can be accepted as preferable.

This, at any rate, appears to be the common opinion. No one, for example, can seriously suppose that the United States will remain fixed in the particular mold of political, social, and economic relationships which it has attained in 1962. We all look for great changes of one kind or another in the American power structure; but it takes a John Birchite mentality to imagine that violent revolution either will or can accompany them. Much the same is true of the great Communist states. The shifting and uncertain power relations between Moscow and Peking are well advertised in the Western press; but no serious student has been rash enough to predict that they will end in a Sino-Soviet war. It is not the likelihood of armed rebellion in China or the USSR that impresses most, but its apparent impossibility in the foreseeable future.

Thus two-thirds of the population of the globe already live under reasonably stable systems of law and order, so stable that no one predicts violent revolution or collapse for any of them (unless as a result of another world war), yet not so rigid as to be incapable of necessary change and development. By whatever paths of blood and misery the world has attained this result, it has attained it; one must recognize its novelty—for it is a phenomenon almost as unprecedented in history as are the nuclear arsenals themselves—as well as its obvious importance to the general problem of world law and order.

Unfortunately, much of the remaining third of the global population is less well organized. Southern Asia, Africa, and much of Latin America are being swept by the "revolution of expectations," inordinately complicated by nationalism, by racial and class conflict, by differences between the small educated elite groups, with their urban followers, and the peasant masses, as well as by the tendency of the great, stable power centers to exploit these difficulties for the advancement of their own power and influence. Speaking very generally, over much of this area the basic power structures (both domestic and international) are in a fluid state; it is the problem of the new leaderships not so much to "seize power" as to discover the new bases on which a viable power structure may be erected. What rules (law) are available, whether derived from decisions in the UN, from the principles of international law, or from domestic constitutional and institutional arrangements, are clearly out of line with the highly complicated actual power relationships.

Over much of this area no general rule of law and order, even a repressive one like that which the Soviet Union has successfully established over its many different peoples and different conflicts of interest, seems possible. And it would appear that a good deal of violence—whether in the savage form that occurred in the Congo or in Algeria, or simply the military coup d'états that have, with relatively little bloodshed, interrupted the processes of "democracy" in so many parts of the world—is inevitable. No system of law and order can hope to avert all violence, or dispense justice with a hand so even that men, groups, and communities will never seek to "take the law in their own hands." But it is still surprising that so little, not so much, violence and bloodshed has attended the enormous shifts in group, class, and national power relationships which have taken place since 1945.

Such is the situation in which we find ourselves today. We have developed a system of world law and order unprecedented in human experience. It contains no global monopoly of legal force adequate to forbid violent solutions to the problems of nations, classes, communities, and groups, although for the time being the great weapons-systems seem to be providing an effective substitute. Change is certainly proceeding as rapidly as most could wish; yet within an order sufficient to permit the vast majority of the world's peoples to live currently at peace and keep such violence as does continue to occur within tolerable bounds. It is an order efficient to permit even more—to permit the growth of what Robert C. Angell has felicitously called the "interstitial tissue" of global organization: "Actually, an elaborate web of relationships is being woven among the peoples of the world. . . . There is live and growing tissue around us, interstitial tissue, if you will, which is spreading and becoming stronger every year." What would be the effect on this general situation of the assumed excision from it of the organized war system?

This is really the central question. All that we have been asked to assume in this series is an initial abolition of organized war, with the introduction of whatever (only vaguely specified) institutional arrangements may be necessary to maintain the abolition. How, so far as securing necessary social and political change is concerned, would the resultant warless system differ from the existing one? The easy answer is to say that it would differ very little; but there is an obstacle to the easy answer. This lies in the still obscure but clearly intimate relationship which has existed through most of history between domestic violence and revolution and international violence and war. The two have probably been intermingled in most of the major changes in human systems of law, order, and power-organization. Great wars have led to great revolutions; great revolutions have led to great wars. Perhaps the causal relationship was not in fact so simple as this would suggest; but the observation at least inspires an inquiry as to whether, if there are no more great wars, there can be any more great revolutions; or, conversely, if there are to be further great revolutions, will not great wars inevitably be revived?

Our presently existing world order seems to be both sufficiently flexible and sufficiently stable to meet the necessities of change without intolerable concomitants of violence. But so did the Atlantic world appear to its inhabitants on the eve of the French Revolution; so did the Western and the Russian imperial world appear on the eve of World War I. Both the Soviet Union and China today appear to represent stable systems of law and order. But the appearance may prove to be illusory. As power relationships continue to shift within the rigid frameworks of these great socieities, it may be that nothing short of violent and bloody rebellion will suffice to break up the old power structures and institute the new.

Revolutionary violence in France after 1789 not only reorganized the domestic power structure; it fractured the international power structure of the time and led to the first total wars of modern history. Given an initially warless world, a similar violent breakdown of the Russian or Chinese power structures might have similar effects. No presently imaginable system of policed disarmament could deal finally or completely with such a situation. It is hard to picture an international police force endowed with either the physical force or, more importantly, the authority to intervene in a chaotic Russia in order to "restore order." It is easy to imagine the pressures upon the contiguous national police forces to intervene in one way or another in order to preserve their national interests; and to see that these pressures could lead to "escalation," rearmament, and war by processes which the international police would find difficult to control. All that one can say to this is that perfection is unattainable in this world; no system of politics will infallibly meet all the problems that may arise before it. But a politics which starts from a universal and policed disarmament, has a far better chance of meeting this sort of situation than has one which starts with the system of organized war.

There is the opposite case, often illustrated by the Russian Revolution of 1918, in which it is held that great international wars are necessary to break up encrusted and anachronistic power structures inhibiting human development. That wars have had this effect can hardly be doubted, but that major war is a necessary element in political and social advance is much more dubious. In the usual view, the Russian Revolution actually began with Alexander II's emancipation of the serfs in 1861, a voluntary recognition by the autocracy (not unlike the abdication of the Tokugawa Shogunate) that times were changing and that the legally established power structure in Russia would have to be modified accordingly. The process thereafter continued, haltingly, not without a good deal of violence on the part of government and revolutionaries alike, but rather steadily.

Even imperial Russia had within it the potentialities of necessary change; and many believe that the autocracy would have undergone a relatively peaceable "constitutionalization" of the new power relationships—rather as happened in Britain and was happening in Germany—*except* for World War I. The Russo-Japanese War of 1904–05 no doubt pushed the autocracy along the avenues to modernization; but World War I simply paralyzed and finally destroyed it, leaving it as helpless to promote as it was to resist the change which was overdue. Power passed by default into other and more ruthless hands, who built and imposed a new power structure, one which was at least somewhat more responsive to the realities than the Czarist system had been, though hardly an ideal case of political and social evolution. World War I, in this view, was not necessary to political and social change in Russia; all that it did was to distort this change into extreme, and generally inefficient, forms.

Organized war and violent domestic revolution have thus been closely associated, historically, with the processes of political and social change. But the exact nature of the association is not too clear; and it is not easy to be dogmatic about the probable effect of the removal of one, organized war, from the global order. One may hazard some guesses. In the absence of international war, certain processes of violent internal change could not go on as they have done. Revolutionaries, for example, would have less chance of acquiring small arms and financial and propaganda support from rival outside powers than they have today. At the same time, they would have less to fear from outside intervention. To revert to the eighteenth-century examples, another American Revolution could not count on the assistance rendered by France as a strategic move in her war with Britain; another French Revolution would not have to face the coalition of powers joined in defense of the *ancien régime*.

It is not easy to strike a plausible balance between such possibilities; but so far as the present great organized power centers are concerned, it seems reasonable to predict that the abolition of organized war among them would not seriously affect the problem of necessary change. After all, at the end of World War I, the Western Allies attempted to intervene with armed force in the Russian revolutionary situation, in a way they could not do in a world disarmed by assumption. Their lack of success at least suggests that the presence or absence of national armaments would not greatly affect such basic reorganizations of the power structure as were then taking place.

Perhaps the real question lies not with the great and relatively stabilized power systems, but with the less-organized areas. How far will a warless world order try to limit the more sporadic disorder and violence that one must expect here? In a generally disarmed world one may expect the simple absence of the hypertrophied weapon systems to supply an adequate equivalent for a global "monopoly of legal force." The want of the necessary weapons systems will generally forbid resort to violence by any of the great power centers. (The argument, it must be remembered, is based on the assumption that the weapons systems have been *voluntarily* laid aside and destroyed.)

But with the survival everywhere of national police forces, there will be no lack of at least light weapons in the world, accessible to bold or desperate men and to their followers. Riots and mob violence, the more organized use of such weapons as plastic bombs, the even more highly organized forms of guerrilla war, will still be possible. The military coup d'état will still be possible through the manipulation of the national police. (Indeed, most of the "military" forces which have participated in such affairs have amounted to little more than what one would expect the national police in a warless world to be.)

How far will a warless order, through its international police force, attempt to control all these forms of residual violence? It seems improbable that the attempt will go very far. The assumed elimination of major organized war must, after all, eliminate the one great danger in current minor wars and violence—the danger of escalation into a great-power conflict. It seems evident that the warless order must have not merely an international but a supranational (that is, veto-free) police force to control disarmament and to ensure that rearmament does not take place. But a supranational, veto-free police force can take on reality only as its empowerment (authority) as well as the physical force at its disposal is strictly limited to that requisite for its police functions. It is difficult to envisage an international or supranational police force as a great army, capable of coercing the states which must support it and overawing the national police forces which they will retain. One sees this force rather as comparable to the American Federal Bureau of Investigation, which wields very great power within the American system, but does so precisely because its weapons are of negligible importance and its empowerment strictly limited. The FBI obviously could not wage a successful armed battle with any state or municipal police force. It has other means of ensuring its power in state and municipal police circles; and it seems obvious that the real power of the supranational police force vis-à-vis the remaining national police forces with which it must work will rest on similar bases.

The concept of an "international police power" has a long, though generally unfortunate history. Experience seems to demonstrate that while some power of the kind is necessary to avert extremes of savagery, violence, and irresponsibility, it can succeed in this much only if it refrains from itself trying to settle or decide the power struggles out of which the violence arises. One may compare the UN "police action" in Korea with that which it was driven by circumstance to take in Palestine and the Congo. The attempt in the first case was to intervene in a major power struggle, and it ended, as probably it could only have ended, in a fairly major international war. In Palestine and the Congo the attempt has been to limit the savagery as far as possible, without authority to decide the power struggles involved. It seems probable that the patterns along which a supranational police force in a warless world order would tend to develop are to be found in the Congo, not in Korea. For its problems would, in a real sense, be police and not military problems.

Perhaps what was first advanced as the easy answer is the right answer as well. Assuming the removal of the organized war system, the political and social institutions reflecting the underlying power organization of the world, of its peoples, states, classes, communities, and groups, would continue to grow and change much as they are now doing in fact, but without the corroding fear of catastrophe which today complicates and distorts every real problem of international politics.

II

THE CONSTRAINTS OF
INTERNATIONAL LAW

In this chapter, the authors explore the actual issues that confront states-men with respect to problems of international order. This does not mean that they are in agreement. Important differences of perspective will be found in the Kaplan and Falk articles (articles 3, 4, and 5). Both authors agree that the international system is not strong enough to outlaw the use of force. There will be too many occasions on which vital national interests are directly involved and too few acceptable means of resolving the conflict prior to the threat of or resort to force. However, both authors agree that it is very important to regulate and to minimize the resort to force. Falk argues that there is a presumption—albeit a rebuttable one—against the use of force in the existing international order. He is more explicit than Kaplan in his discussion of the constraints that should be applied to the use of force and he is less willing either to accept the validity of arguments related to national interests or to accept the argument that sometimes the resort to force sustains international order. Both authors recognize that the resort to force may threaten the interests of other important states in the international order and that their concern can be used as a constraint on the employment of force but not to outlaw it absolutely. The reader may wish to consider the Middle East crises of 1956 and 1967, the India-Pakistan war of 1971, the India-China war of 1962, and other selected uses of force, from this perspective.

The article by Mr. Butler (article 6) is not explicitly directed toward the same set of questions. He is primarily interested in examining Soviet legal concepts concerning the use of force in interventionary activities within the socialist system. From our standpoint, however, the technical legal aspects are secondary to the major political problem: the potentiality for intervention by the Soviet Union into political processes within other socialist states and the potential impact of such a doctrine upon international order.

This type of intervention is known as the Brezhnev doctrine. In assessing the Brezhnev doctrine, a number of important questions have to be asked. The first concerns the general nature of international order. Is it possible to insulate the socialist system from the rest of the international system, thus permitting "permanent" maintenance of the socialist system within the eastern European bloc, without potentially revolutionary consequences for the rest of the international system? And what is the socialist system? In 1972, during the meeting between President Tito and General Secretary Brezhnev, Yugoslavia and the Soviet Union agreed that each could pursue its own path toward socialism. If the Soviet Union were unilaterally to proclaim that the Yugoslav path was no longer "toward socialism," would this agreement provide the Soviet Union with a claim to an interventionary right? Would the Soviet claim of intervention extend to any state that called itself socialist, even in the absence of an agreement with the Soviet Union? If so, we might then be confronted with a growing socialist sphere within which the normal rules of international law did not apply and within which activities designed to inhibit Soviet intervention would be as nonexistent as they were in the case of Czechoslovakia in 1968.

If the Brezhnev Doctrine should be extended to all socialist states and if France or Italy, for instance, should in the future have socialist governments, this might portend a major redistribution of international "power" that could have very important consequences for American values. Although I do not believe that the probability of such a development is great, its exceptional potential importance relates it directly to the major issue of this section.

It has often been noted that the U.S. also has intervened in the affairs of other governments, as in the Guatemalan and Dominican cases. However, the Guatemalan intervention was indirect, involving only money and supplies. And the Dominican intervention, although it probably saved the government, only separated the rebellious and governmental forces ostensibly, but not actually, to protect American citizens. Moreover, the intervention was followed by an election that even that socialist critic of American policy, Norman Thomas, called free. Could the U.S. have intervened in Latin America in the way the USSR did in Czechoslovakia? If not, does this have implications for Chile? Are these differences in intervention policy and methods—including differences in the use of military force, the duration of intervention, and the ends for which it may be used—important in assessing the prospects for world order?

3.

International Law and the International System

MORTON A. KAPLAN

IT IS GENERALLY ACCEPTED that the social structure of international politics places constraints upon the possible variations in international norms. This assertion implies neither that law can be derived from social structure—for if that were true one could adopt or propose norms consistent with that structure regardless of whether these new norms fit into either the body of existing norms or a framework of legal reasoning—nor that there is a strict determinism between a systematic substructure and a normative superstructure, in which case one would expect the political and social structure to generate the norms of international law almost automatically. The first alternative would make law too much a matter of preference and dependent largely upon the perceived advantages accruing to the actors in adjusting or failing to adjust the law to actual or desired social structures. The second alternative would make law too little a matter of preference; it would derive the law from the political and social structure and divorce it from the values and choices by means of which we interact with the present to create the future.

International law, we can agree, is not a disembodied essence concocted from covenants, treaties, or customs, and unrelated to the social institutions that permit its observance. In the absence of central legislative organs, creative action by the member actors changes the international normative structure. If solemn treaty obligations enunciate intentions based upon rea-

Reprinted by permission from *The Future of the International Legal Order*, Vol. 1, eds., Richard A. Falk and Cyril E. Black, pp. 155–82. Copyright © 1969 by Princeton University Press.

sonable expectation, that fact is a significant element for the process of juridical reasoning. Even when a norm is violated, referral to signs embodied in treaties of the existence of a norm may be important for later restorative actions that help to keep the norm alive and to maintain other important values as well. Sometimes, however, solemnly enunciated norms are based upon expectations that, although reasonable when first formed, are invalidated by later developments. The Charter of the United Nations, for instance, insists upon the outlawry of resort to arms except in self-defense. Yet some might—and I would—argue that the present structure of world politics is as far out of line with such a norm as current state practice would seem to indicate. In such a case—if I have correctly interpreted the situation—the attempt to avow the norm despite repeated and insistent violations may serve only to cast doubt upon the structure of international law generally. Too rigid an insistence upon an absolute ban on force may do a disservice to efforts to regulate the use of force and to maintain other norms that sustain important national and international values, including peace and security. Even within American domestic law judges make law; if wise, their creative efforts will be subsumed within a chain of legal reasoning that establishes a reasonable relationship with existing norms. There is perhaps even more reason in international law not to lose sight of legal logic; it is at least equally important not to become a prisoner of disembodied legal logic. Creative statesmanship that takes into account the (flexible) limits that the international system places on possible international norms retains the likelihood of developing norms constructively—and thus of enhancing important values, including that of a law-abiding international community—even while acquiescing in the demise of a solemnly agreed-to norm, at least in its pure and unrealistic wording.

The present international system seems to be evolving away from the loose bipolar system as we have known it. This will probably provide a number of opportunities for wise political leadership to help "legislate" the direction of change in the international political order and in the international legal order. Before turning to the future and the alternatives it may hold for us, it may be useful to return briefly to the past and to sketch some plausible relationships between the international social and political order and the international legal order. This may serve as a comparative foundation for our speculations concerning the future. To accomplish this purpose we will describe models of the "balance of power" international system and of the loose bipolar system to show the consequences they plausibly have for the international normative order. These models are not intended to be descriptive of reality. They are primarily analytic devices that permit one to test for internal consistency and for logical clarity. These models are abstracted from a much more complex world. This raises questions concerning the application of derivations from the models to the world that cannot be considered here.

However, if appropriate caution is used, models such as these may provide illuminating insights.

"Balance of Power" Model

The "balance of power" model has the following characteristics.

1. The only actors in it are nation-states and thus there is no role differentiation in the model. This is a somewhat counterfactual assumption for there were other organizational forms such as the Danube Authority and the League of Nations during the historical "balance of power."

2. The goals of the major nations of the system are oriented toward the optimization of security. By this we mean that major nations will prefer a high probability for survival as major nations, even though this excludes the possibility of hegemony, to a moderate probability for hegemony combined with a moderate probability for elimination as a major actor. Most analysts would argue that Napoleon and Hitler did not operate according to this assumption. It is possible, although far from obvious, that the model would function differently were the assumption relaxed. There is sufficient factual validity to the assumption for large and interesting periods of history, however, to more than justify its use as a first-order approximation.

3. The weaponry in the system is not nuclear.

4. There are stochastic and unpredictable increases in productivity which, in time, unless compensated for, might destabilize the system. Therefore each actor seeks a margin of security above its proportionate share of the capabilities of the system.

5. There must be at least five major nations in the system. A two-nation system would be unstable. If either of the two nations gained a clear margin of superiority, it would be tempted to eliminate the other in order to guarantee that the other would not eliminate it, if, through some combination of circumstances, the ratio of capabilities was reversed. In a three-nation system, if there were a war of two nations against one, the probably victorious coalition would have some incentive to limit its demands upon the defeated nation. To eliminate the defeated nation would throw the victors into an unstable two-nation system. Under our assumptions, this would be undesirable, unless one nation could gain such an advantage from the elimination of the third that it could eliminate the second nation. But this would also give the second nation an incentive to combine with the third against the first unless it misunderstood its own interests. On the other hand, if the first nation refrains from sacrificing the third nation, that nation may later combine against it with the second nation in a subsequent war. And, if one of the victorious nations in this subsequent war sees some advantage in eliminating the first nation, it is dependent upon the ability of the only remaining nation to recognize that its own interests require it to oppose this. The reasoning here is inconclusive; therefore three is not a clear lower bound for stability.

However, if there are at least five nations, it seems plausible that the argument for limitation in war would hold.

6. Each state, even though of great nation status, is likely to require allies to obtain its objectives. Thus it desires to maintain the existence of potential future alliance partners.

The assumptions specified give rise to the following essential rules of conduct:

1. Act to increase capabilities but negotiate rather than fight.
2. Fight rather than pass up an opportunity to increase capabilities.
3. Stop fighting rather than eliminate an essential national actor.
4. Act to oppose any coalition or single actor that tends to assume a position of predominance with respect to the rest of the system.
5. Act to constrain actors who subscribe to supranational organizing principles.
6. Permit defeated or constrained essential national actors to reenter the system as acceptable role partners or act to bring some previously inessential actor within the essential actor classification. Treat all essential actors as acceptable role partners.

The first two rules follow from the need for a margin of security in a world in which capabilities change stochastically. The third rule is essential for maintaining the availability of future coalition partners. The fourth and fifth rules recognize that deviant actors may destabilize the system by their actions or by the actions of their followers or cohorts within other nations. The sixth rule is also related to the need for potential alliance partners and warns against restricting one's own choices unnecessarily.

These rules are not descriptive rules. They are prescriptive rules. That is, under the governing assumptions, these are rules that states would follow in order to optimize their own security. Thus there is motivation to observe the rules, abstracting from other considerations, but no requirement to do so.

If the major nations follow the specified rules under the specified system conditions, there will be a number of consequences, some of which are obvious and others of which are not so obvious. Alliances will tend to be specific, of short duration, and to shift according to advantage, not according to ideologies (even without war). Wars will tend to be limited in objectives and the rules of war and the doctrine of nonintervention will tend to be observed.

Alliances will tend to be of short duration because permanent alliances would tend to undermine the "balancing" characteristics necessary for the security of the member states. Thus alliances will tend to be for specific objectives as determined by short-term interests. And to use a phrase current in the eighteenth and nineteenth centuries, nations will be disposed to act in terms of interest rather than in terms of sentiment. In short, there is, in this system, a general, although not necessarily consistent, identity between short-term and long-term interests.

The limitation of war in the "balance of power" system requires no further discussion.

We will not go into detail on the expected norms of international law except in a few specifics. One would expect belligerents to behave in ways consistent with maintaining the essential rules of the system since they are required for the security of all essential nations, including belligerents. For instance, behavior during the war or in occupation of territory that infuriated the population of an enemy state would probably preclude the possibility that such a state would be a potential future ally. Although this might not be the only constraint operating to enforce the rules of war, nonetheless it is an important factor tending in that direction.

The rule against intervention in the domestic affairs of another state—a rule violated on a number of occasions—also tends to be sustained under conditions of the model. If the intervention—for instance, in favor of rebels—were successful, there might be a permanent alliance between the states or a tutelage of one over the other. This would injure all other states in the system and thus would tend to draw their active opposition. For this reason the intervention would probably be unwise or unsuccessful. And if, for any reason, the intervention were unsuccessful, the state in which the intervention took place would probably have a serious revulsion for the interventionary state that would tend to make it a permanent enemy of that state. Even if the intervention is successful, the new government may oppose the aiding state to demonstrate its independence. Although these reasons are not absolutely compelling, they are strong enough to make likely rather general observance of the rule of nonintervention in the "balance of power" system.

It should be noted that other states by and large did not tend to intervene on the side of the government in the historic system; rather they merely maintained normal state relations and trade with the government. If the rebels grew strong enough, then the rules of belligerency would apply and other states would behave neutrally toward the belligerents, at least with respect to shipments of the articles of war or the goods of trade. These reasons are not dissimilar to those given above; intervention would have had potentially destabilizing consequences for the system and would have tended to be opposed by the other members of the system.

Recognition, whether of new governments or of new states, tended to follow universal norms in the "balance of power" system. Was there a definite territory? Did the government control the territory? Was there reasonable support on the part of the population or at least the absence of strong overt opposition? If these questions were answered affirmatively, then the government or state would tend to be recognized regardless of the form of internal government or regardless of its friendship or antipathy toward particular states. Although the act of recognition itself was a political act, so that the facts of the case did not absolutely require the act of recognition, nonetheless, with notable exceptions, there was fair concordance between rule and practice. Moreover, since nonrecognition was a political act, its consequences for international law were less than massive, the nonrecognized state merely being denied access to the privileges stemming from comity. Failure to recognize did not remove the duties and obligations under international law that nonrecognizing states had toward the nonrecognized state as a state. Even before the facts were clear that established the legitimacy of a government or a state, this did not imply a reign of anarchy with respect to the non-recognized government or state. Intervention in its affairs would have been contrary to the rules of the system. Recognition may have been a political act and a negotiating tool in getting the new government or state to recognize its obligations under the rules of the international community, but it was not a weapon in a cold war designed to undercut its existence.

The Loose Bipolar Model

A second model—one that has some relevance to present-day international politics—is that of the loose bipolar system. This model contains two blocs, each of which is led by a leading bloc actor. There is role differentiation in this model; in addition to blocs and bloc members, there are nations not joined to blocs and universal organizations as, for instance, the United Nations. The weaponry in this model is nuclear. In an age of efficient logistics and great organizational capacity, this latter feature is an essential element of the system; for, unless factors of scale precluded it, one would expect one of the blocs to overwhelm the other unless deterred by a weapons system such as a nuclear one.

This system operates according to the following simplified set of essential rules:

1. Blocs strive to increase their relative capabilities.
2. Blocs tend to be willing to run at least some risks to eliminate rival blocs.
3. Blocs tend to engage in major war rather than to permit rival blocs to attain predominance.
4. Blocs tend to subordinate objectives of the universal actor to objectives of the bloc but to subordinate objectives of the rival bloc to the universal actor.
5. Non-bloc actors tend to support the universal actor generally and specifically against the contrary objectives of the blocs.
6. Non-bloc actors tend to act to reduce the danger of war between blocs.
7. Non-bloc actors tend to be neutral between blocs except where important objectives of the universal actor are involved.
8. Blocs attempt to extend membership but tend to tolerate the status of non-bloc actors.

The first three rules reflect the uncertainties of the bipolar system and the need for at least a margin of security. Rule 4 is related to the need within the system for mediatory functions. Particularly in the nuclear age, mediatory activities help to coordinate conflicting blocs and to achieve an agreement short of nuclear war. This is similar to other types of bargaining situations in which optimal solutions for both conflicting parties are aided by the mediatory process. On the other hand, although these processes should be supported by the blocs, each bloc should nonetheless attempt to take advantage of any favorable opportunities to obtain better than a "fair" outcome. That is, maneuvering will take place and it will be related to situational advantages. Moreover, it is advantageous, even apart from the concept of mediatory functions, to subordinate the goals of one's opponents to those of the universal organization and to subordinate the goals of the organization to those of the bloc, provided this can be done with minimal inconsistency.

Universal organizations are major supports for the interests of actors not belonging to blocs—the greatest protection for them—insofar as they can be protected by universally applicable rules of conduct. Therefore non-bloc members have an interest in subordinating both blocs to the universal actors. This would become difficult, and probably impossible, in the event of major war; and minor wars might escalate into major wars. Hence, according to Rule 6, non-bloc actors are to reduce the danger of war between blocs. The non-bloc actors cannot properly fulfill these functions unless they remain neutral between the blocs; lack of neutrality would impede their mediatory functions and their support for the universal actor. On the other hand, a neutrality that threatened to undercut the universal actor would injure their interest. Thus Rule 7. Rule 8 emphasizes the fact that although extension of bloc membership is important to the bloc, the mediatory role is sufficiently important to the blocs to tolerate it and even possibly, under appropriate conditions, to support it.

The consequences of the rules are straightforward and for the most part have already been stated. Consequences: Alliances are long-term, are based on permanent and not shifting interests, and have ideological components; wars, except for the fear of nuclear weapons, tend to be unlimited; however, the fear of nuclear war has a strong dampening effect on war; the universal organization tends to support mediatory and war-dampening activities; with respect to international law, there are few restrictions on intervention and these arise mainly out of the fear of escalation.

Some of the reasons for these consequences may now be stated. Alliances tend to be long-term and based on permanent interest; in other words, there is a tendency in the system for bloc members to support the leading member of the bloc even on issues where there is a temporary divergence of short-term interests between them. Moreover, there is a tendency for ideological congruity within the blocs; for the kind of close association involved either requires organizational uniformity, as in the Communist bloc, or the kind of public support and cultural similarity which helped at one time to support NATO. If one bloc were organized according to long-term interests, and other nations were not, the bloc might well gain its way on most issues by splitting the opposition issue by issue.

There would be a tendency in this system for wars to be unlimited; neither bloc would regard the other as a potential coalition partner. The greatest inhibitor of a central confrontation lies in the nuclear component and also perhaps in certain factors of scale that would make administration of the world an extremely difficult, if not impossible, task.

As for the rule of intervention in international law, at least some of the constraint present in the "balance of power" system would not be operative in the loose bipolar system. The opposition to intervention would come from the other bloc and would not have the same massive quality as in the "balance of power" system where most major actors could be expected to oppose it; fear of confrontation and escalation nonetheless would inhibit intervention to some extent. In areas where one bloc had easy access and the other did not, intervention would not be unlikely. Where both blocs had relatively similar access, they might agree to insulate the area from bloc competition or alternatively they might decide to compete for it. The decision would depend upon the specifics of the situation; the model could not be expected to give rise to a specific prediction on this point. One factor inhibiting intervention would be the fear that the erosion of this particular rule of law might tend to undermine the general system of law. Although this fear might be a factor in decisions concerning intervention, the consequence feared is not so direct or so massive that it would be likely to prove overriding; moreover, most interventions would be indirect and covert.

One would expect the use of force to be permissible in this system; the same factors that permit intervention also operate to permit the use of force, the Charter of the United Nations to the contrary notwithstanding. Historically, Palestine, the Congo, Cyprus, Greece, Korea, Vietnam, Suez, Hungary, and various other episodes firmly illustrate the erosion of the so-called rule of law enunciated in the Charter. The bipolarity of the system tends to focus competition between the blocs and to produce a resort to force in those circumstances where one of the blocs has a clear preponderance of capabilities. The rule can to some extent be enforced against non-leading nations, as in the Suez case, or even in the Pakistan-Indian case. But it runs into greater difficulties in cases such as the Indian-Chinese case.

To some extent this stems from the fact that the bloc leaders have no desire for the continuance of a war that neither supports, especially since any armed conflict might lead to a central confrontation even if with low probability; the bloc leaders see no reason to risk even the lowest probabilities of a nuclear war if there is some convenient way of avoiding it and if there is no clear gain for the bloc leaders to be got from the use of force. Where the universal organization tends to dampen the armed confrontations and to mediate quarrels among non-leading nations, it therefore tends to reinforce the interests of the bloc leaders.

Recognition of states or of governments is based not on the criterion of control with reasonable support from the people within a region but is based upon the consequences of the act of recognition for bloc policy. Thus nonrecognition of East Germany, North Korea, or Communist China was, during the height of bipolarity, part of a program of political warfare designed to erode the position of these governments. This does not mean that nonrecognized states or governments are entirely without rights within the system or that unprovoked major acts of military warfare against them are permitted. However, whereas in the "balance of power" system the objective of nonrecognition is to secure the compliance of the nonrecognized state or government with the norms of the system, in the loose bipolar system the objective of nonrecognition is to weaken the international position of the nonrecognized state or government, and under favorable circumstances, to contribute to its demise.

Factors Making for a Change

A number of features of the existing world make for greater divergence from the model of loose bipolarism than would perhaps permit retention of the model in its present form. First, however, mention will be made of those divergences of model from reality that have always been present but that do not clearly invalidate the model. In the model, uncommitted nations are not distinguished from bloc members by internal characteristics. In the real world, most of the uncommitted states are ex-colonies of the members of the NATO bloc. Their historical memories are conditioned by the fight against colonialism and by their fear of a reimposed colonialism, even if in the form of so-called neocolonialism. Their search for identity leads them to distinguish themselves from the former patron state and, even more specifically, from the leader of the NATO bloc, even though the United States has not historically been an imperialist power.

Most of the uncommitted states are also "colored." Although this characteristic should be irrelevant in countries that have values that are universalistic and achievement-oriented, historically this has not been the case. This creates resentment on the part of the uncommitted states against the members of NATO. In their fight against colonialism, most of the uncommitted nations have adopted some form of socialist or Marxist ideology. Although most of the uncommitted countries are not socialist in meaningful applications of that term, they nonetheless accept a number of intellectual corollaries of the socialist or Marxist position. Thus, it is widely believed among them—and even believed by many Western intellectuals—that capitalism is responsible for both colonialism and war.

The uncommitted countries are also by and large underdeveloped. Whereas in the nineteenth century, the newly developing countries, such as Japan, turned to Western Europe or to the United States for their models of development, there has been until recently a tendency among the contemporary developing nations to view either Russia or China as acceptable, or at least as partly acceptable, models.

One consequence of this set of conditions has been the emphasis of the uncommitted nations upon exterminating the remnants of colonialism, mostly through moral pressure or United Nations resolutions, and upon opposing so-called neocolonialist government among the uncommitted states. Thus a government in an uncommitted state that was relatively conservative, bound to NATO nations by treaty, or more concerned with its internal problems than with the export of revolution tended to find itself opposed by the more revolutionary uncommitted states, which at times even intervened in its internal affairs. Rather than lending support to the old rules of nonintervention, which necessarily suffer attrition as a consequence of the shift from the "balance of power" to bipolarity, the uncommitted states have tended to reinforce the shift away from this rule of law and even more narrowly to circumscribe its applicability. Although they have often attempted to distinguish between colonialist intervention and revolutionary intervention—a distinction the Soviet Union has also tried to maintain—and have not been entirely unsuccessful in this effort, nonetheless there has been a further weakening of the rule. These interventions sometimes threatened the stability of the bipolar system and the interests of NATO. A largely revolutionary world would probably be as inimical to American interests as a largely fascist world would have been. Such a world, even apart from conceptions of monolithicity, would confront the United States with strategic military problems and also, and perhaps even more importantly, with political problems that might affect both its systems of alliances and its internal institutional forms.

The above factors, however, would not by themselves necessarily produce instability or invalidate the model. Other factors may, however, invalidate the applicability of the model, although this is not completely clear.

Among the features eroding the loose bipolar system is the recovery, both political and economic, of Western Europe. Until 1948, the Communist parties of Italy and France seemed to pose a possible threat of violent revolution. The national economies of the occupied but liberated nations were slowly recovering from the havoc of war. Without the infusion of massive aid from the United States, social and political upheaval might easily have occurred. With more than six million men in its armies, the Soviet Union seemed to pose a threat of an immediate military nature. Although this threat never objectively existed in the form in which it was visualized, in the absence of the organized Western bloc that developed, Italy, France, or West Germany might have collapsed as Czechoslovakia did. Now that these nations are once again economically vigorous and politically stable and now that the threat of Soviet military action is visualized as only residual, national pride tends to counsel some degree of independent action. Moreover, the failure of Great Britain to join the Common Market upon its formation, the fear that a vigorous Germany might dominate a united Europe without Britain, and the specific policies followed by General de Gaulle that derive at least as much from his own ideology and view of the world as they do from external circumstances, seriously threaten the existence of NATO as an organized bloc and the Common Market as a supranational agency.

If the threat of Soviet military attack seems to have lessened, the likelihood of an American nuclear response to an actual attack by the Soviet Union also seems to have lessened. Before the Soviet Union acquired nuclear weapons, or even while its nuclear force was highly vulnerable to an American first strike, American nuclear retaliation for a Soviet attack was extremely credible. No doubt a massive Soviet attack out of the blue, that is, without provocation—and in the absence of a suitable conventional response—would still in all likelihood incur an American nuclear response. If, however, war were to develop in ambiguous circumstances, in which the Soviet Union suffered a plausible provocation, and after a prelude that gave much time for Americans to consider the potential damage to their own cities in the nuclear exchange, then although an American nuclear response is by no means precluded, neither does it appear quite so credible as it did in the early 1950's. Regardless of the motives that led General de Gaulle to emphasize the development of an independent French nuclear force, the fact that he has seen fit to call attention to the possibility that the United States would not use its nuclear force in defense of Europe is an indication that he felt the argument at least had some merit in securing support for his decisions. The failure of the Western allies to find some solution to this difficulty that satisfied jointly the needs of the United States and of the European nations no doubt has played a role in the weakening of NATO and hence in the growing instability of the loose bipolar system.

Problems of nuclear control may also have played a role, although it is difficult to say how large a role, in the rupture between China and the Soviet Union. Economic aid, personality conflicts, and conflicting national interests in border quarrels, may also have played important roles in this development. The quarrel between them has provided the other satellite parties with alternate founts of authority. The Communist bloc will not soon recover from the demonstration of the extent to which opposition between Socialist states can occur or from the shattering of the myth of the infallible leadership that resulted from Khrushchev's secret speech on Stalin in 1956.

The independence shown by China has had multifarious consequences within the Communist camp. Hungary and Rumania, for example, have been able to resist political pressures from Moscow and to develop at least partly independent policies that increase their support at home and that stabilize their regimes. These developments have increased the appeal of Communism by demonstrating that Communism can be at least in part an indigenous phenomenon and not merely a Moscovite plot. At the same time the world Communist movement has been weakened both by the fact that division exists and by the fact that the two leading Communist actors—Russia and China—must now expend much of their energies on the contest for the leadership of the bloc or, alternatively, in a contest to attract or to neutralize members of the other's bloc. Consequently they must turn much of their management capacity away from problems of international politics; this reinforces the reduction in their external opportunities that has resulted as a consequence of greater political and economic stability in the world. Thus the Communist bloc is no longer seen as a monolithic conspiratorial apparatus—an image that characterized much of the postwar debate.

If the Communist bloc is not seen as an imminent threat and if many believe that further liberalization will occur within the nations of that bloc, the world then will respond to a psychological détente, the logic of which may further reinforce the breakup of bipolarity. The assumption will be that an era of "good feelings" may promote international agreements and help to turn the world from a policy of blocs to one of independent states operating according to a flexible system of alignments.

The belief that détente helps to fragment bloc structure is not entirely wrong. Although the great breaks in the Soviet bloc—those of Yugoslavia, China, Albania, and temporarily of Hungary—did occur during periods of great international tension, the increases in autonomy and collegiality within the bloc are not entirely unrelated to the amelioration of world conflict. To some extent, similar processes are occurring within NATO, although both processes are much more complicated than generalizations concerning the détente imply. Moreover, even if the generalizations concerning the consequences of détente for internal bloc structure have some—but only some— validity, the relationship between détente and international agreement may radically overstate the importance of the psychological variable. The test ban agreement, after all, was reached subsequent to the Cuban missile crisis—a period of great tension in which restrained threat and counter-threat dominated the international scene. To the extent that détente implies moderate external policies and the likelihood of international agreement, the atmosphere of goodwill that is so highly valued in many circles may play only a minor role.

Some would argue—and I believe correctly—that the psychology of the détente mistakes the epiphenomena of international politics for the phenomena. Just as the popular images of the cold war were in part a response to the frustrated hopes of international cooperation that were held during the war period, the psychology of the détente is in part a reaction to the exaggerated fears of the cold war period. According to this view, Stalin's so-called aggressive policies were more likely responses to the opportunities and dangers that the immediate postwar period provided than they were to a generalized policy of expansion. It is also unlikely that Stalin's policies were the product of the uncontrolled nature of his power within the Soviet governmental system. On the other hand, Khrushchev's seemingly more passive policies—it must be remembered that Khrushchev initiated the Cuban missile crisis and sent troops into Hungary although Stalin only threatened Yugoslavia—responded more to lack of opportunity than to a generalized policy of agreement or to the benignity of a more moderate form of internal rule. If this is a correct interpretation, then expressions of goodwill and the amelioration of the internal Soviet regime, no matter how desirable the latter may be on humanitarian grounds, play little role in achieving international agreement. However, even if this view is correct, it is too subtle for the public. Subjective feelings, at least in the West, concerning the alleged fragility of the détente will probably continue to play a role in the formation of international policy and in the erosion of bipolarity.

Thus, the fact that confronts us is the possible, and even probable, erosion of bipolarity. If the loose bipolar system is becoming unstable, perhaps the model of loose bipolarity no longer functions very effectively as a representation of the world. We will, therefore, consider alternative models that, depending upon circumstances, might represent the alternative worlds that might evolve out of the present world. These systems may give us some insights into the kinds of international law that might accompany them.

Unit Veto System

We present here the model of an equilibrium system that conceivably could develop out of the existing international system. The unit veto system is a system in which each nation possesses a nuclear force capable of surviving a first strike by an enemy and of imposing unacceptable damage upon him. We consider this system before considering some more realistic alternatives because these more realistic alternatives do not constitute equilibrium models and because one or more of them are more closely related to the unit veto system than to the loose bipolar system.

Military alliances would be relatively meaningless in this world. Nuclear deterrence would be credible and effective. Conceivably minor military skirmishes would occur within a quite limited framework; presumably a strategy of limited strategic retaliation might be employed where the conventional forces of one side are too limited to halt successfully the armies of an opponent. Catalytic and anonymous wars would lack plausible motivation.

Nonmilitary, that is, political, interventions, would occur with relative frequency in this world. Such interventions could not easily be deterred by nuclear systems; the gap between penalty and transgression would be too huge to bear the burden of credibility; neither aggressor nor victim would likely be convinced by the argument for this kind of response. The universal organization, however, might well be employed by the other nations of the system to dampen such occurrences because of the danger, even if remote, of escalation. Yet, this will be an isolationist world in which the functions of the universal organization are largely underdeveloped. If the revolutionary ambitions of Russia and China, for instance, are likely to be dampened by lack of opportunity, the development of common interests is also likely to play a minimal role in this system. Neither law nor international organization will burgeon in this system. The citizens of the nation-states are likely to be suspicious of foreign nations, uninterested in the morals of quarrels or the morals of other regimes, and lacking in the assurance required for an articulated foreign policy. The dangers in this system may lie in the political deviancy that begins to develop within nations and in the withdrawal of affect from the external world. This will be a system with superficially low entropy that may suddenly flare up.

The systems presented below are not equilibrium models. They are neither highly analytical nor highly theoretical. However, by suitable adjustments at the parameters one might derive them either from the loose bipolar or unit veto models. Although some writers believe that future systems may be variants of a "balance of power" model, I do not agree; in my opinion the introduction of nuclear weapons and changes in scale make variations based on that model less probable than those adumbrated below. These nonequilibrium systems presumably would develop as the consequence of one or more parameter changes inconsistent with the equilibrium models discussed above. If these nonequilibrium systems are not exceptionally stable in their nature, they may nonetheless be maintained by favorable concatenations of circumstances. Most importantly, one can see how any of them could develop out of the present loose bipolar system as a consequence of changes in the parameters of this system. Thus they are useful intellectual tools for considering possible ranges of variation in international norms; we need to think not merely of the desirability of specific norms but also of the ways in which norms interact with international systems. Norms that are desirable when considered independently may either move us toward international systems the other aspects of which are undesirable or turn out to be unenforceable unless still other changes are made in the international system. Alternatively norms that are less desirable when considered independently may (or may not) help to promote international systems more in accord with our values. Perhaps even more important than the possible inconsistencies between specific norms and the development of alternative international systems will be the problem of relating national policy choices to either or both of these problems. We will not—and perhaps cannot—say much that is significant about these problems in one chapter. The systems described below, however, will be useful if they provide a framework within which the relevant policy choices can be discussed. Whether one thinks likely or unlikely the variations discussed, the style of thinking that underlies them may still prove useful.

DÉTENTE SYSTEM

The détente system is one in which the United States and the Soviet Union are the two strongest nations in the system although they are confronted by other national challenges greater than those confronting them in the loose bipolar system. They are still highly competitive but are reasonably relaxed about their competition. The United States no longer finds it necessary to suspect Communist plots in revolutionary movements while the Soviet Union has learned that many of these distant revolutionary movements are so difficult to control and so alien in cultural background that they are not worth more than merely minor risks. China has alienated many of the uncommitted states, such as Indonesia, Algeria, and Cuba. Moreover, she is in her second generation of revolutionary leadership and is becoming more conservative. Nuclear diffusion has not extended beyond the United States, the Soviet Union, Great Britain, France, and China. The test ban has been extended to underground tests. France and China also have become signatories to this pact. Neither the United States nor the Soviet Union is capable of a credible first strike, and as a consequence either they refrain from increasing the size of their nuclear forces or they decrease them somewhat. France has withdrawn its armed forces from integrated NATO control; the pro-French faction in Germany has won a signal victory within German politics. As a consequence NATO becomes, as General de Gaulle demands, a loose alliance without integrative mechanisms. Rumania develops alternate ties to France to counterbalance its dependence upon the Soviet Union. Other signs of increased independence occur in the Communist bloc.

The anticolonial revolution has been carried to completion. The rule of nonintervention has been reestablished in international politics with support from both the United States and the Soviet Union. With both American and Soviet support, the United Nations Security Council condemns efforts by uncommitted nations to interfere in each other's activities. The rule on compensation in cases of expropriation is relaxed. The United Nations begins to play a strong role in the governance of space, celestial bodies, and polar regions. It also sets up a regime for the development of the mineral resources of the seas.

Breaches of the peace—or even wars—occasionally occur in this system but they do not directly involve any of the major nations. These wars are quickly regulated by the United Nations organization; observer teams are sent to prevent continuation of the fighting. A tradition develops of arbitration of major disputes. National courts increasingly apply international law. There are fewer restrictions on this process by either constitutional or legislative requirements within the national systems.

Recognition, as in the "balance of power" system, is based upon universalistic criteria. Recognition policy is no longer part of the arsenal of political warfare as in the loose bipolar system. However, the motivations that uphold recognition policy—as well as those that uphold noninterventionary norms—differ from those of the "balance of power" system. In the détente system these norms are desirable because they reduce those challenges to the existence of a regime or state that could involve the resort to force and increase the dangers of escalation. The mellowing of the Soviet Union—and to some extent of China—reduces the dangers of nonintervention and of universalistic treatment of new regimes and new states. The lack of cohesion of the blocs has similar consequences and also increases the difficulty of gaining support from one's own bloc for interventionary efforts. The rise of major nations either that are not in blocs or that pursue independent foreign policies reduces the pressure on the bloc leaders to assume that security depends upon their initiative in responding to revolutionary change in the world. Small changes no longer seem to threaten cumulative change as seemed to be the case in the loose bipolar system, viz., the case of Korea.

FOUR BLOC SYSTEM

NATO has been dissolved. Western European nations including England have put together a nuclear force with a substantial second strike capability. This force has been integrated in a new organization based on the Common Market and including the Court of Human Rights. Constitutional democratic processes are guaranteed for all the European nations. The United States takes a special responsibility for Latin America and certain areas of Asia. It utilizes the OAS to intervene in Latin America to maintain constitutional processes within that region. It no longer intervenes globally; Europe now also has a capacity in, for instance, the Middle East or Africa comparable to that of the United States in Latin America. Therefore responsibility does not fall inescapably on the United States. The attractiveness of the Western European alternative has reduced the consensus supporting the governments of the Communist satellites in Europe. Consequently for the protection of their own regimes, they are forced to depend more on the Soviet Union. Thus Russian hegemony within the Eastern European bloc is reestablished. Southeast Asia has been neutralized. Communist China has entered the United Nations and has regularized its relationship with the United States. The rule of nonintervention applies in those areas that are not defined as bloc areas. Thus Japan, Africa, India, and certain portions of Southeast Asia fall within this rule. As none of the blocs aspires to control the world and as all now recognize the difficulty of controlling revolutions in developing nations, this rule is reasonably well-enforced.

There are many similarities to the détente system. Space, the Arctic regions, and the seas come under the control of the United Nations, except that the rules according to which this is done are established primarily by bargaining among the four blocs. The rule of expropriation also has been changed to give greater latitude to expropriating states. Some degree of compensation is demanded but not necessarily that amount that corresponds to the market values of the seized assets.

Recognition is usually based upon the criteria of control of territory and support, or at least lack of opposition, by a substantial part of the population. In areas of special sensitivity to the blocs, however, this rule is not followed. Thus, in Latin America, for instance, only republican forms of government

are recognized. Those governments that do not provide for political competition have sanctions applied against them by the Organization of American
States.

Resorts to force are regulated by a United Nations organ. Ad-hoc control,
advisory, or observer groups are employed to separate the combatants. If
these disputes are mediated or arbitrated, the blocs intervene to assure themselves that the principles of settlement are principles not discordant with
their interests.

The influence of the uncommitted states is considerably smaller in this
system than in either the loose bipolar or the détente system. Even in the
détente system, the competition between the United States and the Soviet
Union for the support of uncommitted states is likely to give such states
considerable leverage. In the four bloc system, on the other hand, the existence of a number of alternatives reduces the pressure on any particular
bloc to seek the support of any uncommitted state. As this holds for each of
the blocs, the price to be paid for support is significantly lowered. Although
in order to keep the Organization of American States viable the United States
is quite likely to establish sets of economic arrangements that guard against
violent fluctuations for the single-commodity countries, the global extension
of rationalized procedures is less likely than in a bipolar system.

A variant of the four bloc system deserves consideration. The removal of
the United States from Europe and the development of a united Europe exerts a major attraction upon the Soviet bloc. Instead, however, of clinging to
the Soviet Union for support, the governments of at least some of the East
European states begin to bring into the government only nominally Communist elements in order to foster consensus in the immediate period and
association with the economically more vigorous European community in
the future. As part of this process, they increase their treaty ties with one or
more of the European nations and even enter into what might be regarded as
alliances with them. In some of the Eastern European nations, these transi-
tions take place smoothly. In others regime crises occur, as old guard
Communist elements either rebel against these regimes, while calling on the
Soviet Union for support, or take control of the government legally, while
provoking revolutions against themselves in the process.

Developments past this point depend upon a context that has not been
sketched here and that is obviously contingent in terms of prediction. Some
of the potentialities are, however, obvious. The Soviet Union may also go
through a regime crisis and may either intervene or not intervene with the
consequences these decisions may have for the outbreak of war or the norms
involving the use of force or intervention. Appeals may be made to a united
Europe by either the governments or the revolutionaries, and the decisions
made by Europe will also affect this set of norms. Attempts may be made to
invoke United Nations procedures to pacify the situation. These may succeed, in which case there may be a major enhancement of international

organization and world law. Alternatively the intervention by the United Nations may be so ineffective that the organization is discredited, its mediatory activities paralyzed, and the extension of its control over such areas as space and the seas inhibited. A situation parallel to that of the cold war may develop except that four blocs rather than two play major roles. Great instability may result.

UNSTABLE BLOC SYSTEM

The unstable bloc system is one in which the two major blocs have either begun to fragment or are well along in the process of fragmentation. Arms control agreements are minimal. Third area conflicts are extensive. Local outbreaks of violence are frequent. National liberation movements and internal revolt are rampant in the uncommitted areas. Qualitative aspects of the so-called arms race have made nuclear weapons cheaper and easier to acquire.

Although perhaps ten or fifteen nations have nuclear weapons systems in the unstable bloc system, the United States and the Soviet Union are the only nations with technologically advanced systems. The systems acquired by the United States and the Soviet Union have greatly increased accuracy in delivery, much greater efficiency in the use of warhead materials, and multiple warheads. Although increased mobility of missiles and extensive use of the seas have lowered the vulnerability to first strike of the US and USSR that otherwise would be present in the system in the absence of *these* qualitative improvements, other qualitative improvements, e.g., improved search techniques and increased delivery accuracy, make first strikes much less infeasible than they are at present. The increased instability in the relationships between the Soviet Union and the United States produces further fragmentation of the bloc structure, as the credibility of deterrence has been lessened.

The minor nuclear powers have systems that are good for minimum deterrence only. Their systems are highly vulnerable to first strike. They cannot do serious damage to the nuclear systems of the two major nuclear powers, and they are subject to rapid obsolescence. Alternatively, West Germany and Japan may develop large and sophisticated nuclear systems, while China may utilize its vast territory and large population to offset other deficiencies of its nuclear threat.

This is a system in which the leaders of the two blocs have a strong incentive to insulate themselves from quarrels that might escalate into nuclear war, even at the expense of deserting alliances of which they may be members. Growing recognition of this fact will tend to discredit the value of alliances and will also tend to free the more adventurous nations from the restraints that have previously characterized their behavior. Thus, for instance, a nation such as Rumania might seek support from France as well as from the Soviet Union. Inversely Hungary might turn to the protection of a nuclear-armed West Germany. West Germany, cut off from the support of both the United States and France, might reduce its pressure on East Germany, even to the extent, for instance, of giving tacit support to East German demands on Poland for ex-German territory. This nationalistic West Germany might make a deal with Communist China, in which it uses Chinese territory for nuclear experiments and, in exchange, provides technical aid. This might place great pressure on the Soviet Union, which then might turn either to the United States, or to a deal with either or both Germanies at Polish expense.

This system will be characterized by nuclear blackmail and unstable political coalitions. Although the need to avoid such a potentially unstable system would provide an incentive for the states of Europe to unite within the framework of a supranational organization and for the United States to provide them with the know-how to produce a stable nuclear system, by hypothesis, that alternative has been bypassed. As a consequence, resort to violence is widespread in this system. The United Nations is reduced to a debating body. Arms control agreements are minimal or nonexistent. Outer space, the seas, and the Arctic regions are not governed internationally but are sources of conflict. Recognition is used as a political weapon, and intervention in the affairs of other states is common. The uncommitted states will not be aided by other states to any considerable extent in their development efforts. There will be a general retrogression of international law.

One other variation of the unstable bloc system can be considered. This is a version in which the first strike potentiality of the United States and the Soviet Union is minimal, either because of improvement in antiballistic missile programs or because of failures in search procedures for sea-or-land-based mobile missiles. In this case, alliances would be possible between major and minor nuclear powers or among minor nuclear powers. But the former type of alliance would be inhibited by the small state's possession of nuclear arms. Possession would be a sign of independence and distrust. Moreover the large nuclear state would fear commitment (triggering) by the small nuclear power's use of the weapon. It would desire to insulate itself from a chain of actions that it could not control. And although a general alliance among most of the small states possessing nuclear forces might create a sizable nuclear force, unless there were exceptional political or cultural circumstances, the alliances would be susceptible to nuclear blackmail and splitting tactics.

Wars in this system would tend to be limited but the possibility of escalation would be greater than in the others. Limited direct confrontations between the United States and the Soviet Union might occur in non-European areas. A central confrontation might also occur. But as the danger of escalation beyond the limited war category would be very great, there would be strong pressure to avoid it.

The foreign policies of the United States and the Soviet Union would tend to be interventionist. American policy would tend toward conservatism, that is, toward the support of status quo, conservative regimes. Although one could argue that to retain the support of its own intellectuals, the United States would do better by supporting progressive regimes, American behavior will more likely support regimes opposed to change. There will be a consequent alienation of a considerable portion of the intellectual elite both within the United States and in other NATO states. Soviet policies will support to some extent national liberation movements but in a very cautious way. Additional "Hungaries" may occur that serve to disillusion Soviet intellectuals. Russia will also be torn between a desire to maintain solidarity with China and a fear of the strategic threat and organizational challenge that China presents to the Soviet Union. This will lead to inconsistencies in Soviet policy that conceivably could lead to the fragmentation of the satellite system. This again might produce East German pressure on Poland, depending upon a number of parameters that are too complicated to specify here.

The role of the United Nations will be primarily mediatory and adapted to dampening the consequences of outbreaks of violence. Although each bloc will support political changes contrary to the interests of the opposing bloc, the efforts to secure a constitutional majority in the United Nations will generally prove ineffective. It is not likely that in this system the United Nations will acquire authority over outer space, celestial bodies, or arms control measures. The United Nations will prove ineffective in dampening local outbreaks of violence. Ad-hoc United Nations forces will become difficult to establish. Intervention and recognition policy will not be based on universalistic criteria but will not be used for purposes of political warfare quite as much as in the other variation of the unstable bloc system, as the blocs will introduce some small amount of constraint.

DEVELOPMENT WORLD
The model sketched here goes much further in its optimistic reading of world possibilities than any other of the models. It ignores the failures of development in so many nations, and the even more disheartening apparent failures in nation-building, as in the case of Nigeria, and instead adumbrates the outline of a world in which most of the more optimistic projections from the current world materialize.

In the development world, we would expect that a large number of successful regional groupings would enhance cooperation among the members of the region on both economic and political matters. Success in nation-building has stabilized the national political units. The internal social systems of the nations have developed sufficient infrastructure to provide satisfactory alternatives for those who lose out in political contests and thus to reduce the need for and the frequency of coercive politics. Increased internal political pluralism reduces the costs of political failure, provides alternative career lines and the potentiality for come-backs, and invests amalgamative activities with additional desirable alternative opportunities. Thus Africa and Latin America, for example, would form common markets and would establish the kinds of transportation and communication networks that they presently lack. There is now more intercommunication with Europe and the United States respectively than within the two geographical areas.

We assume that the Common Market flourishes, that with the demise of a general the Seven join the Market, and that the supranational features of the market are emphasized. The Commission on Human Rights becomes a full-fledged court of final constitutional review that sustains political liberalism as well as individual freedom. Although supranational features are less emphasized in Eastern Europe what had been known as the Soviet bloc develops self-regulating agencies in functional areas; these agencies operate either through COMECON or through more specialized and separate arrangements. Although the governments in Eastern Europe do not become democratic and remain, with a few exceptions, one-party systems, individual rights are much more regularized than had been the case in the past; and the freedom to move either within or outside the bloc becomes almost general.

The regime in China has meliorated. Although China has good relations with Korea and Vietnam, and is developing successfully, these nations do not enter into a regional grouping. Japan, which has emerged as the second most industrialized nation on earth, and which is pressing the United States strongly for world leadership, has a very strong aid program toward Southeast Asia. Most nations of this area have entered their own regional association through which Japanese aid and leadership is funnelled. Supranational characteristics of this association are weak, although there are a substantial number of regional cooperative arrangements.

The United States has retreated from global interventionism, although it has become the only "world" power with the incorporation of Australia, New Zealand, and the Philippines as American states. Israel has also joined this new grouping. With the death of the Israeli hope that the Arab states would make peace eventually and with the withdrawal of American protection to foreign states, except under United Nations auspices, incorporation of Israel into the American union remained the only solution for both nations. Cuba has also joined the American nation after a successful democratic revolution, as have the Dominican Republic, Haiti, and the former English West Indies.

The Arab states have formed their own regional association although development is retarded as a consequence of the replacement of oil by other energy sources. Some instability exists in the Arab Middle East as a consequence of internal instability and political extremism. United Nations controls, however, manage to dampen these instabilities.

The United Nations has assumed administration of outer space and the resources of the seas and, in particular, assures that all nations have equitable access to these resources. The United Nations also carries out arms control activities. A United Nations force also has nuclear weapons—to be used only under command of a Standing Committee and upon the authorization from the political organs of the United Nations. England has abandoned her independent nuclear force, as has France, although the European organization possesses a small nuclear force. Only the United States, the Soviet Union, and China possess individual national nuclear forces; and these are far smaller than presently existing forces. Moreover, there has been a widespread distribution of effective ABM systems to other nations and to regional organizations.

In case of civil war, the theories of neutrality and of intervention only in behalf of existing regimes have been discarded in favor of collective intervention organized by or under the terms of resolutions passed by the political organs of the United Nations and consonant with a universally agreed-upon set of standards. Thus interventions against existing governments would be permissible when these governments discriminated among their nationals according to race or religion (or some other unreasonable standard) with respect to their political rights; or when human or essential political rights were denied; or when access to information or freedom of movement was denied. The universal organization, however, would not authorize action prior to the outbreak of organized violence in the absence of a demonstration of widespread support for the demands of those in revolt, or except in circumstances that indicated that change could be brought about according to some reasonable schedule of human costs. When the revolutionaries sought to deny any of the specified values, the universal organization would authorize intervention in support of the existing government. Where the values were unclear or contested, the universal organization would authorize intervention on the side of those who would permit international supervision during a transitional period to help to enforce the stated values. Under these standards intervention under international authorization occurred in South Africa in favor of the blacks, in Kenya in favor of the whites, and in Cuba in favor of the democrats (prior to accession to the United States). In all these cases intervention was against the existing regime. In the cases of Uruguay and Venezuela, intervention occurred in favor of the existing governments.

Where possible, these interventions were organized by appropriate regional groupings whose findings of fact were subject to approval and whose decisions to act were subject to authorization by the universal organization, as in the Kenyan case. Occasionally, the actions were collective actions by the entire universal organization, as in the South African case, and occasionally by one or a few states, as when the United States, Mexico, and Brazil organized the action against Cuba. The case of Hungary was the only instance in which the United Nations authorized intervention against both the existing government and the findings of the appropriate regional body. In this case action was organized by the Western European organization when the Eastern European unit supported the Hungarian government in its repressive measures.

DISCUSSION

These models obviously are not exhaustive of the alternatives that the future may provide. Also even within the models, depending upon variations in the parameters, there are multiple complications we have not even begun to sketch. As mentioned earlier, these are not equilibrium models. They are intended merely to permit discussion of the range of variation potentially inherent in the existing world situation. Despite these deficiencies in the models and in the discussion necessarily based upon them, it should nonetheless be apparent that national decisions seemingly unrelated to normative consequences may have extremely important side effects with respect to these normative consequences. For instance, present American policy designed to prevent nuclear diffusion may perhaps permit maintenance of a bipolar world with the prospects for world order inherent in that bipolarism. It may alternatively fail to prevent diffusion and also fail to encourage such alternatives as a European system, thus bypassing either a stabilized bipolarity or a four bloc system for a nonstable bloc system in which the restraints of international law are poorly developed. Even though bipolarity may provide a less stable legal structure than a "balance of power" system there are not improbable alternatives even less favorable for the development of international law than loose bipolarity. Even the détente, which is commonly regarded as one of the foundations of an expanded world legal order, may have the opposite consequences. It may help destabilize bipolarity at a time when the possible alternatives are worse from the standpoint of world order.

There are possible conflicts between the policies best designed to secure law-abiding behavior and those best designed to maintain the strategic interests of the United States. For instance, every time the United States engages in a Bay of Pigs, a Guatemalan coup, or even in bombing north of the seventeenth parallel in Vietnam, it weakens the already loosened fabric of international law. The failure to engage in such actions may injure American strategic interests. Yet American strategic interests, although not identical with the prospects for world order, are not unrelated to them. Sacrifice of these strategic interests may impede the development either of any kind of universalistic system of norms or of one consonant—or at least not inconsistent—with our values and interests. Questions of this kind are always difficult to assess; they involve choices at the margin, large uncertainties, and competing values. None is susceptible to dogmatic or facile answer such that one can assert "policy A builds law and policy B tears law apart," even with respect to the particular norm at issue. The argument that the best way to build law is to act lawfully, although not entirely incorrect, obviously rests on a form of legal determinism that will not withstand serious analysis. Moreover, there are interests and values other than those that flow from the development of a system of international law.

Thus the truism that the United States has an interest in upholding, maintaining, and enlarging the area of international law obscures as much as it clarifies. There can be little doubt that if the United States could choose that world of all possible worlds in which it wished to participate as a nation, it would be a world organized according to strong principles of international law. It would be a world that maintained freedom of political choice for the peoples of the various nations; access to supranational tribunals in cases of violations of human rights by national governments; noninterference in the affairs of individual nations except perhaps in pursuit of an international bill of rights; the outlawry of the use of force except in the pursuit of recognized common interests; objective standards for recognition; international governance of space, the seas, and Arctic regions; international control of violent fluctuations of the commodity markets; and developed supranational law in those geographic regions and functional areas where a common framework of customs, values, and economic development permit a highly developed set of common legal rules. Yet it defies at least this writer's imagination to project an institutional development that would support this kind of body of law. In a world in which we must choose from among a set of bad alternatives the least bad, we will continue to be confronted with hard and ambiguous choices. Some policies may seem best adapted to supporting the development of international institutions, others to implementing one or another international norm (perhaps at the expense of still some other international norm), others to promoting American strategic interests or political values. Some policies may seem to provide the greatest opportunity for the development of world order if they succeed. These may possibly create the greatest risks for maintaining even that minimal degree of world order we presently have should they fail.

No discussion at this level of generality could hope to provide any hard answers to such questions. The choices that will face our statesmen will be choices defined by the actual sets of circumstances that confront them—circumstances that are at best only vaguely predictable now. A discussion at this level of generality, however, may reveal some of the reasons why the choices are hard, what alternatives may compete for our attention, and what factors may play a role in our decision. It may also provide a framework within which our thoughts about the matter can be organized in advance, so that the choices may be perceived in terms of their intermediate as well as of their immediate contexts and consequences.

We have recently passed through an episode in which the United States sought to have the United Nations punish the Soviet Union for refusing to contribute toward the support of institutional measures that were incompatible with perceived Soviet interests. Suspension of Soviet membership obviously would have been incompatible with the functioning of the United Nations in a bipolar world. Yet in the absence of a genuine world consensus on institutions and values, was it not perhaps unreasonable to expect the Soviet Union to use its scarce resources to support measures designed to bring about a world community not in accord with Soviet values? Was not Soviet recalcitrance at least in part the consequence of an effort to shift the burden of intervention from the United States and its allies to an international organization whose useful functions in the international system were different from those which we attempted to impose on it? No doubt from the standpoint of the values of the United States wanted to implement, United Nations ventures in the Congo, among others, were perceived as helpful. No doubt American and Western European intervention in the Congo was made easier by reason of United Nations cover. Perhaps failure to act would have produced chaos in the Congo and the disintegration of the Congolese state. Perhaps alternatively, though not surely, UN intervention prevented successful revolution by a radical Congolese grouping that would have squandered the resources of the Congo and that would have fettered the Congolese people with a bloodthirsty and inefficient tyranny. Surely, however, the actions taken were not designed to secure Soviet support for the peace-keeping activities of the United Nations, or for the role of the Secretary-General; nor were they even designed to demonstrate to the Asian and African nations the development of "objective" and impartial enforcement procedures by the United Nations.

The UN has recently taken measures against the Rhodesians. It has yet to take measures against the Soviet bloc or other authoritarian nations for violations of human rights within national territory. Should action against Rhodesia be opposed on the ground either that it is a violation of domestic jurisdiction or that the Asian and African states will not support actions against violations of human rights when these involve the rights of white people? Alternatively should such actions be supported because they are politically expedient, because they constitute a first step toward widespread UN jurisdiction in the area of the violation of human rights, or because any good that can be supported constitutes an appropriate basis for action? How do such decisions affect the structural processes of international law and interact with other decisions to promote one or another of the alternative possible international systems?

We have not begun to discuss these questions; yet clearly they deserve systematic discussion. Generally laymen and also scholars have argued in terms of simplistic notions and of projections of existing lines of development. If scientific answers to these important questions cannot be obtained and if intuition will prove more important than quantification, symbolic logic, and sustained argument, yet systematic discussion is likely to reveal interconnections, turning points, and unconsidered alternatives that are essential to informed intuition and to selected empirical investigations that are related to these informed intuitions.

We have adumbrated the truism that law and international organization, if pursued too single-mindedly, may undercut the development of both law and organization. We can all agree that it would be unwise either to overstress the impact of the social and political structure of world politics on the normative structure of the international system or to fail to recognize the relationship between the two. We know that placing our ambitions too low forsakes the possibility of progress and that placing our ambitions too high may assure retrogression. What we lack is a sense of ordered relationship between national policy, international organization, international norm, and international system. In short, we are ignorant where we need knowledge and full of abstract generalization where we require articulated theory.

4.

Quincy Wright: On Legal Tests of Aggressive War

RICHARD A. FALK

QUINCY WRIGHT's central concern during his long and remarkably productive life was with the status of war in human affairs. As a scholar he studied the subject ceaselessly, and from many angles. As a human being he worked with steadfast effort to promote a peaceful world. In these multiple roles as scholar/activist/humanitarian Quincy Wright placed great stress on the importance of international law, and he wrote often and influentially on the relevance of law to war. One exemplary feature of Quincy Wright's achievements as man and scholar involved his extraordinary capacity to separate realms of scholarly analysis from realms of emotional commitment and fortuitous affiliation. In his legal analysis, Quincy Wright embodied the spirit of science, relying upon impartial inquiry into rules and facts so as to produce "the right answer."

In this sense, Quincy Wright, better than many of his professional contemporaries, reconciled his views about foreign policy with his judgment about the requirements of international law on specific occasions of controversy within his nation of affiliation. He believed profoundly that world peace depended on conforming foreign policy to guidelines set forth in binding instruments of international law. He believed that patriotism (as well as idealism) required all governments, including his own, to abide by legal prohibitions upon recourse to force in international society. At the same time, Quincy Wright was neither a "legalist" nor "moralist," nor did

Excerpts reprinted by permission from the *American Journal of International Law,* Vol. 66, No. 3, July 1972. Copyright © 1972 by the American Society of International Law.

he underestimate the complexity of international conflict. Indeed, it was his awareness of the extra-legal setting that shaped his conviction that *clear rules* were needed; otherwise, each side acts as it wishes, and finds sufficient comfort in a self-serving selection of facts, arguments, and justifications that are always available in the wider contexts of choice and action to support partisan claims to wage war.

I. First-Order Constraints

In this comment I would like to consider Quincy Wright's views on the legal status of force in relation to some other leading positions, and then reflect on its relevance to contemporary problems of world order. It seems helpful to anchor the discussion by reference to the relevance of law in a specific situation of controversy. I have chosen a celebrated panel of the American Society of International Law held in 1963 to consider the legal status of the "Cuban Quarantine," the American interdiction in 1962 of Soviet efforts to deploy nuclear missiles in Cuba.[1]

Quincy Wright concluded that the unilateral imposition of the quarantine by the United States

> cannot be reconciled with its obligations under the United Nations Charter to settle its international disputes by peaceful means and to refrain from use or threat of force in international relations (Article 2, paragraphs 3, 4), except for individual or collective self-defense against armed attack (Article 51), under authority of the United Nations (Articles 24, 39), or on invitation of the state where the force is to be used (Article 2, paragraph 1)[2]

Professor Wright explained his reasons for reaching this legal conclusion, and acknowledged that "The quarantine proved to be a means for pursuing what the United States regarded as a defensive policy, not out of proportion to the feelings in the United States that the missiles constituted a dangerous threat," but he did regard the quarantine as a violation of Article 51 because self-defense was legal under the Charter only if a prior armed attack occurred.[3] In essence, Quincy Wright believed that the rules of law should be construed in accordance with their natural meaning and by canons of impartial construction such as one would expect from a third party. In this sense, Quincy Wright felt that a scholar had a primary mission to be as scientific as possible about the relationship between law and policy and that it was much more important for the citizen-scholar to insist that his

1. "Cuban Quarantine: Implications for the Future," 1963 Proceedings, Am. Soc. Int. Law 1–18.
2. Wright, "The Cuban Quarantine," *ibid.* 9–10, at 9.
3. *Ibid.*, at 10; by implication also Professor Wright rejected the claim of regionalist prerogatives relied upon by Abram Chayes.

government abide by international law than to bend the law to suit the momentary needs of the prince. Professor Wright's deeper position, of course, was that the prince—indeed that all princes—needed above all a reciprocally effective system of war-restraining law, and that such a system, given the absence of any international government, depended on rule-oriented patterns of behavior.

Abram Chayes, who had been Legal Adviser of the Department of State at the time of the Cuban missile crisis and was continuing to serve in that capacity, also appeared on that Panel with Professor Wright. Chayes said that the Department of State was his "client," and it was to be expected, particularly since he had helped frame the official position on the missile crisis, that he would argue that the imposition of the quarantine had been legal, specifically that it was a valid exercise of power under regional security arrangements that existed in the Western Hemisphere.[4] It seems equally clear that, if the Soviet Union had sought a regional basis for the validation of its coercive policies in Eastern Europe and if the United States Government was eager to oppose those policies on legal grounds, then Chayes, as Legal Adviser, would have produced a legal denunciation based on the Charter's prohibition on non-defensive uses of force. In other words, international law serves to generate arguments in support of foreign policy postures, and the policy adequacy of a given action has to be assessed by criteria other than law—did it work? Was it repudiated by international or regional organs? Will it be respected as a basis for national action in the future? Does it commend itself as a constructive initiative to men of reason, stature, and good will?[5] Unlike Quincy Wright, Chayes regards the relevance of the Charter as problematic to specific undertakings:

> The normative provisions of the Charter are expressed in general language. Their content is not self-evident or immanent in the words themselves . . . Content and meaning are built up by accumulating experience, by developing public attitudes, and by the action of political bodies and other organs charged with the vindication of the norms.[6]

On a more jurisprudential level, Chayes felt that discussion of the central issue "Was the quarantine legal?" was "bound to elicit over-generalized and useless answers." He instead applauded the tendency of American lawyers "to think of norms only in relation to remedy," which serves "to refine,

---

4. Professor Chayes developed his position on legal prerogatives more fully in "Law and the Quarantine of Cuba," 41 Foreign Affairs 550 (July, 1963), and "The Legal Case for U.S. Action on Cuba," 47 Dept. of State Bulletin 763 (1962).

5. Professor Chayes makes no distinction, it seems, between the communication of claims to act in specified ways and the assessment of the legal status of these claims in terms of norms of restraint. What assessment is possible involves the effects of policy on the objectives of law (*e.g.*, minimization of violence, maintenance of freedom of the high seas, discouragement of aggression, etc.), but not the policy itself.

6. Chayes, "Remarks," note 1 above, at 13.

focus, narrow, and ripen questions so that they can be raised and decided within a professional framework, by professional techniques, and, more important, with due regard for the limitations of law as an instrument of social order and control."[7] And in this sense, the role of law involves shaping policy in a variety of ways, to quote Chayes once more: "For instance, broad legal notions, such as the principle of least possible use of force, were obviously among important considerations which argued for the quarantine rather than more drastic measures."[8] I have quoted Chayes at some length to develop some aspects of a position in American legal thinking, which he well exemplified, which has tended to exert much more influence in the United States than the approach to law and force that I have attributed to Quincy Wright.[9]

Why is this the case?

—Chayes' view dissolves the tension between the international lawyer *qua* scientific scholar and international lawyer *qua* citizen, or even more, *qua* public servant;[10]

—Chayes' view permits the international lawyer to conceive of the relevance of international law to policy in a more realistic way, as marginal and implementing rather than as decisive, and therefore avoids a widespread tendency within American society and elsewhere to dismiss international law altogether because governments violate it whenever vital interests are at stake;

—Chayes' view concentrates on the policy nexus, the process of decision by government leaders, and therefore avoids the static bias of detached judgment;

—Chayes' view, however unintentionally, serves the interests of a principal government such as the United States, which relies on its military power to sustain its dominant position in world affairs and wants to have maximum discretion to use force without altogether renouncing its claims to idealism.

What are the costs of rejecting Quincy Wright's approach to these matters?

—International law tends to be diminished in its capacity to enable judgment of the legal status of controversial government action;

—International law tends to become politicized by its primary presentation as a means for implementing a government policy and the international lawyer becomes a servant of the prince rather than his independent auditor;

7. *Ibid.*, at 11–12.
8. *Ibid.*, at 11.
9. Of course, the basis of this influence is an overall view of the relation between law and change that has prevailed in the United States, especially with regard to the discretion available to judicial decision-makers. The "openness" of the law in other decisional settings is a natural sequel.
10. There is, of course, a strong psychological impulse to harmonize these distinct roles played by an international lawyer.

—Restraints on the use of force in international life tend to be weakened as a government can always find some legal reasons to accompany claims to act and, therefore, the whole struggle to confine force to circumstances of defensive necessity is severely curtailed.

It was Quincy Wright's view that the best course of action, on almost every occasion involving the use of force, involved respect for the Charter prohibitions:

> . . . law itself, by formulating rules of order and principles of justice, can be a powerful aid to statesmen and others who wish a peaceful world, in which fair competition in ways of life, forms of government, and systems of thought and economy can make for human progress.[11]

Professor Wright also regarded the meaning of the Charter as "fairly clear" despite the generality of the norms and the failure of the United Nations (or other legal bodies) to reach an agreed definition.[12] In this sense, Quincy Wright is affirming the capacity and duty of the international lawyer to answer the big question (Is the quarantine legal?) that Chayes dismisses with cultivated disdain. In essence, Wright stands for the view that international law is more significant if it stresses its relevance to *realms of order* rather than to *realms of action*.

At that same Panel meeting, Dean Acheson posited an extreme disjunction of the relationship between law and policy as it applied to the Cuban missile crisis:

> I must conclude that the propriety of the Cuban quarantine is not a legal issue. The power, position and prestige of the United States had been challenged by another state; and law simply does not deal with such questions of ultimate power—power that comes close to the sources of sovereignty.[13]

With this single rhetorical flourish, Acheson virtually nullifies the entire Charter enterprise, and confirms as fact and precept the discretionary basis of the use of force in world affairs. Mr. Acheson was most candid in saying that he

> would be surprised if practical men, trained in legal history and thought, had devised and brought to a state of general acceptance a principle condemnatory of an action so essential to the continuation of preeminent power as that taken by the United States last October. . . .

11. Wright, The Role of Law in the Elimination of War 43 (Manchester, Manchester University Press, 1961).

12. *Ibid.*, at 64.

13. Acheson, "Remarks," note 1 above, 13–15, at 14; a perceptive critical discussion of the Acheson position is found in Henkin, How Nations Behave 251–271 (New York, Praeger, 1968).

No law can destroy the state creating the law. The survival of states is not a matter of law.[14]

We are never told by Mr. Acheson why the survival of the United States was threatened by the prospect of missile deployments in Cuba, and so the invocation of a survival context is itself a matter for unilateral appreciation. We are never told, a reality to which Quincy Wright was always attuned, what are the reciprocal implications of such an approach (when an interdiction claim is invoked by a rival on the basis of *its* images of survival rather than by ourselves). Quincy Wright was keenly aware of the extent to which world tensions and conflict arise out of contradictory appreciations of reality that result from distorted perceptions of ideological predispositions.[15] This awareness made him deeply suspicious of self-serving rhetoric of the sort relied upon by statesmen justifying force and for the imperative need to posit and support clear rules of order, even if some sacrifice in the pursuit of justice took place. More specifically, Professor Wright pointed out to the audience that Nikita Khrushchev, the Soviet Premier at the time, had stated that the deployment of Soviet missiles in Cuba had a purely defensive intent, being deployed against threats and plans for attack originating in the United States.[16]

Certainly one of the most fundamental policy issues of the day involves the choice among these three legal positions on the status of national claims to use force in international affairs: I—Quincy Wright: claims are subject to sufficiently clear legal guidelines that should be adhered to by all governments on all occasions; II—Abram Chayes: claims are subject to secondary legal guidelines that help limit national uses of force and minimize disruptive effects on world order; III—Dean Acheson: claims are subject only to extra-legal considerations of prudence and conscience.

The choice of position and rationale remains one of the central issues confronting international lawyers at the present time. It may be that the most compelling position is midway between I and II involving a general presumption of clear guidelines, rebuttable by a context of exceptional circumstances that make the dominant recourse to force serve "defensive" or "humanitarian" purposes. My own shift in recent years from adherence to I to a position midway between I and II arises from a consideration of the Israeli position in the Middle East war of 1967 and the Indian position in relation to the Indo-Pakistan war of 1971.[17] In both instances position I

14. *Ibid.*
15. See, *e.g.*, Boulding, The Image (Ann Arbor, University of Michigan Press, 1956); White, Nobody Wanted War: Misperception in Vietnam and Other Wars (New York, Anchor Books, rev. ed., 1970).
16. Note 6 above, at 16; see also comments on p. 17.
17. My shift in position relates only to *initiation* of border-crossing war by striking the first blow. Such temporal priority does not, I am now convinced, provide an adequate test of aggression. The adoption of a qualified contextual approach on initiation of war does not imply the extension of this approach to the legal status of territories acquired by force, or to the permissibility of retaining such territories.

tends to induce an inference of illegality, whereas the claim to use force seems justified by reference to a variety of *objective* features of the context: major provocation, justifiable necessity, consequential harm of inaction. In adopting a position I/II it is important to exclude ideological factors associated with normative preferences of the claimant government; as such, the sort of claims made by the United States in the Dominican Republic in 1965 or the Soviet Union in Czechoslovakia in 1968 were not of a character that could overcome the presumption of illegality associated with the use of force across an international boundary.[18] In my view, to clarify position I/II it will be necessary to specify, to the extent possible, the contextual factors that overcome the presumption of illegality and create the legal basis for recourse.[19] These factors would then provide guidelines for planning and judging governmental action.

To further clarify position I/II it would also be necessary to relate the claim to act with the process of its implementation.[20] In this second context of decision and judgment relevant considerations include proportionality, minimum use of force necessary to achieve legitimate objectives, adherence to conduct rules and standards embodied in the laws of war, limitation of claims to the correction of abuses and deference to international procedures.

We need a carefully delineated view, in accordance with the ideas set forward in the last two paragraphs, of position I/II. Two things are to be noted relevant to Quincy Wright's contributions: first, that position I/II is really a deviation from position I, as most clearly set forth in his work, rather than a compromise between I and II;[21] second, that the essential feature of position I/II is to accept position I as the standard basis of guidance and judgment; the orientation of position II becomes operative

18. For a useful appreciation of the tendency by rival Superpowers to erode Charter prohibitions on the use of force, see Franck, "Who Killed Article 2(4)?", 64 A.J.I.L. 809 (1970).

19. Among the important efforts to specify or avoid contextual factors are Bowett, Self-Defence in International Law (Manchester, Manchester University Press, 1958); Brownlie, International Law and the Use of Force by States (Oxford, Oxford University Press, 1963); McDougal and Feliciano, Law and Minimum World Public Order (New Haven, Yale University Press, 1961); J. Stone, Aggression and World Order (Berkeley, University of California Press, 1958).

20. I would differentiate between four principal phases on the international force continuum relevant for legal analysis:

I	II	III	IV
Recourses and Threats	Conduct and Execution of Claim	Termination of Violence	Assessment of Responsibility and Punishment

Each of these phases could be analyzed in relation to the three main positions taken by the quarantine panelists.

21. This assertion intends to emphasize the clarity of the prohibition (Position I) that can be qualified only by sustaining the burden to establish exceptional qualifying circumstances. Therefore Position I/II is defined exclusively by reference to I, and does not attempt to take contextual factors routinely into account as an offset to the clarity of the Charter prohibitions on threats or uses of force.

only when exceptional features of the context specified in advance overcome the presumption of illegality attaching to the initiating user of international force.

II. Second-Order Constraints

Professor Wright's views on recourse to force were complemented by a very clear and consistent analysis of what international law contributed in the peacekeeping context when war was under way. He set forth these views in an important article published in this journal in 1935, and reiterated them in numerous contexts, perhaps with most impact in his article "The Prevention of Aggression."[22]

The essence of Quincy Wright's position was to clarify the League's notion that the aggressor was the actor that refused to stop fighting and to obey the provisional measures enacted by community organs. He was advancing an interpretation of the League Covenant as clarified by League practice in conflict situations. In these situations the fundamental test of aggression is the acceptance by the parties of a proposal for armistice, or as it is now generally called, cease-fire. The government that refuses to accede to the armistice proposal becomes the aggressor, independently of responsibility for initiating hostilities in the first instance. Wright pointed out that this effort to restore peace had been successful in several League cases: ". . . the Greco-Bulgarian affair of 1926, the Shanghai affair of 1932, and the Leticia affair of 1932." Specifically, "an invitation to both parties to stop fighting . . . resulted in a suspension of hostilities and an eventual pacific settlement of the controversy."[23] In Manchuria and the Chaco cases, the League approach had failed, but Wright persuasively discounts these instances. Wright's endorsement of this cease-fire approach is based on its operational clarity. As he puts it,

> It is seldom difficult to determine whether armed force is actually being employed. It also is not difficult to determine whether the proposed armistice has been accepted, and, in case an impartial commission has been dispatched to the spot, whether it is being observed.[24]

In a sense, one is dealing with functionally distinct issues: confining recourse to war within legal boundaries; assuring termination of ongoing hostilities.[25]

Quincy Wright makes it clear that the effectiveness of the cease-fire ap-

22. "The Concept of Aggression in International Law," 29 A.J.I.L. 373 (1935); "The Prevention of Aggression," 50 *ibid.* 514 (1956).

23. Note 22 above, 29 A.J.I.L. 373, 389 (1935).

24. *Ibid.*, at 391.

25. Quincy Wright also acknowledges a third category of concerns involving the assessment of responsibility for a wrongful use of international force.

proach depends on a *rapid* crystallization of an armistice proposal by the League. In Wright's view the speed of issuance assures that the momentum of war will not have proceeded so far as to give one of the parties a major stake in continuing with it or securing the fruits of military success already achieved. There are, according to Wright, several elements of obtaining rapid results: an agreed definition of aggression that commands widespread respect; a set of notions that combines cease-fire with measures promoting its observance, including a line of separation and the provision of a supervisory presence.[26]

In the Charter context, Wright accepts the notion of collective security on behalf of the victim of aggression as more fundamental than it was in the League context. Therefore, more stress is placed on identifying which side is the aggressor as the basis of response in the face of ensuing hostilities. For Wright, even without the political fissures that emerged after World War II, the Charter approach could not be applied effectively and authoritatively without a clear definition of aggression that was acceptable to and taken seriously by principal governments.[27] However, Professor Wright notes that the idea of provisional measures has been carried forward in Article 40 of the Charter, and in a number of instances of ensuing conflict the Security Council and General Assembly have suspended judgment on responsibility for recourse in order to mobilize a consensus as to provisional measures relating to cease-fire and withdrawal from occupied territory.[28]

It is Wright's view that "the value of such measures . . . depends upon the speed with which they are applied." He goes on to observe that

> Clearly, if hostilities have resulted in considerable changes in the *de facto* possession of territory . . . a cease-fire order based upon the territorial situation before hostilities, might be difficult to enforce. Thus the justice and effectiveness of provisional measures depends upon the speed with which they are ordered. They should be issued before hostilities have changed the situation.[29]

Again we have here a clear position on the problem of second-order constraints where there is no consensus as to responsibility for initiating hostilities, either for reasons of confused facts, perceptions or interests. Professor Wright, therefore, accepts the difficulty of applying even an agreed

26. *Ibid.*, at 395.
27. Note 22 above, 50 A.J.I.L. 514, 519 (1956) (". . . a suitable definition of aggression seems central in the entire work of the United Nations."). *Cf.* recent concerns of comparable character from most diverse sources: Ferencz, "Defining Aggression as a Means to Peace" (pamphlet) (New York, B'nai B'rith International Council, 1972); *idem*, above, p. 491; Chkhikvadze and Bogdanov, "Who is Hindering Progress in the Definition of Aggression," International Affairs 22 (Oct. 1971).
28. Note 27 above, 50 A.J.I.L. 514, 530 (1956).
29. *Ibid.*

definition of aggression "during active hostilities" and suggests that "it appears to be wise, as indeed the experience of the League and the United Nations suggests, to utilize a simpler test of aggression dependent upon response to 'provisional measures.'"[30] Thus India became the aggressor after it failed to adhere to the General Assembly resolution calling for an immediate cease-fire and withdrawal from occupied Pakistani territory; similarly, Israel in relation to the cease-fire resolution issued in the course of the 1967 war.[31]

Wright's views on cease-fire follow from according the maintenance of peace absolute primacy as a world order value. As I have indicated in discussing recourse norms, position I/II acknowledges the possibility of legal recourse to war under carefully defined exceptional circumstances. Therefore, a claimant government might be entitled to use force *until* it has accomplished its mission, and the international community might be obliged to shape provisional measures accordingly. But suppose there is a conflict between adherence to position I by the voting majorities in the political organs of the United Nations and adherence to position I/II by the claimant government? Or suppose the relevant consensus in the Security Council or the General Assembly rejects the contention that recourse to force is justified by the exceptional circumstances? Or suppose that the political organs fail to act rapidly in accordance with Professor Wright's stress on this element of effective provisional measures?[32]

As with issues of recourse, the basic need is for a fundamental position, such as that initially evolved by Professor Wright in relation to League norms and practice, softened by guidelines identifying exceptional circumstances. It is not at all clear that, if the claim to use force qualifies under position I/II, it is necessarily desirable to obtain a rapid call for provisional measures or to ignore the need to rectify manifest abuse of a flagrant character. For instance, if the recourse to force is based in large part on an effort to prevent genocide or to relieve national territory from a burden of extreme provocation, then the reason for recourse needs to be embodied in

---

30. *Ibid.*

31. There are obvious difficulties that arise from the employment of diverse tests of aggression. For instance, India and Israel are "aggressor" states in relation to provisional measures, but not in relation to the initiation of hostilities. There is also the question as to whether on each occasion of armed conflict at least one actor is responsible for its initiation. Put more concretely, does it follow from sustaining the burden of exceptional circumstances to overcome Charter prohibitions that the other side is guilty of aggression? By upholding Israel's recourse to force first in 1967 is one necessarily suggesting that the Arab governments were guilty of prior aggression? This is a difficult problem area that requires detailed analysis.

32. Clearly, the effectiveness and authorizativeness of UN initiatives are an important dimension in the overall assessment of national behavior. Deference to third-party procedures depends, in all social orders, on their capacity to implement their decisions and the degree to which these decisions generate respect. The transition from a self-help to a police system depends heavily on such considerations, especially if the transition is accomplished contractually by voluntary action.

the substance of the call for cease-fire.[33] In this sense, the emphasis on speed may be too mechanical or, put differently, speed of action may be relevant only in those situations in which the presumption of invalidity attaching to a claim to initiate or use force is not overcome nor is there present a practical basis for organizing an effective form of collective security. That is, the approach to provisional measures urged by Professor Wright seems best conceived of as a third-order constraint: first-order constraints—prevention; second-order constraints—indulgence of limited claim to use or threaten force or collective security on behalf of victim of invalid claim to use or threaten force; third-order constraints—provisional measures to restore peace as quickly as possible.

III. Concluding Comment

Professor Wright's views on these issues will have an enduring relevance for international lawyers concerned with the central war/peace issues. His approach to these issues combined the technical virtuosity of a master craftsman with the essential clarity of a consistent jurisprudential orientation. Professor Wright's blend of wisdom and jurisprudence led in the direction of formulating clear tests easily applied both to stop wars from starting and to keep them from continuing. It remains controversial among international lawyers as to whether this is an acceptable interpretation of either what the law is or what it ought to be. As I have indicated, my position on the continuum of approaches to these problems is closer to the textualist than contextualist, but intermediate to the extent of allowing exceptional recourse to context so as to overcome textual presumptions.[34]

I hope it is clear that my partial disagreement with Professor Wright's views on these crucial matters is entirely consistent with my admiration for his contributions as a scholar and an activist. Part of Quincy Wright's greatness certainly involved his passionate commitment to serious dialogue, a steady preference for discussion and response over passive and mechanical assent.

As an activist, Quincy Wright symbolized an exemplary tradition by the

33. In this respect I think it is important to move beyond a mechanical view of "peace at any price" to take account of extreme justice considerations. Important insight into this complexity is to be found in the works of Stone and McDougal-Feliciano cited in note 19 above.

34. Position I needs to be more explicitly linked to certain minimum conditions of order within the international system, including peacekeeping capacities and impartial decision-making by the political organs of the United Nations. The non-fulfillment of Charter expectations in Chapter VII certainly has some bearing on the interpretation of rights and duties under Arts. 2(3), 2(4), 33, 51, 54, and so on. The Charter's approach to the control of war was to a certain extent organic, and the failure of a part means the alteration of the status of other parts. Certainly, this is one type of answer, not by any means the only satisfactory one, to Professor Franck's question about who killed Art. 2(4).

extent to which he believed that his own government would serve its own interests best by respecting the emerging law governing recourse to force. His early opposition to the American involvement in the Vietnam war on legal grounds seems vindicated even by reference to the most parochial conceptions of national interests.[35] It was Quincy Wright's most profound belief that guidelines provided by international law were both clear and wise enough for all governments to follow. It may yet be that the cause of peace depends on converting Quincy Wright's vision and scholarly work into operative codes of bureaucratic behavior around the world. In any event, we will need to take account of Quincy Wright's work at every step of the long and arduous path leading to the creation of a peaceful and just system of world order, and if we should get there, we will look back upon Quincy Wright's achievement with even greater gratitude and reverence than is now possible.

35. Quincy Wright was an original member in late 1966 of the Consultative Council of the Lawyers' Committee on American Policy Towards Vietnam and took a characteristically active and significant role in the work of this Council that has used its scholarly resources and stature to oppose the American involvement in the Vietnam war on legal grounds.

5.

The Beirut Raid and the
International Law of Retaliation

RICHARD A. FALK

I

ON THE NIGHT of December 28, 1968, eight Israeli helicopters took part in an attack on the Beirut International Airport. Israeli commandos descended from six of the helicopters (the other two hovered above) that had landed either on runways or at the hangers of the airport. All commercial aircraft belonging to Arab airlines were destroyed by explosives being placed in the nose-wheel well and in the undercarriage well of each plane. The attack resulted in the destruction of 13 planes whose worth has been estimated to be $43.8 million.[1] Additional damage has been reported done to hangars and other airport installations. Lebanese sources report that two Israeli commandos were injured by gunfire from airport guards. There was no loss of life.

The Beirut raid was defended by the Israeli Government as a retaliation for an attack by two Arabs two days earlier, on December 26, upon an El Al

°Work on this article was completed during my period (1968–69) as a Fellow at the Center for Advanced Study in the Behavioral Sciences at Stanford, California. The atmosphere and facilities of the Center are a great encouragement to this sort of scholarly speculation. William W. Bishop, Jr., Gidon Gottlieb, Leon Lipson, Nadav Safran, Oscar Schachter, and Louis B. Sohn, without in any way endorsing my approach to these difficult issues, gave me the benefit of critical comments of an earlier version.

Semantic choices inevitably imply political values in relation to situations of violent international conflict. This issue of characterization is particularly acute in relation to the para-military violence of irregular forces seeking to overthrow the formal government of a

passenger plane at the Athens Airport. The Athens attack was the work of two men, Mohmand Mohammed Issa and Maher Hussein Suleiman, who belonged to the Popular Front for the Liberation of Palestine.[2] The terrorists used gasoline bombs and submachine guns to attack the El Al Boeing 707 as it was preparing to take off with 41 passengers and a crew of 10 on a flight bound for New York City. One passenger, an Israeli engineer named Leon Shirdan, was killed by machine gun bullets that penetrated his plane window. Israeli reports suggest 86 piercing of the fuselage from the cockpit to the tail, with many of the bullet holes through windows at seat level.[3] Greek authorities have charged the two Arabs before a magistrate with first-degree murder, a crime subject to the death penalty in Greece. The Greek magistrate, Nikolas Stylianikis, disclosed that the defendants said, despite the character of their attack, that they had been under orders from a Popular Front official in Beirut to destroy the El Al plane but not to kill any of the passengers.[4] The two

---

foreign country. It is precisely this kind of problem that faces the analyst of Arab-Israeli violence since the end of the June war of 1967. Those who favor Israel's position refer to these para-military endeavors as "terror" or as "guerrilla activity," whereas those who take the Arab side use terms like "liberation movement" and "freedom fighters." There is no very adequate, non-cumbersome neutral terminology available for the analysis of these relationships. I have tried to balance my characterization of this para-military activity by using both sets of descriptive terms.

1. According to the New York Times, Jan. 5, 1969, Sec. 4, p. 1, the owners of the airlines whose planes were destroyed were not only the Arab governments. Middle East Airlines, which lost eight aircraft, is owned 30 percent by Air France, 5 percent by Lebanese individuals, and 65 percent by Intra Company, an inter-governmental corporation constituted by the Kuwaiti, Qatari, Lebanese, and United States governments. The United States is evidently represented by the Commodity Credit Corporation, which is owed money for wheat sales by Intrabank, a predecessor of Intra Company. Lebanese International Airways, which lost three planes, is 58 percent American-owned. Trans-Mediterranean Airways, which lost two planes, is owned by private Lebanese interests. Early reports indicated that British insurance underwriters had agreed to accept $18 million in claims, rejecting claims from policies that did not cover war risks. Note that, aside from Lebanon, none of the interests affected by the Beirut raid involved principal Arab countries. For a detailed inventory of the damage done in the raid, including damage to terminal facilities, see letter of Jan. 14, 1969, from Assad Kotaite, the Lebanese Representative on the Council of the International Civil Aviation Organization, to the Secretary General of I.C.A.O., WP/4945, Jan. 1, 1969.

2. There are several "liberation" groups constituted by Palestinian refugees. The most important group is the Palestine Liberation Organization now presided over by Yasr Arafat. Arafat earned his reputation, and remains, as the leader of Al Fatah, which is the military commando section of Al Asifa. Then there is a group called the Popular Liberation Corps, with anonymous leadership, and associated with the Palestinian branch of the Baath party. Finally, there is the Popular Front for the Liberation of Palestine headed by Dr. George Habbash. It is the Popular Front, a relatively secondary liberation group, that has claimed credit for the attacks on El Al planes. This Popular Front has been weakened by an internal split which led 600 of its estimated 2,000 members to join the Marxist-Leninist Popular Democratic Front for the Liberation of Palestine in late 1968 and early 1969. See note 16.

3. Cf. Ambassador Shabtai Rosenne of Israel, International Civil Aviation Organization, Minutes of Third Meeting of the Extraordinary Session of the Council, Jan. 23, 1969, p. 5.

4. This account of the arraignment proceedings is based on an article in the New York Times, Dec. 31, 1968, p. 3. This contention must be set off against some of the elements

Arabs had traveled from Beirut on Lebanese travel documents provided stateless persons. The Popular Front for the Liberation of Palestine has been operating in Lebanon rather openly since the June war of 1967, with the knowledge and apparent acquiescence of the Government.

On December 29 Lebanon requested an emergency session of the Security Council to consider its charge that Israel has committed a "wanton and premeditated attack" upon the Beirut International Airport. Israel also requested an urgent meeting of the Security Council to consider its counter-charge that Lebanon was "assisting and abetting acts of warfare, violence, and terror by irregular forces and organizations" against Israel.[5] On December 31, after a considerable period of debate, the Security Council, by a vote of 15–0, unanimously[6] adopted a resolution censuring Israel for the Beirut raid.[6] The preliminary language of the resolution emphasized that the attack was "premeditated and of a large scale and carefully planned nature." There were four operative paragraphs in the resolution indicating that the Security Council:

1. Condemns Israel for its premeditated military action in violation of its obligations under the Charter and the cease-fire resolutions;
2. Considers that such premeditated acts of violence endanger the maintenance of the peace;
3. Issues a solemn warning to Israel that if such acts were to be repeated, the Council would have to consider further steps to give effect to its decisions;
4. Considers that Lebanon is entitled to appropriate redress for the destruction it suffered, responsibility for which has been acknowledged by Israel.[7]

On the evening of December 31 a rocket bombardment of Kiryat Shmona, an Israeli town close to the Lebanese border, was presumed to be the work of the Popular Front, in effect a counter-retaliatory use of force. The attack killed two Israeli civilians; a third inhabitant died from a heart attack that appeared to have been provoked by the raid. The rocket bombardment evi-

---

of the attack itself. The assailants evidently could have proceeded more easily to destroy the plane when it was empty and yet chose to wait until it was loaded for take-off. In fact, the semi-official Egyptian newspaper, Al Ahram, praised the members of the liberation group for their willingness to wait at the airport at risk to themselves until their attack would have maximum effect, and exaggerated the damage done by falsely reporting that the El Al plane was destroyed by fire. Al Ahram, Dec. 27, 1968, p. 1.

5. For the text of the two letters, both dated Dec. 29, 1968, requesting an urgent meeting of the Security Council, see S/8945, S/8946.

6. S/Res/262 (1968). For the reactions of various delegations to this resolution, see S/PV. 1462, Dec. 31, 1968, pp. 7–88. The factual circumstances surrounding the Beirut raid, as well as their divergent interpretations, are well stated by the representatives of Lebanon and Israel in their presentations to the Security Council. See S/PV. 1460, Dec. 29, 1968, pp. 6–27, S/PV. 1461, Dec. 30, 1968, pp. 11–20, 43–62.

7. For full text see S/PV. 1462, p. 6; 6 U. N. Monthly Chronicle 19 (January, 1969); also reprinted below, p. 681.

dently originated from Lebanese territory and the nature of the rockets suggested that it was an act of irregular forces. Israel has not brought this attack to the attention of the Security Council. There have been a series of minor incidents along the frontier between Israel and Lebanon, both before and since the Beirut raid, leading to what has been described by both governments as a deteriorating border situation. Shortly after December 28 Lebanon also complained to the U.N. Mixed Armistice Commission about Israeli reconnaissance flights over Lebanese territory, especially those associated with the inspection of the damage done to the airport.

These basic facts surrounding the Beirut raid are, by and large, not in dispute. The relevant context is, of course, both intricate and indefinite, and might be enlarged by either side in contradictory ways. It seems helpful to consider several additional features of the context. The first is an antecedent one. On July 23, 1968, an El Al plane was hijacked by three Arab guerrillas while the plane was subject to Rome air traffic control and, possibly, still in Italian airspace en route from Rome to Tel Aviv. The plane was forced to land in Algiers. The non-Israeli passengers were released, but the Israeli male passengers and crew were held until August 31, when they were released in exchange for some Arab common law criminals imprisoned in Israel, in a transfer arranged under the auspices of the Red Cross.[8]

The second event, a consequence of the Beirut raid, was the formation of a new government in Lebanon that has indicated its intention to join more actively in the struggle against Israel. At the time of the Beirut raid the Lebanese Premier was Abdullah Yaffi, a moderate on Arab-Israeli relations and the leader who assumed responsibility for keeping Lebanon out of the June war of 1967. Yaffi has now been replaced by Rashid Karami, who has a reputation of favoring a somewhat greater Lebanese effort to achieve military preparedness, as well as the acceptance of a more active rôle in opposing Israel.[9] In June, 1967, Mr. Karami was Prime Minister of Lebanon and ordered the army to advance on Israel, but the army refused to obey.

The third event involved the execution of 14 men by the Iraqi Government in punishment for allegedly spying on behalf of Israel. Eleven of these men were put on public display in Baghdad on January 27, 1968, in a very provocative fashion, involving mass demonstrations to celebrate these hangings and intense public displays of anti-Israeli feelings. This gruesome event was accompanied by reports of Israeli concern about the welfare of 3,000 or so

8. Ambassador Rosenne's initial statement in the Security Council specifically invoked this earlier interference with an international flight of El Al Airlines as a part of the context which conditioned the decision to make the Beirut reprisal raid, *cf.* debate of December 29, 1968, in the Security Council, S/PV. 1460, p. 23. Note that Lebanon was not the sole target; all Arab-owned aircraft at the airport were destroyed. See note 1 for specification. As was made clear at various points by Mr. Rosenne and later by Mr. Tekoah, the Beirut raid was intended as a warning directed at all Arab governments.

9. For statistics on comparative arms expenditures in the Middle East, see Nadav Safran, *From War to War: The Arab-Israeli Confrontation, 1948–1967*, pp. 433–434 (New York: Pegasus, 1969).

Jews living in Iraq and intimations from the Iraqi Government that additional spy trials were going to be held. Nine of the men hanged were Jews and so, too, were many of those (reported to be about 60) being held for subsequent trial as Israeli spies.[10]

Israel, although very explicitly disturbed by these events in Iraq, refrained from any action in retaliation. The reason given was that Israel does not engage in reprisals as a punishment for what is past, but only as a warning about what is to come.[11] Such an explanation of Israeli restraint is not altogether convincing on these grounds because of the prospect of future trials and executions. More convincing as an explanation, however, was the apparently influential diplomatic protests received by Iraq from many parts of the world, including the Pope, the dissociation of other Arab countries from the Iraqi action, and the fear that retaliation might jeopardize further the welfare of the Jews still living in Iraq. Despite these considerations, there was speculation that Israel might launch an air attack against Iraqi military units stationed in Jordan.[12] It may be that one further pressure against retaliation was the adverse reaction of the international community to the Beirut raid. This pressure could not be openly acknowledged by Israeli officials without tending to give weight to the deliberations of U.N. organs that have been growing increasingly hostile to Israel's position in the over-all Arab-Israeli dispute.

A fourth event of some significance is the attack on February 18, 1969, also by four members of the Popular Front for the Liberation of Palestine (apparently operating out of the group's headquarters in Jordan) on an El Al plane as it was about to take off from the Zurich airport. Six persons on board were injured and one of the assailants was killed by an Israeli security guard who was on board the plane. Israel refrained from any specific retaliation; its officials blamed the Zurich incident on "the climate of forgiveness" within international society in relation to Arab governmental responsibility for the Athens attack. The Zurich attack was condemned by U Thant, who stressed the seriousness of this new occurrence, especially its terroristic impact on innocent travelers, and appealed to Israel to refrain from retaliation. Both the repetition of the Athens incident after such a short lapse of time and the recollection of the very strong Israeli act of retaliation at Beirut led to much

10. For an account of the Iraqi hangings see The Economist, Feb. 1, 1969, p. 20. Eight more persons, all Moslems, were reportedly executed for similar crimes on Feb. 20, 1969. A further report indicates that in a third Iraqi spy trial seven more persons have been condemned to death, including two or three Jews and a former Premier of Iraq, Dr. Abdel Rahman Al-Bazzaz. New York Times, March 1, 1969, p. 9.

11. "There is still little talk here of an Israeli military reaction to the hangings, in part because this would contradict the Israeli policy of using raids as warnings rather than reprisals, and also because this might do more harm than good." James Feron, "Israeli Consulting on Ways to Assist the Jews of Iraq," New York Times, Jan. 30, 1969, pp. 1–2, at p. 2.

12. See article by James Feron, "Israel Ponders Issue of Reprisal," *ibid.*, Feb. 2, 1969, Sec. 4, p. 1.

greater attention being given to the Zurich incident than had been earlier given to the Athens incident. Israel used its posture of restraint after Zurich to appeal for world support to secure better protection for its international aviation flights. A formal statement attributed to the Swiss Cabinet indicated that the attack at Zurich was viewed by Switzerland as an act of armed intervention for which Arab governments would be held responsible if investigations disclose governmental links with the attack at Zurich;[13] and, in fact, on February 28 the Swiss Government delivered formal notes of protest to Jordan, Syria, and Lebanon in which the attack at Zurich was condemned and in which each of the three governments were urged to take steps "to prevent any new violations of Swiss territory."[14]

A further event occurred on February 24, 1969, when an Israeli air strike was carried out against two major guerrilla camps of Hama and Maisalun located close to the city of Damascus in Syria. There was unofficial speculation in Israel, as a result of the timing, that these camps were attacked in partial retaliation for the Zurich incident; other motivating circumstances were a bombing of a Jerusalem supermarket a few days earlier that had resulted in the death of two Israeli students and an upsurge of Arab commando activity in the vicinity of the Golan Heights.[15] To attack Al Fatah bases in retaliation for activities of its rival organization, the Popular Front, appears at first to be rather surprising, especially as Al Fatah had not been responsible for any of the attacks on El Al and had indicated its determination, in differentiation from the Popular Front, to focus its use of violent means upon military targets.[16] If Israel, however, regards itself as confronted at this point by an adversary relying primarily on a multifaceted liberation strategy employing a variety of terrorist tactics, then responses would seem rational that weaken this over-all para-military capability or that emphasize the collective responsibility of all liberation groups for any acts-of-terror kinds of responses. Also, far less adverse international reaction seems to arise if retaliatory uses of force by Israel are directed at Arab military and para-military targets. Evidently, for instance, the attacks on the Syrian bases resulted in fairly large Arab casualties and yet failed to provoke any sense of international opposition to the Israeli action. An attack of this kind on bases seems well assimilated, unlike the Beirut raid, into the structure of international expectations about tolerable levels of Arab-Israeli violence, given current levels and forms of conflict and hostility.

13. For various accounts of the Zurich attack and reactions to it, see New York Times, Feb. 19, 1969, pp. 1, 2, 3; Feb. 20, 1969, pp. 1, 3.

14. *Ibid.*, March 1, 1969, pp. 1, 14.

15. See James Feron, "New Israeli Strategy Seen in Raid Near Damascus," *ibid.*, Feb. 25, 1969, p. 3.

16. For some discussion of the differences between the activities of these Arab guerrilla groups, see Dana Adams Schmidt, "An Arab Guerrilla Chief Emerges," New York Times, March 4, 1969, p. 6. On the different ideas of tactics between the two main Arab organizations, Al Fatah and the Popular Front, see another report by Schmidt, *ibid.*, Feb. 20, 1969, p. 2.

II. Certain Special Contentions

Both Lebanon and Israel have advanced very special claims in relation to their conduct.

Lebanese officials have denied any specific responsibility whatsoever for the Athens attack, although the work of the Popular Front, including these specific acts, received praise from Lebanese leaders.[17] The Popular Front has freedom of movement in Lebanon and has been allowed officially to recruit members and support in the Lebanese refugee camps containing some 140,000 Palestinians, and to disseminate propaganda throughout the country. Since the June war this activity has been stepped up and the Popular Front has been allowed to carry on its full program, including the planning of commando raids such as the one that took place at Athens. Premier Yaffi described the work of the Arabs who participated in the Athens attack as "legal and sacred."[18]

Both sides have been very displeased with the outcome within the Security Council. The Lebanese had sought more definite action, including a commitment to Chapter VII sanctions that would assure action against Israel, and not just words of censure.[19] The Arab countries and their supporters have argued that Israel has been found guilty of many Charter violations by the Security Council, but that nothing has been done as yet to secure Israeli compliance with the directives of the U.N. organ.

Israel, in contrast, argued that Security Council condemnation is without any significance because the organ is so one-sided in its composition and its

17. Mr. Boutros, the Lebanese representative who appeared before the Security Council, offered a categorical denial of any governmental responsibility for the Athens incident in the following principal language: ". . . Lebanon cannot be held responsible for acts which were committed by Palestinian refugees outside its territory and of course without its knowledge, and which were committed by Palestinian refugees whose intentions were not known to Lebanon." Furthermore, ". . . If Israel really felt that Lebanon was responsible for the incident at Athens, [why] did it not immediately file a complaint against Lebanon in the Council." S/PV. 1461, Dec. 30, 1968, p. 12.

18. See New York Times, Jan. 5, 1969, Sec. IV, p. 1; for further documentation of Lebanese praise for the work of the Popular Front (and other liberation efforts), see release of Israel's Information Office, "The Israeli Action at the Beirut Airport," Dec. 28, 1968. This document included the following quotation attributed to Mr. Yaffi, the Lebanese Prime Minister, on Nov. 2, 1968: "Fedayeen action is legitimate, and no one can condemn the fedayeen for what they are doing. Their aim is to retrieve their homeland and their plundered rights. . . . Thus, I say, fedayeen action is legal." Israeli sources have also quoted specific Lebanese praise for the perpetrators of the Athens incident. See Mr. Tekoah's statement before the Security Council (S/PV. 1461, pp. 52–55), especially the following excerpt: "The attention of the Lebanese Government has been drawn on numerous occasions to the activities of the terror organizations within its borders. The Lebanese Government, however, has not only continued to condone these activities, but has publicly identified itself with them. Prime Minister Al-Yafi has announced several times that his Government supports terror operations against Israel." S/PV. 1461, p. 52.

19. Mr. Boutros indicated that he had "reservations" about the action of the Security Council because "it did not draw the conclusions to which the findings should have led and it hesitated to order the application of Chapter VII of the Charter to Israel." S/PV. 1462, p. 81.

assessment of responsibility.[20] Israeli spokesmen have pointed to the failure of the Security Council resolution even to refer to the earlier Athens raid or to the general Lebanese rôle in tolerating, at the very least, the active use of its territory to mount terroristic activities against Israel.[21]

From the perspective of international law three very important sets of issues are raised by the Beirut raid and its interrelations with the principal contentions advanced by the adversary states:

1. The quality of governmental accountability for terroristic acts that have some link with territory and the rights of response enjoyed by the state that is the target of such terror; this problem is accentuated in the special case where the locus of terror is within a third state and the tactic is to disrupt the security of commercial airline service;
2. The legal status of action by organs of the United Nations in a situation wherein the decisional process is politically one-sided and voting behavior appears less concerned with the specific merits of the disputes;
3. The residual competence of an aggrieved state to use force against a state that persistently refuses to adhere to the recommendations and decisions of the United Nations.

These areas of concern are central to the realization of security and justice in the contemporary world. In particular, in the Middle East the principal antagonists hold sharply contradictory conceptions of the nature of a just outcome. These conceptions govern the perception of any particular sequence of events, such as those surrounding the Beirut raid.[22] Such events provide a rather clear "case" that helps focus an inquiry into the relationship between law and behavior in the Middle East.

Often particular situations, such as the dispute arising out of the Beirut raid, are instances of more general problems of conflict that may arise in several quite distinct settings throughout international society that call for somewhat distinct treatment. The conflict between "territorial sovereignty" and "liberation" is one such contemporary problem that takes several distinct

20. Mr. Tekoah, in reacting to the adverse judgment of the Security Council, said: "Let no one make the mistake of thinking that the people of Israel might be swayed by inequitable pronouncements." Further, ". . . not Security Council resolutions, but the attitude and actions of the Governments in the area will determine the destiny of the Middle East." S/PV. 1462, p. 52.

21. A somewhat more balanced debate took place at I.C.A.O., Minutes of the First, Second, Third, and Fourth Meetings of the Extraordinary Session of the Council, Jan. 20, 21, 23, 31, 1969.

22. For over-all legal perspective, with representative statements by adversary analysts, see the symposium published under the title "The Middle East Crisis: Test of International Law," 32 Law and Contemporary Problems 1–193 (Winter, 1968); W. V. O'Brien, "International Law and the Outbreak of War in the Middle East," 11 Orbis 692, 723 (1967). For general background see Nadav Safran, From War to War. The Arab-Israeli Confrontation, 1948–1967 (New York: Pegasus, 1969); Fred J. Khouri, The Arab-Israeli Dilemma (Syracuse University Press, 1968). On problems of biased and incompatible perception of identical circumstances in relation to international conflict, see Ralph K. White, Nobody Wanted War: Misperception in Vietnam and Other Wars (Garden City, N. Y.: Doubleday, 1968).

forms in different parts of the world. These distinct settings should be borne in mind whenever a legal analysis is made. Otherwise particularities of fact and policy preference may distort the search for more general principles of assessment.

In a legal system as consensual as international law it is especially important to regard particular cases as instances of general problems. For this reason it seems appropriate to mention some of the other settings wherein the broad policy issues at stake in the Beirut raid are presented.[23]

(1) TERROR, LIBERATION MOVEMENTS, AND THE PROCESSES OF SOCIAL CHANGE

In any social system in which strong claims for change are advanced, the threat or use of force is likely to play a major rôle. International society lacks any effective legislative process that might facilitate peaceful adjustment to changes in value and power structures. The idea of national sovereignty, the sanctity of domestic jurisdiction, and the absence of central sanctioning procedures work against the non-violent implementation of the will of the international community on matters of social and political justice. The modern state often enjoys a great technological advantage over its population in a struggle for political control, especially if the struggle assumes a military form.[24] To overcome this disadvantage, social forces favoring change have used techniques of coercion that give a maximum rôle to their distinctive capabilities. Recourse to terror and random violence has been a principal tactic of the dispossessed, insurgent, revolutionary faction seeking to gain control over the machinery of government of a state. The rise of Communism, the rapid collapse of colonialism, the formation of "liberation" movements to deal with racism and residual colonialism in southern Africa, and the predominance of the Afro-Asian outlook in the General Assembly are among the factors that have given prominence to terror as an instrument of political change and as a "legitimate" tactic of military struggle.[25]

23. There are problems of characterization arising from contradictory interpretation of the *facts* (*e.g.*, extent of knowledge by Lebanese officials of the activities of the Popular Front), of the *legal duties* (*e.g.*, extent of obligation to regulate activity of liberation activities within territory), and of *policy issues* (*e.g.*, conflict between security of territory and recourse to retaliatory force).
24. Although variations of terrain, tradition, and political milieu make certain societies very susceptible to internal opposition of an insurgent character; also, of course, in many parts of Asia, Africa, and Latin America the central government is not able to exert its control over the entire expanse of national territory. Of course the logic of governmental control involves the capacity to control liberation activity as well as the incentive to engage in it.
25. There is also absent any consensus as to the character of political legitimacy in international society. The presence of such a consensus induces moderation in the choice of means and ends of political conflict; its absence induces extremist tactics and strategy, making compromises difficult to specify, and giving a prominent rôle to violence and warfare. See Henry A. Kissinger, "Central Issues of American Foreign Policy," in Kermit Gordon (ed.), Agenda for the Nation 585–614, esp. 585–589 (Washington: Brookings Institution, 1968). The sharpest global cleavage related to political legitimacy is concerned with the status of radical socialism as the basis for organizing a sovereign state. The

The use of an external base to mount an insurgent campaign also enjoys a recent tradition of respect in the West. It is relevant to recall the rôle and status of "governments-in-exile" during World War II and the generally heroic imagery used to describe anti-Nazi terrorism in German-occupied Europe. The idea of "liberation" was very strongly endorsed by conservative governments generally committed to the *status quo* in international society, including the leading colonial Powers. And even in more recent times the United States has given "aid and comfort" to anti-Castro exiles who have proposed to liberate their country by violent means, most spectacularly at the Bay of Pigs in April, 1961.[26]

The principal point is that the politics of terror and the use of exile sanctuaries to disrupt "the enemy" society enjoys an ambiguous status in recent international experience. All principal states in the world have in some situations at least, given their support to such practices. Therefore, the approval given to the liberation movements and their tactics of terror by the Arab governments is quite consistent with the behavior of other governments seeking a revision of the jural *status quo,* but unwilling or unable to make an orthodox military challenge or to negotiate a satisfactory diplomatic compromise.

The status of "liberation" movements and their practices has not been dealt with in any systematic and non-polemical fashion by either diplomats or experts in international law.[27] Governments that have been among the most enthusiastic sponsors of recent liberation activity have also been among the most ardent advocates of adherence to the principle of nonintervention in the affairs of sovereign states.[28] Such an apparent contradiction arises from

---

Arab-Israeli conflict that can be expressed in several distinct fashions, perhaps most fundamentally in terms of the status of Zionist claims, is one in which there is almost no consensus as to legitimacy. There is not even a willingness to accept as settled the right of Israel to exist as a distinct sovereign state.

26. One might also mention the psychological support given exile groups from East Europe by the official Congressional celebration of "Captive Nations' Week" each year. For legal critique see Q. Wright, "Subversive Intervention," 54 A.J.I.L. 521 (1960). In Sec. 101 of the Mutual Security Act of 1951 (in similar legislative enactments of several subsequent years) the U. S. Congress appropriated and earmarked 100 million dollars for escapees from Eastern Europe for a Liberation Legion for Eastern Europe, specifically "to form such persons into elements of the military forces supporting the North Atlantic Organization or for other purposes." 46 A.J.I.L. Supp. 14 (1952). For citations see 2 American Foreign Policy, 1950–1955, Basic Documents 3060, 3119.

27. There is some polemical treatment of these issues in relation to the controversy over the legal status of support for various kinds of "wars of national liberation." But there has been no effort to deal with the generality of claims in light of some consistent body of doctrine.

28. In this regard see the Declaration on Inadmissibility of Intervention, adopted as Resolution 2131 (XX) of the General Assembly on Dec. 21, 1965; 60 A.J.I.L. 662 (1966). In recounting the grave concern of the membership with "the increasing threat to universal peace due to armed intervention and other direct or indirect forms of interference," the Declaration "solemnly declares" in its second numbered paragraph that: ". . . Also, no State shall organize, assist, foment, finance, incite or tolerate subversive, terrorist or armed activities directed towards the violent overthrow of the régime of another State,

simultaneously seeking national autonomy for their own society and the drastic revision of certain foreign societies. The pursuit of such a combination of goals tends to undermine the status of rules of restraint, as well as to diminish the force of legislative claims. One or the other priority would be consistent with legal authority, but not both, manipulated to suit specific preferences of a particular government.

(2) REPRISALS, DEFENSE AGAINST TERROR, AND THE MAINTENANCE OF MINIMUM ORDER

The kind of sporadic violence associated with liberation movements presents difficult choices to the target government, especially if its general orientation is unpopular within the regional and world community. For one thing, the terroristic acts are rarely of sufficient salience to command widespread attention from world public opinion. For another, there is normally a partially successful effort to dissociate the liberation movement from the government of the territory wherein exist facilities for training, financing, sanctuary, and guidance. The sponsoring government attempts to minimize its accountability for the conduct of violent operations by the liberation movements, and there does exist a wide range of variation as to the extent and character of control (or even knowledge) possessed by the territorial government over the conduct of specific guerrilla operations and the formation of more general liberation strategy.[29] Finally, the organized international community at the regional and the world level may endorse the objectives of the liberation movement to such an extent as to make censure, much less opposition, impossible for the target state to obtain. The use of terror as an instrument of change is given a certain legitimacy, then, to the extent that its use receives the endorsement of international institutions.[30]

These problems of response are even greater in a situation in which the terrorists' activity involves attacks upon commercial aircraft carried out in a third country. The Palestinian perpetrators of the Athens incident expected, presumably, to be apprehended and punished under Greek law for the common law crimes that they had committed. But this hardly offsets the damage done, by way of real loss of life and inconvenience to passengers; but even more, by way of making people everywhere quite hesitant to fly on airlines

---

or interfere in civil strife in another State." Such a contradiction between Assembly assertion and liberation practice helps discredit the guidance rôle of international norms and to give comfort for those who would dismiss restraints upon violence as "legalisms."

29. Compare Security Council statements of Mr. Boutros and Mr. Tekoah on the issue of responsibility. S/PV. 1461, pp. 12–20, 46–56.

30. A consensus within the General Assembly is strongly supportive of anti-colonial and anti-racist liberation movements. This attitude of support has assumed a quasi-legislative status because of the law-creating rôle of the Organization. See, generally, Falk, The Status of Law in International Society, Ch. VI (Princeton University Press, 1969).

that are likely to be endangered en route. What is the victim government to do? It hardly makes sense to hold the Greek Government accountable in any way, provided it carries out the provisions of its criminal law and, perhaps, issues a protest to the governments giving sanctuary to a liberation movement. The only effective target of response would involve inflicting unacceptable damage upon those governments that can impose limits upon the tactics used by the liberation movements. In the Arab setting, at least since June, 1967, it is not even clear that the Arab governments have much leverage over the activities of the principal liberation groups within their territory. These groups currently enjoy such strong popular backing that some Arab governments (most obviously Jordan) would risk their stability and jeopardize their popular backing if deliberate and over measures to control a liberation movement were undertaken as official policy.[31]

The government of the target state is presented, then, with a difficult choice among options in trying to devise an effective response against terror of this externally-based variety. Its defensive options are much more likely to be limited to regular sorts of military operations. The extremist commitment of terrorist groups means that their leaders are virtually undeterrable by any kind of responsive violence. In fact, responsive violence of an intergovernmental kind, such as the Beirut raid, may actually prove of positive benefit to the liberation movement, inducing the territorial government to declare openly its support. The most generally effective defensive maneuver is to seek and destroy guerrilla training camps and bases. The only other kind of effective defensive measure is one that inflicts injury upon the foreign government such that it will be induced to suppress or curtail the activities of the liberation movement. In both instances, the target state tends to appear to be making a disproportionate response, the scale is large, and the form of operation is overt. In addition, such military action is undertaken by the regular military forces of the government against a foreign state; as such, the *prima facie* indication of a Charter violation seems much more clearly established, and especially so if the state pursues a domestic or international course that is widely unpopular to begin with. Without centralized impartial fact-finding procedures, the state that acts overtly and on a large scale is much more likely to be regarded as the one that has endangered peace and

31. The statement in the text is a very crude generalization. The effect of exerting governmental control of varying degrees over different categories of liberation group activity varies from country to country in the Arab world and through time in each country. In general, Jordan has been most vulnerable to a takeover from the liberation movement as a result of the strong Palestinian influence within the Jordanian armed forces. The Governments of Syria and the United Arab Republic enjoy greater freedom of action, although within each government élite there is a faction strongly committed to the liberation cause that would be deeply alienated by any interference with the freedom of action of the guerrilla group. The same comment also seems true for Lebanon. In all Arab countries the liberation movement seems popular with the masses, and governmental regulation or suppression would be regarded as a very unpopular policy.

initiated "aggression."[32] In effect, traditional legal criteria create a certain asymmetry in favor of the use of more covert and irregular forms of violence across international frontiers. Of course, this asymmetry should be balanced against the central bias of international law in favor of the incumbent government and the absoluteness of its authority over the territory under its control. Such a government can resist with legal "impunity" claims for change, however widely and deeply supported as just and reasonable.

In such a situation there is hardly an alternative to violence for the advocates of change and jural revision. Similarly, a state that is the target of persistent terror has virtually no effective response, in the event that the foreign government is unable or unwilling to suppress the terroristic tactics of a liberation movement, other than recourse to what is traditionally regarded as "aggressive" war. Israel in 1956, and again in 1967, was "provoked," in effect, by its inability to maintain its national security, given its vulnerability to penetration and harassment by externally based terrorists. In the last analysis, protection may involve conquest of the territory from which the terrorism emanates. The logic of self-help which continues to underlie the search for security in a world of sovereign states may encourage this sort of border-crossing military operation, although the provocation does not constitute "an armed attack" and the response is difficult to classify as an instance of "self-defense." The paradoxical relationship between the status of violence and the procedures of social change is a central deficiency of the present structure of international legal order, especially evident at a time of emergent claims for social and political justice.

(3) THE LIMITS OF U.N. AUTHORITY, TRADITIONAL GREAT POWER
    DIPLOMACY, AND NUCLEAR PROLIFERATION

The general problem of curbing this kind of disruptive pattern is accentuated, as has already been suggested, by the character of the United Nations.[33] The United Nations is capable neither of implementing the justice demands of those groups that seek objectives approved by the world community nor of policing compliance with its prohibition upon recourse to violence. The geopolitical and ideological splits in international society generally prevent any kind of operative consensus arising out of U.N. activity. As a consequence, nineteenth-century patterns of alliance diplomacy assume great prominence in the effort to moderate the course of conflicts carried on at the regional

32. For a profound inquiry into these problems, see Myres S. McDougal and Florentino P. Feliciano, Law and Minimum World Public Order 97–260 (New Haven: Yale University Press, 1961). *Cf.* also the French explanation of their refusal to supply arms to Israel, initially as a consequence of Israel's initiation of force in June, 1967, and recently in reaction to Israel's action at the Beirut Airport. New York Times, Jan. 8, 1969, pp. 1, 19.

33. This assertion rests on several considerations: (1) the inability of the U.N. to implement its decisions; (2) the political factors that act to shape such a decision. The problems of control are particularly severe in the Middle East because of the rivalry between the United States and the Soviet Union for influence within the region.

level. Patterns of Great Power competition and co-ordination provide the
fuel for arms races, the incentive for compromise and settlement, and the
basis of uneasy forms of temporary equilibrium. The prospect of easy access
by secondary states to nuclear weapons technology may even mean that a
state unwilling to risk the sacrifice of its interests by a Great Power ally will
seek to develop its own nuclear deterrent.[34]

International society is vulnerable to a series of disruptive conflicts that
involve various kinds of externally-based insurgent operations challenging
the control of an incumbent regime. These conflicts are particularly resistant
to settlement because the stakes of conflict are perceived by participants in
such contradictory terms. Quite often the issue is nothing less than the political identity of the state. Resentments are so deep and bases of power so
divided that reconciliation appears virtually impossible. Victory, defeat,
stalemate, or a temporary truce are the only plausible outcomes.

International law is conditioned in its operation by this international setting. The remainder of this article seeks to clarify the legal situation by
examining two topics: (1) to present briefly the traditional rule-oriented
static analysis of respective rights and duties of parties to such a conflict and
to point out the inadequacies of this approach for these sorts of problems,
and (2) to offer a more process-oriented legal analysis that works toward a
multidimensional conception or test of relative legality.

The Beirut raid will be used as "the case" that illuminates broader issues
of legal approach and disposition. The approach urged is one that could be
adopted either by an official advising a government on the legal implications
of a proposed course of conduct or by a diplomat, civil servant, or expert
seeking to pass judgment on adversary appeals to international law.

III. Traditional Legal Perspectives

ANALYSIS AND APPRAISAL

My purpose is to illustrate the traditional mode of analysis with sufficient
clarity and fairness to provide an adequate background for the proposal of
an alternative mode of legal analysis.

There are several kinds of legal issues that are raised by the Beirut raid:

(1) What is the legal status of a reprisal claim? Under the U.N. Charter?
Under customary international law? What is the relationship between
Charter law and customary international law?

34. *Cf.* speculation to this effect as part of the Israeli reaction to censure by the Security Council and imposition of an arms embargo by France, New York Times, Jan. 12,
1969, pp. 1, 9. A state such as Israel might also seek to avoid inter-regional trade-offs at
her expense if the settlement bargain is achieved by super-Power consensus (*e.g.*, in simplistic terms, the Soviet position on Middle Eastern problems is accepted in exchange for
Soviet acceptance of the U. S. position on South Asian problems).

(2) Does the Beirut raid constitute a reasonable exercise of the right of reprisal?

(3) Does the Security Council resolution of December 31, 1968, constitute a definitive legal assessment of the conflicting contentions of Israel and Lebanon?

THE LEGAL STATUS OF REPRISALS

The prevailing expert view is stated clearly by Ian Brownlie:

> The provisions of the Charter relating to the peaceful settlement of disputes- and non-resort to the use of force are universally regarded as prohibiting reprisals which involve the use of force.[35]

It does seem appropriate to conclude that the U.N. Charter prohibits all forms of forcible self-help other than the exercise of self-defense within the meaning of Article 51.[36] The Security Council clearly confirmed this view of the legal status of reprisals under the Charter when it acted to censure Great Britain for carrying out a reprisal against the Yemeni town of Harib on March 28, 1964, in retaliation for alleged Yemeni support of the anti-colonial struggle in Aden. The resolution passed by a vote of 9–0, with two abstentions, and had as its initial operative clause the Council conclusion that it "*Condemns* reprisals as incompatible with the purposes and principles of the United Nations."[37] Israel has not even claimed that the Beirut attack was an exercise of the right of self-defense, but rather has rested her case on the right to retaliate against Lebanon in view of its alleged connection with "the Athens incident." The Israeli Chief of Staff, General Yetzhak Bar Lev,

35. Ian Brownlie, International Law and the Use of Force by States 281 (and sources cited therein) (Oxford University Press, 1963). Brownlie's statement is supported with additional citations and discussions in R. Higgins, The Development of International Law Through the Political Organs of the United Nations 217–218 (Oxford University Press, 1963). For a general background, see Evelyn Speyer Colbert, Retaliation in International Law (New York: King's Crown Press, 1948).

36. But for more flexible views of what is permitted under the Charter in the name of self-defense, see McDougal and Feliciano, cited note 32, pp. 1–260; see also pp. 679–689; Julius Stone, Aggression and World Order (Berkeley: University of California Press, 1958); D. W. Bowett, Self-Defense in International Law (New York: Praeger, 1958).

37. S/RES/188 (1964). The next clause of the resolution "*deplores* the British military action at Harib on 28 March 1964." And the Charter basis of the condemnation is suggested by language in the preambular section "*Recalling* Article 2, paragraphs 3 and 4 of the Charter of the United Nations." The Security Council resolution here, unlike the one condemning Israel for the Beirut raid, does widen the context and establish some kind of reciprocal obligation on the part of Yemen. For instance, the fourth operative paragraph "Calls upon the Yemen Arab Republic and the United Kingdom to exercise the maximum restraint in order to avoid further incidents and to restore peace to the area." And in the last paragraph, the Secretary General is called upon to use his "good offices to settle outstanding issues, in agreement with the two parties." Thus, although the United Kingdom is censured, the sense of mutual responsibility is stressed in a way that it is not in the December 31 resolution. See also I. F. Stone, "International Law and the Tonkin Bay Incidents," in Marcus G. Raskin and Bernard B. Fall (eds.), The Viet-Nam Reader (New York: Vintage, 1965).

has been quoted as saying that the Beirut raid was a reprisal the purpose of which "is to make clear to the other side that the price they must pay for terrorist activities can be very high."[38]

It seems clear that on the doctrinal level Israel is not entitled to exercise a right of reprisal in modern international law. Such clarity, however, serves mainly to discredit doctrinal approaches to legal analysis. International society is not sufficiently organized to eliminate forcible self-help in either its sanctioning or deterrent rôles. Therefore, each reprisal claim needs to be appraised by reference to these two rôles. Israel contended that the Beirut raid was a sanction imposed as a consequence of Lebanese responsibility for the Athens incident. Assessing the reasonableness of these claims involves a complex inquiry into the over-all factual context. The legal rules of prohibition isolated from context offer very little guidance for the conduct of such an inquiry, except to the uncertain extent that they embody various policies

38. See New York Times, Jan. 5, 1969, Sec. 4, p. 1; General Bar Lev said that "the large-scale operation" against the fedayeen bases of Karameh and Es-Salt in Jordan during 1968 "were not reprisals." He went on to say that "these were actions intended to strike directly at the heart of the terrorists." As an earlier example of a reprisal General Bar Lev cited the Israeli commando attack upon Egyptian bridges and upon a transformer station serving the Aswan Valley, the destruction taking place in the Nag Hamadi area. This reprisal was in retaliation for alleged Egyptian violations of the cease-fire along the Suez Canal. For a summary of the meetings of the Security Council devoted to this question on November 1 and 4, 1968, see 5 U.N. Monthly Chronicle 3–16 (November, 1968). Another prominent Israeli reprisal action occurred in October, 1967, after Eyptian rockets sank an Israeli destroyer, *Elath*, leading to the death of most of the crew. Israel alleged that the *Elath*, the largest ship in the Israeli Navy, was on "a routine patrol" and sailing in international waters, more than twelve miles from the Egyptian shore. Egypt contended that the *Elath* was only ten miles from shore and heading for Port Said in a "provocative" manner. The *Elath* was sunk on October 21 and the Israelis retaliated three days later with a heavy artillery barrage directed at the City of Suez situated near the cease-fire line. One result of the barrage was to destroy or badly damage the two most important oil refineries in Egypt that supplied 80 percent of the country's gasoline and cooking fuel. The *Elath* reprisal contrasts with the Beirut raid because the provocative action—sinking the ship—was clearly governmental in character. Hence, there was no issue as to whether Egypt was responsible, if in fact it was "illegal" to sink the *Elath*, itself a complicated issue of both fact and law. A resolution in the Security Council condemned both acts of violence as violations of the cease-fire and called for strict adherence by all governments in the future. Account of the *Elath* incident is based on Khouri, note 22 above, p. 279.

The principal purpose of retaliatory uses of force by Israel is to influence decision-making by Arab governments, especially with respect to their encouragement of terroristic tactics on the part of liberation groups located on their territory. Mr. Tekoah's conclusion of his final statement in the Security Council makes the centrality of this objective very clear. He says: "Israel's action in Beirut, taken in defense of its rights, should bring the Arab Governments to understand the full depth of Israel's determination to ensure its right to peace and security. When the Arab States realize that determination, become persuaded by its tenacity and draw the appropriate conclusions, there will be peace in the Middle East." S/PV. 1462, p. 52. Arab spokesmen, in contrast, refused to treat the Beirut raid as raising any issue that was broader than the permissibility of such an attack by the Israeli Government, given the absence of any prior governmental act of provocation on the part of Lebanon. Both the Beirut and the *Elath* reprisal raids seemed to include an element of punitive action, a policy of inflicting losses on Arab governments that exceed those inflicted upon Israel by prior action.

about the minimization of violence in the adjustment of international disputes.

THE RIGHT OF REPRISAL IN CUSTOMARY INTERNATIONAL LAW

In view of the inadequacy of Charter doctrines either to provide authoritative guidance or to give insight into the comparative merits of legal positions in the Beirut context, it would seem appropriate to consider the question by reference to pre-Charter legal conceptions contained in customary international law on the subject of reprisals.[39] For a valid exercise of the customary right of reprisal it is necessary to satisfy three main requirements:

1. That the target of the reprisal be guilty of the commission of a prior illegal act directed against the claimant state;
2. That the claimant state make an effort to obtain redress from the target state;
3. That the damage inflicted in retaliation be roughly proportional to the damage initially inflicted.[40]

In relation to the controversy over the Beirut raid it is difficult to apply these standards. It is especially difficult to determine whether the Lebanese Government should be properly held responsible for the commando acts of the Popular Front at Athens. Does the Lebanese failure to take reasonable steps to suppress the activity of the Popular Front on its territory establish a sufficient link to make it responsible for the specific acts of the organization?[41] Can the failure of the Lebanese Government to disavow the terrorist

39. As a technical matter, Charter law is properly accorded priority over inconsistent rules of customary international law. Therefore, the clear rejection of the right of reprisal in U.N. practice seems to establish the general authority of this conclusion in positive international law. However, the inability of the United Nations to impose its views of legal limitation upon states leads to a kind of second-order level of legal inquiry that is guided by the more permissive attitudes toward the use of force to uphold national interests that is contained in customary international law. This point has considerable jurisprudential importance, as it suggests the usefulness of a method of successive legal approximations. If the Charter status of reprisals exhausted legal inquiry, then there would be no prospect of moderating force in retaliatory settings wherein the Charter approach was ineffectual. Specifically, in the Arab-Israeli setting it appears useful to maintain second-order levels of legal inquiry so as to retain criteria of reasonableness in a situation that threatens at many points to deteriorate into intense and limitless forms of violent conflict. The customary international law of reprisal is a very important illustration of such second-order legality. Note, especially, that this kind of inquiry is associated with the contention of Israel that the purpose of a reprisal is not to inflict a punishment, but to communicate a claim with respect to future behavior. Even second-order legal inquiry may be ill-adapted to the kind of retaliatory claim being made by Israel, see above, Sec. II, and a third-order legal inquiry involving the specification of considerations bearing on the relative legal status of a particular retaliatory claim, see below, Sec. IV.
40. A useful short discussion of the background and character of the right of reprisal is given by Gerhard von Glahn (ed.), Law Among Nations 498–501 (New York: Macmillan, 1965).
41. Many international documents that formulate governmental duties of conduct include the responsibility to prevent the use of territory as a base for liberation activities

acts or warn the Popular Front to cease such acts be used to constitute a post-facto ratification that establishes the link? The need to make this kind of demonstration would appear strong in view of Lebanon's especial effort, unlike that of any other Arab state,[42] to remain at peace with Israel.[43] Israel's reprisal claim seems to fall short of satisfying the test for the first legal requirement.

Israel did not protest to Lebanon in any public forum about its responsibility for the Athens incident, nor did it demand redress prior to its raid on the Beirut airport.[44] There is no indication that the Israeli Government

---

against a foreign state. For example, the Declaration on Inadmissibility of Intervention, Resolution 2131 (XX) of the General Assembly, Dec. 21, 1965 (see note 28), declares that "no State shall . . . tolerate subversive, terrorist, or armed activities." See also citations in note 69 below, especially Garcia-Mora and Lauterpacht.

42. Note that Israeli representatives in the Security Council indicated that Arab countries other than Lebanon were also intended as targets of the Beirut raid. All Arab aircraft were destroyed, and not only those associated with Lebanese interests. Also the context was defined by Israel to include (1) the Athens incident, (2) the diversion of an El Al plane to Algiers in July, 1968, and (3) the over-all Arab policy of supporting the activities on their territory of the liberation groups. As Mr. Rosenne suggested to the Security Council: "Without in any way belittling the gravity of this terrorist warfare being conducted against Israel's civil aircraft, wherever they might be, the complaint that we are discussing must also be seen in the broader context of the continuation by the Arab States, including Lebanon, of active belligerency and warfare against Israel through the instrumentality of irregular forces and organizations armed, trained and financed by the Arab Governments, including the Government of Lebanon." S/PV. 1460, pp. 24–25.

43. On the comparatively low level of Lebanese hostility toward Israel, see Khouri, cited note 22, pp. 191, 230–231; Safran, cited note 9, pp. 182–185, 245–247. On its more recent increase, however, see "The Israeli Action at the Beirut Airport," Israeli Information Office, undated release, and the statement by Prime Minister Eshkol in Jerusalem on December 29, 1968, bearing the title, "Lebanon Cannot Disclaim Responsibility for Terrorism."

44. The Arab governments, but even more pointedly the Soviet Union, took the position that the Athens incident was a matter for Greek internal criminal law, and of no relevance at all to the debate on the Beirut raid. As Mr. Ghorra of Lebanon said, "In our view, that incident which took place at the Athens airport is a matter of common law, and the Greek courts have sole jurisdiction in the matter." S/PV. 1460, p. 61. Mr. Malik of the Soviet Union put his view as to the territorial, non-governmental character of the Athens incident very forcefully:

"This incident, which took place in Athens, relates to the sovereignty and competence of Greek authorities; it occurred on Greek territory. According to the press reports, the competent authorities of that country are dealing with this matter; they are studying it, and apparently they have taken some measures. They have executive as well as judiciary authorities there. How is this matter at all related to the Security Council? As I have already pointed out in my observations following the adoption of the agenda, if the Security Council were to begin to consider all the terrorist acts which are being perpetrated, no matter where, including even this country [the United States], then the Security Council would simply cease to be a Security Council. . . . The representative of Israel is dragging the Security Council into the consideration of events which took place on the territory of a sovereign power which is certainly entitled to deal with this matter . . . and that country has not appealed to the Security Council." S/PV. 1460, p. 13.

And later on the last day of the debate Mr. Malik reiterated his position in more succinct form:

"It must be stressed that the attack against the Israeli airplane was indeed carried out by citizens of a third State on the territory of yet another State; and, in accordance with

issued a public warning to Lebanese officials that they must take steps to curtail the operations of the Popular Front.[45] The record suggests that the Israeli decision to raid the Beirut airport was not preceded by any reasonable effort to obtain pacific redress. Thus the Israeli claim also appears to fall short of the second reprisal requirement.

It is difficult to apply the test of proportionality to specific factual circumstances. How does one weigh the loss of an Israeli life at Athens or the harassment of El Al operations against the destruction of civil aircraft and other equipment valued at more than $43.8 million or the blatant military incursion upon Lebanese territory? In terms of international salience the Beirut raid seems to have been disproportionately greater than the Athens provocation.[46] It was a larger, necessarily spectacular military operation carried out on an inter-governmental basis.[47] It is fair to ask, however, "Proportional to what?" If the Israeli raid is understood as a reprisal for the willingness of the Lebanese Government to tolerate operations by the Popular Front on its territory, then the Beirut raid might be regarded as proportional to inducing greater government control (although probably ineffective to achieve it). The application of this third requirement, and to some extent the first as well, depends on whether the delinquency of the Lebanon Government is regarded as its complicity in the Athens incident or its toleration of the activity of the Popular Front on its territory. Israel did not clearly communicate the character of its claim, although it seemed spe-

---

international law, a State can be held responsible only for acts of its own organs, such as its armed forces or its citizens, on the territory of that given State." S/PV. 1462, p. 22.

Mr. Wiggins, the representative of the United States, did take the position that "Israel was rightly aroused and legitimately concerned about the attack upon an Israeli aircraft in Athens on 26 December" but, nevertheless, he concluded that "[N]othing that we have heard has convinced us that the Government of Lebanon is responsible for the occurrence in Athens." S/PV. 1460, pp. 28–30.

45. Mr. Rosenne did tell the Security Council that "[A]ll through 1968 Lebanon, turning a deaf ear to Israel's appeals has been playing an ever increasing role in the overall Arab belligerency against Israel." S/PV. 1460, p. 21. There is no indication of any specific Israeli effort to persuade the Lebanese Government to exercise stronger control over the Popular Front in view of the Athens incident. Israel's justifications for focusing the attack upon Lebanon rested on allegations involving (1) the departure of the Arab perpetrators from Beirut; (2) the Lebanese toleration of increasing activity by the Popular Front on its territory; and (3) official and semi-official Lebanese endorsement of the use of terroristic methods by the perpetrators of the Athens incident.

46. Mr. Wiggins, the United States representative in the Security Council, made this point forcefully when he said that the Beirut raid was "an unacceptable form of international behavior. In magnitude it is entirely disproportionate to the act that preceded it. It is disproportionate in two ways: first, on the degree of destruction involved; and secondly, in a more fundamental way, in the difference between the acts of two individual terrorists and those of a sizable military force operating openly and directly under governmental orders." S/PV. 1460, pp. 28–30.

47. The visibility of the two occurrences can be gauged by comparing their treatment in newspapers around the world. The Athens incident was reported as a relatively minor terroristic act, whereas the Beirut raid received headlines and the damage done was shown in large photographs.

cifically related to safeguarding the operations of El Al rather than punishing Lebanon or inducing the over-all suppression of the Lebanese activities of the Popular Front.

The reprisal argument turns out to be weak if the events that are appraised concern only the Athens incident and the Beirut raid. The reprisal argument is far stronger, however, if based upon the connection between a Lebanese-based liberation movement operating with government knowledge and approval and the Beirut attack calculated to influence the leaders of the Government to alter this course of policy. The fact that the raid may have produced the opposite effect, moving the Lebanese Government into a position of more overt support for the liberation efforts of the Popular Front, is of no legal consequence; such an effect bears, if at all, on the political perspicacity of Israeli policy-makers. Such a consideration is also of reduced significance if the Beirut raid was directed toward warning all Arab governments, not only Lebanon, that the security of Arab airlines would be disrupted if these governments failed to prevent terroristic acts against El Al Airline. The effectiveness of the Beirut raid in communicating this claim can only be judged after the lapse of a period of time and by evidence of whether the Arab governments do take measures to discourage liberation groups from disrupting El Al.

The customary international law of reprisal does direct inquiry at more specific features of the context than does a mere assessment of the compatibility between the Beirut raid and Charter norms. At the same time, the inquiry is necessarily inconclusive because there is no agreed way to frame the basic issue as to the relationship between liberation activity and the target of a reprisal claim.[48] Furthermore, traditional inquiry relies on far too restrictive ideas about how to assess a particular claim. There is a need to assess a claim by reference to what constitutes reasonable behavior under all of the relevant circumstances.[49] Among the relevant circumstances is the inability to secure territory against terrorism if a neighboring country provides support, or even merely a sympathetic sanctuary.[50]

48. There are underlying the specific allegations of terror and counter-terror the more general allegations about bringing the conflict to an end either by "disintegrating" Israel and replacing it with the secular state of Palestine or by carrying out the provisions of Security Council Resolution 242 of Nov. 22, 1967, or by working out an agreed solution through the good offices of Gunnar V. Jarring, the special representative of the Secretary General, or by accepting a solution for the area that is worked out by guarantor Powers such as the United States, the Soviet Union, France, and the United Kingdom.

49. As pointed out already, Israel, in particular, objected throughout to the effort to restrict the scope of inquiry to the Beirut raid. See note 8.

50. The problem is fully depicted from an Israeli viewpoint in an article: Amnon Rubinstein, " 'Damn Everybody' Sums up the Angry Mood of Israel," New York Times Magazine, Feb. 9, 1969, pp. 24–27, 93, 96–99. See especially p. 98, on which there is a discussion of why Israel does not engage in counter-terror against Arab interests by organizing irregular military forces of its own, thereby cutting the overt link between retaliation and the Israeli Government. A senior officer is quoted as saying " [t]error for terror is the only solution,' " but Mr. Rubinstein writes, "This solution is unacceptable in

A special situation exists, however, when a series of terroristic incidents is undertaken by adversary states to disrupt the security of national society. It becomes somewhat more artificial in such a situation to assess the legal status of a retaliatory act in isolation from this ongoing and cumulative process of incitement through liberation activity. The situation in the Middle East is one of quasi-belligerency in which there is an agreed cease-fire and a *de facto* situation of hostility that frequently results in intergovernmental violence.

We need to evolve a legal framework that is able to deal with a situation of prolonged quasi-belligerency. Such a framework would at least have the advantage of overcoming the dichotomy between war and peace, and would be more sensitive to the continuities of terroristic provocation and retaliatory response such as are evident in the Middle East.[51]

THE STATUS OF THE RESOLUTION OF THE U.N. SECURITY COUNCIL

The Security Council resolution of December 31, 1968, (1) confines the context to the facts of the Beirut raid, and (2) holds Israel responsible for the damage done. The resolution was unanimous after debate by both sides. States normally friendly toward Israel, including the United States, joined in voting with the majority. The resolution is a formal act of the international institution most competent to consider such questions and an authoritative determination of the respective merits of the adversary contentions.[52] There appears to be no valid legal basis for Israel's evident refusal to accept the formal conclusion of the Security Council as entitled to respect by its government.[53]

---

the Israeli Government." He advances three arguments: (1) "The whole philosophy" of Israeli resistance "runs contrary to any suggestion of counter-terror." (2) Recourse to irregular forces would weaken Israel's contention that Arab incitement of irregular forces is a violation of the cease-fire agreement reached at the end of the June war; this reasoning is attributed to Moshe Dayan. (3) Regular troops can be militarily protected in the course of their mission in a way that irregular forces cannot; this view is attributed to General Bar Lev.

51. For somewhat similar suggestions in different circumstances of conflict, see Philip C. Jessup, "Should International Law Recognize an Intermediate Status between Peace and War?" 48 A.J.I.L. 98 (1954); Myres S. McDougal and Florentino P. Feliciano, Law and Minimum World Public Order 97–120 (New Haven: Yale University Press, 1962).

52. The duty of respect arises from the obligation of a Member of the United Nations to accord respect to acts of the Security Council when that organ is acting, as it was here, within its sphere of competence. As the Council was acting under Chapter VI, not VII, its resolution was formally a "recommendation" rather than a "decision." On this point see further discussion in note 59 below.

53. There were extended discussions of the legal consequences of the Beirut raid in the I.C.A.O. These discussions resulted from a Lebanese complaint that the Israeli action was a violation of the Chicago Convention on Air Transport and that Israel should be condemned and made to pay for the damage done. Although questions about the competence of I.C.A.O. to deal with a complaint of this character dominated the debate, the issues were discussed generally in a manner more favorable to the Israeli position than was the case in the Security Council. The outcome of these discussions was a decision *sine die,* which is quite a contrast with the result within the U.N. forum.

The Foreign Minister of Israel, Abba Eban, has suggested that "The UN does not express the idea [of international order] with any effectiveness in its present composition."[54] But one can hardly imagine any alternative composition of the Security Council that would have given a much more favorable review to the claims of Israel. Since the end of the June war of 1967 Israel has been increasingly in an isolated diplomatic position. This isolation is partly a consequence of an Israeli insistence upon securing certain territorial and economic advantages from its military victory in 1967.[55] The attitudes that dominate world community procedures have been oriented against Israel as a consequence of this underlying feature of the conflict, and this orientation shapes the approach of U.N. organs toward specific issues or "events."[56] The failure of the Security Council resolution to widen the ambit of its concern (1) to include the condemnation of Arab terrorism, such as the Athens raid, and (2) to encompass the responsibility of the Lebanese Government for the control of terrorist activity emanating from its territory is probably properly understood as part of the wider judgment that has been passed against Israel by the Security Council.

Under these circumstances, it is to be expected that Israel will contend that the United Nations is not prepared to deal fairly with specific instances of Arab-Israeli charges and countercharges.[57] On another level of response, it is not surprising that spokesmen for Israel point out that some states joining in the resolution of censure have been completely unmoved by U.N. censure of their own conduct. A most obvious and prominent recent example con-

54. An interview published in Time, Jan. 10, 1969, p. 28.

55. In violation of the Nov. 22, 1967, resolution of the Security Council and of the stated objectives of all states other than Israel, there does not seem to be any serious disposition by the Israeli Government to re-establish the *status quo ante* June 5, 1967. In particular, the retention of administrative control over Jerusalem, of the Golan Heights, a strip of Sinai needed to assure control over the Straits of Tiran, and of a portion of the West Bank of the Jordan and of the Gaza Strip seems to be insisted upon by Israel. There is, then, on the Arab side an unwillingness to accept the existence of the state of Israel and on the Israeli side an insistence upon expansion through conquest. For an assessment of Israel's intention to retain conquered Arab lands, see interview with Levi Eshkol published in Newsweek, Feb. 17, 1969, pp. 49–56; see also analysis of these claims by James Feron, "Eshkol Mentions the Unmentionable," New York Times, Feb. 16, 1969, Sec. 4, p. 2. Israel's claims are a mixture of security demands of a defensive nature and of territorial demands of an expansionist nature.

56. The position of Israel before the political organs of the United Nations is coming to resemble that of South Africa in certain critical respects, especially with regard to the degree of its diplomatic isolation. Israel does continue to enjoy some diplomatic support from the United States and from some countries in Western Europe, but, since the end of the 1967 war, even these governments have grown increasingly critical of Israel's expanding demands and exercise of prerogatives.

57. *E.g.*, Julius Stone, "No Peace—No War in the Middle East" (Sydney, Maitland, 1969), especially pp. 4–5. Professor Stone writes on p. 4: "Everyone knows that too many present Security Council Members are committed to voting on the Arab side, for pro-Israel resolutions to be adopted, no less than five of these Members refusing even to maintain diplomatic relations with her."

cerns the failure of the Security Council to censure by formal resolution the Soviet military occupation of Czechoslovakia in August of 1968.[58]

The conclusion seems evident:

1. The Security Council resolution, despite its technical character as a recommendation, is an authoritative pronouncement on the legal status of the Beirut raid;
2. The quality of authority exercised, however, is diluted by the extent to which "the event" was approached with a disposition against Israel arising from the over-all political setting of the Arab-Israeli dispute;
3. The "duty" of Israel to comply with the terms of the resolution is qualified by its status as a recommendation (rather than a decision) and is impaired by the extent to which other states, including Members of the Security Council, have themselves recently acted in defiance of U.N. directives.[59] There is no established tradition of governmental respect for adverse U.N. determinations.[60] Quite the contrary.

It seems proper to conclude, then, that the United Nations has passed judgment against Israel but that this judgment does not mean very much, given the structure and prevailing habits of international society.

IV. Appraising the Beirut Raid: the Search for a Legal Method

Earlier sections of the paper have tried to demonstrate that:

1. the legal rules and standards embodied in international law do not come to grips with the underlying policy setting provided by the Arab-Israeli conflict;
2. the determinations of the Security Council are authoritative, but are nevertheless not very likely to engender respect.

58. Abba S. Eban, Foreign Minister of Israel, suggested that anti-Jewish discrimination is embodied in the recent diplomatic attacks upon Israel: "I have no other explanation for the fact that the Soviet Union, which invaded Czechoslovakia, can condemn alleged Israeli 'aggression' at the UN without the public gallery bursting into laughter." Interview, Time, January 10, 1969, p. 28.

59. There is a certain legal ambiguity created by the status of various actions taken by the Security Council. In a formal sense, the judgments of the Security Council have the status of "recommendations" unless they are made under Chapter VII of the Charter. Except for "decisions" relating to the observation of the cease-fire, the Security Council has relied upon its "recommendatory" powers under Chapter VI. The resolution censuring Israel after the Beirut raid was a "recommendation." As such, it can be argued that Israel has no formal obligation to obey it. On the other hand, a resolution of censure involves an authoritative act of community review that constitutes strong evidence as to the respective rights and duties of parties to an international controversy.

60. Countries that have been the targets of U.N. directives have almost invariably refused to comply. In fact, when an international conflict gets to the point where the U.N. takes sides, it is almost assured that "the losing side" will not voluntarily obey the will of the Organization.

At the same time, it is important to sustain some framework of constraint in circumstances of conflict such as exist in the Middle East. There is, in particular, a need to establish indicators of reasonableness that can be applied to appraise specific flash-points in a setting of continuous conflict. These indicators can influence, above all else, national decision-making processes to adopt a course of conduct that tends to appear reasonable from an objective or third-party point of view. The structuring of expectations, those of the adversary and of the community, are normally the principal purpose of retaliatory uses of force.[61] More specifically, the chief Israeli purpose (presumed and disclosed) in attacking Arab aircraft at the Beirut Airport on December 28, 1968, was to communicate a message about the disruption of Israeli civil aviation to Lebanese government leaders, secondarily to other Arab governments giving support to liberation movements, and thirdly, to other governments concerned with the Middle East.[62] In such a context of conflict, world public opinion can become influential should it crystallize in favor of one party in a dispute; this influence can affect what the parties regard as a reasonable basis of settlement, and hence, the shape and prospects for a negotiated settlement. In this sense, the censure by Pope Paul VI, the imposition of an arms embargo on Israel by France, the replacement of the Yaffi regime by the Karami regime, when added to the unanimous censure of the Security Council, make the Beirut raid a costly act from Israel's point of view. In brief, the reasons why it is costly are as follows:

1. It worsens Israel's diplomatic position within the international community, alienating friendly and more neutral governments and hardening the attitude of more hostile governments.
2. It gives the impression, created by the evidence of censure at the international level, that Israel is relying upon excessive force to impose its will on weaker countries; such an impression creates, in turn, greater toleration for counter-violence, including Arab terrorism.
3. It seems to work against the diplomatic effort to secure a negotiated or agreed-upon settlement of the underlying conflict.
4. It leads Israel to assume a militarily defensive posture in response to international censure, thereby putting itself into an adversary relationship toward the rest of the international community, according greater strength to more militaristic perspectives within its own élite, thereby

61. That is, in strategic parlance, the objective is one of *deterrence* rather than *defense*. The primary effort is to influence decision-making in the target state's government rather than to diminish its capabilities for action. The Beirut raid aimed at shaping the policies of Arab governments with respect, in particular, to terroristic activities directed at the operations of El Al Airlines by liberation movements based within their territory. There was no intention to deprive Arab countries of commercial aircraft, which were obviously replaceable at relatively little cost.

62. Ambassador Tekoah's statements to the Security Council confirm the conclusion that the Israeli Government sought, above all else, to induce Arab governments to prohibit liberation movements operating within their territory from interfering with El Al flights.

inclining the Government to even greater reliance on force (rather than persuasion) in future instance.[63] There is, in other words, a dangerously escalatory cycle generated by any use of force that has been perceived as excessive in third-party contexts.

The principal point is that a retaliatory use of force that is perceived as excessive tends to engender a variety of bad consequences, including some that may be detrimental to the user. The further point is that rules of international law, as traditionally conceived, are too rigidly formulated to give appropriate insight into the factors that shape a decisional process of government and thus does not, in a realistic way, help officials or observers identify when a use of force is "excessive." The excessiveness of a particular use of force depends upon a combination of objective and subjective (value and ideological outlooks) factors, including the effort at justification made by the claimant state.[64] A more useful conception of international law than the specification of categorical rules would be the enumeration of objective factors likely to shape authoritative judgment and expert commentary. Such an enumeration would be useful for legal advisers to the adversary governments and to those passing judgment on contested behavior.

A rule of conduct isolated from context is often too abstract to guide choice and action. The more significant the connection between the overall context that conditions the action and the particular choice and act, the more difficult it is to make beneficial use of rule-guidance. The situation is subject to such a variety of relevant considerations that a generalized rule is unable to offer much guidance for those entrusted with the responsibility of specific governmental policy. A list of policy considerations can be used by the claimant government to shape its course of conduct to assure the achievement of its own ends. These considerations are only part of the input that enters the decisional process. At times, for instance, conduct that appears highly "illegal" by reference to past appraisals might be deemed essential to sustain the security of the state. But if it is demonstrably essential, then the policies supporting defensive force would tend to mitigate or even overcome any perception of "illegality."[65]

63. *Cf.* New York Times, January 12, 1969, pp. 1, 9; see, especially, article by Rubinstein cited in note 50 above. However, the Israeli response to the Zurich incident (see above, pp. 419–420) casts some doubt on the generality of the statement in the text.

64. The objective factors are those that can be formulated in general terms, whereas the subjective factors are those that involve the perceptual framework of the participants in the situation and are subject to wide variation depending on personality, cultural, and ideological considerations.

65. This tendency would be strengthened if the claimant state executed its operation in such a way as to minimize the injury to innocent civilians and third-party interests. The United States claiming pattern in the Cuban missile crisis is a model for this contention. A novel claim by the United States to use force on the high seas was made to appear so reasonable in assertion and execution that critical reaction, even though the Soviet Union was the target of the claim, was kept to a minimum. For two legal arguments by government officials in support of the United States claim, see Leonard C.

The principal objective reasons why the Beirut raid seems illegal are as follows:

1. It involved a governmental use of force by Israel in retaliation against non-governmental provocation.
2. It involved holding the Lebanese responsible for the Athens incident without the production of sufficient evidence establishing a direct link between the Beirut Government and the Arab terrorists.
3. It involved recourse to force without any prior recourse to diplomatic remedies in a situation where no necessity for immediate recourse to retaliation was demonstrated to exist.
4. It involved the destruction of what appeared to involve an excessive amount of property in an unusually spectacular and inflammatory fashion, thereby constituting an affront to the dignity and security of Lebanon.[66]

These elements of the Beirut raid seem to underlie the objective side of the international judgment, explaining, for instance, the hostile reaction of Pope Paul VI and the United States Government to the Israeli conduct.[67] A greater sensitivity to these factors might have shaped the Israeli action in a manner that would have been both more effective to attain the end in view and less at variance with community perceptions of lawful conduct. In the paragraphs that follow, some effort is made to suggest a suitable framework for claims to use force in retaliation against prior terroristic acts.[68] This framework embodies certain general policies concerning the use of force in periods of peace:[69]

Meeker, "Defensive Quarantine and the Law," 57 A.J.I.L. 515 (1963); Abram Chayes, "The Legal Case for U.S. Action on Cuba," 47 Dept. of State Bulletin 763 (1962).

66. I have elsewhere analyzed the reactions of African countries to the so-called Stanleyville operation of December, 1964, in these terms. Falk, *Legal Order in a Violent World* 324–335 (Princeton University Press, 1968).

67. There are certain other factors that explain censure from third-party sources: (1) prior uses by Israel of excessive force in response to terroristic provocation; (2) the selection of Lebanon as the target of retaliation, given the long period of non-involvement by the Lebanese Government in the Arab-Israeli conflict; (3) the growing realization that Israel was insisting upon retaining some of the territorial fruits of the 1967 war; (4) the timing of the Beirut raid seemed to be damaging prospects for either a Great Power or U.N. initiative to bring some measure of stability, if not real peace, to the Middle East.

68. A subsequent article will attempt to evolve a suitable framework for the assessment of acts of violence relied upon by liberation groups to achieve their political ends. Such a framework would involve, necessarily, some assessment of the compatibility between the aims of these groups and appraisal of these aims by regional and global institutions and their conformity with norms of international law. In addition, the choice of means used to pursue such aims requires an innovative legal analysis that reconsiders para-military violence as an instrument of political change. Eventually the two frameworks of legal appraisal will need to be integrated into a single coherent approach to the relevance of international law to this species of international conflict that has assumed such great importance in world affairs.

69. For some relevant legal background see Fritz Grob, *The Relativity of War and Peace* (New Haven: Yale University Press, 1949); Albert E. Hindmarsh, *Force in Peace:*

1. That the burden of persuasion is upon the government that initiates an official use of force across international boundaries;
2. That the governmental user of force will demonstrate its defensive character convincingly by connecting the use of force to the protection of territorial integrity, national security, or political independence;
3. That a genuine and substantial link exists between the prior commission of provocative acts and the resultant claim to be acting in retaliation;
4. That a diligent effort be made to obtain satisfaction by persuasion and pacific means over a reasonable period of time, including recourse to international organizations;
5. That the use of force is proportional to the provocation and calculated to avoid its repetition in the future, and that every precaution be taken to avoid excessive damage and unnecessary loss of life, especially with respect to innocent civilians;[70]
6. That the retaliatory force is directed primarily against military and para-military targets and against military personnel;[71]
7. That the user of force make a prompt and serious explanation of its

---

Force Short of War in International Relations (Cambridge: Harvard University Press, 1933); M. R. Garcia-Mora, International Responsibility for Hostile Acts of Private Persons against Foreign States (The Hague: Nijhoff, 1962); Hersch Lauterpacht, "Revolutionary Activities by Private Persons against Foreign States," 22 A.J.I.L. 105, 130 (1928). For some specification of support given terroristic groups in Egypt and Jordan since the June war, see Stone, note 57 above, pp. 4–6. According to Israeli sources there have been 1,288 acts of sabotage and border incidents between June 6, 1967, and December 31, 1968. 920 of these acts occurred in the Jordanian-Israeli sector, 166 in the Egyptian sector, 37 in the Syrian, 35 in the Lebanese, and 130 in the Gaza Strip sectors. Israeli losses have been put at 234 soldiers and 47 civilians killed and 765 soldiers and 330 civilians wounded. Arab losses are reported by Israel as considerably greater than these figures. See New York Times, Feb. 13, 1969, pp. 1, 4. There are indications of a rising Israeli concern about the growing capacity of the guerrilla groups to impair Israel's security, including especially the character of its administration of occupied territories inhabited largely by Arabs. See James Feron, "Israel Concerned over Guerrillas," *ibid.*, March 9, 1969, Sec. 1, p. 12.

70. Israeli statements before the Security Council emphasized the effort to carry out the Beirut raid without inflicting casualties upon Lebanese citizens. See, *e.g.*, S/PV. 1460, p. 23. And in the official release of the Israeli Information Office in New York, the following language appears: "At great risk to themselves, Israeli troops at the Airport exercised the strictest precautions to prevent civilian casualties. The planes were emptied of passengers and ground crews, and people in the vicinity were led away to safety. Loudspeakers were employed to issue instructions in Arabic and English. The only shots fired were warning shots in the air." Release dated Dec. 28, 1968.

71. Israeli attacks against Arab para-military bases associated with guerrilla activities have occasioned little adverse reaction, especially if "provoked" by an upsurge in miscellaneous incidents of terrorism within Israel. See paragraphs on the air strike against Syrian bases of Al Fatah on Feb. 24, 1969, above, p. 420. To some extent the governmental character of a retaliation against non-governmental provocation is neutralized if the targets are military. This is especially true if the victims of the terrorism were civilians and damage done to non-military targets. The choice of a non-military target for Israeli retaliation after the Athens incident seems to be a very significant element in explaining the strong adverse international reaction to the Beirut raid.

conduct before the relevant organ(s) of community review and seek vindication therefrom of its course of action;

8. That the use of force amounts to a clear message of communication to the target government so that the contours of what constituted the unacceptable provocation are clearly conveyed;

9. That the user of force cannot achieve its retaliatory purposes by acting within its own territorial domain and thus cannot avoid interference with the sovereign prerogatives of a foreign state;

10. That the user of force seek a pacific settlement to the underlying dispute on terms that appear to be just and sensitive to the interests of its adversary;

11. That the pattern of conduct of which the retaliatory use of force is an instance exhibits deference to considerations 1–10, and that a disposition to accord respect to the will of the international community be evident;

12. That the appraisal of the retaliatory use of force take account of the duration and quality of support, if any, that the target government has given to terroristic enterprises.

V. Conclusion

There are several parts of the approach to the kind of legal analysis recommended in this article: (1) a depiction of the central policy issues embodied in the underlying conflict; (2) a check-list of objective considerations relevant to the assertion and appraisal of a claim by a state to make a retaliatory use of force.

The Beirut raid was an event situated in an unusually complicated politico-military setting. Its assessment as a legal act is not a dichotomous "either/or" judgment, nor should its legal appraisal be isolated from antecedent or subsequent conduct. The essential problem confronting Israel is the design of a response against provocative terror carried out by liberation movements enjoying varying degrees of tacit and overt support from various Arab governments. This single problem is related to the over-all search for a resolution or stabilization of the conflict in the Middle East, a conflict that is dangerous to both regional and global stability, containing even some threat of igniting a world war fought with nuclear weapons.[72]

The rôle of legal analysis is to facilitate the process of shaping and judging action: specifically, to promote constructive effects to the actor and to the community. The assumption underlying such an approach is that the primary rôle of international law is to help governments plan *how* to act, rather than to permit some third-party judge to determine whether contested action is legal or not. In fact the function of the third-party judge can be performed

---

72. *Cf.* analysis of Safran, cited note 22 above, at pp. xii–xv, 21–142, in terms of the levels: (1) Arab-Israeli; (2) inter-Arab; (3) U.S.–U.S.S.R.

properly only by attempting to assess *in what respects* and *to what extent* the governmental actor "violated" community norms of a prescriptive nature. Given the present character of international legal order, the essence of law consists of an interactive process of communication among governments and between governments and international institutions as to the character of acceptable behavior. The more this communication is premised upon a consensus as to relevant considerations and the more it reflects the dominance of objective over subjective factors, the more plausible it becomes to say that international law is playing a significant rôle.[73]

The Beirut raid exhibits a failure of the appropriate legal considerations to guide the Israeli Government's claim to use force in retaliation against terroristic provocation. This failure is important because of its bearing on world attitudes toward the relevant merits of the adversary positions of Israel and the Arab states on the underlying issues, including a peaceful settlement on mutually acceptable terms, as well as attitudes toward the whole matter of the existence of the state of Israel. It is also important because retaliation across frontiers against terroristic activity has significance in several other world contexts: Southern Africa, Latin America, and Southern Asia. It is, finally, important because the claim to be acting in a retaliatory capacity is one that involves recourse to self-help that is generally only available to the strong against the weak. As such, the ethics of retaliation is related to the rôle of military superiority in shaping the resolution of international conflict. However, the vulnerability of some states to an externally-based and supported liberation movement points up the artificiality of territorial boundaries. It is arguable that in certain situations actions against terror in the form of striking at the camps and sanctuaries amounts to extraterritorial police enforcement.[74] A reprisal, such as the Beirut raid, seeks to influence the target government to suppress or regulate terrorist activity within its territorial limits; it can be understood as a demand for co-operative law enforcement. If this demand is refused, then the state that is a target of the activity is confronted by a difficult choice. It can either tolerate the foreign sanctuary or it can violate the international boundary. If it does the former, then its enemies often grow stronger and its security diminishes, whereas if it does the latter, then it often puts itself in the position of appearing to be

73. The significance of this rôle, it should be noted, depends on a conception of international law that is wider than one concerned with rules of behavior. Neither the Charter norms nor the norms of customary international law delimiting the right of reprisal, come to grips with the kind of choice that confronts a government that needs to design responses to persistent terrorism directed at the security of its national territory. In such circumstances, the exigencies of response cannot be cast aside by the invocation of legal rules. At the same time, retaliatory claims can be asserted in accordance with a framework of restraint that is designed to minimize disruption, to maximize the clarity of the message conveyed, and to solicit the sympathy of the organized world community.

74. *Cp.* problems associated with the effort by the United States to extend its antitrust regulation to govern the foreign operations of business firms that have an anti-competitive impact on the U.S. economy.

the violator of international peace, the initiator of aggression; in time such a state risks becoming an international pariah. Israel's dilemma in the Middle East is of this sort. The best way out of this dilemma is for Israel to achieve greater sensitivity to world order considerations, especially on matters bearing on the basis for permanent reconciliation. There is a need for reciprocity and mutuality in the course of clarifying the line of ultimate solution, as well as in maintaining a tolerable degree of domestic security during the difficult interim period.

International lawyers can contribute greatly to the quality of world order by working out a systematic framework for the assessment of claims to use retaliatory force. This article is a first step in this direction taken within a limited policy and factual setting.

6.

"Socialist International Law" or "Socialist Principles of International Relations"?

W. E. BUTLER

PROFESSOR TUNKIN'S RECENT volume, *Theory of International Law,* already has been the subject of comment in this journal.[1] His recent lead article in the 1969 *Soviet Yearbook of International Law,* devoted to Socialist international relations and published after the volume on theory, provides additional insight into discussions of the place of international law in the "world Socialist system."[2] Tunkin's concept of Socialist international legal principles as set forth in these publications is highly complex. At the risk of oversimplification, it may be summarized as follows:

The highest principle of relations between workers of different countries is that which is an essential condition for the victory of the proletariat, the principle of proletarian (or Socialist) internationalism. After the October Revolution of 1917, the defense of the Socialist fatherland became an internationalist duty of the Russian working class and the "common cause of the international working class." At this point, proletarian internationalism also became a principle of domestic and foreign state policy of the Soviet Union. The "basic content" of the principle, as applied among Socialist states, is defined as the construction of socialism and communism

Reprinted by permission from the *American Journal of International Law,* Vol 65, No. 5, October 1971. Copyright © 1971 by the American Society of International La v.
   1. G. I. Tunkin, Teoriia mezhdunarodnogo prava (1970); commented upon by John N. Hazard, "Renewed Emphasis upon a Socialist International Law," 65 A.J.I.L 142 (1971), and reviewed *ibid.* 416. Tunkin's book was signed to press on Sept. 26, 1969.
   2. G. I. Tunkin, "V. I. Lenin i printsipy otnoshenii mezhdu sotsialisticheskimi gosudarstvami," Sovetskii ezhegodnik mezhdunarodnogo prava 1969 (1970), pp. 16–29 The Yearbook was signed to press on Nov. 17, 1970.

and the defense of the achievements of socialism in the course of the struggle of the two systems, Socialist and capitalist.

From the principle of proletarian internationalism are derived specific rights and duties for each Socialist state in its relations with other Socialist states. Among these is the duty to pursue close cooperation and mutual assistance in all spheres of the construction of socialism and communism, particularly the economic sphere. Specific reference is made to Socialist economic integration.[3]

The principle of proletarian internationalism also affects several *subordinate* principles, all of which are said to have become Socialist international legal norms and to comprise a new unified system of international legal principles of proletarian internationalism. The subordinate principles listed are:

> (1) respect for the sovereignty of Socialist states, on the basis of which peoples exercise the right to self-determination; (2) non-interference in the internal affairs of another state, which reflects respect for the national peculiarities and expectations of each people; (3) full equality of Socialist states, which reflects the Marxist-Leninist thesis of the equality of nations and of workers' parties.[4]

The above principles are distinguished from those operative in general international law. In their Socialist form, such principles are said to embrace the obligation of ensuring that such rights may be exercised; for example, "the Socialist principle of respect for sovereignty obliges Socialist states not only to respect the sovereignty of other Socialist states, but also to defend Socialist sovereignty in accordance with the demands of proletarian internationalism."[5] The Czechoslovak events of 1968 are considered by Tunkin to have been in full accord with the principle of proletarian internationalism.

Tunkin's exposition makes it clear that Soviet jurists are not attempting to justify the Czechoslovak events as being consistent with general international law. However, the formulation of the three subordinate Socialist principles of international law contains significant qualifications in comparison with their previous definition in Soviet doctrine. All three are made subject to the desires of the "people," who always are assumed to identify with true proletarian internationalism. If the "people" were to accuse their own party or governmental leadership of following policies inconsistent with proletarian internationalism and to appeal for assistance from frater-

---

3. Cautioning against "poisonous nationalism," Tunkin writes: "The events of 1968 in Czechoslovakia have shown how dangerous for the cause of socialism can be manifestations of nationalism in conditions of the activization of anti-socialist forces in a country together with the active support of imperialist reaction." *Ibid.* 25.

4. *Ibid.*

5. *Ibid.* 27.

nal Socialist countries, as forty Czechoslovak party members were alleged to have done, then presumably such assistance might be forthcoming. It could even be said that the fraternal Socialist countries were under a legal obligation to furnish such assistance. Similarly, "respect for national peculiarities and expectations of each people" refers to cultural and ethnic traditions, not to independent nationalist policies pursued to the detriment of the interests of the Socialist bloc.

To Western jurists the doctrine outlined above will appear to be nothing less than an open-ended justification for interference in the affairs of any Socialist country whose domestic or foreign policies threaten "Socialist achievements." A network of agreements authorizing collective intervention to combat an external or internal subversive threat does not exist in the Socialist bloc, as it does for some other regions of the world. The Warsaw Pact plainly contemplated armed attack only from the outside, unless one were to resort to methods of treaty interpretation which have been anathema to Soviet doctrine. Intervention by invitation also failed when the leadership of the then Czechoslovak government and Communist party promptly denied that any such invitation had been extended. International legal doctrine, because it lacks the binding character and the precision of customary or conventional international legal norms, is not a particularly reliable instrument for defining limits which, if exceeded, may give rise to intervention. But doctrinal ambiguity also can have a deterrent effect, unless states which disagree with the doctrine are willing to risk an immediate test of its limits.

As Tunkin himself notes, a question is often asked about the principle of proletarian internationalism in connection with Soviet relations with the People's Republic of China. By describing proletarian internationalism as a *moral and political* principle of the international workers' movement with regard to the PRC, Tunkin has seemingly excluded any prospect that the Socialist countries have a Socialist legal obligation to intervene against the Chinese leadership, although the fundamental interests of the peoples of China and the other Socialist countries are said to coincide.[6]

On the other hand, and in contrast to the impression which may have been left by Professor Hazard's editorial, Tunkin is most circumspect in his use of the phrase "Socialist international law." In fact, the expression is seldom used. Indeed, Tunkin appears to go to some lengths to make clear that he is not suggesting the existence of a separate system of "Socialist international law." The Socialist principles of international law to which he refers are said to be "the basis of a new type of international law, a

6. *Ibid.* 28. The "subjects" of proletarian internationalism in its legal aspect are left open, except for the exclusion of China. The Communist-Party states of Eastern Europe obviously are included, but the status of Yugoslavia, Mongolia, North Korea, North Vietnam, Cuba, and perhaps Albania is unclear. However, the doctrine of Socialist internationalism would not appear to be applicable to non-Communist-Party states.

Socialist international law of the future."[7] The distinction between Socialist principles of international law as themselves comprising a separate system of international law (which Tunkin implies is not yet the case) and as principles of Socialist international relations is an important one in Soviet doctrine, for it emphasizes the political responsibilities of members of the Socialist bloc without raising all of the theoretical dilemmas and practical implications which the posited existence of mutually exclusive systems of international law unquestionably would have.

Even the present formulation is not without its perils, however. In his article Tunkin briefly addresses the problem of the relationship between Socialist principles of international law and *jus cogens.* He argues that *jus cogens*

> cannot be understood as not permitting the progressive development of international law and the creation, on the basis of equality and good will, of local international legal norms which go farther than the norms of general international law in the development of friendly relations and the ensuring of peace, reflecting a higher degree of international integration than general international law.
>
> Also, as the law of peaceful coexistence of states with different social systems, contemporary general international law cannot obstruct the creation of local international legal norms, which are distinguished from norms of general international law by their own social content. In relation to general international law, the international legal principles of proletarian internationalism are just such local norms.[8]

Tunkin's view of *jus cogens* is a considerable revision of that which he expressed in the six-volume Soviet treatise on international law. In the latter, Tunkin referred to ". . . norms possessing the character of *jus cogens,* i.e., norms from which states shall not lawfully deviate in their bilateral or group relations."[9] Indeed, in an article published in the same issue of the *Soviet Yearbook of International Law,* L. A. Aleksidze does not distinguish between Socialist and general international legal principles of *jus cogens.* Aleksidze mentions as generally recognized norms of contemporary inter-

7. *Ibid.* In the volume on theory, this point was not made so carefully: "The principles of proletarian internationalism and other socialist norms arising in relations between countries of the socialist camp are international legal principles and norms of a new, higher type of international law—a socialist international law—the fundamental principles of which are being formed in relations among states of the socialist system and which are going to replace contemporary general international law." Tunkin, Teoriia mezhdunarodnogo prava 503.
8. Tunkin, *loc. cit.* note 2, p. 28. There is presently much emphasis in Soviet media upon Socialist integration, but Tunkin's formulation of *jus cogens* seems to contemplate a body of local norms among states and not, at least at this stage, norms of a municipal character within a federation.
9. 1 V. M. Chkhikvadze *et al.* (eds.), Kurs mezhdunarodnogo prava v shesti tomakh 23 (1967).

national law having an imperative character "principles strengthening the fundamental sovereign rights of states and peoples, equality and self-determination of peoples, respect for state sovereignty and territorial integrity, noninterference, sovereign equality of states. . . ."[10] It may be doubted that many jurists will find the labeling of a particular local norm "higher" than *jus cogens* to be persuasive when the local norm seems intended to permit what *jus cogens* would proscribe.

The debate over the substance and significance of Socialist principles of international relations is far from closed. The suggestion that the principles of proletarian internationalism have less than legal force with respect to the People's Republic of China, the extent and direction of integration within the bloc, and other factors must influence doctrinal views. Eastern Europeans, of course, may derive scant satisfaction from discussions over whether Socialist internationalism is policy, doctrine, or law, for under each notion there remains a residual possibility that intervention may occur. But as international lawyers we must and do constantly distinguish between policies which states may pursue in their discretion, justifications which may be advanced to support their actions, and legal norms said to be mutually binding upon actors. These distinctions are made for a variety of reasons, but partly because the future implications of each position may be different. Socialist jurists do the same. Since the policy, doctrinal, and legal consequences of the Czechoslovak events are not well defined, and in fact are in the process of formulation, Soviet jurists in particular are bound to explore all of them. If their discussion is to be understood, terminological nuances must be followed closely. Much as we would deplore any doctrinal or legal developments which would impair the integrity of general international law, we ought to refrain from announcing the arrival of Socialist international law prematurely when its arrival *qua* law appears to be controversial.

10. L. A. Aleksidze, "Problema jus cogens v sovremennom mezhdunarodnom prave," Sovetskii ezhegodnik mezhdunarodnogo prava 1969 (1970), p. 144.

III

NATIONALISM VERSUS INTERNATIONALISM

Although the following articles by Stanley Hoffmann were written some time ago, the conclusions at which he arrives have in large part withstood the test of time. The voting strength of third world countries in the United Nations has increased significantly since the first article was written and Great Britain has joined the Common Market since the second was written. However, this latter event paradoxically has reinforced the Gaullist conception of the market as a union of nations rather than as a confederation. Many, including the editor, hope that the long-term prospects of the market are stronger and that some day it may constitute a viable political entity in its own right. As yet, the support for this hope is weak.

The first article by Mr. Hoffmann deals with the uses of the United Nations. At the close of the second World War there was great public hope in the United States for the future of the UN. Many, including Eleanor Roosevelt, viewed it as a potential parliament of mankind and as an organization that would make peace and eliminate war. The Charter of the UN seemed to outlaw the use of force. This has not worked out. As Hoffmann tells us, the drafters of the Charter assumed correctly that the organization could operate with effectiveness only if the unity of the big powers were preserved. But the assumption of great power unity was most unrealistic, for these nations were exactly the ones at the close of the war with strongly opposed interests and the means to implement their opposition.

During the early history of the United Nations the United States had effective control of the organization. It was used to support American foreign policy interests in a manner that conflicted strongly with Soviet and other interests. As the organization has been enlarged by the addition of many new states, American control has been attenuated. Now many disputes are carried on within the United Nations that emphasize its inability to provide for peaceful change in a world subject to international quarrels and revolutionary upheavals. The organization has been extremely reluctant, except in the case of Korea, to label the use of force "aggressive," for this makes it more difficult to settle disputes. Moreover, having labelled the Chinese Communists as aggressors, the supposedly universal organization was first forced to negotiate with Communist China on equal terms to settle the Korean war and then, eventually, to admit that nation. The labelling made more difficult the eventual admission of Communist China and, therefore, made more difficult the desired approach to universality of membership.

It seems obvious that the United Nations has certain inbuilt disadvantages as a parliament for mankind. It has been able to condemn South Africa and Rhodesia although its condemnations have been largely ineffective. It has not been exactly even-handed in its treatment of Israel and the Arab states, a conclusion that *a priori* would have been expected from an inspection of its voting list. It is more effective when it doesn't condemn or when it attempts to mediate disputes. It has been misused both by the United States and by third-world countries in pursuit of specific national policies. It surely lacks that degree of consensus concerning international values that would serve genuinely to legitimize voting decisions in its organs and, thus, morally to obligate the member states to support these decisions. It therefore has a real, but only very modest, utility with respect to the issue of world order.

Most of the major decisions of world order will continue to rest on the military power and political alliances of the major states. This was in no instance made clearer than in the Security Council debate at the time of the Cuban missile crisis, when the impotence of the organization in matters of this great import was dramatically revealed.

Hoffman's article on the nation state is the obverse of his article on the United Nations. The article stresses the viability of national organization. Because it was written prior to the emergence of the separatist movement in French Canada, the struggle in Northern Ireland, and the conflict between the Flemings and Walloons in Belgium, it somewhat overestimates the strength of national organization. On the other hand, despite emerging weaknesses in national consensus, no other form of political organization seems remotely viable.

The facts to which Hoffmann points seem clear, but the problems to which the nation state gives rise will not go away that easily. There is some question as to the viability of the nation state in the age of jet planes and fast tanks. Western Europe simply does not have enough military space for maneuver in the face of a possible massive onslaught from the east. Given the predominance of Russian strength on the Eurasian land mass, there is a conflict between the interests invoked by national organization and the military requirement of defense. The argument by General de Gaulle that in the last analysis national armies must be under national command for national security may rest on a false premise. This topic will be further pursued in Part Two (selection 22), where Paul Taylor will suggest a future that diverges sharply from Hoffmann's conclusions. It is obviously closely related to the great issue of Part One: the nature of the international order.

7.

Sisyphus and the Avalanche: The United Nations, Egypt, and Hungary

STANLEY HOFFMANN

THE GODS HAD CONDEMNED Sisyphus to push a rock up the top of a mountain, from which the rock kept rolling down. International organization seems to be a modern illustration of an old myth. After each crisis, new attempts are made to push the rock of peace up again, and no crisis has revealed the frustrating task of international organization more sharply than the recent shock of the Middle Eastern and Hungarian explosions.

First, the crisis has revealed that, in spite of multiple efforts, the mechanisms which the United Nations had established for the prevention and repression of threats to peace did not work well enough to save the organization from having once again to improvise in an emergency. Secondly the crisis has shown that in its policies also, the United Nations was limited to a Sisyphus-like role; the United Nations could not prevent a return to the *status quo* of Soviet control of Hungary, and in the Middle East the strenuous efforts of the organization have not been able to achieve much more than a restoration of a slightly amended but still unsatisfactory *status quo*. Thirdly, the crisis has thrown a strong light over some of the deeper reasons for these procedural and political shortcomings. Fourthly, the split among the leading western powers over the Middle East and the embarrassment provoked in the west by the simultaneity of the Middle Eastern and Hungarian affairs have shown the need for a political strategy common to the western nations

Reprinted by permission from *International Organization*, Vol. 10, No. 3, Summer 1957, pp. 446–69.

(the United States as well as western Europe) for their relations with the United Nations in matters concerning peace and security.

The present article is an attempt to examine briefly the four aspects of the crisis of last fall.

Institutional Weaknesses

Just as after each disappointment the horse in Orwell's *Animal Farm* thought that the happy days would come at last if it only did more work, so after each major incident the statesmen of the world have deplored the chinks in the armor of international organization and have striven for more and better institutional engineering. Thus, the "Uniting for Peace" resolution tried to institutionalize the Korean miracle so that despite the big powers' split, future threats to peace or aggressions would again be handled effectively by the United Nations. The resolution created an impressive series of procedures and organs for preventive and repressive purposes. A more limited but complementary system of alarm bells had been established in such dangerous parts of the world as the Middle East and Kashmir. In last year's crisis, most of these mechanisms proved useless—either because they were simply not used by the very nations that had created them, or because they had been allowed to decay, or because they were not adapted to the circumstances of last fall.

1. Let us look first at the preventive arsenal. The "Uniting for Peace" resolution had established a Peace Observation Commission to "observe and report on the situation in any area where there exists international tension the continuance of which is likely to endanger the maintenance of international peace and security." This Commission has been singularly neglected. It has been used only with reference to the Balkans, where a subcommission was appointed in 1951 by the General Assembly to succeed the United Nations Special Committee which was being discontinued. The subcommission, which submitted no reports of its own—as indeed, there was no need for any, since Greece was now a quiet NATO member. Since 1954, the Peace Observation Commission has been totally lethargic. Thailand requested a subcommission shortly before the end of the Indochina war, but no decision was taken. The Commission was not used in the crisis over the nationalization of the Suez Canal Company. The Security Council, when it discussed the matter in October 1956, was politically in no position to do so. The Egyptian complaint against English and French threats of force and mobilization measures was put on the agenda but never taken up, and Egypt, whose consent or invitation was required under the terms of the 1950 resolution, never asked for a subcommission to be sent into its territory. Indeed, since the threats came from across the sea, a system patterned after Korea was somewhat inappropriate. Thus, only the Anglo-French complaint against Egypt

was discussed, and it was dealt with as an ordinary dispute. The whole emphasis was put on diplomacy and conciliation, not on alarm and prevention.

The Peace Observation Commission was not used in connection with the Arab-Israel dispute either. And why should it have been? Was not this dispute taken care of by an elaborate international machinery? The trouble is that this machinery was in pitiful condition. The Palestine Conciliation Commission was left without instructions ever since the General Assembly, at its seventh session, failed to agree on any resolution. The Commission has long ago acknowledged the impossibility of reconciling the various parties on the fundamental issues (borders, refugees, and Jerusalem) with which it had been asked to deal in those earlier days when the young international organization was setting its hopes very high indeed. The Commission had turned to more modest tasks: the question of Arab accounts blocked in Israeli banks and compensation for abandoned Arab lands in Israel. Such efforts were sure neither to stir nor to calm the troubled waters of Arab-Israel relations.

With no prospect of global settlement, the whole burden of preserving peace in the area fell upon the Truce Supervision Organization (UNTSO). But no mechanism of observers and mixed armistice commissions could forever bear the weight that was put on the UNTSO by the failure to achieve a lasting settlement. Inevitably, a system whose organs could pass judgments on armistice violations but whose condemnations and proposals were ineffective if the parties did not want to accept them was bound to wear down. The strain was increased by a frequently used and complicated circuit. The more important violations were sent by their victims before the Security Council, which in turn called for the Chief of Staff (or his deputies, the chairmen of particular armistice commissions) to report or to appear in person; then after "condemning," "taking note" or "endorsing," the Council dumped the whole matter back into the commanders' laps.

Even more striking, however, was the extraordinary fragility of the mechanism itself, and the passivity of the members of the United Nations who were presiding over its decay. There were so few observers—at one point only five for the whole Israel-Jordan border—that they could intervene only *after* the incidents, waste their energies in post-mortems, and merely maintain a score-board. Ever since the days of the much more numerous truce observers of 1948 the grievances of United Nations representatives in the field have been the same: "the uncooperative attitude" displayed by local authorities, the huge number of complaints by both sides, the violation of the armistice provisions which called for reciprocal reduction and withdrawal of forces, the attempts at limiting the freedom of movement of the observers. Year after year, the Security Council resolutions and the reports of the Chiefs of Staff have monotonously referred to the same sore spots.

The deterioration of the mechanism accelerated in 1955 and 1956. After the Israeli raid into the Gaza Strip in February 1955, General Burns restated a previous proposal for joint patrols, a barbed wire fence, and the manning of outposts by regulars; the Security Council endorsed his suggestions, but no agreement was reached. A new incident occurred in August; the Chief of Staff asked again for an effective physical barrier along the demarcation line. Once more the Security Council backed him. What followed was a series of incidents on the eastern front of Israel. Sisyphus went to work anew; in April 1956, the Security Council asked the Secretary-General to go to the Middle East. Mr. Hammarskjold, when he returned one month later, seemed to believe that he had consolidated the truce mechanism. He had formulated the doctrine of absolute, unconditional observance of each provision referring to the armistice lines; he had obtained an agreement (limited to October 31 by Israel) for the stationing of observers on both sides of the Gaza Strip, and he had hopes for a prompt agreement on the separation of forces, the erection of physical obstacles, and a clearer delimitation of the line. However, he noted that "there is not in all cases an adequate functioning machinery for resolving disputes" over the armistice agreements, and that "no procedure has been established for the handling of conflicts covered by the *general* clauses of the armistice agreements," conflicts over which the mixed commissions had no jurisdiction and which were not usually referred by the parties to the Security Council. He emphasized both the need for such procedures and the impossibility of making any proposals acceptable to the parties. In spite of a new endorsement by the Security Council, which nodded itself back to sleep, the machinery was not repaired and storm signals accumulated.

The hopes of the spring did not materialize, as General Burns reported early in September. Twice the mixed commissions broke down. Mr. Hammarskjold issued a warning to all Middle Eastern states—and not only to them. He stressed that there were limits to what the United Nations could do if the governments concerned did not want to cooperate, and with the same discretion as in his May report he added that "these matters . . . can in no way excuse the United Nations from resolutely pursuing its efforts." The United Nations did not do anything about it, and when the crisis came, the alarm bell was out of order: the Truce Supervision Organization was prevented from investigating the incidents that preceded Israel's attack, and Israel's mobilization and invasion of Egypt came before the United Nations could wake up.

In the weeks that separated Mr. Hammarskjold's warning from Israel's move, and especially after Israel's statement on the Suez Canal blockade, Mr. Ben Gurion's denunciation of Colonel Nasser and Mr. Eban's statements in the Security Council during the discussion of the Jordanian complaint on October 25, the United Nations still had at its disposal one big preventive weapon which could theoretically have been used for the first time: Part A of the "Uniting for Peace" resolution, which provided for an emergency session of the Assembly when "there appears to be a threat to peace," and when the Security Council is paralyzed. But this provision was not used for the same obvious reason which accounts for the failure of Mr. Hammarskjold's warning; the states were either not listening, or they did not want to listen. If a resolution asking for emergency measures had been brought before the Council, an Anglo-French (or French) veto might well have paralyzed the Council, and thus created the conditions for a resort to the 1950 procedure. But no such resolution was introduced or contemplated; on the 25th of October, further debate in the Council was postponed to the 30th.

Thus, the preventive mechanisms had failed. The arsenal was, on the whole, rich enough; but both its exploitation and the repair of those of its weapons that were in bad shape depended on the will and alertness of the United Nations Members. No foolproof set of procedures could ever automatically oblige states to take measures once a certain danger point is reached; and no system would have alerted either the Council or an emergency session of the Assembly about the gravity of the Suez crisis just before the Anglo-French intervention. The Anglo-French ultimatum came at a moment when the dispute apparently had entered a cooler period of bargaining and compromises under the auspices of the Secretary-General. The preventive parts of the "Uniting for Peace" resolution, modelled on the Korean example, can only be operative in cases where the tension is building up gradually and where no party succeeds in concealing its plan to use force. For similar reasons, there was no mechanism which could have prevented the Hungarian crisis.

2. Let us turn next to the repressive equipment of the United Nations. What we find here, paradoxically, is both a poorer and a more useful arsenal. The weapon which was used with great speed and efficiency, contrary to the expectations of the British and the French, was that very Part A of the "Uniting for Peace" resolution which had not been invoked preventively. At the request of the Security Council, two emergency sessions of the Assembly were summoned.

Now, Part C of the 1950 resolution had asked states to take certain initiatives which would facilitate the resort to "collective measures" (including armed force once peace has been broken); and it had established a Collective Measures Committee to study methods of maintaining and strengthening peace. After the failure of the system of Chapter VII, after the watering-down of Mr. Trygve Lie's proposal for "an internationally recruited police force," Sisyphus had been trying again. But this time the rock did not get pushed very high. The states did not react very enthusiastically to the requests of the 1950 resolution, nor to those of the resolution of January 1952 which embodied some suggestions of the Collective Measures Committee's first report. Indeed, the way in which these suggestions were emasculated by the Sixth Assembly was remarkable enough: imperative exhortations for advance preparation (including if necessary legislative changes) were turned into soft recommendations studded with reassuring grants of liberty. The key idea of getting Members to earmark certain elements of their armed forces for service as United Nations units quietly got lost.

The Committee itself based its work on two principles which were probably unavoidable and certainly unfortunate from the point of view of last fall's crisis. First, entrusted with what amounted to a general study of collective security, and realizing that advance commitments to "particular procedures or specific contributions" were unlikely, it tried to design measures that could fit as many circumstances as possible. One of the requirements of collective security is anonymity, but the price one has to pay is vagueness. It is therefore not too astonishing that the efforts of the Committee "were sterile." Secondly, what made them still more surely useless for the Assembly in 1956, even as a mere guide, was the way in which the Committee, just like the "Uniting for Peace" resolution itself, had taken the Korean case as a model—both in order, no doubt, to have at least one island of reference in an ocean of generalities, and because of the permanent tendency of statesmen and generals to prepare meticulously for the previous crisis. This principle had two consequences. The whole effort of the Committee was oriented toward collective enforcement against a transgressor. The Committee thus neglected the cases in which there would be a need for a supervisory force but not for a shooting one, and of course all its efforts were superfluous for a case such as Hungary where what was going to be decided was collective blame without enforcement. Also, the work of the Committee, almost from the first page of its first report, as based on the hypothesis of a clear-cut case of aggression; the other hypothesis (a "breach of peace" which is not a clear-cut aggression) got lost. Now, in the fall of 1956, the United Nations was faced with two baffling situations. One was an armed intervention in a civil war, opposed by one revolutionary government, but called for by the previous cabinet. The other case was a breach of peace composed of two separate invasions. About each of them one could argue endlessly as to whether it constituted a naked aggression, a partly provoked aggression, or a use of force devoid of "aggressive intention" which a well-known international lawyer once stated to be a necessary part of any definition of aggression and then refused to define abstractly. Indeed, the flaw of the Commission's decision to study the suppression of acts of aggression is well indicated by the failure of a host of international bodies to agree on any legally or politically satisfactory definition of aggression. Surely the apex of confusion is reached when a group as serious as the International Law Commission decides that all acts of aggression are crimes against mankind, after having failed to define aggression. Politico-legal concepts should not be defined by lawyers and cannot be adequately defined by politicians either.

At any rate, when the challenge came, the Members of the United Nations had once again to improvise a response in the heat of the moment. Nations condemned to improvisation are rarely willing to go beyond what is immediately needed to save peace, except perhaps for vague promises to think about more stable structures once the danger has receded. Indeed, the history of international organizations is like a graveyard of specialized commissions, or *ad hoc* representatives, who have been more or less gracefully allowed to fade away after finishing their temporary job.

The Policies Followed

We turn now to a brief discussion of the way in which the United Nations used its freedom last fall.

Ever since 1945, the organization has been faced with a series of disputes which were not the traditional quarrels of a stabilized period—quarrels of limited scope which do not challenge the international *status quo* or the internal regimes of states. The United Nations has had to deal with the explosions of a revolutionary period—disputes tainted by violence or at least accompanied by threats of violence. In such circumstances, the neat categories provided for by the Charter ("disputes," "situations," "aggression") often make little sense, and the United Nations has felt free to discard them and to select its course empirically. Last fall the Assembly decided to take a middle road between the two following extremes. On the one hand there is the policy which we might call "pure coercion"; it tries through injunctions, threats or collective enforcement to oblige the transgressors to give up any gains obtained through violations of the Charter; it refuses to subordinate a return to law to concessions asked or conditions raised by the transgressors. On the other hand, there is what might be called a policy of "pure conciliation"; it treats all parties to a dispute as equals and tries to reach a compromise through accommodation without any pressure being put on either side. Of course these two extremes are ideal types, but they have at times been realized. Thus, "pure coercion" was the United Nations policy in Korea, and "pure conciliation" was used during much of the Palestine crisis of 1948, during the first Indonesian conflict (1947–1948), and in the Kashmir stalemate. Now in the case of the Suez crisis, the middle road taken by the Assembly proved to be an increasingly narrow path, and in the case of Hungary, the road soon led to a dead end.

1. In the Middle Eastern crisis, there were excellent reasons for eliminating the two extremes. First, any policy that aimed merely at coercing France, England and Israel back into compliance with the Charter, even if it was not initially accompanied by collective enforcement measures, was risky. If the violators did not choose to obey the injunctions of the United Nations any more than the north Koreans had observed the provisions of the resolution of June 25, 1950, the United Nations would have either to lose face or to turn to sanctions, just as it had on June 27, 1950. Sanctions were both dangerous and questionable. The draft resolution introduced by the United States in the

Security Council after the beginning of the Israeli attack was almost a replica of the resolution of June 25, 1950; England and France were right in pointing out the differences between the cases of north Korea and Israel. After the English and French intervention, any attempt at treating the crisis as a new Korea disappeared. No one was called an aggressor. Consequently, the United Nations on the one hand refused to take up the Soviet appeal for an international mandate to an American-Russian expedition against the invaders—an appeal made, significantly enough, not to the Assembly, where it might have been well received, but to the Security Council, where it was sure to die fast. On the other hand, the United Nations also decided to offer to the parties an instrument that belongs not to the coercive but to the conciliatory arsenal of international organization: the United Nations Emergency Force (UNEF). UNEF is the sort of procedural guarantee which has in previous cases led belligerents to accept a cease-fire. States unwilling to lose face by obeying purely and simply a United Nations call because they do not want to appear to give in to their enemy in the field have often proved more ready to bow to an international mechanism. Seen in this light, UNEF has been playing a role comparable to the role of United Nations commissions and truce organizations in Palestine, Kashmir and Indonesia.

Secondly, however, there were good reasons for discarding a policy of mere conciliation. An organization committed to the defense and illustration of certain principles of international behavior could not accept as *faits accomplis* a series of moves which, however explainable by previous failures of the United Nations itself to redress certain wrongs, nevertheless violated the ban on the use of force against the territorial integrity or political independence of states. Israel had a strong case. The situation that existed before October 29, when Egypt claimed to be still at war with its neighbor but wanted to be protected against it ("unilateral belligerence") was indeed absurd. The need for Israel to defend itself, even through retaliation, against armed Egyptian attacks and against Colonel Nasser's plans for encirclement cannot be dismissed lightly either. But there remain enough arguments on the other side, such as the perils of preventive war, the well established principle that retaliation should not be disproportionate, and the idea that violations of the Charter presented as justified by the opponent's own breaches of treaties can only lead to international anarchy. Mr. Hammarskjold's firm decision to refuse to "condone a change of the *status juris* resulting from military action contrary to the provisions of the Charter" cannot be seriously challenged. Furthermore, in previous cases of disputes in which one side had resorted to military action and which the United Nations had tried to solve through purely conciliatory techniques, the organization had come close to failure; it had been able to remain in control of events only by coming around to Mr. Hammarskjold's doctrine. Consequently, the Assembly aimed some sharp recommendations at the invaders of Egypt; the resolution of November 2 called for their prompt withdrawal. This call had few precedents in the history of the United Nations, outside of the plain collective security case of Korea.

Now, once the two extreme policies had been eliminated, there remained a very broad range of possible "middle roads." Coercion and conciliation can be combined in infinitely varying doses. The crucial question is whether the mixture used after the resolution of November 2 was the best one. The course followed by the Assembly became rather like collective security, with moral and negative political sanctions (the denial of certain claims) substituted for the positive political, economic or military sanctions envisaged by the Collective Measures Committee. In other words, the Assembly and the Secretary-General moved further and further from the pole of "pure conciliation" and closer and closer to the pole of "pure coercion." Instead of achieving both an elimination of illegally obtained advantages and a peaceful settlement of the problems that had led to a violation of the law, the United Nations allowed the first aspect to obliterate the second. In the first place, the issue of "cease-fire and withdrawal" was separated from the underlying substantive issues; consideration of the Suez nationalization problem and of an over-all Arab-Israel settlement was postponed until after the first issue had been disposed of. The two United States draft resolutions which aimed at removing the fundamental causes of tension were shelved. Now, neither during the second Indonesian conflict nor when the Security Council invoked Chapter VII against the Arabs in the summer of 1948 had a policy of strong pressure against one side ruled out consideration of the deeper political issues which explained the breach of peace. In the second place, the elimination of the breach of peace and the restoration or quasi-restoration of the *status quo* became synonymous; Mr. Hammarskjold refused to permit Israel's withdrawal to be accompanied by guarantees over what one might call the "intermediate" issues—issues half way between the return to the *status quo* and a general political negotiation: Gaza, the Gulf of Aqaba, and passage of Israeli ships through the Suez Canal. These two decisions really condemned the United Nations to play the role of Sisyphus; for the crisis had its origins in the precariousness of a *status quo* which was never supposed to last eight years, at least as much as in the bad will of the parties.

Mr. Hammarskjold stated that his proposals tended to restore not the *status quo,* but the *status juris.* But the distinction is a fragile one: indeed, what *is* the *status juris?* The parties disagree, and this disagreement itself explains in part the collapse of the armistice agreements. For the Israelis, the law includes not only the end of border raids, or the scrupulous observance of articles VII and VIII of the Israel-Egypt armistice agreement, dealing with the armistice lines, but also the end of the blockade of the Suez Canal and of the Gulf of Aqaba. For the Egyptians, this is not the case, and in his report of January 24 the Secretary-General (who has constantly refused to answer Israel's questions concerning Egypt's policy of belligerency) was only able to say about the Gulf of Aqaba that "any possible claims of belligerent rights . . .

if asserted, should be limited to clearly non-controversial situations." In his report of January 24, he defined the return to the *status juris* as "a withdrawal of troops, and . . . the relinquishment or nullification of rights asserted in territories covered by the military action and depending upon it." The *status juris* is a return to the *status quo* accompanied by hopes that the parties would in the future respect the law.

A policy should be judged by its results. Mr. Hammarskjold's policy led to an impasse. The Assembly resolution of February 2—the last document adopted by the United Nations—merely endorsed his report of January 24. It asked, as he had done, for a stationing of UNEF "on" the armistice lines— with no length of time suggested. It also called for "the implementation of other measures as proposed in the Secretary-General's report with due regard to the considerations set out therein with a view to assist in achieving situations conducive to the maintenance of peaceful conditions in the area." "It seems very pretty," said Alice in Wonderland after she had read the poem "Jabberwocky," "but it is *rather* hard to understand." If one goes back to Mr. Hammarskjold's report, what one finds is the hope that the parties will let UNEF take over the functions of the Truce Supervision Organization and the familiar wish that the parties will accept at long last "such supporting measures as would guarantee a return to the state of affairs envisaged in the armistice agreement and avoidance of the state of affairs into which conditions, due to a lack of compliance with the agreement, progressively deteriorated." This year's hope for a mined fence replaces last year's hope for a barbed wire one. Sisyphus trusted that the rock would stop rolling down the next time. The Secretary-General, in answer to Israel's request, also stated in his report that "if it is recognized that there is such a need for such an arrangement," UNEF units could be stationed at the entrance of the Gulf of Aqaba. If this was a hint for specific Assembly endorsement, the Assembly, by its wholesale endorsement of Mr. Hammarskjold's "other measures," did not in turn do much more than hint back that it did not mind Mr. Hammarskjold's own hint. It was a tie. It became a deadlock when Israel persisted in asking for more, and Mr. Hammarskjold refused because "adherence to principle and law must be given priority and cannot be conditioned"—an admirable statement that would be even more perfect if the meaning of the law were clear and if Egypt had not, in one instance, defied successfully a principle affirmed by the Security Council.

Therefore, the United States, which until then had left the Secretary-General in charge of all the discussions with Egypt and Israel, had to intervene and to take the matter, in effect, out of the Secretary-General's hands. But it could not, at that stage, contradict him too vigorously. Hence the twists and turns of an "unconditional withdrawal" nevertheless subordinated not to conditions, but to "assumptions," to "hopes and conditions that are not unreasonable." Both because these "assumptions" went a little beyond Mr. Hammarskjold's doctrine, and because they had to be so obscure in order not to clash with it, they became controversial enough to make impossible the drafting of any resolution that would embody them.

It is instructive to establish a sort of balance sheet. By way of documents, we have only the United Nations resolution of February 2, the Secretary-General's report to which it refers, and the "assumptions" of Israel as qualified by the United States and interpreted by Mr. Hammarskjold. (*a*) On the Egyptian side of the former armistice line the United Nations has a police force tolerated by Egypt, but whose mission has not been clearly spelled out. The appeal for a stationing "on" the line, still unheeded by Israel, gives Egypt a most useful political weapon, in addition to Egypt's legal right to ask the Force to leave. (*b*) In the Gaza Strip, Israel's expectations (which Mr. Hammarskjold never encouraged) have proved in great part wrong. The temporary period of United Nations civilian control has been short indeed. Egyptian troops have not returned but they have the legal right to do so. (*c*) At the entrance of the Gulf of Aqaba, a UNEF unit has been stationed. But its duration is shaky, its mission most obscure, and the only solid guarantee seems to be Israel's solemn warning that any interference with free navigation will be considered as an attack giving rise to the right of self-defense. (*d*) As to passage through the Suez Canal, Egypt has not renounced its belligerency. (*e*) Nothing new, except more hatred, has happened with reference to a general settlement between Israel and its neighbors. (*f*) The Suez Canal Company issue has been handled after the Anglo-French withdrawal, and has ended in a *de facto* acceptance of a unilateral Egyptian declaration—with no United Nations pronouncement of any kind.

An abundance of texts calling for a cease-fire and withdrawal had been succeeded by a stunning dearth of authoritative documents covering the present and the future. The interplay between public international debates and secret diplomacy has produced a series of stop-gap agreements differently interpreted by the parties. Some of the multilateral gobbledygook which has replaced the elegant obscurity of nineteenth century diplomacy is still with us—but not much of the authority attached to previous United Nations pronouncements, an authority which has often offset their obscurity. The course followed through the United Nations seems to have led to little more than a temporary reinforcement of the truce system at the Israel-Egypt border. Egypt's present informal acceptance of UNEF can hardly be seen as a big concession. UNEF might prevent new raids, but it also protects Egypt from Israel; and Egypt made sure that the Force would be absolutely weightless in the political balance of power in the Middle East; UNEF is not, as Egypt had feared, an "occupation force," it had served far more, as Egypt wished, as a "fire brigade" called to the rescue of Egypt. Indeed, in an area where all issues *are* linked, the elimination of the breach of peace does not merely restore Egypt's position in the supposed "next phase" (the discussion of the underlying issues). The position has improved. Egypt's right of veto over UNEF provides Colonel Nasser with an instrument of blackmail against any attempt at a solution that he would dislike. We must therefore ask whether another "middle road," a different combination of coercion and conciliation, might not have been *tried* (this is not to say that it would have *succeeded*). For it is one thing to condone violations of the Charter, but it is quite another to refuse to follow a course that makes new violations timely.

It seems that there remained a choice between the Secretary-General's policy of proceeding step-by-step, so that no new issue would be considered before the previous one had been disposed of, and the policy outlined by Mr. Pearson. The Canadian foreign minister wanted to continue the tradition, often used with success, of having the political organs of the United Nations take without delay a stand on all issues involved in the crisis, i.e. suggest procedures for settlement of the deeper underlying problems and define a policy concerning the "intermediate" issues. This would still have upheld the principle that gains obtained by force should not be kept. But it would also have taken into account the fact that the issues raised by Israel's, France's and the United Kingdom's action were linked. After all, the trouble in the Middle East did not begin on October 29, 1956.

It might be argued on legal and on political grounds that Mr. Pearson's "middle course" was not realistic, and that Mr. Hammarskjold's line was the only possible one—except for appeasement or collective enforcement. The legal objections do not seem decisive. One could argue that under international law Egypt's consent was needed at every stage. But Mr. Pearson's proposals did not overlook this requirement. They merely invited the United Nations *first* to define a line of policy and *then* promote negotiations with the parties to get this line adopted. Maybe Egypt's consent would have been hard to get; but Egypt, which had been rescued by the United Nations, which was still partly occupied by a victorious enemy, and which was economically as badly shaken as its opponents, was in no strong position to resist pressure, had it come. One could also object that the resolutions of the Assembly did not leave much leeway to the Secretary-General. Nevertheless, we can observe that Israel did not withdraw "forthwith." Furthermore, the key resolution of November 2 mentioned the problem of raids and the need for observance of "the armistice agreements"—terms which left the door open for arrangements over the "intermediate" issues, as, for instance, Egypt's claiming of belligerency rights, which the Security Council had declared to be in contradiction to the armistice agreements.

In fact, both legal objections do raise far more serious political problems. How could the Secretary-General *himself* exert pressure on Egypt? How much *political* leeway did he have in interpreting the resolutions? It is not enough to state that he probably had much to say in the drafting of the instructions he received from the Assembly, and that the Assembly was unlikely to overrule him if he decided to follow Mr. Pearson's course, at a time when American policy was to praise, paraphrase, and propose whatever Mr. Hammarskjold suggested. For even if he had obtained from the Assembly directives in accordance with Mr. Pearson's program, the success of such a policy depended on one major criterion, which was missing: the willingness of the United States to exert pressure on Egypt in order to gain Egyptian consent. Pressure by the Assembly in the form of resolutions, recommending certain measures was not enough. It had to be accompanied by pressure outside of the United Nations. It was the combination of United Nations and United States pressure which obliged the Dutch to give in in Indonesia—and the Israelis to evacuate Egypt. When it came to the second aspect of the Middle Eastern crisis (the settlement of the deeper and "intermediate" issues) the United States was willing to support the Secretary-General in the Assembly, but Mr. Hammarskjold, had he selected a more vigorous course, would have needed the United States in front of him, in Cairo, so to speak, and not merely behind him in New York.

This objection cannot be dismissed. The decisions of the Assembly and the silence or the United States did condemn the Secretary-General to the following dilemma. He had to take political initiatives that belong to an independent executive rather than to an official with little political power. Or else he had to zigzag between the question marks of ambiguous resolutions. However, it seems to this writer that Mr. Hammarskjold resigned himself to the latter course with such skill, caution and good grace that the dangers of the dilemma were too easily overlooked; the members of the Assembly were encouraged to travel a road which has justly been called a "reversion to the abnormal." Finally, if Mr. Hammarskjold's policy was the inevitable product of the Assembly's feelings and of United States inaction, it becomes necessary to transfer the blame, but not to whitewash the policy.

2. One can argue whether it is Egypt or the United Nations which has been the master in the Middle Eastern crisis. No argument, alas, is possible in the Hungarian one. The road which the Assembly tried to travel was different from the Middle Eastern one; it amounted to an attempt at pure coercion through mere dictation. No collective measures were undertaken, but Soviet military action was condemned far more severely and directly than the Israeli, French and British operation. The call to desist "forthwith" and to withdraw "without any further delay" was not accompanied by the offer of a face-saving international mechanism such as a truce or "nonshooting" police force, or by the offer of a conciliatory device such as a commission of mediation between Hungary and the Soviet Union (such as, for instance, the Balkan Commission). The United Nations merely offered its Secretary-General and observers designated by him, not as peacemakers or mediators, but as investigators, and soon thereafter decided that free elections should be held under United Nations auspices. Conciliation was ruled out. However, when dictation failed, as had all previous attempts in similar circumstances (in the Balkans, in Korea before June 1950, and in Berlin during the United Nations phase of the dispute), the United Nations had to reconsider its policy and to face the dilemma: retreat or toughness. Some Members would have

liked the United Nations to introduce a certain dose of conciliation, by offering its services and by avoiding unilateral definitions of policy. Hence India protested against the call for free elections, and appealed for negotiations with the Soviet and Hungarian governments the sort of discussion of underlying political issues that was being avoided in the Middle East because it seemed to some that such a negotiation would be a reward for aggression! However, the United Nations remained consistent and did not follow Mr. Menon; but it did not change the nature of the pressure exerted on the Soviet Union either. No sanctions of any kind were decided; even one rather mild sort of collective measure that had been suggested was not taken up: the appointment as observers of diplomatic representatives serving in Hungary. The United Nations margin of action was thus quite small. The United Nations could solemnly condemn the violation of the Charter, try to post observers outside of the iron curtain and create an investigation committee which by necessity operated outside of Hungary, but these measures amount to solemn protests, and the formal condemnation has more in common with the Stimson doctrine than with the branding of Red China as an aggressor, which was accompanied by sanctions.

Thus, in effect, the *status quo* was restored everywhere, but it was the Hungarian revolution which was contained, and the Israelis who were rolled back. This apparently paradoxical balance sheet carries with it some important lessons.

Political Limitations of the United Nations

1. The first lesson seems to be that the assumptions of the drafters of the Charter have been vindicated: international organization can operate with maximum effectiveness, i.e. both preserve the political independence and territorial integrity of its members and settle international disputes, only if big power unity is preserved and if the claims to be reconciled do not involve the existence of states or the nature of regimes.

The first of these assumptions was contradicted by the "Uniting for Peace" resolution, which was based on the thought that the organization should not be paralyzed by the cold war and that collective security could be organized even against big powers. Now, it is to a large extent the breakdown of the negative Russian-American concert in the Middle East which led to last year's explosion; between 1947 and the death of Stalin, neither the Soviet Union nor the United States was actively involved in Middle Eastern politics. The Soviets had not intervened in the Iranian oil crisis, and a long series of Security Council resolutions from 1948 to 1953 proved that the two great powers were not on opposite sides of the fence in matters concerning the "Palestine problem." The first Soviet veto came in January 1954—at a time when the British were trying to convince Colonel Nasser to join a Middle Eastern defense organization. What followed is familiar enough: the Baghdad Pact, the Egyptian arms deal, the Aswan Dam affair, and the Soviet veto of the second part of the western resolution over Suez submitted to the Security Council in October. Inversely, it is to a large extent the temporary return to a big power concert which explains the success of the United Nations in getting a Middle Eastern cease-fire and withdrawal without resort to sanctions. The carrot of UNEF was accompanied by the stick of combined (although antagonistic) Soviet and American pressure. Soviet threats of resort to "collective measures" increased in effect the weight of American pressure. Finally, it is of course the existence of a "bi-polar" world which explains the failure of the United Nations to achieve any comparable result in Hungary.

The "Uniting for Peace" resolution provided only a procedure for acting in an emergency such as the Hungarian one. The success of the Korean experiment in collective action was misleading; there, the Russian armed forces were not *directly* involved, and the Chinese were not a military power of the first magnitude. It has been said quite rightly that the "Uniting for Peace" resolution, to be effective, supposes that the world is "divided for war" and ready to fight. To fight north Korea, indeed; far less ready to fight Red China and not at all to fight the Soviets. On the one hand, in 1950 and again in 1956 certain small or medium-size Members of the United Nations have been most unwilling to go beyond the original Charter and to envisage any form of coercion (even purely verbal) against a great power. On the other hand, the United States itself adopted toward the Soviet Union a policy which in effect does not have much use for the United Nations. The doctrine of massive retaliation "by means and at places of our own choosing" implies that when the United States decides to strike at the Soviet Union, the main American action will take place outside of the United Nations, which is too slow, militarily unprepared, and anyhow heavily compelled by its own principles to fight on the field chosen by the enemy. The doctrine also means that, when the United States decides that there is no point in striking back, as it did last October, the United Nations can only hurl rhetorical thunderbolts at the Soviets.

As for the other original assumption of the Charter, it seems that the very inability of the United Nations to do much more than restore the *status quo* in the Middle East shows the limitations of the policy of collective assertion, parliamentary debates and majority votes with which the United Nations has tried to tackle the problem of change and the anticolonial revolution. Various factors contribute to the deadlock. In the first place, if the majority tries to accelerate the process, the nation whose sovereignty is infringed by United Nations policies still has the legal power to resist—as the Union of South Africa has shown and as Israel shows now in connection with the stationing of UNEF. In the second place, if, on the contrary, nations adversely affected by the nationalist revolutions try to reverse the trend, the states that owe their existence to these revolutions, those that stand to gain by encouraging the trend and those that are afraid of resisting it are numerous enough in the

Assembly to prevent any such move. The new nations of Asia and Africa can therefore save the territorial *status quo* of any one of them, when it is threatened from the outside. They tend to favor or accept a measure such as the nationalization of the Suez Canal Company because it is presented politically as a victory over colonialism and legally as the mere exercise of territorial sovereignty. (Far less concern is shown over matters involving persons.) Thus, the "new United Nations" can operate as a boomerang against countries like England, France or Israel—a western bridgehead in the Arab world.

Thirdly, there is a deeper reason which explains why it is so difficult for international organization to provide peaceful change in a revolutionary world. Most of the causes of trouble and change are completely beyond the reach of the United Nations. The United Nations in this respect is both restricted and anachronistic. It approaches dynamic forces such as pan-Arabism or communism with nineteenth century concepts such as the duty of non-intervention of states. It approaches the crucial problem posed by the different behavior of different regimes—dictatorships, totalitarian governments, democracies—with the old liberal concept according to which the type of government has to be discounted in international affairs, as if ideologies and national politics really did stop at each border or at "the water's edge." It ignores the submerged part of the iceberg of world politics, such as the techniques of subversion or the struggle for control of raw materials and sources of energy. By its occasional attempts at concentrating on the technical aspects of a dispute so as to make it less explosive, the United Nations can be led to underestimate such imponderable elements as those without which the Suez crisis can hardly be understood: the issue of national prestige, the fear of humiliation, the defensive nationalism of France and England (a reaction to the triumphant nationalism of Asia and Africa) the Anglo-French instinctive Munich reaction in the summer of 1956, or the fear of colonialism which explains why Asian countries reacted more violently to Suez than to Budapest. The United Nations tries to play Hamlet with Fortinbras alone.

2. Even though the original assumptions of the Charter have been vindicated, the United Nations has to operate in a world in which those assumptions simply do not apply. Hence there has appeared in the debates and policies of the United Nations a number of inequities and discrepancies which the last crises have put into clear focus and which weaken the influence of the organization. There is first of all the problem of the use of force. The ban of the Charter seems either too rigid or too narrow; it has led in practice to a different treatment of *faits accomplis* without armed violence, or of the subtler forms of pressure or subversion, and of "coups" accomplished by armies. Now, if the first category is tolerated, the ban on the second cannot be interpreted as an absolute. The Charter was an attempt at providing states with a better alternative to the solution of international disputes. If this alternative does not work, if states' claims of great emotional or political importance are either not taken into account by international mechanisms or

are merely dragged or gradually compromised away from one conference to the next, we will have more Suez expeditions. The alternative to collective adjustment is certainly not collective sainthood and it cannot be individual suicide. The successful suppression by the United Nations of a big scale attempt at solving disputes by armed force in the Middle East might merely encourage states caught in such a dilemma to resort to all kinds of force except armed force, or to attack anything (through subversion, blockade, embargoes, etc.) as long as it is not someone's territory. Even the resort to armed force has often been successful. It has been unpunished when it was decided by the Soviet Union within its zone of influence; it has also been unpunished when the dose of force used each time has been small although it was administered frequently, such as in armistice line violations, or when the theater of operations was not a vital one in world politics (such as in the case of Hyderabad and to some extent Kashmir), or when the plea of domestic jurisdiction still has some authority (as in Algeria).

Inconsistencies in United Nations attitudes have also been criticized with reference to the power of the states which the United Nations has challenged. Messrs. Pineau, Lloyd and Spaak have complained about the differences between the United Nations' "kindness" toward the Soviets and harshness toward England, France and Israel. Here some distinctions must be made. If one looks at the documents, this accusation is quite unfair. It is not the United Nations which has treated the transgressors differently; it is the transgressors who have reacted differently to United Nations resolutions; to whitewash violations of the Charter in one part of the world because they cannot be remedied elsewhere is a policy of chaos. Similarly, if one looks at the problem from the point of view of the preservation of world peace, it could be argued that the failure of the United Nations in Hungary and its success in Egypt contributed equally to the safeguarding of peace. Those who would have liked the United Nations to send a UNEF to Hungary forget among other things that UNEF was sent to Egypt with the consent of all parties and that any other kind of force would be not a supervisory unit but an international fighting army. As for non-military sanctions (economic reprisals or the suspension or expulsion of Mr. Kadar's United Nations delegates), they would merely have assuaged the nerves of United Nations members—and further demonstrated the lack of effective United Nations power in that area. However, if one looks at the problem from the point of view of "justice" rather than of "peace," and if one considers the actual amount of pressure that was put respectively on the Soviets and on Britain, France, and Israel, rather than the texts voted upon, Messrs. Pineau, Lloyd, and Spaak do have a very real point. The contrast in the amount of pressure, however justified by power considerations, is shocking precisely because the principles of the Charter are supposed to apply equally to all. "Two wrongs don't make one right," said Mr. Eisenhower. In a way, this is true; but in another way, one wrong (the Soviet refusal to budge) and one right (Israel's unconditional

withdrawal) do finally make two wrongs: the Soviet immunity and the difference in pressure. Through some perverse law, it also seems that the more a
state resists the United Nations, the more this state gets away with: the Soviets, and Egypt on the issue of the Suez blockade, have emerged scot free;
Israel has finally saved a bit more than England and France, which agreed
faster to withdraw.

A final discrepancy was alluded to by Barbara Ward, when she defined
international agencies as "mechanisms for making other nations do what one
would not do oneself." There have been admirable examples of this during
the recent crises. The Israelis have insisted that UNEF should not be stationed on Israeli soil or on any territory controlled by Israel, but at the same
time they have protested against the Secretary-General's reminder that all the
requests made by Israel concerning Gaza or UNEF required the consent of
Egypt. Yugoslavia refused to accept United Nations observers who would
investigate about Hungary because this would be "a dangerous precedent,"
whereas for years similar investigations were conducted about the Union of
South Africa's *apartheid* policies. India protested against mere "propaganda"
resolutions condemning the Soviets, but she also wanted to see maximum
pressure put on Israel, as though blame became propaganda only when the
recipient was not easily influenced by outside pressure. The states which
have used the United Nations most effectively as an instrument for the advancement of their cause are the ones which have insisted most constantly
upon the limited and temporary role of UNEF. The main common bond
among the members of the United Nations is the defense rather than the
moderation of their sovereignty; that there should be growing cynicism or
skepticism as a result is not surprising.

The West and the United Nations

Nevertheless, the United Nations is here to stay, and western powers should
adopt a policy or strategy toward the United Nations. The Soviets have one;
so do the new nations. We have just mentioned some inconsistencies; we
could add here the example of the United States, which last summer showed
no enthusiasm whatsoever toward bringing the Suez Canal issue to the
United Nations, and which after October 30 emphasized vehemently its
reliance on the United Nations in all Middle Eastern problems except the
fight against "international communism."

1. An obvious starting point would be the fact that the western nations
cannot put the United Nations at the center of their foreign policies. This is
as true with reference to the competition for the "uncommitted" world as it
is in relation to straight east-west issues. The predominance of small states
in the Assembly and the sort of "bloc veto" or diluting power of the African-
Asian nations when they are allied with the Soviet group have somewhat
tarnished Mr. Morganthau's vision of "new United Nations" as a field in

which the United States could multilateralize its national interest. On the contrary, given the rules of the Assembly, the interests of the Africans and Asians (and, at times, through the intermediary of these nations, the interests of the Soviet group) might receive American naturalization. When the weight of multilateral restraint on American or western interests is such that these interests emerge quite unrecognizable, how acceptable is such a restraint, and how useful the mechanism in which this alchemical process takes place. In certain cases, a tail constituted by a few small states, whose support is needed, can wag the American dog.

But there is a second and equally obvious starting point. The west has a tremendous interest in keeping the United Nations alive and in good health—even in political matters. The United Nations provides the west with an indispensable, although too lofty, set of ideals and with a necessary, although too narrow, set of procedures. It is not merely because the United Nations has defended the national sovereignty of non-western countries that so many of the latter have applauded the American attitude in the crisis of last fall. It is also, as Hugh Gaitskell has recognized, because the Charter constitutes the only hopeful international ideal for most nations of the present world, as well as a code of behavior which represents the maximum that anyone has a right to expect. The way in which the Soviets have in turn exploited this ideal and this code in the Middle Eastern crisis should be a warning.

The crisis of last fall demonstrated that the United Nations plays a legitimizing role of increasing importance—at least negatively. The United Nations does not quite have the strength to *initiate*, but it has the authority to prevent certain things and to stop others, and it has enough moral force to legitimize what it endorses. Consequently, actions (other than the construction of regional or functional organizations, or action aimed directly at the Soviet bloc) which are undertaken outside and without the *imprimatur* of the United Nations risk losing part of their value. The two London conferences over Suez last summer suffered somewhat from that risk. It is easy to show how shaky this international legitimacy is and to denounce "international majoritarianism." But every state today, however grudgingly, gropes for the former and wants the benefits of the latter. It was a majority which England and France were trying to get behind their (and Mr. Dulles') scheme at the first London conference. When Mr. Dulles stated that "it is one thing for a nation to defy one or two nations but it is quite another thing to defy the sober and considered judgment of many nations," England and France approved, since the defiant nation, then, was Egypt. The Menzies mission did its best to impress Colonel Nasser with the importance of majority rule. In September and October, when England and France first began to lose that majority, then decided to go it alone, the fact that an overwhelming number of nations decided against them did influence their policy. The legitimacy of the United Nations is bound to be fragile, given the political limitations and inconsistencies imposed by a revolutionary period, as well as such structural defects as the right of veto and the egalitarian voting formula. But any kind of legitimacy in such a period is a blessing and a guide for future stabilization.

No western nation can afford to define the national interest so narrowly that such an asset would be left to others. Nor can any western nation afford deliberately to put the United Nations to a test which the organization will lose, so as to use this failure as a pretext for Charter violations; for if this nation's bold attempt should go wrong, it will be only too happy if there is an international mechanism available to rescue it from the mess. "In an inflammable world, it is no mean achievement of international organization to serve as a candle snuffer so as to minimize the necessity for relying upon an unreliable fire department." If there were no United Nations that could offer a United Nations Emergency Force to a suspicious Egypt, the alternative would be a clash between Soviet "volunteers" and Anglo-French "policemen." The nations' almost hysterical emphasis on sovereignty explains both why the candle snuffer can do so little and why only an international organization can be the candle snuffer. Anything else would smell of "intervention," neo-colonialism, or gunboat diplomacy.

2. With these two opposed starting points, we can at least suggest certain lines of policy. No doubt, it is uncomfortable for the west to have to live in two rather conflicting eras at the same time: The traditional era of "power politics," sovereignty, and unilateral action, which is still with us, and the emergent era of the "rule of law," symbolized more by ideals than by acts. The Soviets have the advantage of living almost exclusively in the first. The underdeveloped nations are carried by a "wave of the future" or "stream of history" which allows them to use quite naturally the principles and purposes of the Charter as a tool of national policy. The west has done the same thing in the cold war but finds it far more difficult with respect to the anti-colonial revolution; nevertheless, a way must be found to bridge the gap between the two eras.

A first precept would be to avoid any head-on clash with the ideals which the west professes (and profits from). This involves, first of all, in cases where attempts at conciliation or peaceful change have failed, the duty to defend one's interests by methods which are not internationally regressive. The use of armed force, except for collective security, in self-defense and perhaps in circumstances as tragic as Israel's position after years of encirclement and insecurity, is to be avoided. Israel itself has not brought lasting peace any nearer either by its former massive retaliatory raids or by last fall's war. The case of England and France is even clearer. It could be shown quite persuasively that Colonel Nasser's nationalization of an international public service accompanied by statements which expressed a will to use this service for national purposes and which presented the move as an act of retaliation was going against the direction which international society is bound to take if complete disintegration is to be avoided. Thus, England and France had a number of perfectly "progressive" arguments. Legally, Egypt could exploit the letter of international law and invoke the narrowest interpretation of rather ambiguous provisions, but the western powers could resort to an interpretation in which the spirit and purposes of the law rather than the textual arguments served as criteria. In fact, a number of Asian and African nations did agree with the western reasoning in the first London conference. If a special session of the United Nations Assembly had been summoned at the time instead of the Conference, as the British Labor Party had suggested, the west might have obtained the legitimizing seal of the United Nations. However, this "progressive" case was destroyed by the use of military force in circumstances that seemed to combine the perils of a plot and the imprudence of an improvization. Such a move immediately provoked a clear opposition by Asia and Africa against the invaders—the very kind of alignment that threatens to wreck both the United Nations and the international politics of the west, and that had been miraculously avoided in the Suez crisis until then. The only justification is that the wavering of Mr. Dulles seemed to shut out all the more subtle forms of pressure on Egypt. But perhaps Mr. Dulles would have been less anxious to stress "peace" so absolutely if there had been fewer war noises in Paris and London. The arsenal of coercion is rich enough for western states to find in it other weapons than bombers and tanks.

Our precept also involves the duty to prevent situations in which a head-on clash between the Charter and western nations seems like a lesser evil. Whenever the United Nations is unable to provide adequate procedures of peaceful adjustment, or whenever the only possible decisions of the United Nations would conflict with western interests, other mechanisms must be tried. The United Nations as a set of procedures is not necessarily the best means toward the ideals for which these procedures stand. In such cases to avoid the United Nations altogether is far more respectable than the tactic which consists in finally bringing to the United Nations disputes which many previous attempts have failed to solve and which have reached such a temperature that they can only explode in the faces of the United Nations Members. The United Nations should be a hospital, not a morgue. Nor can western policymakers let it become a force which would weaken or increase the weaknesses of the west in world affairs. A second precept would be to use the United Nations in such a way that United Nations ideals and western interests would be brought together without too much strain. This involves, first of all, the need to strengthen as much as possible those very alarm bells and mechanisms whose weaknesses we have deplored in the beginning. The more fragile the *status quo* and the smaller the chance of peaceful adjustment, the more necessary it becomes to repair the institutional deficiencies described last year by the Secretary-General and to equip the Assembly with devices which will allow it, should the crisis recur, to react more smoothly instead of staggering "from crisis to crisis improvising in haste."

Our precept involves, secondly, the need at least to try to find ways in which the United Nations could play a more active role in efforts toward peaceful change. The hope is dim, as recent failures in Kashmir have confirmed. However, attempts at substituting small negotiating bodies for unruly parliamentary debates or at restoring the League of Nations system of rapporteurs might be fruitful. As the Assembly works now, it is far more capable of creating subsidiary organs than of providing conciliation, and it would be good to use more of the former in order to gain more of the latter.

Our precept also requires a thorough effort at leadership by western nations in the United Nations in order to obtain the necessary two-thirds majority for proposals which are in the interest of the west. The crisis of last fall has shown that only such political leadership can produce results. For a great power such as the United States to "leave to the United Nations" matters of great concern to itself or to its allies is a mistake, whenever it means that this great power has no policy of its own to propose to the United Nations. Abandoned without such leadership to the free play of voting blocs, the Assembly will inevitably tend to pass the buck to the Secretary-General, and no civil servant, national or international, however subtle and dedicated, will ever tend to take bold initiatives in a political vacuum. Mr. Acheson has wisely reminded us that in the minds of the authors of the "Uniting for Peace" resolution, the Assembly was supposed to execute, not to frame, policy. Such leadership should imply a will to refuse excessive dilution of vital proposals for the sake of getting a text on the books, and a readiness to take matters out of the United Nations if necessary (as last February). The alternative to a "bloc veto" in the Assembly does not have to be a weak compromise where important interests are lost and only sponsors gained. Western nations have enough voting power of their own to block any proposals that would conflict with their policies; chess can be played by more than one group. In the long run no non-communist member of the United Nations has anything to gain either by refusing institutional improvements or by opposing efforts at coping with the problem of change in areas where the *status juris* has all the marks of a powder keg.

Our precept means, finally, that such leadership must not only be exerted within the United Nations but must also be extended outside of the United Nations. Precisely because many factors in world affairs are beyond the control of the organization, and because it is not a world government with an executive branch entrusted to the Secretary-General (even though the Assembly tries to act as a legislature), the Members of the United Nations have the duty to supplement and not just to echo the calls of the United Nations for peaceful adjustment. This is another major lesson of the crisis.

To sum up, the tragic events of Hungary have confirmed the powerlessness of the United Nations in the zone under Soviet control; there, a change of the *status quo* cannot be obtained by the United Nations and it is anyhow hard to see how other mechanisms can obtain it at a price acceptable to the west.

In the Middle East a general settlement satisfactory to all parties was and still is probably impossible either in or outside the United Nations; but no efforts were made at all. A considerable "intermediary" improvement was probably far less impossible; but it was not achieved. Diplomatic efforts that might have been aimed at a settlement will have to be devoted instead to a consolidation and improvement of the *status quo*. Because of the very limitations and inequities revealed by the crisis it is not possible to expect the United Nations itself to contribute much in the future to a settlement of the more explosive Middle Eastern issues. This imposes upon the statesmen of the west the triple duty to see that such a settlement be attempted within or outside the United Nations by all means compatible with the Charter; to avoid moves and maneuvers that imperil the principles upon which the United Nations rests; and to strengthen those United Nations techniques whose purpose it is to postpone or to limit explosions until a deeper settlement has been achieved.

Already the Middle East in the United Nations has become disturbingly similar to the Turkish question in the Concert of Europe. There too, the main powers of the world had for years agreed only on the maintenance of the *status quo* and on the need to prevent the peoples of the area from disturbing peace by trying to settle their own fate violently. When the hands-off policy of the big powers disappeared and when the nationalities so long contained began to lift the lid and to exploit their guardians' rivalries, the first world war put an end to the game. The Concert was institutionally and politically too weak to prevent the catastrophe. A war temporarily averted or repressed is not a world restored—it might simply mean a bigger blast prepared.

Thus Sisyphus has survived the avalanche. He will have to stay on the job. To be sure, if other mortals do not come to help him, his rock will never remain on top of the mountain and the next landslide might crush him. But if he does not try again, however clumsily, with their help, the gods of war and want will have won a remarkable victory.

8.

Obstinate or Obsolete? The Fate of the Nation-State and the Case of Western Europe

STANLEY HOFFMANN

I

THE CRITICAL ISSUE for every student of world order is the fate of the nation-state. In the nuclear age, the fragmentation of the world into countless units, each of which has a claim to independence, is obviously dangerous for peace and illogical for welfare. The dynamism which animates those units, when they are not merely city-states of limited expanse or dynastic states manipulated by the Prince's calculations, but nation-states that pour into their foreign policy the collective pride, ambitions, fears, prejudices, and images of large masses of people, is particularly formidable.[1] An abstract theorist could argue that any system of autonomous units follows the same basic rules, whatever the nature of those units. But in practice, that is, in history, their substance matters as much as their form; the story of world affairs since the French Revolution is not merely one more sequence in the ballet of sovereign states; it is the story of the fires and upheavals propagated by nationalism. A claim to sovereignty based on historical tradition and dynastic legitimacy alone has never had the fervor, the self-righteous assertiveness which a similar claim based on the idea and feelings of nationhood presents: in world politics, the dynastic function of nationalism is the constitution of nation-states by amalgamation or by splintering, and its emotional function

Reprinted by permission from *Daedalus, Journal of the American Academy of Arts and Sciences,* Vol. 95, No. 3, 1966.

1. See Pierre Renouvin et Jean-Baptiste Duroselle, *Introduction a l'histoire des relations internationales* (Paris, 1964).

is the supplying of a formidable good conscience to leaders who see their task as the achievement of nationhood, the defense of the nation, or the expansion of a national mission.[2]

This is where the drama lies. The nation-state is at the same time a form of social organization and—in practice if not in every brand of theory—a factor of international non-integration; but those who argue in favor of a more integrated world, either under more centralized power or through various networks of regional or functional agencies, tend to forget Auguste Comte's old maxim that *on ne détruit que ce qu'on remplace:* the new "formula" will have to provide not only world order, but also the kind of social organization in which leaders, élites, and citizens feel at home. There is currently no agreement on what such a formula will be;[3] as a result, nation-states —often inchoate, economically absurd, administratively ramshackle, and impotent yet dangerous in international politics—remain the basic units in spite of all the remonstrations and exhortations. They go on *faute de mieux* despite their alleged obsolescence; indeed, not only do they profit from man's incapacity to bring about a better order, but their very existence is a formidable obstacle to their replacement.

If there was one part of the world in which men of good will thought that the nation-state could be superseded, it was Western Europe. One of France's most subtle commentators on international politics has recently reminded us of E. H. Carr's bold prediction of 1945: "we shall not see again a Europe of twenty, and a world of more than sixty independent sovereign states."[4] Statesmen have invented original schemes for moving Western Europe "beyond the nation-state,"[5] and political scientists have studied their efforts with a care from which emotional involvement was not missing. The conditions seemed ideal. On the one hand, nationalism seemed at its lowest ebb; on the other, an adequate formula and method for building a substitute had apparently been devised. Twenty years after the end of World War II—a period as long as the whole interwar era—observers have had to revise their judgments. The most optimistic put their hope in the chances the future may still harbor, rather than in the propelling power of the present; the less optimistic ones, like myself, try simply to understand what went wrong.

My own conclusion is sad and simple. The nation-state is still here, and the new Jerusalem has been postponed because the nations in Western Europe have not been able to stop time and to fragment space. Political unification could have succeeded if, on the one hand, these nations had not been caught

2. In a way, the weaker are the foundations on which the nation rests, the shriller the assertions become.

3. On this point, see Rupert Emerson, *From Empire to Nation* (Cambridge, Mass., 1962), Ch. XIX; and Raymond Aron, *Paix et Guerre entre les Nations* (Paris, 1962), Ch. XI.

4. E. H. Carr, *Nationalism and After* (London, 1965), p. 51. Quoted in Pierre Hassner, "Nationalisme et relations internationales," *Revue française de science politique,* Vol. XV, No. 3 (June 1965), pp. 499–528.

5. See Ernst B. Haas' book by this title (Stanford, Calif., 1964).

in the whirlpool of different concerns, as a result both of profoundly different internal circumstances and of outside legacies, and if, on the other hand, they had been able or obliged to concentrate on "community-building" to the exclusion of all problems situated either outside their area or within each one of them. Domestic differences and different world views obviously mean diverging foreign policies; the involvement of the policy-makers in issues among which "community-building" is merely one has meant a deepening, not a decrease, of those divergences. The reasons follow: the unification movement has been the victim, and the survival of nation-states the outcome, of three factors, one of which characterizes every international system, and the other two only the present system. Every international system owes its inner logic and its unfolding to the *diversity* of domestic determinants, geo-historical situations, and outside aims among its units; any international system based on fragmentation tends, through the dynamics of unevenness (so well understood, if applied only to economic unevenness, by Lenin) to reproduce diversity. However, there is no inherent reason that the model of the fragmented international system should rule out by itself two developments in which the critics of the nation-state have put their bets or their hopes. Why must it be a diversity of nations? Could it not be a diversity of regions, of "federating" blocs, superseding the nation-state just as the dynastic state had replaced the feudal puzzle? Or else, why does the very logic of con-flagrations fed by hostility not lead to the kind of catastrophic unification of exhausted yet interdependent nations, sketched out by Kant? Let us remember that the unity movement in Europe was precisely an attempt at creating a regional entity, and that its origins and its springs resembled, on the re-duced scale of a half-continent, the process dreamed up by Kant in his *Idea of Universal History*.[6]

The answers are not entirely provided by the two factors that come to mind immediately. One is the legitimacy of national self-determination, the only principle which transcends all blocs and ideologies, since all pay lip service to it, and provides the foundation for the only "universal actor" of the international system: the United Nations. The other is the newness of many of the states, which have wrested their independence by a nationalist upsurge and are therefore unlikely to throw or give away what they have obtained only too recently. However, the legitimacy of the nation-state does not by itself guarantee the nation-state's survival in the international state of nature, and the appeal of nationalism as an emancipating passion does not assure that the nation-state must everywhere remain the basic form of social organization, in a world in which many nations are old and settled and the shortcomings of the nation-state are obvious. The real answers are provided by two unique features of the present international system. One, it is the first truly *global* international system: the regional subsystems have only a re-

6. See on this point my essay "Rousseau on War and Peace," in *The State of War* (New York, 1965).

duced autonomy; the "relationships of major tension" blanket the whole planet, the domestic polities are dominated not so much by the region's problems as by purely local and purely global ones, which conspire to divert the region's members from the internal affairs of their area, and indeed would make an isolated treatment of those affairs impossible. As a result, each nation, new or old, finds itself placed in an orbit of its own, from which it is quite difficult to move away: for the attraction of the regional forces is offset by the pull of all the other forces. Or, to change the metaphor, those nations that coexist in the same apparently separate "home" of a geographical region find themselves both exposed to the smells and noises that come from outside through all their windows and doors, and looking at the outlying houses from which the interference issues. Coming from diverse pasts, moved by diverse tempers, living in different parts of the house, inescapably yet differently subjected and attracted to the outside world, those cohabitants react unevenly to their exposure and calculate conflictingly how they could either reduce the disturbance or affect in turn all those who live elsewhere. The adjustment of their own relations within the house becomes subordinated to their divergencies about the outside world; the "regional subsystem" becomes a stake in the rivalry of its members about the system as a whole.

However, the coziness of the common home could still prevail if the inhabitants were forced to come to terms, either by one of them, or by the fear of a threatening neighbor. This is precisely where the second unique feature of the present situation intervenes. What tends to perpetuate the nation-states decisively in a system whose universality seems to sharpen rather than shrink their diversity is the new set of conditions that govern and restrict the rule of force: Damocles' sword has become a boomerang, the ideological legitimacy of the nation-state is protected by the relative and forced tameness of the world jungle. Force in the nuclear age is still the "midwife of societies" insofar as revolutionary war either breeds new nations or shapes regimes in existing nations; but the use of force along traditional lines, for conquest and expansion—the very use that made the "permeable" feudal units not only obsolete but collapse and replaced them with modern states often built on "blood and iron"—has become too dangerous. The legitimacy of the feudal unit could be undermined in two ways: brutally, by the rule of force—the big fish swallowing small fish by national might; subtly or legitimately, so to speak, through self-undermining—the logic of dynastic weddings or acquisitions that consolidated larger units. A system based on national self-determination rules out the latter; a system in which nations, once established, find force a much blunted weapon rules out the former. Thus agglomeration by conquest or out of a fear of conquest fails to take place. The new conditions of violence tend even to pay to national borders the tribute of vice to virtue: violence which dons the cloak of revolution rather than of interstate wars, or persists in the form of such wars only when they accompany revolutions or conflicts in divided countries, perversely respects borders by infiltrating under them rather than by crossing them overtly. Thus all that is left for unification is what one might call "national self-abdication" or self-abnegation, the eventual willingness of nations to try something else; but precisely global involvement hinders rather than helps, and the atrophy of war removes the most pressing incentive. What a nation-state cannot provide alone—in economics, or defense—it can still provide through means far less drastic than hara-kiri.

These two features give its solidity to the principle of national self-determination, as well as its resilience to the U.N. They also give its present, and quite unique, shape to the "relationship of major tension": the conflict between East and West. This conflict is both muted and universal—and both aspects contribute to the survival of the nation-state. As the superpowers find that what makes their power overwhelming also makes it less usable, or rather usable only to deter one another and to deny each other gains, the lesser states discover under the umbrella of the nuclear stalemate that they are not condemned to death, and that indeed their nuisance power is impressive—especially when the kind of violence that prevails in present circumstances favors the porcupine over the elephant. The superpowers experience in their own camps the backlash of a rebellion against domination that enjoys broad impunity, and cannot easily coax or coerce third parties into agglomeration under their tutelage. Yet they retain the means to prevent other powers from agglomerating away from their clutches. Thus, as the superpowers compete, with filed nails, all over the globe, the nation-state becomes the universal point of salience, to use the new language of strategy— the lowest common denominator in the competition.

Other international systems were merely conservative of diversity; the present system is profoundly conservative of the diversity of nation-states, despite all its revolutionary features. The dream of Rousseau, concerned both about the prevalence of the general will—that is, the nation-state—and about peace, was the creation of communities insulated from one another. In history, where "the essence and drama of nationalism is not to be alone in the world,"[7] the clash of non-insulated states has tended to breed both nation-states and wars. Today, Rousseau's ideals come closer to reality, but in the most un-Rousseauan way: the nation-states prevail in peace, they remain unsuperseded because a fragile peace keeps the Kantian doctor away, they are unreplaced because their very involvement in the world, their very inability to insulate themselves from one another, preserves their separateness. The "new Europe" dreamed by the Europeans could not be established by force. Left to the wills and calculations of its members, the new formula has not jelled because they could not agree on its role in the world. The failure (so far) of an experiment tried in apparently ideal conditions tells us a great deal about contemporary world politics, about the chances of unification movements elsewhere, and about the functional approach to unification.

7. P. Hassner, *op. cit.,* p. 523.

For it shows that the movement can fail not only when there is a surge of nationalism in one important part, but also when there are differences in assessments of the national interest that rule out agreement on the shape and on the world role of the new, supranational whole.

The word nationalism is notoriously slippery. What I suggest is the following threefold distinction, which may be helpful in analyzing the interaction between the nation-state and the international system:

1. There is *national consciousness* (what the French call *sentiment national*)—a sense of "cohesion and distinctiveness,"[8] which sets one off from other groups. My point is that this sense, which tends to have important effects on international relations as long as it is shared by people who have not achieved statehood, is rather "neutral" once the nation and the state coincide: that is, the existence of national consciousness does not dictate foreign policy, does not indicate whether the people's "image" of foreigners will be friendly or unfriendly (they will be seen as different—nothing else is implied), nor does it indicate whether or not the leaders will be willing to accept sacrifices of sovereignty. One cannot even posit that a strong national consciousness will be an obstacle for movements of unification, for it is perfectly conceivable that a nation convinces itself that its "cohesion and distinctiveness" will be best preserved in a larger entity. Here, we must turn to the second category.

2. For lack of a better phrase, I shall call it the *national situation*. Any nation-state, whether pulsing with a strong "national consciousness" or not—indeed, any state, whether a true nation-state or a disparate collection of unintegrated groups—is, to borrow Sartre's language, thrown into the world; its situation is made up altogether of its internal features—what, in an individual, would be called heredity and character—and of its position in the world. The state of national consciousness in the nation is one, but only one, of the elements of the situation. It is a composite of objective data (inside: social structure and political system; outside: geography, formal commitments) and subjective factors (inside: values, prejudices, opinions, reflexes; outside: one's own traditions and assessments of others, and the other's attitudes and approaches toward oneself); some of its components are intractable, others flexible and changeable. Any statesman, whether he is a fervent patriot or not, must define the nation's foreign policy by taking that situation into account; even if he is convinced of the obsolescence of *the* nation-state (or of *his* nation-state), the steps he will be able and willing to take in order to overcome it will be shaped by the fact that he speaks—to borrow de Gaulle's language this time—for the nation as it is in the world as it is. He cannot act as if his nation-state did not exist, however sorry its shape may be, or as if the world were other than it is. The national situation may facilitate unification moves, even when national consciousness is strong. It may prove a

8. Karl Deutsch, *Nationalism and Social Communication* (Cambridge, Mass., 1953), p. 147.

formidable obstacle, even when national consciousness is weak. The point is that even when the policy-maker tries to move "beyond the nation-state" he can do it only by taking along the nation with its baggage of memories and problems—with its situation. I do not want to suggest that the situation is a "given" that dictates policy; but it sets complicated limits that affect freedom of choice.[9]

3. I will reserve the term *"nationalism"* for a specific meaning: it is one of the numerous ways in which political leaders and élites can interpret the dictates, or rather the suggestions, of the national situation, one of the ways of using the margin it leaves. Whereas national consciousness is a feeling, and the national situation a condition, nationalism is a doctrine or (if one uses a broad definition) an ideology—the doctrine or ideology that gives to the nation in world affairs absolute value and top priority. The consequences of such a preference may vary immensely: nationalism may imply expansion (that is, the attempt at establishing the supremacy of one's nation over others) or merely defense; it may entail the notion of a universal mission or, on the contrary, insulation. It may be peaceful or pugnacious.[10] It is less an imperative determinant of choice than a criterion of choice and an attitude which shapes the choices made. But whatever its manifestations, its varying content, it always follows one rule common to all the former, it always pours the latter into one mold: the preservation of the nation as the highest good. Nationalism thus affects, *at least* negatively, the way in which the freedom of choice left by the national situation will be used; indeed, it may collide with, and try to disregard or overcome, the limits which the situation sets.

The relation between nationalism and the two other factors is complicated. Nationalism (in the sense of the will to establish a nation-state) is triggered by, and in turn activates, national consciousness in oppressed nationalities; but nationalism, in colonial areas as well as in mature nation-states, can also be a substitute for a still weak or for a fading national consciousness. In nation-states that are going concerns, national consciousness breeds nationalism only in certain kinds of national situations. The national situation may be assessed by a nationalist leader exactly in the same way as by a non-nationalist one; however, nationalism may lead the former to promote policies the latter would have rejected and to oppose moves the former would have undertaken. That bane of international relations theory, the national interest, could be defined as follows:

9. A more systematic and exhaustive analysis would have to discriminate rigorously among the various components of the national situation; if the purpose of the analysis is to help one understand the relations between the nation-state and the international system, it would be particularly necessary to assess (1) the degree to which each of these components is an unchangeable given (or a given unchangeable over a long period of time) or on the contrary an element that can be transformed by will and action; (2) the hierarchy of importance and the order of urgency that political élites and decision-makers establish among the components.

10. See Raoul Girardet, "Antour de l'ideologie nationaliste," *Revue française de science politique, op. cit.,* pp. 423–45; and P. Hassner, *op. cit.,* pp. 516–19.

N.I. = National situation × outlook of the foreign policy-makers.

It is obvious that the same situation can result in different policies, depending in particular on whether or not there is a nationalist policy-maker. It is obvious also that national interests of different nations will not be defined in easily compatible terms if those respective outlooks are nationalist, even when the situations are not so different. But the same incompatibility may obtain, even if the outlooks are not nationalistic, when the situations are indeed very different.[11]

II

Let us now look at the fate of the nation-states in the part of Europe occupied by the so-called Six, that is, the continental part of Western Europe, first by examining the basic features of their national situations, then by commenting upon the process of unification, later by discussing its results, and finally by drawing some lessons.

Western Europe in the postwar years has been characterized by three features which have affected all of its nations. But each of those features has nevertheless affected each of the six nations in a different way because of the deep differences that have continued to divide the Six.

1. The first feature—the most hopeful one from the viewpoint of the unifiers—was the temporary demise of nationalism. In the defeated countries—Germany and Italy—nationalism had become associated with the regimes that had led the nations into war, defeat, and destruction. The collapse of two national ideologies that had been bellicose, aggressive, and imperialistic brought about an almost total discredit for nationalism is every guise. Among the nations of Western Europe that were on the Allied side, the most remarkable thing was that the terrible years of occupation and resistance had not resulted in a resurgence of chauvinism. Amusingly enough, it was the Communist Party of France that gave the most nationalistic tone to its propaganda; on the whole, the platforms of the Resistance movements show an acute awareness of the dangers of nationalist celebrations and national fragmentation in Western Europe. The Resistance itself had had a kind of supranational dimension; none of the national resistance movements could have survived without outside support; the nations whose honor they had saved had been liberated rather than victorious. All this prevented the upsurge of the kind of cramped chauvinism that had followed the victory of World War I, just as the completeness of the disaster and the impossibility of putting the blame on any traitors crushed any potential revival in Germany of the smoldering nationalism of resentment that had undermined the Weimar Republic. There was, in other words, above and beyond the differ-

---

11. As will be stated more explicitly in part V, what matters is not the "objective" difference detected by scholars or outsiders, but the "felt" difference experienced by political élites and decision-makers.

ences in national situations between indubitable losers and dubious winners, the general feeling of a common defeat, and also the hope of a common future: for the Resistance platforms often put their emphasis on the need for a union or federation of Western Europe.

However, the demise of nationalism affected differently the various nations of the half-continent. On the one hand, there were significant differences in national consciousness. If nationalism was low, patriotic sentiment was extremely high in liberated France. The circumstances in which the hated Nazis were expelled and the domestic collaborators purged amounted to what I have called elsewhere a rediscovery of the French political community by the French:[12] the nation seemed to have redeemed its "cohesion and distinctiveness." On the contrary, in Germany especially, the destruction of nationalism seemed to have been accompanied by a drop in national consciousness as well: what was distinctive was guilt and shame; what had been only too cohesive was being torn apart not by internal political cleavages, but by partition, zones of occupation, regional parochialisms blessed by the victors. The French national backbone had been straightened by the ordeal, although the pain had been too strong to tempt the French to flex nationalistic muscles; the German national backbone appeared to have been broken along with the strutting jaw and clenched fist of Nazi nationalism. Italy was in slightly better shape than Germany, in part because of its Resistance movements, but its story was closer to the German than to the French.

However, there were other elements in the national situation, besides patriotic consciousness, that also affected differently the various nations' inclination to nationalism. The defeated nations—Germany in particular— were in the position of patients on whom drastic surgery had been performed, and who were lying prostrate, dependent for their every movement on the surgeons and nurses. Even if one had wanted to restore the nation to the pinnacle of values and objectives, one could not have succeeded except with the help and consent of one's guardians—who were not likely to give support to such a drive; in other words, the situation itself set the strictest limits to the possibility of any kind of nationalism, expansive or insulating. The lost territories were beyond recuperation; a healing period of *"repli"* comparable to that which had marked the early foreign policy of the Third Republic was not conceivable either. One could not get anything alone, and anything others could provide, while limited, would be something to be grateful for.

On the other hand, France and, to a lesser extent (because of their much smaller size), Belgium and Holland were not so well inoculated. For, although the prevalence of the nation meant little in the immediate European context, it meant a great deal in the imperial one: if the circumstances of the Liberation kept national consciousness from veering into nationalism in one realm, the same circumstances tended to encourage such a turn with

12. See "Paradoxes of the French Political Community," in S. Hoffmann, *et al., In Search of France* (Cambridge, Mass., 1963).

respect to the colonies. Cut down to size in Europe, these nations were bound to act as if they could call upon their overseas possessions to redress the balance; accustomed, through their association of nationalism with Nazi and Fascist imperialism, to equate chauvinism only with expansion, they would not be so easily discouraged from a nationalism of defense, aimed at preserving the "national mission" overseas. The Dutch lost most of their empire early enough to find themselves, in this respect, not so different from the German and Italian amputees; the Belgians remained serene long enough not to have nationalistic fevers about the huge member that seemed to give them no trouble until the day when it broke off—brutally, painfully, but irremediably. The French, however, suffered almost at once from dis-imperial dyspepsia, and the long, losing battle they fought gave rise continuously to nationalist tantrums of frustration and rage. Moreover, the French inclination to nationalism was higher because of an internal component of the national situation as well: there was in France one political force that was clearly nationalist, that had indeed presided over the Liberation, given whatever unity they had to the Resistance movements, and achieved in the most impressive way a highly original convergence of Jacobin universalist nationalism and of "traditionalist," right-wing, defensive nationalism—the force of General de Gaulle. His resignation had meant, as Alfred Grosser suggests,[13] the defeat of a doctrine that put not only a priority mark on foreign affairs but also a priority claim on *Notre Dame la France*. The incident that had led to his departure—a conflict over the military budget—had been symbolic enough of the demise of nationalism referred to above. But his durability, first as a political leader, later as a "capital that belongs to all and to none," reflected a lasting nostalgia for nationalism; and it was equally symbolic that the crisis which returned him to power was a crisis over Algeria.

2. The second feature common to all the West European national situations, yet affecting them differently, was the "political collapse of Europe." Europe did not merely lose power and wealth: such losses can be repaired, as the aftermath of World War I had shown. Europe, previously the heart of the international system, the locus of the world organization, the fount of international law, fell under what de Gaulle has called "the two hegemonies." The phrase is, obviously, inaccurate and insulting: one of those hegemonies took a highly imperial form, and thus discouraged and prevented the creation in Eastern Europe of any regional entity capable of overcoming the prewar national rivalries. Nothing is to be gained, however, by denying that U.S. hegemony has been a basic fact of life. American domination has indeed had the kinds of "domination effects" any hegemony produces: the transfer of decision-making in vital matters from the dominated to the dominator breeds a kind of paternalism in the latter, and irresponsibility (either in the form of abdication or in the form of scapegoatism) in the former. But the consequences of hegemony vary according to its nature. The peculiar nature of this

13. *La politique extérieure de la V République* (Paris, 1965), p. 12.

domination has also had unique consequences—better and worse than in the classical cases. One may dominate because one wants to and can; but one may also dominate because one must and does: by one's weight and under the pressures of a compelling situation. This has been America's experience: its hegemony was "situational," not deliberate.

The effects have been better than usual, insofar as such hegemony restricted itself to areas in which European nations had become either impotent or incapable of recovery by self-reliance. It left the dominated with a considerable freedom of maneuver, and indeed prodded them into recovery, power recuperation, and regional unity; it favored both individual and collective emancipation. But the effects have been worse precisely because this laxity meant that each party could react to *this* common feature of the national situations (that is, American hegemony) according to the distinctive *other* features of his national situation, features left intact by the weight and acts of the U.S., by contrast with the U.S.S.R. American domination was only one part of the picture. Hence the following paradox: both America's prodding and the individual and collective impotence of Western European nations, now reduced to the condition of clients and stakes, ought logically to have pushed them into unity-for-emancipation—the kind of process Soviet policy discouraged in the other half of Europe. But the very margin of autonomy left to each West European nation by the U.S. gave it an array of choices: between accepting and rejecting dependence, between unity as a weapon for emancipation and unity as merely a way to make dependence more comfortable. It would have been a miracle if all the nations had made the same choice; the diversity of national situations has ultimately prevailed. To define one's position toward the U.S. was the common imperative, but each one has defined it in his own way.

At first, this diversity of domestic outlooks and external positions did not appear to be an obstacle to the unification movement. As Ernst Haas has shown,[14] the movement grew on ambiguity, and those who accepted American hegemony as a lasting fact of European life as well as those who did not could submerge their disagreement in the construction of a regional entity that could be seen, by the former, as the most effective way for continuing to receive American protection and contributing to America's mission and, by the latter, as the most effective way to challenge American predominance. However, there are limits to the credit of ambiguity. The split could not be concealed once the new entity was asked to tackle matters of "high politics"— that is, go beyond the purely internal economic problems of little impact or dependence on the external relationship to the U.S.[15] It is therefore no sur-

14. *The Uniting of Europe* (Stanford, Calif., 1958).
15. See my discussion in "The European process of Atlantic cross-purposes," *Journal of Common Market Studies* (February 1965), pp. 85–101. The very success of internal economic integration raised those external issues far earlier than many expected. (Cf. Britain's application for membership, the problem of external commercial policy.)

prise that this split should have disrupted unification at two moments—in 1953–54, when the problem of German rearmament was raised; and in 1962–65, when de Gaulle's challenge of the U.S. became global.[16]

This is how the diversity of national situations operated. First, it produced (and produces) the basic split between those I would call the resigned ones, and those I would call the resisters. The resigned ones were, on the one hand, the smaller nations, aware of their weaknesses, realizing that the Soviet threat could not be met by Europeans alone, accustomed to dependence on external protectors, grateful to America for the unique features of its protection, and looking forward to an important role for Europe but not in the realm of high politics. Italy had, in the past, tried to act as a great power without protectors; yet not only were those days over, but also the acceptance of American hegemony provided the creaky Italian political system with a kind of double cushion—against the threat of Communism, but also against the need to spend too much energy and money on Italian rearmament. For the smaller states as well as for Italy, the acceptance of U.S. hegemony was like an insurance policy, which protected them against having to give priority to foreign affairs. On the other hand, Germany accepted dependence on the U.S. not merely as a comfort, but as a necessity as vital as breathing. West Germany's geographical position had turned it into the front line, its partition has contributed to imposing security as the supreme goal, the staunch anti-Communism of its leadership had ruled out any search for security along the lines of neutrality. There followed not only the acceptance of U.S. leadership but also the need to do everything possible in order to tie the United States to Western Europe. Moreover, in West Germany's helpless position, the recovery of equality was another vital goal, and it could be reached only through cooperation with the most powerful of the occupying forces. Defeat, division, and danger conspired to making West Germany switch almost abruptly from its imperialistic nationalism of the Nazi era to a dependence which was apparently submissive, yet also productive (of security and status gains) under Adenauer.

As for the resisters, they, like the West Germans, gave priority to foreign affairs—only not in the same perspective. The French reading of geography and history was different.[17] To be sure, the present need for security against the Soviet Union was felt. But there were two reasons that the "tyranny of the cold war" operated differently in France. One, French feelings of hostility

16. The latter case is self-evident; the first, less so, since the crisis over E.D.C. was primarily an 'intra-European" split, between the French and the Germans over the return of the latter to arms and soldiery. However, there was more to it than this: E.D.C. was accepted mostly by those who thought that Europe could and should not refuse to do what the U.S. had demanded—that is, rearm in order to share the defense of the half-continent with the U.S., and to incite the U.S. to remain its primary defender; E.D.C. was rejected by those who feared that the Defense Community would freeze existing power relationships forever.

17. There was, however, in France, a minority of "resigned ones," like Paul Reynaud.

toward Russia were much lower than in Germany, and, although it may be too strong to speak of a nostalgia for the wartime grand alliance, it is not false to say that the hope of an ultimate détente allowing for European reunification, for a return of the Soviets to moderation, and for an emancipation of the continent from its "two hegemonies" never died. The French time perspective has been consistently different from, say, the German: the urgency of the threat never overshadowed the desire for, and belief in, the advent of a less tense international system. This may have been due not only to France's location, but also to other elements in France's national situation. Whereas Germany's continuity with its past was both wrecked and repudiated, France (like England) looked back to the days when Europe held the center of the stage and forward to the time when Europe would again be an actor, not a stake: the anomaly was the present, not the past. Also, on colonial matters, France (more than England) often found little to distinguish America's reprobation from Soviet hostility. Two, France continued to worry not only about possible Soviet thrusts but also about Germany's potential threats: the suspicion of a reborn German national consciousness and nationalism has marked all French leaders. An additional reason for fearing the perpetuation of American hegemony and the freezing of the cold war, for hoping for a détente that would help Europe reunite, was thus provided by the fear that any other course would make Germany the main beneficiary of America's favors. Germany looked East with some terror, but there was only one foe there; when the French looked East, they saw two nations to fear; each could be used as an ally against the other—but for the time being the Soviet danger was the greater, and, should Germany be built up too much against the Soviets, the security gained by France in one respect would be compromised in another.[18]

There was a second way in which the diversity of national situations operated. As I have suggested, situations limit and affect but do not command choices. A general desire for overcoming the cold war and American hegemony did not mean a general agreement on how to do so. What I have called "the resistance" was split, and it is this split that has become decisive for an analysis of the obstacles to European unification. Had all the resisters calculated that the best way to reach France's objectives was the construction of a powerful West European entity, which could rival America's might, turn the bipolar contest into a triangle, and wrest advantages from both extra-European giants, the "ambiguity" of a movement led by resigned as well as resisting forces might not have damaged the enterprise until much later. However, there was a sharp division over methods between those who reasoned along the lines just described—like Jean Monnet—and those who feared

18. There is an impressive continuity in French efforts to preserve the difference between France's position and Germany's: from the préalables and protocols to E.D.C., to Mendès-France's Brussels proposals, to de Gaulle's opposition to any nuclear role for Germany.

that the sacrifice of national sovereignty to supranational institutions might entail a loss of control over the direction of the undertaking. The latter consisted of two kinds of people: on the one hand, the nationalists who, as indicated above, were still very much around, exasperated by the colonial battles, anxious to preserve all the resources of French diplomacy and strategy in order, in the present, to concentrate on the fronts overseas and, later, to promote whatever policies would be required, rather than let a foreign body decide; on the other hand, men like Mendès-France, who were not nationalists in the sense of this paper, but who thought that the continental European construction was not France's best way of coping with her situation—they thought that priority ought to go to more urgent tasks such as the search for a détente, the liberalization of the Empire, the reform of the economy.[19]

The success of the European movement required, first, that the "resisters" suspicious of European integration remain a minority—not only throughout the six but in the leadership of every one of the six, not only in Parliament but above all in the Executive, the prime decision-making force in every state: a requirement which was met in 1950–53 and in 1955–58, but not in the crucial months for E.D.C. in 1953–54, and no longer after 1958. The movement proceeded after 1958 because of the dialectic of ambiguity; however, there was a second requirement for success: that the "minute of truth"—when the European elites would have to ask themselves questions about the ultimate political direction of their community—be postponed as long as possible; that is, that the cold war remain sufficiently intense to impose even on the "resisters" a priority for the kind of security that implied U.S. protection—a priority for the *urgent* over the *long-term important* as they saw it. This is precisely what was already, if temporarily, shaken by the brief period of nervous demobilization that followed Stalin's death, in 1953–54, and then gradually undermined by the third basic feature of Europe's postwar situation. But before we turn to it, one remark must be made: in French foreign policy, "resistance by European integration" prevailed over "resistance by self-reliance" only as long as France was bogged down in colonial wars; it was this important and purely French element in France's national situation whose ups and downs affected quite decisively the method of "resistance."[20]

19. France's "integrationist resisters," like Jean Monnet himself, often chose not to stress the "resistance" aspect of their long-term vision, but nevertheless aimed ultimately at establishing in Western Europe not a junior partner of the U.S. but a "second force" in the West. Mendès-France's political vision never put the nation on top of the hierarchy of values; however, in 1954 (especially in his ill-fated demands for a revision of E.D.C. at the Brussels meeting in August) as well as in 1957 (when he voted against the Common Market), his actual policies did put a priority on national reform over external entanglements.

20. It is no coincidence if E.D.C. was rejected six weeks after the end of the war in Indochina, if the Common Market was signed while war raged in Algeria, if de Gaulle's sharpest attack on the "Monnet method" followed the Evian agreements. The weight of the situation affected and inflected the course of even as nationalist a leader as de Gaulle,

3. The divisions and contradictions described above were sharpened by the third common feature, which emerged in the mid-1950's and whose effects have developed progressively since: the nuclear stalemate between the superpowers. The impact of the "balance of terror" on the Western alliance has been analyzed so often and well[21] that nothing needs to be added here; but what is needed is a brief explanation of how the two splits already discussed have been worsened by Europe's gradual discovery of the uncertainties of America's nuclear protection (now that the U.S. could be devastated too), and how some new splits appeared. For to the extent to which the stalemate has loosened up a previously very tight situation—tight because of the threat from the East and the ties to the U.S.—it has altogether sharpened previous differences in national situations *and* increased the number of alternatives made available to élites and statesmen. Greater indeterminacy has meant greater confusion.

First, the split between French "resistance" and German "resignation" has become deeper. The dominant political élites in Germany have interpreted the new national situation created by the balance of terror as merely adding urgency to their previous calculation of interest. The nuclear stalemate was, given Germany's position, deemed to increase the danger for the West: the U.S. was relatively less strong, the Soviet Union stronger, that is, more of a threat. Indeed, the Socialists switched from their increasingly more furtive glances at neutrality to an outright endorsement of the Christian Democratic interpretation. If America's monopoly was broken, if America's guarantee was weakened thereby, what was needed—in a world that was not willing to let Germany rearm with nuclear weapons, in a continent that could not really develop a nuclear force of its own capable of replacing America's and of matching Russia's—was a German policy so respectful of America's main concerns, and also so vigilant with respect to the Soviet Union, that the U.S. would both feel obligated to keep its mantle of protection over Germany and not be tempted into negotiating a détente at Germany's expense. German docility would be the condition for, and counterpart of, American entanglement. The German reaction to a development that could, if General Gallois' logic were followed, lead to the prevalence of "polycentrism" at bipolarity's expense was the search for ways of exorcising the former and preserving the latter. On the whole, the smaller nations and Italy, while not at all fearful

---

between 1958 and 1962. Even he went along with the "Monnet method," however grudgingly, right until the end of the Algerian War. It is not a coincidence either if the French leaders most suspicious of the imprisoning effects of the community of the Six from France were the ones who labored hardest at improving the national situation by removing the colonial burdens (Mendès-France, de Gaulle)—and if those French rulers who followed Monnet and tried to place the pride of a nation with a sharp but wounded patriotic sense in its leadership of a united Europe were the men who failed to improve the national situation overseas (the M.R.P., Mollet). The one French politician who sought both European integration and imperial "disengagement" was Antoine Pinay.

21. Especially by Henry Kissinger in *The Troubled Partnership* (New York, 1965).

about the consequences of polycentrism (on the contrary), were nevertheless not shaken out of their "resignation"; the mere appearance of parity of nuclear peril was not enough to make them anxious to give, or to make them domestically capable of giving, priority to an active foreign policy.

In France, on the contrary, the balance of terror reinforced the attitude of resistance: what had always been a goal—emancipation—but had in fact been no more than a hope, given the thickness of the iron curtain, the simple rigidity of the superpowers' policies in the days of Mr. Dulles, and Europe's inability to affect the course of events, now became a possibility; for the giants' stalemate meant increased security for the less great (however much they might complain about the decrease of American protection and use it as a pretext, their lament coexisted with a heightened feeling of protection against war in general). What the Germans saw as a liability was an opportunity to the French. Germany's situation, its low national consciousness, incited most German leaders to choose what might be called a "minimizing" interpretation of the new situation; France's situation, its high national consciousness and, after 1958, the doctrine of its leader, incited French political élites to choose a "maximizing" interpretation. The increasing costs of the use of force made this use by the superpowers less likely, American protection less certain but also less essential, Europe's recovery of not merely wealth but power more desirable and possible—possible since the quest for power could be pushed without excessive risk of sanctions by the two giants, desirable since power, while transformed, remains the moving force and *ultima ratio* of world politics. This recovery of power would help bring about the much desired prevalence of polycentrism over bipolarity.[22]

Secondly, as this feud shows, the balance of terror heightened the split over method among the "resisters." On the one hand, it provided new arguments for those who thought that emancipation could be achieved only through the uniting of Western Europe: individual national efforts would remain too ridiculously weak to amount to anything but a waste in resources; a collective effort, however, could exploit the new situation, make Western Europe a true partner of the U.S., and not merely an economic partner and a military aide-de-camp. On the other hand, those who feared that the "united way" could become a frustrating deviation reasoned that the theory of graduated deterrence justified the acquisition of nuclear weapons by a middle-sized power with limited resources and that this acquisition would increase considerably the political influence as well as the prestige of the nation. The increased costs of force ruled out, in any case, what had in the

22. One should not forget that the original decisions that led to the French force de frappe were taken before de Gaulle, or that the French opposition to a national deterrent came from men who did not at all object to his argument about the need for Europe as a whole to stop being a client of the U.S., and who thought that, indeed, America's nuclear monopoly in the alliance was obsolete.

past been the most disastrous effort of the mushrooming of sovereign states—a warlike, expansionist nationalism—but they simultaneously refloated the value of small or middle-sized nations, no longer condemned by the cold, bipolar war to look for bigger protectors or to agglomerate in order to assure their security. Moreover, the "united way" would be a dead-end, since some, and not exactly the least significant, of the associates had no desire for collective European power at the possible expense of American protection. Not the least significant reason for the prevalence of the second line of thought over the first has been one important element of the national situation—the army: almost destroyed by its Algerian experience, it had to be "reconverted." In the circumstances of 1962, this meant inevitably a conversion to French atomic concerns. Its success builds up in turn a vested interest in the preservation of the new establishment—and increases the difference in national situations between France and a non-nuclear Germany.

Thirdly, the new situation affected European unification negatively not only by sharpening those splits but in two other ways as well. On the one hand, until then, opposition to a supranational entity had come only from a fraction of the "resisters"; in the early 1950's the U.S. had strongly—too strongly—urged the establishment of a European defense system which was not considered likely to challenge America's own predominance in the military area. In the 1960's, the U.S. no longer urged the West Europeans to build such a system. American leadership has developed a deep concern for maintaining centralized control over the forces of the alliance, that is, for preserving bipolarity, and a growing realization that Europe's appetite would not stop short of nuclear weapons. As a result, some of the "resigned ones," instead of endorsing European integration as unreservedly as when the situation of a dependent Europe in a cold-war-dominated world did not allow Europeans to entertain thoughts of genuine military "partnership" with the U.S., now for the first time showed themselves of two minds—they were willing to pursue integration in economic and social fields, but much less so in matters of defense, lest NATO be weakened. It is significant that the Dutch resisted de Gaulle's efforts, in 1960–62, to include defense in his confederal scheme and that the German leaders, in their quest for security, put their hopes in the MLF—a scheme that ties European nations one by one to the U.S.—rather than in a revised and revived E.D.C. Inevitably, such mental reservations of those who had been among the champions of supranationality could only confirm the suspicions of those "resisters" who had distrusted the "Monnet method" since the beginning. Thus, the national situation of Germany in particular—a situation in which America's own policy of reliance on Germany as the anchor of U.S. influence on the continent plays a large role—damaged the European movement: the German leaders were largely successful in their drive to entangle the U.S., but found that the price they had to pay was a decreasing ability to push for European integration. European integration and dependence on the U.S. were no longer automatically compatible.[23]

On the other hand, even that minority of German leaders who began to read Germany's national interest differently did not really compensate for the weakening of the majority's integrating ardor. Increasingly, in 1963 to 1965, suspicions about the value of the policy of docility-for-entanglement were voiced by a group of Christian Democrats, led by Adenauer and Strauss. They still read the German situation in terms of security first; but their faith in America's aptitude to provide it was shaken, and they saw that Germany had sufficiently gained from America's support not to have to behave as a minor any longer. Their nickname of German Gaullists is however totally unsuitable. To be sure, these men are "resisters" in the sense of turning away from America; they are close to the French "integrationist resisters," insofar as they propose a European defense effort and a joint European nuclear policy (rather than a purely German one). Nevertheless, their foreign policy goals are quite different from those of all the French resisters, integrationist or nationalist. The national situation of France made most French leaders agree on a common *vision,* described above, that can be summed up as the end of the cold war and a continent reunited with a Germany placed under certain wraps. That common vision coexists with the split on *policies* already discussed—the "European" policy (in which the wraps are organic, that is, the net and bonds of integration) *vs.* the "national" policy (in which the wraps are contractual). The national situation of Germany has made most German leaders, after the Social Democratic switch,[24] agree on a common *vision* deeply different from the French—a perpetuation of the cold war, hostility to the Soviet Union, the hope for a reunification tantamount not merely to the thawing of the Eastern "camp" but to its disintegration, and with as few concessions as possible. Since 1963, this vision has coexisted with two different *policies:* the majority policy of reliance on the U.S., the minority policy of substituting a strong, tough Europe for an increasingly less reliable, increasingly détente-happy U.S. At present, "resisters" are thus split not only on methods (French integrationists *vs.* French anti-integrationists) but also on objectives (French *vs.* German).

This long discussion of the different responses to common situations has been necessary in reaction to the dominant approach to European integration which has focused on process. The self-propelling power of the process is severely constrained by the associates' views and splits on ends and means. In order to go "beyond the nation-state," one will have to do more than set up procedures in adequate "background" and "process conditions." For a procedure is not a purpose, a process is not a policy.

23. Hence the rather vague or embarrassed formulas used by Jean Monnet's Action Committee for the United States of Europe with regard to defense in the past two years.
24. The case of Erich Mende's Free Democrats is more complicated.

III

However, since it is the process of European integration that is its most original feature, we must examine it also.[25] We have been witnessing a kind of race, between the logic of integration set up by Monnet and analyzed by Haas, and the logic of diversity, analyzed above. According to the former, the double pressure of necessity (the interdependence of the social fabric, which will oblige statesmen to integrate even sectors originally left uncoordinated) and of men (the action of the supranational agents) will gradually restrict the freedom of movement of the national governments by turning the national situations into one of total enmeshing. In such a milieu, nationalism will be a futile exercise in anachronism, and the national consciousness itself will, so to speak, be impregnated by an awareness of the higher interest in union. The logic of diversity, by contrast, sets limits to the degree to which the "spill-over" process can limit the freedom of action of the governments; it restricts the domain in which the logic of functional integration operates to the area of welfare; indeed, to the extent that discrepancies over the other areas begin to prevail over the laborious harmonization in welfare, even issues belonging to the latter sphere may become infected by the disharmony which reigns in those other areas. The logic of integration is that of a blender which crunches the most diverse products, overcomes their different tastes and perfumes, and replaces them with one, presumably delicious, juice. One lets each item be ground because one expects a finer synthesis: that is, ambiguity helps rather than hinders because each "ingredient" can hope that its taste will prevail at the end. The logic of diversity is the opposite: it suggests that, in areas of key importance to the national interest, nations prefer the certainty, or the self-controlled uncertainty, of national self-reliance, to the uncontrolled uncertainty of the untested blender; ambiguity carries one only a part of the way. The logic of integration assumes that it is possible to fool each one of the associates some of the time because his over-all gain will still exceed his occasional losses, even if his calculations turn out wrong here or there. The logic of diversity implies that, on a vital issue, losses are not compensated by gains on other (and especially not on other less vital) issues: nobody wants to be fooled. The logic of integration deems the uncertainties of the supranational function process creative; the logic of diversity sees them as destructive past a certain threshold: Russian roulette is fine only as long as the gun is filled with blanks. Ambiguity lures and lulls the national consciousness into integration as long as the benefits are high, the costs low, the expectations considerable. Ambiguity may arouse and stiffen national consciousness into nationalism if the benefits are slow, the losses high, the hopes dashed or deferred. Functional integration's gamble could be won

25. See my previous discussion in "Discord in Community," in F. Wilcox and H. F. Haviland, Jr. (eds.), *The Atlantic Community* (New York, 1963), pp. 3–31; "Europe's Identity Crisis," *Dædalus* (Fall 1964), pp. 1244–97, and the article listed in reference 15.

only if the method had sufficient potency to promise a permanent excess of gains over losses, and of hopes over frustrations. Theoretically, this may be true of economic integration. It is not true of political integration (in the sense of "high politics").

The success of the approach symbolized by Jean Monnet depended, and depends still, on his winning a triple gamble: on goals, on methods, on results. As for goals, it is a gamble on the possibility of substituting motion as an end in itself, for agreement on ends. It is a fact that the trans-national integrationist élites did not agree on whether the object of the community-building enterprise ought to be the construction of a new super-state—that is, a federal potential nation, *à la* U.S.A., more able because of its size and resources to play the traditional game of power than the dwarfed nations of Western Europe—or whether the object was to demonstrate that power politics could be overcome through cooperation and compromise, to build the first example of a radically new kind of unit, to achieve a change in the nature and not merely in the scale of the game. Monnet himself has been ambiguous on this score; Hallstein has been leaning in the first direction, many of Monnet's public relations men in the second.[26] Nor did the integrationists agree on whether the main goal was the creation of a regional "security community,"[27] that is, the pacification of a former hotbed of wars, or whether the main goal was the creation of an entity whose position and might could decisively affect the course of the cold war in particular, of international relations in general. Now, it is perfectly possible for a movement to feed on its harboring continental nationalists as well as anti-power idealists, inward-looking politicians and outward-looking politicians —but only as long as there is no need to make a choice. Decisions on tariffs did not require such choices. Decisions on agriculture already raise basic problems of orientation. Decisions on foreign policy and membership and defense cannot be reached unless the goals are clarified. One cannot be all things to all people all of the time.

As for methods, there was a gamble on the irresistible rise of supra-national functionalism. It assumed, first, that national sovereignty, already devalued by events, could be chewed up leaf by leaf like an artichoke. It assumed, second, that the dilemma of governments having to choose between pursuing an integration that ties their hands and stopping a movement that benefits their people could be exploited in favor of integration by men representing the common good, endowed with the advantages of superior expertise, initiating proposals, propped against a set of deadlines, and using for their cause the technique of package deals. Finally, it was assumed that this approach would both take into account the interests of the greater powers

26. See, for instance, Max Kohnstamm's "The European Tide," in Stephen R. Graubard (ed.), *A New Europe?* (Boston, 1964), pp. 140–73.
27. See K. W. Deutsch, *et al., Political Community and the North Atlantic Area* (Princeton, N.J., 1937).

and prevent the crushing of the smaller ones. The troubles with this gamble have been numerous. One, even an artichoke has a heart, which remains intact after the leaves have been eaten. It is of course true that a successful economic and social integration would considerably limit the freedom governments would still enjoy in theory for their diplomacy and strategy; but why should one assume that they would not be aware of it? As the artichoke's heart gets more and more denuded, the governments' vigilance gets more and more alerted. To be sure, the second assumption implies that the logic of the movement would prevent them from doing anything about it: they would be powerless to save the heart. But, two, this would be true only if governments never put what they consider essential interests of the nation above the particular interests of certain categories of nationals, if superior expertise were always either the Commission's monopoly or the solution of the issue at hand, if package deals were effective in every argument, and, above all, if the governments' representatives were always determined to behave as a "community organ" rather than as the agents of states that are not willing to accept a community under any conditions. Finally, functional integration may indeed give lasting satisfaction to the smaller powers, precisely because it is for them that the ratio of "welfare politics" to high politics is highest, and that the chance of gaining benefits through intergovernmental methods that reflect rather than correct the power differential between the big and the small is poorest; but this is also why the method is not likely *à la longue* to satisfy the bigger powers as much: facing them, the supranational civil servants, for all their skill and legal powers, are a bit like Jonases trying to turn whales into jellyfish. Of course, the idea—ultimately—is to move from an essentially administrative procedure in which supranational civil servants enter a dialogue with national ministers, to a truly federal one in which a federal cabinet is responsible to a federal parliament; but what is thus presented as a linear progress may turn out to be a vicious circle, since the ministers hold the key to the transformation, and may refuse it unless the goals are defined and the results already achieved are satisfactory.

There was a gamble about results as well. The experience of integration would entail net benefits for all, and bring about clear progress toward community formation. Such progress could be measured by the following yardsticks: in the realm of interstate relations, an increasing transfer of power to the new common agencies, and the prevalence of solutions "upgrading the common interest" over other kinds of compromises; in the realm of transnational society, an increasing flow of communications; in the area of national consciousness—which is important both for interstate relations, because (as seen above) it may set limits to the statesmen's discretion, and for transnational society, because it affects the scope and meaning of the communication flows—progress would be measured by increasing compatibility of views about external issues. The results achieved so far are mixed; negative on the last count (see below), limited on the second, and marked on the first by features that the enthusiasts of integration did not expect. On the one hand, there has been some strengthening of the authority of the Commission, and in various areas there has been some "upgrading of common interests." On the other hand, the Commission's unfortunate attempt to consolidate those gains at de Gaulle's expense, in the spring of 1965, has brought about a startling setback for the whole enterprise; moreover, in their negotiations, the members have conspicuously failed to find a common interest in some vital areas (energy, England's entry), and sometimes succeeded in reaching apparently "integrating" decisions only after the most ungainly, traditional kind of bargaining, in which such uncommunity-like methods as threats, ultimatums, and retaliatory moves were used. In other words, either the ideal was not reached, or it was reached in a way that was both the opposite of the ideal and ultimately its destroyer. If we look at the institutions of the Common Market as an incipient political system for Europe, we find that its authority remains limited, its structure weak, its popular base restricted and distant.[28]

It is therefore not surprising if the uncertainty about results already achieved contributes to uncertainty about future prospects. For the very divisions among the partisans of integration make it hard to predict where the "Monnet method" would lead, if the process were to continue along the lines so fondly planned by the French "inspirator." Would the enterprise become an effective federation, gradually turning the many into one, or would it lead to a mere facade behind which all the divergences and rivalries would continue to be played out? It is at least remarkable that Gaullist and American fears should converge in one respect: de Gaulle has consistently warned that the application of the supranational method to the area of high politics would lead not to a strong European entity, but to a dilution of national responsibility whose only beneficiary would be the U.S.; incapable of defining a coherent policy, the "technocrats" would leave the decisions in vital areas to the U.S., at least by default. On the contrary, many Americans have come to believe, on the basis of some of E.E.C.'s actions in the realm of tariffs and trade, that a united Europe would be able to challenge U.S. leadership much more effectively than the separate European states ever could. The truth of the matter is that nobody knows: a method is not a policy, a process is not a direction; the results achieved so far are too specialized, and the way in which they have been reached is too bumpy, to allow one to extrapolate and project safely. The face of a united Europe has not begun to emerge; there are just a few lines, but one does not know whether the supranational technique would finally give to Western Europe the features of a going concern, or those of a Fourth Republic writ large—the ambitions of a world power, or the complacency of parochialism. The range of possibilities is so broad, the alternatives are so extreme, that the more the Six move into the

28. Under authority, I include three distinct notions: autonomy (the capacity to act independently of the governments, and particularly the financial capacity), power (control over acts of others), and legitimacy (being accepted as the "rightful" center of action).

stormy waters of high politics, the less not only they but also the outside powers, such as the U.S., which may be affected by their acts are willing to extend the credit of hope and to make new wagers: neither Gaullist France nor the present U.S. leadership is willing to risk a major loss of control. Contrary to the French proverb, in the process of functional integration, only the first steps do not cost much.

There are two important general lessons one can draw from a study of the process of integration. The first concerns the limits of the functional method: its very (if relative) success in the relatively painless area in which it works relatively well lifts the participants to the level of issues to which it does not apply well any more—like swimmers whose skill at moving quickly away from the shore suddenly brings them to the point where the waters are stormiest and deepest, at a time when fatigue is setting in, and none of the questions about ultimate goal, direction, and length of swim has been answered. The functional process was used in order to "make Europe"; once Europe began being made, the process collided with the question; "making Europe, what for?" The process is like a grinding machine that can work only if someone keeps giving it something to grind. When the users start quarreling and stop providing, the machine stops. For a while, the machine worked because the governments poured into it a common determination to integrate their economies in order to maximize wealth; but with their wealth increasing, the question of what to do with it was going to arise: a technique capable of supplying means does not *ipso facto* provide the ends, and it is about those ends that quarrels have broken out. They might have been avoided if the situation had been more compelling—if the Six had been so cooped up that each one's horizon would have been nothing other than his five partners. But this has never been their outlook, nor is it any more their necessity. Each one is willing to live with the others, but not on terms too different from his own; and the Six are not in the position of the three miserable prisoners of *No Exit.* Transforming a dependent "subsystem" proved to be one thing; defining its relations to all other subsystems and to the international system in general has turned out to be quite another—indeed, so formidable a matter as to keep the transformation of the subsystem in abeyance until those relations can be defined.

The model of functional integration, a substitute for the kind of instant federation which governments had not been prepared to accept, shows its origins in important respects. One, it is essentially an administrative model, which relies on bureaucratic expertise for the promotion of a policy defined by the political authorities, and for the definition of a policy that political decision-makers are technically incapable of shaping—something like French planning under the Fourth Republic. The hope was that in the interstices of political bickering the administrators could build up a consensus; but the mistake was to believe that a formula that works well within certain limits is a panacea—and that even within the limits of "welfare politics" administrative skill can always overcome the disastrous effects of political paralysis or mis-management (cf. the impact of inflation, or balance of payment troubles, on planning). Two, the model assumes that the basic political decisions, to be prepared and pursued by the civil servants but formally made by the govern-ments, would be reached through the process of short-term bargaining, by politicians whose mode of operation is empirical muddling through, of the kind that puts immediate advantages above long-term pursuits: this model corresponds well to the nature of parliamentary politics with a weak Execu-tive, for example, the politics of the Fourth Republic, but the mistake was to believe that all political regimes would conform to this rather sorry image, and also to ignore the disastrous results which the original example produced whenever conflicts over values and fundamental choices made mere empiri-cal groping useless or worse than useless (cf. decolonization).[29]

The second lesson is even more discouraging for the advocates of func-tionalism. To revert to the analogy of the grinder, what has happened is that the machine, piqued by the slowing down of supply, suddenly suggested to its users that in the future the supplying of grinding material be taken out of their hands and left to the machine. The institutional machinery tends to become an actor with a stake in its own survival and expansion. The same thing happens often enough within a state whose political system is ineffec-tive. But here we deal not with one but with six political systems, and the reason for the ineffectiveness of the Council of Ministers of the Six may be the excessive toughness, not the weakness, of the national political systems involved. In other words, by trying to be a force, the bureaucracy here, in-evitably, makes itself even more of a stake that the nations try to control or at least to affect. A new complication is thus added to all the substantive issues that divide the participants—one that provides them with a whole trunkful of screens and masks. Thus, the agricultural problem is one that could have been solved "technically," since the governments had previously reached basic compromises, and more or less agreed on the relations between Common Market and outside agriculture. But the way in which these accords had been reached left scars, and the nature of the agreement meant a victory for one state (France) over another (Germany). The whole issue has been reopened, due not to the states' but to the Commission's initiative. In the crisis of 1965, the Commission's overly bold proposal of a common agricul-tural policy (along pro-French lines) cum supranationality (against French determination) has, on the one hand, allowed some of the Six, hostile in fact to the substantive proposals, to endorse the Commission's plan and stand up as champions of supranationality, while knowing that the French would block the scheme; the French have been able to use the Commission's rashness as a pretext for trying to kill supranationality altogether; a German government not too kindly disposed toward a Commission whose initiatives and economic

29. Along similar lines, see Francis Rosenstiel, *Le principe de "Supranationalité"* (Paris, 1962).

inspiration were hardly in line with Mr. Erhard's views has found itself defending the Commission, whose head, now under French attack, is a German; a French government anxious to get its partners committed to a protected agricultural market has preferred to postpone the realization of this goal rather than let the Commission's autonomy grow. The states have found something more to disagree about, and the Commission, in an attempt to push the car out of the bog, has stopped the motor for months. To be sure, the Commission's dilemma had become acute: either its members resigned themselves to being merely patient brokers to their quarreling clients, and letting them set the pace; or else they tried to behave both according to the ideal-type of the Monnet method, and as if a genuine community had already been established; but if prudence meant sluggishness, anticipation has meant delay. In the immediate future, the settlement of the various substantive issues—"the uniting of Europe, what for?"—is likely to be postponed while the Six try to repair the damaged machinery; in a way, haggling about the kind of grinder one wants is a polite method for appearing to want to keep grinding together, while really disagreeing completely on what one wants to put in and get out.

IV

We must come now to the balance sheet of the "European experiment." The most visible aspect is the survival of the nations. To be sure, they survive transformed: first, swept by the advent of the "age of mass consumption," caught in an apparently inexorable process of industrialization, urbanization, and democratization, they become more alike in social structure, in economic and social policies, even in physical appearance; there is a spectacular break between a past which so many monuments bring to constant memory, and a rationalized future that puts these nations closer to the problems of America's industrial society than to the issues of their own history. Second, these similarities are promoted by the Common Market itself: it is of no mean consequence that the prospect of a collapse of the Market should have brought anguish to various interest groups, some of which had fought its establishment: the transnational linkages of businessmen and farmers are part of the transformation. Third, none of the Western European nations is a world power any longer in the traditional sense, that is, in the sense either of having physical establishments backed by military might in various parts of the globe, or of possessing in Europe armed forces superior to those of any non-European power.

And yet they survive as nations. Let us go back to the criteria of integration listed above. On foreign and defense policies, not only has no power been transferred to common European organs, but France has actually taken power away from NATO, and, as shown in part two, differences in the calculations of the national interest have, if anything, broadened ever since the advent of the balance of terror. As for intra-European communications, research shows that the indubitably solid economic network of E.E.C. has not been complemented by a network of social and cultural communications;[30] the links between some of those societies and the U.S. are stronger than the links among them. Indeed, even in the realm of economic relations, the Common Market for goods has not been completed by a system of pan-West European enterprises: enterprises that find themselves unable to compete with rivals within E.E.C. often associate themselves with American firms rather than merge with such rivals. Finally, views about external issues, far from becoming more compatible, appear to reflect as well as to support the divergent definitions of the national interest by the statesmen. French élite opinion puts Europe ahead of the North Atlantic partnership, deems bipolarity obsolete, is overwhelmingly indifferent or even hostile to the U.S., and is still highly suspicious of Germany; only a minority comes out in favor of a genuine political federation of Western Europe and thinks that U.S. and French interests coincide. German élite opinion puts the North Atlantic entente ahead of Europe, believes that the world is still bipolar, is overwhelmingly favorable to the U.S., deems U.S. and German interests in agreement, is either favorably inclined toward France or at least not hostile, and shows a majority in favor of a European federation. There is no common European outlook. Nor is there a common "project," a common conception of either Europe's role in world affairs or Europe's possible contribution to the solution of the problems characteristic of all industrial societies.

It is important to understand where the obstacles lie. To some extent, they lie in the present condition of national consciousness. I mentioned earlier that there were at the start considerable differences from country to country. In two respects, similarities have emerged in recent years. There has been a rebirth of German national consciousness, largely because the bold attempt at fastening Germany's shattered consciousness directly to a new European one did not succeed: the existence of a German national situation has gradually reawakened a German national awareness, and thus reduced the gap between Germany and France in this area. Moreover, all the national consciences in Western Europe are alike in one sense: they are not like Rousseau's general will, a combination of mores and moves that define with a large degree of intellectual clarity and emotional involvement the purposes of the national community. Today's national consciousness in Europe is negative rather than positive. There is still, in each nation, a "vouloir-vivre collectif." But it is not a "daily plebiscite" *for* something. It is, in some parts, a daily routine, a community based on habit rather than on common tasks, an identity that is received rather than shaped. Thus Germany's sense of "cohesion and distinctiveness" is the inevitable result of the survival and recovery of a West German state in a world of nations, rather than a specific

30. I am using here unpublished studies done under Karl Deutsch, especially by Donald J. Puchala.

willed set of imperatives. In other parts, national consciousness is a daily refusal rather than a daily creation, a desire to preserve a certain heritage (however waning, and less because it is meaningful today than because it is one's own) rather than a determination to define a common destiny, an identity that is hollow rather than full and marked more by bad humor toward foreign influences than by any positive contribution.

To be sure, the negative or hollow character of national consciousness need not be a liability for the champions of integration: general wills *a la* Rousseau could be formidable obstacles to any fusion of sovereignty. However, the obstacle resides partly in the common nature of the present state of national consciousness, partly in the remaining differences. A patriotic consciousness that survives in a kind of nonpurposive complacency may not be a barrier to efforts at transcending it, but it is a drag: it does not carry forward or push statesmen in the way in which an intense and positive "general will" prods leaders who act on behalf of national goals, or in the way in which European federalists have sometimes hoped that enlightened national patriotisms would propel Europe's national leaders into building a new European community, into which those enlightened patriotisms would converge and merge. Moreover, two of the "national consciences" have raised obstacles: the French one because it remains too strong, the German one because it remains too weak. The French may not have a sense of national purpose, but, precisely because their patriotism has been tested so often and so long, because the pressures of the outside world have continued throughout the postwar era to batter their concerns and their conceits, and because modernization, now accepted and even desired, also undermines traditional values still cherished and traditional authority patterns still enforced, French national consciousness opposes considerable resistance to any suggestion of abdication, resignation, *repli*—so much so that the "Europeans" themselves have had to present integration as an opportunity for getting French views shared by others instead of stressing the "community" side of the enterprise.[31] Germany's national consciousness, on the other hand, remains marked by a genuine distaste for or timidity toward what might be called the power activities of a national community on the world stage; hence a tendency to shy away from the problems of "high politics" which a united Europe would have to face and whose avoidance only delays the advent of unity; a tendency to refuse to make policy choices and to pretend (to oneself and to others) that no such choices are required, that there is no incompatibility between a "European Europe" and an Atlantic partnership. In one case, a defensive excess of self-confidence makes unity on terms other than one's own difficult, and obliges integrationist leaders to use cunning and flattery and deceit (with often lamentable results—like the E.D.C. crisis); in the other case, an equally defensive lack of self-confidence projects itself

31. On this point, see Raymond Aron and Daniel Lerner (eds.), *France Defeats EDC* (New York, 1957).

into the external undertakings of the nation and weakens the foundations of the common European enterprise.

And yet, if the "national consciousness" of the European nations could be isolated from all other elements of the national situation, one would, I think, conclude that the main reasons for the resistance of the nation-state lie elsewhere.

They lie, first of all, in the differences in national situations, exacerbated by the interaction between each of the Six and the present international system. Earlier, we have looked at concrete instances of such differences; let us return to them in a more analytic way. One part of each national situation is the purely *domestic* component. In a modern nation-state, the very importance of the political system, in the triple sense of functional scope, authority, and popular basis, is already a formidable obstacle to integration. It is comparatively easier to overcome the parochialism of a political system which, being of the night-watchman variety, has only a slender administrative structure, whose power consists of punishing, rather than rewarding, with the help of a tiny budget, and whose transmission belts to the mass of the people are few and narrow, than it is to dismantle the fortress of a political system which rests on "socially mobilized" and mobilizing parties and pressure groups, and handles an enormous variety of social and economic services with a huge bureaucracy. To be sure, it was the hope and tactic of Monnet to dismantle the fortress by redirecting the allegiance of parties and pressure groups toward the new central institutions, by endowing the latter with the ability to compete with the national governments in the setting up of social services. In other words, the authority of the new European political system would deepen as its scope broadened and its popular basis expanded. The success of this attempt at drying up the national ponds by diverting their waters into a new, supranational pool depended on three prerequisites which have not been met: with respect to popular basis, the prevalence of parties and pressure groups over Executives; with respect to scope, the self-sustaining and expanding capacity of the new central bureaucracy; with respect to both scope and popular basis, the development of transnational political issues of interest to all political forces and publics across boundary lines. The modern Executive establishment has one remarkable feature: it owes much of its legitimacy and its might to the support of popularly based parties and pressure groups, but it also enjoys a degree of autonomy that allows it to resist pressures, to manipulate opposition, to manufacture support. Even the weak Fourth Republic has evaded pressure toward "transnationalism" and diluted the dose of "bargaining politics" along supranational lines. The civil servants' careers are still made and unmade in the national capitals. Above all, each nation's political life continues to be dominated by "parochial" issues: each political system is like a thermos bottle that keeps warm, or lukewarm, the liquid inside. The European political process has never come close to resembling that of any Western European democracy because it has been starved of common and distinctive European issues. It is as if, for the mythical common man, the nation-state were still the most satisfying—indeed the most rewarding—form of social organization in existence.[32] As for what it can no longer provide him with by itself, the state can still provide it without committing suicide, through cooperation, or the citizens can go and find it across borders, without any need to transfer their allegiance—or else there is, in any event, no guarantee that any form of social organization other than a still utopian world state could provide it. If we look at the issues that have dominated European politics, we find two distinct blocs. One is the bloc of problems peculiar to each nation—Italy's battle of Reds *vs.* Blacks, or its concern for the Mezzogiorno; Belgium's linguistic clashes; Germany's "social economy" and liquidation of the past; France's constitutional troubles and miraculously preserved party splintering. Here, whatever the transnational party and interest group alignments in Luxembourg, the dominant motifs have been purely national. The other bloc of issues are the international ones (including European unity). But here is where the *external* component of the national situation has thwarted the emergence of a common European political system comparable to that of each nation.

It is here that the weight of geography and of history—a history of nations —has kept the nation-states in their watertight compartments. It is no accident if France, the initiator of the process, has also been its chief troublemaker: for in those two respects France's position differed from everyone else's in the community, and was actually closer to England's. Historically first: for Germany, integration meant a leap from opprobrium and impotence, to respectability and equal rights; for the smaller powers, it meant exchanging a very modest dose of autonomy for participation in a potentially strong and rich grouping. France could not help being much more ambivalent, for integration meant on the one hand an avenue for leadership and the shaping of a powerful bloc, but it also meant on the other the acceptance of permanent restrictions to an autonomy that was indeed quite theoretical in the late 1940's, but whose loss could not be deemed definitive. For a once-great power, whose national history is long, and therefore used to rise and fall, inherits from its past a whole set of habits and reflexes which make it conduct its policy as if it were still or could again become a great power (unless those habits and reflexes have been smashed, at least for a while, as completely and compellingly as were Germany's); for this once-great power showed, as described above, a still vigilant national consciousness, often the more virulent for all its negativism; for the international system itself seemed to open vistas of increased freedom of action to middle-sized states. In other words, integration meant an almost certain improvement in the national situation of the other five, but for France it could be a deterioration or an adventure.[33]

32. See Rupert Emerson, *op. cit.*, Ch. XIX.

33. England's refusal to join European integration, before 1961, could not fail to increase French reticence, for integration thus meant equality with Germany, and a clear-cut

There is no better example than the nuclear problem: integration here meant, for France, giving up the possibility of having a force of her own, perhaps never even being certain that a united Europe (with no agreement on strategy and diplomacy in sight) would create a common deterrent, at best contributing to a European force which would put Germany in the same position as France; but the French decision to pursue the logic of diversity, while giving her her own force, has also made a European nuclear solution more difficult and increased France's distance from Germany. Moreover, a geographical difference has corroborated the historical one: France had lasting colonial involvements. Not only did they, on the whole, intensify national consciousness; they also contributed to France's ambivalence toward European ently tried to tie their partners to the prevalence of France's overseas plight became, the more integration was preached as a kind of compensatory mechanism. But, on the other hand, this meant that integration had to be given a "national" rather than a "supranational" color, to be presented as a new career rather than as a common leap; it meant that the French consistently tried to tie their partners to the prevalence of France's overseas concerns, much against these partners' better judgment; above all, it meant that there was a competition for public attention and for official energies, between the "load" of integration and the burden of the overseas mission. The great power reflex and the colonial legacy combine today in the policy of cooperation with the former imperial possessions, despite its costs: cooperation is presented as a transfiguration of the legacy, and a manifestation of the reflex.[34]

Thus, the national situations have multiplied the effects of differences between the shapes of the various national consciences. But the resistance of the nation-state is not due only to the kind of loan of life that its inevitable entanglement in international affairs and the idle motion left by its past provide even to nations with a low national consciousness. It is due also to the impact of the revival of nationalism in France. Even without de Gaulle the differences analyzed above would have slowed down integration and kept some fire in the nation's stoves. But the personal contribution of de Gaulle to the crisis of integration has been enormous. Not only has he raised questions that were inescapable in the long run, earlier and more pungently than they would have been otherwise, but he has also provided and tried to impose his own answers. His impact is due to his style as well as to his policies. The

---

difference between France's position and England's, that is, a reversal of French aspirations and traditions. England has on the whole rejected the "resignation-resistance" dilemma—and as a result, both the aspects of its foreign policy that appeared like resignation to U.S. predominance and the aspects that implied resistance to decline have contributed to the crisis of European integration: for France's veto in January 1963 meant a French refusal to let into Europe a power that had just confirmed its military ties to the U.S., but Britain's previous desire to play a world role and aversion to "fading into Europe" encouraged France's own misgivings about integration.

34. See Alfred Grosser, *op. cit.*, Ch. IV.

meaning of de Gaulle has been a change in French policy from ambivalence toward supranational integration to outright hostility; from a reluctance to force one's partners to dispel the ambiguities of "united Europe" to an almost gleeful determination to bring differences out into the open; from a tendency to interpret the national situation as oppressively difficult to a herculean effort at improving all its components in order to push back limits and maximize opportunities. The meaning of de Gaulle has also been a change in the national situations of the others, leading to a sharpening of antagonisms and to a kind of cumulative retreat from integration. Each one of those meanings must be briefly examined.

Insofar as France is concerned, the key is provided by de Gaulle's concept of grandeur.[35] Greatness is a mixture of pride and ambition—the nation shall not at any point leave the control of its destiny to others (which does not mean that he does not acknowledge the existence of irresistible waves with which the ship of state must roll, lest, precisely, it fall in the hands of others who would rush to a predatory rescue or to a plunder of the wreck). The nation must try at any point to play as full a role in the world as its means allow. The consequences are clear: First, the kind of supranational integration which would leave decisions on vital issues to majority votes or to executive organs independent of the states is out of the question; even if the interests and policies of France should happen to prevail for a while (as indeed they did as long as the Commission, in its drive for economic integration, remained very close to French ideas), there would be no assurance against a sudden and disastrous reversal. Second, extensive cooperation is not at all ruled out: on the contrary, such cooperation will benefit all participants as long as it corresponds to and enhances mutual interests. Third, however, it is part of the very ambition of grandeur that in such schemes of cooperation which aim not merely at exchanges of *services* but at the definition of common *policies*, France will try to exert her leadership and carry out her views: the degree of French cooperativeness will be measured by the degree of responsiveness of the others.

It is true that the General is an empiricist, and that his analysis of the European situation is to a large extent irrefutable. What could be more starting from what exists—the nation-state—refusing to act as if what does not yet exist—a united Europe—had already been established, and refusing to forget that each of the European nations is willy-nilly engaged in an international competition that entails a fight for rank and power? But pragmatism is always at the service of ends, explicit or not (the definition of a bad foreign policy could be: that which uses rigid means at the service of explicit ends, as well as that whose flexible means are not serving clearly-thought-out ends). De Gaulle's empiricism is a superb display of skill, but on behalf of a thoroughly non-empirical doctrine. It is obvious that his distrust of supra-

35. For a more detailed analysis of this concept, see my article: "De Gaulle's Memoirs: The Hero as History," *World Politics*, Vol. XIII, No. 1 (October 1960), pp. 140–155.

national integration, which, within Europe, could submit French interests to the dictates of others, and could expose Europe to the dictates of the "hegemonists," while it is perfectly comprehensible as a starting point, nevertheless results in a kind of freezing of integration and perpetuation of the nation-state. If his chief foreign policy objective were the creation of a European entity acting as a world power, his "empirical" *starting point* would be a most unrealistic *method*. But the fact is that such a creation is not his supreme objective, and Europe not his supreme value.

His supreme value remains the nation-state; his supreme political objective is the creation of a world in which the "two hegemonies" will have been replaced by a multipolar international system, whose "first floor" would be the numerous nations, endowed with and entitled to political integrity and independence, and whose "second floor" would be inhabited by the nuclear powers, in a role comparable to that of the late European concert. Again, the implications are clear: de Gaulle's doctrine is a "universalist nationalism," that is, he sees France's mission as world-wide, not local and defensive, but this means that Europe is just one corner of the tapestry; Europe is a means, not an end. "Things being what they are," it is better to have separate nation-states (whose margin of freedom is undoubtedly smaller than when the use of force was not so costly, whose capacity to shape history is also undoubtedly limited if their size, population, and resources are mediocre, but whose ability to behave as self-determined actors on the stage is enhanced precisely by the blunting of force and by the opportunities opened to other instruments of power and influence) than it is to have a larger entity, undoubtedly more able to act as a forceful competitor in the world's contests should it be coherent, but more likely to be incoherent, given the divisions of its members and the leverage interested outsiders possess over some of the insiders. The size of the unit is less important than its "cohesion and distinctiveness," for its effectiveness is not merely a function of its material resources: if the unit has no capacity to turn these to action, because of internal cleavages and strains, the only beneficiaries would be its rivals. In a contest with giants, a confident David is better than a disturbed Goliath. This is a choice that reflects a doctrine; the refusal to gamble on European unity goes along with a willingness to gamble on the continuing potency of the French nation-state; the determination to accept only the kind of Europe that would be France writ large[36] corresponds to a conviction that French policies could be made to prevail whether Europe contributes its support or not: "with Europe if they follow, without Europe if they do not," Europe is just a card in a global game. Schumpeter had defined imperialism as an objectless quest; de Gaulle's nationalism is a kind of permanent quest with varying content but never any other cause than itself.

As I suggested above, a nationalist leader is one whose reading of the

---

36. Grosser, *op. cit.*, pp. 112–113, draws attention to Prime Minister Pompidou's statement: "France is condemned by geography and history to play the role of Europe."

national situation is likely to be quite different from the reading other leaders would give. De Gaulle's brand of nationalism being what it is—universalist, aimed at overcoming the "two hegemonies," exploiting both of the somewhat contradictory trends that dominate the present world (the conservation of the nation as its basic unit, the concentration of what one might call "final power" among the nuclear states)—it is not surprising that he has altogether liquidated a colonial burden that kept France away from every one of the routes he wanted to travel, and replaced it with an ambitious policy of cooperation with the "Third World." In a way, it is true, as some critics have charged, that this policy is a kind of self-consolation prize for the failure of his European policy; but in another sense it conforms deeply to his most vital designs and to his most constant habit of never relying on one line of policy only: In the first place, cooperation manifests France's universal destiny; in the second, it aims at consolidating a system of independent, if cooperating, nations; in the third, it tries to use the prestige thus gained as an elevator to the floor of the "big five," to which access has been denied so far by the "big two." It is clear that the first two missions rule out a concentration on Europe alone, that the second prevents in any case his putting any passion into overcoming the nation-state in Europe, that the third is precisely a substitute for the "elevator" Europe has failed to provide. As a result, all that has made France's historical heritage and geographic position distinctive has been strengthened.

Every great leader has his built-in flaw, since this is a world in which roses have thorns. De Gaulle's is the self-fulfilling prophecy. Distrustful of any Europe but his own, his acts have made Europe anything but his. Here we must turn to the impact of his policy on France's partners. First of all, there is a matter of style: wanting cooperation not integration, de Gaulle has refused to treat the Community organs as Community organs; but, wanting to force his views about cooperation on partners still attached to integration, and attempting to impose his views about a "European Europe" on associates who might have settled for cooperation but only on behalf of another policy, de Gaulle has paradoxically had to try to achieve cooperation for a common policy in a way that smacked of conflict not cooperation, of unilateralism not compromise. Thus we have witnessed not just a retreat from the Monnet method to, say, the kind of intergovernmental cooperation that marks O.E.C.D., but to a kind of grand strategy of nonmilitary conflict, a kind of political cold war of maneuver and "chicken." With compromises wrested by ultimatums, concessions obtained not through package deals but under the threat of boycotts, it is not surprising if even the Commission ended by playing the General's game instead of turning whatever other cheek was left; its spring 1965 agricultural plan was as outright a challenge to de Gaulle as de Gaulle's veto of January 1963 had been an affront to the Community spirit. Just as de Gaulle had tried to force Germany to sacrifice her farmers to the idea of a European entity, the Commission tried to call de Gaulle's bluff by forcing him to choose between French farmers' interests and the French national interest in a "European Europe" for agriculture, on the one hand, and his own hostility to supranationality and the French national interest (as seen by him) in the free use of French resources, on the other. Playing his game, the Commission also played into his hands, allowing him to apply the Schelling tactic of "if you do not do what I ask, I will blow up my brains on your new suit," and in the end buying his return at the price of a sacrifice of integration.[37] In other words, he has forced each member to treat the Community no longer as an end in itself; and he has driven even its constituted bodies, which still insist it is that, into bringing grist to his mill.

Second, his impact on his partners is a matter of policy as well. Here we must examine Franco-German relations. As long as he hoped that Germany would follow his guidance and provide the basis for the "European Europe" of his design, his attitude toward West Germany was one of total support of her intransigence toward the Communists. As soon as the increasing clarity of his own policy (half-veiled until the end of the Algerian ordeal and his triumph in the constitutional battle of October-November 1962) provoked German suspicion and reticence, as soon as the U.S., in response to his challenge, consolidated its ties with a still loyal Germany and even promised her substantial rewards for her loyalty, he applied to Germany the shock tactics so effectively used on Britain and the U.S. during World War II: he made his own opening to the East and gradually shifted away from the kind of celebration of a "new Germany" (heir to her greatness in her past but now willing to take her place as France's aide in the new "European Europe"), so characteristic of his German visit in the fall of 1962. He now resorts to carefully worded reminders to the Germans of their past misdeeds, of the risk which their loyalty to the U.S. entails for their reunification, and of the interest France and the Eastern states (including Russia) share in keeping Germany under permanent restrictions. Had Germany been willing to follow France, he would have given priority to the construction of a "half-Europe" that would thereafter have been a magnet (as well as a guarantee of German harmlessness) to the East. Germany's refusal leads him to put the gradual emergence of a "Europe from the Atlantic to the Urals"—indeed from the British Isles to the Urals[38]—if not ahead of at least on the same plane as the development of the "European Europe" in the West; for the containment of Germany, no longer assured in a disunited Western Europe of the Six, may still be obtained in a much larger framework. The implications are important. First, there is a considerable change in Germany's national situation. On the one hand, its external component has been transformed. Whereas for more than fifteen years both the U.S. and France carried out tacitly Robert Schuman's recommendation—"never leave Germany to herself"—the Franco-American competition for German support, the Gaullist refusal to tie Germany to France in a federal

37. See Thomas Schelling's *Strategy of Conflict* (Cambridge, Mass., 1960).
38. See de Gaulle's reference to England in his press conference of September 9, 1965.

Europe so to speak for the knot's sake (that is, unless Germany follows France), America's disastrous emulation of the sorcerer's apprentice in titillating Germany's interest in nuclear strategy or weapons-sharing, in the belief, or under the pretext, of anticipating her appetite, all of these factors have contributed to loosen the bonds between Germany and the West: to the European part of the West, because of the slump in integration, and even to the U.S., because of America's failure to follow up after raising in Germany hopes that should not have been raised, but which, once raised and frustrated, are unlikely to fade. On the other hand, and consequently, the domestic component of Germany's national situation has also been affected: Still concerned with security as well as with reunification, but less and less capable of believing that loyalty to their allies will deliver any goods, the German leaders and élites may well come to feel less dependent and less constrained. Of course, objectively, the external constraints remain compelling: a policy of self-assertion may not lead anywhere; an attempt at bypassing the nuclear restrictions of the Paris agreements is not likely to make the East Europeans and the Soviets any more willing to let East Germany go; and the price the Soviets may want to exact for reunification is not likely to increase German security. But the fact that Germany's ties to Western powers are weakening means at least potentially that the capacity to test those constraints by unilateral action may well be used. To be in a cell with a chain around one's ankles and the hope of being liberated by one's jailers is one kind of situation. To be in that cell without such a chain and with such hopes gone is another situation, although the cell has not changed.

In other words, although the impact of de Gaulle on Germany so far has not been a rebirth of German nationalism, it has been a transformation of the situation that gives to nationalism some chances—chances if not of external success, given the nature of the cell, then of being at least "tried." The temptation to use one's economic power and potential military might in order to reach one's goals and the example of one's allies competing for accommodation with one's foe are not resistible forever, especially if one's past is full of precedents. To be sure, a nationalist Germany may well find itself as unable to shake the walls or to escape through the bars as Gaullist France is unable to forge the "European Europe." But the paradox of a revisionist France, trying to change the international system to her advantage despite her complete lack of "traditional" grievances (lost territories, military discrimination, and so forth), next to a Germany full of such grievances, yet behaving in fact like a *status quo* power, may not last eternally. Of course, a less aggressively ambitious France might not have prevented Germany from trying to follow her own path one day: the possibility of someone else's imitative *hubris* is no reason for one's own *effacement;* but precisely because the "essence and drama" of nationalism are the meeting with others, the risk of contagion—a risk that is part of de Gaulle's gamble—cannot be discarded.

Thus the nation-state survives, preserved by the formidable autonomy of politics, as manifested in the resilience of political systems, the interaction between separate states and a single international system, the role of leaders who believe both in the primacy of "high politics" over the kind of managerial politics susceptible to functionalism, and in the primacy of the nation, struggling in the world of today, over any new form, whose painful establishment might require one's lasting withdrawal from the pressing and exalting daily contest.

V

This long balance sheet leaves us with two sets of questions: What are the prospects in Western Europe? What generalizations can one draw from the whole experience? As for the prospects, what precedes reads perhaps too much like a post-mortem. Is there no chance for the European Community? Is it condemned to be, at best, a success in the economic realm but a fiasco in "high politics," something like a hydra with one single body but a multitude of heads?

It would be presumptuous indeed to read hope out of court. One of the decisive elements in the movement's "spillback," de Gaulle's nationalism, may not outlive him. His successors may have a less sweeping vision and may make exactly the opposite gamble from his—that is, prefer the risks of the common enterprise, whose rewards might be high if it works, to the dividends of national action; they could indeed attempt to revive the Monnet concept of Europe, and even to overcome the deficiencies of functionalism by a leap into more genuinely federal institutions. Moreover, whereas de Gaulle has had the backing of a parliamentary majority hostile to supranational integration and has exerted the kind of rule that parties and pressure groups do not affect much anyhow, his successors may depend for domestic support and survival precisely on those parties and pressure groups which had started to weave a transnational fabric. Should this be the case, the "Europe of the Six," instead of being as close as it now is to the traditional model of interstate relations, might move again toward the other ideal-tpye, that of political community-building, so well described by Ernst Haas, who sees in it the wave of the future.[39]

Whereas in the case of a revival of German nationalism, the prospect of failure may not be enough to deter an attempt, here I would maintain that an attempt would not be tantamount to success. In the first place, while nothing (not even the Common Market) is irreversible, no important event leaves the world unmarked, and after the event one can never pick up the pieces as if nothing had happened: this, which is true of the Common Market, is true also of General de Gaulle. It will not be easy to sweep under the rug the curls of dust he has willfully placed in the sunlight; it will not be easy to ignore

39. See his essay "Technocracy, Pluralism and the New Europe," in Stephen R. Graubard (ed.), *op. cit.*, pp. 62–88.

the kinds of questions he has asked, even if his answers are rejected, precisely because they are the questions any European enterprise would have faced sooner or later. Second, even the passing of his nationalism might not transform the national situations of the European nation-states so deeply that all the cleavages discussed here would suddenly disappear. For, even if all the political leaders of Western Europe had once again the same non-nationalist approach, the differences in the national situations would still lead to divergent definitions of the national interests. In particular, the problem of nuclear weapons control and command in a grouping divided between nuclear "have-nots" and nuclear "haves" may prove to be as intractable, and to raise as much of an obstacle to community-formation among Western Europeans, as in the Atlantic alliance. The ideal conditions not merely for the resumption but for the success of a forward march would be a transformation of Germany's external situation and of France's domestic one. If the search for a détente should lead the U.S. to put a rapprochement with the U.S.S.R. ahead of its bonds to West Germany, and if it became clear in West Germany, as a result, both that security is neither the most urgent problem nor entirely provided any more by the U.S., and that reunification cannot be obtained from and through the U.S.; if, in addition, such disappointment with the U.S. does not encourage West German leadership to follow a nationalist path, or if an attempt by West Germany to obtain for itself from Moscow what its allies had failed to provide for her should end in frustration, then—at last—West Germany might be willing to accept a foreign policy close to de Gaulle's "European Europe" with its indifference to regimes and ideologies, its repudiation of the cold war outlook, its opening to the East, and its cautious promise of eventual reunification at the cost of border limitations and arms restrictions. In other words, on the German side, what would be required would be a "polycentric," yet non-nationalist, reading of the external situation. This would be likely to happen if at the same time France had given up her nationalist interpretation of "polycentrism," and become again more humble, more willing to trust the Community organs, more in need of adopting European integration as a goal in itself. Such a possibility would exist if, domestically, the impervious stability of de Gaulle's regime were to be replaced not merely with a political system whose Executive would lean on an "integrationist" party majority, but with the kind of instability that both prevents political leaders from acting on the world stage as if they were its managers and pressures them into seeking a European solution, or alibi, for their difficulties. Europe as Germany's least frustrating framework, Europe as the best compensation for France's domestic troubles, a Europe following Monnet's approach toward de Gaulle's objectives:[40] it may appear like a

40. As Grosser points out in his book and the presidential election campaign of 1965 confirmed, even the opposition to de Gaulle's foreign policy accepts his notion of a "European Europe" and rejects American "hegemony" (with the exception of a very few men like Reynaud or perhaps Lecanuet). There is disagreement about methods and style rather than on objectives.

dream; it cannot be dismissed. But whether it has a chance depends essentially on *when* the General's nationalism will pass from the scene, on *what* degree of cooperation among the nations of Western Europe there will be at that time, on *whether* a new attempt by Britain to join the Community would introduce additional complications, on *what* the U.S. policy in Europe will be; the chance depends on the timely convergence of too many variables to be counted on.

IV

THE PROLIFERATION OF NUCLEAR WEAPONS

The possible proliferation of nuclear weapons necessarily has profound import for international order. Mr. Yuter is a firm advocate of nuclear non-proliferation, and his article makes unmistakably clear the close relationship between non-proliferation and bipolarity. It also indicates the extent to which his position contains an inbuilt anti-Chinese orientation.

The major public incentive for preventing nuclear proliferation is the belief that the more nuclear powers there are, the greater the danger of war. The incentives to the Soviet Union and the United States include preventing the rise of nuclear competitors. The Soviet Union is particularly interested in preventing West Germany and China from becoming major nuclear powers. I doubt that the dangers of proliferation are as great as stated and in my essay I argue that a non-proliferation policy would likely be more effective if based on a criterion more rational than being a nuclear power on the date of the treaty.

There are a number of considerations inhibiting the spread of nuclear weapons, particularly to Germany and Japan, including primarily the danger of the transition process. But very serious questions arise as to the nature of the subsequent international order as American power diminishes, if other nations remain deprived of their own nuclear deterrence against attacks on their homeland.

Nuclear disarmament would be one answer to this problem, for the absence of nuclear weapons from all countries would leave all on an equal footing. However, it seems clear that neither the Soviet Union nor the

United States is moving in this direction. SALT—the strategic arms limitation talks between Russia and the U. S. that resulted in the agreements of December 1971 that are discussed in chapter X—may help to control the arms race but it is not a disarmament measure. It set a temporary upper limit on the number of offensive missiles that leaves all other nations far behind and that has caused serious concern in China and some concern in Europe.

If we were moving toward an era of much greater international order, this issue might not become crucial. If, however, power is becoming dispersed, as appears to be the case, thus reducing the incentive for the United States to intervene as it did in Korea, some nations may have to face a problem of nuclear blackmail in the future. Whether there will be countervailing mechanisms including economic interdependencies that minimize this risk is a subject on which current analysis in international relations is weak. However, this topic is very important for its linkage to the entire problem of world order.

9.

Preventing Nuclear Proliferation through the Legal Control of China's Bomb

SEYMOUR C. YUTER

THE SPREAD of nuclear weapons poses a serious threat to the survival of mankind. If proliferation is not halted, the probability of their eventual use will increase through a variety of incalculable contingencies: mistakes in predicting the response of an enemy to a limited war or blackmail; failure to exercise effective control over nuclear arsenals and their operators, increasing the chance that these weapons will fall into unauthorized and irresponsible hands; errors in tracing the source of a nuclear attack, leading to an inappropriate response; an attack launched by a country whose leaders are ignorant of, or unconcerned with, the consequences of their action. One can imagine other equally tragic scenarios.

Fortunately, the two nuclear-armed superpowers seem to be convinced that further proliferation would work against their best interests. They must now demonstrate that their concern is matched by the will to cooperate in establishing and enforcing meaningful arms control measures. This raises the possibility of a Washington-Moscow global condominium, a prospect that does not upset historian Arnold Toynbee:

> . . . I believe that peace and affluence are what most people desire, and we cannot have these without order in the age of mechanization. I therefore believe that the human race would submit to a Russo-American . . . dictatorship if it believed that, at this price, it could have affluence and

Reprinted by permission from *ORBIS*, Winter 1969, pp. 1018–41. Copyright by the Trustees of the University of Pennsylvania.

peace. . . . Of course, if nuclear weapons were limited to Russia and America, there wouldn't be democratic government of the world. A Russo-American world government would probably be very authoritarian, but it would at least ensure the survival of the human race—and that is the first consideration, to my mind.[1]

Raymond Aron agrees that the two nuclear giants must collaborate for their own safety, but dismisses the possibility of joint authoritarian rule:

> The governing idea by which I interpreted the diplomatic situation was that of the solidarity of the two great powers—the warring brothers—against a total war of which they would be the first victims. Inevitably enemies by position and by the incompatibility of their ideologies, the United States and the Soviet Union have a common interest not in ruling together over the world (of which they would be quite incapable), but in not destroying each other.[2]

Even if the United States and the Soviet Union agree to arms control and nonproliferation measures, they cannot damp the arms race unless these measures can be made universally binding. Above all else, the superpowers must support arms control arrangements that can effectively freeze Communist China's nuclear development program; otherwise, Chinese progress will probably drive India, Japan and eventually West Germany into the nuclear club. While it is unlikely that West Germany would be the sixth nuclear power, she might well follow India and Japan in "going nuclear."

China's nuclear capability could be stunted by a universally-binding test ban which is either observed voluntarily by China or forced on her by both superpowers or by one superpower with at least the tacit support of the other. However, in the absence of a traumatic event, such as an accidental nuclear exchange, universal arms control measures do not appear to be feasible. In this case, the nuclear club will be expanded to admit, among others, West Germany, a development foreseen by Professor Morton A. Kaplan:

> Although the United States and the Soviet Union do have a common interest in not destroying each other, the Soviet Union has not learned to be satisfied with its present resources and influences. A nuclear-armed Federal Republic is in the best interests of the United States as a buffer against the Soviet Union; in any event nuclear proliferation to West Germany and other states is most likely regardless of U.S. policies. When the U.S.S.R. first learns that West Germany is acquiring nuclear weapons, the U.S. will deter the Soviet Union from forcibly disarming the West Ger-

1. Interview with Arnold Toynbee, *Playboy*, April 1967, pp. 68, 70; confirmed in a private memorandum received by the author on August 16, 1967. Also see Arnold Toynbee, *Change and Habit: The Challenge of Our Time* (New York: Oxford University Press, 1966), p. 157.
2. Raymond Aron, *Peace and War: A Theory of International Relations* (New York: Doubleday, 1966), p. xi.

mans. After West Germany has an operational nuclear arsenal which poses at least a minimal threat to the major Soviet cities, reunification with East Germany will not improbably follow. A reunited nuclear-armed Germany would in that case play a leading role in Europe and would provide an effective buffer to Soviet expansion and influence. The Soviet Union would then be sandwiched between a reunited nuclear-armed Germany and a nuclear-armed mainland China. Even if nuclear proliferation to West Germany and other states leads to small nuclear wars, the world will survive. The remaining practicable alternatives to this world are worse.[3]

II

The perils of proliferation which we will examine in this article lead me to conclude that the United States is currently faced with three difficult alternatives: (1) accepting a nuclear-proliferating world, in which a confrontation with the Soviet Union over a nuclear-arming West Germany could easily lead to general nuclear war; (2) attempting, with at least the tacit support of the Soviet Union, to prevent further nuclear proliferation by freezing or destroying the Chinese nuclear program, which might lead to a nuclear exchange in the Far East; or (3) withdrawing in isolation behind a heavy anti-ballistic missile system, leaving the rest of the world to be dominated by the Soviet Union and China—a policy that could lead to U.S. surrender or a nuclear war if and when the noose got too tight.

My analysis also leads to the conclusion that the Soviet Union is faced with three similar and difficult choices: (1) accepting a nuclear-proliferating world in which a confrontation with the United States over a nuclear-arming West Germany could easily lead to nuclear war; (2) attempting, with at least the tacit support of the United States, to prevent further nuclear proliferation (particularly to West Germany) by freezing or destroying the Chinese nuclear program; or (3) withdrawing in isolation behind a heavy anti-ballistic missile system, leaving the rest of the world to be dominated by the United States, China and Western Europe (probably led by a nuclear-armed and unified Germany), with the likelihood of having to relinquish former German territory to the Germans and former Chinese territory to the Chinese.

If Professor Kaplan is correct, the Soviets will back down in the confrontation with the United States over the nuclear arming of West Germany; and later, in a second crisis with the United States over the attempts of a nuclear-armed West Germany to force reunification, the USSR will back down again. The ultimate result will be a truncated "fortress Russia." But if Kaplan is wrong and the Soviets resist, the danger of an escalating crisis leading to general nuclear war is real. The Soviet invasion of Czechoslovakia, partly to counter a perceived military threat from West Germany, evidences strong Soviet resolve to prevent a nuclear-armed West Germany; and U.S. policy in

3. Morton A. Kaplan, private memorandum, received by the author June 15, 1967.

Viet Nam (at least prior to President Nixon's inauguration) seems to indicate that the United States would not risk nuclear war over the right of West Germany to go nuclear.

The least undesirable of the alternatives listed above is a joint attempt by the United States and the Soviet Union to prevent further nuclear proliferation by attempting to freeze or destroy the Chinese nuclear program. Such a plan is worth exploring if one agrees with Toynbee that the human race would submit to a "Russo-American dictatorship" in order to have affluence and peace. Nor is a Russo-American condominium, designed to minimize the threat of nuclear war, inconsistent with Aron's view. Such a condominium might take the form of an international organization to administer a universally-binding nuclear test ban law, i.e., an international nuclear peacekeeping law recognized by a large majority of states, including the United States and the USSR, and expressing an intent to bind nonassenting states.

India advocated a universal test ban during the UN disarmament debate in November 1965,[4] presumably to control the Chinese nuclear threat. The Nonproliferation Treaty not only fails to deal with the Chinese nuclear threat, but probably encourages the Chinese to consider giving nuclear weapons to "socialist" countries, which could include Syria and the UAR. On the other hand, a universal test ban could result in the removal *under law* of the Chinese nuclear threat and thus prevent further nuclear proliferation.

III

Kaplan's prognosis that in all likelihood West Germany will go nuclear and then reunite with East Germany, notwithstanding the resistance of the Soviet Union, might produce one, or perhaps two, dangerous crises: the first, when the Soviet Union learns about the Federal Republic's plans to go nuclear (the transition crisis), and a second, if and when a nuclear-armed West Germany attempts to force reunification from a position of nuclear strength (the reunification crisis). In the transition crisis, the Soviets will have an option to conduct a preemptive or disarming strike against the embryonic nuclear-weapon manufacturing capability of the West Germans, whether located in West Germany or elsewhere. Less dangerous Soviet responses would include blocking Western access to West Berlin, seizing West Berlin, or giving nuclear weapons to the East European allies, perhaps Poland and East Germany.

Washington could react to such Soviet moves by temporizing and taking no substantive action, meeting the escalating crisis by effectively countering each Soviet move, or leaving West Germany and therefore Europe to their fate and withdrawing behind an anti-ballistic missile system. Kaplan believes the United States could not afford to adopt an isolationist posture and permit

4. General Assembly, Official Records, Twentieth Session, First Committee, pp. 169–170 (November 24, 1965).

the Soviets to dominate Europe; therefore, Washington will counter each Soviet move, preventing the Soviets from disarming the West Germans—i.e., Moscow will back down. The U.S. government would have little choice but to oppose Soviet moves, since the alternatives would lead to a substantial change in the world balance of power against the United States, with a consequent threat of nuclear conflict when Soviet pressure became intolerable.

Under almost any conceivable circumstance the transition crisis presents a serious threat of a nuclear holocaust, since a confrontation between the United States and the USSR is likely to occur. In light of the strong Soviet resolve shown in the invasion of Czechoslovakia and the lack of comparable U.S. resolve in Viet Nam, the United States might not succeed in forcing the Soviets to back down over the German problem, and instead might leave Europe to Soviet domination rather than risk nuclear war over the right of the West Germans to go nuclear. Therefore, Washington might well prefer to take action to avoid a transition crisis that could lead to nuclear war or an adverse change in the world balance of power.

A reunification crisis could also lead to a confrontation between the United States and the Soviet Union, since a move by a nuclear-armed West Germany to force reunification against the will of the USSR is likely to be countered by the Soviets and any threat by the Soviets against the West Germans will probably be countered by the United States. This pessimistic prediction is based on the reasonable assumption that the Soviets oppose a reunited Germany as inimicable to their interests; therefore, reunification will not be achieved by peaceful means in the foreseeable future. A forced reunification could result from an uprising in East Germany against the Soviet overlords, whether or not sponsored by the West Germans, or even by a national liberation war, directly or indirectly supported by the Federal Republic, to free the "Soviet-occupied zone of Germany" (the jungles and mountains of the communist-style liberation war being replaced by nighttime sabotage and terrorism against Soviet installations, personnel and sympathizers).

The people of a nuclear-armed West Germany, after many years of unsuccessful attempts to reunify peacefully, and in a state of increasing frustration, might elect a neo-Nazi or other radical nationalist government dedicated to reunification by force if necessary. These radical leaders might engage in an escalating crisis with the Soviets in the belief that a smaller West German nuclear capability could neutralize Soviet nuclear strength and force the Soviets ultimately to back down. While the outcome of such a crisis is difficult to foresee, it seems likely that if the United States remained a power in Europe, it would have to back the West Germans, thus setting up a second U.S.-USSR confrontation and threat of nuclear war.

There appears also to be a direct connection between a nuclear-arming mainland China and a U.S.-USSR confrontation leading to nuclear war. A plausible scenario can be constructed along the following lines:

(1) India continues to refuse to sign the Nonproliferation Treaty because of the Chinese nuclear threat and the failure of the superpowers to give credible guarantees to defend her against that threat. At an opportune moment, India goes nuclear,[5] on the pretext of developing an anti-ballistic missile system for protection against mainland China. However, such a defensive nuclear program would probably initially pass through a stage where the Indians would mount offensive missiles as a deterrent against Chinese nuclear blackmail. A nuclear missile program would probably have to be pursued in a joint venture with either West Germany or Japan.

(2) Japan, also because of the Chinese nuclear threat, either reserves the option to go nuclear by refusing to sign the Nonproliferation Treaty, or signs and later opts out for substantially the same reasons as the Indians. Japan could join with India to develop a ballistic missile defense system, the Indians providing the nuclear warheads and the Japanese the missile vehicles.[6] The Japanese have a sophisticated electronics capability and have had valuable experience in designing and manufacturing high-altitude rockets. Their rocket technology could probably be supplemented with the electronic guidance system necessary to develop a ballistic missile with sufficient range to threaten most of the major Chinese cities from either Japan or India, and ultimately to develop an ABM system. The Indian civilian nuclear capability could easily be converted to military purposes to produce the nuclear warheads.

(3) When India and Japan acquire nuclear weapons for defense, it will be difficult to deter such countries as Israel and Sweden from going nuclear, again nominally in order to deploy an anti-ballistic missile system against potential nuclear threats. Pakistan and the UAR are quite likely to go nuclear shopping in Peking in order to counter threats from India and Israel, respectively.

(4) Increasing nuclear proliferation and the threat from Soviet missiles targeted on West Germany will certainly force the Bonn government to acquire nuclear weapons, previous commitments notwithstanding. After all, why should the Federal Republic be discriminated against when Great Britain, France, India and Japan have found it necessary to defend themselves against nuclear threats and blackmail?

Paradoxically, the USSR is making it easier for the West Germans to go nuclear because of its deployment of an ABM system. This action offers India and Japan a good excuse to acquire ABM systems and will most probably

5. In the UN debate in May 1968 concerning the Nonproliferation Treaty, India explicitly stated that it could not subscribe to it. (UN Document A/C.1/PV. 1567 [May 14, 1968], p. 82.) By 1966 India was in a position to produce about two atomic bombs a year; additional facilities were being constructed to provide an increased atomic bomb capability.

6. As of February 1969, Japan, India and West Germany had not yet signed the Nonproliferation Treaty.

encourage the West Germans to do the same. After all, would the Soviets deploy a system which was not effective against a Chinese nuclear attack? While the answer to this question might well be yes (since an ABM cannot be fully tested today, its effectiveness even under light nuclear attacks cannot be proved), how could the Indians and Japanese be persuaded, in light of the Soviet deployment, that ABM systems are not worthwhile? Ironically, then, the Soviets may be deploying an *ineffective* ABM system, yet indirectly encouraging the West Germans to go nuclear, and thus defeating one of the most important goals of Soviet foreign policy.

The failure of the two superpowers to deal effectively with the developing Chinese nuclear threat, coupled with the Soviet deployment of an anti-ballistic missile system probably chiefly deployed against the threat from the East, seems likely to result in the further proliferation of nuclear weapons, eventually to West Germany. Kaplan believes the resulting containment of the Soviet Union between a nuclear-armed West Germany and a nuclear-armed mainland China is in the best interests of the United States—even though small nuclear wars may occur. He sees no better practicable alternatives. However, for those of us who hope that he is wrong about practicable alternatives, a *limited* U.S.-USSR condominium aimed at containing the Chinese nuclear threat and preventing further nuclear proliferation (particularly to West Germany) must be explored as a feasible alternative to a nuclear confrontation between the two superpowers.

Such a condominium is unlikely to be abused to the detriment of the nonnuclear-weapon states, given the fundamental ideological and power dispute between the superpowers. It would work only when vital selfish interests coincide, as is the case with the superpowers' common desire to prevent further nuclear proliferation. Understandably, some have asked what gives the United States and the USSR the right to set up a condominium, no matter how limited. The clearest answer is that the American and Soviet peoples have the most to lose in a nuclear war stemming from nuclear proliferation.

IV

Aron's view of the two superpowers' mutuality of interests in preventing a total war in which they would be the major victims was supported by the circumstances surrounding the Arab-Israeli war of June 1967. Notwithstanding what appeared to be its firm support of Israel's right of passage through the Straits of Tiran and of Israel's claim that the Aqaba Gulf was an international waterway which could not legally be blockaded by the United Arab Republic, the United States temporized in fear of a possible confrontation with the Soviet Union. On the other side, the Arabs thought they had a firm promise on the part of the Soviets to provide effective support for them against "Israeli aggression." Yet, in the face of an overwhelming Israeli military victory, Moscow joined with Washington in calling for a cease-fire which effectively confirmed the new territorial status quo, with Israel occupying vast sections and strategic areas of former Arab territory. As soon as it appeared to Soviet leaders that they might be heading for a possible confrontation with the United States, they got on the hot line to Washington to assure President Johnson that they had no intention of meddling in the Middle East war if he would give similar assurances, which he quickly did. Thus, the United States and the USSR appeared ready to sacrifice what most observers thought were firm guarantees to their "client" states in order to avoid a possible confrontation with each other.

The Arab-Israeli war demonstrated that both superpowers would go to great lengths to avoid a face-to-face encounter, providing vital interests were not involved. On the other hand, the Cuban missile crisis of 1962 proved that dangerous confrontations are possible when vital interests *are* involved— in that case the vital interests of the United States. Similarly, it is surely against the essential interests of the Soviet Union to have a nuclear-armed "revanchist" West Germany on its western flank or to have a strong reunified Germany in Europe. If there is a potential crisis which could produce a U.S.-USSR confrontation and lead to nuclear war, it would be a West German decision to go nuclear or a West German decision to force reunification against the will of the Soviet Union. It was not surprising then that, despite continued U.S. bombing of the socialist state of North Viet Nam, the Soviets continued to negotiate with the U.S. government in an attempt to obtain a nonproliferation treaty that would hinder what the Soviets perceive to be West German nuclear ambitions. The Soviets fear that some West German leaders want to acquire nuclear arms one way or another, and there is fairly persuasive support for their fears:

> Former Chancellor Adenauer expressed dissatisfaction late in 1965 with the prospect that Germany's NATO allies, Great Britain and the United States, as part of a "select club" of nuclear powers, might negotiate at Geneva an agreement deleterious to German interests. This prospect led Adenauer to announce he could not commit himself "forever" to German nonacquisition of nuclear weapons. Similarly, Franz-Josef Strauss has warned that "a new Fuhrer-type" who "would promise and probably also acquire nuclear weapons" might emerge if Germany were subjected to continued nuclear discrimination within the Atlantic Alliance.

> . . . .
> The renunciation by the Federal Republic of the production of atomic weapons on its territory would not necessarily preclude German participation in an Atlantic or European nuclear force.[7]

A foreign policy adviser to Franz-Josef Strauss, one of the most influential

7. Diane A. Kressler, "Germany, NATO and Europe," ORBIS, Spring 1966, p. 234.

members of the current West German coalition government, made the following statement:

> The Federal Republic will only gain its national independence and full
> political sovereignty if it abandons the demand for the creation of a larger
> national . . . entity in favor of promoting the reunification of the German
> people *within the process of European integration.* . . . A West European
> confederation would have every right in law and ethics to state and to
> pursue its purpose, namely, to end the division of Europe and to create a
> European community extending from the Atlantic to the present borders
> of the Soviet Union.[8]

Some influential German politicians appear to believe that German reunification should be pursued from a position of strength provided by a
European nuclear force. Despite the evidence that the vast majority of the
West German people and their political leaders have no present desire to
acquire a national nuclear force,[9] a future West German government,
whether or not led by a "Fuhrer-type," may decide to go nuclear in the face
of fading hopes for a European nuclear force and continued frustration
caused by the division of the German people. Nuclear proliferation to states
such as India and Japan could readily provide the excuse for Bonn officials
to take this step.

V

What is the likelihood that India would change its policy and sign the
Nonproliferation Treaty and forego nuclear arms? Mason Willrich has summarized India's conditions:

> Would a guarantee against nuclear blackmail help India decide to forgo
> the chance of developing a nuclear capability? Since Communist China
> began setting off nuclear blasts, India has raised its price for making an
> unequivocal renunciation; it indicates that it wants considerably more
> than a simple guarantee. An undertaking "through the United Nations"
> to safeguard the security of nonnuclear nations is only part of its demand.
> Also included are an agreement by the nuclear powers not to transfer
> nuclear weapons to other powers, a comprehensive nuclear test ban and a
> freeze on further production of nuclear weapons and delivery systems,
> coupled with substantial reductions in existing inventories. Moreover,
> India had not excluded Communist China from the list of required sub-
> scribers to a nonproliferation agreement. It seems clear that a "paper"
> guarantee other than one by the United Nations, or conceivably one given

8. Klaus Bloemer, "Germany and a 'European Europe'," Orbis, Spring 1966, pp. 245–
246.

9. Karl Deutsch, *Arms Control and the Atlantic Alliance* (New York: John Wiley, 1967),
p. 52.

jointly by the United States and the Soviet Union, would be unacceptable as contrary to India's commitment to nonalignment.[10]

Any guarantee to defend India against Chinese nuclear blackmail and attack would probably be unsatisfactory to India since it would have to depend on joint U.S.-USSR action, which could be undermined by a credible Chinese nuclear threat to the superpowers or their allies, or even by a Moscow-Peking realignment after the passing of Mao from the Chinese scene. In any case, India was not satisfied by the Security Council Resolution of June 17, 1968, jointly sponsored by the United States, the Soviet Union and Britain, which recognized "that aggression with nuclear weapons or the threat of such aggression against a nonnuclear-weapon state would create a situation in which the Security Council, and above all its nuclear-weapon state permanent members, would have to act immediately in accordance with their obligations under the United Nations Charter."

Therefore, if India is to remain nonaligned, New Delhi must deal sooner or later with the Chinese nuclear threat, unless it is removed by one or both of the superpowers or by some unforeseen upheaval in China itself. The Chinese nuclear threat could be minimized by an effective anti-ballistic missile system supplied to India by either or both of the superpowers, or independently developed in cooperation with Japan or perhaps West Germany. However, since an ABM system, to be effective, most likely requires nuclear warheads, and since these and the system as a whole have not been proven and probably cannot be proven under the restrictions of the Test Ban Treaty, a more likely option is an independent Indian nuclear deterrent. Either option is incompatible with an Indian signature on the Nonproliferation Treaty.

Unless the Chinese nuclear threat is removed by a disarming strike, or is otherwise dealt with to the satisfaction of India, a voluntary Indian signature seems unlikely. Of course, India may bow to joint pressure by the superpowers, particularly from a U.S. threat to terminate grain shipments. But such an involuntary signature is unlikely to be meaningful after the first good Indian harvest, and the consequent long-term damage to U.S.-Indian relations should hopefully deter the U.S. government from using such tactics to obtain an Indian signature.

There is the slight possibility that a Chinese misstep in connection with the Vietnamese conflict may provide the Pentagon with sufficient reason to preempt the Chinese nuclear capability, but the Chinese are no doubt aware of this possibility and have been careful not to give the United States such an excuse. The past policy of both superpowers has obviously been not to launch a preemptive strike even under severe provocation, and it seems unlikely that this policy will change. Further, Soviet deployment of an ABM system, prob-

10. Mason Willrich, "Guarantees to Non-Nuclear Nations," *Foreign Affairs*, July 1966, pp. 689–690.

ably aimed chiefly at China, supports the belief that Moscow has decided to live with the Chinese nuclear threat.

Unless the Chinese threat can otherwise be dealt with to the satisfaction of India, or India gives up its nonaligned status and moves under the American nuclear umbrella (a very remote possibility), it is likely that New Delhi will not sign the Nonproliferation Treaty and will eventually go nuclear.[11] If West Germany follows the Indian example, as it well might, a U.S.-Soviet confrontation is almost inevitable and a nuclear exchange cannot be ruled out. The prospect of continuing enmity in the Middle East coupled with nuclear proliferation to Israel and the United Arab Republic (not to mention India and Pakistan), could set off small and disastrous nuclear wars. While all evidence seems to indicate that the superpowers will not become involved in minor nuclear wars, every effort should be made to avoid them, notwithstanding Professor Kaplan's suggestion that there are no better practicable world alternatives.

Even if India and other nonnuclear-weapon states do not sign the treaty, this does not mean that it would not be beneficial—at least to the Soviet Union. From the Soviet view, a treaty bearing American and West German signatures is desirable, since such a commitment might hinder the United States in coming to the aid of the West Germans if they decide to abrogate the treaty and acquire nuclear weapons, and are then confronted by determined Soviet opposition, including the possibility of a disarming strike. A U.S. decision to counter Soviet threats might not be popular with the American people, who believe treaties should be observed and who still have residual fears of German militarism. But if the alternative is to allow Europe to be dominated by the Soviet Union, as it probably would be, then a dangerous superpower confrontation would be likely. In this light, it is not surprising that many West German leaders resisted signing the treaty, while the Soviets promoted the treaty—despite Peking's accusations of U.S.-Soviet collaboration, the irritations caused by the war in Viet Nam, and the expressed opposition of India and other nuclear club candidates.

Several other complications connected with the treaty should be noted briefly. It has been stated on high authority that the treaty will prevent the spread of nuclear weapons because mainland China, although denouncing the treaty, is not able to offer its weapons for export.[12] China's position, in reality, is that the more socialist countries with nuclear weapons the better,[13] and Syria or the UAR might meet the ideological qualifications. A Chinese

11. A 1968 report by India's government-sponsored Institute of Defense Studies and Analyses made the case for India's ability to afford the bomb by noting that she has the tenth largest gross national product in the world, and argued that India should "develop its nuclear option." *New York Times*, September 8, 1968, p. 34. An Indian ambassador put it to the author more simply, saying: "If China can afford the bomb, so can India."
12. Former U.S. Ambassador to the UN, Arthur J. Goldberg, *New York Times*, October 5, 1968, p. 34.
13. Morton Halperin, *China and the Bomb* (New York: Praeger, 1965), p. 47.

transfer of even a few nuclear weapons to Syria or the UAR could instantly and radically change the balance of power in the Middle East, and a U.S. treaty obligation not to transfer nuclear weapons to Israel to redress the balance actually encourages such Chinese action. Further, should Washington attempt to pressure Bonn to sign the treaty, many top West German political leaders will be alienated, and the same is probably true with respect to the Japanese. Also, some U.S. allies, not likely to go nuclear in any case, will want additional guarantees of nuclear security, thus increasing U.S. obligations.

Thus, the treaty hardly seems worth ratifying if it does not deal effectively with the principal cause of proliferation, namely, mainland China. And the treaty may not survive its first five years if the superpowers continue to escalate the nuclear arms race. Atmospheric or space testing of anti-ballistic missiles by the superpowers would kill the Nonproliferation Treaty and the Test Ban Treaty.

VI

Is there an international arms control alternative which might deal with the Chinese nuclear threat to the satisfaction of India and thus lead to a voluntary Indian signature on the Nonproliferation Treaty? In September 1965, I proposed that the Partial Nuclear Test Ban Treaty, agreed to by the United States, the United Kingdom and the Soviet Union in Moscow in 1963 and later signed or acceded to by the vast majority of states (with the notable exceptions of mainland China and France), be made universally binding. This proposal was set forth in a privately circulated memorandum to U.S. and foreign arms control specialists, including Ambassador V. C. Trivedi, the Indian delegate to the Eighteen Nation Disarmament Committee. I later discussed it in detail with Ambassador Trivedi, and on November 24, 1965, during the disarmament debate in the First Committee of the UN General Assembly, the Ambassador, referring to Chinese atmospheric tests, stated that:

> The first priority is the task of making the Moscow Test Ban Treaty universally binding. We have requested and we have urged, we have deplored and we have condemned; but neither our displeasure nor our appeals have borne any fruit. The international community cannot, I submit, continue to remain helpless and impotent in the teeth of such defiance and will be obliged to examine what it can do to ensure that the health of humanity is not periodically attacked by the death-dealing debris of radioactive fallout.[14]

14. General Assembly, Official Records, Twentieth Session, First Committee (November 24, 1965), pp. 169–170.

On February 15, 1966, Ambassador Trivedi told the Eighteen Nation Disarmament Committee:

> As the Indian delegation said in New York during the last session of the General Assembly, the first priority in this field is thus to be accorded to the task of making the Moscow Test Ban Treaty universally binding. This is not a treaty which is subscribed to by a few powers with vested interests and their allies; it is a treaty which the non-aligned and nonnuclear nations have urged from the beginning and have signed in overwhelming number.[15]

Again, on June 30, 1966, he said:

> When we talk of nuclear weapons tests, therefore, it is essential that we talk comprehensively of all nuclear weapon tests, that we talk of tests in all environments and that we remember the terms of United Nations resolution 2032 (XX) of the last session, namely, "arrangements to ban effectively all nuclear weapon tests in all environments". . . .
>
> In working out those arrangements, the first priority should logically and coherently be given to the task of making the Moscow Test Ban Treaty universally applicable.[16]

However, in October 1966 China exploded on target a nuclear weapon carried by a guided missile; on December 28 China conducted another explosion; and on June 17, 1967 she successfully detonated her first hydrogen bomb. Apparently the disruptions of the Cultural Revolution had not slowed the Chinese nuclear weapon development program.

After the Chinese guided-missile test of October 1966, some observers thought India had lost interest in a universally-binding test ban and had turned her attention to acquiring an ABM system, presumably from one or both of the superpowers—an action that would have been incompatible with an Indian signature on the nonproliferation treaty. If this was New Delhi's intention, it may have been based on a belief that it was too late to freeze Chinese nuclear development, or on the U.S. failure to respond to India's suggestions for a universally-binding test ban. The United States presumably believed that it was not politically feasible to force compliance with arms control agreements, particularly on mainland China and possibly on France, the only states that have not signed or acceded to the 1963 Test Ban Treaty and continue to conduct atmospheric tests.

It is highly unlikely that France would risk a confrontation with the superpowers if they decided to support and enforce a universal test ban, but it must be assumed that China would challenge the ban. If that conclusion is correct, then we are face-to-face with a tragic dilemma: If the Chinese

15. Conference of the Eighteen-Nation Committee on Disarmament, Document ENDC/PV.240 (February 15, 1966), pp. 9–10.
16. *Ibid.*, Document ENDC/PV.269 (June 30, 1966), p. 12.

nuclear threat is not checked or removed, the likely result is a dangerous superpower confrontation over a West German decision to go nuclear, which could lead to general nuclear war. On the other hand, if an attempt is made by one or both of the superpowers to check or remove the Chinese nuclear threat, then a dangerous confrontation with China is likely—one that could lead to Chinese nuclear threats, and possibly nuclear and conventional attacks on neighboring areas, such as Japan, India, South Viet Nam, South Korea, Taiwan and Siberia. The danger of such attacks depends on whether the Chinese have an operational nuclear capability at the time of the confrontation; in view of Chinese nuclear progress, such a capability might be achieved in a few years. While China may even now have a small number of atomic bombs, she does not have long-range bombers. Chinese leaders seem to be counting on mating a hydrogen warhead to an intercontinental missile delivery system. But there is some danger that in a confrontation in the near future, China might be able to deliver atomic bombs by aircraft, triggering a nuclear response by one or both of the superpowers or even by a missile-supplied Taiwan.

Because of China's nuclear progress, Washington decided to deploy a "thin" anti-ballistic missile system originally estimated to cost about four to five billion dollars. A similar system will probably have to be supplied to Japan, Taiwan and other U.S. allies at comparable costs. It would be difficult to turn down an Indian request for a similar system. Thus, the initial cost of deploying extensive "thin" ABM systems would be in the order of tens of billions of dollars, and such "thin" systems would have to be periodically "thickened" to keep up with increasing Chinese nuclear capabilities. Eventually, "heavy" ABM systems would exist in many areas of the world at a cost reaching into the hundreds of billions of dollars. Under such circumstances we would have little money left for the global war on poverty.

But even a worldwide ABM deployment would not prevent the foreseeable superpower confrontation over West Germany. Indeed, it may even increase the chances for a confrontation since the United States and the Soviet Union may believe the danger of mass destruction has been lessened by their ABM systems. The resulting arms race would be catastrophic in cost and potential danger, for advances in ABM systems would force the superpowers simultaneously to deploy more advanced offensive missile systems. The effect would be to render arms control measures completely meaningless.

It is the author's view that—to paraphrase Gresham's Law that bad money drives out good money—arms race measures drive out arms control measures. In their syndicated column ("Inside Washington") of December 9, 1966, Robert S. Allen and Paul Scott reported:

> U.S. authorities are gravely concerned by an authoritative warning that Russia may use Red China's next atomic test as the pretext to withdraw from the [nuclear test ban] treaty. The State Department has been in-

formed that this alarming possibility was clearly intimated by Deputy Foreign Minister Vasily Kuznetsov during a long talk with UN Secretary-General U Thant last week.

Kuznetsov, the highest ranking Soviet official to visit the UN in two years, observed that abrogation of the 1963 test ban pact may become necessary because of the growing threat to Russia's security from Peking's unrestricted development of nuclear weapons.

If a way isn't found soon to curb China's atomic activity, Kuznetsov maintained, the Soviet would have no other recourse but to resume atmospheric testing.

Significantly, Goldberg was directed by President Johnson to find out whether the Russians or U Thant have recommendations on how the Chinese nuclear program could be curbed without triggering a war.

This report may still have validity for today. The probable reason for a Soviet abrogation of the 1963 Test Ban Treaty would be to test the ABM system it is deploying. This would require atmospheric nuclear explosions. It is unlikely that the Soviets would spend tens of billions of rubles on an untested ABM system. Thus, the 1963 treaty is likely to become a casualty of Chinese nuclear developments, in much the same way as the Nonproliferation Treaty will become a casualty if some of the leading candidates for the nuclear club go nuclear in response to the Chinese threat.

Given these dismal prospects, the political feasibility of a universally-binding test ban, designed to freeze or permit the destruction of the Chinese nuclear capability, seems worth serious consideration. Such a universal test ban should be comprehensive, that is, include all types of nuclear tests, especially underground tests. Otherwise, the Chinese could continue their development program by testing underground. But nuclear weapons specialists in both the United States and the USSR may be counting on underground shots to perfect and test warheads for anti-ballistic missiles, even though extensive underground tests already conducted by both superpowers may have solved most of the foreseeable problems. In any case, determined and probably successful opposition from the military and their supporters in both countries against a universal comprehensive test ban is reasonably predictable.

It should be remembered, however, that the primary reason for deploying a "thin" ABM system is to defend against a Chinese attack. If a universal comprehensive test ban is successful in halting or eliminating the Chinese nuclear development program, a "thin" ABM system would not be required, and the Soviets might readily agree to remove their probably unproven ABM system in order to avoid an expensive arms race escalation with the United States—particularly if there was little likelihood that the West Germans would go nuclear. One would certainly hope that underground testing could be safely suspended until the effectiveness of a universal ban was determined; this would not require a long period of time, because as the Chinese nuclear arsenal becomes more and more advanced, the likelihood that an attempt would be made to enforce a universal test ban decreases.

VII

The following feasibility analysis assumes that a universal test ban rider has been attached to the Nonproliferation Treaty with U.S. and Soviet approval to induce India and possibly other nuclear club candidates to sign. The rider would prohibit all nuclear tests by a party or a nonparty, and would obligate all parties, particularly the nuclear states that signed the treaty, to exert appropriate efforts, consistent with the UN Charter, to prevent any banned activities by a nonparty.[17]

(1) *France would probably not challenge the rider.* A major obstacle to U.S. acceptance of a universal test ban rider is the possibility that it could further strain U.S.-French relations. However, France would probably avoid a confrontation with the United States and would either await challenge of the rider by mainland China or would accept the Nonproliferation Treaty with the rider, for the following reasons: (a) France continues to rely on the U.S. nuclear umbrella, which could be removed as a consequence of a U.S.-French confrontation over effective arms control measures. (b) The French *force de frappe* is so far only a political device to help France achieve world power status; it could be politically neutralized by a Soviet anti-ballistic missile system deployed primarily against a Chinese nuclear threat. (c) Continued testing would probably not significantly improve the sophistication of the French nuclear arsenal or enhance French prestige and status as a world power. Thus, France does not really need to conduct a lengthy series of tests and may be ready to sign the treaty with a rider. (d) French tests could be prevented by blockading their Pacific test islands or by surrounding the islands with ships of many states. (e) The treaty and rider would require the establishment of an organization to administer and enforce the test ban, and France could be given equal world status with the United States and the USSR in the organization's peacekeeping activities.[18] (f) Washington could offer other concessions to France to induce her to sign a treaty with a rider.

17. Such a rider would be similar to Article X of the Antarctic Treaty which provides that "Each of the Contracting Parties undertakes to exert appropriate efforts, consistent with the Charter of the United Nations, to the end that no one engages in any activity contrary to the principles or purposes of the Present Treaty." Paragraph 1 of Article V specifically prohibits any nuclear explosions in Antarctica. December 1, 1959 [1961], 12 U.S.T. 794; T.I.A.S., No. 4780; 402 U.N.T.S. 71 (effective June 23, 1961).

18. According to a leading French nuclear strategist, "It is a pretty safe bet that at the latest when ['democratization' of the nuclear weapon] happens, the nuclear powers will close their ranks in face of this common danger and will be forced to conclude between themselves a control agreement which they will not hesitate to enforce, more or less politely, on the rest of the world." André Beaufre, *Deterrence and Strategy* (New York: Praeger, 1966), p. 99.

(2) *Mainland China would probably challenge the rider.* A universal test ban rider would probably be challenged by mainland China for the following reasons: (a) Continued testing is essential if China is to develop a credible nuclear weapons arsenal. (b) Testing produces important political gains, both domestically and abroad. (c) The rider would be a precedent for other universal arms control measures likely to be opposed by mainland China, such as a universal nonproliferation treaty. Therefore, a Chinese challenge of the rider and a confrontation with the international community is probable, although a prudent government in Peking could postpone such a confrontation for a long time and might even terminate its expensive nuclear weapons development program.

(3) *Probable U.S. position.* If the U.S. government believes that the rider is acceptable to the USSR and that France is willing to cooperate by signing or at least by postponing additional tests until the Chinese have challenged the rider, then it could be acceptable to Washington. If France postponed testing to await the Chinese challenge, and the international community then failed to compel Peking to abide by the rider, France could safely resume her testing program. In any case, French cooperation is probably attainable, particularly if the French are led to believe that the United States will accept the rider and attempt to enforce it against the French if challenged. In view of the long series of anti-American actions taken by France, particularly with respect to NATO, Viet Nam and the Middle East, it should not be difficult to convince her leaders that the United States would actively help to enforce such a test ban against her. If mainland China postponed testing or terminated its nuclear weapons development program, France would almost certainly follow suit.

(4) *Probable USSR position.* The Soviet Union would sign the Nonproliferation Treaty with a universal test ban rider for the following reasons: (a) An overriding Soviet goal is to prevent the Federal Republic of Germany from acquiring nuclear weapons, and this goal would be closer if the United States and West Germany signed the Nonproliferation Treaty. (b) If India and Japan refused to sign the treaty without a universal test ban rider, then the Federal Republic might not sign; even if Bonn did sign, it is likely that it would eventually opt out rather than suffer discrimination. (c) There is reason to believe that India would sign the Nonproliferation Treaty with a rider, and would opt out only if the rider were not successfully enforced against the Chinese. (d) Another Soviet goal is to prevent the proliferation of nuclear weapons generally; if India refused to sign the Nonproliferation Treaty, or signs and then opts out at a convenient time, that goal would be unattained. (e) The Soviets would like to diminish the severe worldwide criticism of their invasion of Czechoslovakia. (f) The Soviet Union seems to have many reasons to freeze or reduce the Chinese nuclear weapon capability. Since the Soviet inva-

sion of Czechoslovakia, a fellow socialist state, was probably motivated by a strong Soviet resolve to prevent a West German military threat, the Kremlin in all likelihood is prepared to take even more direct action, if necessary, against the more immediate and more dangerous threat from a nuclear-armed China. Maoist China will probably soon be formally ejected from the socialist camp, thus reducing the political cost of Soviet action against China.

(5) *Both the United States and the USSR might accept the rider.* In the face of New Delhi's insistence on the rider, the USSR might accept it in order to obtain India's signature and to freeze or reverse the Chinese nuclear development program. Washington might accept the rider for substantially the same reasons. Certainly, neither superpower would agree to the rider without acceptance by the other, but the possibility of mutual agreement could be secretly explored prior to their taking public positions on it.[19]

(6) *Probable consequences of a rider.* If the United States, Great Britain, the Soviet Union and a large number of other states agreed to adding the universal test ban rider to the Nonproliferation Treaty, the burden would fall on the United States (with the help of the Taiwan Chinese) and the USSR to enforce it against any mainland Chinese challenge, preferably before an international enforcement organization was established in order to avoid unnecessary delay and additional political obstacles. It seems unlikely that the superpowers would accept the rider unless both were prepared at least tacitly to support its enforcement. Each superpower would probably maneuver to place the enforcement burden on the other. However, it is likely that both superpowers would at least tacitly support Taiwan in enforcing the test ban against the mainland Chinese (for example, by enabling Taiwan to destroy Chinese nuclear facilities), or both would accept substantially equal responsibility for enforcing the test ban *in the name of the law* with the help of other volunteers, such as the Taiwan government.[20] While Peking's short-term reaction would obviously be one of great anger and bitterness, the Chinese are unlikely to respond with offensive thrusts and risk nuclear attack on their major cities. The long-

19. Paradoxically, the chances for meaningful arms control agreements have probably increased as a result of the Soviet invasion of Czechoslovakia and the election of Richard Nixon. The invasion symbolized Soviet interest in maintaining the global status quo and generated a Soviet need to lessen the adverse reaction by agreeing to further arms control agreements. President Nixon probably has a freer hand to negotiate than Johnson had because he need not fear attack from the right; and "hard-liners" in Washington and Moscow will probably be able to do business together on the basis of coinciding selfish interests (with respect to mainland China, for example), since to some extent they think alike.

20. Such an enforcement action might be carried out successfully through conventional bombing, but some ground action, similar to the British commando action against the Nazi heavy water plant in Norway during World War II, might also be required. If the mainland Chinese were to rebuild their nuclear weapon facilities, enforcement action would have to be repeated if they resumed nuclear tests.

term Chinese reaction might also be one of revanchism; yet it should be kept in mind that, although the United States dropped atomic bombs on Japanese cities and fire-bombed German cities, within a few years the Japanese and Germans were among America's best allies.

(7) *Universal observance or enforcement of the rider could lead to world peace through law.* If the rider were universally observed or successfully enforced, *nuclear* peace could probably be maintained through law as long as the superpowers cooperated; in view of the alternatives, this might be for a long time. In any event, the danger of a nuclear war would be minimized and a giant step taken toward the goal of attaining peace through law.

Whether or not there is any logic in this feasibility analysis, the ineluctable fact remains that neither superpower is likely to support arms control measures that might require enforcement against noncomplying states—even though the long-term alternative may be a nuclear war over West German acquisition of nuclear weapons. Only an extremely dangerous crisis which thoroughly alarms the world, such as an accidental nuclear missile exchange, might alter the nuclear powers' outlook. Therefore, the Chinese quite likely will be able to create an operational nuclear missile arsenal which will eventually pose a credible threat to the United States, the USSR and other countries resisting Chinese political objectives. A Chinese announcement of June 1967 looked forward to the day when the superpowers' nuclear blackmail tactics would no longer be effective:

The success of China's hydrogen bomb test has further broken the nuclear monopoly of United States imperialism and Soviet revisionism and dealt a telling blow at their policy of nuclear blackmail.

It is a very great encouragement and support to the Vietnamese people in their heroic war against United States aggression and for national salvation, to the Arab people in their resistance to aggression by the United States and British imperialists and their tool, Israel, and to the revolutionary people of the whole world.[21]

A major purpose of China's nuclear arsenal is to neutralize the nuclear advantage of the superpowers, leaving her mass army free to accomplish its goals. These goals are, at the very least, the ejection of U.S. influence from the Western Pacific, Southeast Asia and Japan, the acquisition of Taiwan, and the recovery of former Chinese territory in Siberia. Additionally, China wants to dictate formation of pro-Peking governments in New Delhi and the capitals of Southeast Asia, and to gain recognition as a superpower, with the expectation that her views would have to be taken into account in connection with the settlement of all international disputes and the allocation of resources. Last, but not least, Peking wants to be free to lend active sup-

21. *New York Times,* June 18, 1967, p. 3.

port to revolutionary peoples throughout the world so they may be liberated from "Western imperialism" and "Soviet revisionism."

The envisioned failure to deal with the Chinese nuclear threat is likely to produce a threat of nuclear conflict over a nuclear-arming West Germany, small nuclear wars between countries such as India and Pakistan and Israel and the UAR, and the expenditure of many tens, even hundreds, of billions of dollars in ABM systems at the expense of the world war against poverty. Additionally, both the United States and the USSR can expect to be involved in escalating crises caused by what China believes to be legitimate complaints—Taiwan, U.S. military bases, and former Chinese territories in Siberia. Considering the commitment of present Chinese rulers to violence, revolution and turmoil, Peking's acquisition of a sizeable nuclear arsenal before the end of the 1970's threatens to create instability over large portions of the globe—and possibly nuclear conflict. It is not hard to envision the Chinese winning "nuclear chicken" games and thus acquiring Taiwan and bordering Soviet territories; they may also influence establishment of pro-Peking governments in New Delhi and Tokyo, Seoul and Saigon. The Chinese would probably be emboldened to support "wars of national liberation" in Venezuela and even Mexico, and the developing countries of Africa and Asia. It is not comforting to envision Vietnamese-type "liberation wars" in our own backyard. Many undeveloped countries have masses of discontents, potential "revolutionary patriots" whom the Chinese might actively support by supplying arms and by neutralizing "imperialist nuclear blackmail." Also, China, mischievously or in an effort to replace Soviet influence, might give nuclear weapons to countries such as the UAR, thus instantly creating a dangerous situation likely to involve the two superpowers. China could no doubt find many ways to trigger a nuclear war between the superpowers.

It has been argued that her increasing affluence might diminish China's present revolutionary fervor—along the lines of the Soviet experience—so that these dismal predictions might not come true. But there is a fundamental difference between China and the Soviet Union. The Soviet Union is reasonably satisfied with the territorial status quo, at least to the extent that her leaders are unwilling to take grave risks. China is not willing to settle for the status quo.[22]

The prospects for the Soviet Union are not much better. If, as predicted by Kaplan, the Soviets cannot prevent China and West Germany from gaining access to nuclear arms, they may not be able to stop these two states from reacquiring their former territories in Siberia and Central Europe. A some-

22. The Soviet invasion of Czechoslovakia, which upset nearly all communist parties in the West and many nonaligned states, is evidence of the Soviet desire to maintain the status quo of the "Socialist Commonwealth" at the expense of extending its control to other states. It will be more difficult now, for example, to persuade the people of France and Italy to elect a communist party to power and thus put their country into the communist bloc.

what truncated Russia surrounded by unfriendly nuclear-armed powers might be forced into isolationism and a "fortress" mentality.

VIII

Arms control measures cannot be effective if they are binding only on those states which assent to be bound. This is particularly true with respect to nuclear arms. Chinese nuclear arms progress apparently has forced the Soviet Union to deploy an anti-ballistic missile system, and it is unlikely that the Soviets will expend the vast sums needed to complete the system until they are sure of its effectiveness. Since an anti-ballistic missile will almost certainly use a nuclear warhead, the testing of the system will require atmospheric and space test explosions which will force the Soviet Union to withdraw from the 1963 Nuclear Test Ban Treaty. Further, Chinese nuclear arms progress is likely to prevent the attainment of an *effective* nuclear nonproliferation treaty.

Arms control measures can prevent arms race measures only when they are universally binding, i.e., by virtue of being accepted by assenting states and imposed on nonassenting states. A universally-binding nuclear test ban in all environments which had enforcement credibility could be effective in preventing further Chinese work on nuclear weapons if Peking observed the ban or if it were forced on the Chinese by a threat to destroy, or the actual destruction of, their capability.[23] The failure to freeze or terminate the Chinese nuclear program is likely to lead to a superpower confrontation with its danger of a general nuclear war, to small nuclear wars, and to the expenditure of vast sums of money on ABM systems of questionable effectiveness.

But is there a legal basis for binding nonassenting states against their will? In my view, *generally-recognized* international peacekeeping laws can be relied on to bind nonassenting states because they are recognized by a large majority of the states. These laws are limited to international peacekeeping purposes, express an intent to bind nonassenting states, and are adhered to by a large majority of the states, specifically including the United States and the Soviet Union. They can be relied on to bind nonassenting states because the international community says they are universally binding.

The UN Charter is the principal example of a generally-recognized international peacekeeping law. Article 2(6) of the Charter makes its peacekeeping provisions applicable to nonparties against their will. The UN action in repelling the North Korean invasion of South Korea is just one example of UN actions against nonparties deemed to have violated the Charter.[24]

23. A universally-binding *partial* nuclear test ban (forbidding tests in the atmosphere, in outer space and under water, as the present ban does) might be a more feasible first step. It would also be a precedent for a universally-binding test ban in all environments, as well as other universal arms control measures such as a universal nuclear nonproliferation treaty, and could bring a halt to the Chinese nuclear arms development program.

24. For an excellent survey of the precedents for binding nonassenting states, see Louis B. Sohn, "Enforcement of Disarmament Controls with Respect to States which have

184 : *The Proliferation of Nuclear Weapons*

If enforcement measures are to be carried out by volunteering states, then generally-recognized international peacekeeping laws will have enforcement credibility to the extent that a nonassenting state, desiring to conduct the activity banned by the law, believes that at least one volunteering state with adequate capability would punish it. For example, if the Nationalist Chinese had an enforcement capability, such as a fleet of long-range bombers, the mainland Chinese might believe that Taiwan would volunteer to punish them for conducting the banned activity.

An organization established to administer these peacekeeping laws could be controlled by a small number of responsible powers and develop into an "upper house" to the United Nations, particularly if the government of mainland China is admitted to the world body and takes the Chinese seat in the Security Council.

It is the task of the political leaders of the United States, the Soviet Union, the United Kingdom, and other states to determine whether, as a practical matter, universal nuclear arms control laws can be enforced against nonassenting states. If they conclude that it is feasible to enforce compliance of these laws, a significant step toward the goal of maintaining nuclear peace through law may be taken. If enforced compliance is not feasible, arms control agreements such as the Nuclear Test Ban and the Nonproliferation Treaty will inevitably be "driven out" by arms race measures such as a Chinese missile deployment, ABM defenses and ABM-penetrating offensive missile systems.[25] To put it plainly, if the Chinese are able to deploy an effective nuclear missile system, there will be no effective nuclear arms control measures.

---

not Ratified a Disarmament or Arms Control Treaty," in Donald G. Brennan and Robert Maxwell, editors, *Arms Control and Disarmament* (Oxford: Pergamon Press, 1968), p. 99. It should be noted that most states, including the United States and the USSR, also agree that both customary law and peace treaties settling wars can bind states against their will. Based on my discussions with some Soviet international law experts in August 1968, a universal test ban, if politically acceptable, would present no legal problems to the Soviets with respect to binding nonassenting states. The U.S. position on this legal issue is not publicly known.

25. This view is supported by the result of the London Naval Agreement, signed on March 25, 1936 by Great Britain, France and the United States, which provided for restrictions on the size of certain types of naval vessels and the caliber of guns of the signatories. The treaty also had an "escalator clause" allowing signatories to exceed the restrictions in the event of competitive building by another state. Within two years, the United States and Great Britain announced that they were resuming competitive building due to the accelerated naval construction of Japan, a nonsignatory. Historical Evaluation and Research Organization, *Responses to Violations of Arms Control and Disarmament Agreements* (Washington: HERO, April 1964), p. 152, and in the Annex, Volume II, p. A-161. This report was prepared for the Arms Control and Disarmament Agency under ACDA Contract GC-17, March 29, 1963, and is on file in the ACDA library in Washington.

10.

The Nuclear Non-Proliferation Treaty: Its Rationale, Prospects and Possible Impact on International Law

MORTON A. KAPLAN

I.   Introduction

THE TREATY on the Non-Proliferation of Nuclear Weapons, proposed at the twenty-second session of the United Nations General Assembly, was signed by sixty two nations on July 1, 1968. The treaty essentially prohibits each nuclear-weapon State, defined as one which had manufactured and exploded a nuclear weapon or other nuclear explosive device prior to January 1, 1967, from transferring any nuclear weapons or nuclear devices to any other nation, and it commits any non-nuclear weapon State to a policy of not accepting or producing these weapons or devices. Additional provisions seek to establish safeguards through international inspection of the non-nuclear weapon States by the International Atomic Energy Agency based on agreements to be negotiated with that Agency. The treaty is clearly intended not to affect the rights of the parties to the treaty to continue research and development in the production and use of nuclear energy for peaceful purposes, and it provides that the benefit of peaceful applications of nuclear energy which one party derives are to be made available to the other parties. The Preamble declares that it is the intention of the parties to the treaty to achieve at the earliest possible date the cessation of the nuclear arms race and eventual nuclear disarmament. Yet the only provision in the treaty for accomplishing such a goal is the agreement of the parties to pursue negotiations in the future, and only the non-nuclear weapon States are subject to the safeguards in the treaty.

Excerpted and Reprinted by permission from the *Journal of Public Law*, Vol. 18, No. 1, 1969, pp. 1–20 and from *ORBIS*, Winter 1969, pp. 1042–1057.

While history will be the ultimate judge of the success or failure of the treaty, it is both possible and justifiable at this time to evaluate the effectiveness of this attempt at international cooperation in reaching certain international goals.

II. Rationale

Interest in a non-proliferation treaty represents part of a larger interest in the subject of nuclear arms control. The history of arms control and disarmament conferences extends back for more than two thousand years and the control and banning of certain weapons has received much international attention in the last one hundred years, but the development of nuclear weapons has greatly intensified the concern with this problem. The reasons for this increased concern are fairly obvious. In the first place, nuclear weapons can be used to destroy modern civilization with a speed and efficiency that was unknown to any previous weapons system. Although Douhet's theory of air warfare[1] presented a similar view on the advent of military aircraft which was criticized by his contemporaries, the realization now by governments and heads of state that weapons systems exist which actually can be used to end life on earth (but not as easily as many believe) has had an enormous impact upon state behavior. This growing concern with the problem of nuclear weapons properly manifests an urgency that earlier weapons systems did not justify.

Another reason for concern lies in some conceptions concerning the nuclear arms race. Although it has been asserted incorrectly that arms races produce wars—a conclusion for which there is little empirical or theoretical justification—the nuclear arms race is still believed to increase the dangers of proliferation and of destruction.[2] Actually, this conception of the problem is much oversimplified. The early stages of the nuclear arms race were highly dangerous, but also contained some stabilizing elements. The early nuclear weapons carriers—airplanes and liquid-fuelled missiles—were slow reacting and highly vulnerable to surprise attack. A nuclear accident, an unauthorized attack, or misinterpreted radar indications under such conditions of vulnerability increased the probability of a preemptive strike during times of crisis to a greater level than prudent statesmen found acceptable. While the danger of such preemptive strike was clearly a reality, this does not necessarily imply

1. *See* G. DOUHET, THE COMMAND OF THE AIR (D. Ferrari transl. 1942). General Giulio Douhet was an Italian strategist who argued that military aircraft were weapons designed for offensive action of incomparable destructive potential, against which no effective defense could be foreseen. Any nation which attained command of the air could then proceed to shatter the enemy's military potential and will to wage war by direct aerial bombing.

2. For a good discussion of the nuclear arms race and its accompanying dangers, see Kahn, *The Arms Race and Some of its Hazards*, in 1 THE STRATEGY OF WORLD ORDER 17 (R. Falk & S. Mendlovitz eds. 1966). *See also* Boulding, *The Prevention of World War III*, 38 VA. Q. REV. 1 (1962).

that the probability of its occurrence was very high. On two occasions, for example, radar "blips" were recorded which, if indicative of enemy action, would have led to the initial deployment of Strategic Air Command (SAC) forces to the positive control point to await presidential authorization for a strike under the "failsafe" procedure. In both instances, however, the forces were not activated. SAC leaders had decided that it was extremely unlikely that the radar indications represented a possible Russian attack since there was no present international crisis. Thus, the early dangers of a preemptive strike were apparently stabilized by the hesitancy of nuclear powers to respond prematurely under such conditions in the absence of a full-blown international crisis. Nevertheless, the dangers still existed and the possibility that misinterpreted blips might occur during an actual crisis could not be ruled out.

A second stabilizing factor in the early stages lay in the peculiar mathematics of a missile arms race itself. Depending upon the specific characteristics of the weapons systems, a larger number of missiles possessed by a defending nation requires a greater proportional superiority on the part of an enemy in order to launch an effective first strike. This consequently makes it more difficult for the enemy to acquire the necessary striking superiority, makes it more difficult to maintain secrecy in the attempt to achieve superiority, and makes it easier to respond successfully to the effort to reach such superiority. Thus, although increases in the nuclear arsenals of the major nations increased the potential amount of damage that each side could do to the other, the resultant danger was at the same time stabilized by these very increases, and the likelihood became less that the large-scale use of nuclear forces would be made. As systems were improved both quantitatively and qualitatively with the introduction of solid-fuelled, quick-reacting missiles with hardened bases, it became even more likely that a prudent and responsible national leadership could maintain a militarily non-responsive posture, even in times of crisis.

It is, however, no longer true that the qualitative arms race is mutually stabilizing. Multiple Independent Re-entry Vehicles (MIRV), Fractional Orbital Ballistic Systems (FOBS), orbital weapons, and the early stages of the deployment of Ballistic Missile Defenses (BMD) are reintroducing some of the dangers of the early stages of the arms race, such as the possibility of preemptive strikes, without any of the corresponding stabilizing elements. While the Nuclear Non-Proliferation Treaty does not meet this new problem directly, it is intended, at least in part, to prevent an unstable arms race from multiplying in intensity as even increasing numbers of nations attempt to acquire nuclear forces.[3]

The nuclear systems now being developed by nations other than the United States and the Soviet Union have many of the hazardous characteris-

---

3. G.A., Res. 2373, 22 U.N. GAOR____, U.N. Doc. A/7016/Add. 1 (1968).

tics of the early qualitative stages of the arms race. The French *force de frappe* is an example of such a force. This system is based on the *Mirage*, a very effective plane which, because it does possess the capability of reaching Moscow or Leningrad, except insofar as the Russians improve their low altitude radar control from overhead sources, is sufficiently provocative to raise a serious possibility of a Russian preemptive strike during an intense crisis. Indeed, the force is sufficiently provocative to act as a self-deterrent for the French. They probably would not actually dare to use it in a first strike, for, although they might destroy Moscow or Leningrad, all of France could be obliterated in retaliation. On the other hand, possession of the force during an escalating crisis, with the possibility of its irrational use, might tempt the Russians to strike first in order to protect their own national security. Therefore, possession of the force would seem to weaken, rather than strengthen, the resolve of a prudent French leadership during a time of crisis.

If this type of force is so provocative and inherently dangerous, why should France or any other country wish to have such a system? One possible explanation is national pride and grandeur. A more sound reason, however, lies in the lack of the credibility of the United States' nuclear commitment to NATO. The United States has never given an ironclad nuclear "guarantee" to Western Europe.[4] America's persistent and wise declaratory war policy which delays the application of an immediate nuclear response to an attack on Western Europe has raised serious, even if not entirely justified, questions in the minds of many Europeans concerning the credibility of the American nuclear guarantee. If Russia were to strike without provocation, the United States in all likelihood would respond nuclearly. A crisis that developed over a period of time, however, and in which the equities were not clear would provide the United States with alternatives to the use of nuclear weapons. Under these circumstances, the United States would have an opportunity to consider the potential damage to American cities from a nuclear exchange and would probably pressure European nations to make concessions which they would view as inconsistent with their interests and security. If the Europeans did not yield to these pressures, they would be left defenseless. Although the American nuclear guarantee would not entirely lack credibility in this situation, that credibility would be limited and political costs would be involved. From this standpoint, then, it is not difficult to see why European countries would consider possession of an independent nuclear system to be an essential part of their national defense and security.

Moreover, the Russian invasion of Czechoslovakia has taught those Europeans who did not previously understand this issue that one important function of nuclear weapons is to deter conventional attack and that conven-

4. *See generally* Agreement Between the Parties to the North Atlantic Treaty for Cooperation Regarding Atomic Information, June 18, 1964, art. I, [1965] 1 U.S.T. 109, 111, T.I.A.S. No. 5768; North Atlantic Treaty with Other Governments, April 4, 1949, art. 5, 63 Stat. 2241, 2244 (1949), T.I.A.S. No. 1964.

tional rather than nuclear attack might well be the danger they face. Many Europeans are asking themselves whether the Soviet Union would have invaded Czechoslovakia if that nation had had in its possession even the most primitive nuclear weapons and delivery systems. In order to allay the fears of non-nuclear weapon States, the United States, Great Britain and the Soviet Union offered identical security guarantees pertaining to attacks on signatory nations.[5] The guarantees are, of course, not self-enforcing and, apart from the reliability or unreliability of the pledgers, will no doubt prove subject to interpretation depending upon the conditions of particular cases. In any event, however, Czechoslovakia demonstrated that it is not merely nuclear strikes but also conventional attacks that must be deterred.

These thoughts may appear inconsistent with the arguments concerning the self-deterrent quality of unstable nuclear forces. This will not be the case, however, if a distinction is made between a crisis that escalates out of control and a crisis in which a deliberate decision is made to escalate its intensity. In the first case, the possessor of the unstable nuclear system will likely suffer a failure of resolve. In the second case, the aggressor State will more likely decide that the risks of escalation are not worth the potential gains.

One might ask whether nuclear proliferation might not have advantages that compensate for its defects. If the proliferation of nuclear systems reduces the likelihood of deliberate aggression across national borders, then perhaps the increased risk of inadvertent, unauthorized or accidental war might be sufficiently compensated for. Yet this is not simply the case. The sheer proliferation of the number of unstable nuclear systems intuitively seems to increase the risks beyond reasonable limits. There is, however, an additional and even more basic reason for mistrusting the extensive spread of nuclear weapons. Both the United States and the Soviet Union, as well as China, Japan, West Germany, France, Great Britain and other developed nations, have decision-making systems that ensure bureaucratic delays, the rational and systematic calculation of alternatives, and the adjustment of military means to responsible, even if conflicting, national goals. In the hands of countries with governmental decision-making processes such as this, the presence of nuclear weapons does not immediately raise the threat of irrational deployment. But the possession of nuclear systems by nations that are subject to intense and recurrent regime crises, that regard themselves as being in such bad situations that they would have nothing to lose by becoming involved in a nuclear conflict, or that have romantic notions of the world and their role in it, is less than reassuring. The leader of such a country might

5. S.C. Res. 255, 23 U.N. SCOR, 1433d meeting____, U.N. Doc. S/8631 (1968). The text of the resolution adopted by the Security Council may also be found in 7 INT'L LEGAL MATERIALS 895 (1968). While not included as a part of the treaty, these guarantees were designed to win adherence to its provisions by assuring non-nuclear States that, although they would not be able to acquire their own systems, they could rely on the response of the guarantors, through the United Nations, in the event of attack.

not hesitate to use nuclear-weaponry in a crisis, and while he would probably not be able to destroy the world, he could still inflict considerable material, moral and political damage. The idea of the proliferation of nuclear systems to nations of that kind is distinctly frightening. One does not have to believe that these nations would necessarily use nuclear weapons in an irresponsible way, but the probability that they might is still too large for comfort and causes concern about the unchecked spread of nuclear arms.

It is not difficult to see where further pressures for nuclear proliferation will come from in the future. Although many Japanese are still bitterly opposed to a nuclear system in their country, they must sooner or later end their nuclear reliance upon the United States. As the second leading industrial power in the non-Communist world, Japan must eventually acquire a military and political authority commensurate with her economic power. The Japanese are known for their one hundred eighty degree turns in policy, so it is quite possible that their views on the nuclear issue will change. They must also cope with the Chinese problem and someday their feelings of guilt toward China may turn to resentment. India also faces a problem of potential aggression from China and the pressures within India for the development of nuclear forces are constantly increasing. West Germany is presently fearful of acquiring nuclear weapons, but the invasion of Czechoslovakia by the Soviet Union has made it clear to many Germans that they may soon face a greater danger if they do not acquire a nuclear system. These and other nations can be expected to press for nuclear arms with any increase in cold war tensions and conflicts.

III.   Prospects

Prior to promulgation of the treaty, there had been a number of occasions when nuclear proliferation might have been halted, or at least slowed, by the use of military measures.[6] Since such steps would have been diplomatically and politically infeasible,[7] the adoption of a multilateral instrument designed to impede the expansion of nuclear arms appears to be the only effective means of reaching this desired result. The question must remain, however, whether or not such a treaty will indeed be effective. The Nuclear Non-Proliferation Treaty, assuming it is signed by the requisite number of States, will depend for its effectiveness upon several factors. To begin with, the

6. In 1946, for example, the United States could have delivered an ultimatum to the Soviet Union that a single testing of a nuclear weapon would lead to a strike against Soviet nuclear facilities. In the 1960's, similar measures might have been taken by the Soviet Union against China or by the United States against France.

7. The attempted establishment of an American world dictatorship, even though rigidly limited to restricting the possession of nuclear weapons, would have been misunderstood by the American public and bitterly resented by Russia and the West European nations. The almost certain attempts to evade this dictatorship could only have resulted in the United States taking increasingly more onerous and unpopular measures to preserve its role as a nuclear policeman.

Chinese threat to Japan and India must be minimized before these nations can be expected to acquiesce in the provisions of the treaty. It is difficult to see how this might be done short of removing China's nuclear capability. At this point in time, such a step seems extremely difficult, if not impossible. Like Japan and India, other nations on the threshold of nuclear arm acquisition may also resist the treaty on the grounds that it constitutes a danger to their national integrity and security. Without the acceptance of the treaty by those countries with the capability of developing nuclear weapons, it "will become little more than a pious declaration of intention."[8] Furthermore, the success of the treaty will depend upon the Soviet Union, the United States and France maintaining constant pressure upon West Germany not to acquire nuclear weapons. Neither the removal of China's force nor the prevention of West Germany's acquisition of nuclear arms seems likely. The Chinese system cannot be neutralized and West Germany cannot be impeded in its effort to obtain nuclear forces in the absence of an United States— Soviet Union condominium that extends at least to the nuclear weapons issue. It is quite difficult to believe that the coincidence of American and Soviet interests is sufficiently great so as to enable them to maintain the requisite joint pressure over a significant period of time. The Russian invasion of Czechoslovakia is only one illustration of how the conflict of interests between the United States and the Soviet Union could interfere with the efforts of the two countries to act jointly in a manner to prevent proliferation. In fact, the two nations have been unwilling to coordinate, let alone to collaborate, on other measures against China that would be necessary in order to maintain the effectiveness of the treaty. In addition, such a condominium would raise serious moral issues. It would impose upon the other nations of the world a Soviet-American leadership that would not be justified by diplomatic skill, culture, economic power or any other reasonable criterion. Moreover, one might always ask the question that if the United States and the Soviet Union can be trusted to control nuclear weapons, why cannot Japan, India, Italy or any other country be trusted? If the success of the Nuclear Non-Proliferation Treaty must depend upon extended Soviet-American cooperation, then its effectiveness will be severely limited.

I am grateful to Dr. Yuter (see his article in this issue of ORBIS) for making intellectually clear one of the most significant conditions necessary for success of a nuclear nondiffusion treaty: a universal nuclear test ban. Politicians or statesmen obfuscate the conditions requisite for a successful treaty in an effort to secure support for the NPT by hiding its weaknesses; they dissemble its blemishes, its dangers and its immoralities. Three major conditions requisite for the treaty's success are a universal test ban, as Yuter notes; a condominium between the United States and the Soviet Union; and a guarantee by the nuclear powers to nonnuclear powers against aggression by countries possessing nuclear weapons.

8. 114 CONG. REC. S. 11785 (daily ed. Oct. 1, 1968).

It is important not to ignore one of the purposes of the universal test ban that Yuter advocates. Although a universally binding test ban would operate to prevent any nation from testing nuclear weapons, one of the main purposes of such a ban is to legitimate an attack on China's nuclear facilities if China continues to develop her nuclear arsenal. Peking is well aware that the Geneva negotiations on nuclear diffusion, although addressed to the general problem of the spread of nuclear weapons, were also directed against China and West Germany. The failure to include an explicit universal test ban in the treaty—largely the result of a failure of nerve on the part of the United States and the Soviet Union—or alternatively to provide India with ironclad guarantees against aggression, accounts for stubborn Indian resistance to the NPT. Unless the Indians can be induced to sign, the prospect that the treaty will hold for the twenty-five years of its life is slight.

Of course, unexpected changes in world politics leading to the peaceful settlement of disputes, the reduction of issues among nations, and enormous increases in international cooperation and international governance might confound this prediction. Yet, it is doubtful whether even supporters of the treaty, at least those in official positions, would expect such developments.

IV.   The China Problem

Consider the enormity of a decision to destroy China's nuclear facilities. The United States refrained from carrying out a similar attack on the Soviet Union at a time when to do so would have maintained the American nuclear monopoly. That monopoly cannot be restored by destroying the fledgling Chinese arsenal. If many regard the war in Viet Nam as a racist war, a conclusion from which this writer vigorously dissents, an attack on Chinese nuclear facilities would seem to most of the world to be unmistakably of that character. Such an attack, even if it succeeded, and this cannot be assumed, would not end China's nuclear ambitions. The resentment accumulated within that sleeping giant would likely produce both political and military disturbances and eventually a resumption of nuclear production. The shock generated by the initial attack would more likely deter those who undertook it than those who suffered from it. Moreover, the message conveyed to other nations in Asia, regardless of whether they thought they wished to see the Chinese facilities destroyed, would be that the United States or the Soviet Union can intervene in Asia affairs without provocation—hardly a reassuring message or one the United States should desire to convey. Even those who believe, mistakenly in my opinion, that we are morally capable of carrying out such an attack on China would not be able easily to contemplate a similar attack on a nuclear-armed India or a nuclear-armed Japan—an outcome an attack on China would do more to promote than forestall.

Furthermore, unless the attack were carried out by the United States and the Soviet Union in concert, which would not be easy to manage considering how difficult it is to secure cooperation on much less momentous issues, the single nation mounting it might drive China into the arms of the other. Only the most reckless of American administrators would entertain the prospect of thus reunifying the communist world, for, even though the Soviet Union might wish and might secretly encourage a U.S. attack on Chinese facilities, Moscow would denounce us for it with the utmost vehemence. We would be foolish to do otherwise were circumstances reversed.

One can discount the possibility that such an attack could be carried out by an international administration. The attempt to bring an international body to such a decision, by means of sophisticated arguments concerning the binding quality of a treaty on a nonsignator nation, would stir up so much horror in contemplating the act that the consensus necessary for carrying it out could not be achieved. A decision to attack China's nuclear facilities requires secrecy, stealth and guile. The nature of this decision-making process leading to an attack would help to discredit it. In any event, such secrecy is not genuinely possible for an international administration under contemporary circumstances.

Since it is most improbable at this late stage of China's program that purely conventional military operations would suffice, the attack on the Chinese facilities would have to be nuclear. It would thus constitute the first use of nuclear weapons since the Second World War. The resort to nuclear weapons toward the end of that war did not sociologically or psychologically set a precedent for the post-World War II period. To employ them now in the absence of a cause for war, other than nuclear testing by China, would demonstrate the shocking uses to which nuclear weapons could be put in the world; it would instruct nations in their utility in a way not favored by the present leaders of the United States or by any intelligent leaders who might later take office. It would at the same time legitimize the use of nuclear weapons. The impact on the structure of world politics would be one I would contemplate with the greatest concern.

V. A Russo-American Condominium

That an effective nuclear nonproliferation treaty would require a Soviet-American condominium appears beyond question. The process of securing passage of the treaty in the General Assembly of the United Nations demonstrated the power of such a condominium, as threats, promises and pressures were employed against reluctant nations in a way not seen since Stalin's ham-handed rule of the Soviet satellites—except for Moscow's attempt to halt the liberalization process in Czechoslovakia in 1968. Although U.S. pressures and threats were less harsh and more veiled behind superficial politeness than those used by the Soviet Union, the episode is a shameful chapter in recent history, falling far short of the quality of behavior we have a right to expect between supposedly friendly and nearly equal nations.

But whence comes the warrant for such a condominium? Where is the moral authority for it? What right does either the United States or the Soviet Union have to such a role, apart from the present possession of massive nuclear systems, that would not pertain equally to Great Britain; France, West Germany, India, Japan or Communist China? At the very time when the Soviet and American blocs are breaking up and when the superiority of these two nations over the other nations of the world is diminishing, what reason is there to believe that their military ascendancy will be accepted for the next twenty-five years? What warrant is there for believing that this condominium will not be resisted, revolted against, subverted and challenged in ways that might prove even more destabilizing than the diffusion of nuclear weapons? Are we prepared to maintain this condominium by such brutalities that we would interfere with the independent political life going on in the various nations of the world? Are we ready and willing to take on the enormous responsibilities entailed? And are such responsibilities really in our own interest?

What is there in the nature of Soviet-American relations in the past twenty-five years, in the social and political systems of the two nations, in their goals in the world, in the means they use to achieve these goals, that leads us to believe they could maintain this harmony of interest in face of the unexpected problems virtually sure to arise in the near and intermediate future? Upon what basis can we believe that the national regimes in the two countries will find such harmony consistent not merely with external interests but with their interests in winning elections or maintaining regime continuity? What reason is there to believe that maintenance of such a condominium will so overshadow all other values, beliefs and commitments that the governments of both nations will maintain it with single-minded purpose? And, even were all these other doubts to be overcome, what reason is there to believe that the two regimes could overcome problems of bargaining among themselves in such a way that agreement upon spoils and responsibilities would continue to be reached over so long a time?

The condominium, in effect, did not even survive the process of negotiating the treaty, for the terms of the treaty failed to meet the minimum requirements for effective implementation over the intermediate period. Thus, faith that such a condominium could be established and maintained for a quarter-century constitutes a touching reaffirmation of the simplistic nature of politics, to wit, that the most complicated events can be manipulated from the right vantage points. This is a charming notion, but it gives more credit to social engineering than is warranted and ignores the complexities, ambiguities, absurdities and novelties that help to make up the historical process. The treaty represents a flight from reality.

VI. The Nuclear Guarantee

The third item required for the success of a nonproliferation treaty is a guarantee by the United States and/or the Soviet Union to defend the victims of aggression. This guarantee must be not merely against nuclear attack but also against conventional attack, for one virtue of a nuclear arsenal is its deterrent effect against attack by a conventionally superior foe. The United States and the Soviet Union have restricted their guarantees to other nations to cases of nuclear attack, but even these guarantees are less than automatic. India asks for a guarantee going far beyond anything we have extended to our NATO allies. And our NATO allies interpret the American "pause" strategy as a retreat from the restricted nuclear guarantee we have offered them.

The guarantee issue has been buried beneath a web of deceptive verbiage. At this point in time nuclear attacks are unlikely and, with few exceptions, wars designed to exterminate another nation are almost equally unlikely. For most situations that could arise either the U.S. or Soviet nuclear force would constitute a sufficient deterrent, apart from any question of guarantee. As long as our image of the threat is one of criminals huddling behind closed doors, plotting conquest, and preparing their massive attack in secrecy and without provocation, we will misunderstand the nature of the problem. If such a threat ever existed, and it is doubtful whether this image correctly describes even the Nazi aggressions or the Japanese attack on Pearl Harbor, then the guarantees being offered by the Soviet Union and the United States should suffice; for, although it is not clear that the guarantees would be honored in all cases, the risk that they would be honored would seem to outrun any conceivable gain "criminal" aggressors might achieve in their strikes out of the blue.

It is the unanticipated crisis, in which the equities are mixed or unclear and in which regimes or international interests arise in a not entirely controllable manner, that lies at the root of the concern of other nations. Such crises develop slowly, although they may accelerate rapidly toward the end, and provide opportunity for the guaranteeing powers to conclude that their guarantees were not meant to be extended under the prevailing conditions. This would place the guaranteed power under enormous pressure to make concessions to which it might object for legitimate national reasons, as in the case of Czechoslovakia during the Munich crisis. Otherwise the guaranteeing power would in all likelihood attempt to withdraw from its commitment in consideration of the damage that might occur to its major cities as a result of action in support of a state not vital to its interests, a regime of which it might not entirely approve, or a bargaining sequence it had come to believe, under pressure of events, was stubborn, unintelligent or unrealistic.

Surely the United States does not desire to give a blank check to other states for nuclear wars. Blank checks almost invariably work out poorly, as the Kaiser learned during the First World War and as Britain learned after its blank check to Poland in 1939. They may increase rather than decrease the prospect of war, improper political demands, and risks that no reasonable U.S. government would desire to subject the American population to. Yet, in the absence of a blank check, a conditional and vague guarantee of the sort being offered to other states by the United States and the Soviet Union may only constitute a source of pressure against the victimized or weaker state, as at Munich. Torn by our ambivalence over the concept of the guarantee, we make a weak guarantee that entails the worst of the possible political prospects. We are led into deceit, as we were when we proposed the MLF. Such deceit is not often a sound basis for policy.

It is ironic that this particular form of guarantee, deceitful though it may be, is being offered at a time when the American public is threatening to return to a new version of its prewar isolationism. The 1967 Middle East war demonstrated the extent to which the events in Viet Nam have produced a cautious response in our highest official circles with respect to crises elsewhere. The slogan of reducing U.S. commitments has gained great popularity, and most of our leading political figures vie in proclaiming their adherence to that slogan. Yet we ask the rest of the world to believe that we are making the most momentous, and grave, and risk-bearing, form of commitment, that will cover circumstances we cannot begin to visualize. We fool only ourselves, for our self-deception is transparent to most other nations of the world; the latter temporarily cooperate with our policy and with that of the Soviet Union only because of the enormous pressures we have brought to bear against them.

Worst of all, we are attempting to force vigorous countries, with proud histories and dignified cultures, to accept the position of international wards. Were they to accept such an ignoble role, there would doubtless be unfortunate domestic political repercussions. Were they to resist the role, international problems might be worsened by the very existence of the treaty we are forcing upon them. At a time when important political pressure is being applied to lower the voting age to eighteen in the United States, and when university students are demonstrating in favor of increasing autonomy in control of their institutions, we are trying to force proud nations led by civilized and intelligent adults into the role of international juveniles. Does anyone really believe that such a solution could be maintained for long?

VII. The German Problem

The treaty involves the additional danger that it will not halt the spread of nuclear weapons but will only force the spread to occur under the worst possible auspices. The Germans endorsed the MLF not because they thought it a viable military force but because they thought agreement to the plan was the most practicable method for maintaining U.S. support and because they hoped it would evolve so as to give them a potential finger on the American nuclear trigger. They have since come to fear that German interests are being sacrificed by the United States to the concept of American-Soviet détente. This may (or may not) be a reasonable policy for the United States to follow but at least the decision concerning it should be made with a view to the potential consequences. Eventually it will become clear to the Germans that the French as well as the Americans have been playing games with German interests, and that the French are also opposed to German reunification.

It is now twenty-four years since the end of the Second World War. Germans who were fifteen years old at the conclusion of the war in 1945 are now thirty-nine. In five years all Germans under age forty-four will have been fifteen years old or less when the war ended. These Germans rightly feel no guilt for the crimes of the Nazis, and, to the extent that they may recognize the complicity of older German citizens, a complicity that is somewhat less than crystal clear, they do not recognize that any of this bears upon themselves. Although the NPT superficially applies to all nonnuclear states, Germans as well as Chinese are aware that it is particularly directed against them. They are sure to resent this unequal treatment of their great nations.

Granted that such speculations are hazardous, I would not expect the pressure for German nuclearization to become severe before 1975. The change of generations both in Germany and in her neighbors, as well as the changes in international circumstances, will by then allow what is now only latent to become manifest. In this respect it is interesting to note that resistance to Germany's signature on the NPT includes such distinguished crusaders for peace as Carl von Weizsacker, ostensibly because the treaty would interfere with Germany's peaceful uses of nuclear energy. Yet this reason, cited by many Germans, seems so weak intellectually that we must suspect latent motivations perhaps not understood by those who advance it.

If the present generation of responsible and democratic German leaders is forced to accept the onus for Germany's signature on the nuclear nonproliferation treaty, as now appears likely, the nationalistic reaction of betrayed German youths toward the nations that have treated Germany as an inferior and toward the democratic politicians who have accepted such a role could inspire a movement leading to the development of a German nuclear force under the direction of a radical regime. Acquisition of the force would not be difficult, for Germany will in the near future have the capability of producing several hundred nuclear weapons a year. Were it to be acquired during a period that is fairly quiet on the international scene, I do not believe Moscow would do more than bluster. Moreover, were the Soviets to attack in an effort to destroy Germany's nuclear force, the impact upon world politics would be shattering and the prognosis for the future less than sanguine. Neither of these projected outcomes would be consonant with American national interests, and a Soviet attack would be particularly threatening.

VIII. Thoughts on Czechoslovakia, 1968

The preceding sections of this article were written just before the invasion of Czechoslovakia by the Soviet Union, Poland, East Germany, Hungary and Bulgaria. It would have been possible to revise the entire article to remove inconsistencies between the statements made here and those made in the body of the article, but this would indicate a degree of prescience that is not warranted. I had stated several times during the crisis that, were I a dedicated communist and a member of the Soviet Politburo, I would vote for the invasion of Czechoslovakia, but that I thought the Soviet leadership was sufficiently conservative to make that course of action less than a 50/50 contingency. The events of August 1968 showed that the Kremlin leaders were able to mobilize their courage for a vicious assault upon the freedom of the Czechoslovakian people.

Although the bloc is far from monolithic and was less than monolithic even under Stalin, the unity of the five invading powers has been forged anew. Rumania remains defiant and recalcitrant, but shows no signs of defecting. China pursues its lonely path, but, when Mao dies, it is not inconceivable that Chinese military leaders may turn to the USSR as the only power capable of supplying them with modern arms, and attempt to repair the rupture between the two countries and diminish the distance between their policies. If the Soviet Union can hold to this new tough course, it is possible that even Rumania and Yugoslavia may be brought into line. This is speculative, however, and much depends upon the events of the near future.

The situation in Czechoslovakia remains uncertain. The Soviet Union has been unable to find the kind of "stooge" government it was able to set up in Hungary under Janos Kadar. It cannot administer and run Czechoslovakia without aid from at least some remnants of the Communist Party. The truce between the Dubcek Government and Moscow is uneasy, but the prospects for Czechoslovak freedom and independence are dim. As to the reaction of the United States to the Soviet intervention, the story dispatched from Warsaw by Jonathan Randal to the *New York Times* on August 21 remains pertinent.

> Eastern Europeans find it difficult to understand why the Johnson administration chose to negotiate a number of important deals with the Soviet Union during the height of the Czechoslovak crisis. Many Eastern Europeans feel that the United States is more interested in fostering its relations with the Soviet Union than in exerting influence in the area of Europe that since 1956 the United States has accepted as a Soviet sphere of influence. "The inaugural flights between New York and Moscow, the signing of the treaty to halt proliferation of nuclear weapons, and the bilateral cultural exchanges may have led the Soviet Union to intervene militarily," an

Eastern European diplomat said recently, "because the Kremlin calculated that the United States was not even morally concerned with Czechoslovakia."

Comments of this kind manifest how some East Europeans engaged in the art of international politics interpret the significance of American behavior. The Soviets by analogy may reason in the same way. Moreover, since these diplomats have many contacts with their Soviet colleagues, their observations may possibly represent some of the expressed opinions of highly placed Soviet personnel. It is not inconceivable that their advice on how to bargain with the Soviets is preferable to the generalizations about projection and the theories about mirror images that Senator Fulbright obtains from his consulting psychiatrists.

The quotation from the Randal news story confirms what intelligent observers already knew: that it was not the example of the Viet Nam conflict that led to Soviet action in Czechoslovakia, but rather the combination of the danger of internal liberalization in the Soviet Union and the threat to the bloc, particularly to East Germany. These serious problems motivated the Soviet Union to act at a time when the United States was showing an indecent desire for détente with the USSR. For the past several years, and particularly during the crisis, Washington has displayed enthusiasm for measures that are of more importance to the Soviet Union than to the United States. The nuclear nonproliferation treaty is a prime example. After having made the mistake of agreeing to the NPT, the United States might have deterred the invasion of Czechoslovakia by informing the Soviet Union privately that such an invasion would lead to the immediate cancellation of the pact and the possible nuclear armament of West Germany. That intelligent and sensible step was not taken because the Johnson Administration was in fact, despite the attacks upon it by the doves, inclined to the same sort of flabby sentimental enthusiasm for détente that motivates such people as Senators Fulbright and McCarthy.

The present sequence of events dims the prospects for the continued gradual dissolution of the Soviet bloc, although this possibility still cannot be ruled out despite the vigorous action taken against Czechoslovakia. We cannot exclude the possibility that the Soviet Union might some day attack West Germany. Although this probability is not very great, no doubt many Germans today feel less secure, as indeed they should, than they did before the Czech crisis. The fact that West Germany is a member of NATO and Czechoslovakia is a member of the Warsaw Pact does not entirely invalidate the conclusion some Germans might draw that the U.S. guarantee, either under NATO or under the nuclear nondiffusion pact, is somewhat less than certain. The innocent expressions in Washington that there is, after all, nothing we can do but accept a *fait accompli*, undercut seriously the value of both guarantees. Few Germans will miss this point, and those Germans who have been particularly associated with the concept of détente and with acceptance of the nuclear nondiffusion treaty, such as Willy Brandt of the Social Democratic Party, will be seriously injured in their political prospects because of it. The changing German viewpoint increases greatly the likelihood that Germany will some day seek nuclear weapons and that if the democratic politicians do not lead this move, radical nationalists will. Let us hope that Washington will understand this message.

One cannot draw the conclusion that the Germans will be deterred from acquiring nuclear weapons by fear that the United States will desert them during an acquisition crisis. If assurance concerning the U.S. guarantee in a political crisis is not strong enough for Germans to rely on it firmly, still their acquisition of nuclear weapons in time of tranquillity, particularly if Japan or India has already taken similar action, would hardly justify a resort to force by the USSR—except in a way threatening to the United States and world stability and therefore invoking the possibility of an American nuclear response. This probability need not be high to deter the Soviets. Their hesitancy about Czechoslovakia before the decision to invade was obvious enough that they might have been deterred by expressions of American opposition or even by indications of a Czechoslovak willingness to fight.

Thus we are confronted by the apparent (but not genuine) paradox that a U.S. guarantee which is not fully credible for a political crisis might nonetheless be sufficient to dissuade the Soviets from creating a crisis over the German acquisition of nuclear weapons. This need not be the case and much will depend upon circumstances. Included in such circumstances will be the speed with which Germany acquires at least some nuclear weapons, either through clandestine production—she will have the fissionable materials required to produce several hundred bombs a year in the 1970's—or through collusion with another nation. German possession of only a few bombs, even if they do not constitute an otherwise viable nuclear force, would probably be adequate to deter the Soviets, apart from the American deterrent. Would the Soviets have invaded Czechoslovakia if that nation had possessed a few bombs and even the most primitive kind of delivery capability? Germans are likely at some time in the future to ask themselves this question.

Assuming any initial resistance is overcome and the treaty is signed by the requisite number of States, will this automatically insure its success? Although signatures on a treaty do constitute some kind of moral obligation and thus give rise to the possibility of treaty success, the probability that the treaty will fail still remains substantial.

If the Nuclear Non-Proliferation Treaty fails to accomplish its objectives, does this necessarily imply that there were no measures against proliferation which might have been successful? On the contrary, there were alternatives. One such alternative was a joint NATO nuclear system, the nuclear force of which could have been used by the military command under, for example, two criteria: a nuclear attack by the Soviet Union or a Soviet conventional invasion and failure to withdraw after a stated interval upon demand. The proposed Multi-Lateral Force was a hypocritical substitute for such a measure and fooled no one in Europe, since the system was ineffective when compared with SAC and would have been subjected to six vetoes, including the American veto that exists with respect to the American nuclear force. As a second alternative to the treaty, the United States could have helped to build a joint European nuclear force to which it would not have been a party. Such a force might have satisfied the legitimate security needs of western European nations, and neither it nor a NATO system would have served as an incentive for smaller countries to acquire nuclear weapons. By supplying "know how" to Europe, Japan and perhaps even India, the United States would have established the lesson that nuclear forces are very difficult and expensive to acquire and depend for their acquisition upon the cooperation of one of the nuclear superpowers.

Although future qualitative developments in nuclear systems may produce nuclear proliferation anyway, even with the existence of alternatives to the treaty, one of these proposals might have delayed or possibly halted nuclear proliferation. The Nuclear Non-Proliferation Treaty, however, is being adopted too late in the process of nuclear expansion to have an even chance of success. It attempts to exclude too many nations from the acquisition of nuclear weapons, a decision that will make it even more difficult to halt proliferation because it is more likely to produce an early violation of the treaty. Moreover, the treaty negotiations themselves have forced other nations to consider nuclear policy much more systematically than they have before, and have also whetted the appetites of many other nations concerning nuclear weapons in a way that likely would not have occurred in the absence of negotiations. This increased awareness of nuclear arms and development can only make enforcement of the treaty among signatories more difficult. A further obstacle to complete acceptance of treaty obligations can be found in the certain degree of hypocrisy present in the positions of both the United States and the Soviet Union by their rejection of the demands of other nations to link specific nuclear disarmament measures with non-proliferation provisions.

If the treaty fails, its demise will lead to a number of results. It will provide an example that arms control treaties in the present world situation are ineffective. It will induce a system crisis by leading to proliferation under circumstances that involve violations of the spirit, if not the letter, of the treaty. A failure can, in all probability, induce a law-enforcement crisis.

IX. Impact on International Law

The Nuclear Non-Proliferation Treaty raises several problems concerning the enforcement of its provisions on an international level. Each signatory to the treaty, for example, has the right to withdraw from its coverage on three months notice upon a unilateral finding and statement that extraordinary events related to the subject matter of the treaty have jeopardized the supreme interests of its country,[9] but there are no procedures in the treaty for validating this claim or for asserting a counterclaim. Suppose that a State were to withdraw on grounds that appeared to others as not related to extraordinary events or failed to give the three month notice before withdrawing because it wished to avoid counter-pressures that might produce security dangers. Some States would no doubt view such technical violations as requiring some type of enforcement action, even though none is provided for in the treaty. Suppose a non-signatory State acquired nuclear weapons. This act could well lead to demands for enforcement action under the tenuous claim that the treaty, like customary international law, binds nonsignatory as well as signatory States.[10] Yet if non-signatory States are really not covered by the treaty or any enforcement measures pertaining to it, the acquisition of nuclear weapons by non-signatories would only further emphasize the unreasonable inferiority of non-nuclear signatory States.

Consider the problem of enforcement under ambiguous circumstances. Could such enforcement take place through the United Nations? If there were a formal sanction for treaty violations, it might prove difficult to pass such a measure through the Security Council without a veto. Moreover, since many nations might not wish to establish a precedent that might be directed against them in the future, it is conceivable that two-thirds of the states in the General Assembly would not support an enforcement action. If the ultimate decision were defeated by the General Assembly, would this improve general attitudes toward the effectiveness of international law?

Suppose claimed treaty violations were not brought before the United Nations but were enforced by the United States and the Soviet Union, acting either individually or in concert. Would this be a good example for the world? Would an invasion by either nation designed to destroy nuclear facilities increase confidence in international law or would it constitute instead a lesson that the nuclear super-powers intended to maintain their monopoly? In the absence of a political and military crisis, would the threat of using nuclear force merely to prevent the acquisition of nuclear weapons by another State—on the unilateral claim that its behavior is contrary to the treaty and despite the fact that a number of other States with no superior right except prior possession are exempted—induce respect for the law? This type of enforcement procedure would appear to be unjustified and only an exercise of naked power. Either an invasion or the use of nuclear power as a means of enforcement would constitute an incredibly powerful lesson concerning the

9. Treaty on the Non-Proliferation of Nuclear Weapons, *opened for signature* July 1, 1968, art. 10, [1968]____ U.S.T. ____, T.I.A.S. No. ____, ____ U.N.T.S. ____.
10. *See* Sohn, *Enforcement of Disarmament Controls with Respect to States Which Have Not Ratified a Disarmament or Arms Control Treaty*, in 1 ARMS CONTROL AND DISARMAMENT 99 (M. Miller ed. 1968).

advantages of acquiring a nuclear system, provided this could be done under circumstances that did not invite attack. Even if the treaty violation were unambiguous and if the treaty had an enforcement clause, would not either enforcement method present a shock to the entire political and social fabric of the world?

Are non-enforceable treaties that conflict with the clear interest of major States really good ideas? Perhaps the no-strike clause in labor contracts—a much less sensitive area of law—provides a valid precedent for the Nuclear Non-Proliferation Treaty. The treaty does not contain—and the United States and the Soviet Union were unable to write into it over the resistance of the other negotiating States—the definite enforcement procedures contained in some no-strike clauses. Instead, the treaty merely emphasizes the unequal positions of the signatories. Its effectiveness thus rests in part upon its morally compelling character, although the distinctions between signatory States do not conform to any reasonable system of classification. It is inherently capricious and arbitrary; in this respect, as in others, it sets a bad precedent for international law.

The probable failure of the treaty can only induce disrespect for international law by those who do not appreciate either that the treaty may not have been violated in a precise technical sense or that it was not meant to be enforceable. While in operation, it will undermine respect for the law because of its arbitrary system of classification. Contrary to delaying proliferation, the treaty may only hasten this result. Moreover, if the treaty eases the path of radical nationalists into government office, these regimes are likely to become disruptive elements to the stability of international law. If the treaty is simply used as a pretext to forcibly prevent other nations from acquiring nuclear weapons, still further damage to the bases of international law can be expected. In an era of nuclear development, a stable international legal system is needed. Some method of checking the spread of nuclear arms must be found which will, at the same time, preserve the integrity of the international system. The Nuclear Non-Proliferation Treaty appears to be misconceived for both these purposes and actually presents a threat to the prospects for a successful system of international law.

Part Two
Great Issues of Foreign Policy

Introduction

It is a great issue of foreign policy to determine what type of international order we wish to build and how to respond to the emerging framework of international order. However, in Part Two we concentrate on more specific problems of foreign policy: those to which statesmen traditionally direct their attention, sometimes, unfortunately, to the exclusion of the great issues considered in Part One.

As the reader already knows, the international system is a decentralized order. If an attack occurs, the victim cannot run to the police or the courts. Self-help is the primary mode of activity in the international system. Thus, the statesman wants to know if he possesses anything that others covet sufficiently to attack him. If so, who are the potential enemies? If the potential enemies are strong or have many allies, the statesman will want to know who may come to his aid and under what conditions. He will be concerned about changes in foreign areas that threaten his potentiality for alliances.

During the dynastic era, many of the wars in Europe were concerned with problems of succession in other countries. For instance, during the war of the Spanish succession Austria feared that the inheritance of the Spanish throne by a Bourbon, for instance, might threaten its interests. In the early nineteenth century, the spread of French revolutionary ideals nearly permitted Napoleon to take over all of western Europe. Somewhat later, the spread of democratic ideals threatened monarchial regimes. During the 1930's, the spread of fascism threatened the democracies. In the postwar period, the spread of communism seemed to portend similar dire conse-

207

quences for the democratic and capitalist powers. Since then, the dispute between China and the Soviet Union has started a controversy over whether world communism remains a major threat or not.

The statesman is also interested in whether non-aligned areas are viable. If NATO did not exist, could Europe fend off Russian pressure that might lead to its Finlandization? This leads directly to the next question: does it matter whether Europe can defend itself or not? In other words, would American national security be threatened if Europe fell to communism?

The same issue arose in a different form before World War II. Interventionists often argued that if the Nazis conquered all of Europe they would move into Africa. Then maps would be taken out and the small distance between the bulge of Africa and Latin America noted. It was then argued that the Nazis and other Fascists would move from Africa into Latin America, and then up into North America. Herbert Hoover demolished these particular arguments, by demonstrating that they were based on military nonsense. Many contemporary arguments that if the Communists take over Southeast Asia they will next be threatening the Hawaiian Islands and then the west coast of the United States are also likely nonsense.

However, it did not follow from the foolishness of the argument for intervention that isolation was a viable policy for the United States in the 1930's. In the first place, fascism was viewed as the wave of the future. Thus, even without Nazi conquest, fascist movements were spreading in Latin America. Moreover, they had spread to the United States, so there was a threat from within as well as from without.

In a world that was everywhere hostile, presumably we would have retreated to a "Fortress America." Now as then this probably would involve a garrison state. In addition, many sources of supply and trade patterns would be vulnerable to the hostility of other nations. Our intellectual communications with others would diminish and this might well have a direct impact upon the rate of scientific advance in the United States. This is particularly important in an age that is nuclear and in which technological change is rapid. New laser technologies, for instance, might undercut the basis of U.S. deterrence. Sheer physical security is potentially far more fragile than it was in the 1930's.

Of course, none of this is provable in any hard scientific sense. But it does raise a serious question as to the validity of the national security of the United States in isolation. I do not believe that American national security would long exist if the U.S. were isolated in a world of authoritarian regimes. Moreover, I believe that we do have an interest, even if not an overriding one, in helping others defend their freedom.

Another great issue to which the statesman may address himself is whether the international system is one that responds to reason, friendliness, and unilateral concessions, or one that responds to hard bargaining, cynical manipulation, and the threat and use of force. This will later tie in directly to Part Three, where we will ask whether reductions in military force will lead to reciprocal reductions by other nations or whether military programs are required, at the minimum as bargaining chips, to restrain others in the pursuit of an arms race. The question here is eminently practical: What is the form of behavior that produces desirable results in the existing international system?

These great issues are intimately involved in all the specific issues of national policy, such as whether we should assist the Israelis, intervene in the India-Pakistan dispute, realign ourselves with Communist China, pursue détente with the Soviet Union, and so forth. However, they are not involved in any simple sense, for each particular issue of policy involves each of these great issues in a complicated and interlocked way. Thus, it is extremely difficult to disentangle them from the specific circumstances in which they are involved. Moreover, given the great dependence of political matters upon contextual elements, these issues come out more clearly in the concrete examination of specific issues of foreign policy than they do in a purely analytical and abstract discussion. And in any event, it is only in this concrete form that they appear to the statesmen who may hold our destiny in their hands.

V

ADVERSARY FOREIGN POLICY: THE SOVIET CASE

In the first article in this chapter, I argue that an important change between the late 1940's and the 1960's occurred in the international system rather than in the motivation of states and that public views of both periods involve overinterpretations and overreactions against previous beliefs. The close of the Second World War found Europe "up for grabs," and I believe that neither the United States nor the Soviet Union could have viewed with equanimity the major uncontrollable changes that might have occurred in the absence of their intervention in the extremely important European peninsula. Thus, I view much of the immediate postwar period as one of consolidation that minimized risk, even though it was ideologized in terms of enemy aggressiveness and war dangers. However, as the European nations recovered from the war, as political stability returned, as the Soviet bloc was consolidated, as the Soviet Union recovered from the ravages of the Second World War, the risks of radical change became minimal while the overwhelming economic and political power of the Soviet Union and the United States diminished, thus causing extremely important changes in the world political context.

Although the terms of his explanation are somewhat different, G. A. Arbatov (article 12) produces essentially a mirror image of my theme. The nature of American diplomacy has changed, he says, because of the internal and external constraints that now face American policy. Although he insists upon characterizing American policy as aggressive and imperialistic in line with Soviet dogma, his argument that the situation prevents the implementation of aggressive, imperialistic policies and his citations from

President Nixon indicating peaceful shifts in American policy are designed to reenforce the view that agreements with the United States are both possible and desirable. Unlike Senator Fulbright, neither Kaplan nor Arbatov talks of détente in general. Both recognize important conflicts of interest between the United States and the Soviet Union. They advocate agreements on those issues that can be settled within the present framework of circumstances, and recognition of remaining and genuine conflicts of interest that need not be driven to the point of ultimate hostility.

The student will note seeming discrepancies between Arbatov's article and that by R. Judson Mitchell on Soviet "two camps" doctrine (article 13). Under Stalin, this doctrine was a mirror image of the old John Foster Dulles doctrine: conflict was inevitable and neutrality was impossible. Khrushchev altered this Stalinist view and recognized a third camp, including national democratic regimes. Because of this change in world politics, he believed, the imperialist powers would be unable to carry out their aggressive plans. The reader will see a similarity to Arbatov's explanation, and this position provided an ideological framework for Khrushchev's agreements with the United States. Mr. Mitchell cites the reversion under Brezhnev to a new "two camps" doctrine that seemingly is inconsistent with what Arbatov suggests. Yet Secretary General Brezhnev is believed to be the patron of the Institute that Arbatov heads. Thus, the question arises as to whether the Soviet sources cited by Mitchell accurately portray Brezhnev's views or that of a more right-wing faction in the Kremlin to which concessions were made. Or have Brezhnev's views changed since 1968? To what extent is this "two camps" doctrine a recurrent theme in Soviet diplomacy, which merely get submerged during particular periods in which more moderate views are in the ascendant?

Even if the cold war images of the Soviet Union were in error, it does not follow that there was no real threat. It may not have been primarily military as in Korea or Hungary, but danger did arise from political pressure or even blackmail by the Soviet Union—for instance, during the Berlin blockade and Khrushchev's threats against Berlin in the mid- and late-1950's. Moreover, whatever the truth may be about Russian policy at any particular time, it does not follow that it will remain consistent over time. Brezhnev seems committed to the policy of détente. Russia has a long frontier with China. It has internal economic problems. It badly needed wheat from the United States. Brezhnev may even be concerned about the apparent unpredictability of President Nixon.

On the other hand, the United States appears to be in a period of retreat from its world responsibilities. Thus, a policy of détente also assists this development. If NATO weakens or if the United States withdraws from Europe, Soviet pressure on Europe may be reasserted. If this were the actual Soviet intention, it would fit Mitchell's hypothesis concerning the new "two camps" Soviet doctrine. However, even if Mitchell is wrong, a new Soviet leadership may see such a policy as viable. In other words, this potential Soviet policy remains a hazard for the United States and affects any policy it may have in the world in general and toward Europe in particular.

In this respect, the reader may take into account the fact that Soviet policy in the past has never operated on mere sentiment, and it is unlikely to do so in the future. Maxim Litvinov stated that "We Marxists are the last who can be reproached with allowing sentiment to prevail over policy." Or, as another spokesman put it, "Our security does not depend upon paper documents." After the Munich settlement in the autumn of 1938, Potemkin, the undersecretary of the Soviet foreign office, said to Coulandre, the French ambassador to Moscow, "This means the fourth partition of Poland." The Russians obviously were not put off by the anti-Comintern pact or by the vicious vituperation—for instance, calling them inhuman beasts— that was put out by the Berlin radio.

We have emphasized the Soviet Union as a potential enemy because the cold war was primarily an American/Soviet confrontation. The major lines of American policy were established by the nature of this confrontation. Moreover, any single case can be used to make explicit the problem of interpreting the policies of a potential adversary. On the other hand, the Korean war involved a direct American/Chinese confrontation. Moreover, much of American policy in Southeast Asia, including our fateful intervention in Vietnam, was motivated by official perceptions of a Chinese threat. This issue is touched upon in my review of Senator Fulbright's book, where I take a view of Chinese motivations sharply contrary to that held by official Washington. Later, in chapter VIII the article by Ian Clark assumes new conceptions of Chinese intentions that were relevant to President Nixon's détente with the Communist government.

Because the Chinese/Soviet issue is relevant to this chapter as well as to chapter VIII, and to the settlement of the Vietnam war also, a few words on the diplomacy that led to this new structure of relations may be useful. This diplomacy created a political climate in which both the Soviet Union and Communist China had strong incentives to bring pressure to bear upon the North Vietnamese to accept a negotiated settlement that did not destroy the South Vietnamese government or humiliate the United States. This was foreshadowed in statements by Richard Nixon even before he became president; his 1968 article in *Foreign Affairs* indicated his desire for a rapprochement with Communist China, and statements subsequent to his inauguration reinforced this posture.

But the readjustments were not easy. Although 1969 was the year of greatest Russian pressure upon China—including hints of nuclear attack— it was to take two years before the Chinese responded to Richard Nixon's overtures. The internal politics of China are murky and we cannot be certain of the reasons. However, there were apparently strong internal resistances to the American opening as well as possible misinterpretations of

Nixon's policy. In any event, the inauguration of ping-pong diplomacy by Chou En-lai in 1971 began the process. As the Chinese now had opted for an American connection, rather than seeking reassurance through concessions to the Soviet Union, they had an incentive to help avoid a humiliating defeat for the United States. More than this, they required an American presence in Southeast Asia to offset the Soviet Union and a continued American presence in western Europe to complicate any Russian considerations of harsh pressure—or even a nuclear strike—against them.

On the other hand, the Chinese opening to the United States produced fear in the Soviet Union. By the end of 1971 Russian suspicions were so great that the American/Soviet détente might have been jeopardized. It was necessary for the Nixon administration, in a display of diplomatic flexibility, to limit its connection with China in a way that did not worry the Chinese and at the same time inhibited Soviet fears of a Chinese-American alliance. As part of this process, the United States continued to engage in measures of détente with the Soviet Union, including successful SALT negotiations, and thus reassured the Soviet leadership of a relatively coequal role with the United States in world politics—an outcome of great importance to the Soviet Union. Economic pressures and a desire not to drive the United States into the feared Chinese-American alliance gave the Soviet Union an incentive to help arrange a peace in South Vietnam.

For the first time, then, both China and Russia had more of an incentive to assist the United States than to struggle over their comparative influence in North Vietnam, although this last consideration continued to play a minor role in their policies. Yet this dénouement was not an automatic response to world politics. Might not a weaker American posture in western Europe, as proposed by some, have encouraged the Soviet Union to solve its problems by Finlandization of western Europe? Would a scuttling of the American position in South Vietnam have convinced the Chinese of the unreliability of an American connection and have strengthened those forces in China seeking safety through concessions to the Soviet Union? Careful balance was required or the entire basis of American security in both Europe and Asia might have been jeopardized. Thus the diplomacy of the Nixon administration may account for the temporary stability that characterizes the present international system, and may be more than simply a result of inevitable tendencies in the world system.

11.

Changes in United States Perspectives on the Soviet Union and Détente

MORTON A. KAPLAN

Nature of the Détente

What is meant by *détente*—a term generally used in an exceedingly obscure and ideological fashion? In what ways may the détente affect the normative structure of the world? My conclusion, which I now anticipate, will be that the term implies too great a disjunction with the immediate past, at least in terms of objective conditions, if not of attitudes toward these conditions, and that, although conditions have changed, our attitudes toward them have changed even more, and perhaps in some misleading ways.

The term *détente* is, of course, contrasted with the term *cold war*. No doubt if one reads newspaper editorials, public speeches by our political leaders, and memoirs these contrasts have real meaning. Use of these terms, however, has obscured certain kinds of fundamental political processes and has confused short-term system needs, which produced consonant policies on the part of the blocs, with longer-range national motivations which would be extremely difficult to substantiate.

The American cold war image of the Soviet Union was that of a conspiratorial octopus engaged in a program of world-wide revolutionary activity and preparing for ultimate world conquest by military means. No doubt the objective of military conquest was not entirely excluded by Stalin. He is quoted by Djilas as saying, "The war will soon be over. We shall recover in 15 or

Reprinted by permission from the Hudson Institute, Martin Marietta Report. © 1965 by Morton A. Kaplan.

20 years, and then we'll have another go at it."[1] Although a nation can prepare for an event 15 or 20 years in the future and although this quotation tells us something of Stalin's mentality, there is an enormous gap between that kind of long-term objective and the meaningful decisions of foreign policy in a short-range time scale. Indeed, if anything, the quotation helps to discredit the notion widely held in the West in the late 1940's to the effect that an unprovoked Soviet military attack was imminent or, if deterred, was deterred by the American nuclear monopoly. The evidence would seem overwhelming that Stalin had no such short-term objectives, that despite the superiority of Soviet conventional forces, Stalin's main immediate objectives were rebuilding the Soviet Union and re-establishing Russian spheres of influence in zones bordering on the Soviet Union. Stalin strongly resisted Yugoslav demands for Soviet support on the question of Trieste. The Communist parties in France and Italy cooperated in holding down demands for wage increases to rebuild both countries until after the Trotskyite-inspired Renault strike in France. Only after Communist expulsion from the cabinet in both countries (following Marshall Plan proposals) did Communist Party behavior in both countries become consistently disruptive for the economy. The Greek civil war was largely supported by Yugoslavia and Bulgaria and, to the extent that we can trust Yugoslav accounts, was resisted to some extent by Stalin. The Soviet Union gave little aid to the Chinese Communists.[2] In 1949, the Russian embassy was the only major embassy to follow the Kuomintang nationalists from Peking to Canton, while the American and British embassies remained in Peking. Even during the retreat, the Soviet Union was carrying on complicated diplomatic negotiations with the Kuomintang régime.

This is a picture which runs counter to the cold war images of the 1950's. The alternate picture—the one generally accepted in the United States—cites the Soviet presence in Iran in the postwar period and support for the Tudeh party, the civil war in Greece, the economic disruption that occurred after late 1947 in France and Italy, the formation of the Cominform in the fall of 1947, the Communist take-overs in eastern European countries in 1947 and 1948, the coup in Czechoslovakia in 1948, the spy trials, the Berlin blockade, and finally, the Korean war of 1950. All of these moves fit in with the conspiratorial hypothesis, as do the revolutionary efforts, including the coup attempt in Indonesia, in Southeast Asia beginning in 1948.

The Communists, of course, present a different picture. They point to the shutting off of lend-lease by the United States before the end of the Second

1. Milovan Djilas, *Conversations with Stalin*, New York, Harcourt, Brace & World, Inc., 1962, pp. 114–115.
2. They did permit the Chinese Communists to seize the Japanese arms piles in Manchuria. It is quite conceivable that Stalin simply remembered the fiasco of Shanghai in 1927, when the Comintern ordered the Chinese Communists to bury their weapons and the Kuomintang took advantage of the situation to execute as many of the Communist leaders as they could capture.

World War, to the exclusion of the Russians from the Japanese occupation,[3] to our recalcitrance on the problem of Poland, to the Marshall Plan and the consequent elimination of the Communists from the governments of Italy and France, to the rehabilitation of the German economy and Bizonia, to the Truman Doctrine, and, finally, to the Brussels pact and NATO to which, in their account, the Cominform and the Warsaw Pact were mere responses.

Both these pictures—and indeed the current picture of détente—overlook the situational components of policy. The immediate postwar period left Europe in a state of rapid flux, without social, political, or economic stability. This fluidity created risks and also provided opportunities for both the United States and the Soviet Union. Rapid shifts—too rapid—in the constellation of political forces were possible. The instability of the external environment required reactive and interventionary policies.

That interventions or reactions were required by the situation lest too drastic a shift in the required constellation of forces occur does not imply that every action which was taken can be fully accounted for by this need. The situation provides a constraint on policy; it does not preclude alternative decisions or consonant decisions taken for different reasons. Nonetheless, even if this gross constraint cannot fully account for the policies followed and the positions taken, it is true that no explanation eliminating this factor can begin to explain the history of the postwar period. One could thus view the 1945–1950 period as one in which situational factors created opportunities for bloc formation and bloc consolidation. The period 1945–1950 was the period of the growth of structure of the emerging international system.

The period 1945–1950 was also the period in which the wartime images of the world and, in particular, of the Soviet Union had to be readjusted. The main wartime image was an image in which the victorious and "democratic" allies would reconstruct a new world while holding down the vicious fascist states. This simple-minded picture could not survive the end of the war, for, at the end of the war, the United States and the Soviet Union discovered a fact that could no longer be ignored. Each was the greatest potential threat to the other, to its image of the world, and to its own internal stability. And each faced a highly unstructured world which was susceptible to rapid change if either nation did not quickly counter the moves of the other. Thus the hopes for postwar cooperation of the victorious allies were frustrated. Frustrated hopes rarely find their expression in realistic analysis. If the cooperative image of the world had to be rejected, then a villain had to be discovered. And it was not sufficient to discover a real villain—that is, a nation with a totalitarian political system—but a villain whose every move represented an unprovoked step in a cynical and aggressive plan to conquer the world.

3. These, of course, countered what the Russians did in late 1944 and 1945 in the occupied eastern European nations.

Seen more realistically, two processes were going on. One was a process of bloc development and consolidation which was necessitated by the structure of the postwar period; accompanying it was the new structure of belief that to some extent functioned not as a representational picture of the world as it was, but as an explanation or rationalization of the frustrated hopes of the war period.

There was a third process that helps to place the other two in better perspective. This is accounted for by the internal structure and organization of the Soviet Union. If the image of the Soviet Union in the late 1940's as a nation striving for world conquest through subversion and military war is a caricature, there are, nonetheless, aspects of the Soviet Union that give some credence to a more moderate version of this analysis. The goals pursued by any actor function both with external opportunity and with internal resources. The average citizen, for instance, does not attempt to buy the world's leading newspaper, but if he possessed enough money he might develop this ambition. It is a well-known phenomenon, and one that really should not require further explanation (were it not for the crudity of the literature on the subject) that latent or even entirely unanticipated goals rise to the level of consciousness and attempted implementation upon the concatenation of favorable opportunity and internal potentiality.

In the 1940's the Soviet Union possessed a party apparatus that permitted a genuine degree of international direction. No doubt if a Deminform were possible, the United States might find itself giving directions to satellite parties in uncommitted areas of the world. This means is not available to us and we must proceed, where we desire to influence events, through other instrumentalities. That kind of instrumentality—the party instrumentality—was open to the Soviet Union; it does not require any devil theory of history to infer that upon suitable opportunities it was used. It is one thing, however, to acknowledge the existence and even the use of such instrumentalities, and it is quite a second thing to derive the conspiracies that occurred merely from the existence of that apparatus.[4] We are always faced with the question of why an event occurred when it did.

For instance, why did the Czech coup take place in 1948 and not in 1945, even though the Soviet Union could have maintained military control in 1945? Obviously, motivations other than merely the motivation to create a Communist state in Czechoslovakia operated upon the Soviet leadership. In cases of complex motivation, where perhaps no single motive is sufficient to produce the event that occurred, historical evaluation and explanation is more difficult. One thing does seem plausible though: the explanation that these events had long been planned in advance is not good enough. That

---

4. See Morton A. Kaplan, *The Communist Coup in Czechoslovakia,* Research Monograph No. 5, Center of International Studies, Princeton University, January 4, 1960, for an analysis of the way in which external circumstances and opportunity possibly combined to bring about the Czech coup in 1948.

Soviet ideology and Communist organization might create certain kinds of latencies toward activities of this kind may be accepted, but latency is not manifestation. The thesis being argued here is that the disorganization of the world system moved these latent objectives into the manifest area. The frustrated hopes of the war years gave rise to the overinterpretation of this behavior. If this explanation is plausible, it would then follow that although the democratic centralist nature of Communism played a major role in the kinds of disvalued activities in which the Soviet Union participated, Stalinism or terror as such, even though an internal component of the Soviet régime, did not. If this is so, one runs the risk of deriving from putative ameliorations of Soviet internal politics an amelioration of foreign policy that may be unrelated, at least in a direct way.

There are two qualifications that I would like to make. The first is that although the change, or the seeming change, in Soviet foreign policy was not to any great extent a direct product of evolution in the internal structure of the government, an internal crisis which produced a hardening of the régime might produce a temporary hardening of Soviet foreign policy. This would be difficult to predict, however, for the very opposite might occur. The new Soviet régime might need increased détente to secure internal public support, particularly with respect to the hardening of internal practices. Although the example is no precedent because Beria appeared to have been committed to internal liberalization in terms of the apparent drift of his policy, Beria—perhaps because of his bad reputation—apparently was prepared to go farther toward a solution of the German problem that would have been acceptable and even desirable to the West than was any subsequent Soviet leader.

The other qualification involves the relationship between latent and manifest goals. The order in which Hitler's conquests were carried out, and even to some extent the fact that they were carried out at all, depended upon circumstances. However, his goals were well articulated and he was actively searching for and attempting to create circumstances which enabled him to execute his expansionist objectives. This does not imply that he wanted the world war he got. He much preferred to pick and choose among his adversaries, to eliminate them one at a time, and to achieve his objectives systematically. He may even have been sincere in promising to protect the British Empire after Germany's territorial and colonial objectives were satisfied, although this would have meant not a genuinely independent Britain but a satellite Britain. Still, even if Hitler's plans for war were not those of immediate world war, they were of a nature which perhaps did call for world war as a defensive reaction by the other powers. Again, when the Arab states look at Israel, they recognize that they are in no position to launch a military attack against Israel today. They would be beaten. However, by maintaining a state of formal war and of armed incidents and tension, by refusing to regularize relationships, and by keeping their own people stirred up, they are keeping high the probability that should, in the future, circumstances arise which strengthen them or weaken Israel, they will be able to seize the opportunity to attack.

Therefore, the question arises, apart from the favorable character of circumstances, what the nature of the latency in Soviet objectives was. Under Stalin one could argue that extreme conservatism and caution prevailed. Despite the reputation of the Soviet Union for disruptive external activities, the Soviet Union, unlike Nazi Germany, was not engaged in a campaign of chemical dissolution and disruption of adjacent areas. Its conspiratorial apparatus seized opportunities in those areas where disruption and chaos already existed and where the alternatives would have been dangerous to the security of the Soviet Union. Stalin's objectives were long-term objectives. He did not attempt to force fate. His system, no doubt, was different from and more dangerous than the bourgeois state apparatus, for a conspiratorial apparatus was indeed an intrinsic part of the system. But it was used cautiously. Even his talk of another go in 15 or 20 years involves a timetable that was a generation distant. The operational consequences for current policy were extremely peripheral. Even the one apparent gamble he took—and this toward the close of his life—the Korean War, may be put into perspective. The operation was carried out by a third team, the North Koreans. It was an area the United States had apparently written off; American forces had been withdrawn and the area had been placed outside our defense perimeter. Congress had voted against arms aid to Korea and had overridden this vote by a margin of a single vote only after a plea from both President Truman and Secretary of State Acheson. Moreover, the operation took place when the United States was virtually disarmed. The Soviet Union apparently was so surprised by the American reaction that it was not able to attend Security Council meetings of the United Nations before the crucial votes were taken. The Soviet Union clearly had no scruples about taking over independent nations and transforming them into satellites, as the case of Czechoslovakia indicates. But its political strategy was a slow-motion strategy adjusted to its philosophy of conservatism and the limitation of its ambitions to "ripe" situations.

To state that Stalin was cautious, however, and had no intention of engaging in a frontal military assault does not mean that the situation lacked danger. Economic turmoil, political disillusionment, and lack of American military commitment would have had profound effects upon the politics of Western Europe. Those who viewed Communism as the wave of the future would have begun to make their compromises with it. And the local Communist parties and the Soviet Union likely would have begun to put brutal pressure on the Western European nations—one at a time, and after real or manufactured provocations. The Truman Doctrine, the Marshall Plan, and NATO were inspired and necessary responses to a weakness in Western organization without which Western Europe might have been lost to Communist pressure. The beliefs as to the nature of the Soviet threat, however, were awry. The Czechoslovak coup of 1948 was likely the better metaphor. Even Hitler had not intended a bold massive assault against the west, although he had contemplated war with more readiness than did Stalin.

It is important to consider some of the changes in the Soviet system that have occurred since Stalin's death and the ways in which these may affect the nature of the détente and of the processes of conflict resolution and norm formulation in the contemporary world. Before doing so it is well to state that the theme of coexistence—a theme that does imply active political conflict—was Stalin's theme, that Stalin declared that war between the Soviet and capitalist states was not inevitable, and that the Soviet Union as early as 1949 was sponsoring world-wide peace movements. Moreover, under both Lenin and Stalin, the Soviet Union had supported bourgeois nationalist revolutions, for instance, in Turkey and in China. The changes in Soviet policy to which I refer, therefore, do not affect these elements as such. They refer to the internal structure of the Communist world as it affects the implementation of foreign policy goals. I can only adumbrate these changes.

Just as the partners of the United States in the West recovered from their postwar states of destitution, so in the Soviet zone the states recovered from the ravages of war and the régimes began to gain a modicum of consent, if only in the sense that the régimes were viewed by the local population as not so bad as some of the probable alternatives. Moreover, to meet production goals, in view of the resentment of the Soviet Union by the populaces of a number of the satellite nations, some degree of nationalism and independence was required. The secret speech by Khrushchev at the 20th party congress denouncing Stalin shattered for many of the committed intellectuals of the Communist parties the myth of the infallibility of the leadership, just as the demotion of Khrushchev later further helped undermine this myth.

The consequences of the shattering of this myth have been overstated in some quarters and insufficient differentiation has been made as to which groups both in the populations and in the leaderships were affected by disillusionment, for not all were. Moreover, the degree of subsequent polycentrism can also be overstated. China always was for practical purposes a genuinely independent member of the bloc. China was further irritated by Russian refusal to give China substantial economic aid, by Russia's reneging on its pledge to aid China's nuclear development, and by other Russian activities within the bloc that ran against Chinese interests. This resulted in the split between China and Russia and helped to increase polycentrism and independence within the bloc itself. The consequences of this have not been entirely bad from the standpoint of world Communism, for the demonstration that a nation can be Communist and not completely subservient to the Soviet Union undoubtedly reduces the resistance to involvement with the Communist nations and with local Communist parties by a number of elites in underdeveloped and uncommitted nations. This same development undoubtedly increases the problems of the Soviet Union in using the bloc as a mere instrument of Soviet foreign policy. However, because the only kind of appeal China can make to the other members of the bloc is in terms of ideological dogma and revolutionary Communism—despite the extremely conservative nature of China's own foreign policy—the Soviet Union is almost required by the nature of this conflict to adhere to a more revolutionary policy than it otherwise might, even though the bloc is no longer in some ways the effective instrument of Soviet foreign policy that it once had been.

Furthermore, at least under Khrushchev, the actions of the Soviet Union were influenced by the non-conservative personality of the ruling figure in the régime. The installation of Soviet missiles in Cuba, for instance, created both a political and military threat for the United States. It threatened actively to create opportunities for revolution and intervention to Latin America, both through positive action and symbolically through the demonstration of American inability to counter this move. This action was much closer to Hitler's style of policy than to Stalin's. Unlike the situation at Munich in 1938, however, the leadership of the democratic countries still retained military superiority and also had the will to exercise the superiority. Khrushchev's gambit did not work any more than his earlier attempted nuclear blackmail in Europe. In this sense, Khrushchev's policy was even more radical and reckless than any of Hitler's between the Rhineland reoccupation of 1936 and the outbreak of war in 1939. The military occupation of Hungary in 1956 also contrasted strongly with Stalin's inaction with respect to Yugoslavia in 1948.

Thus, the Soviet Union is pictured as a nation whose bloc structure no longer created the opportunities for external intervention which existed in the immediate postwar period and whose environment also dampened these possibilities. It nonetheless behaved in a more radical way than Stalin had ever behaved. However, this attempt by Khrushchevite Russia to follow this provocative course was frustrated by American resistance. And the possibilities for aggressive foreign policy were reduced both by lack of external opportunity and by a decline in the utility of the Communist apparatus. Much Russian attention necessarily was given to rivalry with China and the struggle over control of the world Communist movement. Thus, the immediate likelihood of direct conflict between the Soviet Union and the United States was greatly diminished. The so-called détente was to a considerable extent a consequence of these factors. This does not mean that the potentialities for cooperation in some areas cannot be developed or are insignificant any more than an assessment of Soviet motivation in the late 1940's, different from the then current one, would have implied that conflict was unreal or unimportant. Yet in each case reactive public—and occasionally governmental—images have misrepresented the situation and have produced mis-estimates of the dangers, opportunities, and probable outcomes that the situation presents.

It could be argued that a similar and perhaps even more stable détente was in fact beginning to develop under Stalin's régime, despite Korea. The détente was created largely by the nature of the changes in the world, that is, by the stabilization of nations other than the Soviet Union and the United States, the reduced opportunities for external intervention in these stable areas, and the changes in the nature of the two blocs. Attitudes were changing too. It is a generation since the close of the Second World War. We no longer remember the hopes we had and the ways in which they were frustrated. Therefore, there is a tendency—almost surely wrong—to interpret the present change as a radical change. As a consequence we may tend to overestimate the nature of the change and to underestimate the potentiality for continued indirect clashes in the underdeveloped areas of the world and elsewhere.

12.

American Foreign Policy on the Threshold of the 1970's

G. A. ARBATOV

FOR ALL THE POLITICAL worries, big and small, that concerned Americans in 1969, the question of the 1970's was central to many debates and discussions. And it would appear that the matter is not merely one of some kind of calendar magic.

The transition from one decade to the next coincides this time with a certain turning point in the development of the United States, when the domestic and foreign policy problems facing the country require a reevaluation of many established notions and a search for a way out of the impasses in which American policy has found itself. This is why the words, "the seventies," constantly recurring in the titles of numerous American pamphlets and articles, are something more than a device to catch the reader's eye. Behind these titles are the profound malaise and despair of a considerable part of the American public, which is beginning to realize that it is impossible to go on living in the old way, and is seeking, anxiously and with hope, to peer into the future.

The United States is a power whose policy influences the destiny of not just its own people. The general course of events in the international arena depends significantly on its policy. Therefore, the course taken by the U.S. in the 1970's is truly an international problem; and it naturally attracts the attention of Soviet specialists in American studies.

Any attempt to look into the future must include at least two components:

First, an interpretation of the policy changes that the objective situation,

Reprinted by permission from *Soviet Law and Government*, Vol. 9, No. 1, 1970. Published by International Arts and Sciences Press, Inc., White Plains, New York.

the real course of events, demands and probably will demand; and

Second, an interpretation of the degree to which these objective needs are capable of influencing the formation of foreign policy.

These are the questions to which the present article is devoted.

I

The fact that the foreign policy of U.S. imperialism has encountered major difficulties, and is even in crisis, is beyond question. This is recognized even by many American researchers. Differences among them begin, basically, over another question: What are the causes of these difficulties? A great number of different opinions are expressed on this question. Some believe the causes lie in the loss by the United States of its "overwhelming military superiority" and in insufficient decisiveness. Others believe the causes stem from tactical errors; still others, from unskilled practical implementation of a political course that, in their opinion, is basically correct. But the voices of those who cast doubt not only upon individual manifestations but upon the very foundations of Washington's foreign policy are heard ever more loudly.

Thus, the dispute over the nature of the present difficulties comes down to determining what underlies them: faulty tactics or an untenable strategy?

It seems to us that whereas, at the end of the 1950's or early in the 1960's, there still might have been grounds for such a debate among American political theorists (as well as among practical politicians), by the beginning of the 1970's a discussion of this problem has become essentially meaningless: the debate has been decided by life, by the entire experience of the preceding decade. This experience has demonstrated rather clearly what can, and what cannot, be gained by improving the tactics and means of struggle within the bounds of U.S. political strategy since World War II.

The sources of this strategy are obvious. On the one hand, there was a sense of omnipotence in the Power that had emerged from the war, with hegemony over the capitalist world and with a monopoly of atomic weapons. This not only whipped up the imperialist pretensions of the United States but caused *its strategy in foreign policy to be linked indissolubly with the use of military force and with the threat to use it.*

On the other hand, there is a fear, penetrating ever deeper, of the changes that have come over the planet, destroying the old structures familiar and dear to imperialism, and establishing new ones, alien and hateful to it. This fear gave rise to the *political psychology of the world policeman,* defender of outdated systems, guardian and protector of reaction throughout the world, and engendered the claim of the right to impose upon other peoples a way of life and thought, a political system, and even leaders pleasing to American capital.

However, the plans to employ military force to reorganize the world in the manner desired by the Washington guardians of human destinies were not fated to be realized.

The rapid recovery and further advance of the Soviet economy dissipated the expectations of "economic collapse" of socialism. The atomic monopoly of the United States, one of the cornerstones of all American military-political plans, did collapse. The testing of a thermonuclear weapon in the USSR in 1953 was of decisive significance in this regard. A second blow against American plans, no less powerful, was dealt by the Soviet successes in rocketry, which put an end to the illusion of the "invulnerability" of the United States and to the advantages that it enjoyed at the time thanks to its geographic position. Another world war, which the imperialist circles of the United States were even recently able to see as a natural continuation—"the ultimate argument"—of their policy, now became equivalent to suicide.

Other principles of U.S. foreign policy strategy also proved to be undermined. One of them was the bogey of the "Communist threat," with the aid of which Washington wished to unite its allies and mobilize the American people for an anti-Soviet crusade. But the "general mobilization" of the peoples for the struggle against communism broke down ingloriously.

In the first place, the attitude toward socialism underwent a basic change in many parts of the world. A number of countries irrevocably took a new path of development, and a worldwide socialist system came into being. Socialism became increasingly popular.

In the second place, the consistently peaceloving policy of the USSR and the other socialist countries convincingly demonstrated to all peoples, including those of countries allied with the United States, the absurdity of the propagandistic fairy tale of the "communist threat," with which American political figures sought to justify military preparations.

The carefully erected structure of "global" policy broke down under the impact of new realities of world history.

The dichotomy between the foreign policy strategy of U.S. imperialism and the conditions of the contemporary world was already generally apparent by the end of the 1950's and the beginning of the 1960's. As early as that time, a broad discussion of the root problems of foreign policy developed in the United States. Even in government circles, people began to understand that the gap between the premises of the foreign policy strategy of the U.S. and the actual conditions of the rapidly changing world was constantly widening. However, it soon became clear that the reorientation engendered by this basically amounted to a modernization of means and tactics, but did not touch upon the objectives and strategy of foreign policy.

In all fairness, it must be noted that divergent views were advanced in the debates. As an example, one can cite the outlook of Senator Fulbright, presented in his book *Old Myths and New Realities*, published as early as

1964. Even at that date, he posed the question of the need for a fundamental reexamination of many time-hallowed bases of U.S. foreign policy, and for bringing them into accord with changing reality. Senator Fulbright directed particular attention to the "paradoxical contradiction between the increase in national military might and the decline in the degree to which national security is guaranteed." [All non-Russian quotations are retranslated—Editors.] "To equate security and the quantity of arms," he wrote prophetically, "can only drag us into an accelerating arms race, lead to a rise in international tension and, accordingly, to a decline in security. Nor is it out of the question that we might possess overwhelming military superiority and still face erosion of our power and influence in the world."[1]

It was not only spokesmen of the "traditional" opposition in Congress and some political theorists who called many aspects of U.S. foreign policy strategy into question. Analogous views were also expressed by certain figures who played a role of considerable importance in shaping the country's course in foreign policy. President Kennedy, for example, not only declared that thermonuclear war was unacceptable to the United States, and spoke for reduction of tension in Soviet-American relations; he also came to recognize that no "American solution" of international problems was possible and that no single country could govern worldwide processes. However, it was the other trend that won out in the internal struggle within the ruling circles of the United States.

In the classical style of imperialist politics, reliance upon military might remained the point of departure in the search for new solutions. Nor could it be otherwise, once the ruling circles of the United States refused to consider abandoning their "global" pretensions. Under such circumstances it was difficult to withstand the temptation to seek new military means in the struggle to enforce these claims. One after another, studies by military and political theorists (Maxwell Taylor, Henry Kissinger, and others) made their appearance, with the very latest formulas for employing the armed might of the United States. Finally, the new doctrine, initially presented by General Taylor in 1956 to the Joint Chiefs of Staff, gained official adoption in 1961. It gained fame as the doctrine of "flexible response."

Officially, the essence of this doctrine consists in bit-by-bit application of force, i.e., of varying dosages of it, to correspond with the needs dictated by the struggle for American objectives in one or another theater of war. Proceeding from a recognition of the impossibility of achieving success by a blow directed at the principal enemy, the Soviet Union, the creators of this policy placed reliance on limited, local wars, military actions political in nature, and also on large-scale use of various kinds of subversion. Their purpose is either to prevent sociopolitical changes in various parts of the world or to proceed to the attack, "nibbling" at the socialist camp and at

---

1. W. Fulbright, *Old Myths and New Realities* (New York, 1964), pp. 49–50.

the zone of countries liberated from colonialism, at their periphery, in places where, for one reason or another, a weak link can be found (or created).

Many welcomed this doctrine, seeing in it a sign of a move toward realism, an abandonment of the prior doctrine of "massive retaliation" that suspended over the world the sword of thermonuclear war, which was to be dropped in case of any turn of events undesirable for the United States. But the realism of the "flexible response" doctrine was in many respects no more than apparent. In fact, the adventurism characteristic of earlier U.S. foreign policy doctrines is inherent in it as well.

Above all, it soon became clear that the new military doctrine did not negate, but rather supplemented, the old one. This is seen particularly in the very program of the U.S. military buildup since the beginning of the 1960's. It is undeniable that, under this program, intensified deployment began of "conventional" armed forces, with the objective of providing "small" and "medium" doses of application of force (according to this doctrine, conventional arms had to be sufficient to wage "two and a half" conflicts: two large and one small). But at the same time, the biggest leap ahead occurred in the development of strategic forces—nuclear weapons and various (primarily rocket) means of delivery—i.e., the weaponry of "massive retaliation" that was necessary primarily for the so-called "central war" (i.e., the war with the USSR).[2]

To justify this staggering program, a wide-scale propaganda campaign was launched on the "missile gap" by which the USA lagged behind the USSR. In evaluating it several years later, Robert MacNamara, former Secretary of Defense, admitted that the program for building the strategic forces of the United States was an "overreaction" and was not justified by the actual situation.

However that may be, the strategic arms race was whipped up, and the consequences of that step are to be seen to this day. An unmistakable contradiction appeared between certain political steps taken by President Ken-

2. The following table is based on the data of the Institute of Strategic Studies in London.

	Type of weapon	
Year	Intercontinental ballistic missiles	"Polaris" missiles aboard submarines
1961	63	96
1962	294	144
1963	424	224
1964	834	416
1965	854	496
1966	904	592
1967	1,054	656

nedy, testifying to his readiness to normalize relations with the USSR, and the rapid growth of those forms of arms that could only be destined for the notorious "central war."

This emphasis on armaments manufacture essentially far from contradicts the doctrine of "flexible response." If one gives it some thought, that doctrine is by its very mechanism unthinkable without a large arsenal of nuclear rockets and without blackmail—including adventurist acts as an inherent component. Never mind the carefully worked-out system of "escalation" of conflicts, the ultimate stage of which is always world war; the very possibility of conducting "local" wars and broad operations of a police character involves bluff, intimidation, and balancing on the brink of thermonuclear war. It is precisely these elements in the policy of "flexible response" that are called upon to assure that the instigators of "local" and "police" wars will go unpunished.

Many American political figures made no attempt to hide this. Walt Rostow, who was President Johnson's Special Advisor for National Security Affairs, once wrote, for example, that the job was to make the other side refrain from action, "fearful" that a given act would lead to a nuclear conflict. "To make this credible," he adds, "is as difficult a task as man has ever faced . . . . The only means that can instill such a conviction is if the President of the United States is prepared to anticipate a nuclear war and has in fact moved along that road."[3]

Another innovation of American foreign policy strategy in the 1960's was the policy of "bridge-building." At the time it was announced, it could still be regarded by many as a kind of response to the challenge of peaceful coexistence hurled by the socialist states. It is no accident that, at the outset, it was subjected to a fire of criticism by the extreme Right in the USA itself (it should be said that certain liberal spokesmen interpret this policy in this way to the present day).

However, the "bridge-building" policy soon presented itself in different dress: essentially as a platform for extended subversive activity aimed at dissolving the socialist commonwealth and undermining the socialist social system.

The inspirers of this policy demonstrated a remarkable capacity to distort and pervert any ideas they touched. Even generally accepted forms of international communication, which had enjoyed a good reputation for centuries—such as trade, cultural and scientific-technical ties, etc.—when put through the meat-grinder of the thinking of such people, are immediately transformed into their opposites, into evil weapons of subversive activity.

Z. Brzezinski has particularly distinguished himself in that walk of life. On his lips, the undermining of world socialism would be facilitated by no

3. *Look*, December 12, 1967, p. 30.

less than . . . peace and the normalization of the world situation. "Only in an international atmosphere free of tension," he declares, "can the hidden rough spots and contradictions from which the East suffers become politically important." A moderation of international tension, he says, "would unquestionably challenge" communism.[4]

One must approach such statements and declarations very soberly. In the first place, it should be seen that they simply contain a good deal of irresponsible propaganda chatter. It is especially irresponsible because questions having a direct bearing on such enormous contemporary political problems as the preservation of peace and normalization of Soviet-American relations become objects of petty and quite unscrupulous gambles.[5]

At the same time, statements such as those adduced here speak rather eloquently about the notions with which the policy of "bridge-building" was associated by many of its inspirers—profoundly antisocialist notions having the purpose of undermining the socialist system and doing harm to socialism.

Thus, the "updating" of foreign policy carried out by Washington in the 1960's came down to the following:

An attempt was made to perfect methods to politically utilize military force on a global scale (i.e., as a means of political pressure and blackmail); and chosen as targets for direct application of force were opponents with whom clashes would not have suicidal consequences for the United States;

With respect to those whom Washington regards as its primary adversaries (the Soviet Union and other socialist countries), attempts were made to find and put in motion a set of other "instruments" of policy for the purpose of accomplishing what cannot be achieved by military means under present circumstances: the weakening of socialism, the undermining of its foundations and, in the final analysis, its destruction.

One of the results of the 1960's lies specifically in the fact that attempts to "modernize" the foreign policy of the United States suffered failure in both these directions.

Above all, efforts to put into practice the policy of subverting socialism were particularly unsuccessful. The events of recent years have shown the

4. Z. Brzezinski, *Alternative to Partition* (New York, 1965), p. 121.
5. Efforts to stake its own claim to all ideals and demands enjoying the broad support of the masses have become one of the principal tendencies in imperialist propaganda. It attempts, by all possible means, to instill the notion that not only peace, the easing of international tension, and the development of economic, scientific-technical, and cultural contacts with the West, but improvement in the well-being of the working people, the rise in education and culture of the peoples of the socialist countries, and the development of socialist democracy run counter to the interests of socialism and contribute to its "erosion." The intent of such ideological diversions is obvious: to appropriate to themselves and to depict as foreign and even hostile to socialism those very ideals and principles that strengthen the power of attraction of that social system and arouse increasing millions of people to the struggle against imperialism.

unsoundness of calculations that the Socialist countries and Communist parties would be indifferent observers of the efforts of internal counter-revolution and international reaction, designed to "erode" socialism and return the lands of socialism to the bosom of the capitalist system. It turned out that efforts of that kind yield the United States nothing but an increase in international tension.

Nor did Washington succeed in finding a means of implementing its former policy of "from a position of strength" in a manner that would bring real dividends and at the same time eliminate the risk of major international complications endangering the United States itself. There is no way of doing this. The threat of world thermonuclear war today lies not only in that some lunatic may "press the button"; it is in the very policy of "local" military adventures, nuclear blackmail, an unrestrained arms race, and high-handed intervention in the affairs of other countries.

This policy is itself capable of directing the development of international relations into a channel in which it will no longer be possible to retain control over events.

In this sense there can no longer be any purely "local" conflicts and wars in today's world; they all have far-reaching international consequences. This is testified to by the experience of the U.S. adventure in Vietnam, which frustrated the relaxation of tension then under way, complicated the international situation, whipped up the arms race, and produced growing instability in the world arena.

The principal consequence of the 1960's for the United States consisted in the fact that its policy not only did not help it advance in the struggle for the strategic goals set by Washington, but actually undermined the country's international position and complicated the situation at home.

Of course, in recent years, the process of sociopolitical development in the world has been complex and contradictory. While the revolutionary, anti-imperialist forces have on the whole had major successes, certain difficulties have come to light in their ranks—due not only to the stance taken by Peking but also to objective complications arising in the creative tasks of the revolution in a number of countries, and due to mistakes committed by individual detachments of fighters against imperialism.

But the "slyness" of history lies in the fact that, in our times, even individual failures and losses of one of the sides—in this case, the anti-imperialist front—do not assure victories and "profits" to the other side. In today's world, events are determined not by the arithmetic of the traditional political game of the great powers, but by the algebra of the complex sociopolitical struggle that has engulfed our planet. This is why, for all the complexities and contradictions of the historical process, the net balance has proved not at all to favor imperialism. Recent years have brought the United States a further weakening of its political positions, and the collapse of all efforts to stop the profound processes under way in the world.

II

The shameful war of the United States in Vietnam is a real catalyst of these phenomena. Many factors revealing the bankruptcy of the "innovations" in foreign policy thinking in the U.S. in recent years have been concentrated in the Vietnam war, as if by a focusing lens. Vietnam has served to test both the doctrine of "local" and limited war, the most recent discoveries in the sphere of counterinsurgency, the notorious concept of "escalation," and attempts to play upon differences in the socialist camp. On this level, the Americans have attempted to transform Vietnam into a proving ground not only for new military equipment but for new political techniques. The results have proved to be sad.

When it took the path of aggression in Vietnam, the U.S. counted on a quick, small war. Even in October 1963, the White House announced that "most of the military undertakings by the United States will be completed by the end of 1965."[6] Instead, the U.S. got a protracted, bloody war, perhaps the most difficult of any it has ever had occasion to wage.

The United States wished, in Vietnam, to give an object lesson to all peoples by demonstrating its readiness and capacity to employ force. No such lesson was given. On the contrary, the entire world saw that even the mightiest of all capitalist countries was incapable of performing the mission of policeman it had taken upon itself when it encountered the will and heroism of a revolutionary people reinforced by broad international sympathy and support.

The war in Vietnam produced enormous tension in the entire U.S. military machine and had severe economic consequences. It worsened the negative balance of payments and contributed to a weakening in the international position of the American dollar and to an acute international currency crisis. The war in Vietnam accelerated the growth of a budgetary deficit and of inflation and taxes, and led to a cutting of appropriations for social needs. The widely advertised program of building a "great society" ran aground; moreover, as is now obvious, it was adopted not out of good intentions but as a response to rising domestic pressure. Social contradictions within the country are intensifying, and the most acute of them are already breaking to the surface in the form of serious shocks.

The aggression in Vietnam seriously undermined the political position of the United States in the international arena. Whereas the Americans had succeeded in using the war in Korea to strengthen their military alliances, the war in Vietnam has shaken them. The economic expansion and foreign political adventurism of the United States has produced a sharp exacerbation of interimperialist contradictions.

Washington's gamble on differences in the socialist system also was

6. E. Weintal and C. Bartlett, *Facing the Brink* (New York, 1967), p. 90.

trumped. The geographic remoteness of Vietnam from most of the socialist countries and the refusal of the Chinese leadership to engage in joint actions did not prevent the socialist states from giving effective support to the heroic people of Vietnam.

The war in Vietnam, we know, is by no means the first imperialist adventure engaged in by the United States. Nor is it the first unsuccessful adventure: one might recall the failure of the armed intervention in Cuba in 1961, not to speak of a series of earlier examples. But in at least one respect the significance of the failures that have overtaken U.S. imperialism in Vietnam goes beyond everything it ever had to encounter before. This time there was revealed the untenability not only of the plans for the "local" adventure next on its list, but of Washington's entire "global" political strategy.

The basis of this strategy has always been reliance on military force. The war in Vietnam demonstrated that military might alone is no longer able to bring the United States victory not only in the struggle against its "major" enemy but even on the periphery, in a struggle against an opponent which, by all the traditional canons of military art, might have been evaluated as far inferior to the United States. It turned out that even the enormous military power created by the United States has its limits, and that these limits are considerably narrower than required by Washington's political plans.[7]

No less important a foundation of U.S. foreign policy is the mission of "world policeman" it has taken upon itself. It is clear today that Washington no longer has the strength to carry out that mission, and that the attempt to implant and preserve regimes satisfactory to it everywhere in the world has less and less support both in the United States and beyond its borders.

The present President of the United States recognized this during the election campaign, albeit in guarded form. In an article published in the October 1967 issue of *Foreign Affairs*, he wrote: "I am not arguing that the day is past when the United States would respond militarily to a commu-

7. At the end of 1968, the volume *Agenda for the Nation,* something of an admonition to the incoming Administration, was published in the United States. One of its authors was Henry Kissinger, who apparently had no inkling, when the book was written, that he was fated to occupy one of the key foreign policy posts in that Administration. He wrote: "Throughout history, military might has been regarded as an absolute value. Statesmen have held it to be a primary and essential task to bring about the further growth of this power. As recently as twenty-five years ago it would have been impossible to conceive that a country might dispose of entirely too much military might, such as to be inapplicable for political purposes. . . . The paradox of contemporary military force lies in the fact that the gigantic increase in force has undermined the possibility of employing it for political purposes. . . ." "In other words," Kissinger emphasized, "power is no longer automatically convertible into influence." *Agenda for the Nation,* The Brookings Institution, Washington, 1968, p. 589.

nist threat in the less stable parts of the world, or that unilateral actions in response to unilateral requests are out of the question. But other countries must recognize that, in the future, the role of the United States as world policeman is limited. They can count on rapid and effective help from the U.S. only if they themselves create machinery meeting two requirements: (a) the states of the region will have undertaken rapid collective military efforts to liquidate, with their own forces, the potential threat, and these efforts have failed to yield the necessary result; and (b) a collective request to the United States for assistance follows."[8]

The undermining of these foundations of U.S. global strategy has had far-reaching political consequences. The yawning chasm has been revealed between goals and capabilities, between aspirations and potentialities, between a policy shaped over many years and the realities of the contemporary international situation. Many prominent American researchers come to the same conclusion.[9]

Thus, on the threshold of the 1970's, an objective situation has developed that imperatively demands serious changes in the foreign policy pursued by the United States. The course of events is taking such a turn that delay in making changes or, even more, attempts to reinforce the previous line of policy will inevitably deepen the crisis of Washington's foreign policy and engender more and more new problems and difficulties.

And here we move to the second question: To what degree will these demands of the situation influence the course of U.S. foreign policy in the 1970's?

One would wish, naturally, to answer this question as concretely as possible—not in the sense, of course, of attempting to divine precisely and in all details the forms and time periods within which possible changes in U.S. foreign policy will occur. Another question is involved: determination of the most likely direction of such changes, basing our analysis on the actual situation.

To do otherwise would mean to give the simplest kind of answer: that the U.S. remains, and will for the foreseeable future remain, an imperialist power, which will of course pursue an imperialist policy. But the point is that imperialism, despite all the tendencies built into that system and its policy, is able, both within the country and on the international arena, to

8. *Foreign Affairs*, October 1967, p. 114.
9. For example, one of the "patriarchs" of political science in the United States, Hans Morgenthau, wrote in 1969: "If one were to attempt to describe American foreign policy in a single sentence, it might be said that during the past decade or so it has lived on the intellectual capital accumulated during the famous fifteen weeks in the spring of 1947, when the concept of containment, the Truman Doctrine, and the Marshall Plan laid the foundations of the new American policy, and that today this capital has been exhausted. . . . This policy has become obsolete, and the United States has thus far been unable to develop a new policy, capable of grappling successfully with the problems of this century." H. Morgenthau, *A New Foreign Policy for the United States* (New York, 1969), p. 3.

go only so far as it is permitted to—permitted by the objective situation and by the strength of the resistance of its adversaries.

It is precisely this understanding of political reality that underlies the tactics of the communist movement and of all anti-imperialist forces at the present stage. Their program of struggle against the omnipotence of monopolies, fascist reaction, colonialism, and national oppression, against aggression and war, takes as its point of departure that many democratic demands can already be successfully implemented under the conditions existing today, and that, to accomplish this, there is no need to wait for fundamental sociopolitical changes throughout the world.

The validity of such an approach has long been demonstrated. The change in the world relationship of forces in favor of socialism, and the consistent and determined struggle of the working masses, have created serious obstacles to imperialist aspirations and have made it possible to achieve many major successes. These successes include the fact that it has been possible to prevent acute conflicts from turning into a new world war, and in many cases to cut short or prevent imperialist aggression.

Serious obstacles to the imperialist policy of the United States appeared in the international arena as early as the 1950's. In the 1960's, the relationship of forces in the world arena continued to change in the same direction. In dealing with the essence of these changes and their influence upon the policy of imperialism, Comrade L. I. Brezhnev, in his speech at the International Conference of Communist and Workers' parties in Moscow in June 1969, emphasized: "The rising might of socialism, the abolition of colonial regimes, and the onslaught of the workers' movement are wielding a constantly increasing influence on the internal processes and policy of imperialism. Many important features of contemporary imperialism are to be explained by the fact that it has been compelled to adapt itself to new conditions, to the conditions of the struggle of the two systems."[10]

The matter at issue is essentially that of further limiting the freedom of action of imperialism—above all, U.S. imperialism.

In this regard, the development of events in the 1960's was marked by still another very serious change. Earlier, Washington's foreign policy had encountered obstacles of a purely international nature (the might of the Soviet Union and of the other lands of socialism and their determination to resist aggression, the opposition of the peoples of other countries to Washington's imperialist aspirations, the unwillingness of the allies of the United States to be drawn into risky adventures, and so forth). Now serious obstacles to this course have arisen within the country as well.

The present domestic situation in the United States is a major and important subject deserving special examination. In the present situation, we

10. *Mezhdunarodnoe Soveshchanie kommunisticheskikh i rabochikh partii*, Politizdat, Moscow, 1969, p. 44.

are interested in only a single aspect of it: the influence that the exacerbation of domestic problems has on Washington's foreign policy. There can hardly be any difference of opinion. The worsening of many of these problems was associated, directly or indirectly, with "excesses in foreign policy"—costly transoceanic adventures and the extravagance of the arms race. It means that solution of these problems demands at least a partial reduction in such "excesses."

This holds for inflation, which is intensified by the enormous expenditures for military and foreign policy purposes; it holds even more for the problems of the black population (one important aspect is the serious economic position of the Negroes), of poverty, and of the cities (to overcome the crisis of American cities would alone demand tremendous capital investments). Of course, the U.S. has managed to live with these problems for a long time. But what is new in the present situation is that it is becoming more and more difficult to do that. Many old problems are today arising anew in the sense that they are generating extensive sociopolitical manifestations and are threatening serious internal upheavals.

It was only in the 1960's that Americans became convinced that even so rich a country as the United States could not simultaneously have both "guns" and "butter." Under these conditions, demands for "butter" merged with demands to limit the production of "guns." This intensified the protest campaign against the war in Vietnam, a war that is costing American taxpayers about $30 billion per year. This has also changed the attitude toward the arms race, which not long ago was regarded by many as an economic blessing, one that saved the country from a depression. The argument that the arms race is an instrument for undermining the Soviet economy also ceased to be operative. In this connection, McGeorge Bundy, former advisor to the President and now head of the Ford Foundation, concludes: "The course of the discussion about the ABM indicates that that notion will apparently never gain popularity."[11] Disclosing the reasons for this change in the thinking of many Americans, the prominent American specialist on problems of arms control, Professor G. Rathjens, writes: "It would be an error to assume that by making the appropriate expenditures for arms, the U.S. could compel the USSR to accept the status of a second-rate power because of its lower economic and industrial potential. Long before such a situation was reached, the development of the U.S. itself would slow down, and the demands for new military projects would have serious consequences for American society."[12]

It is important to emphasize something else. Aside from economic considerations, moral and political factors have begun to play a more noticeable role in the stands taken against the arms race and an expansionist

11. *Foreign Affairs*, October 1969.
12. G. Rathjens, *The Future of the Strategic Arms Race: Options for the 1970's* (New York, 1969), p. 31.

foreign policy. The policy of recent years was unsuccessful not only from the standpoint of its practical results. It helped to dispel, in the eyes of a considerable part of the American public, myths that had been used to conceal imperialist aspirations. Faith in the "nobility" of the mission that the U.S. is carrying out—according to American propaganda, "defense" of democracy and freedom—proved to be seriously undermined. An increasing number of Americans are ceasing to believe that the arms race and the rise in militarization are a necessary response to a "threat from without." Thus, it is not only the economic and military resources but the moral "resources" of American policy that prove to have been stretched too far. The youth and black movements, whose participants deny the very right of the U.S. to dictate its will to other peoples, provide especially clear evidence of this.

A situation has arisen in which continuation or, beyond that, further activation of a policy aimed at strengthening the military might and international influence of the United States is beginning, in the opinion of many sober Americans, to threaten serious domestic complications and the undermining of the foundations of the "national power of the USA." From this derive the deep differences in the ruling circles themselves, in the "political elite" as such.

Its liberal component is speaking out more actively than before for a serious review of foreign policy, including the speediest possible end to the war in Vietnam, limitation of the arms race, and reduction of the scale of American obligations abroad. The demands of these political forces are taking an increasingly anti-militarist direction.[13] Also noteworthy is the fact that even some conservative political figures, seriously frightened by growing domestic difficulties, are beginning to express similar viewpoints.

The marked activation of the opposition has provided the basis for diverse and often contradictory evaluations of the political situation in the U.S. Some observers have hastened to declare that serious changes in the political course of the USA are an accomplished fact, and have predicted a reduction in the military and diplomatic obligations of Washington abroad for the immediate future. Others, on the other hand, hold that essentially nothing has changed or can change, and that the course of the United States will remain what it was.

It seems to us that both extreme evaluations of the present political situation in the United States are unjustified.

The former overlooks the fact that, simultaneous with the activation of the opposition, the pressure of opposing forces has also grown, above all that of the so-called military-industrial complex, of reactionary groups inti-

13. Thus, Professor Galbraith recently offered a complete program for combating the militarists and the military-industrial complex, a program to which, as far as one may judge, there has been a broad response in the country. J. Galbraith, "How to Control the Military," *Harper's Magazine,* June 1969.

mately connected with the Pentagon and with war industry, and of the right-wing elements in both bourgeois parties (these groups have their representatives in the present Administration and exercise no small influence upon it). The results of the 1968 elections, in which about 10 million votes went to Wallace, indicate that the most extreme reaction consolidated its position. The voices of those who call for accelerating the arms race and intensifying the aggressive, expansionist course of foreign policy—essentially for a return to the period of the most acute "cold war"—are being heard today perhaps more loudly than in the recent past. Facts confirm that what has happened in the political life of the United States has not at all been a shift "to the left," but rather a polarization of forces and an exacerbation of the struggle.[14]

At the same time, one must not underestimate the importance of the activation of the opposition calling for a revision of American foreign policy. Its strength lies not only in having a considerable number of votes in the Senate and in the support it has from many political and public figures and scholars with great prominence and authority in the United States. Even more important is the fact that the line taken by this opposition expresses the objective needs of the situation and is finding response among the broad public. This is transforming it into a political factor capable, to one degree or another, of influencing the formation of Washington's foreign policy.

It may be stated that a complex and, it would appear, not very stable balance of political forces has now taken shape in Washington. The struggle between these forces is becoming sharper, and its course will largely determine the further development of American foreign policy.

These aspects of the situation influence the policy of the present Administration. In the opinion of many American observers, the Administration is aware of the serious difficulties that U.S. foreign policy has encountered ("As the new Administration has apparently understood," writes Professor Stanley Hoffmann, forecasting U.S. policy in the 1970's, "the former political course led us into a dead end").[15] However, the passing months have not yet shown that serious practical conclusions are being drawn from this.

14. The struggle between the two trends is also under way with respect to fundamental questions of domestic policy. One of them is the line aiming at reforms designed to prevent further exacerbation of the most "explosive" problems of contemporary America (the problems of the Negroes, poverty, the cities, etc.). The measures proposed by the proponents of the other line tend rather to be aimed at the symptoms instead of the genuine causes of today's social difficulties and problems, whether they involve "tightening the screws," repression of the Negro movement and of the youth "rebellion," etc. These are the two typical responses of the bourgeoisie to any serious economic or sociopolitical crisis (both these trends appeared in what might be called polished form in the 1930s; the same severe crisis brought Roosevelt to power in the United States, with his reformist New Deal platform, and Hitler to power in Germany, with his attempts to solve all problems by fascist repression and war).

15. *Life*, April 14, 1969, p. 66.

Spokesmen for the present Administration, both in the election campaign and after coming to power, have spoken more than once, for example, of the need to reduce the "involvement" of the United States in the affairs of other countries (particularly the kind of "involvement" that might result in being drawn into such serious military conflicts as the war in Vietnam). However, there are virtually no real steps to be seen along this line. As far as Vietnam is concerned, in the positions taken on that question, there have been essentially no changes capable of opening the door to political settlement of the conflict.

The leaders of the present Administration entered the election with the demand for achieving decisive "superiority" over the Soviet Union in armaments. Subsequently, however, the term "superiority" was replaced by "sufficiency." But the leaders of the Pentagon are, as before, planning to force the arms race. The actions of the Nixon Administration in that regard are highly contradictory: on the one hand, it is making certain reductions in the current arms budget (small, and in matters of secondary importance); on the other, it takes decisions to build new and expensive weapons systems (the Safeguard ABM; the MIRV multiple, individually targeted warheads).

On the matter of relations with the USSR, the leadership of the new Administration has announced a change "from the era of confrontation to the era of negotiation." However, in practice, this change is making slow progress. It took more than six months for the new Administration to agree to conduct strategic arms limitation talks. Contacts with respect to the Near East began sooner; but because of the position taken by Washington, no prospects for settlement of that situation have as yet opened up. What is most important, no changes whatever have occurred in the practical politics of the United States pointing to a real desire to improve relations with the USSR.

Of course, the new Administration has been in power for only a year. However, many observers note "slowness" in the process of its getting down to work and developing a policy. But it would appear that this is not simply a matter of the difficulties of the "initial period." What is most important is the sharpness of the struggle that has developed around fundamental questions of policy, and the strength of the resistance to policy changes of a positive nature.

In the book already cited, *Agenda for the Nation*, the present Presidential Advisor on National Security Affairs, H. Kissinger, wrote the following with respect to the problems facing the new Administration: "Even under the happiest concatenation of circumstances, the new Administration will face crises. In virtually every corner of the world we have spent our fixed capital—we have rarely dealt with underlying problems and have warded off only the most immediate problems. The difficulties will probably multiply when it becomes clear that one of the consequences of the war in Vietnam will be a stubborn unwillingness on the part of Americans to be drawn into conflicts overseas.

"The new Administration has the right to demand understanding and sympathy from the American people. But it must base its demands not upon smooth superficial answers to hard questions. It must, in the first place, ask the right questions. The Administration must understand that in the sphere of foreign policy we will never be able to promote the establishment of a stable and viable world order if, to begin with, we do not draw up our notions about that order."[16]

As far as one can judge from the American press, Kissinger did not abandon this standpoint after he took his official post. As early as the summer of 1969, the following statement by him appeared in the press: "An important task facing the government is that of creating a new foundation of theory for the foreign policy of the United States. We have reached a time when the notions by which we were guided in the postwar period are dying away."[17]

Statements such as these, however, leave many questions unanswered. And this is not only because it is unclear whether those who may have a decisive influence upon the development of Washington's foreign policy share Kissinger's viewpoint. Even more important is whether the feeling of a need for changes will be embodied in actual policy. And even if this is the case, in what direction will these changes proceed: in the direction demanded by the objective situation or once again in the direction of perfecting the methods and means of fighting for goals that have long since demonstrated their unreality?

Many years ago the German military theorist Clausewitz presented a classical analysis of an international situation with a certain similarity to the present. It was the situation brought about by the Great French Revolution, which the monarchs of Europe attempted to crush by force. Clausewitz explains that these efforts failed because the forces of the old world "sought to use customary methods to create a counterbalance to new and overwhelming forces. All these are errors of policy. Is it possible to foresee and correct such errors if one continues to think in terms of a purely military understanding of events?" "Of course not," was his answer to that question.[18]

This evaluation of the actions of the forces of the old world in the period of bourgeois revolutions is even more pertinent in our era—the era of transition from capitalism to socialism, of national liberation revolutions and broad democratic movements. Under these conditions, serious changes in international relations have occurred. To the changes resulting from

16. *Agenda for the Nation,* p. 614.
17. *The New York Times Magazine,* June 1, 1969, p. 54.
18. K. Clausewitz, *On War,* translation from the German (Moscow, 1934), p. 565.

World War II, there have been added the profound social and political changes of the postwar quarter-century.

Against the background of these changes, the goals of the United States have become manifestly unattainable and untenable: there is no Power that can contain the pressure for changes associated with social progress. Even less can it turn back the course of history. Nor has reliance on the use of force, whether "total" or "limited," justified itself. And still another fact has become apparent: the United States has quite enough problems not only in the international arena but within the country. And the old foreign policy is only rendering their solution more difficult.

A great deal depends, both for the U.S. itself and for the international situation as a whole, upon the conclusions that will be drawn in Washington from all these facts.

The decade now beginning opens many new opportunities. For the United States, they will consist primarily in the fact that a growing portion of its public is beginning to understand—more deeply and better than before—the problems facing their country, the reasons for its failures, the real sources of its weaknesses and strengths.

But the 1970's can also be years of serious dangers. The decade that has passed provides a certain notion of the possible nature and scale of such dangers.

The choice America must make is quite serious, perhaps too serious to be determined entirely by the wishes of the group now at the helm of power or by the advice of the experts helping them—be they the most highly qualified and farseeing. The answer to the question as to which path that country will follow in the 1970's will, in the final analysis, depend upon the course of the complex political struggle in the United States itself, a struggle that is developing under the influence of both domestic and foreign policy factors.

13.

The Revised "Two Camps" Doctrine in Soviet Foreign Policy

R. JUDSON MITCHELL

THE DECADE OF THE 1960's appears, in retrospect, to have been a crisis period for the Soviet Union and the socialist commonwealth, marked by a number of spectacular failures in foreign policy, most of which were associated with the initiatives of Nikita Khrushchev. Eight major areas of Soviet failure may be pointed out: (1) the economic decline which affected the entire East European subsystem in the early 1960's; (2) the political fragmentation of the East European subsystem, featuring the cases of Rumania and Czechoslovakia; (3) the alienation and withdrawal of China from the Soviet bloc; (4) the general breakdown of cohesion in the world communist movement; (5) setbacks in Soviet relations with the Third World, especially in Africa south of the Sahara; (6) the Cuban missile crisis and the subsequent loss of Soviet prestige in terms of both great-power and world revolutionary politics; (7) the absence of payoff by way of a political settlement in Central Europe from Khrushchev's pressure tactics vis-à-vis Berlin (although this situation was somewhat stabilized by erection of the Berlin Wall); and (8) the disastrous outcome of the Arab-Israeli conflict of 1967 for Soviet aspirations in the Middle East.

The Soviet leadership, not surprisingly, subjected its foreign policy to an "agonizing reappraisal"; the second half of the decade was marked by a gradual, although sometimes violent, reorientation of policy. The main lines of the resulting new approach are now clear. Its most striking feature is a

Reprinted by permission from *ORBIS*, Spring 1972, pp. 21–34. Copyright by the Foreign Policy Research Institute.

much stronger emphasis on military power as an instrument of foreign policy. There are several notable indications of this: the impressive rise in military expenditures in the Soviet budget since 1965; strenuous and apparently successful efforts to establish nuclear parity with the United States; expansion of the Soviet navy and, particularly, development of Soviet naval power in the Indian Ocean and the Mediterranean; the deployment of nearly one million men along the Sino-Soviet frontier; the suppression of the Czechoslovak experiment by military force; and the increasing coordination of, and reliance upon, the Warsaw Treaty Organization.

The Soviets have also sought to restore the lost cohesion of the world communist movement. They have had some moderate success in this endeavor, highlighted by the 1969 Moscow meeting of parties and the establishment of closer contacts with some of the nonruling parties, especially that of France, where the expulsion of Roger Garaudy has pointed toward a closer rapport with the Moscow line. More important initiatives during this period include the alliance with India, which prepared the way for the favorable outcome of the recent Indian-Pakistani war; overtures toward normalization in Central Europe, culminating in the 1970 treaties between the German Democratic Republic and Soviet Union and the Federal Republic of Germany and the 1971 four-power Berlin agreement; and the continuation of certain aspects of peaceful coexistence policy, mainly in regard to nuclear non-proliferation and control and the attempted expansion of technical and trade contacts with the United States and other Western countries. The only other major area of interest has been the Middle East, where the USSR has gone to great lengths to redress the Arab-Israeli military balance and where the Soviets' continued presence exacerbates tensions in what is perhaps the world's most sensitive trouble spot.

Soviet policy and behavior over the last seven years thus gives much credence to Chinese charges that the Soviet Union's motivations are simply those of a great power and lacking in revolutionary substance. Moscow's approach to international politics during this period involves a mixture of conflict and accommodation and appears on the surface to be geared more to a somewhat restrictive conception of Soviet national interest than to the promotion of world revolution. This, of course, would be nothing new, as amply demonstrated by the "socialism in one country," Popular Front and Nazi-Soviet Pact phases of Stalinist foreign policy. But while this rather superficial interpretation, which is favored both by Peking and by many Western circles, may indeed have validity, it can at best demonstrate only the continuities in Soviet policy and could, perhaps, be utilized in developing a cyclical theory of Soviet international behavior. Such an interpretation can tell us nothing about what, if anything, is new in Soviet motivations governing foreign policy. For answers to questions of this sort we must turn to Soviet ideology.

Soviet policymakers operate within the framework of general systemic norms that require the justification of behavior in terms of Marxist-Leninist ideology. The ideology does not, however, simply serve a legitimating function; it also provides operational guidelines. The policymaker or ideological spokesman must relate a continuously changing social reality to the constants of the ideology. From a purely theoretical standpoint; the only constant in Marxism-Leninism would appear to be the dialectic. But from a broader ideological perspective, the constants would include the contradictions of capitalism and the historical progression toward the worldwide achievement of socialism and communism. The practical task of the Soviet interpreter is to analyze the changes in development of the socialist system, the capitalist system and the general world political system and relate these to the broader ideological perspective. Major foreign policy departures are then explained on the basis of that analysis. It is thus the Soviet analysis of social development that provides coherence for the general foreign policy line in any given period. Since that analysis varies from period to period, innovative ideological inputs are a common feature of Soviet foreign policy.[1]

In the last several years Soviet foreign policy analysis has been dominated by a revised "two camps" doctrine which differs both qualitatively and quantitatively from the old Stalinist formulation of "two camps" and offers a striking contrast to the "three camps" and "peace zone" analysis of the Khrushchev era.

The "two camps" doctrine of Stalin's day was intimately connected with the concept of "capitalist encirclement": it expressed the reality of the precarious and isolated position of the Soviet Union in a world where capitalism maintained an overwhelming hegemony. When Soviet isolation was most pronounced, as in the "class against class" Comintern period, 1928–1935, "two camps"—the idea of two hostile, implacable, irreconcilable forces confronting each other—was most strongly emphasized. During the early cold war period, starting with the Cominform's campaign against the Marshall Plan in 1947, the "two camps" doctrine was again given pointed emphasis. The balance of forces in the world, while undergoing change, was still favorable to the capitalist camp; "capitalist encirclement" was regarded as a continuing reality.

Khrushchev, in 1959, declared that "capitalist encirclement" of the Soviet Union had ended and that the victory of socialism in the USSR was both "complete and final," with no possibility for the restoration of capitalism.[2]

---

1. Cf. Richard Lowenthal, "Development versus Utopia in Communist Policy," *Survey*, Winter-Spring 1970, pp. 3–27; Robert G. Wesson, "Soviet Ideology: The Necessity of Marxism," *Soviet Studies*, July 1969, pp. 64–70; Vera Pirozhkova, "The Recent Events in Czechoslovakia and the Fundamentals of Soviet Foreign Policy," *Bulletin of the Institute for the Study of the USSR*, October 1968, pp. 5–13.

2. *Pravda*, January 28, 1959, p. 9.

A year later, the end of "capitalist encirclement" was proclaimed for the East European states in the Soviet bloc.[3] The announcement that "capitalist encirclement" had come to an end was based on Khrushchev's analysis of the change in the world balance of forces; from this also he conceived his major theoretical innovations relative to world politics.

Khrushchev made three significant, interrelated contributions to Marxist-Leninist analysis of the relationship between social systems: the concept of "three camps"; the reformulation of the doctrine of "peaceful coexistence"; and the new doctrine concerning the possibility of the "peaceful transition to socialism." According to his reasoning, a vastly enlarged and powerful socialist camp had emerged from the Second World War, to which had been added the anti-imperialist, newly liberated countries which formed a "third camp." Not only were the countries of the "third camp" strongly opposed to imperialism; their developmental needs would necessarily incline them toward socialism. The two camps together constituted the formidable "peace zone." Under these circumstances it would be madness for the imperialists to unleash war. "Peaceful coexistence" was therefore not merely a matter of temporary respite and stabilization, but a quasi-permanent feature of international politics, pending the final collapse of capitalism.[4] Also, as Khrushchev saw it, the changed balance of forces in the world favorable to socialism and unfavorable to imperialism now made possible, in some countries, the "peaceful transition to socialism": here existing democratic institutions could be utilized for the transfer of power and the establishment, in one form or another, of the dictatorship of the proletariat.[5]

It should be noted that Khrushchev did not rule out an eventual polarization of social forces; such a polarization would seem to be implicit in his expectation that "peaceful coexistence" would prepare the way for the triumph of communism. However, his formulation did nullify the *necessity* for a final cataclysmic struggle, and consequently provided an ideological basis for tactical flexibility surpassing any previous development in Marxism-Leninism. But tactical flexibility yielded a low payoff in strategic successes, and the record of foreign policy failures outlined above surely was a major reason for Khrushchev's ouster. In view of that record, it is not surprising that Khrushchev's successors have produced a new formulation of Soviet international relations theory. Still, there appears to be nothing inevitable about the reversion toward the idea of "two camps." The current version of the "two camps" doctrine seems in certain important respects to be less optimistic than the old Stalinist model.

3. Dan N. Jacobs, *The New Communist Manifesto* (New York: Harper, 1961), p. 19.
4. *Pravda*, February 15, 1956, pp. 2–3; *Program of the Communist Party of the Soviet Union* (New York: Crosscurrents Press, 1961), pp. 60–66; W. W. Kulski, *Peaceful Coexistence* (Chicago: Henry Regnery, 1959), pp. 127–137.
5. *Program of the Communist Party of the Soviet Union, op cit.*, pp. 44–45.

The Brezhnev Doctrine

The experimentation of the "Prague Spring," the Soviet intervention in Czechoslovakia, and the repercussions resulting from the crisis triggered the new Soviet formulation, although the Czech crisis was only one of the developments requiring a general theoretical reorientation.

S. Kovalev's front-page article in *Pravda* on September 26, 1968, which initiated the so-called Brezhnev Doctrine, pointed toward a renewed emphasis on "two camps":

> Each Communist Party is free in its application of Marxist-Leninist and socialist principles but it cannot deviate from these principles if it is to remain a Communist Party. This signifies concretely that each Communist Party must, above all, take cognizance of such a crucial fact of our time as the conflict between two antithetical social systems—capitalism and socialism. This conflict is an objective one not dependent upon the will of the people and is determined by the division of the world between two antithetical social systems.

Kovalev also maintained that every Communist Party is responsible not only to its own people but to all socialist countries and to the entire movement of world socialism, which is "indivisible." The sovereignty of any particular socialist country cannot be placed above the interests of the world revolutionary movement. "The weakening of any link in the world socialist system" affects the entire system and this must always be taken into account.

L. I. Brezhnev, in his November 12, 1968 Warsaw speech, further pursued the concept of the "weakest link of socialism" and the idea of "two camps":

> They [the imperialists] are seeking out the weak links in the socialist front, pursuing a course of subversive ideological work inside the socialist countries, attempting to slow dissension, drive wedges between them and encourage and inflame nationalist feelings and tendencies, and are seeking to isolate individual socialist states so that they can seize them by the throat one by one. In short, imperialism is trying to undermine socialism's solidarity precisely as a world system.[6]

The "weakening of links" in the socialist system was attributed to what Brezhnev called "difficulties."[7] This euphemism, subsequently employed by all Soviet spokesmen in references to the "weakest link" problem, was used to describe social phenomena that are otherwise universally identified in

---

6. *Pravda*, November 13, 1968, p. 1. Quoted in *Current Digest of the Soviet Press*, December 4, 1968, p. 3.

7. *Ibid.*

Marxist theory as "contradictions." Marxist theoreticians have in the past made a distinction between antagonistic and nonantagonistic contradictions, the socialist system allegedly being free of the former.[8] It is clear from Brezhnev's account of the "difficulties," however, that he was referring to antagonistic contradictions. Moreover, these contradictions were appearing not at the inception of socialism but at an advanced stage of socialist development.

This critical situation is diagnosed as providing an opening for the imperialists, whose basic strategy is determined by the shift in the world balance of forces. As the contradictions of capitalism increase in intensity, the imperialist camp grows progressively weaker relative to the socialist camp, and the capitalists become desperate. Unable to resort to open warfare due to the nuclear balance and the overall strength of the socialist camp, they must resort to more subtle tactics, variously described by Soviet spokesmen as "peaceful infiltration," "peaceful counter-revolution" and "creeping counter-revolution." If successful (and their failure is not claimed to be historically inevitable), such tactics will result in bourgeois restoration, "reversing the course of history."[9] Such a capitalist offensive is feasible, with the outcome presumably in doubt, "even after creation of the foundations of socialist society."[10] Although the immediate target is the "weakest link of socialism," the capitalist counteroffensive is really aimed at the Soviet Union, the center of the world socialist system.[11]

Brezhnev's prescription for the crisis produced by the "weakening of links" and the capitalist counteroffensive is a fourfold program that indicates clearly the content of the new variant of the "two camps" idea. It calls for:

(1) Intensification of ideological warfare against bourgeois ideology—i.e., revisionism and ideological nonconformity[12]—with renewed emphasis on Lenin's dictum that there are only two ideologies, the bourgeois and the socialist.[13]

(2) Strengthening the role of the Communist Party throughout the socialist commonwealth.

(3) Fostering increased coordination of the activities of the socialist countries in all fields—according to Brezhnev, the "sharper the contra-

8. See Sh. Sanakoev, "The Basis of the Relations Between the Socialist Countries," *International Affairs* (Moscow), July 1958, p. 27.
9. See Brezhnev's speech to the International Parties Conference, *Pravda*, June 8, 1969, pp. 1–4, and A. Sovetov, "The Present Stage in the Struggle Between Socialism and Imperialism," *International Affairs*, November 1968, pp. 3–9.
10. I. Oleinik, "Leninism and the International Significance of the Experience Gained in Socialist Construction," *International Affairs*, February-March 1970, p. 30.
11. Sovetov, *op. cit.*, p. 4.
12. *Pravda*, June 8, 1969, p. 4.
13. See V. I. Lenin, *What Is to be Done?* (New York: International Publishers, 1929), p. 41.

dictions between the new and the old world," the greater becomes the importance of such coordination.[14]

(4) Applying coercion on an international or interparty basis to meet immediate crises caused by the "weakening of links," through a strengthening of the socialist commonwealth's primary coercive arm, the Warsaw Treaty Organizations.[15]

At the Twenty-fourth Congress of the CPSU, Brezhnev stated that the Warsaw Treaty Organization "has been and continues to be the main centre for coordinating the foreign policy activity of the fraternal countries."[16] Earlier, following the restoration and consolidation of system control in Czechoslovakia, he had affirmed the efficacy of coercion under the WTO aegis in dealing with the "weakest link" problem. "Czechoslovakia has been and remains a socialist country," the CPSU leader said in October 1969. "Czechoslovakia has been and remains a firm link in the socialist commonwealth."[17]

It can scarcely be imagined that the events in Czechoslovakia alone, important as they were, produced this toughening of the Moscow line and a major reordering of the Soviet approach to international politics. The Soviet leadership was threatened on various fronts, especially the Chinese; under the circumstances, it was essential to tighten control of the inner bloc.[18] Justifying the tightening in terms of the ideology was equally necessary. What is most interesting about that justification is the centrality of the admission of developmental crisis within the socialist system.

The admission of a developmental crisis points up the difference between the Brezhnevian approach and those of Stalin and Khrushchev. Stalin's "two camps" and "capitalist encirclement" formulation justified internal coercion under conditions of a seriously unfavorable world balance of forces. Although he maintained that contradictions increase during the building of socialism, his projections were based upon progressive and unilinear development: the contradictions of capitalism remained the definitive element in the struggle. Under Brezhnev, the vision of unilinear development has all but vanished and, in any case, is no longer deterministic; the contradictions of socialism now open up the possibility of capi-

---

14. *Pravda*, June 8, 1969, p. 2.

15. "In Defense of Socialism and Peace," *International Affairs*, September 1968, p. 5.

16. *24th Congress of the Communist Party of the Soviet Union: Documents* (Moscow: Novosti Press Agency Publishing House, 1971), p. 11. See also Sh. Sanakoev, "Socialist Foreign Policy: Coordination and Effectiveness," *International Affairs*, June 1971, pp. 8–9, and O. Selyaninov, "Internationalism of Soviet Foreign Policy," *ibid.*, July 1971, p. 12.

17. *Pravda*, October 28, 1969, p. 1.

18. See Michel Tatu, "L'Invasion de la Tchecoslovaquie et la Détente en Europe," in Jerzy Lukaszewski, editor, *Les Democraties Populaires Après Prague* (Bruges, Belgium: De Tempel, 1970), pp. 95–106.

talist victory. Although the world balance of forces has allegedly changed decisively in favor of the socialist system, neo-Stalinist methods must be employed because contradictions reappear at an advanced stage of socialist development. Thus, from the perspective of historical development, Brezhnev offers a more pessimistic view of the world than did Stalin.

Against the Khrushchevian reliance on natural processes (perhaps only on the theoretical level), Brezhnev poses the necessity for coercion. Khrushchev's concepts of "three camps," the "peace zone" and "peaceful coexistence" reflected a facile assurance that the processes of history were moving inexorably in a direction favorable to the world communist movement. Brezhnev obviously takes a less optimistic view, which has been expressed in a new formulation of the "two camps" doctrine. Over the past three years, the Soviet leadership has moved gradually to integrate all major areas of foreign policy into this revised interpertation of world politics.

The Third World and National Liberation Movements

Khrushchev regarded national liberation movements as being secondary to the relationships between the capitalist and socialist camps:[19] the progressive decay of capitalism and the growing strength of the socialist camp were the decisive variables in his historical equation. Nevertheless, the "third camp" was acknowledged to be vitally important in the world balance of forces. While communist power was viewed as the agent primarily responsible for the end of colonialism,[20] the newly emerging countries were considered as an independent and—even though they were noncommunist for the most part—progressive force. Khrushchev identified four elements in the "national front," all of them progressive: the working class, the peasantry, the national bourgeoisie, and the democratic intelligentsia.[21] These varied forces, following their own interests, would combine to defeat feudal and neo-colonial elements; this combination born of the realities of social development was tilting the world balance more and more in favor of socialism: "The national states become ever more active as an independent force on the world scene; objectively, this force is in the main a progressive, revolutionary, and anti-imperialist force."[22]

Khrushchev thus stopped short of designating the third camp as the decisive element in world revolution. That possibility had posed a crucial

19. Bernard S. Morris, *International Communism and American Policy* (New York: Atherton Press, 1966), p. 145.

20. Michael P. Gehlen, *The Politics of Coexistence* (Bloomington: Indiana University Press, 1967), p. 45; Karen Brutents, "The Doom of Colonialism," *New Times* (Moscow), October 1961, p. 10.

21. *Program of the Communist Party of the Soviet Union, op. cit.*, p. 51.

22. *Ibid.*, p. 54.

issue for the world movement since the early Comintern days and was at the heart of the "weakest link of imperialism" concept. The principal after-the-fact justification for the occurrence of revolution in Russia, in defiance of Marx's analysis, had been this "weakest link" doctrine.[23] Mao was thus in the great Leninist tradition, dating back to Lenin's 1916 pamphlet, *Imperialism: the Highest Stage of Capitalism*, when he posited the centrality of the "Third World." However, in the 1960's Mao developed his own "two camps" doctrine; when he depicted a conflict between the "world town" and the "world village," he was turning the "weakest link" concept against Moscow itself. This was too much for the Soviets. The Kremlin's reply to this Maoist thrust featured those same elements seen earlier in its response to developments in Eastern Europe: polarization and subjectivism.

Soviet analysts now divide the newly free countries into three categories: those with a socialist, noncapitalist orientation; those with a capitalist orientation; and those that have not yet made their final choice. Even among the first group there are two possibilities: "either a gradual change, to the positions of scientific socialism or desertion of the originally proclaimed socialist goals and movement along the road of bourgeois nationalism."[24] Missing is Khrushchev's description of a diversity of progressive social forces; there is no middle ground. Moreover, the outcome lies in the realm of contingency and not in that of historical determinism: "Which of these two tendencies will triumph depends on a number of factors, among them whether a close alliance and proper ties are set up between the revolutionary-democratic parties and all the progressive forces, including Marxist-Leninists. . . ."[25]

To Mao's contemptuous classification of the Soviet Union among the forces of the "world town," the Soviets have responded with protestations that "the World Communist Movement is the vanguard of anti-imperialism"[26] and "the Soviet Union is the decisive force of the Socialist community and the reliable mainstay of the world revolutionary and liberation movement."[27] This seems to amount to a claim that the USSR is the center of both the socialist camp and the anti-imperialist movement. It might well be recalled that Khrushchev maintained that there was not even a single center for the socialist commonwealth. "At present," he said in 1961, such a center "is both impossible and unnecessary."[28]

23. *Ibid.*, p. 15.
24. A. Iskenderov, "New Stage in the Development of the National Liberation Movement," *Partiinaya Zhizn'*, August 1971, p. 12.
25. *Ibid.*, p. 13.
26. Brezhnev's speech, *24th Congress of the Communist Party of the Soviet Union: Documents, op. cit.*, p. 26.
27. Sovetov, *op. cit.*, p. 4; cf. Brezhnev's speech to the International Parties Conference, *Pravda*, June 8, 1969, p. 2.
28. N. S. Khrushchev, "For New Victories in the World Communist Movement," *Kommunist*, January 1961, p. 34.

China

It is surely no exaggeration to regard China as the major area of concern in Soviet foreign policy today; therefore, the perceived Chinese threat must be central to the reformulation discussed here. How does China fit into the revised "two camps" doctrine? The answer is obvious: in an extraordinary application of the Leninist principle on the polarization of ideology, the Soviets have placed the Chinese, although accused of "Leftism," in the capitalist camp.

The Soviets proceeded slowly and somewhat fitfully toward this stark exclusion of the Chinese. In 1968 Brezhnev was accusing the Chinese of "revisionism," "Leftist adventurism," "nationalism" and "chauvinism," but he still included the Chinese Communist party as a "detachment of the Communist movement."[29] In April 1969 two Soviet analysts, Yu. Alimov and V. Polyansky, writing in *International Affairs,* appeared to place China in a separate category, independent of the two camps:

> The Mao group in its efforts to intensify the struggle against the socialist community is trying to profit from the contradictions between the two systems. It has openly set itself up in opposition to the World Communist Movement and is trying to organize an international "Maoist" movement.[30]

The following two years witnessed armed conflict on the Ussuri, the restoration of diplomatic relations between Moscow and Peking, and the signing of a trade agreement. This mixed record was reflected in Brezhnev's remarks on China to the Twenty-fourth CPSU Congress. There he denounced Maoism as a distortion of Marxism-Leninism and rejected the "slanderous inventions concerning the policy of our Party and state," but he again included China within the ranks of the world communist movement and called for the normalization of relations with the People's Republic.[31]

Moscow ended its hesitation in September 1971, following the partial Sino-American détente of that summer. A *Pravda* editorial made definite the relegation of China to the opposition camp and denounced Maoism as a "petty-bourgeois ideological movement basically alien to Marxism-Leninism." More specifically, Chinese theories of "the Superpowers" and of "town versus village" were ascribed to nationalistic, great-power motives as opposed to the class approach of Marxism-Leninism. The "Superpowers" theory was particularly condemned as "class betrayal"; according to *Pravda,* Peking plays down the confrontation between two world systems, thus

29. *Pravda,* November 13, 1968, p. 2.
30. "The Struggle Against Imperialism and Anti-Imperialist Unity," p. 21.
31. *24th Congress of the Communist Party of the Soviet Union: Documents, op. cit.,* pp. 15–16.

avoiding the struggle against imperialism. Because the Maoists, by their anti-Soviet policies and their ideological deviations, had placed themselves beyond the pale of Marxism-Leninism, the editorial proceeded to the damning conclusion: they had "objectively" placed themselves in the other camp.

> . . . Maoism, in its present struggle against Marxist-Leninist theory, against the communist movement and the socialist community, objectively converges with all the various political forces hostile to socialism —the imperialists and racists, the Trotskyites and reformists—forming a kind of united front with them.[32]

Relations with the Capitalist Camp

The new "two camps" approach involves an intensification of struggle between systems. However, the basic strategic considerations governing Khrushchev's formulation of "peaceful coexistence" are still applicable. Nuclear war must be avoided and any moves tending to lower tensions that might escalate into nuclear confrontation serve the interests of both camps. But, as indicated above, the capitalists, faced with increasing contradictions, have adopted more subtle tactics of subversion. The struggle now becomes, more than ever before, one of ideological conflict.[33] Since the "objective factors" have receded into the background (these allegedly favor the socialists but are no longer necessarily decisive), the strength of the socialist camp vis-à-vis the capitalist is today largely determined by the degree of its ideological uniformity and internal organizational cohesion.

The continuing efforts to reach agreements with the United States under "peaceful coexistence" have been integrated with this analysis. Such measures as the nuclear limitation and control treaties are referred to under the rubric "diplomatic struggle of the two worlds."[34] Significant international agreements with the countries of the capitalist camp reflect recognition by "Western ruling circles" of the "existing balance of world forces."[35]

The concrete political meaning of this interpretation becomes clearer when our focus turns to Soviet efforts toward "normalization" in Europe. Here the major Soviet emphasis has been the "inviolability of frontiers."[36] Since it was the East European bloc, not the Western, that was most sub-

---

32. "The Word and the Deed: China's Leadership in Action," *Pravda,* September 4, 1971, p. 2.

33. See Philip Bart, "Two World Systems Today and Tomorrow," *World Marxist Review,* January 1971.

34. Sanakoev, "Socialist Foreign Policy: Coordination and Effectiveness," *op. cit.,* p. 10.

35. *Ibid.*

36. *Ibid,* p. 11.

ject to fragmentation and disintegrative tendencies in the 1960's (admitted by the Soviets in their "weakest link of socialism" dicussions), it seems unmistakable that with respect to Europe the "diplomatic struggle of the two worlds" is designed to secure the stabilization and consolidation of the socialist camp.

The New "Two Camps" Doctrine

The polarization concept that forms the core of the revised "two camps" doctrine was well summarized by a Soviet analyst in the August 1970 issue of *International Affairs:*

> Since the world has been split into two opposing social camps, the decisive factor in the foreign policy of every state has been first of all its membership of one of these camps. Neither the geographical position of a state nor any other specific can deprive this social, and, in the final analysis, class factor of its determining role.[37]

That statement could easily have been written during the Stalinist era. But the developmental analysis of the present period and the conclusions drawn by the Soviet leadership add a significant element and yield a substantially different "two camps" doctrine. The main outlines of the revised version may be summarized as follows:

(1) The world is divided into two hostile and irreconcilable camps, the capitalist and the socialist. There is no possibility of a "convergence" between the two social systems.[38]

(2) The center of the socialist camp is the Soviet Union; the center of the capitalist camp is the United States.

(3) The criterion for membership in the socialist camp is adherence to Marxist-Leninist ideology as interpreted by the CPSU. Third World political systems that are tending in this direction may be provisionally included. All others are "objectively aligned" with the capitalist camp.

(4) International agreements with countries of the capitalist camp are feasible and desirable but they reflect the "diplomatic struggle of the two worlds" and are designed to strengthen the position of the socialist camp in the "world balance of forces."

(5) Soviet military power is the guarantor of the security of the socialist camp against overt attack by the capitalists.

(6) Since the strategic balance precludes overt conflict between the camps and since the "difficulties"—i.e., the contradictions of socialism—

---

37. O. Selyaninov, "The International and the National in the Policy of the Socialist States," pp. 14–19.

38. See O. Selyaninov, "Proletarian Internationalism and the Socialist State," *International Affairs,* November 1969, p. 10.

in the socialist camp make possible capitalist restoration, the struggle is now primarily an ideological one, with the outcome open-ended. The crucial variables for the outcome are the ideological dynamism and organizational cohesion of the socialist camp.

(7) Application of coercion across state boundaries on an interstate and interparty basis is a legitimate and sometimes necessary method for providing favorable conditions in the ideological struggle and promoting cohesion in the socialist camp.

Several important inferences may be drawn from the above formulation. First, it reflects the virtual shattering of Soviet confidence in historical determinism. Subjective factors are given a precedence heretofore unknown in Marxism-Leninism. It is ironic that the Soviet response to the Chinese challenge has been built around a subjectivism akin to Maoism, although there remain other significant differences between the two ideological approaches.

Second, the new "two camps" doctrine involves a certain narrowing of Soviet concerns and goals, at least for the short run. That narrowing can perhaps best be understood as expressed in William Riker's concept of the "blocking coalition."[39] The struggle is still conceptualized in zero-sum terms and there remains the possibility of Soviet expansionism, as in India and the Middle East, but there is a definite movement away from the high-risk confrontations of the Khrushchev era and toward the husbanding of what Riker calls "fixed assets." The main emphasis now is clearly on protection of the organizer's base bloc and on the denial of victory to the other side.

Finally, the current emphasis on coercion as a legitimate method for promoting bloc cohesion points up the continuing fundamental weakness in the Soviet approach to integration of the socialist commonwealth. Amitai Etzioni's proposition that "the relation between the application of coercive power and the success of unification is curvilinear"[40] appears to be highly relevant for this system. If that proposition is valid (and the history of the socialist commonwealth provides ample empirical evidence in its support), we might reasonably predict continuing crises of integration at high levels of development for the socialist system. In that case, the Soviet theoretical response to the integration crises of the 1960's would itself be a major contributing factor to the integration crises of the 1970's.

39. William H. Riker, *The Theory of Political Coalitions* (New Haven: Yale University Press, 1962), pp. 103–104, 211–246.
40. Amitai Etzioni, *Political Unification* (New York: Holt, Rinehart and Winston, 1965), p. 94.

14.

The Foundations of
National Security

J. WILLIAM FULBRIGHT

THERE IS NO LONGER any validity in the Clausewitz doctrine of war as "a carrying out of policy with other means." Nuclear weapons have rendered it totally obsolete because the instrument of policy is now totally disproportionate to the end in view. Nuclear weapons have deprived force of its utility as an instrument of national policy, leaving the nuclear powers with vastly greater but far less useful power than they had before. So long as there is reason—not virtue, but simply reason—in the foreign policy of the great nations, nuclear weapons are not so much an instrument as an inhibition on policy.

By all available evidence, the Russians are no less aware of this than we. The memory of their 20 million dead in World War II is still fresh in the minds of most Russians. In a speech on July 19, 1963, Chairman Khrushchev castigated the Chinese Communists as "those who want to start a war against everybody. . . Do these men know," he asked, "that if all the nuclear warheads were touched off, the world would be in such a state that the survivors would envy the dead?" Or, commenting again in Hungary in April, 1964, on the equanimity with which the Chinese Communists spoke of nuclear war, Khrushchev expressed his opinion that "it is not from an excess of brains but from an absence of them that people say such things."

In the pursuit of its ambitions, whether by militant or peaceful means, the Soviet Union, like any other nation, is subject to the unending pressures for

From *Old Myths and New Realities*, by J. William Fulbright, pp. 56–78. Copyright © 1964 by J. William Fulbright. Reprinted by permission of Random House, Inc.

change imposed by time and circumstance. "Man," it has been said, "the supreme pragmatist, is a revisionist by nature."[1] Those who attribute to the Soviet leaders a permanent and unalterable determination to destroy the free societies of the West are crediting the Soviet Union with a strength and constancy of will that, so far as I know, has never been achieved by any nation.

There is, in fact, every reason to anticipate change, both within the Communist nations and in the relations between the Communist and the free nations. If there is any "law" of history, it is the inevitability and continuity of change. It is sometimes for the better, but often for the worse, and we cannot assume that the future evolution of the Communist world will be toward moderate and peaceful policies. But neither are we helpless and passive spectators to the course which the Communist nations follow. We have the means and resources to influence events in the Soviet Union and in other bloc countries. Our ability to put those means to effective use depends in no small measure on our willingness to go beyond a rigidly ideological view of communism and to deal with the Communist countries as the national entities which they are, each with special national interests and aspirations.

If we look at the Communist bloc objectively, and not through the distorting prism of ideological hostility, we can see that important and encouraging changes have already taken place. We perceive that Soviet society and the Soviet economy are becoming highly complex, too complex to be completely and efficiently controlled by a highly centralized dictatorship. We perceive that under the pressures of growing complexity a degree of economic decentralization has taken place, that the police terror of the Stalin era has been abated, that the Central Committee of the Communist Party may even be developing under Khrushchev into a kind of rudimentary parliamentary body. And most important of all, as I pointed out in Chapter I, the unity of the Communist bloc has been disrupted, and we find ourselves confronted with a growing diversity of national outlooks and policies, ranging from the harsh orthodoxy of Communist China to the pragmatism of the Soviet Union, the nationalism of Poland and Hungary, and the astonishing diplomatic independence of Rumania.

There are those who maintain that the only valid test of altered Soviet policies must be the explicit repudiation of those tenets of Marxist ideology that call for world revolution and the universal victory of communism. To ask for overt renunciation of a cherished doctrine is to expect too much of human nature. Men do not repudiate the doctrines and dogmas to which they have sworn their loyalty. Instead they rationalize, revise, and reinterpret them to meet new needs and new circumstances, all the while protesting that their heresy is the purest orthodoxy.

Something of this nature is now occurring in the Soviet Union. Khrushchev has not repudiated Marx and Lenin; on the contrary, he vows his fealty to

---

1. Eric Hansen, "Revisionism: Genesis and Prognosis" (unpublished paper).

their doctrines at every opportunity. But his "orthodoxy" has not deterred him from some striking interpretations of the scriptures. Contrast, for example, the Marxist-Leninist emphasis on discipline and self-sacrifice and revolution with Khrushchev's famous words in Budapest in April, 1964: "The important thing is that we should have more to eat—good goulash—schools, housing, and ballet. How much more do these things give to the enlargement of man's life? It is worth fighting and working for these things." Or contrast the Marxist-Leninist principle of relentless struggle for the universal victory of communism with Khrushchev's answer to his own rhetorical question as to whether the Soviet Union should help the French working class to take over power. "Who asked us to mix in their affairs?" was his reply. "What do we know about them?"

The attribution of an unalterable will and constancy to Soviet policy has been a serious handicap to our own policy. It has restricted our ability to gain insights into the realities of Soviet society and Soviet foreign policy. It has denied us valuable opportunities to take advantage of changing conditions in the Communist world and to encourage changes which would reduce the Communist threat to the free world. We have overestimated the ability of the Soviets to pursue malevolent aims, without regard to time or circumstances, and, in so doing, we have underestimated our own ability to influence Soviet behavior.

A stigma of heresy has been attached to suggestions by American policymakers that Soviet policy can change or that it is sometimes altered in response to our own. But it is a fact that in the wake of the failure of the aggressive policies of the Stalin period, the Soviet leaders have gradually shifted to a policy of peaceful, or competitive, coexistence with the West. This policy confronts us with certain dangers but also with important opportunities if we are wise enough to take advantage of them.

The abrupt change in the Soviet position which made possible the signing of the nuclear test ban treaty in 1963 appears to have been motivated by the general failure of competitive coexistence as practiced in the last few years and by a number of specific problems, both foreign and domestic. The most conspicuous of these is the public eruption of the dispute with Communist China. In addition, the Soviet leaders have been troubled by economic difficulties at home, particularly in agriculture, by the increasingly insistent demands of the Russian people for more and better food, clothing, and housing, and by difficulties between the regime and Soviet intellectuals and artists; by increasing centrifugal tendencies in Eastern Europe, aggravated by the dismaying contrast with an increasingly prosperous and powerful Western Europe; and by the negligible rewards of Soviet diplomacy and economic aid in Asia and Africa.

The most crucial failure of Soviet policy has been in its dealings with the West. Contrary to Soviet expectations of a few years ago, it has proven impossible to extract concessions from the West on Berlin and Central Europe by nuclear diplomacy. Thwarted in Europe, Khrushchev embarked in the fall of 1962 on the extremely dangerous adventure of placing missiles in Cuba, hoping, it would seem, to force a solution in Berlin and an unfreezing of Central Europe. The debacle in Cuba led the Soviet leaders to a major reappraisal of their policies.

That reappraisal has apparently resulted in a decision to seek a relaxation of tensions with the West. The nuclear test ban treaty and subsequent limited agreements with the West were clearly calculated to serve that purpose. In addition, the tone of Soviet diplomacy has changed; in matters ranging from Cuba to Vietnam, vituperation has been muted and the Russians have passed up a number of opportunities to quarrel with the United States.

From the Soviet point of view, a limited *détente* with the West appears to offer certain clear advantages. Three reasons for seeking improved relations with the West seem of major importance. First and foremost is the genuine fear of nuclear war which the Soviets share with the West, all the more since the United States demonstrated in the Cuban crisis that it was prepared to use nuclear weapons to defend its vital interests. Secondly, in the mounting conflict with the Chinese, the Soviet Union can claim a success for its policies of "peaceful coexistence" and, more important, can use the world-wide popularity of the test ban and other arms-control measures to strengthen its position both in the Communist bloc and in the non-Communist underdeveloped countries, thereby further isolating the Chinese. Thirdly, Khrushchev appears to be interested in measures which will permit a leveling off, and perhaps a reduction, of weapons expenditures in order to be able to divert scarce resources for meeting some of the demands of the Russian people for a better life.

In an article written shortly after the signing of the test ban treaty, Professor Zbigniew Brzezinski, Director of Columbia University's Research Institute on Communist Affairs, interpreted the Soviet adherence to the test ban treaty as follows: "Khrushchev's acceptance of an 'atmosphere-only' test ban strongly suggests a major Soviet reassessment of the world situation and an implicit acknowledgment that Soviet policies of the last few years have failed. The Soviet leaders have evidently concluded that the general world situation is again in a 'quiescent' stage. Instead of dissipating Soviet resources in useless revolutionary efforts, or missile adventures of the Cuban variety, they will probably concentrate on consolidating their present position."[2]

If the relaxation of tensions is conceived by the Soviets as an interlude in which to consolidate their position, strengthen their power base, and then renew their aggressive policies against the West, is it wise for us to grant them this interlude? It is indeed wise, for two main reasons: first, because it will provide the West with an identical opportunity to strengthen the power base of the free world; and secondly, because it will generate conditions in

2. Zbigniew Brzezinski, "After the Test Ban," *The New Republic*, August 31, 1963, p. 18.

which the Soviet and Communist bloc peoples will be emboldened to step up their demands for peace and a better life, conditions which the Soviet leadership will find it exceedingly difficult to alter.

From the point of view of the West, an interlude of relaxed world tensions will provide a splendid opportunity to strengthen the foundations of the security of the free world—if only we will use it. First of all, we can use the opportunity to bring greater unity and prosperity to the Atlantic community— by seeking means of resolving our differences over the control of nuclear weapons and by negotiating extensive tariff reductions under the terms of the American Trade Expansion Act of 1962. Secondly, we can re-invigorate our efforts to strengthen the free nations of Asia, Africa, and Latin America by providing a more discriminating and intelligent program of economic assistance and by encouraging co-operative free-world aid programs through such agencies as the International Development Association. Finally, we can use a period of relaxed tensions to focus energy and resources on our long-neglected needs here at home—on the expansion and improvement of our public education, on generating greater economic growth and full employment, on the conservation of our resources and the renewal of our cities.

All of these lines of action have a direct and vital bearing on our national security. If we pursue them with vigor and determination, I think it can be confidently predicted that the free world will be the major beneficiary of a period of relaxed world tension, with a power base so strengthened that the margin of free-world superiority over the Communist bloc will be substantially widened.

The other great advantage to the West of a period of relaxed tensions is that it may release long-suppressed pressures for peace and the satisfaction of civilian needs within the Soviet bloc. Public opinion, even in a dictatorship like the Soviet Union, is an enormously powerful force which no government can safely defy for too long or in too many ways. Russian public opinion is overwhelmingly opposed to war and overwhelmingly in favor of higher wages, of better food, clothing, and housing, and of all the good things of life in a modern industrial society. The Russian *people* may well turn out to be a powerful ally of the free nations, who also want peace and prosperity. It is quite possible that a thaw in Soviet-American relations, even though conceived by the Soviet leadership as a temporary pause, could lead gradually to an entirely new relationship. Motives have a way of becoming lost as the actions to which they give rise generate new attitudes and new and unforeseen motives. Pressed by the demands of an increasingly assertive public opinion, the Soviet leaders may find new reasons to continue a policy of peace and accommodation with the West. Step by step their revolutionary zeal may diminish, as they find that a peaceful and affluent national existence is not really so tragic a fate as they had imagined.

No one knows whether Soviet society will actually evolve along these lines, but the trend of Soviet history suggests that it is by no means impossible.

"Indeed, the most striking characteristic of recent Soviet foreign policy," Professor Shulman has pointed out, "has been the way in which policies undertaken for short-term, expediential purposes have tended to elongate in time, and become embedded in doctrine and political strategy."[3]

It is possible, I believe, for the West to encourage a hopeful direction in Soviet policy. We can seek to strengthen Russian public opinion as a brake against dangerous policies by conveying accurate information about Western life and Western aims, and about the heavy price that both sides are paying for the cold war. We can make it clear to the Russians that they have nothing to fear from the West so long as they respect the rights and independence of other nations. We can suggest to them at every possible opportunity, both by persuasion and by example, that there is no greater human vanity than the assumption that one's own values have universal validity, and no enterprise more certain of failure than the attempt to impose the preferences of a single society on an unwilling world. And finally, we can encourage them to recognize, as we must never fail to recognize ourselves, that adventures born of passion are soon severed from their lofty aims, turning idealism into barbarism and men into demons.

On November 14, 1860, Alexander Hamilton Stephens, who subsequently became Vice-President of the Southern Confederacy, delivered an address to the Georgia Legislature which bears wisdom for our own time. Appealing to his colleagues to delay the withdrawal of Georgia from the Union, Stephens said of the prospective secession: "It may be that out of it we may become greater and more prosperous, but I am candid and sincere in telling you that I fear if we yield to passion, and without sufficient cause shall take that step, that instead of becoming greater or more peaceful, prosperous, and happy—instead of becoming Gods, we will become demons, and at no distant day commence cutting one another's throats. This is my apprehension. Let us, therefore, whatever we do, meet these difficulties, great as they are, like wise and sensible men, and consider them in the light of all the consequences which may attend our action."[4]

The purpose of a realistic foreign policy is not to end the cold war but to modify it, not to resolve the conflict between communism and freedom—a goal which is almost certainly beyond the reach of the present generation—but to remove some of the terror and passion from it. The progress thus far achieved and now in prospect has been small in substance, in the sense that it has brought us scarcely closer to a solution of such great problems as the arms race and the division of Germany. But in another sense—the extremely important psychological sense—it may be that we are doing better than we

3. Statement by Professor Marshall Shulman, August 26, 1963, Hearings before the Committee on Foreign Relations, United States Senate, 88th Congress, First Session, *Nuclear Test Ban Treaty* (Washington, D.C.: U.S. Government Printing Office, 1963), p. 797.

4. Alexander Hamilton Stephens, "Secession," in *Modern Eloquence* (New York: P. F. Collier & Sons, 1928), Vol. II, p. 203.

know. The ultimate criterion of the importance of any issue is its implications for war and peace. The division of Germany is a most important issue in itself, but its global and historical significance, like that of the arms race, is that it has a critical bearing on whether we shall have war or peace. If, by a series of agreements on issues which in substance are much less important than the division of Germany and the arms race—such agreements as the test ban treaty, reductions in the output of fissionable materials, or the opening of consulates and airline connections—we succeed in creating a *state of mind* in which neither side considers war as a likely eventuality or as a real option for itself except under radically changed conditions, then in fact we will have progressed toward precisely the same objective which a German settlement or a general disarmament agreement would help to achieve—a world substantially free of the threat of nuclear incineration.

The point which I am trying, imperfectly, to make is that in our quest for world peace the *alteration of attitudes* is no less important, perhaps more important, than the resolution of issues. It is in the minds of men, after all, that wars are spawned; to act upon the human mind, regardless of the issue or occasion for doing so, is to act upon the source of conflict and the potential source of redemption and reconciliation. It would seem, therefore, that there may be important new things to be learned about international relations through the scholarship of psychologists and psychiatrists.

When all is said and done, when the abstractions and subtleties of political science have been exhausted, there remain the most basic unanswered questions about war and peace and why we contest the issues we contest and why we even care about them. As Aldous Huxley has written: "There may be arguments about the best way of raising wheat in a cold climate or of re-afforesting a denuded mountain. But such arguments never lead to organized slaughter. Organized slaughter is the result of arguments about such questions as the following: Which is the best nation? The best religion? The best political theory? The best form of government? Why are other people so stupid and wicked? Why can't they see how good and intelligent we are? Why do they resist our beneficent efforts to bring them under our control and make them like ourselves?"[5]

In our search for answers to the complex questions of war and peace, we come ultimately to the paradox of man himself, which I have never heard better expressed than in a one-page essay called "Man," written by an American hill-country philosopher whose writings suggest strongly the style and thought of Mark Twain. It reads as follows:

> Man is a queer animal, like the beasts of the fields, the fowls of the air, and the fishes of the sea, he came into this world without his consent and is going out the same way.

5. Aldous Huxley, "The Politics of Ecology" (pamphlet, published by The Center for the Study of Democratic Institutions, Santa Barbara, California, 1963), p. 6.

At birth he is one of the most helpless creatures in all existence. He can neither walk, talk, swim nor crawl, and has but two legs while most other animals have four legs. Unlike other animals he has no covering for his body to protect it against the bite or sting of poisonous insects, tooth or claw of ferocious beasts save a little hair which appears about his body only in patches.

With all his limitations he yet has one advantage over animals—the power of reason, but history shows that he often discards that for superstition. Of all the animals on earth, man has shown himself to be the most cruel and brutal. He is the only animal that will create instruments of death for his own destruction.

Man is the only animal on all the earth that has ever been known to burn its young as a sacrifice to appease the wrath of some imaginary deity. He is the only one that will build homes, towns and cities at such a cost in sacrifice and suffering and turn around and destroy them in war.

He is the only animal that will gather his fellows together in creeds, clans, and nations, line them up in companies, regiments, armies, and get glory out of their slaughter. Just because some king or politician told him to.

Man is the only creature in all existence that is not satisfied with the punishment he can inflict on his fellows while here, but had to invent a a hell of fire and brimestone in which to burn them after they are dead.

Where he came from, or when, or how, or where he is going after death he does not know, but he hopes to live again in ease and idleness where he can worship his gods and enjoy himself, watching his fellow creatures wriggle and writhe in eternal flames down in hell.

The root question, for which I must confess I have no answer, is how and why it is that so much of the energy and intelligence that men could use to make life better for themselves is used instead to make life difficult and painful for other men. When the subtleties of strategy and power and diplomatic method have all been explained, we are still left with the seemingly unanswerable question of how and why it is that we *care* about such things, which are so remote from the personal satisfactions that bring pleasure and grace and fulfillment into our lives.

The paradoxes of human nature are eternal and perhaps unanswerable, but I do think we know enough about elemental human needs to be able to apply certain psychological principles in our efforts to alleviate the tensions of the cold war.

In this connection, I would suggest that a great deal—more than one would suspect—depends upon the *manner* in which we seek to negotiate reasonable agreements with the Russians. We must remember that we are not dealing with automatons whose sole function in life is to embody an ideology and a party line, but with human beings—people who, like ourselves, have special areas of pride, prejudice, and sensitivity. I have found, for example, as have others who have discussed current issues with Soviet officials and citizens, that the whole trend of a conversation can be influenced by the way in which you begin it. If you confront them at the outset with an attack on the harshness of their ideology, the shortcomings of their economy, or the excesses of their dictatorship, you are likely to be rewarded with an outburst of chauvinism and vituperation about American policy and practices. There are those who find such encounters emotionally satisfying, but no one can deny that they are singularly barren of productive results.

If, on the other hand, you start out with a compliment about the successes of Soviet society—and there have been a few—or with a candid reference to the shortcomings of our own society—and there have also been a few of these—then it often happens that the response is surprisingly expansive and conciliatory. You are likely to hear an admission that everything, after all, is not perfect in the Soviet Union, and that there are even a few things about America that are admirable and worthy of imitation.

The compliments in themselves are of little importance. But the candor and the cordiality are of great importance. As any good businessman knows, they set a tone and an atmosphere in which emotion gives way to reason and it becomes possible to do business, to move on from cordial generalities to specific negotiations. They generate that minimum of mutual confidence which is absolutely essential for reaching concrete agreements. Under existing circumstances, no one can expect such agreements to be more than modest accommodations which are clearly in the mutual interest; but they are at least a start toward more significant arrangements, and as I have already suggested, the critical question of war and peace may have less to do with the specifications of agreements than with the attitudes they engender and the attitudes they dispel.

"Frightened, hostile individuals tend to behave in ways which aggravate their difficulties instead of resolving them," says the distinguished psychiatrist Dr. Jerome D. Frank, "and frightened, hostile nations seem to behave similarly."[6] A nation, like an individual, Dr. Frank suggests, is likely to respond to a feared rival by breaking off communications, by provocative behavior, or by taking measures which promise immediate relief, regardless of their ultimate consequences.

Among the psychiatrically constructive techniques which might be used to cope with the destructive emotions of the cold war, Dr. Frank suggests the following: that we give Russian views our respectful attention as one way of making the Russians more receptive to ours; that we enormously increase communications between the Communist and the free worlds through cultural, scientific, agricultural, and student exchange programs; that we engage in co-operative activities that will enable both sides to achieve desired goals

6. Letter from Dr. Frank to the author, September 13, 1960.

neither can as readily achieve alone—such activities as joint projects in space exploration or in building health services throughout the world, or such enterprises as the possible Central American canal consortium referred to in Chapter I.

Through such means we may strive to break through the ideological passions and national animosities that fill men's minds with destructive zeal and blind them to what Aldous Huxley called the simple human preference for life and peace. Through such means we may strive to build strong foundations for our national security and, indeed, for the security of all peoples.

We must bring to bear all the resources of human knowledge and invention to build viable foundations of security in the nuclear age—the resources of political science and history, of economics and sociology, of psychology and literature and the arts. It is not enough to seek security through armaments or even through ingenious schemes of disarmament; nor is it enough to seek security through schemes for the transfer of territories or for the deployment and redeployment of forces. Security is a state of mind rather than a set of devices and arrangements. The latter are important because they contribute, but only to the extent that they contribute, to generating a *psychological process* in which peoples and statesmen come increasingly to think of war as undesirable and unfeasible.

It is this *process* that has critical importance for our security. Whether we advance it by seeking a settlement on Berlin or a new disarmament agreement, by the opening of consulates or by a joint enterprise in space, is less important than that the process be advanced. Our emphasis at any one time should be on those issues which seem most likely to be tractable and soluble. As long as we are by one means or another cultivating a world-wide state of mind in which peace is favored over war, we are doing the most effective possible thing to strengthen the foundations of our security. And only when such a state of mind is widely prevalent in the world will the kind of unprecedented political creativity on a global scale which has been made necessary by the invention of nuclear weapons become possible as well.

The cold war and all the other national rivalries of our time are not likely to evaporate in our lifetimes. The major question of our time is not how to end these conflicts but whether we can find some way to conduct them without resorting to weapons that will resolve them once and for all by wiping out the contestants. A generation ago we were speaking of "making the world safe for democracy." Having failed of this in two World Wars, we must now seek ways of making the world reasonably safe for the continuing contest between those who favor democracy and those who oppose it. It is a modest aspiration, but it is a sane and realistic one for a generation which, having failed of grander things, must now look to its own survival.

Extreme nationalism and dogmatic ideology are luxuries that the human race can no longer afford. It must turn its energies now to the politics of survival. If we do so, we may find in time that we can do better than just survive.

We may find that the simple human preference for life and peace has an inspirational force of its own, less intoxicating perhaps than the sacred abstractions of nation and ideology, but far more relevant to the requirements of human life and human happiness.

There are, to be sure, risks in such an approach. There is an element of trust in it, and we can be betrayed. But human life is fraught with risks, and the behavior of the sane man is not the avoidance of all possible danger but the weighing of greater against lesser risks and of risks against opportunities.

We have an opportunity at present to try to build stronger foundations for our national security than armaments alone can ever provide. That opportunity lies in a policy of encouraging the development of a habit of peaceful and civilized contacts between ourselves and the Communist bloc. I believe that this opportunity must be pursued, with reason and restraint, with due regard for the pitfalls involved and for the possibility that our efforts may fail, but with no less regard for the promise of a safer and more civilized world. In the course of this pursuit, both we and our adversaries may find it possible one day to break through the barriers of nationalism and ideology and to approach each other in something of the spirit of Pope John's words to Khrushchev's son-in-law: "They tell me you are an atheist. But you will not refuse an old man's blessing for your children."

15.

Old Realities and New Myths

MORTON A. KAPLAN

SENATOR FULBRIGHT's recent excursion into the analysis of foreign policy has been hailed as a breath of fresh air that sweeps away the cobwebs of cant and misunderstanding. The history of post-war foreign policy explains why such a study is needed. The inspiring successes and inventive genius of the first Truman Administration—an era unparalleled in American history for resourceful and courageous adaptation to changing circumstances—have been succeeded by disarray and confusion in American foreign policy. Both the early postwar stereotypes and the grand design of policy are breaking down. Thus the Senator's objective—an objective of unmasking old myths and clarifying new realities—is necessary and salutary.

But has the Senator reached his goal or has he rather obscured old realities and created new myths? Has he clarified the failings of our foreign policy since 1950 or is he preparing the way for the mistakes of the late 1960's? Has he analyzed the mistaken assumptions, the lost opportunities, and the changed contours of the problems or has he compounded the set of errors? Has he exorcised true myths or instead ghosts—pale reflections of positions that have been rejected for a decade? Has he correctly outlined the differ-

An early draft of this review article was circulated as a discussion paper at the Hudson Institute. Discussion papers are written at the initiative of the author and are not subject to review. They do not necessarily reflect the views of the Hudson Institute.

Reprinted by permission from *World Politics*, January 1965, pp. 334–67.

ences between the foreign policies of Stalin and Khrushchev or has his analysis falsified both positions? Has Senator Fulbright's use of social science produced deeper understanding of the problems of statecraft or has it produced misleading oversimplifications and erroneous generalizations?

Matters that are very important and also very complex, such as international politics, naturally produce passionate dispute. One therefore often wants to write circumspectly in order to lower the fever of the debaters. There is also a proper role for the deliberately controversial piece. This is sometimes an important means for forcing re-examination of beliefs that are very deeply held. Senator Fulbright's book essays such a role. So does this review article.

I

All political structures require myths in order to operate. These myths provide unity and direction in a disorderly world. Thus the myth of the monolithic nature of the Soviet bloc and of the imminent danger of a premeditated and unprovoked Soviet attack in the West, although factually inaccurate even for the 1947–1950 period, did serve the purpose of mobilizing energies for the Truman Doctrine, the Marshall Plan, and NATO.

No doubt the myth structure had dysfunctional consequences, even during this early period. It fostered a premature effort to achieve German rearmament—an effort that probably delayed German rearmament and that would not in any event have produced German forces during the putative crucial period. It undoubtedly was responsible for other blunders of a more serious nature during the Korean War. Its functional aspects, however, outweighed the dysfunctional in the period up to Korea. The excessive rigidity of the myth and the requirement for policies not completely in harmony with it after this period called for a re-evaluation.

A number of students of international politics were alert to the problem. This reviewer included in his first professional paper in 1952 the caution that more than one interpretation of Soviet policy was possible and that Soviet policy might change in important ways after "an old and sick man dies."[1] But even John Foster Dulles, rigid as he was in his policies, had some understanding of the myth of monolithicity. By 1954 (and in some cases earlier) most officials of the United States government had learned that the Soviet bloc was not monolithic and that the threat of Soviet attack was quite hypothetical. They did not, however, respond appropriately to the recovery of Western Europe, to the growing strains (as opposed to mere lack of monolithicity) in the Soviet bloc and in NATO, and to the consequences of nuclear military weapons, particularly after the Soviet system also had such weapons.

1. "An Introduction to the Strategy of Statecraft," *World Politics,* IV (July 1952), 570.

These developments produced alliance difficulties which Senator Fulbright apparently still does not understand and which he attributes to a greater extent than is reasonable to the real—and unfortunate—foibles of General de Gaulle. We will return to this subject, but first we must turn to the analysis which Senator Fulbright makes of the changed Soviet system and of other world problems and to the conclusions he draws.

II

Senator Fulbright states that the Soviet world is hostile to the United States but that the nature of its threat has changed radically: "It has shown a new willingness to enter mutually advantageous arrangements with the West and, thus far at least, to honor them. It has therefore become possible . . . to deal with the Soviet Union, for certain purposes, as a normal state with normal and traditional interest. . . . How the Soviet Union organizes its internal life, the gods and doctrines that it worships, are matters for the Soviet Union to determine. It is not Communist dogma as espoused within Russia but Communist imperialism that threatens us and other peoples of the non-Communist world" (pp. 9–10).

Senator Fulbright here certifies the myth of the contrast between Stalin and Khrushchev (as elsewhere he certifies Khrushchev's myth concerning China). It is true that Stalin had greater control over bloc affairs than Khrushchev had and that this permitted Stalin to follow some lines of policy that were not available to Khrushchev. But it is not true that Stalin's policy was one of utter and implacable hostility to the non-Soviet world or that Khrushchev's policy was one of wholehearted accommodation. Senator Fulbright noted in an earlier book that Stalin was not incautious, as was Hitler.[2] Indeed, one might argue that Stalin showed greater caution in foreign policy than Khrushchev. Stalin rejected the opportunity to support Yugoslavia over Trieste. He was far from enthusiastic about the Greek civil war, which was supported largely by Yugoslavia and Bulgaria. Until the Communists were thrown out of the French and Italian governments in 1947, they were under instructions to hold down strikes in order to facilitate economic recovery. The claims of Soviet support for a Communist takeover in China are apparently mythological. Stalin did support the Korean War and the Communist coup in Czechoslovakia. But these were proxy operations. Khrushchev put down the Hungarian revolution by the direct use of Soviet armed forces and he put Soviet nuclear missiles and Soviet crews into Cuba ninety miles off U.S. shores. Stalin, on the other hand, denounced Yugoslav and Bulgarian plans to recognize the Greek rebels as a Comsomolist preventive war policy. And, as for the keeping of treaties, were any treaties more abjectly kept than

2. J. William Fulbright, *Prospects for the West* (Cambridge, Mass., 1963), 8.

was the Nazi-Soviet Pact by Stalin? As for the support of national democratic revolutions, as opposed to Communist revolutions, had not both Lenin and Stalin supported such revolutions in Asia, particularly in China?

The myth of the contrast between Stalin and Khrushchev with respect to foreign policy is one of the most pervasive in American politics today. And it receives full support from Fulbright. On the other hand, none of the examples of Soviet moderation, either under Stalin or under Khrushchev, establishes the "normality" of the Soviet state. Undoubtedly real states have never conformed exactly to the concept of the normal state. There are too many economic, social, and political organizations or systems that cut across national boundaries. But in a world in which virtually all differences are differences of degree, the number of degrees can assume crucial importance. The difference between the Soviet Union and the "normal" state lies only partly in Communist ideology (which under Stalin, Khrushchev, and Mao did and still does involve the "burial" of democracy). To a greater extent, it lies in the nature of Soviet political organization which provides the means for the implementation of Communist doctrine and Communist state objectives. The Communist parties in other nations have in the past constituted organizations responsive to directives from Moscow in ways that impeded normal diplomatic processes. These organizations made more difficult concerted action against Soviet expansive actions, made easier Soviet pursuit of diplomatic objectives, and provided a cover for intervention in the internal affairs of other states. The existence of this type of apparatus created opportunities that would not otherwise have been present, and confronted "normal" states with weaknesses in their positions that otherwise it would not have been so important to guard against.

The existence of Communist China as an alternative center for communism undoubtedly complicates the picture of an organized bloc directed, if not ordered, from a single center. Even so, world politics today cannot be understood without an understanding of communism and Communist organization. For instance, it is just as wrong to regard the Viet Cong merely as a local uprising—a new myth perhaps—as it is to view the Viet Cong merely as the product of an international Communist conspiracy, whether spawned in North Vietnam, China, or Moscow. To assert that Russia can be treated as a normal state, for the reasons which Senator Fulbright gives, is to obscure important aspects of the nature of current world politics and to sponsor a countermyth.

It is worth remembering that the three great threats to the stability of world order in modern times—Napoleon, Hitler, and communism—have represented revolutionary rejections of the existing state structure and have utilized groups within other nations in support of their objectives. It was not mere expanionism—dangerous as that might have been—but expansionism combined with ideology and, in the case of nazism and communism, party organization that built the threat to its most serious dimensions. Of the three, the Communist threat possesses the best organization and the most attractive ideology. If the Soviet bloc continues to weaken and if communism is transformed, the threat may be mitigated. But it likely will not be eliminated. And present trends may be halted or even reversed.

Despite Senator Fulbright's endorsement, George Kennan's thesis concerning the possibility that United States policy can affect the liberalization of the Soviet bloc is dubious. According to Kennan, "It could well be argued . . . that if the major Western powers had full freedom of movement in devising their own policies, it would be within their power to determine whether the Chinese view, or the Soviet view, or perhaps a view more liberal than either, would ultimately prevail within the Communist camp."[3] This analysis raises more questions than it answers. The lion's share of American aid within the Soviet bloc since 1956—aid that has been justified as a support for liberalization and autonomy—has gone to Poland, which, of all the Russian satellites, has backslid most since 1956 in terms of internal freedoms and autonomy. Hungary and Rumania have been virtually ostracized by the United States until recently. Yet these two nations have made the greatest advances since 1956 in liberalization and autonomy. Perhaps American aid prevented even greater backsliding in Poland. But it seems more likely that the commitment of the United States to the Gomulka regime disarmed the internal opposition and stifled the incentives for changes which, in terms of American values and interests, would have been highly desirable. It is striking that the Senator quotes Mr. Kennan's comment when, to the extent that there is any evidence, it would appear to support the opposite point of view. Here the Senator supports one of the State Department's new myths—a myth that lacks the functional values which the old myths did support.

In principle it would be possible to find a path among the strains of the Communist bloc and to structure a policy that advanced American interests by discriminating among the Communist nations. It is difficult, however, for one who has watched the divagations of the State Department to have any confidence in its attempts to do so. Nor do the leakings of incidental intelligence from the State Department concerning its image of the Communist world lessen the fears of the external observer.

The Department of State and Senator Fulbright have bought Khrushchev's myth of the great changes in Soviet foreign policy since Stalin. This myth invokes a picture of Khrushchev as more moderate and of Stalin as less moderate than either actually was. Khrushchev also sold to the United States his myth concerning the contrast between the peaceful Russians and the war-mongering Chinese. (Undoubtedly it was the boldness of Chinese attacks on Hong Kong, Macao, Quemoy, and Matsu that led us to accept this point of view.) Another aspect of this myth—one to which Senator Fulbright subscribes—is that the Chinese advocate the reckless use of nuclear weapons

3. George Kennan, "Polycentrism and Western Policy," *Foreign Affairs*, XLII (January 1964), 178; quoted in *Old Myths and New Realities*, 13.

(p. 57). Yet, as the Chinese have pointed out, it was Mr. Khrushchev who was reckless. The Chinese have said: "We have always maintained that socialist countries must not use nuclear weapons to support the peoples' wars of national liberation and revolutionary civil wars. . . . A socialist country absolutely must not be the first to use nuclear weapons, nor should it in any circumstances play with them or engage in nuclear blackmail and nuclear gambling. . . ."[4]

At least Senator Fulbright does not seem to subscribe to the emanations from some sources in Foggy Bottom that the United States and the Soviet Union will reach an accommodation that will enable them jointly to stem the aggressive designs of the Communist Chinese. Could any myth be better designed than this one to undermine American interests and values? Russia fronts on an area that is of urgent value to the United States. The skills, resources, and industry of Europe are such that the loss of the area to the Soviet Union would be a disaster. China does not front on any areas of reasonably comparable interest. Moreover, China diverts Russia from Europe. In addition, an alignment of the United States, Western Europe, and the Soviet Union against China would produce a racial confrontation that might undermine the values that characterize our institutions. Even though this notion is still not official policy, it is nonetheless deeply disturbing to hear talk of a U.S.-Russian alignment against China.

Even where Senator Fulbright speaks sensibly of the possibility that the United States and China might eventually cooperate on some issues, he builds into this position the myth that the problems between the two nations stem from China's "implacable hostility toward the United States" (p. 38). Undoubtedly the Kremlin would like us to believe this, but why should we play into his hand? And where is the evidence for this hostility? Korea? We threatened legitimate Chinese national interests when we marched to the Yalu. Our disclaimers that China should not have regarded this as a threat would have been worthless even had our action in marching to the Yalu not repudiated earlier statements by the Secretary of State that our only objective in Korea was to restore the *status quo ante.* There was no excuse for this action on our part unless we intended to have a showdown with one or both of the Communist powers. Taiwan? Undoubtedly we have a moral commitment to the inhabitants of Taiwan not to surrender them to Communist tyranny. But since we cannot expect the Communists to admit that their regime is immoral, our position is weak on the basis of the more traditional criteria. India? The border region is ill-defined. Even where the Indians have a treaty claim, they undermined it themselves by the rationale of their attack on Goa. The Indians consistently refused peaceful negotiations. They en-

4. From *Jenmin Jih Pao,* November 19, 1963, as translated and published by the BBC Monitoring Service in *Summary of World Broadcasts: Part III, The Far East,* 2nd Series (November 20, 1963), C9–C11.

gaged in deep military probes and were preparing an attack when the Chinese beat them to it. The Senator is right that we have nothing to gain now from recognition and much to lose, but why cloak this conclusion in false moralisms? It only confuses the real issue of international politics—namely, that specific interests may be incompatible. And it reinforces the myth that our problems stem from misunderstandings. They may instead stem from proper understanding.

Senator Fulbright thus structures a world in which the Russians show great moderation and the Chinese are reckless. He therefore finds it possible and desirable to achieve a general detente with the Russians, even if he does not advocate an alliance with the Russians against the Chinese. But has he really built his case properly? We have already considered many aspects of that case. We may now consider the final ingredients—ingredients which this time do exist but whose combination in a stew may not produce an edible dish. I agree with the Senator that it is unlikely that we can win the cold war completely or end it immediately and that good and evil are not absolutes. But I do not understand what relevance these comments have. Hitler was good to his dogs. One could even argue for some of his social policies. Genghis Khan undoubtedly had some redeeming features. No doubt St. Francis of Assisi had some very undesirable characteristics. Evil will never be eliminated from the world nor will good ever reign supreme. But not even Barry Goldwater wanted to unleash SAC against Moscow. And if a new Hitler had a big nuclear force, we undoubtedly would think twice about unconditional surrender.

Occasionally one gets a student in the classroom—never one of the best, although rarely one of the worst—who discovers that all nations behave selfishly and who therefore thinks that no interesting or important differences in national behavior can be articulated. On the continuum of national behavior there are significant differences. It makes good sense to recognize the Soviet system as an evil system. This does not mean that we must attempt to suppress the system by force. Even apart from the existence of nuclear forces, such an attempt might only unleash still greater evils. Surely, however, we are and ought to be hostile to the Soviet system and to its existence, just as we should be hostile to the evils of racism within our own system. Would not our policies be better adapted to their proper ends if we did recognize that each agreement with the Soviet system is strictly limited to some specific objective and that no purpose is or could be served by a general spirit of detente?

In addition, there is no significant evidence that a spirit of detente will in fact increase the probability that specific agreements will be reached and maintained in those areas where joint interests outweigh the detestation which the leaders of each system feel for the other. Would not Senator Fulbright's own recognition that American strategic superiority was a necessary element in the partial victory we won in the Cuban missile crisis (p. 5) imply that the Soviets do respond to hard realities and not to expressions of good will? And, although I distrust facile generalizations from history, does not the history of postwar negotiations with the Soviet Union indicate the same?

When Senator Fulbright speaks of the Central Committee of the Soviet Union as developing into a rudimentary parliamentary body (p. 58), he reinforces the new myths in a particularly dangerous way. The development of which he speaks might occur in the Soviet Union. To assert its plausibility on the basis of existing evidence is indefensible. The rarity of genuinely parliamentary regimes in the world, even where conditions are less unfavorable than in the Soviet Union, militates against this hypothesis. The least one would expect is an analysis of the micro-structure of Soviet society and political organs to indicate the factors that give plausibility to this type of development.[5] One would not like to think that major political orientations were based on superficial and fleeting analogies. The Wilsonian myths have long been discredited, and for reasons that are substantial.

Senator Fulbright undoubtedly makes some pertinent specific comments about the nature of the Soviet system, the changes in it, and the implications of these for world politics and American policy. These remarks are surrounded by other less cogent remarks in such a way that in effect a new myth is created—one in which the Soviet system withers away, the bloc disintegrates, the appetite of the Soviet Union diminishes, and it becomes little different from Britain or France. Culturally different perhaps, and a little more boorish, but essentially a member of the club. Although wishful thoughts sometimes come true, wishful thinking is not an adequate guide for policy.

As this review article is going to press, word has just come through of the purging of Khrushchev from the Soviet Russian leadership. This event, which caught official Washington by surprise, underscores the inadvisability of basing American policy upon the supposed attributes of particular Soviet leaders or upon inspired guesses concerning the future transformations that Soviet society and foreign policy are likely to undergo. This is so for three reasons. In the first place, the matter of the particular persons in charge of the Soviet Union may not be critical; that is, Soviet policy may not change in major ways or for the worse under the new leadership. In the second place, our policies may be largely irrelevant in influencing either change or stability in the Russian leadership. In the third place, we may be—and are likely to be—poorly informed concerning the alternatives. Although I do not believe we are likely to be so naïve as to credit information fed to us from Soviet sources as to the nature of internal Soviet quarrels (obviously such accounts

5. For a cogent analysis which indicates the implausibility of this hypothesis, see Allen Kassof, "The Administered Society: Totalitarianism Without Terror," *World Politics*, xvi (July 1964), 558–75.

serve multiple functions), we may become overcommitted to our own Krem-linological hypotheses.

It is much too early to evaluate the present shift in the Soviet high command. The new leadership is not yet consolidated and the struggle for control is likely to continue. Although the new leadership may be more effective in implementing Soviet policy than was the bumbling Khrushchev, we are less likely to be confronted with the kind of impulsive gambling that he engaged in. In any event, pragmatic policies based on specific coincidences of American and Soviet interests are likely to serve American interests better than a general commitment either to detente or to inflexible hostility. During the succession crisis of 1953, we may have missed an opportunity to negotiate the German question advantageously because of our commitment to inflexible hostility. It would be a shame if this time a commitment to detente made us so unwilling to disturb the new situation that we again failed to explore the negotiation space available to us.

III

Senator Fulbright attacks several other "myths" of U.S. foreign policy. "We Americans," the Senator says, "would do well to divest ourselves of the silly notion that the issue with Panama is a test of our courage and resolve. . . . It takes stubbornness but not courage to reject the entreaties of the weak" (pp. 18–19). If the Senator were merely saying that the United States can afford to be magnanimous in its treatment of Panama, I would not disagree with him. I favor revision of the treaty, increased benefits for Panama, and even a different type of regime for the administration of the Canal. Our past policy has been governed at least by inattention and perhaps also by pettiness and stupidity.

President Johnson, however, exercised sound judgment when he refused to "negotiate" a change of the treaty under pressure. For once, in recent years, the United States refused to quail when subjected to "blackmail" by a smaller power. And, in this instance, particularly, given the history of our past attitudes toward the Canal and the irresponsible statements of the Panamanian representatives, the failure to conform to a "stubborn" line, to use the Senator's word, probably would have had extremely unfortunate consequences elsewhere in the world.

For years the United States has paid blackmail to petty and unpopular dictators who have threatened us with the alternative of communism. We have played with the simple-minded notion that we can "buy off" Nasser and Sukarno with our largesse, not merely with respect to temporary expediencies, but with respect to long-term goals. Part of this policy has rested on the liberal myth that the troubles of the world stem not from incompatible goals but from mutual suspicions. Another part of it rests on characterological weakness and the inability to take a stand. This weakness was demonstrated for all the world to see when the Secretary-General of the United Nations made the outrageously false charge that we discriminated against Japan in the use of nuclear weapons, as contrasted with Germany, because Japan was a colored nation. The *New York Times* did not record even the weakest kind of official rebuttal, even by a lesser official, let alone by our chief representative to the UN.

On the other hand, I do not understand why we demanded that Bolivia break relations with Castro. I thought that we approved of the present Bolivian government. Since the breaking of relations with Castro by Bolivia does not weaken Castro's regime in any way, but may weaken the Bolivian regime, it would seem to have little to commend it.

Senator Fulbright, however, is dealing with a straw man when he attacks administration policy on Cuba. Of course, it is ridiculous to try to enforce a boycott in ways that we cannot enforce, that only antagonize allies, and that do not do much to hurt Castro. The real alternative, however, is not to remove those measures that do strain his regime and that put an extra burden on the Russians, but to support the exiles in ways that would further harass and weaken the regime.

Since Castro could not have taken over without at least tacit official support from the United States, we do have a moral obligation to the Cuban people to remove his tyrannical regime. The effective arguments against this course lie not in its impossibility in terms of resources but in the demonstrated incompetence of the United States when it comes to implementing programs of this sort. The Bay of Pigs episode demonstrated not only military incompetence and failure of will but also political ineptitude of an egregious nature. We did not have any good idea of what to do with Cuba after Castro was gone or we could not possibly have supported the Cubans we did. We could, if necessary, bring down the Castro regime today, using direct American military force, without risking a nuclear confrontation or political disaster in Latin America, if we possessed the requisite political skills. This undoubtedly would not solve our problems elsewhere in Latin America, but it might give us a respite which we could then utilize. In any event, however, we seem capable only of a policy of pinpricks which seems to satisfy our national ego but which produces little in the way of practical results and at a price which is unnecessarily high. And the opposition party seems only to desire to use the Marines to nursemaid the water taps.

Much the same kind of paralysis affects our Vietnamese policy. It was apparent for years that the Diem regime lacked the political skills to win the war against the guerrillas. It was and is also clear that no other regime can win that war unless the war is extended against the North. Even though much of the Viet Cong support is genuinely indigenous, so that perhaps it could not be halted by simple orders from the North, Viet Cong morale is sustained by the immunity of the Northern bastion. And the morale of the

South is depressed by that same immunity. The present position is completely one-sided.

The fear that extension would merely unleash the North and the Chinese overlooks the difficulty the Chinese would have in intervening, the immense logistic advantages possessed by the United States, and the great reluctance of the North Vietnamese to encourage Chinese intervention. Such intervention would undermine Viet Minh autonomy and create the conditions under which a vigorous guerrilla war against the Viet Minh, utilizing the traditional techniques of such ventures, could be launched. If the United States is unwilling or unable to adopt a winning strategy, which should include the negotiation of definite and moderate political objectives, it might instead cut its losses by withdrawing. This is a less desirable policy, but it is better than the inept policy that is being pursued.

Indeed, one wonders if the present course can be called a policy at all. Whom did the Department of State believe it was fooling by sending General Taylor to Vietnam? Surely the Chinese were not deceived into believing that the sending of General Taylor heralded a potentially tougher policy, when it was transparent that he was sent only because the United States intended nothing that went farther than its current line. One is inclined to believe that the American response in Tonkin Gulf reflected the President's gut reaction, not State Department policy. This is reinforced by the almost unbelievable report in the *New York Times* that some officials recommended that the response be made by the South Vietnamese.[6]

IV

Senator Fulbright fails to understand the legitimate European concern about the nature of the American nuclear commitment. "It is," he says, "clearly understood in the United States that a successful Soviet attack on Europe would almost certainly be followed by an attack on the United States, and that even if it were not, the loss of Europe to the free world would leave the United States so weakened and isolated as to put its security, its economy, and probably its survival as a free society in the gravest jeopardy. Nor is it possible to imagine that the Russians would take the incredible risk of leaving the United States out of the conflict with its forces intact and able to intervene whenever it chose" (p. 99). This position is a ritual incantation in Washington. And among the greatest of myths are ritual incantations.

Possibly if the Soviet Union struck Western Europe in a massive onslaught out of the blue, the American response would approach the certainty of which Senator Fulbright talks. This is perhaps the least plausible way in which a European conflict is likely to begin. Most observers believe it would start slowly, as the consequence of an unplanned incident, in which the

6. James Reston, *New York Times* (August 6, 1964), 8: "One view was that the retaliation should be done by the South Vietnamese to minimize the risk."

equities and objectives of the states involved would be less than clear. We probably would have lots of time to overevaluate the equities on the Russian side and to consider the potential casualties on our own.

The Europeans are most familiar with very interesting public statements by our highest officials. At the hearing to consider his nomination as Secretary of State, Christian Herter said, "I cannot conceive of any President involving us in an all-out nuclear war unless the facts showed clearly we are in danger of all-out devastation ourselves, or that actual moves have been made toward devastating ourselves."[7]

European qualms are increased by comments on the horrors of nuclear war. On July 26, 1963, President Kennedy asserted: "A war today or tomorrow, if it led to nuclear war, would not be like any war in history. A full-scale nuclear exchange, lasting less than 60 minutes, with the weapons now in existence, could wipe out more than 300 million Americans, Europeans, and Russians, as well as untold numbers elsewhere. And the survivors—as Chairman Khrushchev warned the Communist Chinese—'The survivors would envy the dead.' For they would inherit a world so devastated by explosions and poison and fire that today we cannot even conceive of its horrors."[8]

President Kennedy may have overemphasized the likelihood that a nuclear exchange would escalate into a full-scale nuclear war. But if the President makes such a statement, are not Europeans right to fear that Americans may fear nuclear war even more than the loss of Europe? After all, the dangers of nuclear war would be clear and immediate. Those that Senator Fulbright speaks of are indirect and remote. It seems likely that some Americans would be inclined to use the escape clause Senator Fulbright elsewhere invoked: "Our commitment to the defense of Europe is absolute and irrevocable—so long as the critical decisions that led to war or peace are not removed beyond our influence or responsibility."[9] Might we not soon find that that was the case? Moreover, Europeans fear that we might object to military action in a situation that appeared vital to them, and consequently fear that we would then disclaim responsibility for action taken by them.

I do not disagree with Senator Fulbright's analysis of the value of Europe to the United States, although I believe he greatly overestimates the probability that a Soviet attack on Europe would necessarily be part of a plan to attack the United States. The threat to us would likely be indirect and would require great sophistication on the part of the public and high policymakers for its understanding. The Senator is correct when he asserts that that threat would be to our way of life.

Shortly after Sputnik the American guarantee seemed to lose its effectiveness—thus anticipating military developments that had not yet taken place—

7. Committee on Foreign Relations, U.S. Senate, *Hearings on the Nomination of Christian A. Herter to be Secretary of State*, 86th Congress, 1st Session, 1959, 9–10.
8. J. F. Kennedy, "The Nuclear Test Ban Treaty: A Step Toward Peace," *Department of State Bulletin*, XLIX (August 12, 1963), 236.
9. *Prospects for the West*, 60–61.

and the Russian threat also seemed less imminent. Thus the incentives for independence of foreign policy and the development of independent nuclear systems seemed to increase. Many Americans—some of them most influential —began to welcome the latter development in this period. Since this seemed to me to be the wrong policy, I began to circulate in 1958 what I believe to have been the first proposal for a joint NATO nuclear force.[10] The proposal was presented to a conference at Princeton University in 1959. A Bowie-Knorr study group later incisively recommended to the Eisenhower Administration a joint NATO nuclear force based on Polaris submarines. This was followed by a somewhat similar Eisenhower Administration proposal for a NATO Polaris nuclear force which, although inadequate, was nonetheless desirable.

When the Kennedy Administration came into office, it was so thoroughly committed against nuclear diffusion that it pigeonholed the proposal for a NATO force. Only after it became clear that diffusion could not be prevented did it consider an alternative to national diffusion. Unfortunately, when it did consider alternatives, its proposals were gimmicks that attempted more to persuade than to cope with the legitimate problems that the European nations faced. Since the proposals were ineffective in satisfying the needs of the Europeans and were advanced by an administration that had shown hostility to the idea of a real NATO force, most Europeans viewed them as frauds. It is probable that the Germans have backed MLF not because they like it, but because they need American support and hope that present support for the United States may later produce American support for a nuclear force that the Germans can use in their vital interests. In addition, the clearly appropriate technical decision on Skybolt was implemented with peculiar political ineptitude at Nassau. NATO is still paying the penalty for these mistakes. Perhaps even the most sincere, adequate, and judiciously presented proposals would have been scuttled by de Gaulle. But the United States gave de Gaulle every excuse to follow his current policy.

The French force will soon confront the United States with a dilemma. It does not do so yet only because the force does not yet exist. Inspired stories from Washington to the effect that the French force will not be able to penetrate Soviet airspace either are inaccurate or the Soviets have much better low-level radar and anti-aircraft capabilities than we have. The trouble with the French force is that it is a first-strike force highly vulnerable to attack on the ground and therefore provocative. It cannot be integrated into a strategy of limited nuclear strikes. It may deter in all situations except the most provocative. But our nuclear force would be equally deterring for these situations, since the Russians would not run even a small chance of our nuclear intervention unless the provocation were gross. In the most provocative situations, however, the Russians might have to decide whether an attack on the French of such scope that it would eliminate the French force—

10. Subsequently published in revised form under the title, "Problems of Coalition and Deterrence," in Klaus Knorr, ed., *NATO and American Security* (Princeton 1959), 127–50,

an attack that would therefore produce large civilian casualties—would trigger the American force. Although the probability that they would attack the United States as a consequence of such a calculation may not be very high, it nonetheless may be higher than we want to risk. After all, we are building a controlled force because we do not want to run the risks involved in an uncontrolled force—even one that is much better than the French *force de frappe*. It would largely negate this policy for the United States to remain in NATO while the French possess the *force de frappe*. Even those who may think the problem somewhat less drastic must still recognize that it is very serious. The incentive for the United States to remove itself from NATO is reinforced by the fact that even if NATO were dissolved, the existence of an American nuclear force likely would deter the Russians from an attack on Western Europe under all conditions except the most provocative.

We have been much too unwilling as a nation over the last twelve years to recognize that Western Europe has emerged from the period of American tutelage and that it has necessarily become restive about American dominance in the area of foreign policy. We have been unwilling to make concessions when those concessions would have been appreciated and perhaps effective. We have refused to admit that the Europeans have a legitimate problem with respect to our nuclear guarantee, or that those under threat of annihilation have some right to representation in the making of the decisions that might lead to it. We have been unwilling to admit that there are conditions under which it may be legitimate to surrender our nuclear veto or that conditions might develop which would make it desirable for us to leave NATO.

We have been caught within a system of rigid myths. Our paralysis of policy has permitted General de Gaulle to constrain our alternatives for us. We have neglected the opportunities to constrain his alternatives for him. This is demonstrated most clearly by the impotence of our policy with respect to the *force de frappe*. If we had told de Gaulle that if he went ahead with the French force we might leave NATO and drop the American nuclear guarantee, and if we had provided some reasonable alternative for the French, he might have found his alternatives constrained. And there would likely have been political opposition in France to the *force de frappe*, for many Frenchmen have been convinced that the *force de frappe* is a supplement, not an alternative, to American nuclear force—a supplement that increases French independence. If the French had to face the added prospect that the United States might sponsor a German nuclear force if the United States withdrew from NATO, the French might feel even more constrained. If we then suggested, as an alternative, that we would help the Europeans to develop a joint European force, considerable support for it might develop. Although this is less desirable than a joint NATO force, it is better than the likely consequences of the present situation. And this may perhaps be the period in which we have our last opportunity to encourage this development.

The creation of a controllable joint European nuclear force would remove the incentive for American withdrawal from NATO. Thus the United States could maintain its conventional forces in Europe and in this way NATO could retain the conventional superiority that is so important for stability. On the other hand, complete American withdrawal, perhaps coupled with the nuclear offer suggested above, may be the only way to shock Europe into unity—a unity that would have a powerful attractive force for the Soviet satellites. And the existence of such a Europe might clarify for the United States the advantages of a larger Atlantic Union. This plan, however, seems too much to hope for under likely circumstances.

Senator Fulbright, however, believes that NATO is a viable organization. The consultation on nuclear strategy which Senator Fulbright calls for is a requirement for viability, although it is probably too late. But it is not enough. If the reduction of NATO to impotence is to be averted and if we do not desire a joint European nuclear force, actual control of a NATO nuclear system must be devolved from American control under clearly stated conditions. In "Problems of Coalition and Deterrence," the conditions suggested were Russian first use or a massive Russian incursion in Western Europe, followed by a refusal to withdraw upon notice. Given the change in conventional force balances that has recently occurred in Europe, the latter condition may not be so important any more.

Of course, solving the military problem will not solve the real problem of NATO. It could at best provide time for a political solution. Since it may already be too late to form a joint NATO force, serious attention should be given to the alternative of a joint European nuclear force, lest we also be too late in sponsoring this plan.

V

Senator Fulbright is not a social scientist and it is not legitimate to hold him to the standards of social science. It is, however, saddening to see him discard the conventional wisdom of diplomacy, with its virtues as well as its vices, for social science generalizations that come from the bottom of the heap.

"There is," says Senator Fulbright, "perhaps some instruction for us in the experience of Europe before 1914. None of the great powers of that era actually planned a major war, but each of the two major groupings . . . was beset by fears of attack by the other. . . . Mutual fear generated the arms race, which in turn generated greater fear, until almost by accident Europe was plunged into general war" (p. 51). This assertion lacks any kind of historic depth. The system of mobilization of the great powers obtaining at the time may have played a role in the First World War, but not the arms race. The major factors were political; and the fears that existed, both warranted and unwarranted, were not generated by the arms race. The almost insoluble problem of the Austro-Hungarian Empire lay at the center of this problem.

Accidents did play a role, but again not accidents closely connected with an arms race. Moreover, what evidence does the Senator have for his assertion that "a continuing arms race, accompanied by mounting fears and tensions, has frequently led to war in the past" (*ibid.*)?

If one thing is clear about the present, it is that some aspects of the arms race have improved the stability of peace in the world we live in, have diminished the probability that a nuclear accident or a provocative situation will produce war, and have made it possible to control nuclear war, if it occurs. Perhaps much of the "detente" which we perceive can be attributed to this greater military stability. Whether a continued arms race would have similar felicitous consequences or whether these would be overbalanced by unfavorable aspects of the arms race is a matter for sober and cautious analysis.

Matters get even worse when the Senator decides that psychologists have a big contribution to make toward understanding the problems of peace and war. The Senator quotes Gordon Allport to the effect that "The crux of the matter lies in the fact that while most people deplore war, they nonetheless *expect* it to continue. *And what people expect determines their behavior. . . .* the indispensable condition of war is that people must expect war, before, under war-minded leadership, they make war."[11] Fulbright says that war is a habit and that one must create the expectation of peace.

It is not possible in this review article to make a full analysis of the kind of muddle-headed thinking that underlies these propositions. The reference terms are completely undefined with respect to their boundary conditions and reflect an ideology rather than intellectual analysis. One might instead argue that if Chamberlain and his group had expected that war was possible, they might have avoided it. The fact is that there is a range of ways in which to settle conflicts; these extend through diplomacy, economic and political moves, armed reprisals, and war. Any intelligent diplomat knows they are all possible, and he attempts to resolve conflict in the least costly way consistent with the set of goals and values that he is trying to implement. The knowledge that a more costly way is possible—that is, that war is possible—reinforces the likelihood of peace. A statesman aware of this is more likely to avoid cornering his opponent or foreclosing all other alternatives than is one who does not believe in the possibility of war.

Some wars may have been started because the rulers of the nations involved believed in war as the most appropriate method of settlement of disputes. Bismarck's small wars in fact did follow this pattern, although, contrary to the expectations of Allport and Fulbright, these wars were expeditious, paid off, and did not produce very large war cycles.[12] The

11. Gordon W. Allport, "The Role of Expectancy," in Hadley Cantril, ed., *Tensions That Cause Wars* (Urbana, Ill., 1950), 43 and 48; quoted in *Old Myths and New Realities*, 144–45 (italics in original).

12. It could be argued that Bismarck's seizure of Alsace-Lorraine did indirectly have the last-named consequence. This does not affect the principle of the discussion, for the issue of the series is too remote to fall within the terms of the generalization.

generalization is an unsatisfactory explanation of the First World War, except in the tautological sense that it is impossible to fight a war without the expectation that war is possible. This is hardly a startling insight. Moreover, it is foolhardy and costly to believe that peace is probable if faced with a revolutionary opponent who believes in war. In this kind of situation, the expectation of war may improve the chances for peace; and the expectation of peace may increase the probability of war. In any event, the proposition that it is the expectation of war that produces war makes central what is at best peripheral and simple what is surely very complex. To borrow a psychological term, it denies the real problems that produce war and maintain peace and runs to a comforting womb in which all will be well when all think good thoughts.

Senator Fulbright quotes a statement in a letter from Dr. Jerome D. Frank to the effect that "Frightened, hostile individuals tend to behave in ways which aggravate their difficulties instead of resolving them, and frightened, hostile nations seem to behave similarly" (pp. 74–75). This generalization is not very helpful with respect to individual behavior, let alone with respect to state behavior. For instance, I have my students read the psychological literature on paranoia, which points out that trying to satisfy the demands of paranoidal individuals does not satisfy them, but may drive them into making even greater demands. According to much of the literature, the only way to handle such people is to keep paranoids closely controlled. The parallel with Hitler—and, some would think, with the Soviet Union—is obvious. My better students, however, recognize that such generalizations can do more harm than good, for they can divert attention from the concrete aspects of the case to abstract theoretical aspects which, even if they were better validated than psychological theory is, would still apply only statistically, and then only to individual behavior. And one would still need to know that the individual really belonged in the category.

Such psychological theories—and one could find a theory that would support any conceivable pattern of response—have value only when they reinforce analyses made on more relevant grounds. That is, an analysis in depth is made of behavior patterns and situational components. Then, if the theory of personality that seems to apply in the individual case supports the conclusion, it tends to reinforce and corroborate judgment. Even so, it probably has only marginal value. Many of the best analysts state privately that the Freudian categories can be used predictively or prescriptively only when the analyst is familiar with the life history and circumstances of the patient in great detail and in context. This is a kind of knowledge we will not have for the relevant political cases.

If prediction, or prescription, is so difficult for individuals, the problem is even worse when we deal with national entities. The individuals who represent these entities are constrained by colleagues, decision-making processes, and role expectations. They respond to regime pressures we know little about; and much of what we know is probably wrong or out of context. We do not understand either the insulating mechanisms or the triggering devices that operate in these circumstances. The psychological generalizations which have at best only minimal utility when dealing with individuals are worse than useless—indeed, are dangerous—when dealing with matters of high international politics.

Moreover, Dr. Frank's generalization would seem to conflict with well-known information about Russian Bolshevik leadership. The Russians—in the past at least—were concerned with concrete results as opposed to "pride." They found it easier to bargain with hostile enemies whose positions they "understood," and with whom they could make limited and temporary agreements that were mutually advantageous, than with opponents who exuded "good will" and whose motives they could neither understand nor trust. Even where the hostility was overwhelming, as in the case of Hitler, Stalin responded by backing down step by step, even to the extent of not mobilizing adequately at the frontier. If I were incautious, I could assert that the way to deal with the Russians is to keep confronting them with threats. This might be true in individual cases; as a generalization, it is dangerous.

It is better to trust the intuition of the experienced participant than vague psychological generalizations. It is, however, true that the intuition of the trained participant may break down when he operates in a different environment. Roosevelt, for instance, did not really recognize that the techniques of persuasion which worked so well in domestic politics were not very useful when dealing with Stalin and de Gaulle. As a consequence, where agreement seemed essential, he may have repressed the evidence that it did not exist— e.g., in the case of Stalin. Where agreement did not seem essential, he likely recognized disagreement and responded with pique, as in the case of de Gaulle. (Is a repetition of history possible?) The psychologist and anthropologist could help by alerting the practitioner to the range of possible variations and the conditions under which the variations are likely to occur. Dr. Frank, however, does not attempt to open the practitioner's mind to the range of variations but to persuade him of the accuracy of a set of dangerously oversimplified generalizations that have only limited applicability at best. This perverts the utility that a knowledge of psychology might have for the practitioner. Unfortunately, Dr. Frank is not merely a bad example. In general, the psychologists who have been talking loudly about international politics make ridiculous and misleading assertions that they attempt to cloak beneath a certificate of professional skill.

If one treated these generalizations with care, it would be apparent that no conclusions could be drawn from them. For instance, Senator Fulbright's quotation from Dr. Frank does not state that friendly behavior on our part would reduce Russian hostility or that Russian hostility would produce difficulties for us. Practitioners would do well to avoid the half-digested contributions of psychologists, anthropologists, and sociologists to the problems of foreign policy. As bad as common sense and conventional wisdom may be, it is much better than what these men have to offer.

VI

There were a number of myths which Senator Fulbright might have dealt with but did not. Why foreign aid, for instance? Except for Marshall Plan aid to Western Europe and for aid to a few selected countries, such as Israel and Taiwan, there is little evidence that our aid has done any good and some that it has done harm. If aid is to be provided primarily as a gesture of sympathy—a not unworthy reason—perhaps we should understand this. If there are other reasons, it is time to discover what they are.

Why support for India? Successful development in democracies in Asia is taking place in Japan and Malaya, but not in India. If we are looking for a counterexample to China, India is the wrong place. Would it really hurt us if India drifted into the Russian orbit in some respects at least? Such a development might support rather than hinder American foreign policy requirements. It might worsen the strains between Russia and China and increase the drain upon Russian resources.

Our relations with Japan are much better now that Ambassador Reischauer has replaced Ambassador MacArthur, but why jeopardize these fine relations by maintaining bases which are an irritant and which probably could not be used in any serious crisis? If the Japanese government is not adding its voice to the attack against the bases, this probably stems more from its fears concerning Congress and trade than from lack of resentment. We conceivably may pay a high penalty for not anticipating this problem and resolving it on our own initiative.

We pay lip service to the problem of German unity. In fact, we do not want such unity any more than the French or the Russians. Yet the division of Germany is by far the most plausible cause of central war or of several other extremely uncomfortable developments. Russia's own interests, if she understood them, would lie in the resolution of the issue as long as the fake government of East Germany could be eliminated in a face-saving way. The failure to understand this and to press the issue may be the neatest ostrich trick of the century.

As for the UN, it undoubtedly is a valuable institution that we would do well to support. However, we overload and overvalue the institution in a whole series of ways that cannot be recounted here. There is more cant than wisdom in our attitudes toward the organization. (This is also true with respect to our position on Russian dues.) And this may in fact help more to undermine the UN than to support it. In the same way, the enormous amount of cant on the subject of disarmament may do more to undermine than to support peace, let alone other values.

Does the United States have the will and the skill to act resourcefully in various areas of the globe? Events in Vietnam, Cuba, Africa, Latin America, and Asia call this into question. We lack the will to act, the coldness to engage in counterterror, and the skill to discriminate among contenders for favor. The Congo is a prime instance of the last-named failing. Perhaps we would be much better advised to cut our commitments—not, as Senator Fulbright contends, because we lack the power, but rather because we lack the will and the skill.

I believed that the development of Atlantic Union was the hope of mankind. I would still believe so if it could be made to work. But is not the evidence now against it and even against smaller designs such as NATO? Perhaps we should still try palliatives like the parliamentary union suggested by Senator Fulbright, but perhaps we should also think seriously about more relevant and feasible objectives. What about union with Australia? The Australians like us; they are far enough away not to fear our embrace, but to fear its lack. If they joined the union as a State, the Canadians might follow suit. We would then unify much of the northern half of the hemisphere and also would have an outpost in Asia which we could use to protect the Philippines and other interests in that part of the world. If the British later joined, we might eventually link up with a Europe that had united in the meantime. This new American union should not be limited to those of white skin and English tongue, but English-speaking white nations are the more likely early entrants.

We can draw one further inference from the disarray of our alliance structure. Our alliances are no longer sufficiently functional for us to worry excessively about the reactions of our alliance partners to our policies. Our concern for Allied reactions serves more to inhibit policy than the existence of the alliance structure serves to support policy. Although we should not be entirely indifferent to the opinions of our allies, it is plausible that our present hobbled policy further undermines our external support and that a more active and determined policy might create new support when its effectiveness has been demonstrated. Perhaps we should allow support to coalesce, as we did at the time of the missile crisis in Cuba, and not worry even about those cases where it is lacking in the immediate event. Just as every case of Soviet economic aid and of revolution somewhere in the world tends to be feared by the United States, we tend to fear any disruption of the existing alliance structure. This may be far too negative a position. And it likely contributes to the existing paralysis of United States foreign policy.

More examples might be given, but they cannot be developed here. Our criticisms of Washington and of Senator Fulbright have been severe. Perhaps to some extent this has been a one-sided account. There are intelligent, dedicated, courageous, and hard-working individuals who have responsibilities for the conduct of U.S. foreign policy and who carry out these responsibilities in the Department of State and in the Executive Office of the President. Still, these organizations do not function well, at least in the top echelons. The contrast with the intellect, sparkle, and skill of the Department of Defense is all too obvious. We have learned the art of war much better than the art of peace. By the most important operational tests, U.S. foreign policy is bankrupt.

At least some of the blame for this bankruptcy of policy can be attributed to the new dysfunctional myths that Senator Fulbright espouses. We do not need these myths. We do need a new analysis that will provide new directions for American foreign policy that are more in harmony with American possibilities, resources, ideals, and will than is present American policy. Undoubtedly it is unpleasant to admit the failures of one's hopes and expectations. But mere denial will not change any of the facts. To succeed in an adverse world, we require the courage to view the world as it is and to mold it, so far as lies within our powers and skills, as we would have it. Now is the time for a real great debate—the debate that Senator Fulbright did not provide for us.

VI

THE THIRD WORLD
AND REVOLUTION

The articles included in this section cover a variety of topics related to a number of the major issues we have already discussed. I group them here, however, primarily for the emphasis they place on a related set of specific great issues. Are the disturbances in third-world nations—guerrilla wars, coups, and revolutionary movements—of significance for American national security? Senator Church (article 17), for instance, suggests that these changes pose no threat of injury to the United States and are in the interest of the peoples of the countries in which they occur. The statement by Eqbal Ahmad (article 18) carries the argument further and asserts that American intervention will injure American interests. Both articles rest upon a premise that is implicit: a reduced need for American allies abroad, a lesser incentive to intervene in the affairs of other nations, a relative independence of American security from turmoil in the external world, and—a subject that will be treated at greater length in chapter IX on national style—a belief that cooperative and friendly policies will reduce whatever remaining dangerous potential there is in the world situation.

I argue in my article against ritualistic support for reactionary or stagnating regimes, but Senator Church and Eqbal Ahmad seem to argue for support for all revolutionary regimes on the ground that such regimes are necessary for development and, thus, are desired by the people. For instance, according to Senator Church, "With our support, repressive governments in Brazil and Greece and a conservative government in the Dominican Republic, to cite but a few examples, have successfully held down popular aspirations for social and economic change."

If the reader wishes to assess this argument, he may compare the growth rate in properly paired countries. For instance, the growth rate in South Korea should be compared with that in North Korea. The growth rate in the Dominican Republic or Brazil should be compared with that in Cuba or Chile. The growth rate in Iran should be compared with that in neighboring Iraq. The growth rate in Taiwan should be compared with that in Communist China. Even if these pairs of nations are not precisely comparable, a variety of examples of this kind at least might suggest that "revolutionary" regimes are not required for economic development.

Is there any evidence to support the view that the masses of people in underdeveloped nations desire revolutionary change? If the reader believes this, how would he explain the failure of the Viet Cong's Tet 1968 offensive and their spring offensive of 1972 to draw significant popular support in Vietnam? Did the absence of popular uprisings during the 1972 spring offensive, when they would have undermined the basis for continued American support (given the attitude of Congress), suggest popular opposition to Communist control? What of the sustained efforts of the An Quang Buddhists to prevent uprisings, despite their opposition to the Thieu government?

Is the charge correct that the United States has always supported reactionary regimes that have not advanced the economic and the libertarian interests of the populations? What of land reform? The reader may compare the effective land reforms in Japan and on Taiwan with the collectivization of land in Communist China and North Vietnam that turned the peasants into state employees.

There may be legitimate choices for the U.S. to make. Even if democracy as we know it is not possible in some nations because the prerequisites for it do not exist, we may be able to distinguish between authoritarian and totalitarian regimes—between regimes that permit some degree of formal opposition even if they do employ repressive techniques, and some degree of press and educational freedom even though they are severely restricted, and those regimes that suppress all formal opposition and allow no dissent in the press or in the educational system.

I believe that we should take into account the fact that authoritarian regimes based on right-wing elites are less efficient than Communist regimes based on highly organized mass parties and, therefore, that their tyrannies are more easily reversible. Ambassador Reischauer suggests below that we should also take into account American security interests, our need for allies and bases, and our practical capability to produce change.

However, even if the reader agrees that the American record has neither been always reactionary nor always opposed to the wishes of the populace of threatened areas, it does not follow that American intervention is necessarily wise or effective. The high costs of the Vietnam war make intervention a dubious political prospect in the future. Moreover, there is a further question that may dominate the others: whether the U.S. is capable of effective intervention in the post-Vietnam period. The reader may agree with all the previous distinctions and still argue that ineffective intervention would be worse than nonintervention, even in pursuit of worthy values. Article 19 by Earl C. Ravenal on the Nixon Doctrine in Asia makes the major point that Nixon's acceptance of a one-and-one-half war strategy, as opposed to the previous two-and-one-half war strategy, provides the United States with a force structure that is inadequate to Nixon's commitments in the third world and in Asia in particular. Thus, Ravenal argues, Nixon's policy perhaps deters war somewhat in that area but increases the probability of an American involvement if war occurs. He suggests that if involvement occurs, it would be unsuccessful because of the reduced capability of our armed forces, thus leaving us only with a nuclear alternative, a strategy that I assume Mr. Ravenal neither advocates nor expects the United States to use. On the other hand, in defending his policy, Mr. Nixon argues that the major job of defense will need to be accomplished by local national forces and that the United States will offer only advice and some military assistance, including perhaps naval and air support.

If one is thinking of the type of involvement in which President Johnson engaged in Vietnam, Mr. Ravenal is obviously correct. If one is thinking, on the other hand, of the scaled-down measures of assistance the United States extended to Vietnam in 1972, possibly with less air support, then the U.S. force posture may be adequate. If the war did not involve direct use of large numbers of Chinese troops (and in Vietnam it did not), if the governments in the areas engaged in the methods of consolidation and reconstruction that Mr. Nixon has recommended to them as a requirement for American assistance, then perhaps these marginal measures of defense would be sufficient. In any event, the reader should study the matter within this framework of analysis.

If the United States is scaling down the scope of its commitment to Asia, does it make any difference whether it is done quickly or slowly? If the American commitment is reduced quickly, would this set off a process of extremely rapid, and perhaps ill-considered, accommodations to the Communist powers by the nations of Southeast Asia, and possibly by Japan and Indonesia as well, or even by Australia? If the reduction is slow, and if the U.S. maintains some bases in the Southeast Asian area, is it possible that the nations of Southeast Asia in particular and the larger Asian nations as well might be provided with the time they require to achieve a more cautious and stable readjustment to the developing Asian scene, including the emergence of Communist China as an actor on the world scene?

The evidence indicates clearly that there is Chinese support for "wars of national liberation" in the southeast Asian area and particularly in northeast Thailand. Does Nixon's new China policy provide the nations of Southeast Asia with time to adjust their own relations with China? If they do this with skill, would continued Chinese support of national liberation movements become more costly for China than a cooperative policy, especially if the alternative may be a greatly increased Russian influence in the area? In this respect, is it likely that during a deliberative readjustment of national policies, China may discover a requirement for some degree of American presence in order to offset potential Russian influence? I do not suggest that the answers to these questions are foreordained, although my own tentative answers are probably evident. Regardless, however, of how we answer these questions, they constitute the great issues that demand the reader's attentive concern. Finally, the reader will also note that President Nixon made the required readjustment in the case of China that Mr. Ravenal doubted could be made, in much less time than Ravenal thought possible, and at a lower price in terms of the sacrifice of American commitments.

16.

United States Foreign Policy in a Revolutionary Age

MORTON A. KAPLAN

I Introduction

The following essay is necessarily oversimplified. In the first place, it attempts to deal briefly with many broad-ranging topics of foreign policy. The complexities of the problems involved in American foreign policy can barely be adumbrated. In the second place, the general line of policy recommended represents a striking departure in many respects from general postwar policy as practiced under both the Truman and Eisenhower administrations. The effort to outline the nature of the policy and to relate it to the structural features of contemporary world politics can best be carried out if the policy is presented in its most stark and simple form.

Of course, no policy can be implemented in this simple fashion, for it is not possible to obtain sufficient domestic or allied agreement. In addition, particular features of individual situations almost always require qualification of generalized prescriptions, regardless of the nature of the prescriptions, unless they are so general as to be meaningless or inapplicable. General formulations are better for establishing frameworks of attitudinal responses than for deriving detailed policy. This essay is intended primarily to indicate the changes in attitudes toward foreign policy that are desirable in today's revolutionary world.

There are many difficulties with the pursuit of American foreign policy, and it is, of course, much easier to criticize than to undertake the responsi-

Reprinted by permission from *The Revolution in World Politics*, pp. 255–257 and 431–456. Copyright © 1962 John Wiley & Sons, Inc.

bility for formulating and executing national policy. If I were to single out, however, two general criticisms, they would be: (1) that the policy of the recent past has been more appropriate to a "balance of power" system than to a bipolar system; and (2) that policy has been more appropriate to an era in which society is static than to one in which there is rapid and revolutionary social change.

II   Bipolarity and Revolutionary Change

With respect to the first criticism, that past policy has been more appropriate to a "balance of power" system, several brief observations may be made. The "balance of power" system operates on the basis of short-term alignments of a flexible nature. It is a system in which alignment preferences are based on specific and limited interests. Thus, the enemy of today may be the ally of tomorrow. The nature of regimes and of internal social conditions are indifferent to alignment decisions. And, hence, morality or sentiment, as contrasted with "interest," plays a subordinate role in the decision process. Although the system can tolerate neutrals, neutrals as such do not play an essential role in the system. Indeed, if important states essayed such a role as permanent, their decision might be quite inconsistent with the stability of the system and with their own long-range interests.

The loose bipolar system, on the other hand, depends upon the formation of blocs based upon considerations of long-term interest. The closer the value patterns of the bloc members, the easier it is to maintain the solidarity of the bloc. Clearly democratic nations could not easily function as members of the Soviet bloc. Although the converse proposition has less force, it still has some validity. NATO solidarity is strong because there are many shared values and institutional practices among most members of the organization. In addition, in the bipolar system it is not desirable to have all nations within the bloc structures. The uncommitted nations play a stabilizing role that, in a nuclear age, is of value to the blocs. The United Nations may also play a mediating role that, within limits, merits the support of the blocs.

For the reasons just enumerated, the policy of building blocs has definite limits in a bipolar age. Also, the distinction between "interest" and "sentiment" is not as compelling as in the "balance of power" age. The kinds of nations one aligns with, and the policies one pursues internationally, ought to be more closely oriented to value—or moral—considerations than was the case in the past.

If we take into consideration that the present age is also a revolutionary one in which change sweeps from nation to nation, sometimes without respect to alignment pattern, the preceding conclusion is strengthened. Blocs cannot obtain generalized support from uncommitted nations, and specific support may very well depend upon what values the bloc stands for and attempts to propagate. The solidarity of the bloc and the willingness of the populace within a nation to take those risks necessary for long-term stability in a nuclear age may depend upon the pursuit of policies that accord with basic ideals.

If we move from the confines of the model of international politics, this conclusion becomes even more compelling. The West, in particular, the United States, is on the defensive. We have become modern Canutes, attempting to hold back the tides, unresponsive to the currents of our time. In an age when new nations have been proliferating and old nations undergoing revolutionary changes, the United States has been implementing a policy designed in general to discourage radical change and to aid governments in power, regardless of the nature of their regimes, provided they are avowedly anti-Communist. The two aspects of the policy, of course, are related, for often the most anti-Communist governments are those which fear radical change at home and which are willing to join American military alliances to receive support that may bolster them against the forces making for internal change. As a consequence, in many areas of the world, the United States seems to represent reaction and a barrier to the hopes and aspirations of large masses of people. It seems to stand for corruption, inefficiency, and maintenance of the status quo. And, at least to many, the alliances it espouses raise the danger of local war for causes not understandable to large masses of the local populations.

The United States has so defined the issues that, for many revolutionary social movements, to pursue what they desire both nationally and internationally is to oppose the United States. This, of course, gives the Soviet Union great leverage. This also makes the bipolar system even more unstable than it otherwise would be. Since, in addition, many Westerners are opposed to the policies that produce these results, it weakens the ability of the United States to counter the Soviet offensive. Coalition problems increase and elements within the United States become disaffected.

The Soviet Union is an active and disturbing foe. Supported by its belief in the historic inevitably of Communism, it challenges the present structure of world politics. It is little inhibited by domestic opinion or by bloc dissidence. It is not associated with colonialism by the new nations and it can support, almost without qualification, actions designed to change the status quo radically. It holds forth the threat of nuclear war and, because it seems impervious to change or to influence, drives those who fear war to put pressure upon the West to make concessions. Along with the threat of war, it advocates disarmament under conditions that are not genuinely acceptable to the West.

Under pressure from the Soviet and Chinese threats, and faced by revolutionary changes in the world, the West retreats. Its alliances become fragile. Compromise and temporization are the order of the day. And, even in the United States, there is difficulty in mobilizing domestic opinion behind policies involving risks. The effort to halt Communism hardly seems worth the risk of nuclear war to many, particularly if a stand must be made in a remote and seemingly unimportant area of the world. It is much easier to postpone risks and to enjoy the luxuries of contemporary American life or to seek scapegoats either on the left or right of the political spectrum. After all, the hard choices can also be avoided by blaming our problems on Communist subversives or on warmongering generals. The witch hunt and the peace march are both symptoms of the breakdown and rejection of political life. They are both symptoms of an essential malaise in the West—of the absence of a unifying political ideal.

Western societies are no longer politically vigorous. Large segments of the public are complacent and desire to preserve what they have rather than to lead crusades that will transform the world. Their attitudes are largely defensive and even the protests against these attitudes are fed more by a gnawing discontent or by impotent anger than by a vision of the future. The bright hopes of the past are transformed into disillusion and bitterness.

There was a day—not too far in the history of the world—when political democratization held forth to most the hopes of redress of past grievances. It was thought that democracy shattered the chains of tradition, made man master of his fate, vanquished ignorance and poverty, and permitted a race of Prometheans to rule the world. Vain hope! It is not that democracy is worse than other forms of government. However futile the hope of self-government and thus of individual dignity, democracy comes closer to reaching these goals than any other form of government. It is consistent with economic vigor, with a standard of living and health higher than any the world has ever known, and with the freedom of man to pursue his own future as he wills rather than as the state dictates. The disillusion does not lie in the comparative lack of achievement of democracy as contrasted with other forms of government. The disillusion stems from the gap between the ideals of the democratic creed and the performance of democratic government.

We have explored the possibilities of democracy and we know that there are limitations on its ability to transform the world. It takes tremendous self-discipline to recognize these limitations as inherent in human organization and to work for limited but possible improvements. For most people, there is a tendency to become complacent about the achievements of democracy and to value personal satisfactions. Such people do not want to sacrifice in the name of an ideal that cannot be achieved. Others find their mission in fighting injustice in some abstract sense. These fasten onto the past and present "sins" of democracy; and, in their desire to punish democracy for its shortcomings, they ignore the immensely larger evils of a creed that still promises abstract justice at some future time if only it can conquer the world.

The essential difficulty of the democratic position is that it seems to deny to many, in democratic nations as well as to those elsewhere, goods that are legitimized by the democratic creed. Any political system must suffer defects. No system can be consistently true to its own ideals. Democracy is challenged in the present age in terms of its own ideals. Its inability to satisfy this challenge by present performance—and sometimes its indifference to real and pressing injustices—creates an internal opposition which cannot be suppressed consistently with the institutions and values it espouses.

Thus, within the democratic nations, there are articulate groups, with some political effectiveness, that are essentially disaffected and that are motivated to inhibit effective political action designed to maintain the security of the NATO bloc. These groups are at basis recriminatory, they are more inclined to view Western policy with suspicion because of its "sins" than they are to view Soviet policy with suspicion. They have a mistrust of capital, which they feel has alienated and exploited man, of military leaders whom they suspect of warlike aims, and of politicians who they believe desire to suppress movements for national freedom and independence. Because many of the articulate intelligentsia belong to these movements, they have a political effect disproportionate to their numerical strength. And, because they are citizens of democracies, their arguments convince many in other nations of the injustice of the democratic nations.

To describe what is necessary to rejuvenate American political life may be beyond the powers of any individual. That subject certainly cannot be considered within the scope of this paper. A few aspects of the problem as it affects the conduct of foreign policy can, however, be mentioned. The goals of American foreign policy must be derived from the basic ideals of the nation if they are to obtain sufficient support for a chance of effective implementation. The United States must begin to think not in terms of specific deals or outcomes but in terms of the kind of world in which American democracy can survive. *Realpolitik* and cynicism may once have been effective techniques for the conduct of foreign policy. If they are resorted to today at the highest levels of policy-making, they will corrode the political faith required for an effective American policy and, if necessary, for the resort to force in support of that policy.

If we enunciate policies merely to gain support and not because we are convinced of their rightness, we encourage others to raise the price of their support. If we assume a posture of strength in support of policies we are not really willing to run risks to implement, the Soviet Union is likely soon to call our bluff and expose our irresolution. If we are to act with hope of success, we must find a source of strength not merely in weapons, but also in our values and ideals.

The United States can no longer afford to be a conservative nation. Conservatism is appropriate when change threatens desirable values *and* when these values can be defended best by defensive measures. There must be an ability to weather the storm. It made sense for Franklin Roosevelt to replace "Dr. New Deal" with "Dr. Win the War." But we are no longer faced with a military conflict of relatively short duration. We are confronted with a revolution of world-wide dimensions, a revolution that cannot be halted by military measures or by temporary defeats. The United States cannot—and should not attempt to—halt this revolution. It can attempt to influence the direction this revolution takes and the values that flourish as it progresses.

Although the "Free World-Communist" dichotomy is grossly oversimplified—witness the authoritarian satrapies of the United States, such as Spain—it points to an essential truth about the present world struggle. Imbedded in the American tradition as it has developed is a belief in the right of each individual to find his own truth, provided only that he respect the rights of others to find their truths. Just as the American political process encourages the enunciation and pursuit of any political goal compatible with the maintenance of a political system permitting such a pursuit for all, the American intellectual system permits an experimental attitude toward beliefs—permits the individual to pursue his thought as best he can. There is no official dogma that circumscribes this process, that must be accepted, that cannot be tested or denied. There is a distaste for official or governmental indoctrination, and a belief that the only dignified beliefs worthy of free men are those that can withstand free and public challenge. There is the belief that the proper goal of society is the mature, free man—and that it is the object of society to provide, or at least to permit, the conditions under which such men can flourish.

The democratic system is one that institutionalizes dissent and that encourages criticism, as long as it does not attack the fundamental principle that others also, even if members of a minority, possess this right. These ideals are imbedded, even if imperfectly, in American institutions. But they are not otherwise related to class, race, religion, or nationality. If we believe in these values, we must believe in them for others as well. And, if we are moral people, within the limits of prudence, we shall not hold to these beliefs passively, but we shall encourage and support those who also subscribe to these values in other lands.

Before examining specific problems, we can summarize the three kinds of major problems facing the United States:

1. The uncommitted states are alienated and act in ways that increase the instability of the bipolar age.

2. The West has no positive set of ideals to generate a confident set of foreign policies. NATO is beset by divisions and fears. The individual member nations complacently desire to protect what they have but lack an image of a world they desire that will induce bold and purposeful programs and policies.

3. The Soviet Union and the Communist bloc constitute an active set of foes. They take advantage of the divisions in the West, and of the fears and complacencies of individual Western nations, to increase the pressure on the West and to force concessions disadvantageous to it. The Communist leaders know the kind of world they want to build and are willing to take risks to achieve their goals. Despite some internal quarrels, they achieve rea-

sonable cooperation and are able to induce reasonable domestic support. The United States must learn how to deal with the Soviet challenge and, to the extent possible, increase the problems facing the Soviet bloc both internally and externally.

There are no complete or easy solutions for these problems. But the United States must learn to cope with them in an adequate way if it is to preserve the values that underlie the American experiment.

III The Uncommitted States and United States Policy

The passion for self-rule, for independence, applies both to groups and to individuals. Colonial existence, no matter how necessary it may seem at some times to promote still further development, is incompatible with human dignity. And although rule by a local dictatorship is far removed from the ideal, it at least extends to the group that which should also be extended to the individual. It is a necessary, if not a sufficient, condition for human dignity, and Americans ought not to be indifferent to the desire for independence, whether that desire be of the black man in Africa, the white man in Eastern Europe, or the yellow man in Asia.

ALLIANCES WITH THE UNCOMMITTED STATES

Most of the new nations are weak and backward. Their leaders remember a period of colonial subjection. They are fearful that their new independence may be compromised and are dedicated to modernizing. The problems of these new nations are enormous, and their leaders desire to insulate them from quarrels they do not recognize as their own. Moreover, they have a genuine interest in attempting to shift the burden of defense against Soviet aggression to others. They will resent any effort to commit them to objectives that divert them from modernizing or that threaten to move them toward the center of the Cold War.

The United States has, fortunately, given up the idea of creating extensive chains of military alliances that depended on the adherence of uncommitted states. This attempt frightened the leaders of many of the new nations. It brought their nations to the center of the Cold War and subjected them to Soviet political attack. The leaders did not desire this—except where internal problems or national divisions, as in Korea or Viet Nam, seemed to necessitate it. Where the populace knew of the commitment, it often misunderstood it. Counterelites opposed to the governments often used the commitments as weapons, as in Iraq. Those who thought the first problem of their nation was development viewed such alliances as a diversion of resources and effort. They much preferred an anticipated insulation from the Cold War and the opportunity to play the East and West off against each other both politically and in terms of access to investment funds.

Where conservative regimes desired alliances to support internal policies, the alliances identified the United States with the policies of these regimes. Where nationalist regimes existed, the attempt to induce them into alliances against their resistance appeared as a threat to their goals, as in Egypt.

In addition, the idea behind these alliances was unsound from the very start. Such nations had little to add in a military sense, although some of them were able to provide bases that temporarily were important. The military aid often unbalanced the economies of these states. In addition, the real and undervalued mediatory role these nations could play when uncommitted was neglected. Where they might have been bulwarks in upholding desirable principles of international law as uncommitted nations, they were instead weak, vulnerable, and temporary members of a Western alliance.

With few exceptions in the present period, military alliances with the new and largely uncommitted states will serve neither their interests nor ours. Alliances or even strong political coalitions are unlikely to work out well. We shall do best if we attempt to commit these nations to the support of universalistic principles of international law or norms of international behavior rather than to specific American interests. Economic aid and the political problems arising therefrom also will constitute an important problem area for American relations with the new and uncommitted nations. This last problem will now be considered.

ECONOMIC DOMINANCE OVER THE UNCOMMITTED STATES

Many of the uncommitted nations believe that the United States, because of its economic power, represents an economic threat to their independence. This fear undoubtedly is greatly exaggerated, but it exists even in our Canadian neighbor to the North. Whatever the economic arguments to the contrary, it would probably make good political sense to encourage at least some other countries, particularly in Latin America, to purchase controlling interests in large local corporations controlled from or owned abroad, especially those which dominate important natural resources such as oil. The United States government should attempt to facilitate the transfer of ownership and control by underwriting it to some extent.[1] This would help to circumvent extremist demands which might force nationalization under conditions that would cause political strains between particular foreign nations and the United States and that would lead to local irrational economic decisions inconsistent with American efforts to support modernization and political liberalism. Moreover, transfers of ownership and control, freely

1. John Kaplan of the Hudson Institute has suggested that this might be accomplished by eliminating tax credits for entirely owned foreign subsidiaries of United States corporations doing business in underdeveloped countries. Although this might possibly have too extensive an effect, it might well be investigated. American business ought to consider such arrangements voluntarily, as well as those in which their interests could be liquidated after a fixed period of years. Business may be deterred from such arrangements more by ideological than economic considerations.

offered, might do much to dampen the entire issue and to forestall extensions of the nationalization principle that would be economically harmful or that would interfere with needed access by developing nations to the American capital market.

SOVIET AID TO THE UNCOMMITTED STATES

The United States has tended to view Soviet aid to uncommitted nations as a calamity, inconsistent with their independence and with American attempts to entice them into political or military alliances or ententes. This has reinforced the auction aspects of American relations with the uncommitted nations and it has debased American generosity. Instead, the United States should welcome Soviet aid as a substitute or complement for American aid even where we may consider the specific forms of aid undesirable. The receiving nations should be depended upon to insist on conditions that preclude major political gains by the Soviet Union. The United States should be prepared to cooperate with such efforts on the part of the uncommitted states. We should insist that the major burden of maintaining independence rest with the uncommitted states; it should not permit these nations to exploit American fears that they might not want to maintain their independence.

American aid offered merely as an alternative to Soviet aid necessarily leads to an auction that cannot be won. The Soviet Union can pick and choose its aid targets. It was always able to breech the wall of aid containment, even at a time when it was relatively weak economically, and was able to force the United States to utilize its aid in ways that were not economically rational. As the Soviet Union grows stronger economically, the problem worsens. If the United States welcomes Soviet aid as an alternative and offers it own aid without regard to securing allies, this vicious cycle can be broken.

PRINCIPLES OF AMERICAN AID—GENERAL

We can now inquire into the principles that ought to govern the extension of American aid to the uncommitted nations. Although the United States may properly give preference to nations that cooperate with it politically and deliberately bail these nations out of political difficulties, it should not attempt to buy outright support and should even discourage such support on the part of those nations where there is no popular local basis for it. In these last cases, failure to follow the suggested principle makes the regimes vulnerable to criticism for forfeiting independence and drives the opposition into an anti-American position. In general, aid should be given because we desire to live in a world where people can look forward to better lives, not because we expect political support, or even because we believe that better conditions will make Communism less likely. Indeed there is little evidence that aid will accomplish these latter objectives.

The United States and the uncommitted states do not have the same community of values or institutions that the United States and Europe have. Except where there are quite specific and compelling common interests—as in the case of South Korea, for instance—we cannot expect the uncommitted states to share our foreign-policy burdens, whatever some abstract ethical system might seem to imply. It would be foolish, therefore, to use aid as a weapon in an attempt to gain foreign-policy support. Within broad limits, aid ought not to be dependent on the external policies of the aided state—unless, of course, that state goes so far as to become a member of the Communist bloc or unless that state acts in a manner consistently disruptive of desirable principles of international order rather than merely in a manner opposed to specific American interests. Attempts to condition aid on foreign-policy support confuse the purpose of the aid, injure the national pride of the aided nations, and eventually undercut the purposes of the aid either by identifying local regimes with the United States in ways that alienate them from their bases of local support, or by driving such regimes into anti-American positions.

However, we should attempt to convince the uncommitted nations that independence and lack of commitment does not imply that they attempt to compromise the differences whenever the United States and the Soviet Union differ. If they really essayed such a role, then it would be strategically advisable for the United States and the Soviet Union to exaggerate their demands and differences; otherwise, the suggested compromises would be disadvantageous to them. And if either failed, or was unable to do this, the other would gain a strategic advantage that might destabilize the international system. The uncommitted nations must be persuaded—but not coerced by aid policy—to the extent possible, to support universalistic normative rules of behavior consistent with the kind of international system in which their own best interests will be protected. It can be argued that opposition to some specific American objectives might be a small price to pay if the uncommitted states could be committed to certain stabilizing norms of international behavior.

In applying its aid, the United States should be concerned with building the kind of world it desires to live in. Modernization, regional cooperation, and democracy undoubtedly are features of the world the United States desires for the future.

SPECIFIC PRINCIPLES OF AID—MODERNIZATION

The leaders of the new nations—in particular the educated elites—desire modernization and independence. These two goals are viewed as inseparable, for it is thought that independence cannot be maintained without modernization and that modernization can be carried out only by independent governments. The existence of dependent colonial areas or of non-modernizing independent states is viewed as a threat to the modernizing regimes.

American exhortations to act moderately, responsibly, or democratically seem, to many modernizing leaders, so irrelevant to their difficult tasks that some believe them to be hypocritical.

The disorder in the Congo and the authoritarian regimes in some of the uncommitted states shock American susceptibilities. But we may be judging these nations by the wrong standards. The historical plays of Shakespeare depict situations no better than those of the Congo; Tudor England was hardly democratic; the Spanish women treated Napoleon's soldiers more cruelly than the *Force Publique* behaved in the Congo; and the Nazi and Ustachi villainies are barely two decades old.

The nations of Europe were not built without bloodshed, corruption, villainy, and misery. But at least these nations did not have modern neighbors to set spectacular expectations for them. They could accept slow progress not only in economic development, but also in the development of a national consciousness and of a state apparatus. Their independence was not seemingly threatened by more developed and more powerful states. In the new nations national consciousness does not exist, except perhaps in inchoate form. There is no state in the European sense. Tribal ties, illiteracy, low levels of resources, production, and skills are inconsistent with the entry into the modern world that their educated elites demand. Even though considerable assistance is available to them, their task is much harder than was the task of the European nations.

Most of the European nations had considerable governmental intervention when entering the modern world. Even in England, Tudor intervention preceded Manchesterian capitalism. Many of the new nations believe they require—and in fact they may be correct—more governmental intervention in the economy than seems proper to us. But we must remember that their economic development is dependent upon political and social revolutions that can be carried out only against the resistance of powerful vested interests. In some of these states, territorial loyalties must replace tribal loyalties. In some, land reform is required. In all, agricultural techniques must be modernized. In many, there is no entrepreneurial class and, even if there were, it could not be expected to take the huge risks required to establish industry, transportation, and communication—without which no contemporary state is viewed as modern. In most, the moneyed interests—where such exist—refuse to use their money productively. Education is essential, but only the state can insure an adequate educational program. These considerations could be multiplied, but that would not be profitable. It is necessary only to point out that these new nations cannot repeat the experience of the United States. If they are to succeed in modernizing at all[2]—and this may be in doubt—there must be considerable intervention in the economy by the state.

---

2. When and if the modernizing elites of some of these countries discover that the attempts to modernize must fail, there may be far-reaching consequences. They may lapse into sloth and corruption. Or, in desperation, they may resort to the most radical of measures.

Economic aid should be related to the ability of the aided area to modernize, to solve its economic problems, and to build a viable and independent nation or areal grouping.

In many of the countries where American aid may be wanted, modernization cannot be carried out without radical social change. This does not mean that existing regimes are always opposed to modernization, any more than were the Shogunate in pre-Meiji Japan or the Nuri as-Said regime in Iraq. But these last two—perhaps unlike the present Thai regime, which is not based on a large landholding class—were unable to carry modernization through without undercutting their bases of political support. In these cases, political revolution was probably a necessary if not sufficient condition for modernization. In some of the Latin American nations the requirements for radical social reform by existing regimes are not so formidable but may still be sufficient to deter the regimes from taking political risks in order to modernize.[3] Where this is the case, American aid is likely to be used ineffectively, and the extension of large-scale aid may even identify the United States with anti-modernist goals.

Intervention in internal affairs to induce modernization is a risky business that may well fail or backfire. Intervention should not be resorted to blithely. On the other hand, the failure of existing regimes to modernize may only insure radical and pro-Soviet revolutions. No specific answers to this problem can be attempted here. There will be cases where intervention may work and others where the risks are too great. But the United States must avoid association with anti-modernist goals. It must display sympathy with modernizing regimes even where specific American economic interests may be affected adversely.

SPECIFIC PRINCIPLES OF AID—REGIONAL COOPERATION

Modernization and cultural independence may be aided by regional cooperation or even by regional integration. The Mahgreb, for instance, is possibly an area where cooperation crossing national boundaries may be feasible and desirable from the standpoint of building a new world order consistent with American principles. Oil-pooling in the Arab Middle East might also be encouraged. Although the Iraq claim to Kuwait could hardly be conceded, the defense of the sovereignty of what is essentially a non-viable political unit demonstrated lack of political foresight.[4]

---

3. This is an exceptionally serious problem for which no clear solutions are in sight. Few ruling groups are sufficiently disinterested to reform themselves out of power, particularly if the reforms are not guaranteed to be workable. Perhaps some of these groups should be bought out or ways discovered to force others to get out or to cooperate.

4. The British were undoubtedly concerned to protect their oil interests. But the present situation is quite unstable. Too much of the Middle East is impoverished and there are too many small oil oases disposing of immense riches. Eventually this situation will change, and the change may be preferable if anticipated and encouraged than if opposed.

The American government presently proposes to set up regional groups in Latin America and Africa with which aid negotiations would be carried on. Little study, however, has been made of the consequences of such a scheme for Africa, in particular, where the question of which states to include would have profound political effects both within the continent and elsewhere. It is at least worth asking whether the political consequences of region-wide economic planning would moderate the policies of the more forward African states, inflame the more moderate states, increase continental harmony, or make worse continental frictions. The inclusion of the United Arab Republic would, of course, have other consequences for American foreign policy.

The commitment of the United States to the OAS leaves little choice except to encourage some kind of regional cooperation in the use of American aid to Latin America. Yet, the program of the Kennedy administration is tied to land reform and to other social and economic reforms. It is doubtful that many of the existing regimes in these countries will, in fact, carry through reforms of a needed radical nature. For this reason, even within the OAS framework, the United States should consider concentrating its aid to those countries that have the desire and ability to modernize themselves. Brazil, Venezuela, Mexico, and Argentina may fall within this category. By committing the major portion of its aid to areas that do modernize economically and socially, the United States would identify itself with such progress. The nations so aided might serve as examples to still others that they need not go the way of the Castro regime in Cuba. On the other hand, by not entirely denying aid to other Latin American countries, the framework of hemispheric solidarity is maintained and American sympathy for the peoples of the hemisphere affirmed. Within this framework, smaller, specific aid programs oriented to other and shorter-term needs could be formulated and carried out. The case for picking and choosing may be even stronger in Africa where the United States lacks historic ties that demand continental solidarity and cooperation. In all cases, major American aid should be conditioned on efforts by the nations involved to help themselves.

The United States should make clear to all that the major purpose of its aid is to help other countries to enter the modern world. Thus, in general, the United States should not commit itself to outworn social or political systems that cannot satisfy aspirations with which it, in terms of its own national values, must strongly sympathize.

SPECIFIC PRINCIPLES OF AID—INTERNAL POLITICS

For reasons specified previously, new nations, in the effort to modernize, must engage in considerable governmental intervention. Efforts to overcome tribalism or to carry through social revolutions necessary for modernization may lead to considerable authoritarianism. The democratic and humane values destroyed in the process may not be properly appreciated by the leaders of the new nations. Many may lack the sophistication of Attaturk, who used authoritarian forms in an effort to create the conditions under which democracy can maintain itself.

Moreover, many of the leaders of the new nations unfortunately have accepted Marxist myths concerning capitalism. Although in fact the socialism of the new states is more pragmatic and accommodates more capitalism than some Americans believe, there is a real danger that the new states may either stifle or fail quickly to create the middle class that stood as a bulwark against governmental despotism in the West (but that took more than a century to develop). Moreover, much of the human misery of the European economic revolution was the consequence of an impersonal market mechanism rather than of a conscious governmental decision. The governments of the new nations, however, largely take responsibility for economic decisions. Resentment, therefore, may crystallize against these governments for the real or seeming failures of governmental policies. And, in their efforts to modernize rapidly and to maintain control of the situation until this is done, the governments may institutionalize repressive mechanisms resistant to change from below although possibly subject to *coup*.

The United States should leave no doubt concerning its sympathy for the efforts of the elites in the new nations to modernize, of its desire to aid them, and of its recognition that modernization cannot be carried through painlessly or according to its own model. On the other hand, we should not be indifferent to the internal politics of the countries that receive economic aid or assistance from it.[5] The effects on American institutions and values, if the United States becomes an isolated island in a totalitarian—even if non-Communist—world, are too complicated to describe here and in any event are moot. But surely Americans prefer not to live in a totalitarian world and even more surely they do not desire to permit their aid to modernizing nations to be diverted toward the maintenance of a totalitarian police state. (Even if the funds are not used directly for this purpose, they permit the diversion of other funds.) If the United States cannot police the world to maintain democracy everywhere—indeed even if it must recognize that the conditions for democracy are not everywhere present or that in some places democracy may be incompatible with modernization—it does not have to close its eyes to the human drama and to resolve political issues in favor of totalitarianism either through a failure of will, or in a fit of absent-mindedness.

In applying a criterion related to the nature of the regime, an effort must be made to make decisions in context rather than in the abstract. Thus, for instance, a distinction can be made between an area where the conditions for some degree of political liberalism are present but repressed by the government and an area where such conditions are not present. For instance, given

5. Unfortunately, until recently the United States did little to support modernizing democracies, particularly when important economic interests objected to their policies. Venezuela under Betancourt was until recently an unfortunate example of this national myopia.

the cultural and social background of Cuba, it is dubious that most of the totalitarian measures of the Castro regime are necessary for—or even consistent with—rapid modernization, although a mere return to the old constitution might have forfeited the possibilities for social revolution.

The situation is quite different in Ghana and Guinea—which, in any event, are authoritarian and not totalitarian—where tribalism must be overcome to create a national state where one did not properly exist previously. A distinction must also be drawn between a Guinea which has had little experience in government and little time to create liberal institutions and a Spain which has made no effort to create such institutions and which seems determined to maintain a rigidly authoritarian regime indefinitely. Moreover, although Guinea or Ghana may be given the benefit of the doubt, because of their brief existence, it is possible to distinguish between those two cases and Nigeria, which seems more inclined, at present, to develop representative institutions.

African single-party systems which seem to permit debate and consent within the single-party structure must also be differentiated from Communist-type single-party systems which prevent national debate or dissent and which restrict debate to centralized and hierarchical party structures. Thus, whether a nation such as Yugoslavia is aided might be made to depend on whether the party structure is sufficiently loosened to permit genuine and general debate and political alternatives not decided on in advance by the party leadership.

Even if the only two criteria for aid were those previously discussed—modernization and regime character—the applications would be subject to some debate. Spain would clearly be excluded, for it is not modernizing, and it is committed to the maintenance of an authoritarian regime. Cuba would not receive aid because, although it is attempting to modernize, it is now doing so within the framework of a totalitarian regime, which applies terroristic methods in case of dissent. Nigeria and some of the French African states are modernizing, but not rapidly, in an effort to avoid harsh political methods. Even so, many of those French African states are one-party states. At this stage of their development they should probably be given the benefit of the doubt on both counts. Ghana and Guinea are attempting to modernize rapidly, are following foreign policies that are unpalatable to the United States, are probably on balance pro-Soviet, and are employing quite harsh political methods. Even so, they are not totalitarian and, within the framework of African political experience, do permit political alternatives. They should probably receive the present benefit of doubt, but the decision might well be re-evaluated after a reasonable period of time. So also should the Jagan regime in Guiana receive the benefit of the doubt unless it shows signs of becoming totalitarian or of entering the Soviet bloc.

The difficult questions will involve the choice between the rapidly modernizing and less liberal and the more slowly modernizing and more liberal

African regimes. No single criterion can be applied here, for policy decisions must rest on prognostications concerning the probable future course of development of these nations. If the judgment is that the more slowly modernizing nations have a reasonable chance to succeed in modernizing with external support, while maintaining relatively liberal institutions, preference should be given to them where emphasis in allocation is made. If, on the other hand, one comes to the conclusion that modern nationhood in any of these areas rests on rapid and forced evolution from tribalized relations to national solidarity or that political demands on the part of the younger educated elite permit no good alternative, then despite dissatisfactions with their external policies and fears concerning their future political development, aid to the more radically modernizing African nations might have higher priority than would otherwise seem desirable.

In any event, although the United States may prefer a particular set of choices for developing nations, based on its own values and prognostications, and may legitimately allocate aid on the basis of these choices, the decisions on modernization affect it only indirectly. Advice may be offered. Attempts to encourage desirable values can and should be made. But in the last analysis, the developing nations must make their own independent choices, for it is their fate that is directly involved. Where the choice that is made involves a destruction of human dignity that offends our most important values and degrades the human beings so manipulated, as in the case of Cuba, we have an obligation to make our opposition clear. But where the differences are based upon tolerable differences in basic values or prognostications concerning the consequences of particular policies, sympathetic understanding would be more appropriate than harsh rejection.

It is inevitable that particular American decisions, even within the framework of clear policy principles, will be misunderstood by some and resented by others. We do not always properly understand or appreciate the actions or intentions of other nations. The new nations require radical change, and the rich United States is not likely to be viewed sympathetically by the harassed leaders and uneducated masses of these nations. Their values, their goals, and their interpretations of policies differ from ours. Popularity is not to be expected. If, however, there is a posture of disinterested support for modernization, social reform, and political liberalism, if American policy is not tied merely to anti-Communism or to attempts to build systems of alliances, there is some hope that American policy will command respect and that it will invite support when it accords with the most important interests of the uncommitted developing nations.

It must be clear that the United States does not seek *direct* political benefits from its aid. Unlike Communism, which, despite its talk of many roads, has a relatively narrow doctrinal content and organizational form, American favoritism for democracy implies little with respect to the content of legislation—apart from support for modernization—and party and governmental structure. It implies support only for organizational forms that permit the institutionalization of dissent and the relatively free play of ideas. Indeed, the democracies do not possess political means by which control can be exercised over other countries, and, as long as the United States does not attempt to force uncommitted nations into pacts for which they are not prepared, it presents no political threat to their independence.

MODE OF AID

The question of whether aid should be given bilaterally or multilaterally is a difficult one to answer. However, proposals to siphon aid through the United Nations according to its normal constitutional procedures would almost surely be unfortunate. As long as the amount of aid handled through the United Nations is small, the temptation to assert the kind of political control that would be inconsistent with the objectives of the aid will be minimal. As soon, however, as large-scale contributions of aid money to be spent by the organization come to be viewed as a tax to be contributed regularly by the richer nations, the kinds of pork-barrel decisions that are often made in the United States Congress will be made in an even more exaggerated form in the United Nations General Assembly. Since economically irrational decisions are also likely to be made at the national level, this compounding of irrationality would be thoroughly inconsistent with the aims of the aid. Multilateral aid, however, might insulate the United States from criticism in the choice of aid recipients. It is true that the history of bilateral aid leaves little room for optimism. But it is at least easier to reform United States aid programs than to reform international political processes.

In sum, therefore, the question of policy, primarily including economic-aid policy, toward the uncommitted states is not susceptible to an easy answer that permits clear applications. The usual reasons given for aid, namely, that it will make friends, produce political stability, and halt Communism, have little evidence to support them. But, in the end, modernization is probably a good thing. It is doubtful if the demands for modernization can be halted in any event. To the extent that modernization is carried through successfully by non-Communist governments, the expansion of the Communist world system will be halted. Political instability is probably inevitable as rising expectations, new organizations, and political counterelites produce accentuated demands on the governments of the underdeveloped nations. The sooner modernization occurs, the fewer the barriers it must overcome, and the more support the West gives to it, the more successful and the less anti-Western it is likely to be. The more the West attempts either to halt modernization, or use it for ulterior purposes, the more radical and the more susceptible to Communist influence modernization is likely to be. The more disinterested the assistance policy of the West, the greater the control of the West over its allocations of resources and the less susceptible the West is to blackmail in various guises.

Undoubtedly, in nations that lack any democratic experience or tradition, some degree of strong political control—even of authoritarianism—will be needed to handle excessive demands on governmental allocations. In others, such as India, the democratic method may be made to work in modernizing the nation and may serve as a model for other nations, if not in the present, then at least with respect to the future. At present, however, democratic values have no appeal for the poor, the backward, the illiterate. They appear to be luxuries or even undesirable. Our best hope is to produce a period of relative stability during which these values can become appreciated. This will not happen until other and prior—even if less important from our viewpoint—values are first achieved. The present period is a crucial one, and the choices made by the West—and primarily by the United States—will play a critical role in determining the shape of world politics for some time to come.

Although specific choices of aid policy or allocations of funds may be responsive to highly particular circumstances, the philosophy that guides the program will be of major importance in determining its effectiveness and acceptability to the aided nations. This guiding spirit in the intermediate run will have more impact on the consciousness of the leaders and peoples of the developing nations than the details of policy. Mistakes will be made and can be overcome with respect to those details. But the failure of the general outlines of policy to accord disinterestedly with the requirement of modernization eventually will lead to major discord between the aims and accomplishments of policy. The aim of the United States must not be popularity or even instrumental alliances. The major aim of American policy must be a structure of world politics in which the most important Western interests can be protected and the democratic form of government survive. The status quo cannot be preserved. The question concerns the shape of the changes to come. It is here precisely that the West and the United States must take their stand as a matter of principle rather than as a matter of expediency.

IV   United States General Alliance Policy

The United States should begin to overhaul its alliance system along with its program of aid. Unfortunately, it is not always wise to scrap alliances that it was initially unwise to form. Withdrawal from an alliance may too easily be interpreted as withdrawal from an obligation to defend and, thus, may set in motion other undesirable events. For instance, withdrawal from SEATO might encourage Chinese aggression and might also encourage political deals favorable to Communism by local political elites. Opportunistic political elites, convinced that withdrawal from the alliances signified withdrawal from an interest in the independence of the area, might then begin to make "hedging" internal political deals. Moreover, some areas literally require an

17.

The Global Crunch

FRANK CHURCH

For all their immense physical power, the two dominant nations in the world—the United States and the Soviet Union—suffer from a neurotic sense of insecurity, although neither regards itself as being in imminent danger of attack by the other. At tremendous cost, their nuclear armories keep them at bay and, even if each were foolishly to add a new inventory of ABM missiles to the awesome stockpile, the delicate equilibrium will hold, leaving the two rivals in a state of chronic but only low-grade anxiety over the danger of attack by the other. It is a costly and desperately dangerous way of keeping the peace, but it is all we have shown ourselves capable of thus far.

The immediate threat that each superpower perceives from the other is its ideological impact on third countries, most particularly those that it regards as its protective buffers. It is one of the supposed realities of international politics—a kind of higher law transcending such legal documents as the United Nations Charter—that great powers are allowed to have spheres of influence made up of "friendly" neighbors. In the case of maritime powers such as the United States, the neighborhood may extend to the fringes of distant continents; but, whether or not the buffer is contiguous, the principle is the same: In order to guard itself against even the most remote or hypothetical threat to its security, a great power is held entitled to intervene in the affairs of its small neighbors, even to the extent of making the basic decisions as to how they will organize and run their own societies. This is where ideology comes in. Neither the Soviet Union nor the United States seems to regard itself as being in danger of *direct* ideological subversion by the other, although there have been times—the period of Stalinism in the Soviet Union and of McCarthyism in the United States—when they did. In more recent years, the focus of great-power apprehension has been on their small-power buffers. Over these, each great power displays frenzied determination to exert ideological control. Within its sphere, the Soviet Union insists on the maintenance of Communist governments, inaccurately described, for the most part, as socialist; the United States, on the other hand, insists on the maintenance of non-Communist governments that we, for the most part, incorrectly call free.

Starting with the assumption that ideology is an instrument of foreign policy through which the rival great power will establish its political domination over others, whenever and wherever the opportunity arises, each great power seems to look upon its own buffer states as peculiarly susceptible to ideological subversion by the other great power. It is further assumed that the ultimate aim of this subversion is to isolate and undermine the great power itself; that ideology, being contagious, is singularly suited to this purpose; and that, like a disease, it must therefore be isolated and destroyed before it can spread. These assumptions lead to the conclusion that it is no more than an act of self-defense for a great power to take such measures as it judges necessary to preserve the ideological purity of its sphere of influence.

Seen in this way, the various interventions of the United States and the Soviet Union are explained not only as legitimate defensive measures but as positive services. Thus, in the case of the intervention in the Dominican Republic in 1965, American policy makers were untroubled by the fact that the U.S. actions violated both the Rio Treaty and the Charter of the Organization of American States and that the revolution the U.S. suppressed was on behalf of a freely elected government that had been expelled by a coup. These were judged only superficial considerations when weighed against the need to defend America from the specter of a "second Cuba" while rescuing th Dominicans from their foolhardy flirtation with communism. Similarly, in the case of Vietnam, far from wishing to impose anything on anybody, the United States, in former Secretary of State Dean Rusk's view during a 1967 press conference, seeks only to save the world from being "cut in two by Asian communism."

It remained for the Russians to devise a doctrine of ideological justification for the policy of interventionism. In a document that has come to be known as the Brezhnev doctrine, published in *Pravda*, the Soviet government pointed out that, in invading Czechoslovakia, the Soviet Union and its protégés were doing no more than "discharging their internationalist duty toward the fraternal peoples of Czechoslovakia" and defending their own "socialist gains" against "anti-socialist forces" supported by "world imperialism" seeking to "export counterrevolution." Turn this phraseology around, substitute "anti-democratic" for "anti-socialist," "world communism" for "world imperialism," "revolution" for "counterrevolution," and the resultant rationale differs little from the official explanation of our own interventions in recent years.

Whether or not the Russians actually believed their excuse I would not venture to guess. At any rate, I don't believe it; I believe that the Russians—even if they persuaded themselves otherwise—suppressed the liberal government of Czechoslovakia because they feared the contagion of freedom for the rest of their empire and ultimately for the Soviet Union itself. Nor do I believe that, in suppressing revolutions in Latin America and in trying to suppress revolution in Vietnam, the United States is acting legitimately in its own self-defense. There are, God knows, profound differences between the internal orders of the United States and the Soviet Union—ours is a free society and theirs is a totalitarian society whose leaders have shown themselves to be terrified of freedom—but, in their foreign policies, the two superpowers have taken on a remarkable resemblance. Concerned primarily with the preservation of their own vast hegemonies, they have become, in their respective spheres, defenders of the *status quo* against the pressures of revolutionary upheaval in which each perceives little but the secret hand of the other.

The Impotence of Power

Suppressing revolution in its own immediate vicinity is an easy if embarrassing task for a superpower. Suppressing it on a distant continent is more difficult; and, as we have learned in Vietnam, beating down a strongly motivated, capably led and well-organized indigenous force is a virtual impossibility. Confronted with rising nationalistic movements, the superpowers, to their own astonishment, sometimes find themselves muscle-bound. Their nuclear power, though colossal, is so colossal as to be unusable except for keeping *each other* terrified. But in dealing with the unruly third world, as Presidential advisor Henry Kissinger pointed out in a Brookings Institution symposium called *Agenda for the Nation*, "Power no longer translates automatically into influence."

Nor, one might add, does influence translate readily into desirable or usable power. In Europe before World War One, there was a significant relationship between influence and power and between territory and power—though perhaps even then, the correlation was less than it seemed. Yet, by conquering territory or forming alliances, a nation could hope to gain material resources and political predominance. Accordingly, the balance of power was maintained—more or less—by isolating and denying opportunities for territorial expansion to the most powerful or ambitious nation. In our own time, the balance of power is determined far more by economic and technological developments *within* countries than by alliances and territorial acquisition. China, for example, has gained far greater power through the acquisition of nuclear weapons than if it had conquered all of Southeast Asia.

Nonetheless, the great powers struggle to establish their influence in neutral countries. Guided by a ritualized, anachronistic, 19th Century concept of the balance of power, they seek influence for its own sake, as if it were a concrete, negotiable asset. I am thinking not only of Vietnam, but of India, where we worry about Soviet economic aid, and to whom the President once even cut off food supplies because the Indian prime minister had sent birthday greetings to Ho Chi Minh. I am thinking of Laos, where we are not only fighting a proxy war against the Communist Pathet Lao but are engaged in an agitated rivalry with the French for the control of secondary education. And I am thinking of the global propaganda effort of the United States Information Agency, with its festivals and exhibits and libraries carefully pruned of books that seriously criticize America, all aimed at manufacturing a favorable image of the United States.

All this, we are told, is influence, and influence is power. But is it really power? Does it secure something valuable for either the other country or ourselves? If so, I have never heard a satisfactory explanation of what it is; and that, I strongly suspect, is because there is none. The real stake, I apprehend, is not power at all, but a shadow that calls itself power, nourishing an egotism that calls itself self-interest.

Vietnam, in this context, is a showcase of bankruptcy, a hopeless war fought for insubstantial stakes. As a war for high principle, Vietnam simply does not measure up: The Saigon government is neither a democracy warranting our support on ideological grounds nor a victim of *international* aggression warranting our support under the United Nations Charter. As an effort to contain Chinese power, the war in Vietnam is irrelevant as well as unsuccessful; even if a Communist Vietnam were to fall under Chinese control, as I do not think it would, the gains to China would be trivial compared with those accruing from her industrialization and acquisition of nuclear weapons.

The case on which Vietnam must stand or fall—if it has not already fallen—is the theory of an exemplary war, a war fought not so much on its own intrinsic merits as to demonstrate something to the world, such as that America will always live up to its alleged commitments or that "wars of national liberation" cannot succeed. The stake, then, is ultimately a psychological one—influence conceived as power.

Knocking down the case for an exemplary war is at this point very nearly belaboring the obvious. How we can demonstrate faithfulness to our commitments by honoring dubious promises to the Saigon generals while blatantly violating our treaty commitments in the Western Hemisphere—as we did in the covert intervention against the Arbenz government in Guatemala in 1954, the Bay of Pigs in 1961, the Dominican Republic in 1965—is beyond my understanding. As to proving that wars of national liberation cannot succeed, all that we have proved in four years of bitter, inconclusive warfare is that, even with an Army of over 500,000 Americans, we cannot win a victory for an unpopular and incompetent regime against a disciplined, nationalist insurrectionary force. In the harsh but accurate summation of Peregrine Worsthorne, a British conservative who was once a supporter of the war, writing in the *New Republic:*

> Instead of the Americans impressing the world with their strength and virtue, they are making themselves hated by some for what they are doing, and despised by the remainder for not doing it more efficaciously.

At least two prominent members of the Nixon Administration have explicitly recognized the bankruptcy of our Vietnam strategy. Henry Kissinger wrote in *Agenda for the Nation:*

> Whatever the outcome of the war in Vietnam, it is clear that it has greatly diminished American willingness to become involved in this form of warfare elsewhere. Its utility as a precedent has therefore been importantly undermined.

President Nixon's ambassador to the United Nations, Mr. Charles Yost, made the point in *Foreign Affairs* as forcefully as possible:

> The most decisive lesson of Vietnam would seem to be that no matter how much force it may expend, the United States cannot ensure the security of a country whose government is unable to mobilize and maintain sufficient popular support to control domestic insurgency. . . . If indigenous dissidents, whether or not Communist, whether or not supported from outside, are able to mobilize and maintain more effective popular support than the government, they will eventually prevail.

Vietnam is only one—albeit the most striking and costly—instance of a general, if not quite invariable, American policy of opposing revolution in the developing world. In some instances, this policy has been successful, at least for the short term. With our support, repressive governments in Brazil and Greece and a conservative government in the Dominican Republic, to cite but a few examples, have successfully held down popular aspirations for social and economic change. Through our support of reactionary governments in Latin America and elsewhere, we are preserving order in our sphere of influence and momentarily, at least, excluding revolution. But it is order purchased at the price of aligning ourselves with corruption and reaction against aggrieved and indignant indigenous forces that by and large are more responsive to popular aspirations than those that we support.

This policy of preserving the *status quo* is an exceedingly shortsighted one. Sooner or later, there can be little doubt, the rising forces of popular discontent will break through the brittle lid of repression. So, at least, historical experience suggests. We did it ourselves in 1776 and much of the history of 19th Century Europe consists of the successful rebellion of nationalist movements—German, Italian, Belgian, Greek and Slavic—against the powerful European order forged by the Congress of Vienna in 1815. In the 20th Century, we have seen the great European empires—British, French and Dutch—break up in the face of nationalist rebellion in hardly more than a decade after World War Two.

Since then, the revolutionary tide has continued to swell across Asia, Africa and Latin America, and it seems unlikely that even the immense resources of the United States will prove sufficient to contain the tide much longer. We have all but acknowledged our failure in Vietnam. What would we do if Souvanna Phouma's government in Laos should collapse, as it probably would if we terminated our counterinsurgency efforts and as it may, anyway? Or if a popular rebellion should break out against the military dictatorship in Brazil? Or if a Communist-Socialist government should come to power in Chile through a free election, as it could in 1970? Would we send armies to these large countries, as we did to South Vietnam and the small Dominican Republic? With aid and arms, we have helped delay the collapse of regimes whose very existence is an obstacle to social and political justice. Eventually, there seems little doubt, they will collapse, the more violently and with greater upheaval for having been perpetuated beyond their natural life span.

.   .   .

Thus far, I have been writing of the fragility and shortsightedness of our policy of repressing revolution. Something should be said about its morals as well. "Order" and "stability" are antiseptic words; they do not tell us anything about the way human beings live or the way they die. The diplomatic historians who invoke the model of Metternich's European order in the 19th Century usually neglect to mention that it was an order purchased at the cost of condemning millions of people to live under the tyranny of the Russian czar, the Turkish sultan and other ignorant and reactionary monarchs. The absolute primacy of order over justice was neatly expressed by Metternich in his assertion that "Barbarous as it is, Turkey is a necessary evil." In a similar vein—if not, let us hope, with equal callousness—when we speak of "stability" and "order" in the developing countries, we neglect to note that in more than a few instances, the order purchased by our aid and by our arms is one that binds millions of people to live under a feudalism that fosters ignorance, hunger and disease. It means blighted lives, children with bellies bloated and brains stunted by malnutrition, their parents scavenging food in garbage heaps—a daily occurrence in the omnipresent slums of Asia and Latin America. Only the abstractions of diplomacy take form in high policy councils; to see its flesh and blood, one must go to a Brazilian slum or to a devastated village in Vietnam.

Besides being shortsighted and immoral, our policy of perpetuating the *status quo* has a third fatal defect—a defect that represents our best hope for formulating a new foreign policy: It goes against the American grain. That is the meaning of the dissent against Vietnam and of the deep alienation of so many of our youth. It is their belief in the values they were brought up to believe in—in the idea of their country as a model of decency and democracy—that has confounded the policy makers who only a few years ago were contending that we could fight a limited war for a decade or two without seriously disrupting the internal life of the United States. What they overlooked in their preoccupation with war games and escalation scenarios was the concern of millions of Americans not just with the cost but with the character of wars they fight and their consequent outrage against a war that—even at what the strategists would consider tolerable cost—has made a charnel house of a small and poor Asian country. In this moral sense, there is hope—hope that we will recognize at last that a foreign policy that goes against our national character is untenable.

An Act of Faith

The question to which we come is whether order, in the sense in which we now conceive it, is, indeed, a vital interest of the United States, or whether, in this revolutionary age, we can accommodate ourselves to a great deal of disorder in the world. My answer, as I am sure will be clear by now, is that we must and can learn to live with widespread revolutionary turmoil. We *must* because it is not within our means to stem the tide; we *can* because social revolution is not nearly so menacing to us as we have supposed—or at least it need not be. If we can but liberate ourselves from ideological obsession—from the automatic association of social revolution with communism and of communism with Soviet or Chinese power—we may find it possible to discriminate among disorders in the world and to evaluate them with greater objectivity, which is to say, more on the basis of their own contest and less on the basis of our own fears. We should find, I think, that some revolutionary movements—including even Communist ones—will affect us little, if at all; that others may affect us adversely but not grievously; and that some may even benefit us.

All of which is to say nothing about the *right* of other peoples to settle their own affairs without interference by the great powers. There is, after all, no moral or legal right of a great power to impose its will on a small country, even if the latter does things that affect it adversely. Americans were justly outraged by the Soviet invasion of Czechoslovakia, not primarily because we thought the Russians could have endured Czech democratization without loss to themselves but because we thought the Czechs had a *right* to reform their system, whether it suited the Russians or not. Ought not the same principle apply in our relations with Latin America and, indeed, with small countries all over the world?

I believe that it should. I would go even further and suggest that we re-dedicate ourselves to the Good Neighbor Policy enunciated by President Franklin Roosevelt 30 years ago. There is, of course, nothing new about the principle of non-intervention: We have been preaching it for years. What I suggest as an innovation is that we now undertake to *practice* it—not only when we find it perfectly consistent with what we judge to be our interests but even when it does not suit our own national preferences. I suggest, there-fore, as a guiding principle of American foreign policy, that we abstain hereafter from military intervention in the internal affairs of other countries under any circumstances short of a clear and certain danger to our national security—such as that posed by Castro's decision to make Cuba a Soviet mis-sile base—and that we adhere to this principle whether others, including the Russians and the Chinese, do so or not.

Surely, it will be argued, we cannot be expected to refrain from interfer-ence while the Russians hold eastern Europe in thrall and the Chinese foster wars of national liberation in Asia and both seek opportunities to subvert non-Communist governments all over the world. Would this not throw open the floodgates to a torrent of revolutions leading to communism?

Setting aside for the moment the question of whether Communist rule else-where is invariably detrimental to the United States, experience suggests a policy of nonintervention would *not* throw open the floodgates to commu-nism. Communist bids for power have failed more often than they have succeeded in countries beyond the direct reach of Soviet military power—Indonesia and Guinea, for example. Of all the scores of countries, old and new, in Asia, Africa and Latin America, only four are Communist. There is, of course, no assurance that an American policy of nonintervention would guarantee against new Communist takeovers—obviously, our abstention from Cuba in 1959 was a factor in the success of Castro's revolution. But neither is there a guarantee that military intervention will defeat every Communist revolution—witness Vietnam. Neither abstention nor military intervention can be counted on to immunize against communism, for the simple reason that neither is of ultimate relevance to the conditions that militate for or against revolution within a country in the first place.

We have, in fact, had positive benefits from pursuing a policy of non-intervention. There is no country in Latin America more friendly to the United States than Mexico, which expelled American oil interests 40 years ago, while seemingly enthralled with Marxist doctrines, and which even now pursues an independent foreign policy, including the maintenance of cordial relations with Cuba. The thought presents itself that a policy of noninterven-tion could now serve as well to liberate us from the embrace of incompetent and reactionary regimes, which ignore popular aspirations at home out of confidence that, if trouble develops, they can summon the American Marines, while holding us in line by the threat of their own collapse.

The critical factor is nationalism, which, far more than any ideology, has shown itself to be the engine of change in modern history. When an ideology is as strongly identified with nationalism as communism is in Cuba and Vietnam and as democracy is in Czechoslovakia, foreign military intervention must either fail outright or, as the Russians have learned in Czechoslovakia, succeed at such cost in world wide moral opprobrium as to be self-defeating. My own personal feeling is that, in a free market of ideas, communism has no record of achievement to commend itself as a means toward rapid modernization in developing countries. But, be that as it may, it will ultimately succeed or fail for reasons having little to do with the preferences of the superpowers.

We could profitably take a leaf from the Chinese notebook in this respect. The Lin Piao doctrine of "wars of national liberation," often mistaken as a blueprint for world conquest, is, in fact, an explicit acknowledgment of the inability of a foregin power to sustain a revolution without indigenous support. This is what Lin Piao said in the *Peking Review:*

> In order to make a revolution and to fight a people's war and be victorious, it is imperative to adhere to the policy of self-reliance, rely on the strength of the masses in one's own country and prepare to carry on the fight independently even when all material aid from outside is cut off. If one does not operate by one's own efforts, does not independently ponder and solve the problems of the revolution in one's own country and does not rely on the strength of the masses, but leans wholly on foreign aid—even though this be aid from socialist countries which persist in revolution (i.e., China)—no victory can be won, or be consolidated even if it is won.

One hears in this the echo of President Kennedy, speaking of South Vietnam in 1963: "In the final analysis, it is their war. They are the ones who have to win it or lose it." Or, as Theodore Draper summed it up in *Commentary,* "The crisis in 1965 in South Vietnam was far more intimately related to South Vietnamese disintegration than to North Vietnamese infiltration."

Nationalism is not only the barrier to communism in countries that reject it; it is a modifier and neutralizer of communism in those few small countries that do possess it. As Tito has demonstrated in Europe and as Ho Chi Minh has demonstrated in Asia, a strongly nationalist regime will defend its independence regardless of common ideology; and it will do so with far greater effectiveness than a weak and unpopular regime, also regardless of ideology. It is beyond question that the Tito government has been a vastly more effective barrier to Soviet power in the Balkans than the old pre-War monarchy ever could have been; and, as Edwin O. Reischauer wrote in *Look:*

It seems highly probable that Ho's Communist-dominated regime, if it had been allowed by us to take over all Vietnam at the end of the war, would have moved to a position with relation to China not unlike that of Tito's Yugoslavia toward the Soviet Union.

If freedom is the basic human drive we believe it to be, an act of faith seems warranted—not in its universal triumph, which experience gives us no particular reason to expect, but in its survival and continuing appeal. The root fact of ideology to which we come—perhaps the only tenet that can be called a fact—is that, at some basic level of being, every man and woman alive aspires to freedom and abhors compulsion. It does not follow from this—as, in the rhetorical excess of the Cold War, it is so often said to follow—that communism is doomed to perish from the earth as a distortion of nature, or that democracy, as we know it in America, is predestined to triumph everywhere. Political forms that seem to offend human nature have existed throughout history, and others that have seemed attuned to human needs have been known to perish. All that can be said with confidence is that, whatever is done to suppress them, man's basic aspirations have a way of reasserting themselves and, insofar as our American political forms are attuned to these basic aspirations, they are a long leg ahead in the struggle for survival.

Faith in the viability of freedom will not, in itself, guarantee our national security. But it can and should help allay our extravagant fear of communism. It should enable us to compete with confidence in the market of ideas. It should free us from the fatal temptation to fight fire with fire by imitating the tactics of a rival who can*not* be as sure of the viability of his ideas in an open contest. The Russians, when you come right down to it, have better reason to fear freedom in Czechoslovakia than we have to fear communism in Vietnam. Appealing as it does to basic human aspirations, the contagion of Czech liberty very likely *is* a threat, at least in the long run, to the totalitarian system of the Soviet Union; by no stretch of the imagination can Ho Chi Minh's rule in Vietnam be said to pose a comparable threat to democracy in the United States.

The greatest danger to our democracy, I dare say, is not that the Communists will destroy it, but that we will betray it by the very means chosen to defend it. Foreign policy is not and cannot be permitted to become an end in itself. It is, rather, a means toward an end, which in our case is not only the safety of the United States but the preservation of her democratic values. A foreign policy of intervention must ultimately be subversive of that purpose. Requiring as it does the maintenance of a huge and costly military establishment, it must also entail the neglect of domestic needs, a burgeoning military-industrial-academic complex, chronic crises and marathon wars—all anathema to a democratic society. Every time we suppress a popular revolution abroad, we subvert our own democratic principles at home. In no single instance is the self-inflicted injury likely to be fatal; but with each successive occurrence, the contradiction and hypocrisy become more apparent and more of our people become disillusioned, more become alienated or angry, while a few are simply corrupted.

Being gradual and cumulative, the malady went largely undetected for too long a time. Now, however, a hue and cry has been raised, and for that we may be grateful, because the great debate in which we are engaged can, if we wish, be corrective as well as cathartic, by laying the foundations for a new approach in our foreign relations.

The shape and content of a new foreign policy are still beyond our view. For the moment, all that comes clearly into focus are the contradictions of our present approach and a few basic inferences that can be drawn from recent experience, notably: that we need not rely on military intervention to give freedom a chance of surviving in the world; that, indeed, we cannot do so without compromising our own freedom; and that only by being true to our traditional values and our own best concept of ourselves can we hope to play a decent and constructive role in a revolutionary world.

18.

The Lessons of Vietnam

EQBAL AHMAD AND EDWIN REISCHAUER

EQBAL AHMAD: [American policies] are a mixed bag of welfare imperialism and relentless optimism. They reflect that strange compound of assumptions and attitudes which characterizes American policy in the "third world" and which invokes among those of us from the "third world" feelings of bewilderment and fear. The policy-makers in Washington will be pleased by [the] earlier assertion that Vietnam may not after all be regarded as a failure when there is a "reckoning of the benefits of the intervention." The worried doubters, however, are assured that the uniqueness of Vietnam makes unlikely a duplication of the Vietnamese situation. The acknowledgment of the risks of historical analogies should please the modernistic social scientists who object to this form of analysis. Yet the more traditional among us should have no great cause for complaint after the prescience of a prophetic cycle theorist has been praised. The invocation of the Klingberg cycle must gratify the isolationists and the pacifists with the knowledge that America has reached the end of its twenty-seven-year period of "extroversion." But the cold war liberals ought to be soothed by the intimation that while America may have to eschew military involvements of Vietnamese proportions, it cannot disengage from its responsibilities to the underdeveloped. The hawks, of course, can look forward to the next cycle of extroversion, sometime after 1984. Finally, those most vociferous of all Americans—the sociologists and political scientists—must rejoice over

Abridged from pp. 232–41 and 267–71 of *No More Vietnams?* by Richard M. Pfeffer. Copyright © 1968 by The Adlai Stevenson Institute of International Affairs. Reprinted by permission of Harper & Row, Publishers, Inc.

the promise of their promotion to an unquestionably lucrative and highly challenging role as engineers and architects of political ideologies, parties, and participation—modern day philosopher-kings engaged and anointed by a super CIA. Only the New Left radicals may find it difficult going, unless, of course, they derive a vicarious satisfaction from the speculation that in the event of a fourth major military involvement (the earlier three being World War II, Korea, and Vietnam) the "constitutional structure of the Republic could well be shaken."

The phased modernization of West European countries, the United States, and even Japan enjoyed the luxuries of time, superior psychological, economic, and cultural resources, plus the opportunity of channeling to the colonies and the expanding frontier the tensions and ambitions produced by technology and social change. Yet they had their share of excesses, civil wars, revolutions, disorders, and ideological aberration. Today, the "third world" countries must undergo a triple transformation—social, economic, and political—simultaneously, in telescoped time and under the multiple pressures of colonial heritage and growing population. In the circumstances, our relative calm should surprise observers. We may hope to avoid the extremes of excesses—regression into colonial, racist, fascist, or Stalinist aberrations. Yet we shall inevitably experience conflicts and disorders in the process of reformulating our values and reconstructing our societies. If a superpower enters our world committed obsessively to orderly change and with an interest in maintaining stable clients, it will necessarily distort our development, sharpen our conflicts, and will also render itself vulnerable to the perpetual temptation of intervening militarily in behalf of its losing protégés.

Our formal independence has given us, at best, an unenviable position as pawns in the game of high politics. That is why we react in fear when one superpower serves notice on a country, as America has done in Vietnam, that it will cajole, coerce, and finally conquer a people that would not conform to its inverted image of freedom and democracy; and another great power insists, in the name of justice, on subverting a people driven by want and search for dignity, so that the attainment of justice becomes an excuse for the strangling of human freedom. Vietnam is important to us only because it has dramatized our agony and exacerbated our fears. And it leads me to conclude that unless there is a drastic change in Western attitudes toward a transforming world, the underdeveloped countries which stand in agony today at the threshold of the twentieth century could become the greatest suckers in history. But then who knows what price we may exact from the world for the destruction of our dignity, not to mention our lives and property, and our right to formulate our destiny without gross foreign interference?

The jealous nationalism of the underdeveloped countries is not simply a question of mood. It is a matter of survival. To the extent that even communist states like Cuba, North Vietnam, and North Korea, not to mention China, assert their independence from the dictates of the protecting power despite their acute dependence (on Russia) and their encirclement (by the United States), it is a measure of their responsiveness to this national need. It is curious, indeed, that in a discussion focused in great part on political development in underdeveloped countries, [there has been] no reference to this primary fact in our political life. I suspect that this omission, though unintentional, is not accidental. It reflects the anti-nationalist thrust of the United States, which, as suggested earlier, is related to certain aspects of the American political culture.

When a nationalist movement acquires a radical content, when it threatens to nationalize property and socialize national resources, when it becomes diplomatically assertive and neutralist, it initially elicits an unfavorable response from the United States. Its programs threaten potential or actual American investments; its diplomatic posture involves the loss of a potential or actual ally in the cold war; its revolutionary doctrine appears dangerously congruent with the communist enemy's. If a country threatened by such a nationalism happens to be a client state, then a United States-mounted coup d'état or sharp, swift military intervention seeks to restore the status quo. Interventions of this type include Guatemala, the Dominican Republic, and Iran. In nonclient underdeveloped states such a radical nationalist movement is tolerated by the United States if it comes to power unexpectedly, or turns radical gradually and without serious challenge under a legitimate and popular leader—although relations with such regimes remain intermittently reserved if not restrained. Egypt is an example of the first type, Tanzania of the second.

American tolerance toward these countries appeared to be increasing in the Kennedy Administration; neutralists were not regarded invariably as allies of communism. There was even a tendency actively to encourage their radical posture, especially in the zones of French influence (Tunisia became an AID showpiece during this period and has since shown unabashed loyalty to the United States). The unusual popularity in the "third world" of the Kennedy Administration was due, not so much to actual change in United States policy, but largely to the feeling among us that America was beginning to understand the nature of our nationalism, that the puppeteer view of the world was giving way to a more sophisticated understanding of our drive toward sovereignty. But only among the East European clients of the USSR has American policy consistently welcomed and, where possible, encouraged reactive nationalism.

. . . in the American alliance with conservative nationalism, the interaction between United States economic aid and desire for reform promotes the expansion of American presence and finally ends in intervention. Military assistance produces much the same, if more dangerous, symbiosis between the United States and the recipient indigenous elites. The more a foreign power involves itself in native problems, the greater becomes its economic and psychic investments. As the relationship gets more institutionalized, it becomes harder to extricate itself from the commitment. The tendency then is to blame individuals and not the system, which inherently lacks the capacity to maintain and enhance its legitimacy. Hence one gets rid of a dictator only to inherit a worse one. United States-supported Latin American coups provide innumerable examples of this vicious cycle.

The case of Vietnam is also illustrative. There is now a general tendency in America to blame Diem, who had once been billed as a democratic alternative to Ho Chi Minh. Yet it is not fair to blame him for failing to introduce meaningful reforms and thus driving the Vietnamese to desperation. It was morbid optimism to expect an absentee aristocrat to substitute for a heroic leader who had devoted a lifetime to the liberation of his country, and to bypass a leadership and cadres whose organic ties with the peasants were cemented by the bitter struggle for independence. Given his situation, Diem had no choice; his only possible weapons were a power apparatus to regiment the population, all-out support of minorities and the privileged, and widespread terror. These were not the aberrations of a program, but the program itself. And his assassination left the United States at the mercy of the musical-chair generals, who had earlier collaborated with France and who further degenerated into sanctioning the systematic destruction of a country they claimed to govern.

I do not question . . . that the achievement of consolidation of power by a regime followed by advances in the area of social reforms and political institutionalization will reduce the chances of United States military intervention. Yet [the] belief that the United States should actively engage in fostering political development is fraught with risks and is likely, at best, to be self-defeating.

No foreign power has the ability to equip a native government with legitimacy (the essential quality of rulership) nor with the will and capacity to open channels for peaceful change—unless it is the case of a military occupation which for some historical or psychological reasons is accepted by the population. In fact, the reverse is truer: identification with a foreign power erodes the legitimacy of a regime. And the correlation between growing legitimacy and willingness to open new domestic channels for participation is known to be positive. Even if I were to accept the questionable premise that the United States has not been involved in aiding and influencing political and administrative development in Vietnam, I should at least question the efficacy of such involvement. Given the absence of legitimacy and the reactionary character of the Diem regime, I doubt that a timely and firm American involvement in political development would have led to the creation of legitimate and popular institutions in Vietnam, thus preventing the insurrection from spreading.

The primary factor in promoting political institutions is not improved professionalism, as is largely true of the army, navy, hospitals, etc. Rather it involves a vision of society, the choice of values and goals. These are not exportable goods or skills that can form part of foreign aid programs. It is incorrect, therefore, to put political parties in the same category as hospitals and armies. Political institutions unsupported by operative values become mere formalities or else turn into bureaucratic instruments of control rather than of participation. The dramatic failure of the American mission in Vietnam should at least have laid to rest this kind of technocratic evangelism and culture-centered optimism.

Legitimate rulers who have a value commitment to maintaining a measure of accountability to the populace and to creatively confronting the crises of participation, development, and distribution are unlikely to need foreign help in creating and running political institutions. The recent history of underdeveloped countries provides ample evidence that their leaders do not lack organizing skills, nor are they in need of advice on institution building. If they do not promote political participation, it is because they do not wish to do so. The Algerians, many of whom are in power today, created one of the most powerful and, under assault, indestructible political institutions of this century. Yet the FLN, unlike the Neo-Destour party of Tunisia or the Istiqlal of Morocco, did not really survive independence, and not for lack of foreign advice or pressure. Potentially it is still a revivable institution, for many of the old cadres and an eager populace are longing to be active participants again. What is lacking is the incentive on the part of Algeria's military leaders, who perhaps perceive in the development of popular institutions a threat to the power of the army.

Similarly Pakistan's Muslim League degenerated into factions and Ghana's Convention party turned into a bureaucratic behemoth, not for lack of organizing skill nor because of ignorance on the part of politicians about the meaning and importance of political institutions. They weakened as popular institutions because the leaders perceived them as threats, or at least as useless for wielding power after independence had been achieved. These leaders lacked the radical commitment to social and economic transformation, on the basis of which they could continually communicate with the majority a consistent and functioning ideology which could provide guidelines against which political behavior could be tested and upon which political institutions could be based. They lacked an operative commitment to accountability which could ensure their adherence to institutionalized norms and practices.

These commitments are seldom acquired through pressures from allies. They result from social conflict or social movements, in response to continual, often violent pressures from below, or as a consequence of revolutionary upheaval. Unless an elite is already committed deeply and operatively to a set of political values, it is not likely to become so under foreign pressure. In fact, protective foreign involvement may only harden its unwillingness to distribute its privileges and power.[1]

. . . The interaction between economic aid and United States pressures for social reforms produces the expansion of American presence as well as its frustration; the combination leads eventually to intervention. . . . Similar involvement in political development will produce the same result. In fact, the very forces which lead to a positive relationship between economic reform and intervention are likely to have a stronger correlation between political involvement and intervention. Political participation is even more difficult to sell to an entrenched ruling class than economic reforms, because it involves the sharing of power as well as resources. It is bound to produce greater resentment and truculence on the part of native allies, more frustration, greater psychic and material involvement, and more intervention on the part of the United States. Politics and power, more than economics, command the passions of men—especially well-fed men.

[The] suggestion that the escalation of political involvement into military intervention can be avoided by keeping political commitments "conditional and/or covert" suffers from bad history no less than poor principles. Commitments, even conditional ones, have a vicious logic of proliferation. History is replete with examples of conditional commitments giving birth to unconditional ones. Vietnam itself is a case in point; need one recall that American boys were never committed to fighting the battle of Asian boys? As for covertness, how does one keep political activities of this magnitude covert in a democracy—or in a dictatorship, for that matter? And how does the professed commitment to the principles of participation and democracy square with the systematic denial to people of information on the nature of institutions to which they belong and to which they contribute?

If my earlier analysis of American political culture has any validity, it points out the danger of continued United States interventionism, especially in the client states. By way of summary, it seems (1) that the United States is not yet able to tolerate, much less encourage, radical nationalism in client states; the tendency to accept and encourage nationalism as a vehicle for social transformation has been proportionately greater in the countries where the United States does not command direct influence; (2) that the United States expects of the underdeveloped countries a style and norms of politics which are unlikely to be fulfilled at this stage of their development; (3) that in countries where its involvement is significant,

---

1. For this reason I believe in the "domino theory," in reverse. If the United States "wins" in Vietnam, it may have the effect of assuring the Thai rulers (whose propensity to promise elections has become proverbial) and the Filipino elite (who have the reputation of being the most corrupt in Asia) that the United States will save them from their people. The defeat of United States objectives in Vietnam, on the other hand, may have a salutary effect on their willingness to reform.

failure to conform to American expectations produces a vicious cycle of expanding American role in domestic affairs, erosion of the legitimacy of United States-supported elites, radicalization and enlargement of civil conflict, and military intervention in behalf of the *status quo*; while seeking order and stability, in fact the United States contributes to more disorder; (4) that the deeper its involvement in a country, the less flexible it becomes in dealing with diverse political groupings and the more it develops a vested interest in defending friendly governments against revolutionary forces; (5) that a colonial style, perhaps acquired in Latin America and reinforced by evangelism as well as incipient racism, persists and produces a relationship of dependence and protectiveness between native elites and the United States.

From these conclusions it should follow that if the dialectic of intervention is to be broken, scholars and policy-makers have to give attention to the manner in which the United States must disengage from direct involvement in underdeveloped countries. Such a disengagement need not be the result of isolationist sentiments. It must envisage a new role for the United States and new styles of relationships which will take into account the interest of America as well as of the underdeveloped. Yet such a change in policy must necessarily be preceded by not only an examination of America's assumptions but also a redefinition of its goals.

There is a preoccupation with success; we are given a "useful reminder that consequences are all that count." The criteria of success, however, are left unclear. Restoration of order, successful arbitration between conflicting native factions, organizing "honest elections" which the "right man" wins, and promoting reforms are cited as achievements of the Dominican intervention. [It is also argued] that the "judgment that United States policy in the Vietnamese crisis was ultimately unsuccessful tends to be based upon an incomplete, perhaps misleading reckoning of the benefits of the intervention." [This] defers a discussion of whether or not it was a salutary case of intervention.

One is led to ask, "benefits" for whom? For the United States? For the Thai and Filipino clients of the United States? For the men in Saigon who once collaborated with France and are now collaborating with America? Or for the people of Vietnam and Southeast Asia? If one judges from the point of view of the Pentagon or the White House, many benefits are already perceptible and more can be discerned for the future. For example, military officials are reportedly happy over the unusual opportunity to test and develop new weapons both for conventional and irregular warfare; a new generation of officers and men have gained combat experience in unfamiliar terrain; lessons learned in Vietnam have led to improved techniques of counter-insurgency and pacification in the other client states of Southeast Asia and Latin America. Domestically the war may have served as a safety valve for absorbing thousands of young blacks, the most aggressive of whom opt to extend their service in the military. And insofar as the intentions of the United States are still unclear, it is possible that, unwilling to negotiate withdrawal (the *status quo* being the *casus belli* is nonnegotiable), it will eventually acquire a piece of strategic real estate near China, inhabited by the beaten and sunk remainder of a once brave and proud people—a sort of modern Indian reservation in the heart of Asia. The ruling elites of Thailand, the Philippines (and elsewhere), and other war profiteers may also have reasons to extol the benefits of the intervention, especially if the United States can demonstrate its willingness to commit a genocide in order to save its clients.

EDWIN REISCHAUER: The "central lesson" of Vietnam—at least as the American public perceives it—is already, I believe, quite obvious and . . . widely applied, whether rightly or wrongly, . . . We may still re-escalate the present war if the negotiations fail; but assuming that some sort of Vietnam settlement is achieved, I find it hard to believe that even a relatively strong "sellout" case would produce "irresistible demands for renewed and escalated intervention" in other parts of the world. Vietnam may be a "less than conclusive test of anything much," but at least it has shown the limited ability of the United States to control at a reasonable cost the course of events in a nationally aroused less developed nation. That this "lesson" has sunk home in this country can be seen in the strongly anti-interventionist reaction in the Administration, in Congress, and among the public to the Indonesian, Congo, and other recent disturbances.

This "lesson" can and, I believe, will lead to the broader conclusion that no external power can control (and thus exploit to its own advantage) less developed nations which are large enough in population and have enough national consciousness to be real national entities. I believe that we are moving away from the application to Asia of the "balance of power" and "power vacuum" concepts of the cold war, and in the process we no doubt will greatly downgrade our strategic interest in most of the less developed world. This is the direction in which we are moving, I believe, but just how far and fast we move is still to be determined by the specific outcome in Vietnam.

At this point "neoisolationism" becomes a real question . . . . Those who have used the term have never meant to suggest a return to the 1930's type of isolation from Europe and the other advanced parts of the world. This indeed is unthinkable and impossible. Nor have they meant a more cautious attitude toward intervention in internal instabilities in less developed nations. This is coming and will not, I feel, be labeled as isolationism. Their fear is the very realistic one that the United States will move, not just to greater caution about intervention in the affairs of less developed nations, but far beyond this position to virtual unconcern with their fate. The result could be a dismantling of the capacity to intervene in the cases where intervention may indeed be in our national interests and an unwillingness to give economic aid or take other measures that would contribute to the long-range development of the less developed nations.

This, I feel, is no idle fear. Past aid programs have been wheedled out of Congress largely on the basis of our alleged great strategic stakes in the less developed world. Cold logic, however, will increasingly show that we have few if any immediate, vital, national interests in the less developed world, either strategic or economic. And added to logic will be the emotional responses to our present crises at home and abroad. The Vietnam fiasco is beginning to produce the conservative response that if Asians do not appreciate our efforts in their behalf and are not willing to do their share, they deserve to be left to "stew in their own juices." The liberal response is that we should concentrate first on the great ills of our own society (the beam in our own eye) before trying to help distant people with their ills. Cultural (possibly even racial) biases strengthen both positions, . . . "The Congressional revolt against foreign aid seems an ominous harbinger."

I would suggest two reasons why the United States has very real interests in the stability and development of the less developed nations. The first is that no clear line exists between our very immediate interests in the security and stability of the advanced nations (such as those of Europe, Japan, and Australia) and conditions in the less developed world. For example, a complete disruption of all the oil lands of the Middle East might spell catastrophe for Europe and Japan. Spreading chaos which reduced the capacities for trade of the countries of South and Southeast Asia would be hard on a country like Japan, for which trade with these regions is important. While we can guarantee the defense (both nuclear and conventional) of Japan and Australia from across the Pacific Ocean, we cannot defend from such long distances the sea lanes on which both depend. Neither could we so defend South Korea, the loss of which to a hostile power might seriously affect Japan's stability. If basic unconcern with the less developed areas led to an abandonment of our capacities or will to intervene on occasion in those parts of the world, this might have a serious secondary effect on areas of the world that are immediately important to us.

The second reason is very long range and less easily defined but probably more important. In a rapidly shrinking, ever more closely integrated world in which interrelations and mutual influences grow constantly stronger, vast discrepancies of wealth and opportunity between various regions and nations and the resentments and hostilities these breed become increasingly dangerous to world stability as a whole. The problem actually is a new one—in a sense only a cloud on the horizon—but predictably it will grow to dangerous proportions, just as the discrepancies in wealth and opportunity in our own nation, which in a simpler day constituted no great problem, have through neglect produced an explosive crisis in this more complicated age. If we fail to work toward closing the international gap in wealth and opportunity, we may some day face an insoluble problem.

I thus come to an advocacy of [a] middle course between overinvolvement and complete unconcern. I am less [than] sanguine, however, that we will be wise enough to take this middle course. The arguments for it are either complicated or very long range, while the arguments for the "neoisolationism" of unconcern are clear-cut and emotionally appealing.

On the optimistic assumption, however, that we will attempt to find our way down the middle course, . . . I would formulate the basic principles to be followed [as]:

(1) We should distinguish clearly between our capacity to intervene and our commitment to do so, maintaining the former (at least to some degree) but minimizing the latter. For example, we should maintain the Seventh Fleet in the western Pacific, thus protecting the freedom of the seas and giving us the option to intervene against aggression, thereby probably inhibiting it to some extent, but without committing ourselves in advance. Prior commitments to less developed nations may be necessary in some cases (in East Asia, South Korea probably needs such a commitment, and Taiwan and the Philippines are also possible exceptions because of a long historical involvement on our part and their easy defensibility, as islands, from aggression), but such commitments should be regarded essentially as liabilities rather than assets.

(2) As a general rule, intervention in internal instability or civil war should be avoided. Exceptions might be countries that are both very small and highly strategic, if such exist. If a regime—with our aid, in case it is worthy of it—cannot handle internal problems of this sort itself, we probably could not do it for them. The chief problem we would face is to be sure that we maintain a strict line between aid to a beleaguered regime and intervention in a civil war. Depending on the case, the line beyond which we should not go might be (a) purely economic aid, (b) weapons, (c) military and constabulary training and advice.

(3) As another general rule, we should attempt to assure that any intervention against aggression is international in character, but we cannot assume that this can always be achieved and there may be cases where we would have to intervene unilaterally. For example, a North Korean invasion of South Korea, a definite possibility, might not elicit an international response but might demand a unilateral American intervention.

(4) No intervention should be allowed to become open-ended. As Vietnam has shown, we must retain the ability to stop the escalation of our involvement if our initial efforts do not produce the expected results.

(5) Economic and technological aid—which to my mind should be the main thrust of our policies toward the less developed nations, rather than military defenses—should be handled in such a way as to avoid our own political and emotional commitment to specific regimes and to minimize

their fears of our domination. For both purposes the internationalization of aid mechanisms and the use of semipublic foundations would be helpful. I would also add the concept of divorcing planning and operations in the development process from the providing of funds and materials, putting the former completely under the control of the aid recipient and relegating the aid giver to the role of banker, who provides the funds and materials for development programs and, when needed, the funds for hiring the necessary planning and operations staff, but who is not himself directly involved in drawing up plans or implementing programs.

19.

The Nixon Doctrine and
Our Asian Commitments

EARL C. RAVENAL

EIGHTEEN MONTHS after its enunciation at Guam the Nixon Doctrine remains obscure and contradictory in its intent and application. It is not simply that the wider pattern of war in Indochina challenges the Doctrine's promise of a lower posture in Asia. More than that, close analysis and the unfolding of events expose some basic flaws in the logic of the Administration's evolving security policy for the new decade. The Nixon Doctrine properly includes more than the declaratory policy orientation. It comprises also the revised worldwide security strategy of "1½ wars" and the new defense decision-making processes such as "fiscal guidance budgeting." These elements have received little comment, especially in their integral relation to our commitments in Asia. But the effects of this Administration's moves in these areas will shape and constrain the choices of the United States for a long time to come.

The President's foreign policy declaration of February 1970 promised that "our interests, our foreign policy objectives, our strategies and our defense budgets are being brought into balance—with each other and with our overall national priorities."[1] After a decade of burgeoning military spending and entanglement in foreign conflict, the nation has welcomed the vision of lower defense budgets balanced by a reduction in American involvement overseas, particularly in Asia. Actually, however, the Admin-

Reprinted by permission from *Foreign Affairs*, January 1971, pp. 201–17. Copyright © 1971 by the Council on Foreign Relations, Inc., New York.

1. Richard Nixon, "U. S. Foreign Policy for the 1970's, A New Strategy for Peace" (Washington, D. C., U. S. Government Printing Office, February 18, 1970).

332 : *The Third World and Revolution*

istration's new policies and decision processes do not bring about the proposed balance; in fact, they create a more serious imbalance. Essentially we are to support the same level of potential involvement with smaller conventional forces. The specter of intervention will remain, but the risk of defeat or stalemate will be greater; or the nuclear threshold will be lower. The fundamental issues of interests, commitments and alliances are not resolved.

II

The objectives of close-in military containment and the forward defense of our Asian allies present us with a series of bleak choices:

With regard to deterrence: (1) perpetuation of a high level of active conventional forces, conspicuously deployed or deployable; (2) fundamental and obvious reliance on nuclear weapons; or (3) acknowledgment of the higher probability of an enemy initiative.

With regard to initial defense: (1) maintenance or rapid deployment of large armies in Asia; (2) early recourse to tactical nuclear weapons; or (3) acceptance of the greater risk of losing allied territory.

With regard to terminating a war: (1) large commitments of troops and heavy casualties; (2) use of nuclear weapons, either tactical or strategic; or (3) resignation to an indefinite and wasting stalemate, tantamount to defeat.

The only solution that transcends the triangle of unsatisfactory choices is to reevaluate our interests in Asia; restate those objectives that implicate us in the possibility of war on the Asian mainland and diminish our control over our actions; resist the grand and vapid formulas of our role in Asia—such as the existential platitude that "we are a Pacific power"—that perpetuate the illusion of paramountcy; retreat from the policy of military containment of China; and revise the alliances that have come to represent our commitment to containment.

But this course the President has consistently rejected: ". . . we will maintain our interests in Asia and the commitments that flow from them. . . . The United States will keep all its treaty commitments." Thus the root problem of the Nixon Doctrine is its abiding commitment to the containment of China. In the furtherance of this policy our government hopes to maintain all our present Asian alliances and de facto commitments, profiting from their deterrent value but avoiding their implications. Yet it also intends to scale down our conventional military capability. The result is that the Nixon Doctrine neither reduces our potential involvement in Asian conflicts nor resolves the resulting dilemma by providing convincingly for a defense that will obviate reliance on nuclear weapons.

Let us examine the prospect of the Nixon Doctrine as a relief from involvement in Asian contingencies. The trauma that has resulted from our inability to win decisively in Vietnam has caused our policy-makers to suggest a limitation of future involvement on the basis of a distinction between external or overt aggression on the one hand, and insurgency, political subversion and civil war on the other. The President attempts in this way to avoid the strategy dilemma by altering the criteria for intervention and thus understating the probability of involvement:

> . . . we cannot expect U.S. military forces to cope with the entire spectrum of threats facing allies or potential allies throughout the world. This is particularly true of subversion and guerrilla warfare, or "wars of national liberation." Experience has shown that the best means of dealing with insurgencies is to preempt them through economic development and social reform and to control them with police, paramilitary and military action by the threatened government.

But this is nothing more than a postulation that the unwished contingency will not arise. The hard question remains: What if these "best means" are not successful? Under *those* conditions what kind of solutions does the Nixon Doctrine envisage? Might the United States be impelled to intervene with combat forces? The President states:

> . . . a direct combat role for U.S. general purpose forces arises primarily when insurgency has shaded into external aggression or when there is an overt conventional attack. In such cases, we shall weigh our interests and our commitments, and we shall consider the efforts of our allies, in determining our response.

But this formula for discrimination and discretion seems both unclear and unrealistic. At what point does an insurgency become "external aggression"? A definition sometimes proposed is the introduction of enemy mainforce units, rather than mere individual fillers. But, even apart from the difficult question of verification, this event might be well beyond the point where our intervention became critical to the situation. The paradox is that in critical cases we might not wish to define the situation to preclude intervention; in less than critical cases we would not need to invoke nice distinctions to justify it. In any case, relying on formulas and distinctions misses the point: it is simply not credible that we would sacrifice our still-held objectives to the vagaries of circumstance.

Indeed, as long as our policy remains the containment of China and the repression of Asian communism, we are inclined to view even largely indigenous revolutions as objective instances of the purposes of Peking or Hanoi or Pyongyang. Consequently, if an insurgency in an allied or even a neutral country began to succeed, we would probably first increase logistical aid, then extend the role of advisers and provide air support. Since such moves might bring a countervailing response from the Asian Communist sponsors of the insurgency, we might have to choose between sending ground forces and allowing an ally to lose by our default. In certain extremities we might be forced to the final choice among unlimited conventional escalation, defeat of our own forces, or "technological escalation" to the use of nuclear weapons.

Thus, with our formal or implied commitments and the President's openended prescription, the United States might yet be drawn into a land war on the Asian mainland or have to confront equally dire alternatives. In this respect the Nixon Doctrine does not improve on the policy that led to Vietnam. And, of course, our exposure to involvement in the case of more overt aggression, such as a Chinese-supported invasion in Korea or Southeast Asia, remains undiminished.

The only proposition that has become clear about the Nixon Doctrine is that its most advertised hope of resolving the strategy problem—both reducing the forces we maintain for Asian defense and avoiding involvement in conflict—is Asianization, i.e. the substitution of indigenous forces, equipped through enlarged U.S. military assistance, for American troops. The case for expanded military assistance has been stated with unprecedented urgency by Secretary Laird in preparation for vastly increased Military Assistance Program (MAP) budget requests for 1972 and succeeding fiscal years. Secretary Laird has characterized MAP as "the essential ingredient of our policy if we are to honor our obligations, support our allies, and yet reduce the likelihood of having to commit American ground combat units."[2]

But the Secretary recognizes the declining level of popular and Congressional support for military assistance. His solution, considered perennially within the Defense and State Departments but proposed for the first time in a Secretarial posture statement to the Congress, is that "military assistance should be integrated into the Defense Budget so that we can plan more rationally and present to the Congress more fully an integrated program." Military aid for certain "forward defense countries," including South Vietnam, Thailand and Laos, and consisting of about 80 percent of the total category "Support for Other Nations,"[3] is already meshed into the Defense Budget. This legislative ploy has not yet been applied to Korea or Taiwan, though the reduction of our troops in Korea and the insurance of Taiwan against Communist pressure depend, in the judgment of this Administration, on the freedom to substitute U.S. matériel for manpower.

To merge military assistance entirely into the regular functional appropriation categories of the Defense Budget would be to institutionalize the dual rationale for military assistance that has become traditional in debate within the Department of Defense. The first element in this rationale is the argument from "trade-off"—a calculus that compares the costs of equal units

2. Melvin R. Laird, "Fiscal Year 1971 Defense Program and Budget" (Washington, D. C., U. S. Government Printing Office, March 2, 1970).

3. $2.443 billion out of $3.127 billion in the President's budget for fiscal year 1971.

of effectiveness of U.S. and foreign troops. This is essentially an assertion of "absolute advantage" and is the basic and obvious sense of Secretary Laird's statement: "A MAP dollar is of far greater value than a dollar spent directly on U.S. forces."

The second element is the argument from "comparative advantage," borrowed from the economic theory of international trade: "Each nation must do its share and contribute what it can appropriately provide—manpower from many of our allies; technology, material, and specialized skills from the United States." The proponents of military comparative advantage assert, by analogy, that the cooperating and specializing defense community can "consume" security at a higher level. It may be, however, that they can only consume more of the tangible intermediate trappings of security, i.e. the forces and arms. The essence of security, especially for the United States as the senior partner, might depend more on certain qualitative factors. In fact, there are several difficulties in the Administration's ostensibly neutral and technical arguments for military assistance.

First, both trade-off and comparative advantage assume and confirm the inevitability and relevance of the shared mission—that is, the forward defense of the ally's territory. But only if we cannot avoid this mission is it proper to confine the debate to the optimal distribution of roles and costs.

Second, the argument from comparative advantage, like the economic theory at its origin, stresses specialization. But the concomitant of specialization is interdependence. Thus a policy of selective reliance on allies, in order to be effective, implies automatic involvement from the earliest moments of a conflict.[4]

Third, early experience indicates that U.S. ground forces cannot simply be traded off with precisely calculated increments of military assistance. They must be politically ransomed by disproportionate grants, more conspicuous deployments and more fervent and explicit confirmations of our commitment.[5]

Fourth, from the diplomatic standpoint the substitution of massive infusions of modern arms for U.S. troops is anything but neutral. To the North Koreans and their sponsors, for example, the one and one-half billion dollars of support and new equipment we now intend to give South Korea might look very provocative and destabilizing. A new phase of the penin-

4. After the decision to reduce the ceiling on U.S. troops in Korea from 63,000 to 43,000, our government moved to base permanently there a wing of F-4 fighter-bombers. An American official explained: "Our aim is to reassure the Koreans during this difficult period. Despite budgetary cuts, it shows we intend to maintain our relative air strength here. They know that the minute an air attack starts, we're involved." (*The New York Times,* August 17, 1970.)

5. The Administration proposes special budget requests of $1 billion over a five-year period for Korean force modernization, in addition to about $700 million likely to be provided in the regular military assistance budget. Even then, the Republic of Korea is demanding $2–3 billion, plus public assurances of no further troop withdrawals until after five years and the actual completion of the promised modernization program.

sular arms race could be the result, with a net loss to regional and U.S. security.

Finally, the legislative tactic of integrating the Military Assistance Program into the Defense Budget would remove military assistance as an object of the broader concerns of foreign policy and assign it to the jurisdiction of more narrowly defense-oriented Congressional committees. The debate would be less political and more technical. The focus would shift from the question of involvement to the question of relative costs. Thus Asianization, which is the keystone of the Nixon Doctrine, would substitute some Asian forces and resources, but along the same perimeter of interest. It affords a pretext for reducing expense, but it does not enhance our security or relieve us from involvement.

III

The basic question is whether the Nixon Doctrine is an honest policy that will fully fund the worldwide and Asian commitments it proposes to maintain, or whether it conceals a drift toward nuclear defense or an acceptance of greater risk of local defeat. The most obvious change in our military posture is that the new formula provides conventional forces to counter a major communist thrust in Asia or Europe, but not simultaneously. As the President has explained:

> The stated basis of our conventional posture in the 1960's was the so-called "2½ war" principle. According to it, U.S. forces would be maintained for a three-month conventional forward defense of NATO, a defense of Korea or Southeast Asia against a full-scale Chinese attack, and a minor contingency—all simultaneously. These force levels were never reached.
>
> In the effort to harmonize doctrine and capability, we chose what is best described as the "1½ war" strategy. Under it we will maintain in peacetime general purpose forces adequate for simultaneously meeting a major Communist attack in either Europe or Asia, assisting allies against non-Chinese threats in Asia, and contending with a contingency elsewhere.

What will be the ultimate force levels associated with the new 1½-war strategy, and how can we assess their implications for Asian defense? Peacetime forces are obviously entailed by the extent of our commitments, but in no precisely determined way. A most important intermediate term—which could account for wide differences in strategy and forces—is the probable simultaneity of contingencies.[6] The Nixon strategy of 1½ wars is explicitly founded on the improbability of two simultaneous major contingencies.

___

6. Other sources of uncertainty and wide variation are: the readiness of our reserve divisions, the amount of available airlift and sealift, and the effectiveness of allied forces.

Thus demands on the planned general purpose forces are to be considered alternative rather than additive.

Can we then expect a force reduction equivalent to the requirement for defending against the lesser of the major contingencies? To support the previous strategy of 2½ wars, the Baseline (or peacetime) Force Structure was thought to provide seven active divisions for Southeast Asia, two for Korea, eight for NATO, and two and one-third for a minor contingency and a strategic reserve—a total of 19-⅓. Since the present 1½-war doctrine includes only one major contingency, in NATO *or* Asia, one might derive an active ground force as low as 10-⅓ divisions.

Such a literal expectation, however, is confused by the President's desire to insure "against greater than expected threats by maintaining more than the forces required to meet conventional threats in one theater—such as NATO Europe;" the fact that certain types of divisions are inherently specialized for certain geographical contingencies, so that all eight of our armored and mechanized divisions will probably remain oriented to NATO and inapplicable to Asian defense; and finally, the judgments of both the President and Secretary Laird that the force levels necessary to implement the previous 2½-war policy "were never reached."

But it seems clear that the ultimate Baseline Force Structure under the Nixon Doctrine will contain even fewer divisions for the Asian requirement than the minimal proposals for a conventional defense.[7] The reduced conventional force is most significant as a reflection of the altered concept of Asian defense embodied in the Nixon Doctrine. The constituent propositions of this concept are: (1) the most likely threats to our Asian allies do not involve Chinese invasion, and (2) with greatly expanded military assistance our allies can largely provide the ground forces to counter such threats.

There is a third proposition, strongly implied by the logic of the problem and markedly signaled in the President's foreign policy statement: in a future Asian conflict, particularly if it does involve China, United States intervention is likely to carry with it the use of tactical nuclear weapons.

—the nuclear capability of our strategic and theater nuclear forces serves as a deterrent to full-scale Soviet attack on NATO Europe or Chinese attack on our Asian allies;

—the prospects for a coordinated two-front attack on our allies by Russia and China are low both because of the risks of nuclear war and the improbability of Sino-Soviet cooperation. In any event, we do not believe that such a coordinated attack should be met primarily by U.S. conventional forces.

7. About five to seven divisions have been considered the minimum to blunt and delay an attack along the main access routes in Southeast Asia, then fall back to a defensible perimeter. Against a communist invasion of Korea it was thought that the South Korean army alone could hold initially north of Seoul until reinforced by Korean reserves or U.S. units to be mobilized or diverted from other requirements.

Though the "coordinated" attack described by the President is improbable, it should be noted that "theater nuclear forces" are prescribed as deterrents against the *single* contingency of a "Chinese attack on our Asian allies." Also, there are more plausible scenarios that would, in terms of their potential to immobilize U.S. forces, be the functional equivalent of a major attack: a Soviet military build-up and political pressure in central or southern Europe; or China's rendering massive logistical support to one of her Asian allies to the point where that ally could release overwhelming forces against a neighboring country; or the imminent entry of China into a war where we or one of our allies might have provided the provocation. It is conceivable that two such lesser contingencies could arise, in Europe and Asia, and that one of them could develop to the point of a conflict. In that event we would be reluctant to consider our conventional forces for either theater available for the other. Motivated by illusions of decisive action and immunity from retaliation, we might be tempted to dispose of the Asian conflict by technological escalation.

Therefore, if we remain committed to the defense of interests in both theaters, but maintain conventional forces for only one large contingency, our strategy is biased toward the earlier use of nuclear weapons. Of course, there is no necessary continuum of escalation from conventional war to tactical nuclear war. But the 1½-war strategy provides the President with fewer alternatives and renders the resort to nuclear weapons a more compelling choice, as well as making nuclear threat a more obvious residual feature of our diplomacy.

And so the "balance" promised in the new security policy is achieved—but not by adjusting our commitments, restricting our objectives or modifying our conception of the interests of the United States. Rather, budgetary stringencies inspire a reduction in force levels; a "1½-war strategy" is tailored to fit the intractable realities; and a series of rationalizations is constructed to validate the new strategy—rationalizations that simply stipulate a reduced threat, count heavily on subsidized and coerced allied efforts at self-defense, and suggest an early nuclear reaction if our calculations prove insufficiently conservative.

Thus the Nixon Doctrine reveals an apparent contradiction between objectives and strategy. Are we seeing the beginning of a return to the defense posture of the 1950's, with unabated commitments to a collection of front-line client-states, but with limited options and a renewed flirtation with the fantasy of tactical nuclear warfare?

IV

The new security policy not only shifts substantively down to a 1½-war strategy but also changes the model for determining defense requirements. Instead of the classic progression from the definition of foreign policy interests to the formulation of objectives, to the prescription of strategies, to the calculation of forces and their costs, we now see a constrained calculus that proceeds in reverse from limited budgets to trimmed forces to arbitrary strategies. The implications are not transmitted through the system to include a revision of objectives and interests. At best the system is balanced back from resources through strategies; the imbalance is shifted to a point between strategies and objectives.

But even the strategies and the forces may be out of balance. For the budget-constrained strategy revision is complemented by a fundamental change in the defense planning process. The previous system was requirements-oriented: there was, in theory, no prior budgetary restriction. Rather, planning began with the stated worldwide defense objective and resulted in forces and a budget which were recommended to the President and the Congress as systematically entailed by our defense objectives. Of course, the ideal system foundered on the institutional realities of weapons-systems and force creation. Indeed, the philosophy of unconstrained implementation of security objectives—"buy what you need"—encouraged inflated requirements within the framework of 2½ wars. And the attempts of the Secretary to limit forces only led the military to attempts to goldplate those prescribed forces, while keeping a ledger on the "shortfall" between the imposed strategy and the imposed force structure. But at least the direction and scope of the planning process compelled attention to the relevance and adequacy of the forces, and allowed the possibility of reasoning back from the rejection of excessive requirements to the questioning of overambitious strategies, extensive commitments and artificial interests.

By contrast, the new defense planning process begins simultaneously with "strategic guidance" and "fiscal guidance," established by the President and the National Security Council. The new procedure has attained certain efficiencies in managing the Pentagon budget cycle. But from the policy standpoint it is another matter: within the fiscal ceilings we will get the forces and weapons systems that the organization tends to produce—not the ones we might need. Of the two kinds of guidance, the fiscal is quantitative and unarguable; the strategic is verbal and elastic. If there is a coincidence of those forces and systems tailored to the fiscal guidance and those derived from the strategic guidance, it will be either accidental or contrived.

More likely, the Services will interpret the new guidance as a set of parameters within which they can promote self-serving programs. Under conditions of budgetary stringency they will skimp on manpower, supplies, war reserve stocks, maintenance and transport, while preserving headquarters, cadres of units, research and development of large new systems, and sophisticated technological overhead. In effect they will tend, as in the 1950's, to sacrifice those items that maintain balance, readiness and sustainability of effort, and to insist on those items that insure morale, careers and the competitive position of each Service.

Thus the Administration's defense planning procedure allows a second contradiction: between strategy and forces. This country may well end the 1970's with the worst of both worlds: on the one hand, a full panoply of commitments and a strategy that continues to serve an ambitious policy of containment; on the other, a worldwide sprinkling of token deployments and a force structure that is still expensive, but unbalanced, unready and irrelevant to our security.

V

The disabilities of the Nixon Doctrine follow from its insistence on the containment of China in face of budgetary pressures that arise not out of absolute scarcity of resources, but out of the nation's unwillingness to make large sacrifices for objectives that cannot be credibly invoked by its leadership. If the Administration is to be consistent in revising our defense posture and limiting defense budgets, it must consider a commensurate curtailment of our foreign policy objectives in Asia. Adjusting the intermediate-term strategies will not effect the reconciliation and will permit an honest implementation of the force and budget cuts.

But the Nixon Doctrine does not resolve the Asian defense problem in this fundamental way: rather, it appears as another formula for permanent confrontation with China. What are the issues that elude the perennial expressions of interest, by several administrations, in accommodating China? During the Johnson Administration the policy of containment ceded to a variant characterized as "containment without isolation." The shift, however, was accompanied by no tangible initiatives and induced no reciprocity from China. President Nixon entered office with a mandate—which he had created largely himself through his campaign emphasis—to bring about a reconciliation with China. His Administration has relaxed certain restrictions on trade and travel and revived the Warsaw ambassadorial talks. But such moves, though impressive as indications of enlightenment, do not touch on the essential concerns of China. However we ultimately conceive our interests, we might as well be realistic about the eventual price of a real accommodation with China.

This price would include three kinds of consideration: (1) diplomatic recognition and admission without qualification to the United Nations and the permanent Security Council seat; (2) affirmation of a one-China policy, even allowing the eventual accession of Taiwan to the mainland; (3) removal of the U.S. military presence on the mainland of Asia, without substituting a naval cordon, a ring of nearby island bases, a host of Asian mercenary armies, or a nuclear tripwire. The components of such a withdrawal would be: liquidation of the Vietnam war and removal of all U.S. forces there; retraction of all U.S. troops from other mainland Asian countries and Taiwan and closure of all bases; termination of military assistance to mainland states and cessation of efforts to create proxy forces to continue our mission; and dissolution of our security alliances with the "forward-defense" countries of Thailand, Taiwan, and Korea.

Such a program would amount to a major diplomatic revolution. It might take a quarter of a century to implement, even with the most sophisticated public and political support within the United States. It would alienate client régimes, unsettle for long intervals our relations with the Soviets, and tax the understanding of major allies such as Japan and Australia. It would signify the renunciation of our efforts to control events in Asia; henceforth we would control only our responses to events.

But it is fair to ask whether we will not arrive at this disposition of affairs in Asia at some point, whether we will it or not. Should this occur after a quarter of a century of tension and devastation, or political maneuver and diplomatic search? It is also fair to speculate that a more neutral, or even positive, relationship with China might give us a new scope of advantages. We might benefit eventually from a commercial relationship with China, rather than conceding the economic penetration of the mainland by Japan and Western Europe while we remain frozen in our historic impasse. We might also, simply through the dissolution of predictable enmity with China, make it more difficult for the Soviets to challenge us in other areas of the world. And we might find it useful to have a counterpoise to Japan, which is still our principal Pacific competitor, economic and potentially military, and a possible future partner of the USSR in such common interests as counterbalancing China and developing eastern Siberia.

The tangible expression of containment is our security alliances and the other strong, though less formal, military commitments around the periphery of China. These commitments, it can be argued, create the threat to us by transforming otherwise neutral events into situations of relevance to our interests; perpetuate the confrontation with China that gives substance to the threat, by frustrating the essential motives of China; lock us into a posture of forward defense on the mainland of Asia; and dictate the requirement for large general purpose forces or equivalent means of deterrence and defense.

Our alliances in Asia do not form a coherent and comprehensive system such as NATO. Rather they are a collection of bilateral agreements, plus the multilateral SEATO pact, contracted separately from 1951 through 1962. Even the purposes served by these alliances, as seen at the time of their negotiation, were diverse. Containment of China might have been a concurrent motive, but it did not uniformly inspire the creation of the pacts. Quite apart from containing our enemies, several of the treaties exhibit motives of containing our allies as well.

The ANZUS and Philippine treaties of 1951, though signed against the backdrop of the Korean War, related more to the fear of Japan which these allies derived from World War II. The 1953 agreement with the Republic of Korea was, among other things, a price for Syngman Rhee's restraint from attempting to reunify the peninsula by force. Similarly the treaty with the Republic of China in 1955 was in part a *quid pro quo* for Chiang's acceptance of "re-leashing" during the Straits crisis of that year. The SEATO alliance of 1954, which extended protection to South Vietnam, Laos, and Cambodia, arose less from the vision of true collective defense than the desire of the United States to have a legal basis for discretionary intervention under the nominal coloration of "united action." The bilateral U.S.-Thai adjunct to SEATO, negotiated by Rusk and Thanat in 1962, reassured the Thais, during the events that led to the Laos neutralization accords, that the U.S. would respond to a threat to Thai security, regardless of the reaction of other SEATO signatories; this agreement, too, was a price to secure the acquiescence of an ally in an arrangement that suited the interest of the United States. The 1960 Security Treaty with Japan, revising the original treaty of 1951, reaffirmed U.S. administration of Okinawa and perpetuated our use of bases in the Japanese home islands, subject to prior consultation for nuclear or direct combat deployments. (The Nixon-Sato communique of October 1969 pledged reversion of Okinawa to Japan by 1972, a status that implies removal of nuclear weapons and submission to the "homeland formula" for consultation on the use of bases.)

Though deterrence has always been the primary function of our alliances, their military content has changed profoundly from the time they were contracted. The Dulles policy, in the pacts of 1953–55, did not emphasize the actual defense of allied territory or contemplate the dispatch of U.S. ground forces to any point where the Communist powers chose to apply military force. Rather, it aimed at nuclear deterrence of overt aggression. In this concept the alliances served to establish a territorial definition. The implied countermeasure was the discretionary application of American nuclear force against communist airfields, supply centers, ports and perhaps industries and cities. The concept was not clearly resolved: it was semi-strategic and semi-tactical, partially punitive and partially for direct military effect. Also, cases short of obvious aggression, such as subversion and support for internal revolutionary struggles, were acknowledged to be imprecise and difficult. In Indochina in 1954 the Eisenhower Administration could not identify an appropriate enemy or target to fit the massive nuclear response and narrowly declined to intervene. Of course, it also sensed the lack of formal alliance protection over Southeast Asia as an impediment to intervention and moved to create SEATO within two months of the partition of Vietnam.

The refinement of tactical battlefield nuclear weapons in the middle and later 1950's made conceivable the notion of actual nuclear defense confined to the theater of conflict. The Kennedy-McNamara policy of flexible response, including counter-insurgency techniques and large balanced conventional forces, provided the practical means of containing a wider spectrum of Chinese or Chinese-supported initiatives. Thus the policy of close-in containment of China—involving the actual forward defense of allied territory—acquired its content.

There is a set of propositions that qualifies military deterrence: the more explicit and obvious our commitment, the more effective in preventing war, but the less effective in preventing our involvement in war; conversely, the more attenuated our commitment, the less certain our involvement, but the more probable a hostile initiative.

An Administration with a more relaxed view of Asia might take the risk of the second proposition and look more neutrally on a communist probe. But this Administration appears likely to maintain its deterrent stance and take its chances on involvement in conflict. This would mean that it will not overtly diminish any commitment; indeed it is likely to reaffirm and reinforce any commitment that is beset by doubt. But to maintain the deterrent effect of our commitments in the face of reductions in budgets, forces and deployments, the Administration must replace deleted capabilities with some equivalent, such as increased rapid deployment ability or nuclear threat. This Administration could not count entirely on the mobility of our forces, which can be evidenced only by massive exercises and adequate lift resources, which are far from certain to be appropriated. Residually, it is forced to rely on nuclear deterrence, which need only be hinted. The point is that our mode of deterrence and our provisions for defense will now progressively diverge from the preferences of our treaty partners. Our proposed substitution of technology and threat for our manpower and presence might be equivalent from our point of view, but not from that of our allies.

None of our Asian defense arrangements is specific about the tangible support that might be evoked by an act of aggression. No joint defense force with agreed war plans and command structures exists. Our military concept could become, rather than the forward defense of all territory, a mobile defense, an enclave strategy, or even a nuclear tripwire. In another dimension, our commitment might be satisfied by various types of support, such as logistical, tactical air or nuclear fire. U.S. contingency plans are essentially unilateral and subject to uncommunicated change. And implementation of all treaties refers to our constitutional procedures, which are themselves in a phase of more stringent interpretation.

Because of this scope for maneuver or evasion, our Asian allies will be correspondingly more sensitive to interpretive commentary by U.S. officials and to shifts in our military posture. Already they sense that the substantive content of our alliances is affected by the President's choice of worldwide strategy. The selected strategy is described as defending both Europe and Asia—though alternatively. But it is clear that Europe holds priority and claims virtually as many resources as previously; the major war case associated with the reduction in active forces is Asia. Although no alliances are formally disturbed, our Asian allies, as they count our divisions and analyze our posture statements and policy declarations, have cause for concern that behind the façade of ritualistic reiteration we might have altered our capability and specific intent to fulfill our treaty commitments.

Thus we can devalue the diplomatic and deterrent effect of our alliances without even gaining immunity from involvement, simply by shifting strategies, debating criteria for intervention and making arbitrary adjustments in force levels. In view of the liabilities of this course—which is the course of the present Administration—we might as well face the problem more directly and begin to consider the broader alternatives to containment, with their full implications for our alliances in Asia.

VII

As long as we assert interests in Asia that (1) entail defending territory, (2) could plausibly be threatened by hostile actions, and (3) are evidenced by alliances that dispose us to a military response, we are exposed to the contingency of involvement. If we maintain this exposure through insistence on our present Asian commitments, while adopting budget-constrained strategies, we risk a future defeat or stalemate, or we allow ourselves to be moved toward reliance on nuclear weapons.

To avoid these alternatives, two courses are available. One is heavy dependence on allied forces to fulfill defense requirements. This is the hope of Asianization, offered prominently by the Nixon Doctrine. But this policy binds us closely to the fate of our Asian clients and diminishes our control over our involvement; and there is still the liability that U.S. forces might be required to rescue the efforts of our allies.

The other course is a process of military readjustment and political accommodation that would make it far less likely that we would become involved every time there is some slippage in the extensive diplomatic "fault" that runs along the rim of Asia. This course is arduous and complex, and as little under our unilateral and absolute control as a course of military deterrence. But the consequences of not budging from our present set of ambitions and illusions—or by trifling with the unalterable purposes of China by limiting ourselves to insubstantial diplomatic initiatives—are far bleaker.

The situation calls not for a symbolic shift in strategy—such as the 1½-war doctrine—which is founded on the hope that the contingencies that would test it, to which we are still liable, might not occur. The situation is not amenable to purely instrumental solutions, such as the calculated equippage of allied armies or the reliance on technological escalation. The situation requires a fundamental questioning and revision of the containment of China.

The confusion that surrounds the Nixon Doctrine is appropriate to its conflicting message and incomplete intent. While pledging to honor all of our existing commitments, the President has placed them all in considerable doubt. While offering promise of avoiding involvement in future Asian conflicts, he has biased the nature of our participation. Thus, in the attempt to perpetuate our control of the destiny of Asia, the Nixon Doctrine may forfeit control of our own destiny in Asia.

VII

RELATIONS WITH EUROPE

The articles in this chapter address themselves to the central issue of whether the United States needs allies in the contemporary world, whether its most powerful allies—the nations of western Europe belonging to NATO—will continue to be U.S. allies, and whether Europe can evolve into an entity capable of defending its own interests against the Soviet bloc.

NATO was formed to provide Europe with confidence that the U.S. would come to its defense if the Soviet Union attacked. The original NATO theory was that of the trip-wire. The NATO ground forces were insufficient for defense but the presence of small U.S. forces would trigger massive retaliation by the U.S. nuclear forces. As the Soviet Union developed its nuclear weaponry and the U.S. homeland became vulnerable, NATO had less confidence that massive retaliation was sufficiently deterring to the Russians because the danger to the U.S. made its use less credible. Therefore, NATO sought greater assurance in shield forces—ground forces that could hold for a significant length of time and perhaps that could even defeat a Russian or Warsaw Treaty Organization invasion. As détente developed, the perception of a Soviet threat diminished both in Western Europe and the United States. Correspondingly the willingness to pay for adequate conventional forces diminished. Pressures developed for a European Security Conference and a Mutual Balanced Forces Reduction Conference. However, as these pressures continued, some Europeans began to fear that the American commitment might weaken and that this might subject them to Soviet pressure. This is producing the present debate both in Western Europe and in the United States on the role of U.S. relations with Europe.

Is Europe vital to the security of the United States? Simon Serfaty suggests below that it is not, that we could defend ourselves behind our own frontiers. But is this correct? Would a United States isolated behind its frontiers and perhaps confronted with a Europe dominated by the Soviet Union and an Asia dominated by China (or by Russia) remain firm in its libertarian values, or would it become suspicious, conservative, and militaristic? If, as a result of an isolationist political decision, our enemies would be enabled to cut off our access to much of the world's supplies and interfere with our intellectual communications with other important areas, would we soon become relatively poor and backward? Would we then be susceptible to insecurity as a consequence of technological breakthroughs elsewhere? Serfaty does not intend his question to be more than provocative, although others are perhaps more serious in suggesting that the Finlandization of Europe would not seriously injure U.S. national security. Clearly my implied negative answer is subject to dispute and U.S. isolationism need not produce a Europe dominated by Russia. However, the question is one the reader should consider at some length if he is to take neo-isolationism seriously.

Even if one agrees that Soviet domination of Europe would be dangerous to American security, he need not agree that a reduction of American forces in Europe would produce that result. This belief might be based on confidence in détente or an expectation that the Europeans will find an effective alternative for themselves if the American presence is reduced.

Many Europeans, as well as Americans, rest their faith on détente and deterrence. Yet, if readers consider the major political events of the last ten years, they will discover that most knowledgeable political observers were surprised by them. Examples include the Czechoslovakian liberalization, which clearly surprised western observers; the Soviet invasion of Czechoslovakia in 1968, which clearly surprised the Czechoslovak leadership; and the Nixon rapprochement with China, which appeared to surprise everyone. It is reasonable to work to improve détente. Is it reasonable to depend for security primarily upon détente?

Serfaty is less concerned than Duchêne that a reduced American presence would injure European defensibility. However, even the present NATO defense posture is problematic. Although a few observers argue that the NATO forces have defensive superiority, others strongly deny this, and the latter is the generally accepted position. The noted French analyst, General Beaufre, argues that Warsaw Treaty Organization forces would be at the Rhine in 2 or 3 days. Most analysts who disagree with him extend this defensibility only to 2 or 3 weeks.

Serfaty and Duchêne suggest a European nuclear force as an alternative to deterrence by the United States, although Duchêne obviously sees the need for an interim solution prior to such a European development. Yet how can there be a European force without a Europe? And how are Europe and NATO to be related in the immediate future?

Even the recent hopeful developments in the Common Market recounted in the article by Paul Taylor fail to suggest strongly the potential for Europe to become a major military power. In some NATO countries the length of national service is being reduced, and there are strong pressures for reductions in military budgets. The crucial European question may well be a nuclear one. There have been suggestions, still far short of implementation, that the British and French forces be pooled as the foundation for a European force. Yet neither the British nor the French are likely to permit any German finger on the nuclear trigger. And, in the absence of such a role, the Germans would be in the same insecure position toward the suggested European force that France was toward the American force when it decided to produce its own nuclear armaments. This is precisely why the Germans prefer an American nuclear guarantee to a European one.

Contrary to what Professor Kolodziej suggests below, French leaders have been unreceptive to mutual balanced force reductions precisely because any reduction of the American presence on the continent of Europe would increase German strength relative to French. This consideration obviously affects French considerations of a genuinely supranational Europe divorced from the United States. The demise of NATO, and the consequent reduction of the value of the American nuclear guarantee to Germany, would isolate Germany and subject her to Soviet pressure. Moreover, even if the Europeans were genuinely willing to form a supranational Europe and to develop a nuclear force in which Germany had a genuinely coequal role, is it likely that the Congressional Joint Committee on Atomic Energy would permit those transfers of information that would make the venture economically feasible?

In the absence of an adequate conventional defense, Europe must rest its security upon deterrence by the U.S. However, the reliance upon deterrence overlooks much of the political context of the European problem, which revolves around the great issue of crisis stability. It is important to prevent a war in Europe (or anywhere), and therefore it is of major importance also to prevent the initiation of any major crisis in Europe, particularly in circumstances in which the strategic position of NATO is weaker than that of the Warsaw Treaty Organization. If the Soviet position is militarily superior, and if important Soviet interests are being threatened by events partly beyond Soviet control, the Soviets might be tempted to initiate or to escalate a crisis in a situation in which they have strategic superiority. Even if they have no intention of attacking anyone, we will never be sure of this. And if we are not sure of this, will not we and our NATO allies be forced to take steps to de-escalate the crisis—such as removing provocative weapons systems from Germany or troop concentrations from frontier regions—in an attempt to maintain the peace, even if this involves concessions? The greater NATO's military inferiority is, the greater this temptation will be, as in the case of Russian concessions during the Cuban missile crisis.

Strategic inequality may well produce dynamic political instability. Therefore, given the risks inherent in the current American European posture, is it unlikely that adoption of the proposals of Senator Mansfield and others for a reduction of American forces in Europe would set off a search for alternative European policies? Prime Minister Heath of Great Britain suggested in February 1973 that some western European states would accommodate themselves to Soviet policy in this event.

Some argue that it is the maintenance of military blocs in Europe that prevents the development of a new, pacific, international system in the European area. However, once NATO is disbanded, it could not quickly be put together again. The Soviet presence would be overwhelming. Major reductions in armed forces might set in motion disintegrative forces in the European area that might be beyond the control of either Europeans or Americans. The great importance of continued stability in Europe is emphasized by the report in the *New York Times,* of October 17, 1972, according to which Chou En-lai stated to Walter Scheel, the Western German foreign minister, his objection to mutual balanced force reductions in the west or a deterioration in the NATO posture. Thus, Chou sees a potential major impact of European instability upon China's security. Is it unlikely that its impact on American security would be minor?

20.

America and Europe in the Seventies: Integration or Disintegration?

SIMON SERFATY

I. The Setting

"THE MOST CONSTRUCTIVE American foreign policy since the end of World War II has been the development of Atlantic relationships." Thus wrote Henry Kissinger in 1965. Yet, he went on, the promises which stemmed from such a policy were "flawed by increasingly sharp disputes among the Allies." As America dealt with these disputes, Kissinger warned further, it would have to avoid the "danger of becoming mired by the prudent, the tactical or the expedient" and, in the process, "confuse creativity with a projection of the present into the future."[1] Shortly afterward, the coming of a new era in Americano–European relations was heralded in the first presidential state of the world message.

Significantly, this "genuine partnership" was not expected to extend to such key areas as the preservation of a nuclear deterrent and the maintenance of a balance of conventional power. There the uniqueness of America's contribution was still accepted as a self-evident feature of the "new" relationship. But these were precisely the unresolved issues of the sixties: instead of discussing situations in which there might be real differences of assessment, and even differences of interests among the allies, the Nixon administration continued to assume that such differences would be muted

This article was written under the auspices of the California Arms Control and Foreign Policy Seminar. Reprinted by permission from Dr. Serfaty.
1. Henry Kissinger, *The Troubled Partnership* (New York 1966), pp. 4–5, 248–9 (Anchor Book edition).

by the same dominant set of vital and mutual interests which had linked America and Europe since World War II. In doing so, it adopted, in Hans Morgenthau's words, "the solution of business as usual, of the continuation of institutional arrangements and procedural routines."[2] Such a solution, it will be argued here, is no solution at all as it fails to deal with the changing realities of America's and Europe's security requirements and interests.

Admittedly, the area of permissible changes cannot be defined and constricted by the dominant power only. It is also sharply defined by states other than the superpowers whose ambitions and fears make them hesitate between a desire for change and a need for security. Obviously, changes in the status quo bring about new situations which are more or less secure depending on developments which cannot always be easily predicted. Thus, what makes the security of Europe relatively stable is an implicit recognition of the status quo. Yet, it is precisely because of this resulting sense of security that the status quo is being challenged, thereby releasing, however timidly, forces for change which may themselves lead to security problems. This is what Pierre Hassner has called the paradox of self-denying security, whereby the main threat to security is to take it too easily for granted.[3]

Such paradoxes, of course, abound, and we now see nations which seek security even though they already have it, nations which gain insecurity as they gain power, and nations which advocate change in the name of the status quo (and, for that matter, vice versa). West Germany, for example, advocates change in at least three major areas of German interests: frontiers (for purposes of reunification), alliances (to pull East Germany out of the Warsaw Pact), and status (for regaining an international equality still denied to her). Yet, West Germany can succeed in her revisionist endeavor only to the extent that she accepts the status quo; too much revisionist *elan* might bring about a reaction from foes and friends alike. Hence the paradox of a West German state which seeks revisionist objectives and advocates a status quo policy.

China is another state whose revisionist ambitions (vis-à-vis frontiers, her military encirclement, and her international status) can be expressed only within a framework which recognizes the legitimacy of the existing status quo. China must speak both a language of power which she does not have and a language of harmony which she does not want. Nor can either language be expected to improve substantially with time. To other nations, harmony implies status quo; to China, harmony requires change. To force change, China must display her power. Today, China's power stems essen-

2. Hans J. Morgenthau, *A New Foreign Policy for the United States* (New York, 1969), pp. 5–6.
3. Pierre Hassner, "Change and Security in Europe," Part I, "The Background," *Adelphi Papers*, Number 45, February 1968.

tially from her ability to bridge the technological gap with human masses; however effective in the short term, this is in the long term a most fragile bridge. But as this technological gap is filled more substantially, China's deterrent posture may become even weaker as, while becoming industrialized, she becomes increasingly sensitive to a nuclear attack which would presently be relatively harmless.

Standing at the verge of a "new era," America registers the departure of old fears but somehow fails to record the arrival of new realities. Thus, we periodically dismiss the threat of a Soviet military aggression in Western Europe as unlikely. President Kennedy noticed it as early as 1963 when he told Spaak of Belgium, "the whole debate about an atomic force in Europe is really useless, because Berlin is secure and Europe as a whole is well protected. What really matters at this point is the rest of the world."[4] Yet, we still hold on to the notion that such an aggression, regardless of Soviet intentions, is being deterred primarily by the Atlantic Alliance and the troops stationed in the area. There may be here another form of self-denying security—a self-induced insecurity whereby the main source of insecurity is a stubborn refusal to recognize security where it presently exists.

Although all would agree with President Nixon's assertion that we are now deep into the age of conciliation, most would also agree with an implicit corollary that the tools of coercion must nevertheless be preserved, almost untouched. Senator Mansfield, for example, is in favor of a troop withdrawal from Western Europe. Yet, even though this is an issue which he has been raising for the past twelve years, the Senator from Montana remains remarkably patient and defensive about his request. He would not go so far as to recommend a full withdrawal. "I am not advocating," he emphasizes, "and I have not advocated that all U.S. troops be removed from Europe."[5] At most the debate is one of numbers. The principle of a considerable military presence in Western Europe is not at stake: "A U.S. presence should remain," although a "smaller" one. Why? Because today like before "our vital interests in what transpires in Europe remains. In this day and age," continued Mansfield, "an armed attack on Western Europe will certainly involve us almost from the start." But would it? The answer appears to be so self-evident that it is usually not necessary to go beyond the laconic assertion, as Secretary Rogers last put it in March 1972, that ". . . we must not forget for a moment that Western Europe's security is indivisible from our own."[6] How could one forget it when it is repeated as often as it is by foreign policy critics and apologists alike? Yet, wouldn't it be helpful, as a reflection of the undisputed transformation of America's

4. Arthur Schlesinger, Jr., *A Thousand Days* (Boston, 1965), p. 872.
5. Congressional Record, daily ed., January 24, 1970, p. S496.
6. *United States Foreign Policy, 1971: A Report of the Secretary of State* (Washington D.C., 1972), p. viii.

354 : *Relations with Europe*

and Europe's physical and economic interests, to examine more critically this notion of Atlantic inseparability and, in the process, raise the question of whether or not, in the seventies, the Atlantic Alliance must remain the instrument most likely to satisfy America's and Europe's interests?

II. Strategic Realities: The Limits of Atlantic Integration

Through the years it has been argued that the Atlantic Alliance is necessary to deter the Soviet Union from, at most, a military invasion of Western Europe, and, at least, the extension of its influence to the point of totally excluding the United States from Europe. Concurrently, a secondary (and understandably less publicized) objective of the alliance has been that of containing Germany from within by serving as a railguard against any potential revival of German militarism. What made such Atlantic integration credible was therefore the desirability, from the viewpoint of both sides of the Atlantic, of the alliance. There could be no security for America—it was argued in 1949 and it continues to be argued today—if there was no security for Europe, as Europe's industrial base, population, and institutions remained essential to the physical security and economic and spiritual health of America.

Leaving Germany aside for a moment, it must be noted that this security equation prevailed even though the perception of the Soviet threat was not evenly felt within the Atlantic Alliance. It was usually strongest in the United States and West Germany, usually weakest in France and even Great Britain. To the French particularly, Atlantic integration, like European integration, was accepted reluctantly as a means toward other ends which included the security of American assistance (not just military but also, and perhaps above all, economic and political) and the handcuffing of Germany. In Britain, too, the perception of the Soviet threat was increased in the aftermath of World War II by imperial rather than national considerations.

In the United States proper, the perception of the threat peaked in the summer of 1950 when, rightly or wrongly, the invasion of Korea was seen as the prelude to a large-scale invasion of Western Europe. "From now on," emphasized Secretary Dean Acheson at the time, "it is action which counts and not further resolutions or further plans or further meetings."[7] Thus the misgivings of the other allies were put aside, and Washington's perception of the Soviet threat became the basis upon which the military integration of the Atlantic area was undertaken.

A more limited perception of the Soviet threat reemerged in Western Europe in the early sixties. Especially evident in Gaullist rhetoric, the

7. News conference of December 22, 1950. *Department of State Bulletin*, vol. XXIV, p. 3.

"decline" of this threat was explained in terms of Western Europe's political and economic recovery, the displacement of the focal point of superpower confrontation away from Europe and toward such peripheral areas as Southeast Asia and the Middle East, and, in the aftermath of the Cuban missile crisis, the military ascendancy of the United States. Even the 1968 invasion of Czechoslovakia failed to revive significantly East-West tensions in Europe.

Throughout this period, however, America continued to reason that given this waning of the Soviet military threat, and even given the Kremlin's willingness to discuss the specific modalities of the resulting stalemate, it was more urgent than ever to preserve the cohesion of the alliance at a time when serious negotiations were about to begin. There remained doubts that, possibly based on intended deception, détente was no more than Moscow's application of the old technique of dividing to conquer better. Obviously, discord within the Atlantic Alliance would create opportunities that Soviet diplomacy might conceivably exploit for political advantage. Such discord might be further increased by the Soviets if they abandoned, as they did, their threatening posture. They could then achieve peacefully what their hostile behavior had failed to secure. This was in essence Washington's answer to those who, in the pre-Vietnam days, were already forecasting the end of alliances.

The case for the alliance rested then—and it still rests today—on the assumption that first, despite détente, Moscow's ultimate objective remains the control of the rest of Europe; and second, that despite its recovery Western Europe remains impotent in the face of such a Soviet attempt at communization. Even if these two assumptions were justified, we would still have to measure the contribution of the alliance in terms of making up for Europe's lack of power and containing Moscow's persistent ambitions. Thus, a key contribution is said to be the 310,000 American troops stationed in the area. These troops, it is argued, play the same essential roles as they played throughout the fifties. On the one hand, they symbolically assure the Europeans (and the Russians) that should a war break out in Europe, America will be involved from the start of hostilities. On the other hand, these troops reinforce Europe's non-nuclear capabilities, thereby fulfilling two related objectives: first, prevent a conventional *fait accompli,* and second, raise the nuclear threshold.

There is no need here to discuss once again whether such assurances were ever needed or such objectives were ever realistic. Assuming they were, one may still question whether it is still necessary today to have America station troops in Europe as a means of assuring Europe of its good faith and Russia of its commitment. Even if such hostages continue to be required, can they not be found in the tens of thousands of tourists and other American citizens who are in Europe at any time of the year or in the billions of dollars which America has invested in Western Europe over the past twenty years? And if a trip wire is needed, is it America's role to provide it? Conventional forces in Europe are not expected to fight a non-nuclear war; they are merely expected to contain a potential aggressor for a limited amount of time. Can't the Europeans themselves fulfill this minimal objective? With regular armed forces amounting to approximately half of the Soviet forces, and with military expenditures equal to about half of the Soviet expenditures, a "Europe" limited to its four major states (France, Great Britain, Italy, and West Germany) already has the required means. All that it lacks, apparently, is the will. But then, why would it be willing to assume the burden of conventional defense (which it does not believe in anyway) as long as Washington, its bitter complaining notwithstanding, agrees to assume such a burden itself?

What is surprising about such questions is that having been raised as often and for as long as they have, they continue to be dismissed by a majority of policy-makers and analysts alike. Things have worked this way up to now, it is said, why change them? Fear of the future appears to be based on the unshakable premise that an American withdrawal from Western Europe cannot be considered, let alone be implemented, without jeopardizing America's and Europe's security and other vital interests. Given the obvious international changes which have taken place the past ten years the persuasiveness of such a premise appears today very much in doubt.

The end of America's nuclear monopoly, followed by the end of its nuclear supremacy, and combined with successive technological revolutions in nuclear weaponry and their means of delivery, have sensibly modified the security relationship between America and Europe. It was possible for Europe to rely on America's nuclear weapons as an instrument of policy as long as America's superiority in such weapons was unchallenged. But when such superiority receded and America's threat of retaliation was balanced with a Soviet counterthreat of similar reprisal, both Europe and America asked whether any nation could and should risk destruction for the sake of another nation. And, assuming that America was willing to risk its cities for the defense of European cities, was such a commitment credible to partners *and* potential enemies alike? Thus, the question is no longer whether or not the alliance is necessary; it is also whether or not what might make the alliance necessary also makes it desirable and credible.

Of course, even the uncertainty of America's guarantee may contribute to Europe's security. For Moscow does not have to be sure of America's retaliation to be deterred. All that it needs is to be in doubt. To this extent, de Gaulle's former complaint about such uncertainty reflects, paradoxically, the very reason why deterrence works.[8]

8. "No one in the world," noted de Gaulle on May 15, 1962, "particularly no one in America can say if, or where, or when, or how, or to what extent American nuclear weapons would be used to defend Europe." This is true, of course: no one can say—especially no one in the Soviet Union.

In a general vein, alliances in the nuclear age go in contradictory directions. For one, national commitments, if they are to be credible, must be made within a more "integrated" framework, that is to say a framework which automates the implementation of the commitment. In Thomas Schelling's words, this is being "rationally irrational": an irrational policy which calls for the potential destruction of one's national self in defense of another is made rational if alternatives to the irrational option are simply preempted, for example, by making automatic through one device or another, nuclear retaliation against an aggressor. At the same time, alliances tend to be disintegrative precisely because of the practical irrationality of the commitment; nuclear or otherwise, war is divisible in the nuclear age because destruction might otherwise be indivisible. A nation is not going to commit itself to destruction merely so that another nation might live. To argue differently may be neither credible nor desirable to potential victims as well as to potential aggressors.[9]

This dilemma—imperial convictions vs. national responsibilities—is especially acute in the case of the Atlantic Alliance where the security gap is broadened even further by conflicting defense requirements. Thus throughout the past few years many in Europe have argued that toughening the terms of deterrence through a strategy *à la* massive retaliation increases the security of Europe by decreasing the likelihood of war. Yet, such a reasoning implies that the irrational is rationalized into a national policy; what is wanted is the paralyzing of the other side with fear. It is then assumed, of course, that a rationally irrational policy will not be met with a similar dose of irrationality. Yet, what if irrationality does prevail on the other side as well? In other words, what if deterrence fails? Can the question of defense still remain a collective question, or should it become instead everyone to himself? To make deterrence possible, Washington must pledge its national body to the nuclear defense of Western Europe. But to make defense possible, Western Europe may have to give its continental body so that America might survive a non-nuclear war. What is rational on one side of the Atlantic may be irrational on the other.

Although it stressed deterrence, massive retaliation was a policy of minimum deterrence calling for minimum involvement in world affairs, inasmuch as the situations where the use of such retaliation would be acceptable and credible were by definition strictly limited. On the other hand, and even though it stresses defense, flexible response is a policy of maximum deterrence because making retaliation as minimal as possible permits maximum involvement in international crises. Yet, the fact that the European allies would have been generally disturbed by flexible response is not surprising as it reflects a real deterrence gap between America and Europe. Obviously enough, what seems controlled on one side of the

9. Much of what follows is adapted from my *The Elusive Enemy* (Boston, 1972), pp. 136–142.

Atlantic does not look quite the same on the other side. Conventional or nuclear, a war waged in Europe will be limited only from a non-European viewpoint.

But is there any American (or European) strategy which will ever gain Europe's (or America's) favor? If the Soviet Union's capabilities are overlooked and the devastating nature of a thermonuclear war ignored, Europeans may regard the military status quo as satisfactory and thus decrease further their defense expenditures. If, conversely, Soviet capabilities are "realistically" estimated and the horrors of nuclear war correspondingly emphasized, Europeans may well feel constrained to develop their own nuclear forces to ensure a security for which, they may think, America will not fight. If Soviet conventional (non-nuclear) capabilities are conceded to be large, Europeans argue that their contribution in the field of conventional weapons is useless in shifting the balance. If these capabilities are thought to be small, Europeans might argue that any contribution of theirs is unnecessary. In the fifties, Europe found massive retaliation highly dangerous because it implied the potential escalation of any armed confrontation in Europe into a total nuclear war. In the sixties, Europe found flexible response no less dangerous because it might encourage Soviet aggression in Western Europe through the implied reduction in scope of America's retaliation, hence increasing its acceptability. Europeans, who charge both Moscow and Washington with the intention of confining a war over Europe to Europe, would like to see such a war confined to American and Soviet territories. In the age of flexible response, the European allies in effect complained that the United States had achieved additional security at the expense of Western Europe. Yet the inescapable fact is that regardless of America's strategy, Western Europe remains more insecure than America by definition—the obvious implication of Europe's geographical location. Situated between both superpowers, Europe holds the same position as Poland held in the past, located between two of the great powers of the time (Prussia and Russia). Ultimately, a war between the two superpowers could remain "limited" to Europe while their own territory would be totally spared, and the only balance which America can restore between itself and Europe is a balance of *insecurity*. "Who can say," asked de Gaulle at his apocalyptic best, "that if the occasion arises . . . [the Soviet Union and the United States] while each deciding not to launch its missiles at the main enemy so that it should itself be spared, will not crush the others. It is possible to imagine that in some awful day Western Europe should be wiped out from Moscow and Central Europe from Washington."[10] No one can say, to be sure. Yet Western Europe's reluctance to be wiped out from Moscow, possibly for the sake of Washington, can only be matched by Washington's own reluctance to be wiped out from Moscow,

10. de Gaulle's news conference of November 10, 1962.

possibly for the sake of Western Europe. Herein lie the limits of Atlantic integration.

III. Other Realities: The Limits of Atlantic Disintegration

What transpires from such discussions is a security gap between the United States and Europe. The search for security within the Atlantic Alliance is being transformed into a zero sum game wherein America's security is sought, in part at least, at the expense of its European allies, and vice versa. In other words, while both sides can do much damage to one another (either Europe or America can force the other into a war which it did not want for the sake of interests which it did not share), it still remains to be seen whether either side can do much to enhance its partner's security and other related interests. Is Western Europe indispensable to America's security? Or to put it differently, in the most extreme case of one state gaining imperial control of Europe, would America's physical security be directly threatened?

The only current threat to a European balance of power is obviously raised by the Soviet Union. Any threat to such a balance that would not come from Moscow would undoubtedly be contained by Moscow itself. Thus what Washington is concerned with is Soviet control of the European continent. Yet, one is technically tempted to ask, "So what?" Deterrence is not based on resources only, though clearly Soviet control of Western Europe's resources would greatly enhance Soviet capabilities."[11] Deterrence is based on the ability to retaliate and destroy. Thus Soviet control of Western Europe would affect America's physical security only to the extent that it would reduce America's retaliatory capability. Such a situation is not an easy one to foresee. It might be speculated, of course, that Moscow would then use the resources found in Western Europe to accelerate the arms race with America until America is reduced to economic exhaustion. Yet, even a comparison of America's economic resources with those of a joint Europe-Soviet condominium leaves the outcome of such a race highly doubtful.

Of course, the above assumes both Moscow's desire to overrun Western Europe and Western Europe's impotence in the face of it. Granting Moscow's desire it is the latter assumption which is said to make the Atlantic Alliance necessary. All technicalities aside, this notion of Western European impotence is surprising given Western Europe's capabilities, real and potential. Indeed, America's protection of as powerful a group of states is without precedent in history. Ultimately, does American policy in Europe today aim at containing the Soviet Union *or* Western Europe—or even

11. For a refreshing and stimulating analysis of the requirements of America's physical security, see Robert W. Tucker, *A New Isolationism: Threat or Promise?* (New York, 1972).

both? Couldn't deterrence of whatever Soviet threat there is be achieved more effectively on a nuclear and regional basis? Clearly, the Europeans have the resources—human, financial, and technological—to attain a credible level of deterrence (which is not to say, of course, that they could attain a level of nuclear parity with either superpower). On the face of it, the key problem is said to be one of political organization. But an effective Western European nuclear deterrent does not necessarily require a political integration of Europe. At most it assumes a coordination of national nuclear strategies, a coordination justified by the assertion that in the nuclear age a war in Europe cannot be limited to any one state but is likely to spread in space to all key European states. The point here is that if France or Great Britain can deter the Soviet Union, either separately or in common, then it follows that Europe can deter the Soviet Union. The perception of a Soviet invasion of Germany, for example, in the face of the threat of a substantial French and British retaliation, as well as the fact of an always possible American retaliation, makes sense only in the case of a major threat raised by West Germany against Soviet interests, in which case it is likely that Moscow would not be the only party interested in pre-empting such a threat. Thus, America might someday soon quietly invite the Europeans, nationally or regionally, to replace American leadership in the containing of the Soviet Union. To gain time, Washington might even grant the Europeans the technical assistance in the field of nuclear weaponry which it gave London but denied Paris. To be sure, nuclear proliferation would take place in the process, not only in Western Europe but possibly in other areas of the world as well. What is less sure is whether nuclear proliferation is automatically harmful to American interests. Again, the self-evident assumptions here are twofold. First, nuclear proliferation increases the risks of nuclear war. Second, any nuclear war is likely to affect America's physical security by making America an active participant in the conflict. The first one of these assumptions is probably true—not because the prudence and rationality of the nuclear states are in doubt but because the risks of irrationality and accidental wars are quantitatively increased through proliferation. The latter assumption is based on the more dubious notion that a nuclear peace is indivisible; in what precedes, this notion was rejected as it was suggested instead that a nuclear peace may prove at least divisible along narrowly defined regional lines.

Still, a militarily independent Western Europe, it will be argued, might seek an economic independence as well and erode America's economic interests on the continent. Two assumptions underline such fears. First, it is implicitly suggested that military and economic links go hand in hand so that as America's military presence in Western Europe is rolled back, so is America's economic presence. There does not appear to be much logic in such an argument. The rollback of America's economic empire can be expected to take place regardless of the evolution of its overall foreign policy.

The question is not so much whether it will occur but how far it will go. Hence the second assumption, namely that Western Europe's political and military dependence on America are the safest guarantee against excessive economic nationalism in Europe.

One wonders. In the realm of trade, for example, America's best guarantee is less geared to Europe's security requirements than it is to Europe's economic requirements. Of course, the American economy would suffer somewhat should international trade dry up. But America's partners might suffer even more. Consider the following figures. In 1970, the 8.4% of the U.S. gross national product was comprised of international trade. But foreign trade accounted for 33.7% in Great Britain, 23.1% (1969) for France, 34.3% for Western Germany, and 29.3% (1969) for Italy. For the EEC as a whole it was 35.3%. For exports only these figures were 4.3% for the United States, as compared to 15.8%, 10.7% (1969), 20.7%, and 14.2% (1969), for Great Britain, France, Western Germany, and Italy respectively.

The extent of such economic dependence between Western Europe and America is even more evident if we consider the export relationships between the two areas. Thus in relation to America's total exports the percentage of American exports to Great Britain, France, Western Germany, and Italy were 5.9, 3.4, 6.3, and 3.1 respectively. In turn, the percentages of the four states' exports to the United States were 11.5, 5.3, 9.1, and 10.2 respectively. Notice that the disymmetry of such dependence has grown in the sixties despite the growing emergence (and alleged related independence) of Western Europe as a bloc.

The point here is fairly obvious. It has been made before, and it has been ignored before: an American military withdrawal from Western Europe does not need to be accompanied by an economic withdrawal. It need not be so because it is not in America's interest to end such a relationship, and, perhaps more importantly, because it is even less in the interest of Western Europe to end it. Such a reasoning still holds even in the farfetched case of a Soviet-dominated Western Europe. If nowhere else, herein lie the limits of Atlantic disintegration.

IV. A Non-Aligned Europe?

Ambiguity is the main characteristic of a period of transition. Clearly, the seventies can be expected to be a period of transition as the structure of a new multipolar system slowly takes shape. Yet, certain patterns appear to be easily predictable. Thus, in the years to come, both halves of Europe will be moving away from the formerly hegemonic states. To be sure, they will do so in a disymmetrical fashion, slower in the East, faster in the West. But still, neither the United States nor the Soviet Union can now maintain the same control they exerted at a time of tight bipolar confrontation. With particular reference to America such a situation is heartening since it indicates that, in part at least, America's post World War II policy in Europe has succeeded. Nevertheless, this process of de-Americanization of Western Europe must still unfold primarily with, rather than primarily against, America.

As such detachment takes place, several situations may emerge in Europe, all of which, however threatening they may appear to be to American interests, are nonetheless matters best left to Western Europe alone: a *relance communiste* in several Western European states, particularly in Italy, but also in France; a renewed wave of anti-Americanism in the field of American investments in Europe; increasing flirtation between Western and Eastern Europe, even as Eastern Europe remains under Soviet "protection"; and finally, an even closer rapprochement with the Soviet Union independent of American participation.

Western Europe itself can go many directions, between the two extremes of supranational integration and national disintegration. These extremes, though, are themselves highly unlikely. Since the days when the perception of Soviet imperialism combined with a fear of German militarism to give birth to Pleven's call for a united European army, the prospects of Europe's political unification have been at best unrealistic, notwithstanding predictions to the contrary—predictions which, needless to say, have been especially frequent on the American side of the Atlantic. Nor is a dismemberment of the existing institutions likely to occur. All ten states have too much to lose from such a breakdown now that the many obstacles that paved the way to economic integration throughout the sixties have been overcome. Thus, what is in store for Western Europe is probably a situation of "status quo plus," the "plus" relating to further economic integration among the West European states.

Now, notwithstanding assertions to the contrary, such a Europe cannot be expected to have serious claims as a global power. For here, too, to assume that in the seventies European statesmen will pursue in concert a global and far-reaching foreign policy in unrealistic. They have neither the power nor the interest to do so. What will come with such an economic "plus" is more likely to be increased political non-alignment. Such non-alignment need not be international abstentionism. In certain areas Western European states, alone or as a group, may, in Anthony Hartley's words, "play the honest broker or the candid friend—both of them ungrateful enough roles to be undertaken with considerable caution."[12]

However preferable they might be, nuclear weapons would not be essential to the institution and defense of Western Europe's non-alignment. From a European viewpoint, the states with imperial designs over Europe clearly stalemate one another. In case of confrontation between these two super-

---

12. Anthony Hartley, "Western Europe in the 1970s: Possible Roles," *Europe and America in the 1970s,* Part I, Adelphi Papers, No. 70, November 1970, pp. 24–31.

states it is highly doubtful first, that Europe would be spared and second, that Europe's contribution would be considerable. If Western Europe as a whole was to opt for nuclear status there would still be little room left for defense once and if deterrence failed. A non-aligned Western Europe, nuclear or not, could still have close relationships with the two island powers —the United States and Japan—as well as with the two land powers—the Soviet Union and China—and, of course, Eastern Europe, too. Its advantages, from a European viewpoint, would be manyfold. Remaining disengaged from international ideological confrontations might prove to be a useful tool for further domestic unity; internal support for such a policy would be furthered by the economic gains which would result from lesser defense spending; economic influence—free of political ambitions—would be more readily acceptable, especially in Third World countries.

The withdrawal of American troops and a serious appraisal of the Atlantic Alliance of its goals and of its objectives, increase the likelihood that such a Europe would emerge. They do not, however, leave Western Europe at the mercy of Soviet intentions. For Soviet intentions would still remain shaped by their perception of American intentions. A withdrawal on the part of America would not mean that when the chips are down, America would not find it possible to return. What we have argued here is that the alliance proper adds little to Western Europe's security. What we have also argued is that in terms of its physcal security and economic interests America could afford not to return. Implicit in such arguments was a certain trust in Soviet intentions. Yet, this trust need not be a matter of conviction alone. A withdrawal of American power from Europe would not preempt the retaliatory potential of such power. The credibility of America's retaliation might be affected. But it would not be affected to the point of *in*credibility—at least not significantly more than it is now. Whether or not this de-Atlanticized Western Europe chooses to go nuclear, or whether it moves closer toward supranational integration are questions to be left to the Europeans. America's rapprochement with the Soviet Union and the end of the Cold War in Europe are taking place in spite of the Atlantic Alliance and not because of it. It is time to cope with the realities of the seventies, encourage new evolutions and define new relationships not because the old ones have failed but because their very success finally preempted their previous need.

21.

A New European Defense Community

FRANÇOIS DUCHÊNE

AT THE MOMENT WHEN East Asia is emerging as the new center of great-power confrontation, the old one, Europe, is showing signs of settling down. Eighteen years of almost glacially imperceptible movement have elapsed between the post-Stalin "thaw" of 1953 and the wary "era of negotiations" of 1971. But now the whole constellation of talks between the Soviet Union and its major Western adversaries, around the Strategic Arms Limitation Talks (SALT), the *Ostpolitik*, Berlin, force reductions, and the convocation of a security conference, look like ratifying the stalemate between the two blocs painfully reached in Europe over the years. Since this recognizes in particular the frontiers between the contestants, it amounts not only to a virtual settlement of the cold war but to the nearest approximation one can expect of a peace treaty ending the Second World War. Moreover, this development coincides with another of great importance. The likely enlargement of the European Community from six to ten member countries, including Britain, is bound to open a new phase in the integration of Western Europe. With two such changes, European security in the middle and later 1970's will necessarily be very different from the patterns that have grown familiar during 20 years.

On the whole, the natural expectation is a shift away from the quasi-military confrontation of the cold war to civilian and political processes gradually increasing the interdependence of industrial societies with potentially complementary interests. If so, it will probably be the first time that an area vital to the world balance, without being itself a great power, is brought under control not as a victim of rival masters but as a field of co-operation sought keenly by the weaker states. It could be almost the equivalent in nuclear and international terms of the King's Peace which brought the European nation-state out of feudal chaos. This is an intoxicating hope and it is not surprising that one of the questions it inspires is whether the time has not come to lower the heavy military guard which has succeeded in stabilizing Europe. Russia is not to be feared because it is increasingly preoccupied with East Asia and with consumer demands at home; and because the last thing the declining ideological metropolis of Moscow would want would be a Communist Germany, let alone Western Europe, to dethrone it altogether from its already precarious monopoly. The economic and political cohesion of an integrating Western Europe, sheltered by America's nuclear deterrent, could compensate for the superior military power of the Soviet Union.

Talk of a new European security system rests upon such presuppositions. As pressed by reformers in the establishments of the smaller East European states, such a posture even becomes a Western duty. Only if Russia loses all fear of Western military power, they argue, will conservatives in the Soviet Politburo be stripped of their great alibi and forced to concede the experiments in liberal communism essential to lighten the Russian imperium in Eastern Europe. That the ultimate aim should be to deemphasize military confrontation as much as possible is already virtually beyond controversy. It is the gospel after President Nixon's "U.S. Foreign Policy for the 1970's," which declares: "There is a growing impatience with confrontation. We and our allies seek a . . . détente."

The question is no longer the objective but the means, and in particular the means in terms of the requirements of security. Revisionist American historians of the cold war tend to deny that today's stability in Europe owes much to the security balance. This is impossible, with today's knowledge, to prove one way or the other. What can hardly be denied is that peace has been strong and not weak in the most heavily armed of all the continents; and that the acceptance of the existence of two blocs has led not to a widening rift but to closer contacts in the last ten years. The tragic expression of this was the way in which the Soviet occupation of Czechoslovakia was followed almost immediately by the unfurling of the *Ostpolitik*. It has been demonstrated, as far as such things can be in politics, that the security control of the European situation has been basic to the confidence needed for cooperation.

This does not necessarily mean that an emphasis on security helps to accelerate cooperation now. It is conceivable that the Soviet Union might move rather faster to a consumer society if it discounted the West as a military force in Europe and that this might help economic cooperation between East and West. But Western attitudes are patently far from the only factor in Soviet attitudes. Yugoslavia is regarded as a thorn in Russia's flesh in its own right. *A fortiori*, China is a powerful reason for Russia to tighten its control over, for instance, Rumania. It is often claimed in Eastern Europe that fear of NATO played a large part in the Soviet decision to suppress the Dubček regime. But it is highly questionable whether the Politburo would have allowed what it regarded, probably rightly, as a loss of control in Czechoslovakia by the Communist party even if NATO had been irrelevant to its discussions.

Common to all these questions, as indeed to the change in internal planning, or to Comecon integration, is the desire of a rigid bureaucratic structure to maintain and enhance its power. NATO is tangential to this obstacle, which is rooted in the domestic situation of the Soviet Union and which is likely to set the ultimate limits on the speed of East-West cooperation. This is particularly so because of the Czech crisis itself, and since then pressures to reduce forces in both America and Europe have been monuments to the military passivity of the West. It will be hard in the future to argue seriously that military confrontation is a major factor in Moscow's attempts to maintain socialist orthodoxy as the Communist party and the Soviet Union understand it. The political confrontation is harder to dispose of because it cannot disappear so long as Western Europe fulfills aspirations indigenous to East European societies themselves and these aspirations are thought to threaten the Soviet power structure. The only circumstances under which that could disappear would be if internal developments in Russia or the West led to the convergence of societies, or if the Soviet Union established a hegemony over Europe as a whole and treated it as a backyard. In the former case cooperation is largely a product, not the sole or even primary cause, of convergence, and Western security policies, though relevant, are secondary; in the latter, the security of Western Europe itself is involved.

II

In practice, therefore, Western strategies must not drop security for cooperation but seek to combine the two, rather as in another phrase of President Nixon's which calls at once for lower levels of forces and costs and, protesting almost too much, one feels, "a *more* stable military balance" as well. This squares with two psychological postures which have been developing for some time and are likely, barring sharp changes of political direction, to develop further during the coming decade. One is the feeling that if East-West cooperation is to mean anything, it must be possible to lighten the military apparatus in Europe and buy security more cheaply, or to put the East-West balance on a more codified and contractual basis, or both. The other is that Western security policies must be tailored to a situation where the use of force seems remote, and yet to ignore its possibility might in the end raise it up again or at least undermine security and even the long-term hopes for equitable cooperation.

The simplest way to reconcile these aims would be to confirm the superpower control, based on nuclear caution, already established over Europe. It is in some ways the most likely development because it would require the minimum changes in interstate relations and attitudes. It is hard to imagine the Soviet Union, the "elephant" of modern military power, diluting its politico-military primacy in Eastern Europe. There are more doubts about the American "whale," because its insular position gives it an inherent political mobility currently illustrated by the Administration's policies in Asia.

Yet it is in Europe, if anywhere, that American interests are most firmly fixed. This is partly for economic reasons: Europe is not only the great foreign center of U.S. enterprise but still represents 20 percent of the world's annual output, whereas the whole of Asia, including China and Japan (though not Siberia) reaches barely 15 percent. It is also cultural and psychological: the family relationship between the two remains close and may become consciously closer if non-Western influences increasingly shape the world. Everything in the attitudes of the American leadership suggests that in its eyes Europe is indeed as "indispensable as Alaska" and perhaps a lot less forbidding. Moreover, though the relationship between America and Western Europe is very different from the semi-colonial situation in the East, it is hard to see any alternative for years to come to the U.S. nuclear guarantee over West Germany. British, French or European federal nuclear ambitions seem insufficient or remote; and the one subject on which the Soviet Union, fearing that the *Ostpolitik* conceals German ambitions for reunification, and West Germany, aware that the slightest chances for fulfillment of such hopes require Russian assent, are certain to agree on is the non-nuclear status of the Federal Republic.

The danger of real U.S. withdrawal from Europe is probably less likely than is often assumed in a Western Europe nervous of the cold, as the protected always are. The essential structure of the European security balance is likely to subsist. The rising importance of Asia and of domestic priorities should reinforce this tendency. Closer contacts, from SALT to joint production ventures and concern with the environment, could even gradually create constituencies of interest in both East and West concerned to temper rivalry with elements of genuine cooperation. In such circumstances, agreements on force reductions could codify the relationship in security terms and the process of civilian interchange gradually gain more weight and the military confrontation less and the cold war be not ended but left behind. The almost unique character of Europe as a zone of peace in the field of great-power confrontation could well be reinforced and, for the East, improved.

The difficulty with this relatively serene picture is that détente has such a different impact on Eastern and Western societies that it may actually stimulate the dangers of conflict. Given the long history of muffled explosions in Eastern Europe, East-West cooperation, far from diminishing tensions, could ultimately increase them there. Simultaneously, the powerful pressures toward domesticity in the West could lead societies to downgrade defense to the point where excessive risks are taken with security. It is plain that such pressures on governments in the West are far greater than in the Soviet Union, as they were indeed immediately after the war. The way in which the United States has proposed negotiations on force reductions to forestall unilateral decisions imposed upon it by Congress is symptomatic of a situation which also exists in Europe. There will be about 40,000 conscientious objectors in West Germany this year. It is true that the West German laws are very liberal, a reflection of the fact that the authorities have more manpower than they know how to use; but the government has not decreed the fashion sweeping the universities. In Britain, the all-volunteer armed forces shrink year by year (though recruitment tends to rise in a crisis and Ulster has been no exception).

There is a good deal of anxiety that if the United States adopts volunteer forces, whatever is said to the contrary, the sheer contraction of manpower will gradually compel cumulative cuts in American troops in Europe. These tendencies on both sides of the Atlantic raise special doubts because NATO is already weaker in combat forces and, above all, reinforcements, than the Warsaw Pact, and further reductions would compel excessive reliance on nuclear forms of deterrence which themselves inspire trepidation.[1] In psychological terms, and therefore political ones, the balance of security in Europe could become weighted against the West.

The Soviet Union has more freedom of maneuver. Though its many disarmament proposals may be sincere in that Russia would like to economize and perhaps also exorcize as much as it can potential perils in East Asia, it does not seem to be under anything like the internal pressures that beset the West. The priority on consumption figured much more prominently in the platform rhetoric of the 24th Congress of the CPSU than it does in the Five Year Plan. Moreover, troop reductions can hardly be applied to forces within Russia, since these are required by the bad relations within the Communist world. And so long as these forces remain, any reductions in Europe only tend to emphasize the Soviet advantage in reinforcements. In such circumstances, Russian disarmament plans, though worth taking up for the chances they offer of maintaining cheaper security, seem at least partly designed to reinforce political processes which work in favor of Soviet power.

From this point of view, the general style of Soviet military-political behavior in recent years is not particularly promising. For the Politburo, the use of military means to political ends has been highly successful in Czech-

---

1. The Soviet Union alone has about as many combat forces in Central Europe as NATO, and it has 39 divisions in western Russia able to reinforce them in less than 30 days. There is no comparable Western equivalent in Europe or America.

oslovakia. The blatant pressures brought to bear this year on Rumania and Yugoslavia by publicizing maneuvers in Hungary and Bulgaria suggest further reliance on such means. This saber rattling does not mean danger for the West as such, but it does raise the question whether the Soviet Union is really seeking only to stabilize the European status quo in the East or behaving according to the nature of an authoritarian regime which exercises hegemony wherever it prudently can. In that case, the nature of the restraints NATO continues to place on Soviet ambitions remains important.

The main problem is that a West aware of Soviet potential, but unable to do much about such anxieties because of divergent national policies and divisions of opinion about détente, might begin to doubt its capacity to face unforeseen crises. European and American force reductions, economic rivalries and "inward-looking" attitudes in both societies could reduce each country's trust in its allies and particularly that of Europe in an America faced with a potential nuclear crisis. In such circumstances, American opinion might grow increasingly irritated with the European states while an element of appeasement could enter into the policies toward the Soviet Union. "Détente" would then connote mainly a shift in the balance of power in Europe in favor of Russia. The Soviet Union might increasingly interfere in Western policy-making, particularly on security issues, in the name of enlightened East-West relations and be sure to find a party in the West responsive to its arguments. In the long run, it could come to regard itself as the righteous policeman of a European security defined according to its standards and convenience, exercising hegemonic pressure on the policies of West European powers whose very existence, culture, wealth and example make them, willy-nilly, the specter which haunts the domestic politics of Eastern Europe.

Such a Soviet hegemony in Europe would not pose security issues in the extreme form of "freedom or slavery," but it would place West European governments in constant and sometimes acute discomfort. For instance, if the Communists were to enter into a governing coalition in Italy at a time of West European self-confidence, this would be seen as a step in their absorption into the Western system. If confidence were lacking, it could seem laden with the promise of various kinds of subordination to a politically backward superpower. All this remains wildly alarmist, of course, while one assumes the political effectiveness of the American umbrella over Western Europe. If doubts about it spread, the judgment might change. Much depends on the effects of the new doubts which have cropped up between Americans and Europeans.

III

As is the way with dependents, the Europeans have always had doubts about their protectors. The fear that Asia might distract America from Europe is as old as the cold war. Doubts about strategic nuclear parity are not new either. They go back to Sputnik, when it became evident America too was becoming vulnerable at home. These doubts have in the end proved easy to live with. The new one looks more serious. It is rooted not in nuclear parity but in a general impression of potential imparity in political will between the two superpowers, the one all too modern and the other too old-fashioned. Such fears may be excessively tied to short-term modes, like the aftermath of Vietnam, but they are also related to a subtle shift in the European environment which does not look like a passing phase and is no less important for being partly unavoidable.

By 1960, the major European empires were virtually dismantled, but the world system which accompanied them was prolonged and the change disguised by American strategic and economic power, ringing and encroaching on Eurasia. America's retreat from these advance positions is beginning to expose Europe to some of the consequences of its own earlier withdrawal. Strategically, the Soviet fleets are increasingly impinging on Europe's environment in the Mediterranean and Norwegian Seas as well as, more distantly, the oil routes of the Indian Ocean. On land, Yugoslavia is more concerned about security than at any time since 1948. Economically, the United States is no longer able to guarantee European oil supplies, as in 1956, or the monetary and trading context for growth. And Europe is now beginning to feel a little naked in the winds of the larger world.

IV

That the United States reacts as a society rather than as a state to world events, while Russia reacts as a state rather than as a society, poses problems of American purpose. That the United States no longer shapes the environment and perpetuates the European world poses problems of European purpose. This is the basis of a third alternative to superpower control or Soviet hegemony in Europe, the possibility of a West European entity becoming an increasingly significant element in the security balance. The West European Ten together will have total forces numbering over two million men and 300 combat vessels, respectable resources even by superpower standards. They do not mean much without a common political purpose, which is lacking, but even the potentials of power have an effect on that.

A more coordinated West European defense system could not replace the American nuclear guarantee, but it could reinforce it and make it more credible, which would be especially welcome if the totals of West European forces and of American forces in Europe both go down. It could also help in the long run to add a more effective complement to the American navy in the maritime periphery of Europe. This would not replace superpower control over Europe but it would change its inner content and possibly long-term prospects. The European option will be open to West European leaders seeking to face the new and less serene environment or simply perhaps, in the cases of Britain and France, to prolong national ambitions through a collective effort. Without that they will be politically too weak to make their own choices.

The differences between various hypotheses about European security in the coming years presented here (and others one might put forward) are less military than political. Unless forces are maintained at levels very near the current ones, which seems unlikely, military risks have to be taken by the present standards of deterrence. But these risks may be politically acceptable in certain cases, as are the long-standing insufficiencies of NATO today, whereas in others they might seem unbearable. Thus, an agreement on force reductions with substantial cuts on both sides, accompanied by a general climate of cooperation, might maintain the credibility of the NATO structure even if present strategic concepts had to be modified, whereas smaller unilateral Western cuts would sap confidence. Similarly, a West European defense organization would be less likely to increase the number of troops than promise a better use of a smaller number and, even more important, a more cohesive reaction of the Ten to unforeseen eventualities. More depends on political than military factors, not least, timing.

There will probably be a first symbolic cut in forces in 1972; the enlargement of the European Community should take place in 1973. If there are signs of satisfactory agreements on force reductions within a reasonable time scale, security policies may well stick to multilateral approaches both within NATO and in the East-West context. That will raise a minimum of diplomatic problems for the Germans concerned with the *Ostpolitik* and the French and Italians with their Communist parties. It will not force gaullism in France to face a change in national priorities or the Scandinavians to touch the domestically thorny issues of defense. The European Community as it enlarges would seek its new frontier more in common trade and finance policies than in security. Yet East-West negotiations on force reductions are likely to be incredibly complex and, unless things go very well, to raise more anxieties than they allay because of the imparities between NATO and the Warsaw Pact. In that case, the urge to launch the European Community on a more political course might well move into the area of defense.

There are several reasons for this. One is the anxiety about security in the governments of the larger West European countries, which is greater than one might imagine from the atmospherics of the "era of negotiation," and to some extent is a result of them. Prime Minister Edward Heath always mentions security before prosperity as an argument for British entry into the European Community. The West Germans are conscious of a need to anchor the Americans more firmly in Europe and to find a long-term alternative should the effort fail. A collective European effort might help both. To a lesser extent, a European operation would also be attractive as the only way to bring the heirs of de Gaulle back into the Western defense fold without a formal tie to NATO.

A second reason is that if Western disarmament reaches a point where doubt is cast on present doctrines of deterrence, it might well drive a wedge into the triangle between Germany, France, and Britain which is the core of West European relationships. The French and the British would be tempted to stress their nuclear deterrents, and, whether they did so nationally or cooperatively, this would underline what divides them from Germany even if German attitudes to their deterrents are changing as doubts about the United States increase. This could be particularly important if other developments point the same way. Force reductions would tend to apply to Germany, the *terre d'élection* of NATO. Similarly, attempts to meet manpower shortages by raising militia would affect Germany in the front more than France in the rear and still more than Britain behind the Channel. Should these fault lines in NATO-Europe become too marked they could disintegrate it, Britain and France emphasizing nuclear deterrence, Germany the *Ostpolitik*. A European grouping would counter this tendency. Finally, there are existing pressures toward closer organization, notably in joint arms production. Together, these factors could push the major powers in the Community to propose that Europe move into defense.

The most extreme version of the skepticism about a European defense organization one might expect would be that of the French government. That at least is the assumption, and will not be dispelled, since it is in the nature of President Pompidou's style of government that his policies should be expressed in action rather than declared principles. The moment for action cannot come before British entry into the European Community. However, for a Gaullist, M. Pompidou has given hints which suggest his mind may be more open than is supposed. He has stressed the importance of U.S. troops staying in Europe, and his anxiety about withdrawals is well known. In his press conference of January 21, 1971, he proposed that a European confederation should cover the major fields of government including political ones. He stressed that the major decisions should be taken by governments, but did not exclude a role for the Commission in implementing them. All this leaves some room for maneuver and a possibility that M. Pompidou is willing to consider proposals that serve a concrete purpose.

V

Indeed, it should be quite possible to establish effective defense cooperation inside the enlarged European Community on terms the governments will accept. There could be two mutually reinforcing levels of operation: consultation between the governments on broad policies, and contracts to establish joint programs in a few functional areas, like arms production, implemented in ways roughly similar to the Common Market's.

An obvious theme for European consultation would be policy on East-West force reductions and arms control. The same would apply to strategic and tactical concepts—the use of forces, the control of nuclear escalation, and so on—problems which the major NATO allies must discuss in any case when France deploys its tactical nuclear artillery, *Pluton*, in 1973 or 1974 in the only place where it makes sense, in Germany. This should be carried on in a European Nuclear Planning Group (ENPG) parallel to the very successful one which already exists in NATO. Other committees could be set up to discuss manpower and other policies. In themselves, such consultations need not change the attitudes of the countries involved, but, placed in the context of a European grouping with a recognizably separate identity, and associated with functional cooperation at a second level, they almost certainly would have a larger political impact.

The governments would also negotiate contracts, or treaties, establishing common functional bodies mainly in the area of what one might call Defense Support—training, logistics, and the procurement of arms. The governments could set the targets and timing and entrust the implementation to a kind of Common Market system with a Defense Commission proposing policies and the national ministers disposing of them. The lack of a single logistic system is a NATO weakness which could lead to serious confusion in a crisis. In an age of travel, training in a neighboring country and learning a language as well as a trade could be a critical advantage over national systems in the recruitment of otherwise reluctant soldiers. As for procurement, the aerospace industry, which accounts for almost 40 percent of arms spending, looks like being reduced to perhaps three major European consortia in a couple of years' time. If so, the pressure for common production in other arms industries, particularly in electronics, will be increased and the main remaining problem will be to overcome the particularisms of the defense staffs and ministries. One need hardly underline in an American journal that this is never easy even within a single country, but a joint Procurement Agency, proposing criteria for weapons not tarred by a national brush, could help. A related Management Committee to stabilize government-industrial relations would also be useful.

Together, such innovations would establish what would be in effect a European Defense Support Organization. What would still be lacking, apart from the inevitable nuclear absentee, would be a Joint European Command. Its attractions would increase if the troops in Europe declined significantly, because the best counter to small numbers is mobility, i.e. the ability to order troops from any member country to where they are most needed in an agreed area. That might be too much for the governments, particularly the French, to take, though it would in fact allow France to make her point that she will not accept an American Supreme Allied Commander, Europe. For the Europeans to have their own NPG would also imply a grouping outside the NATO equivalent. But in both cases no decisions could be taken without the Americans, so that the changes would in part be more formal than real.

Implicit in them, however, would be the idea of a bilateral relationship between Europe and America. Since the U.S. administration has been favorable to the emergence of a European "caucus" in NATO, this could be turned to good account in renewing the NATO contract between the United States and its allies. A new agreement could be reached under the roof of the Atlantic Alliance in which new pledges for the commitment of American troops in Europe would be given in return for signs of European self-help through integration, and consolidated by a "sense of the Senate" vote. This could invaluably stabilize the European-American relationship for a number of years ahead.

One would expect the Soviet Union to condemn a European Defense Organization, or Community, for much the same reasons as the United States favors it. But there is no force to the idea a Community need hold up East-West cooperation, because this ignores both the time factor and the military and political context. The establishment of a Defense Support Organization, however disliked, could hardly be invoked with success as a provocation; and even a stronger arrangement, a more thoroughgoing Community, would take place against a background of falling forces and possibly agreements on them. The active emphasis of East-West exchanges would in any case be on negotiations and increasing economic contacts. In such circumstances, a West European defense organization would stand for what it was—a minimum security insurance against a breakdown in détente, which the West Europeans of all peoples have an interest in avoiding.

VI

Confidence is, in fact, the key. The problem for Western Europe, in fact for the West *tout court*, with its affluent societies so responsive to hopes of external peace parallel to their own domestic ideals, is how to manage a period of détente which remains full of uncertainty. The problem is a difficult one because it involves opposite movements in the evolution of estimates of "intent" on the one hand and military capability on the other. While political expectations of a Russian invasion are declining to near zero, it makes no political sense to stress the military aspects of security. But to take prospects of peace and cooperation for granted could gradually undermine the security on which an equitable peace and balanced cooperation are based. What is needed is a capacity to meet unexpected circumstances with means relevant to them, and when circumstances mean the Soviet Union, the means can only be American or collective European or both. Such reserves of power are necessary to control détente, maintain confidence and restrain distortions of the political process.

The issue in Europe is an historic one. The nuclear stalemate is making it possible to move away from naked force toward politics and so to civilize conflict in one of the centers of gravity of the balance of power. If this can be done by freeing political forces rather than in the usual way of setting up an empire over them, it will mark a real moment of progress in international twentieth-century society. But, for all that, détente must be carefully controlled and the forces of political backwardness contained as they have already been during the cold war. In some ways the situation is more dangerous because détente can make the process reach into Eastern Europe itself. It is therefore more than ever vital, in a period when attention is directed elsewhere, to maintain a system of security insurance in Europe. This may be possible without new means such as a European Defense Community to bolster up the credibility of the American nuclear guarantee. But if optimism were to prove wrong, it might be too late to correct the political if not military degradation which would have set in. On balance, it seems wiser to control détente by building up in Western Europe a Defense Community to shore up in new circumstances the peace which has made détente possible.

22.

Britain, the Common Market, and the Forces of History

PAUL TAYLOR

THE PERIOD OF THE late 1940's and early 1950's probably represented the peak of achievement for those who favored federal Europe. After the Hague Conference of May 1948 hopes for a more powerful Council of Europe were high: they were dashed mainly on the reef of British functionalism. In the early 1950's, however, several developments among the Six confirmed the prospect of a rapid move toward a high level of institutional centralization. The European Coal and Steel Community had been established and the model of a High Authority of international civil servants, able to take decisions that would be binding directly upon individuals and groups within the state, was in the minds of ambitious Europeans. In 1952 there was some progress toward a European army in a European Defense Community, an integrated force under a European commander-in-chief, and this was soon followed by the proposal for a European Political Community which could exercise political oversight over the other agencies. The European Coal and Steel Community, unlike the later European Economic Community, set up the Common Market in coal, steel and scrap quickly and sought to rectify ensuing difficulties with controlled investment and compensations of various kinds. It seemed likely that these three agencies, each of which had been agreed to in ambitious treaties among the statesmen of Europe, would rapidly bind European countries close together. A federal Europe would soon emerge.

Excerpted and reprinted by permission from *ORBIS*, Fall 1972, pp. 746–58. Copyright by the Foreign Policy Research Institute.

This was not to be the case: the Federalist phase came to an end in 1954. In August of that year the French National Assembly decided, on a procedural vote, not to consider, and therefore not to discuss for ratification, the treaty for a European Defense Community. With this decision the European Political Community was also discarded. The European Coal and Steel Community endured as the one fruit of the efforts and hopes of the early integrationists. It is interesting to note that according to one authority the imminence of institutional and political success in that period was but weakly founded in popular support. Public attitudes in France and Germany betokened little of the community-mindedness that could have sustained the new institutions. By the late 1960's stronger community attitudes had developed[1]—which makes it possible to argue that the action of the French Assembly was in the long-term interest of a united Europe.

Then, in the spring of 1955, statesmen from the Six, meeting at Messina, Sicily, took decisions which led in 1957 to the signing of the Rome Treaty and the establishment of the European Economic Community. This approach involved a gradualist strategy for European integration over a period of twelve years through three transitional phases. Some statesmen, particularly those from France, were much more cautious than they had been in the early 1950's: they could agree about abolishing tariffs on trade between members and the proper way to set up a common external tariff; and they expected agreement about a range of other questions, such as a Community policy for transport, energy, currency, agriculture, and social questions. But the latter proposals were not covered in detail in the treaty; the central organization of the new Community, the Commission, was asked to consider ways in which they could be implemented. The Commission was in effect to act as a generator of proposals for integration which national governments could then consider, approve or reject, through the transitional periods. The whole approach—cautious, gradualist, and tending to avoid premature overcommitment—was Functional in style. This was the Functionalist phase of European integration. It involved the gradual molding of Europe through increasing cooperation from politically less sensitive areas, such as tariffs and trade, to politically more sensitive questions, such as monetary policy and budgetary planning. Some expected that this would be an appropriate strategy by which Europeans could eventually be led to decide together in common structures upon questions of defense and foreign policy.

The Functionalists relied on such procedures as the organization of European pressure groups, adjustment of the attitudes of civil servants, demonstrations that cooperation could be in the short term rewarding. One of the movement's central dynamics was the process of convincing a large

1. See Donald J. Puchala, "International Transactions and Regional Integration," *International Organization,* Autumn 1970, pp. 732–763.

number of people in commerce, industry, and government that the utilitarian benefits of integration outweighed the costs. The Federalists, on the other hand, conceived of an integrated Europe built from the top as a result of decisions taken by enlightened, farseeing politicians who were inspired by the promise of long-term rewards, not all of which were necessarily utilitarian. A typical Federalist strategy involved a Constituent Assembly (the so-called *ad hoc* assembly of 1952–1953 is a good example); a typical Functionalist strategy involved a committee of experts.

But the Functionalist phase was to end in the mid-1960's; it gave way after the 1965 crisis[2] to a period of restraint in which the Commission labored under a mood of pessimism and the states seemed to reassert themselves. Until 1969 there was an effort at stocktaking in which the mounting problems of the new Europe were counted but the main effort was focused on the consolidation of earlier achievements. This may be called the post-Functional period.

The Confederal phase of the European integration process, which followed, bears the hallmark of the summit conference of statesmen from the Six at the Hague in December 1969. This conference was important for the range of new initiatives promising rapid integration in politically sensitive areas. But it was important also because it marked the emergence of Willy Brandt, Chancellor of West Germany, as a statesman who was prepared to take initiatives within the EEC and to pursue a more imaginative West German European policy. Previous German chancellors had been ready enough to work hard for Europe but were usually content to respond to proposals originating elsewhere. Because of this, the French government, particularly under President de Gaulle, was able to establish itself as the agency that decided the pace of integration; German reticence also allowed the French to undertake important new diplomatic ventures such as those in the early and middle 1960's toward Eastern Europe.

Chancellor Brandt's *Ostpolitik* was perhaps the single most important mechanism by which the West Germans established their position in Western Europe in the late 1960's and early 1970's; it is indeed possible to argue that the crucial reason for the *Ostpolitik* was the situation in Western Europe rather than the need to improve West Germany's relations with East Germany and the USSR. The reading of Brandt's mind is now a favorite pastime of political commentators, who usually assume the primacy of East/West détente in his arguments; but it would be just as sensible to assume the primacy of the West European setting. As long as the West Ger-

2. This crisis grew out of the French government's opposition to Commission proposals for transferring control of Community resources, including those of the Agricultural Fund, to the institutions at Brussels, and for increasing the powers of the European Assembly. The French refused to participate in many of the Communities' institutions until January 1966, when they returned following an agreement with the Five. The terms included the postponement of majority voting in the Council and the curtailment of some of the Commission's public relations activities. The earlier proposals were dropped.

Paul Taylor : 379

man government pursued the Hallstein Doctrine it was bound to try to maintain close contacts with the French and to be reluctant to push the French too far lest the latter compromise German interests in Eastern Europe. Toleration of this situation also contributed to a German reluctance to challenge the French on European Community issues and on the question of Britain's accession to the Common Market. It allowed France to monopolize high politics in the Community.

The *Ostpolitik* freed West Germany from an anxious, almost morbid, watchfulness over French activities in Eastern Europe. As the central aspect of a new style of diplomacy for Bonn, it also led the Germans to feel that it was their turn to occupy center stage within the EEC, as they did with great success at the Hague in December 1969. Moreover, by permitting them to be more certain in their advocacy of British membership in the Common Market, it encouraged the French to think of Britain once again as a potentially useful Community partner against West Germany.

The changed character of German diplomacy, the surviving elements of Gaullist ambition in the present French government, the likelihood of British entry—these factors have introduced into the EEC a new awareness of the contending political interests of the member governments. This competitiveness is not the high politics of de Gaulle, but it is certainly a slightly superior and more general level of political engagement than was previously the case. It has produced the essential character of the Confederal phase of European integration. As the *Ostpolitik* has led Bonn to enter into friendly relations with East Germany and to accept a de facto postponement of reunification, so the new style of German diplomacy has contributed in Western Europe both to the taking of new initiatives and to the weakening of supranational political ambitions in the Communities. The fact that the new initiatives toward integration were taken by West Germany and acquiesced in by the French served to consolidate Confederal Europe and strengthen the expectation that national governments would survive.

III

Detectable within the area of political engagements in the early 1970's, however, was the same kind of oscillation noted in British attitudes toward the Communities. On the one hand there was an earnest desire for more centralized European structures: out of the Hague Conference, for instance, came the initiative that led to the Werner proposals for a European Monetary Union to be established by 1980, plans for a more powerful Assembly, and the decision to increase the amount of funds to be allotted to the Communities.[3] These gave high promise of advances which would

3. A subsequent treaty signed in April 1970 allowed the Communities their own resources; from 1975 the Assembly was to exercise a certain minimum control over these resources.

have been more dramatic than any achieved in the 1965–1969 period. The German and French agreement on these matters was again expressed in the EEC Council meeting of February 1971 at which there was unanimous support for monetary union and for the kind of economic coordination in which the Germans were particularly interested as a condition of monetary union. Short-term and medium-term economic and budgetary policies were to be coordinated in meetings between finance ministers and central bankers.

On the other hand, the international monetary crisis and the August 1971 American decision to impose a surcharge on imports revealed serious differences of policy between the West Germans and the French. In May 1971 Germany allowed the mark to float upward against the dollar and in July Franco-German talks on the implementation of monetary reform broke down. The French also opposed the coordination of economic and budgetary policies in the face of German demands. France insisted, with the British, on maintaining the export advantage of existing parities. The lack of a Franco-German agreement on parities and on economic coordination created tensions within the EEC, most seriously by imposing burdens on the common agricultural policy which were bound to be expensive to the French. As Denis Healey pointed out in the London *Sunday Times* of November 21, 1971, "President Pompidou appears to survey the imminent disaster with a complacent *Schaden-freude* at the prospect of a Europe freed from U.S. hegemony in economic and military affairs." While the two governments were agreed about the need for more ambitious steps toward integration, the French were prepared to take risks in relations with Germany that endangered what had been achieved in the Communities.

The surprising thing was that the international monetary crisis of 1971–1972 did not lead to the abandonment of the Werner proposals. The pattern of interaction between the perceived interests of the French and West German governments was such that within two months of the monetary agreements reached at Washington in December 1971 the Werner proposals had been resurrected and were being pursued with full vigor. Such oscillation is characteristic of political relations between governments in this Confederal phase of European integration.

The December 1971 meeting of the Group of Ten in Washington produced agreements to reestablish fixed exchange rates and to devalue the dollar by 7.89 percent against gold.[4] The U.S. government also abolished the 10 percent import surcharge which had been introduced earlier to protect the American balance of payments, and the Japanese and the Germans agreed to revalue their currencies against the dollar. Further initiatives in Europe quickly followed. In January 1972 the Commission of the European

---

4. The devaluation of the dollar was 7.89 per cent when converting foreign currencies to dollars, and 8.57 when converting dollars to foreign currencies.

Communities again proposed measures leading to economic and monetary union. On February 10 and 11 Chancellor Brandt and President Pompidou met in Paris and reached agreement about narrowing the margins of fluctuation among EEC currencies and coordinating policy to control short-term capital flows. The French government also made the important concession of agreeing to the closer coordination of French and German economic policies. The Werner proposals had indeed been revitalized.

They persisted because they were attractive to an unusually wide range of interested parties. Like the proposals for a European Coal and Steel Community in the early 1950's, they had advantages for those who stressed the special political and economic interests of states, for those who favored European integration, and for the problem-oriented who sought the best solution for the perceived problem. The Germans were prepared to consider the proposed union because it would benefit the already strong German economy and was compatible with their interest in a more politically integrated Western Europe. They also had a natural sympathy for a scheme that would strengthen the European contribution to the stability of the international monetary system, improve Europe's position in the management of the international economy, and help to minimize the impact upon European economies of unfavorable developments in the United States.

By the beginning of 1972 the French, too, had come to realize the advantages of monetary and economic union, which may explain the concession at Paris to the German interest in economic coordination. The Werner proposals could prove to be a way of working toward an objective de Gaulle had long sought but failed to achieve: the separation of Germany from the United States and the insulation of Western Europe from undue American influence. (The new proposal for a European unit of currency to replace the Eurodollar—the Europa—would reinforce this independence.) Even within the European system the Werner plan could be seen through French eyes as producing special economic advantages: it would result in the Germans subsidizing French prosperity, despite German caution about economic coordination, by funding regional development and by protecting a vulnerable French currency on the international market.

The Werner proposals for European monetary and economic union were initially challenged but later greatly assisted by the international monetary crisis: the crisis made it clear to statesmen that national interests favored the European proposals and could be conveniently linked with the ideals of those who were in favor of European unification. In 1972 it was too early to judge whether this peculiar convergence of interests would endure or whether intra-European disagreements would again assert themselves. If it could be maintained, important moves toward integration might be forthcoming. Such a powerful alliance of special and general interests was reminiscent of the pattern of support for the European Coal and Steel Community some twenty years earlier. On that occasion the range of political initiatives taken heralded the Federal phase of European integration.

Beneath the political level the functional interdependence established in the 1950's and 1960's continues and in some ways, as Mrs. Camps has suggested, is being strengthened.[5] When attention is focused at the political level it is easy to overestimate the capacity for disagreement among West European governments: as observers, we are faced with the problem of weighting the disagreements we see. European structures now seem strong enough, and popular attitudes sufficiently warm, to make the violent resolution of conflicts between states in Western Europe most unlikely in the future; likewise, the area within which political disagreement takes place is being progressively reduced by the strengthening of the functional systems. That the national governments are reasserting their political roles within Western Europe may be seen as an attempt to defend themselves against the irresistible encroachment of functional systems rather than as another manifestation of the continuing strength of the nation-state. The Confederal phase is marked by both political oscillation and functional encroachment.

IV

It is at this point that the British government has decided to link Britain's fate with that of the Communities. The three phases of integration, Federal, Functional and Confederal, have each left their impact on European structures and European ideas. The Confederal phase, however, is essentially unstable because of the oscillations observed at the political level and the tensions between centralizing and centrifugal forces. The schemes for centralization should be seen in part as a reaction against centrifugal tendencies: the governments want the rewards of cooperation, and are disposed to act to obtain those rewards, but have not fully convinced themselves that they are prepared to pay the price of interdependence. The future facing Britain in Europe will therefore involve a post-Confederal structure, the nature of which will be explained in terms of Federal and Functional elements. An examination of the several conceivable outcomes for European integration should enable decision-makers to formulate an account of the cost of membership in the Communities from the political standpoint.[6] In the process, policy-makers in Britain may obtain a glimpse of the forces of history in the West European context.

5. Camps, *op. cit.*, pp. 676–677.
6. The starting point of my thinking about these outcomes was the interesting article by Ernst B. Haas, "The Study of Regional Integration: Reflections on the Joy and Anguish of Pretheorizing," *International Organization*, Autumn 1970, pp. 607–648.

It is difficult to forecast when these outcomes may be expected; they are not imminent but may appear in the medium-term future. It is also difficult to be precise about the mechanics of the transformation of the existing system into any one of the new forms. I leave this enormous theoretical problem alone. Nevertheless, the outcomes are conceivable. They can be imagined from elements detected in the present situation in the Communities and in Britain, and they reflect concepts which have become part of a tradition of thinking. Certainly the concepts of Federalism and Functionalism will endure as a part of the intellectual apparatus of future students of the European integration process.

The first outcome signifies the ascendancy of the Federalist element. Confederal uncertainties are resolved in favor of the forces of centralization, operating at the political and institutional levels. A new centralized decision-making system emerges out of the existing Brussels institutions, and powers and functions which are at the heart of sovereignty are transferred away from national governments toward the new center. Thus ordained, the United States of Europe is a European superstate, capable of defining a European attitude and a European stance in international society. Within it authority and legitimacy are redistributed to radiate from the central structures; the subregions are definitely subordinate entities and new tasks are allocated to the federal government.

The impact of federal Europe on patterns of diplomacy is interesting. The new state is seen as active and self-seeking by other states, normally in an informal partnership with the United States, but always with the capacity for independence. It is much more capable of initiative, and of pursuing high politics concerned with questions of prestige and linked values, than any of the older units. The present states are all limited to the extent that they are involved in common systems which they are not able to control directly. The new unit would possess far greater potential for self-sufficiency. Functional systems now only loosely contained within the European region would in this superstate be sharply defined within the frontiers of the Federation.

The existence of the new state will, in my judgment, recreate the traditional problems of international society on a larger scale. We can suggest here some of its likely effects. With respect to relations with Eastern Europe it will be divisive. The East European states will be encouraged to protect jealously whatever measure of independence they have won from the Soviet Union. The new Europe's ideological commitment—the projection of a European technocratic capitalist image—will discourage states of a different ideological stance from associating with it; this Europe will repulse rather than attract. In relation to the Third World it will pursue a policy of cautious self-interest, tending to enter into special agreements where appropriate, much like the existing association agreements of the EEC. On the whole its economic policies are not likely to reduce the gulf between the haves and the have-nots: its role will be to act as a jealous guardian of the resources it believes it possesses, and to seek out and exploit those resources it lacks.

In the eyes of other states, particularly in the Third World and Eastern Europe, the armed forces of the new Europe will be viewed as potentially hostile, capable of defending its distinctive interests, even to the extent of using violence. Eventually, the new Europe will probably be able to compete at the nuclear level with the United States and the Soviet Union.

To repeat, the traditional problems of international society are in this outcome manifested on a larger scale. It is extremely foolish to believe that the government of such a federal Europe would be an enlightened actor on the international stage.

The second outcome relies on the strengthening of Functional elements in the existing situation. Governments are persuaded to encourage greater interdependence because of the perception that this is rewarding, but the drive toward centralization is restrained when compared with the Federal outcome. Decision-making is dispersed among the various systems and is not added incrementally to the Brussels institutions. One of the essential conditions of restraint in the forces of centralization is that centrifugal tendencies created by the governments' perception of competing interests are themselves restrained: as governments become increasingly prepared to work together the question of whether formal powers are transferred to the center begins to appear irrelevant. Accordingly, governments remain the focus of authority and legitimacy; they remain intact as initiating and norm-defining agencies. This outcome may be called a *decentralized regional system.*

The closest approximation to it in the 1970's is found in Scandinavia, and the Scandinavian example may be used to illuminate several aspects of the position this new West European system will occupy internationally. The first point is that the surviving governments will not view themselves as prestige-maintaining or as agencies pursuing high politics; their success or failure will be judged increasingly by utilitarian values. Moreover, they will be accepted by outside states as ideologically neutral: there will be a perception of a European point of view, defining not an exclusive European interest but rather a collective outlook on developments in international society. The foreign policies of the new Europe will appear to serve a high moral purpose, rather like Swedish foreign policy today, or the foreign policy of Nehru's India. The European armed forces will not be regarded as upholders of an exclusive interest but will be generally accepted as a suitable source of peacekeeping detachments. The national governments in the new system will be progressively dissuaded from indulging in high politics as they perceive the advantage of a high moral stance and as their success is judged increasingly in economic/utilitarian terms. The usefulness of the Scandinavian model in helping us to understand this outcome is apparent.

From the point of view of the East European states such an outcome seems compatible. It will not create a power challenge on their western frontier; will be less likely to give the impression of an ideologically committed unit in direct conflict with their own recently defined ideology; and will suggest the possibility of joining advantageous systems of cooperation without the immediate risk of political compromise or of compromising politics. In the long run the states of Eastern Europe might be drawn in as full members of the new system.

The dynamic, functional Europe conceived in this outcome is less divisive than the Federalist alternative and is capable of extending from a regional core to wider areas of the international system. It may be judged as morally more desirable but as definitely involving sacrifice of the drama and interest of the nation-state, while preserving something of the state's form.

The third outcome of the integration process may be called the *regional functional system.* For it we have no model. It also requires the ascendancy of the Functional elements in the existing situation, but in this case the national governments must lose all their functions except that of acting as a simple coordinating agency. Authority and legitimacy are neither centralized in new federal structures nor retained in the existing governments: they are dispersed throughout the various functional systems. Each of these has its own field of activity in which it has established competence, and each contains organs that have acquired the right to be taken as final courts of appeal. It is as if the present organs of the Community—the Commission, the Council and the Court—had been recreated in various forms and in overlapping geographic areas to administer a whole range of different task areas. Even so, it could be argued that the problem of coordination in the new system would be less serious than the problems caused by the prerogatives of the nation-state.

This system is indeed beyond the nation-state. The citizens of this new order would respond not to primitive national symbols but to the benefits of cooperation within the various functional systems; within these systems welfare as it is presently understood would also be administered. Stability would be maintained simply by the systems retaining a high level of efficiency in providing rewards to individuals and to subgroups. Because of the absence of what could be recognized as governments with independent status, there would be no need for foreign policy: relations with the outside world would be conducted by particular functional agencies with outside governments and other functional agencies. The use of armed force, where it was necessary, could be administered mainly within the functional agencies: a Securicor or Railway Police type of organization could develop with close links to particular agencies.

Projections of the diplomacy of this new unit are complicated by the absence of a recognizable model in the current situation. But the system is conceivable, and it is worth recalling that the nation-state, which until recently seemed such a permanent feature of the international scene, has in fact existed for a relatively short period of time. It may be that in conditions of advanced economic development, such as obtain in Western Europe, a new type of political organization could emerge; in a post-capitalist, late-industrial society this is particularly likely. We could then talk of political organizations that were "beyond the nation-state."

Of the conceivable outcomes, these three are the most feasible. The survival of nation-states as they are today, while also conceivable, is in my view unlikely. The strengthening of functional systems of interdependence—supported by such factors as the need for economies of scale, research pools, larger markets, regional defense, and the ideological and psychological need to escape from the oppressive structures of the national welfare state—makes some change in the present nation-state system inevitable. There was, it appears, no alternative to closer British participation in European systems of cooperation, though this need not have involved formal membership in the EEC.

The question that arises is whether members of national governments will be able to perceive changes in the conditions of sovereignty and accept the view that high politics must be determined by the environment of political action. For instance, most governments, operating within a regional decentralized system, may yet consider themselves to be protectors of sovereignty and the primary means of enhancing the national image. The observer who knows that sovereignty has changed may see beyond these superficial elements to the reality of a situation in which governments are in fact seriously limited. De Gaulle, who stands as a champion of the unchanging, dominating structure of European politics, the nation-state, may from another perspective be judged as the man who last tried to defend a dying form of political organization.

23.

Changing East-West Relations in Europe: The Bonn-Moscow Treaty of August 1970

DENNIS L. BARK

THAT EAST-WEST RELATIONS in Europe are changing is evidenced most notably by Chancellor Willy Brandt's *Ostpolitik* and its offspring, the Soviet-West German treaty signed in August 1970. To some the treaty, betokening a reconciliation between the enemy of the Second World War and the victor of the East, seems a longed-for dream come true. To others, for various reasons, it appears to be a source of concern and even alarm. This difference of opinion is in no way surprising. Many men of good will in the West have clung for a long time to the hope that the crucial German problem between the West and the Soviet Union can be solved to everyone's satisfaction and that an era of peace and stability can be introduced in Central Europe. Yet the length of time spent in searching for a German settlement may be a substantial part of the reason why some have not greeted the prospective Bonn-Moscow treaty with jubilation. Perhaps critics are wary of claims made by the treaty's proponents that détente has suddenly been achieved on such a vexing and long-standing problem.

Political analysis is a deceptive business. The announcement that a major step has been taken toward peaceful cooperation among all European states, irrespective of differences in their social systems, suggests an enticing vista of "change through rapprochement." The era of injured accusations by the East and replies of righteous indignation by the West may be

Adapted from an address before the Commonwealth Club of California in San Francisco on December 18, 1970. Reprinted by permission from *ORBIS*, Summer 1971, pp. 625–34, 641–42. Copyright by the Foreign Policy Research Institute.

on the wane. An aura of respectability attends the professed desire of the Soviet Union to join the Federal Republic in a common effort to remove the psychological and political barriers sustained by twenty-five years of cold war and its specter of future conflict. But have the problems been solved or merely discounted? If they have been solved, to whose satisfaction was it done? The question is not *whether* to negotiate with the Soviet Union but *how* to negotiate with the Soviet Union and how to measure the results of such negotiations.

Bonn's decision to take the negotiating initiative is praiseworthy. A prolonged West German failure to come to an understanding with Moscow would have had dire consequences, for the Soviet Union is adept at placing the onus for failure to reach agreement on real or imaginary Western inaction. But the awakening of illusory hopes can be equally as detrimental, and it is naive to ascribe legitimacy to an asserted desire to diminish an atmosphere of tension on the international level if this merely reflects a tactical maneuver. The glimmer of détente and the shadow of cold war imply the presence of alternatives, of being able to choose between one or the other, in anticipation that embarkation on a course of détente, were it possible, would end the years of confrontation and render harmless the protestations of the "imperialists"; that the good will and firm resolve thus evinced would produce a lessening of East-West strains throughout the world.

It is said that the conclusion of the Soviet-West German treaty has changed the political mood in Europe. We are told again that the age of cold war has been replaced by the age of détente.[1] The Socialist-Liberal (SPD-FDP) coalition government in Bonn, under Social Democratic Chancellor Brandt, claims to be conducting a policy of "understanding" with the Soviet Union, a policy based on *mutual* recognition of the existing realities in Europe. At long last, in deference to these political and economic realities, the curtain of ideology is being raised, and peaceful coexistence has finally scored a victory.

When Brandt delivered his *Bericht zur Lage der Nation* to the West German parliament on January 14, 1970, three months after he had become the first Socialist Chancellor in West Germany's history,[2] he pointed out that he hoped to achieve the transition of his country's foreign policy toward the East from "confrontation to cooperation." In doing so he paid particular attention to the explanation that "patriotism demands the recog-

1. Back in 1955, for example, *New Statesman and Nation* concluded that "the cold war was suddenly called off at Geneva because both sides recognized that these suspicions [of beginning a new war] were entirely unfounded." See "Problems of the Garden-Party Peace" in the issue of August 13, 1955.

2. In the last national West German election, held in September 1969, 46.1 per cent of the electorate voted for the opposition Christian Democratic and Christian Socialist parties (CDU/CSU). Although the SPD-FDP coalition continues to enjoy a majority of six in the Bundestag, the CDU has a one-seat majority in the 41-member Bundesrat.

nition of what is. . . . It demands the courage to recognize reality."
Brandt's message marked the initiation of his widely acclaimed version of
Ostpolitik, directed in the long term toward establishment of a European
order of peace.

Soon afterward, in March and May, in Erfurt and Kassel, the first postwar meetings between East and West German leaders took place. The next
milestone in Bonn's new *Ostpolitik* was the Bonn-Moscow treaty, termed a
mutual renunciation of force agreement and signed in Moscow on
August 12, 1970 by Chancellor Brandt and Premier Alexei Kosygin. There
followed the Polish-West German treaty of December 7, 1970. Today, a
year after the Moscow ceremonies—and a decade since the building of the
Berlin wall on August 13, 1961—it is time to recapitulate and analyze the
events that have transpired in West Germany's relations with the Soviet
Union and Eastern Europe since the Bonn-Moscow treaty was signed. It
has not yet been ratified by the West German parliament, but it is being
written and spoken about as existing in fact. Indeed, although the Soviet
government continues to press for ratification as a decisive counter to Cold
War advocates in the West—who, for example, opposed the 1970 Mansfield
resolution in the American Congress for a cutback of U.S. forces in Europe—statements appearing in the East European press since early 1971
assert that, because the essence of the Bonn-Moscow treaty is political, it
is in the long term immaterial whether it is ratified or not. The following
considerations are based, not on the assumption that the treaty will or will
not be ratified, but on the situation—*rebus tunc stantibus*—as it exists in
mid-1971.

II

The five articles of the treaty are relatively simple. The two parties affirm
their desire "to maintain international peace and achieve détente." They
agree to further "normalization" in Europe, in accordance with "the actual
situation existing" on the continent. Both parties resolve "to refrain from
the threat or use of force" in all matters affecting international or European
security as well as in their mutual relations, in accordance with Article 2 of
the United Nations Charter. They pledge "to respect without restriction,
the territorial integrity of all states in Europe within their present frontiers," which are declared to be inviolable. Singled out by name in the
treaty are the two borders between East and West Germany and between
East Germany and Poland. Both sides agree to promote economic relations
as well as scientific, technological, and cultural contacts.

Both governments have solemnly voiced their conviction that the treaty
will (1) contribute to European security, (2) contribute to the solution of
existing problems on the continent, and (3) foster peaceful cooperation
among all European states. These goals cannot be criticized. But they are

reminiscent of the scores of bilateral treaties—with Czechoslovakia, for example, or with Poland, or with Hungary—that the Soviet Union has violated unilaterally. They call up also the image of hands across the walls of a divided city. Amid the clamor that West Germany has chosen a path of normalization of relations with the East, as opposed to a policy of cold war, the perspective of what constitutes détente and what determines existing realities is increasingly blurred. Since the easiest way to misinterpret a political document is to confine one's analysis to its text, it would be wise to look not only at the text, but at the various motives behind this acclaimed instrument of détente. All the realities involved must be considered, not merely those leading to a specific interpretation. While the mirror-image analysts of the West may interpret political events interestingly—and sometimes dangerously—a Christmas rush to buy political wares on a selective basis often leads to disillusionment with the merchandise in the New Year.

It is doubtful whether all the realities existing in Europe today are being recognized, either in Bonn or Moscow or the United States. But experience with proclaimed détentes of the past teaches us that West Germany has concluded a treaty with the Soviet Union (1) which will be honored by Moscow only as long as it is compatible with present and future goals of Soviet policy (e.g., compare Soviet adherence to the Potsdam agreement or to those of the European Advisory Commission on Berlin),[3] (2) which aims at consolidating the Soviet power position in Eastern Europe, and (3) which has given West Germany not a single concession on any major European problem.

The West has a legitimate interest in coming to mutually advantageous agreements with the Soviet Union, such as may transpire from the SALT negotiations. But it must be recognized that, just as the SALT talks are not a sign of détente but reflect a mutual U.S.-Soviet interest in limiting strategic weapons competition, so the Soviet negotiations with West Germany reflect Moscow's concern with consolidating the status quo and persuading Germany to grant the USSR the economic and technological assistance necessary to solve her economic difficulties. One cannot read into them a Soviet desire for genuine peaceful accommodation with the West or a willingness to negotiate on a *quid pro quo* basis. A claim to the contrary would be, in the words of Premier Khrushchev on the eve of the 1959 Foreign Ministers Conference convened to discuss the topic of Germany, "a huckster's approach." Khrushchev added, "We do not have any concessions to make, because our proposals have not been made for bartering. . . . [Their] proposals do not contain a single element for negotiation. . . . They are not based on a desire to find a correct solution."

---

3. The incident of Soviet and East German interference with Allied military traffic on the Berlin-Marienborn autobahn that occurred on January 12, 1971 is illustrative. This was the first case of interference with Allied military vehicles since 1963.

The Soviet Union is seeking to strengthen her role in Eastern Europe and at the same time to persuade the West to approve it. The negotiations with Bonn reflect growing Soviet anxiety over China and concern with finding a solution for the economic difficulties plaguing the East European countries, for which West Germany would provide economic assistance. The USSR wishes to receive Western technology, but in turn has offered only visions of détente and mutual trust. She advocates a European Security Conference, which has received West German support, but which aims at creating divisions within the West.[4] Such a conference would possibly sanction the participation of the United States at the outset, but a purely European decision-making body has been proposed for its later stages; in this the Soviet Union, as a European power, would remain a member, and the United States would be excluded. If the United States were to be euchred out of Europe, and if deceptive illusions of détente were to undermine the common bond uniting the NATO allies, a major Soviet goal would be achieved.

The term cold war and the disagreeable image it summons to mind, of querulous discordance bordering on military conflict between East and West, is an effective political weapon in the hands of Soviet tacticians. Overlooking the fact that the cold war, as a manifestation of American power and Western solidarity, has accounted for peace in Europe since 1945, the Soviet Union suggests to the West that the advocacy of détente is a preferable alternative, but neglects to define on what grounds détente should be realized. Thus, by morally disarming confrontation-weary or philosophically-attuned Westerners with eulogies on harmony and peace, the way may be opened for accommodation as Moscow envisages it. In a vacuum created by the hope of détente it could become increasingly easy to sow divisions of interest among West European states and to encourage a reassessment of policy objectives and priorities concerning NATO and its value. As Secretary Brezhnev so carefully reminded his audience during the Twenty-fourth Party Congress of the CPSU on March 30, 1971, Lenin's adage on sowing and reaping remains applicable: "selfless devotion to the revolution and revolutionary propaganda among the people are not wasted even if long decades divide the sowing from the harvest." A disunited Europe could gradually become estranged from the United States. Lacking U.S. leadership and a clear-cut sense of direction or definition of goal, West European countries could become more susceptible to the chimerical assurances of Soviet communism. This possibility is strengthened by spokesmen

4. Brezhnev's proposal in Tbilisi on May 14, 1971, in which he advocated discussions with the West on Mutual Balanced Force Reductions (MBFR) in Europe, can be viewed similarly. It should be remembered that this proposal was initially made by the NATO ministers at their meeting in Reykjavik in June 1968. At that time the idea did not evoke the "great attention" its endorsement by Brezhnev elicited in May 1971.

in the West advocating unilateral withdrawals of American troops from Europe, even before the Europeans themselves increase their cooperation and joint responsibility on the military, political, and economic levels.

A relaxation of tension in Europe needs to be seen in the perspective of the Soviet aim of pushing the United States from the European continent. In Moscow on August 12, 1970, Kosygin assured Brandt that he expected no loosening of Bonn's ties with the West. In the October issue of the Moscow journal, *International Affairs,* the treaty was termed "a tangible result of postwar development in Europe; it has been prepared by the total development of European realities, by the natural course of international relations." On January 2, 1971, Kosygin was quoted by TASS as endorsing an All-European Security Conference, which would (1) serve to "collect and generalize the positive results and experience" accumulated in the wake of the treaties between West Germany and Moscow and Poland, (2) contribute toward "détente in Europe and in the world in general," and (3) aid in overcoming the opposition of those "who are against détente."

The analysis of the relation between détente in Europe and U.S. foreign policy that appeared in the February 1971 issue of *International Affairs* is even more revealing. The author, Anat. Gromyko, not only criticized the "negative" position of the United States toward the consolidation of the status quo in Europe, but concluded: "A further rise in the temperature in Europe will depend on how actively the West European countries themselves decide to take a line independent of the USA in their relations with the USSR and other socialist countries." Subsequently, in a release distributed by TASS on May 16, the *Pravda* correspondent in Brussels, Yuri Kharlanov, declared "the main obstacle to a genuine détente in Europe" to be "the military-industrial complex of the United States and its NATO branch in Western Europe."

III

The Bonn government proclaims with assurance that the Soviet Union recognizes the "realities" of the situation in Europe today. That is beyond question. The Soviet Union recognizes the realities as they are understood in Moscow. But can so much be said of the Brandt Government itself?

One should note that in June 1970, two months before the signing of the Moscow-Bonn treaty, an editorial in *Pravda* stressed the significance of the communiqué released in Moscow in June 1969, during the first international meeting of seventy-five Communist and workers' parties in nine years. In that communiqué communist goals in Western Europe were defined. First on the list was a breakup of NATO and the convocation of an All-European Security Conference. The second imperative was securing "the inviolability of existing frontiers in Europe, in particular the frontier along the Oder-

Neisse" and the frontier between East and West Germany. This goal was attained almost verbatim in Article III of the Bonn-Moscow treaty.

Third, the Moscow communiqué called for West German recognition of East Germany. In the treaty Bonn acquiesced to de facto recognition, and pressure on this point continues. The now departed East German leader, Walter Ulbricht, in his New Year's Eve message for 1971, importuned for the establishment of normal diplomatic relations—in other words, de jure recognition—by the Federal Republic. This demand has been repeated on numerous occasions during the year as Bonn's obligatory contribution toward détente in Europe. Further, the Moscow communiqué sought Bonn's renunciation of its "claim to represent the whole of Germany." Chancellor Brandt's government has renounced the claim, thereby rejecting the mandate given it by free elections according to the preamble of West Germany's Basic Law (*Grundgesetz*). Thus reference in West Germany to a normalization of *Soviet-German* relations twenty-five years after the war is a patent misrepresentation.

The Moscow document of June 1969 also demanded that West Berlin be recognized as "a separate political entity." West Berlin is not a separate political entity, but the Soviet Union made this claim again on a minimum of four occasions in December 1970 alone,[5] has reiterated the assertion frequently during 1971, and will continue to do so in the future. Finally, the communiqué declared that to ensure peace and security in Europe, the European peoples must be guaranteed "their sovereign right to be masters of their continent without interference from the USA" and must be assured "mutually beneficial economic, scientific, and technological cooperation among the European countries and the establishment of relations between them founded on a genuine relaxation of tension and mutual trust."

Descriptions in Moscow and Bonn of the Federal Republic's concessions are deceptively hailed as having created an atmosphere of accord and "understanding," directed mainly toward the world public. The Soviet Union knows well that the justification for alliance (in this case, NATO), in spirit and in fact, is the conviction that a potential (Soviet) threat exists. Create the impression that a threat is nonexistent, and a gradual crumbling of the alliance will follow. How clear this is when we observe the alacrity with which men charmed by the sweet music of promised friendship and cooperation tend to forget the *raison d'être* of alliance against a common foe, typified by such actions as the Soviet invasion of Czechoslovakia. Many people appear to have sudden memory lapses when they are warned that the alternatives in dealing with the Soviet Union are between friendship or a continuation of the cold war.

5. See, for example, *Pravda*, December 6, 1970; Moscow Radio, December 19, 1970; TASS, December 21, 1970; *Izvestiya*, December 22, 1970.

Western optimists, in the Federal Republic and elsewhere, have reminded us time and again that Brandt's *Ostpolitik* relies for its success on
his country's stable, healthy association with the West. In principle this is
no doubt true. But the concessions he made to the Soviet Union in pur-
suance of *Ostpolitik* far outnumber the advantages gained by West Germany—and, hence, by the West as a whole. The significance of the mutual
renunciation of force, for example, is highly questionable. While Soviet
military policies and capabilities are well known, the Federal Republic is
not, has never been, and is not likely to be in a position to attack the Soviet
Union. The Brandt Government signed the Nuclear Non-proliferation
Treaty in 1969 and is also bound to the limitations on armament production
detailed in the protocols to the treaties creating the Western European
Union in 1954 and admitting the Federal Republic to NATO in 1955.
Brandt's trip to Moscow to assure the Soviet government that the Federal
Republic would not attack the USSR would, thus, seem to be nothing more
than a *beau geste*.

Although both the USSR and West Germany agreed in the treaty to refrain from the use of force according to Article 2 of the United Nations
Charter, two important articles of that Charter, Articles 53 and 107, are not
mentioned. In these two articles, which despite claims to the contrary are
in no way invalidated by Article 2, the Allied powers that fought against
the Axis in World War II, in effect against Germany, retain the right of intervention. In short, the Federal Republic has renounced the use of force
in settling international disputes. But the Soviet Union retains its right of
intervention.[6]

Though the treaty declares the "borders of all states in Europe"[7] to be inviolable, two disputed cases were, as mentioned, singled out for special
attention. The Bonn government judged it necessary to acknowledge by
name the inviolability of the Oder-Neisse line with Poland and the border
between East and West Germany. This recognition of the status quo in

6. Controversy on this point has been considerable in the Federal Republic and
elsewhere. In Moscow in March 1971, the newly appointed Soviet Ambassador to
Bonn, Valentin Falin, is reported to have stated that Articles 53 and 107 had not been
"invalidated" but "superseded" by the treaty, as long as West Germany observed the
treaty's provisions.

In April a West German government spokesman indicated that a secret protocol
of the negotiations prior to the treaty's signature contained the Soviet assurance that
Moscow would not unilaterally apply the Enemy States Clause of the UN Charter
against the Federal Republic of Germany. See *Relay from Bonn*, March 19, 23, 25, and
April 15, 1971. See also *Frankfurter Allgemeine Zeitung*, March 19, 20, 23, 1971, and
Frankfurter Rundschau, April 10, 1971.

7. Whether the Soviet Union considers the Berlin Wall an inviolable border is a
disputed question. Every indication would suggest that an assertion to this effect
will not be long in forthcoming. Moscow proclaims East Germany, including its capital
city of "Berlin" (*sic*), to be a sovereign state in Europe. In addition it has stated on
repeated occasions during the last year that the Four-Power discussions on the Berlin
problem, begun in March 1970, are negotiations on the "West Berlin" problem.

Europe, affecting nations not parties to the Bonn-Moscow treaty, is therefore not simply an acknowledgment of reality as the Soviet Union sees it. It is also a tacit acceptance by Bonn of the Brezhnev Doctrine of the limited sovereignty of East European countries.[8] Moreover, whereas the Soviet Union has exacted Bonn's recognition of the division of Germany, it is not prepared to concede to West Germany the right of reunification by peaceful means. No mention of this vital matter is made in the text of the treaty.[9]

VI

What, then, has been the result of the Soviet-West German treaty concluded a year ago? West Germany has conceded much to the USSR, but not one change has been registered on the Berlin problem: new harassments have blocked the air corridors and the interzonal highways. The realities of the Berlin wall, the division of Germany, the occupation of Czechoslovakia, the consolidation of Soviet control of Eastern Europe, continued interference with traffic to and from Berlin, all remain. Since 1950 Moscow has sought recognition of the Oder-Neisse line. Now this has suddenly been achieved. For twenty-one years the Soviets have sought West Germany's surrender of its claim to represent all the German people. This too has now become a reality. For the same length of time the Soviet Union has sought recognition of its East German regime. Chancellor Brandt has provided de facto recognition. The West, for twenty-five years, has sought a solution to the Berlin problem. On August 23 it secured merely a draft agreement. Even if this is eventually approved by all governments concerned, it cannot be guaranteed. Since 1949 Bonn has hoped for an im-

8. It will be interesting to note what justification the Federal Republic can cite for recognizing in a bilateral treaty the borders of third states which, according to the Soviet Union, are sovereign nations, yet are not free to determine what constitutes an infringement of their sovereignty. Since the signing of the treaty considerable dispute has surrounded the interpretation to be given the word "inviolable." See, for example, M. Vulfson, "Problems of European Security," *Kommunist Sovetskoy Latvii,* January 1971.

9. A letter addressed to Soviet Foreign Minister Andrei Gromyko by his West German counterpart, Foreign Minister Walter Scheel, was delivered to the Foreign Ministry in Moscow at the time of the treaty's signature. It stated "that this treaty does not conflict with the political objecives of the Federal Republic of Germany to work for a state of peace in Europe in which the German nation will recover its unity in free self-determination." This letter was accepted at the Soviet Foreign Ministry but was not acknowledged in any form and the point it made is not included in the text of the treaty.

In April 1971 a government spokesman in Bonn announced that the secret protocol to the negotiations, prior to the signing of the treaty, contains a Soviet statement that the existing borders in Europe can be changed by peaceful means. The Soviet government was said to have agreed to publication of the protocols when the treaty is submitted to the West German Bundestag for ratification. See *Frankfurter Rundschau,* April 10, 1971.

provement of relations with East Germany. Relations have not improved. Treaty is not détente. This was made evident in October 1970, just two months after the treaty's conclusion, when *Pravda* again published an enlightening article. Peaceful coexistence was defined anew as "a form of the class struggle between Socialism and Capitalism." "The decisive factor of peaceful coexistence" was declared to be "the economic and military strength of Socialism."

The only predictable element in international relations is change, but it should never be influenced by the political euphoria induced by attractive promises. As Chancellor Brandt has observed on many occasions before and after signing the treaty with Moscow, West Germany needs both "cooperation and consultation" with the West and "understanding" with the East. But Bonn's need for "understanding" does not excuse equivocation on the definition of realities. Only recognition of all the realities can result in a clear-sighted assessment of any political, economic or military situation. A deceptive psychological atmosphere can make unpleasant dilemmas appear to be innocuous. This does not contribute to their solution, but only to the creation of illusions. Moreover, it is naive and hazardous to permit the conduct of foreign policy to be influenced by shifting emotions. It seems apparent that the Soviet Union is bent on recognizing only those realities compatible with her own interests. The West German government's failure to comprehend this and to point it out, as a fact in the portfolio of all existing realities, will produce the kind of change leading to further unilateral concessions, and could pave the way for a united peaceful Europe from the Ussuri to the Atlantic rather than from the Atlantic to the Urals.

The cold war continues as it has for the last twenty-five years under its various cloaks of propaganda and polemic. The minefields still divide Germany. The wall still cuts across Berlin, dividing families and serving as an altar for the death of refugees from the East. The political borders dividing Europe remain. Soviet goals have not changed. Peaceful coexistence has not become détente. It is obviously folly to predict the future course of history, but it is dangerous error to ignore the lessons of the past.

24.

France Ensnared: French Strategic Policy and Bloc Politics after 1968

EDWARD A. KOLODZIEJ

CHARLES DE GAULLE's France made telling points in the debate over bloc politics and American imperial proclivities for more than a decade following the inception of the Fifth Republic. But for all its rhetorical brilliance, and the pleasure it may have given European partners, the Gaullist argument won no professed converts. France's deviant behavior illustrated more than determined the growing diplomatic pluralism of international relations in the 1960's; its efforts alone did little to challenge seriously the bipolarity of global security relations dominated and defined by the Soviet Union and the United States. After 1968, even Gaullist rhetoric ceased to command much world attention. Social and economic turmoil within France and conflicts with America and Germany over monetary policy— and with the Soviet Union over European security in the wake of the Czechoslovakian invasion—exposed the shaky material foundation on which the French critique rested and robbed it of much of its practical, if not all of its theoretical, merit.

It may be instructive to summarize the changed internal and external conditions that prompted a revision of French strategic policy and then sketch and analyze briefly the principal components of the French shift in the post-1968 period.

Reprinted by permission from *ORBIS*, Winter 1971, pp. 1085–1108. Copyright by the Foreign Policy Research Institute.

French Strategic Policy and the Changing Economic and Political Environment

First, student and worker protests throughout France in May 1968 forced a reordering of governmental priorities. However much the workers and students may have approved Gaullist assaults on American hegemony or taken pride in such prestige symbols as the *force de frappe,* they were interested ultimately in more mundane objectives. The workers wanted better housing, lower prices, higher salaries and improved working conditions. The students focused on relevant education for later careers, jobs after graduation, closer student-faculty relations, a greater say in the governing of their universities, access to institutions of higher learning and reforms in conditions of student life and study. Only a minority of Frenchmen could be said to have desired the toppling of the regime.

In bringing most of the country's productive activities to a halt, the student-worker strikes effectively withdrew political support from the regime's foreign and security policies. The majority victory of the Gaullist party, the UDR, in the special parliamentary elections in June 1968, called to produce a new mandate for Gaullist rule, deflected attention from the serious blow struck at President de Gaulle's personal prestige and at his administration. De Gaulle had rested his authority on the French people, not on the National Assembly and still less on the parties. But in the aftermath of the May crisis he had to rely on these previously scorned instruments to cling to the appearances of power. The May events were tantamount to an unscheduled referendum on ten years of Gaullist rule. The rejection in April 1969 of de Gaulle's plan to reform the Senate and decentralize French administration was anticlimactic. "Why did you leave on a question so secondary as that of the regions," asked André Malraux in his last interview with de Gaulle. "Because of the absurdity?" "Because of the absurdity," replied de Gaulle.[1] What a majority of Frenchmen wanted, as Pierre Viansson-Ponté later recognized, was *bonheur,* not *grandeur.*[2]

Second, the May 1968 events triggered an economic and financial crisis that revealed how dependent the ambitious French military program was on the support of its allies. The first casualty was the franc, on which the de Gaulle Government had founded its foreign and domestic policies.[3] A run on France's $6 billion in gold reserves quickly enfeebled the franc. Millions of francs fled the country, seeking refuge in American dollars and German marks. Between May 1 and July 4, reserves dropped $1.8 billion. France's balance of payments position also slipped rapidly. By the end of the year, a deficit of more than $3 billion was registered. Almost overnight the nation found itself suppliant, not solvent.

1. André Malraux, *Les Chênes Qu'On Abat* (Paris: Gallimard, 1971), pp. 40–41.
2. *LeMorde,* May 9, 1971, p. 1.
3. Charles de Gaulle, *Mémoires d'Espoir: Le Renouveau, 1958–1962* (Paris: Plon, 1970).

To halt the downward plunge of its foreign deficits, France instituted selected import quotas and advanced aid to exporters. The EEC subsequently acceded to these *faits accomplis* even though they qualified France's obligation to remove all remaining barriers to the creation of a full customs union by July 1, 1968. On May 30, the French government established exchange controls, and in July a $1.3 billion "swap" was made with European central banks and the Federal Reserve of New York. When another serious attack against the franc was launched in the fall of 1968, the Group of Ten within the International Monetary Fund extended $2 billion in credits to France. The principal donors were the United States and Germany.

American and German help galled French pride. It forced a truce in the "gold war" campaign led by de Gaulle against the credibility of the dollar, the complement to his earlier offensive on the alleged unreliability of the American nuclear deterrent.[4] The Johnson Administration eased the French government's resignation to American financial dominance by minimizing public notice of the dollar's support of the franc. Messages of encouragement were quietly dispatched during the crisis, including a personal exchange of cables between Presidents Johnson and de Gaulle. Johnson's halt of bombing on North Vietnam and his request to establish peace negotiations in Paris, beginning in May, 1968, nursed a cordiality between the two states forced as much by domestic upheaval in both countries as by conscious desire on the part of their governments.

German assistance was also a source of concern. Bonn's help was eventually effective, but the manner in which the aid was furnished unsettled French national sensitivities. The ruling German coalition of Socialists and Christian Democrats was cool to French suggestions and broad American and British hints that the mark be revalued upward. In the fall of 1968, Germany extended credits to France and instituted export controls but went no farther. These positive steps were not strong enough to quell French fears that Germany's assertion of its own economic interests forewarned of future demonstrations of German political independence. New anxieties over a revived Germany, capable of exerting weighty economic and diplomatic influence in the service of German national goals, were by his own accounting uppermost in de Gaulle's thinking during his last months in office.[5] They were no less present in the minds of some French officials in the wake of the April 1971 financial crisis, when Bonn chose to float the mark over the wishes of its EEC partners, and especially France.[6]

Third, the Soviet invasion of Czechoslovakia, in August 1968, underlined how much France depended on the American security guarantee. Moscow's

4. The felicitous phrase is Guy de Carmoy's in "The Last Year of de Gaulle's Foreign Policy," *International Affairs,* July 1969, p. 430.

5. See C. L. Sulzberger's final interview with President de Gaulle, of February 1969, published November 11, 1970 in the *Herald Tribune,* International Edition, pp. 1, 4.

6. Author's interviews, Paris and Brussels, April-May 1971.

action diluted the political utility (not to mention the domestic financial claims) of an independent *force de frappe.* The French nuclear system had been advanced as an indispensable ingredient of a new security framework for Europe in the post-bloc period, marked by the diminishing importance of the NATO and Warsaw organizations and the decreasing presence of American and Soviet forces in Central Europe. Continued polycentrism in Eastern Europe and the gradual liberalization of the totalitarian regime in the Soviet Union were to be the political foundation stones of the new order. The Czech incident dashed French hopes that such a political base could soon be realized. Although the government refused to concede that its détente policy had been seriously damaged—Czechoslovakia was characterized as "an accident along the route"—there were increased signs of a major reevaluation of the strategic threats facing France. Efforts were set in motion, too, to repair sagging alliance fences with Western allies and, specifically, the United States.[7] Attacking the United States was profitable only so long as the threat from the USSR appeared remote. As the Soviet military threat suddenly became real and as America's attention turned from Europe (partly because of engagements elsewhere, partly because of growing impatience with the size of its global burdens) the strategic dilemma became more sharply focused.

Faced with the need to cut back military expenditures, a heightened perception of threats abroad, and an Atlantic partner itself suffering from bloc fatigue—in part brought on by repeated Gaullist attacks—French strategists had to pose a security question that had been conveniently slighted during the heyday of de Gaulle's détente policy toward the Soviet Union between 1965 and 1968: How could France reduce or escape dependency on the United States without reducing the dependability of the United States? In other words, how could she "get away closer" from the American colossus?

Realignment a la Carte

Major operational shifts were soon discernible as France worked at harmonizing the strategic imperatives with political needs and aspirations. Changes could be detected in its announced strategic doctrine, its alliance diplomacy, the size and distribution of expenditures for force levels and weapons systems, and the greater attention devoted to the relation of military spending to economic growth and foreign trade. This reordering began in the final year of the de Gaulle administration and continued into the Pompidou presidency, culminating in the third military five-year plan under the Fifth Republic passed by the National Assembly in November 1970.

7. Sulzberger interview, *op. cit.*

As early as November 1968, less than a year after the announcement of the Ailleret doctrine of an all-horizon defense, criticism of French policy began circulating discreetly within French military circles. The November 1968 number of the prestigious *Revue de Défense Nationale* featured General Edmond Combaux's critique of *"défense tous azimut."*[8] Combaux attacked General Charles Ailleret's strategic recommendations for warping military spending at the expense of conventional forces, for weakening the tie between the nation and national defense in assigning the state's military functions to a professional elite, and, worse, for actually increasing France's dependence on the United States. The latter charge was crucial, for it disarmed Ailleret's argument.

Combaux posited the rule that "the range of the arms always determines the radius of the fortresses or the size of the fortified areas."[9] Thus, the superpowers, acting implicitly on this principle of military logic, created a global alliance network in order to establish their primary defenses as far from their shores as possible. According to the Combaux analysis, Ailleret's strategic notions also implied a defense that would be far from population centers and grounded in large and secure terrain on which to maneuver—which France alone could not provide. Ailleret was unable to accept the conclusion of his own thinking, for it would have led to the recommendation of closer, not weaker, alliance ties. This was precisely what he sought to avoid. Yet only allies could afford France the geographic scope and material possibility of executing Ailleret's strategic notions of national independence.

"It is not sufficient for France to possess rockets of intercontinental range," concluded Combaux. "It is essential to recognize the environment in which these weapons operate and the limitations of their use. They will have value only if they are part of a coherent defense system. Because the dimensions of the system greatly exceed the capabilities of our nation, the need for a permanent defense association between France and her neighbors is inescapable."[10] For Combaux, if Atlantic ties were ruled out by Gaullist fiat, the only feasible alternative open to France to salvage Ailleret's (and the government's official) doctrine was, ironically enough, a global alliance framework based on cooperation with her European partners. Ailleret's (and de Gaulle's) globalism was not so much questioned as was its operational effectiveness if built solely on the limited striking power and territory of the French state.

The confirming signal that France had amended its strategic doctrine was given in May, 1969, in a *Revue de Défense Nationale* article under the

---

8. "Défense Tous Azimut? Oui, Mais . . . ," pp. 1600–1618. See also the useful analysis of Combaux's thought in *Combat*, November 4, 1968, p. 2.

9. Edmond Combaux, "French Military Policy and European Federalism," *ORBIS*, Spring 1969, p. 151.

10. *Ibid.*, p. 152.

signature of General M. Fourquet, Ailleret's successor as commander-in-chief. First, Ailleret's notion of a strategic threat arising from any point in the globe was revised in favor of the traditional view of "an enemy coming from the east."[11] Second, a modified version of NATO's graduated response strategy was substituted for Ailleret's largely all-or-nothing doctrine. Barring a direct enemy strike against France, the first encounter with enemy forces was portrayed as occurring at the conventional level. Once this was breached, the second clash would be at the tactical nuclear plateau. The employment of these weapons would test the intentions of the adversary in order to prevent a premature launching of strategic forces and would manifest France's will to resist. Fourquet also narrowed previous French conceptions of the autonomous use of tactical and even strategic nuclear weapons. Although their independent employment was not ruled out, emphasis was placed on their utilization in coordination with the Western allies, but with more an Atlantic thrust than the European direction indicated by Combaux.

If the French competition of an escalation ladder had few rungs, owing partly to the limited nuclear means disposed by France, Fourquet's formulation was still more in accord with announced NATO strategy. Troop reductions in NATO in the late 1960's induced NATO planners, too, to rely on earlier use of nuclear weapons than had initially been envisioned when the American shift to graduated response had first been proclaimed. These changes had the effect of drawing French and NATO views closer together although for different reasons.[12]

Doctrinal alignments between NATO and French strategy also found practical, albeit limited, expression in what Michel Debré, as Defense Minister in the Chaban-Delmas cabinet, termed a policy of selective cooperation between France and its alliance partners.[13] Even immediately after the 1966 military withdrawal from NATO, France continued to participate in the technical weapons development group at The Hague. French experts increased their membership on NATO technical committees. Ties to the NADGE alert system, indispensable for the protection of France's Mirage forces, were retained; French companies built radar components for the network, and a French general assisted in installing the warning system in Turkey.[14] Likewise, progress has been recorded in coordinating French-NATO air defenses, and France took steps, since proven abortive, to join in the construction of a new NATO communications network. French-

11. General M. Fourquet, "Emploi des Différents Systèmes de Forces dans le Cadre de la Stratégie de Dissuasion," *Revue de Défense Nationale,* May 1969, p. 762.

12. *Le Monde,* April 5, 1969, p. 5.

13. Michel Debré, "France's Global Strategy," *Foreign Affairs,* April 1971, pp. 395–406.

14. *Le Nouvel Observateur,* January 1, 1971, p. 26.

NATO contacts have been multiplied in joint training exercises to improve the efficiency of French conventional forces. As early as the fall of 1968, French naval and air units participated discreetly in NATO maneuvers in the Mediterranean and assumed surveillance functions over Soviet operations in the area.

French authorities insist, nevertheless, that these activities in no way contradict France's decision to quit NATO's integrated command structure or suggest any desire to return to the NATO fold.[15] Such assertions of Gaullist creed do not square easily with some forms of NATO cooperation in which the French have shown an interest. Participation in the NATO communications network or aerial defense, for example, implies French acceptance of NATO priorities under certain defined operating conditions. What passes for integration within NATO has largely been the product of consent arrangements among member states. The French argument over the loss of independence within the alliance has always been overstated. NATO has never achieved the hopes of its public pronouncements in integrating the military capabilities of the member states within a single command structure. The French were not unaware of the difference, but preferred, often solely for reasons of domestic and international consumption, to beat the NATO horse when political opportunity beckoned.

The inadmissibility of France's return to the NATO structure has not precluded gestures of loyalty to the Atlantic Alliance. Apprehensions that France would leave the alliance after 1969, when member states had the right to renounce their treaty obligations unilaterally, were quickly laid to rest. New oaths were taken of the nation's commitment to the Western alliance and specifically to its special security ties with the United States. In a speech before the Ecole Militaire in July 1970, Debré acknowledged the critical defense role played by American military power. "We ought to be aware," he said, "that there exists around us a circle of nations to which we belong and which have in common a cultural and moral treasure as well as a conception of social life. The security of this grouping, in many ways, makes a whole whose principal pillar remains the United States. *It is normal to give a privileged place to Franco-American relations.*"[16] In welcoming Leonid Brezhnev to Paris for an official visit on October 25, 1971, President Georges Pompidou emphasized France's economic and social links "to the Western world" and "its alliances" as "an integral part of her policy."[17]

After 1968, the French security problem was posed less as a matter of blocking American penetration of Europe than of assuring the availability

---

15. Author's interviews, Paris, January-May 1971; Brussels, March 1971.

16. *Le Monde,* July 3, 1970, p. 5. (Emphasis added.)

17. Address delivered by Georges Pompidou at the Grand Trianon on October 25, 1971, Ambassade de France, Service de Presse et d'Information.

of American military power as a calculated hedge against Soviet expansion. The French reaction to the SALT and MBFR talks, discussed below, is partly explicable in these terms.

The Search for Independence

In temporarily acceding to American financial and strategic power, post-1968 France did not abandon the search for independence.[18] It was being pursued at different rates of speed and intensity in at least five areas: (1) the development of national military forces; (2) East-West negotiations; (3) bilateral security ties with Third World states; (4) arms sales; and (5) bilateral security ties in Western Europe.

THE MILITARY PROGRAM

The French strategic and tactical nuclear program continued under tight national control. The third five-year plan for military expenditures, passed by the National Assembly in November 1970, called for maintenance of the Mirage nuclear force until 1976, emplacement of eighteen IRBM's in concrete silos (instead of the twenty-seven first projected), and completion of three Polaris-type submarines by 1974–1975. France was expected to dispose thermonuclear weapons by the middle 1970's.

After a decade of relative neglect, new impetus was given to the development of tactical nuclear forces, based on mobile ground and air delivery systems. Planning for the use of these forces remained national, and no official efforts were made to coordinate them with NATO elements, although informal contacts between French and NATO officers have been reported.[19] What function they would perform in allied defense was not seriously broached. While military doctrine manifested more realism regarding the vulnerability of tactical nuclear forces, the political objections of the Pompidou regime to bloc politics sustained the dubious strategic propositions that France could still act separately in a nuclear war, even in Europe, and that joint nuclear planning inherently weakened overall deterrence between East and West. "Because the nuclear risk is not divisible," wrote Defense Minister Debré in the April 1971 issue of *Foreign Affairs*, "any nuclear cooperation which might have a strategic character is simply not possible. The decision to employ nuclear forces can be made only by a single nation, which is to say that any regulations laid down in advance, which set forth the conditions for employment, diminish the deterrent's credibility."[20] The indivisibility of the nuclear risk partially underlies the

18. Space limitations prevent an explanation of the French criticism of American economic and monetary policy, especially in the wake of the August 1971 dollar crisis. See, for example, *Le Monde*, September 4, 1971, p. 1.

19. Author's interviews, Paris and Brussels, March-May 1971.

20. *Op. cit.*, p. 401. Also of interest is Debré's "Les Principes de Notre Politique de Défense," *Revue de Défense Nationale*, August-September 1970, pp. 1245–1258.

rationale for French refusal to participate in NATO's Nuclear Planning Group.

These assertions of independence are less impressive, however, when the military expenditure program is examined. Pompidou's five-year military plan reinforced the downward trend in military expenditures relative to overall governmental spending and GNP that had been established in the two previous five-year plans of his predecessor. Military spending in proportion to these two factors declined steadily and consistently between 1960 and 1970. In 1960 it composed 28 percent of the government's budget and 5.5 percent of France's GNP. Eleven years later, in 1971, the respective figures were 17.2 percent and 3.27 percent.

The events of 1968, as the Defense Ministry admitted, accelerated this downward slide. While the rate of increase in government spending jumped from 9.4 in 1968 to 16.4 a year later, reflecting increases in social service spending, the rate of growth in military expenditures declined in the same period from 6.1 to 3.9 percent. In 1970 and 1971, for the first time, more funds were devoted to national education than to defense. Higher absolute spending on defense ($5.2 billion in 1971 against $4.2 billion in 1965) was further offset by inflation, the 12.5 percent devaluation of the franc in August 1969, and larger expenditures on military personnel to retain and attract experienced cadres. Consequently, program objectives were stretched out and the combat effectiveness of units, especially among conventional forces, was permitted to lag. Arms purchases and arms development were also reoriented to respond as much to the economic demands of foreign arms competition as to strategic imperatives.[21]

EAST-WEST NEGOTIATIONS

In bloc politics, France strove to distinguish its views on East-West negotiations from those of its Western allies. French policy has been most active and visible in this area. Attention has centered on the American-sponsored NATO proposal for mutual and balanced force reductions (MBFR), SALT, the renewed Soviet call of March 1969 for a European security conference, and Big Four talks over Berlin. Paris showed least enthusiasm for MBFR. It refused to associate itself with the June 1968 NATO resolution proposing force reductions between the Western and Communist military pacts. The grounds of the refusal were not entirely consistent. The proposal was condemned as a reinforcement of bloc politics since multilateral negotiations were envisioned rather than bilateral contacts between states. The French also argued that the Soviet Union was not interested in MBFR, a view later contradicted by Moscow's offer of May 1971 to put East-West talks on just

21. The relevant documents are published by the Comité Interministeriel pour l'Information: *Le Budget de la Défense Nationale* (January 1970); *Le Budget de la Défense Nationale en 1970* (December 1970); and *La Troisième Loi de Programme Militaire* (November 1970).

such a basis.[22] More plausibly, they suggested that if the Soviet Union should accept the NATO proposal there was serious risk that European security would be compromised, since the geographic and military positions of the two superpowers in Europe were asymmetrical. A uniform formula for force reductions applied to both camps would necessarily weaken the Western alliance.[23]

There are indications that, at the military strategic level, France is not interested in any change in the European East-West balance, however much it presses for broader diplomatic, cultural, economic, scientific, and technical exchanges between all European states.[24] Before coming to the United States in early 1970, President Pompidou thought it was "normal that there be an American presence in Europe."[25] He has not departed from this position. The argument against American or allied troop withdrawal before tangible gains have been realized in negotiations with the Soviet Union has instead been strengthened. In his news conference of September 23, 1971, Pompidou implicitly drew a distinction between détente through increased nonmilitary cooperation among European states and détente through changes in the military disposition of member states. Concern for progress in nonmilitary areas was not to interfere with the maintenance of the West's defense capabilities. There has been a shift away from the Gaullist stress on détente over defense.[26] On the other hand, Foreign Minister Maurice Schumann objected before the National Assembly on November 3, 1971 that MBFR was an obstacle to the calling of a European security conference.[27] These conflicting posturings were tantamount to a French call for an armed détente: "Yes" to any nonmilitary moves that would lessen East-West tensions; "No" to any weakening of the West's bargaining position, stemming from a diminution of American troop strength or Western military capabilities.

The French also took a dim view of SALT. Both MBFR and SALT ran counter to their preference for political accords between East and West states. Security arrangements such as SALT had the disadvantage that they would probably suit the economic needs and global security imperatives of the superpowers better than those of the small and middle powers of Europe. De Gaulle had repeatedly warned against a U.S.-USSR agreement over the heads of the European states whose protection depended upon one or the other of these continental powers. The theme continued to be struck in the counsels of the Pompidou regime. Defense Minister Debré,

22. *Herald Tribune*, International Edition, May 15–16, 1971, pp. 1, 2.

23. Author's interviews, Paris and Brussels, January-May 1971.

24. See, for example, "Statement of the Principles of Cooperation between France and the Union of Soviet Socialist Republics, October 30, 1971," Ambassade de France, Service de Presse et d'Information.

25. *U.S. News and World Report*, March 2, 1970, p. 44.

26. *Le Monde*, September 25, 1971, p. 3.

27. Address by Maurice Schumann before the National Assembly, November 3, 1971, Ambassade de France, Service de Presse et d'Information.

pressing the point even further than de Gaulle, contended that a Soviet-American settlement on weapons and military expenditures might actually increase political instability in Europe. French logic dictated that the nuclear balance between the superpowers inevitably made Europe an area of secondary value for them in the event of a nuclear exchange and disposed them to compromise their differences at the expense of the other European states.[28] In the absence of a European political solution, responsive to the views of all affected parties and specifically approved by France, there was the risk that the states whose demands would not have been satisfied would have an incentive to upset the Soviet-American agreement. Precedent could be found in the aerial highjackings undertaken by the Palestinian Arabs in order to assert their interests after having been excluded from the Rogers Plan for the Middle East.[29]

In any event Soviet interest in military disengagement was perceived as considerably less than that of the United States. Either SALT or MBFR or both might leave Europe militarily exposed. After Czechoslovakia, the Gaullist prophecy that the United States could not be trusted to defend Europe began to haunt French policy-makers as much as the possibility that an American-Soviet accord, in the form of a strategic arms agreement, might compromise France's security and political interests. Some, like Debré, clung to the notion that America's commitment to defend Europe depended "on the strategic superiority of the United States."[30] The passing of American strategic superiority, however much due to technological change rather than diminished resolve, could not but heighten doubts about U.S. security guarantees.[31]

The residual hope that a strictly defined military accord between the Superpowers to slow down the arms race might increase the marginal strategic value of the *force de frappe* further complicated the French calculus. But in the renewed realism of the post-1968 period, this expectation was given less weight than before in announced and operational French strategic maneuvering. Officials no longer pretended that the French nuclear force could substitute for the American guarantee in the near future. The most they could hope for was that an enhanced *force de frappe* would strengthen the French bargaining position over a European political settlement.[32] Nuclear weapons were also the entry fee for a prominent place at the world disarmament conference table, a mark of France's status as a global power. Their possession supported her legal position as a member of the Big Four (and therefore an arbiter of Germany's fate) and as a permanent member of the Security Council.

Not surprisingly, the French displayed more interest in a European se-

28. Debré, "France's Global Strategy," *op. cit.*, p. 403.
29. *Le Monde*, September 26, 1970, p. 1.
30. Debré, "France's Global Strategy," *op. cit.*, p. 397.
31. *Le Monde*, October 2, 1971, p. 10.
32. Author's interviews, Paris and Brussels, January-May 1971.

curity conference. Whatever its possible snares—and reinforcement of bloc politics and superpower dominance were high among them—it offered greater room for diplomatic maneuver than military accords. France's strength lay, if anywhere, in its subtly calibrated diplomacy; in military power plays its record since 1940 has been undistinguished. Political, not strategic, understandings with adversary states was the preferred French method.

President Pompidou, like his predecessor, nurtured the Franco-Soviet détente begun in the middle 1960's. The vigor of German Chancellor Willy Brandt's *Ostpolitik* gave new impetus to efforts to keep France in the running as the favored European interlocutor of the Soviet Union. The French President staked out the diplomatic terrain in his first speech at the Kremlin during his eight-day visit to the USSR in October 1970. Expressing optimism that a security conference could promote the independence of European states, he urged active preparation for such a meeting.[33] In his January and September news conferences in 1971 and in his meeting with Brezhnev in October,[34] he called for an early convening of a security conference. The French position was also aimed at responding to the sentiment of the East European states, which looked upon the conference as a means of stabilizing European security and as a diplomatic lever on the Soviet Union, impeding its resort to the Brezhnev Doctrine.

While Pompidou conciliated the Soviets and the East Europeans, his ministers were more qualified in their pronouncements concerning a conference. Within a month of the Soviet proposal Debré, attending NATO anniversary celebrations in Washington, had observed unofficially that the Soviet suggestion might bolster the superpower hold over Europe. French officials privately expressed the same view, emphasizing that a conference could be held only after careful preparations and with the consent of all affected parties.[35] These temporizings were supplemented by a more explicit French qualification: a security conference was contingent on progress in Big Four talks over Berlin. In November 1970, Prime Minister Jacques Chaban-Delmas stated during his official visit to Poland that France could neither agree to the convocation of a security meeting before a Berlin settlement had been achieved nor even engage in multilateral contacts to prepare such a conference in the absence of a Berlin accord.[36] A month later, Foreign Minister Schumann supported a strong NATO resolution citing Berlin in effect as a prior condition for the Soviet-sponsored conference.

President Pompidou attempted to reconcile the divergent views issuing from the Elysée Palace, the National Assembly, the Quai d'Orsay and the

33. Comité Interministeriel pour l'Information, *Visite Officielle du Président de la République en U.R.S.S.* (6–13 Octobre 1970), No. 69, October 1970, p. 8.
34. See *Le Figaro*, January 22, 1971, p. 6.
35. Author's interviews, Paris and Brussels, January-May 1971.
36. *Le Monde*, November 28, 1970, p. 7.

Defense Ministry in his January 1971 news conference. He drew a careful distinction between a juridic prerequisite, which France had not invoked over Berlin, and political prudence which suggested that success in reaching an accord on European security was not likely unless the Berlin question had first been resolved.[37] Schumann's reported remarks at the June 1971 NATO meeting in Portugal lent additional weight to the view that a Berlin accord was the French (and allied) price for a European security conference. By then, the major Western powers of the Atlantic Alliance were agreed that sufficient progress had been made in Big Four talks to soften NATO resistance to the Soviet proposal.[38]

Fall 1971 brought more explicit conditions. Partly in deference to German wishes, these included final settlement of the Big Four Berlin accord signed on September 3, mutual ratification of the Moscow and Warsaw treaties, and the successful conclusion of intra-German talks. The French also have elaborated on the Finnish suggestion of multilateral discussions to be held in Helsinki preparatory to convening the security conference. France would prefer, as Schumann observed, "a conference meeting alternately at two levels: at the level of foreign affairs ministers . . . and . . . at the level of three committees charged with . . . the areas of security, exchange of goods, and also exchanges of ideas or people. . . . It goes without saying that—if the results so justify—a meeting at the highest level could crown the undertaking."[39]

Accordingly, the French have renamed the Soviet proposal the "Conference on Security *and Cooperation* in Europe."[40] The conference might still legitimate Moscow's Eastern empire, but the French expect that it will also elicit Soviet concessions, permitting greater contacts between East and West European states. The Soviet Union might even allow itself to be drawn into an institutional framework growing out of the conference, aimed at encouraging European ties in all nonmilitary sectors and at containing Soviet maneuverability in Europe as much by diplomacy as by military threats. Judging by the communiqués that were issued, institutionalizing the process of East-West cooperation in Europe as an outcome of the conference appeared to be the thrust of Schumann's visits to Hungary and Bulgaria in September 1971.[41]

In French eyes, the oscillations and reservations in governmental pronouncements on a European security conference had political merit. On the one hand, France could assert that in principle it was still in the vanguard of efforts to reconcile East and West. On the other hand, its reservations served as a brake on convening a meeting precipitately. The conflicting French reactions to the security conference, SALT, MBFR, and Berlin were

37. *Le Figaro*, January 22, 1971, p. 6.
38. *Herald Tribune*, International Edition, June 4, 1971, pp. 1, 2.
39. Address by Maurice Schumann, *op. cit.*, p. 6.
40. *Ibid.*, p. 7. (Emphasis added.)
41. *Le Monde*, September 10, 1971, p. 4; September 12–13, 1971, pp. 1, 3.

all of a piece. They evidenced the growing hesitancy of the government to entertain new military proposals for European security. Preserving existing defense arrangements, however unstable they might be, took precedence over initiatives, like MBFR, whose consequences were necessarily uncertain. After 1968, initiatives for defense changes arose elsewhere. Paris lagged behind its Atlantic and European partners, whereas it had once led the search for cheaper, more durable and politically viable security arrangements.

Even the Brandt Government's *Ostpolitik* was questioned increasingly in French ruling circles, although France could justly claim to have been in the forefront of the détente race to win Soviet favor.[42] France had always considered itself the appropriate interlocutor for Germany with the Soviet Union. The Brandt Government, acting on its own advisement in normalizing relations with its Eastern neighbors, offered little opportunity for the French to play their self-conceived intermediary role. However much they might applaud Germany's efforts to improve its relations with Eastern Europe as a confirmation of their own Eastern policy, Brandt's independent brand of *Ostpolitik* could not but reinforce the image of an emergent Germany, progressively beyond French influence, and raise anxieties about the strategic, political, and economic implications of the German-Soviet rapprochement.

Still there was little else for the French government to do than to second the German effort, as Pompidou did at the Kremlin,[43] and to sign a new protocol with the USSR that attempted to match in importance the treaty signed by Germany the preceding August. The Bonn-Moscow treaty recognized the frontiers established by World War II and promised important economic and technological concessions to the Soviet Union.[44] The Franco-Soviet accord, rather than defining new areas of agreement, reaffirmed the allegedly privileged diplomatic relations between the two countries, their special global security responsibilities, especially within the United Nations Security Council, and their determination to enlarge economic ties.[45] The diplomatic tit-for-tat between Bonn and Paris continued into fall 1971, when, partly to counter the German-Soviet communique of September 1971,

42. Useful for a review of French official thinking is the publication of the Comité Interministeriel pour l'Information summarizing President Pompidou's visit to the Soviet Union, *op. cit.* An annex presents Foreign Minister Schumann's analysis of the German-Soviet treaty of August 12, 1970, in which he seeks to quiet French fears of another Rapallo, pp. 37–40.

43. *Ibid.*, pp. 7–9.

44. *L'Express*, August 7–23, 1970, pp. 14–17.

45. *Visite Officielle du Président de la République, op. cit.*, pp. 3–5, 36. France's dubious favor in Soviet circles is raised further into question if one observes the close parallel in language between the protocols signed by the Soviet Union with France and later with Canada in May 1971. Privileged relations have now been reduced to little more than an intent on the part of the consenting states to engage in regular political consultations at fixed intervals. Whereas French-Soviet officials will confer twice a year, Canadian-Soviet representatives will meet only once. *Le Monde*, May 21, 1971, p. 5.

which raised the possibility of two Germanys in the United Nations, France signed not only another economic, technical, and industrial accord with the Soviet Union but a "Statement" of Franco-Soviet principles of cooperation and a "Declaration" of their points of agreement on world issues.[46]

In general, however, the French felt themselves being ensnared against their better judgment—and to some degree their will—in a web of relations principally spun by the United States, the Soviet Union, and West Germany. They seemed often to prefer the part of Penelope, unraveling rather than binding the tapestry of military security relations being woven. Toward the United States, France saw utility in developing limited concrete forms of cooperation with NATO. On the other hand, although it shared some U.S. doubts about a European security conference, it remained skeptical principally over SALT and MBFR. Toward the Soviet Union, French diplomacy temporized over the security conference while citing an expanding series of conditions, in accord with Germany and other Western allies, as a test of Soviet intentions. Toward Germany, maintaining war-won rights still controlled French strategic thinking. The Pompidou regime, like its predecessor,[47] was alert to any move by another power that might dilute France's privileged right to participate with the superpowers on equal terms in settling Germany's future.

Little comfort was drawn from Leonid Brezhnev's suggestion, at the Twenty-fourth Communist Party Congress in Moscow in April 1971, to hold disarmament talks among the five nuclear powers, although due notice was given to the Soviet proposal during Brezhnev's visit to France. Before 1968 the Soviet initiative, which acknowledged France's special responsibilities for global security, would have been recognized as a victory for French diplomacy. After French weakness became apparent in the final year of de Gaulle's rule, the Paris government preferred to hold on to the legal and political gains already secured, as in Berlin and Germany, rather than to gamble for more influence in security matters through initiatives that might change the existing military balance. What remaining capacity France had to influence events bearing on its security interests was seen to lie more in frustrating the designs of other states than in imposing its will on them; its juridic claims and agile diplomatic maneuvering now served it better than its strategic striking power or economic strength.

SECURITY TIES WITH THIRD WORLD STATES

French presence in the underdeveloped world represents the third major element of the search for independence in the post-1968 period, and this is linked closely to the sale of arms abroad. The Pompidou Government's

46. See the issues of *Le Monde,* October 26 to November 1, 1971.
47. De Gaulle was clear on this point in his revealing talk with Sulzberger, *op. cit.,* p. 4: "The real sovereignty of Berlin was awarded to the victors of World War II. . . . The allies—you [the Americans] we, and the British—have the responsibility of sovereignty."

stress on regionalism over Gaullist globalism, symbolized in France's much heralded Mediterranean policy, became the guideline for military planning.[48] "Our zone of privileged action," explained General Mitterand to a group of distinguished defense specialists, "remains . . . the Mediterranean, the Atlantic facade of Brest to Dakar, and Northern equatorial Africa."[49]

France is linked to most of the states of this region in a series of bilateral military assistance accords. Approximately twenty technical military assistance groups were operating in 1970 in Africa and Asia; approximately 12,000 French troops were stationed in various parts of Africa. A small, highly mobile force, capable of intervening abroad in limited engagements to support French interests and treaty obligations, had already been established under the second military *loi-programme*. Direct military support for the government of Chad since August 1968 suggested the kind of intervention contemplated.[50] It followed the Gabon example of February 1964, when French paratroopers reinstated the deposed President.[51] French military planning is oriented toward responding rapidly to prevent the subversion of friendly governments. To carry on a war of attrition, as before in Indochina or Algeria, would quickly sap France's limited conventional capabilities, not to mention domestic political will.

ARMS SALES

Arms sales abroad have represented perhaps the most striking advance in France's relative strategic standing.[52] In 1970, French arms shipments tripled in value over those of the previous year, jumping from $456 million

48. For an elaboration of the Pompidou regime's accent on regionalism, see my article, "French Mediterranean Policy: The Politics of Weakness," *International Affairs*, July 1971.
49. General J. Mitterand, "La Place de l'Action Militaire Extérieure dans la Stratégie Française," *Revue de Défense Nationale*, June 1970, p. 901.
50. Reports on French participation in the fighting in Chad are difficult to find in French or foreign newspapers. For bits of information about the effort, estimated to involve 1,500 troops, see *West Africa*, October 18, 1969 and September 5, 1970; *Herald Tribune*, International Edition, March 31, 1970; and *The Observer*, October 26, 1969. *The Military Balance 1970–71* (London: Institute for Strategic Studies, 1970) lists 2,500 troops in Chad as of June 1970, and 12,500 in Africa. The Chad figures appear high.
51. Useful newspaper accounts of the Gabon expedition are found in *The Guardian*, February 20 and 24, 1964, and *The Sunday Times* (London), February 24, 1964.
52. The annual issue of *The Military Balance* provides a running account of French arms deals. Useful summaries of French arms policy are found in Jean Klein, "Commerce des Armes et Désarmement," *Politique Etrangère*, No. 4/1968, pp. 351–360, and "Les Aspects Actuels de la Règlements du Commerce des Armes," *ibid.*, No. 2/1969, pp. 161–190; and Jacques Isnard, "French Arms Exports," *Survival*, April 1971, pp. 134–135. Also helpful are articles by C. L. Sulzberger, *Herald Tribune*, International Edition, February 22, 1971, p. 4; Josette Alia, *Le Nouvel Observateur*, November 1, 1971, pp. 24–25; Richard Booth, *Le Monde Diplomatique*, April 1970, p. 10; and Georges Chafford, *Combat*, February 5, 1969, p. 7.

to $1.3 billion. France replaced Britain as the third most important exporter of arms, exceeded only by the United States and the Soviet Union, whose respective arms exports were worth $2.7 billion and $2.0 billion. In 1970, military sales totaled 8 percent of all France's exports and 25 percent of its industrial shipments abroad. The bulk of the French success has been in aerospace, where Mirage sales in 1970 alone posted contracts valued at $650 million. The spectacular performance of Mirage in the Six Day War helped to expand sales to almost twenty states around the globe. Helicopters, tanks, missiles, and missile-launching patrol boats composed most of the other attractive sellers.

The French merchandised these military products much like soap chips or automobiles. Easy credit, weak political restrictions, and service contracts were part of each package deal. Even arms fairs were organized to attract customers.[53] They were particularly successful in penetrating American arms markets—from industrial states like Germany (Bonn placed an order for over $200 million in patrol boats in 1970)[54] to less developed states like Colombia, Brazil, Argentina, and Peru, which bought Mirages and, in the case of the latter two South American countries, other arms, including AMX tanks. The expansion of French arms sales to Latin America provides some measure of the vulnerability of the previous U.S. monopoly. Franco-American competition had grown so intense by the spring of 1971 that it elicited presidential notice on both sides of the Atlantic. In a May 1971 report to Congress, President Nixon recommended that military assistance to Latin America be doubled from its base of $75 million a year. Arms manufacturers were also advised to boost sales abroad.[55] On May 23, President Pompidou was reported to have advised the French military to develop simple, cheap, and *exportable* arms.[56]

The motivation for the French marketing effort in arms is varied. While its principal root remains the desire for an independent strategic and diplomatic policy, economic considerations presently predominate. Military sales have maintained France's delicate balance of payments, created jobs and spurred industrial expansion (a high priority of the Pompidou-inspired French VI Plan). In 1970 the number of defense workers engaged in foreign exports doubled over the previous year, reaching a peak of 100,000, or more than one-third of the entire defense work force of 270,000. Arms exports supported an indigenous arms industry that would otherwise have shrunken with the secular decline of conventional forces and thus reinforced French dependency on the United States. It was hoped that these

53. *Le Monde*, September 17, 1970, p. 14.
54. *Ibid.*, October 26, 1970, pp. 1, 2.
55. *Herald Tribune*, International Edition, May 22–23, 1971, p. 3; *Le Monde*, May 19, 1971, p. 32.
56. *Le Monde*, May 23–24, 1971, p. 32.

initial commercial successes would lead to greater military and even civilian sales of French products.[57]

The anticipated political gains of arms exports are difficult to assess. The de Gaulle and Pompidou regimes have had to weather serious internal political storms over their arms policies. Pro-Israeli elements in France sharply attacked the Gaullist embargo on arms to Israel. Their criticisms intensified as French arms sales increased to Arab countries, capped by a contract for 110 Mirages to Libya in early 1970.[58] Black African states have also criticized France for arms sales to South Africa and Portugal, but to date have had to be content with eliciting an Elysée promise that sales would be for defense purposes only and that no arms would be sold to states using them against rebel forces in Africa.[59] Besides the embargo of arms to belligerents in the Middle East and Vietnam, France has reportedly refused to let contracts with approximately twenty countries because of their insolvency, aggressive foreign policies or suspected duplicity in acting as agents for states with which Paris would not deal directly.[60]

SECURITY TIES IN WESTERN EUROPE

There are faint signs of renewed French interest in developing security ties with other West European states, but speculation has easily outdistanced the government's policy in exercising its European options. The negligible progress made in Anglo-French nuclear cooperation despite its tempting prospects is a rough index of the hesitancy of the Pompidou regime to develop closer defense ties rapidly. Greater mutual understanding between the two states, signified by Britain's entry into the Common Market, has been a necessary but by no means sufficient condition for military cooperation, especially in nuclear affairs. With Britain entering the EEC, France can presumably draw to some degree on Anglo-American defense ties to underwrite its security objectives in Europe without being forced into more formally binding relations with the United States within NATO. France's relative strategic standing would also seem to have been enhanced vis-à-vis Germany and the USSR, although it is too early to say what concrete benefits, if any, will derive from what Pompidou indirectly called a new *entente cordiale* during his appearance on BBC in May 1970.

57. Two articles by Paul Balta, Middle East correspondent for *Le Monde*, provide a revealing analysis of French thinking regarding arms sales to Arab states: "La France et le Monde Arabe: Les Réalités Economiques," I, *Revue de Défense Nationale*, May 1970, pp. 813–835; and "La France et le Monde Arabe: Les Réalités Politiques," II, *ibid.*, June 1970, pp. 924–934.

58. The Israeli case is summarized in Uri Dan, *et al.*, *De Gaulle contre Israel: Documents sur l'Embargo* (Paris: Jacques Lanzmann, 1970). The French defense, presented by Prime Minister Jacques Chaban-Delmas, is found in Comité Interministeriel pour l'Information, *La Politique de la France en Mediterranée*, February 1970.

59. *Herald Tribune*, International Edition, October 22, 1970, p. 1.

60. *Le Monde*, May 22–23, 1970, p. 32.

Specific examples of progress in French-British nuclear cooperation are difficult to find. As early as May 1969, Pompidou, during his campaign for the French presidency, floated suggestions that he would be "ready to talk to the United Kingdom about an agreement" on nuclear defense policy which would be the basis for an independent West European effort. Prime Minister Chaban-Delmas a month later echoed Pompidou's views.[61] These probes, which never materialized in concrete proposals, were consistent with de Gaulle's vague hints to the newly arrived British ambassador, Christopher Soames, in February 1969, that France and Britain might form the nucleus of a European grouping to coordinate foreign and defense policies.[62] That little has actually occurred in defense talks between the two states is suggested by the reported French (and British) reluctance to raise defense issues during the Paris summit between Prime Minister Edward Heath and President Pompidou which opened the way for Britain's entry into the Common Market.[63]

On the surface, there would appear to be compelling economic and technical arguments disposing France to favor joint efforts with the British in nuclear policy.[64] The British are far ahead in nuclear weapons development, including multiple warhead technology, penetration devices and hardening techniques. They are especially advanced in the design, manufacture, propulsion and operation of nuclear-powered submarines. France has experienced considerable difficulty making rapid headway precisely in these areas. The nuclear propulsion program got off to a false start, for example, when the French attempt to use natural uranium as a fuel proved abortive after a great deal of money and time had been spent on the project. Throughout the 1960's the nuclear program was plagued by high .and continually mounting costs and slow technological development. In the seven-year period, 1965–1971, an average of 25.5 percent of the French defense budget was devoted to nuclear weapons; approximately half of the expenditures for heavy equipment went into the nuclear program. Furthermore, to speed deployment of the French nuclear fleet and to make it more

61. Quoted in Ian Smart, *Future Conditional: The Prospect for Anglo-French Nuclear Cooperation* (London: Institute for Strategic Studies, Adelphi Paper No. 78, 1971), p. 28.

62. For commentary on the Soames affair, see André Fontaine, *Le Monde*, February 20–21, 1969; Roger Massip, "Complot contre le Marché Commun," *Revue Politique et Parlementaire*, March 1969, pp. 5–8; and extracts from the British parliamentary debates, *The Times* (London), February 25 and 26, 1969.

63. Author's interviews, Paris, May 1971, and *Herald Tribune*, International Edition, May 22–23, 1971, p. 2.

64. See Smart, *op. cit.*, for a searching analysis of the prospects of Anglo-French nuclear policy. Most of the technical and economic data included in this discussion are drawn from Smart's work. Another useful appraisal, more optimistic in forecast, is Andrew J. Pierre, "Nuclear Diplomacy: Britain, France, and America," *Foreign Affairs*, January 1970, pp. 283–301. There is also the proposal of two British MP's, Eldon Griffiths and Michael Niblock, "Anglo-French Nuclear Deterrent," *Atlantic Community Quarterly*, Summer 1970, pp. 196–209.

effective, Britain has much to offer in computer technology, intelligence and satellite systems, navigational equipment, logistics support, management techniques, and command and control data. For its part, France has made appreciable strides in missile technology where Britain is weak. This includes both long-range missiles and tactical nuclear missiles such as Pluton. The common problem facing both states is that work must begin now on planning for a new generation of weapons for the 1980's. Neither country can easily bear the technological and economic costs of this enterprise alone.

The French have an acute short-term problem of strategic vulnerability. The retarded development of a fully operational submarine-launched ballistic missile system saddles them with a highly vulnerable nuclear striking force until the middle to late 1970's. Their thirty-six operational Mirage IVA bombers (the remainder of the sixty-two Mirages is held in reserve) and the eighteen IRBM silos in Haute-Provence are relatively easy targets for Soviet strike forces. Even if the French meet their scheduled projection of three nuclear submarines by 1974-1975, they are not likely to be able to maintain one submarine always on station. Here, too, coordination with the British fleet of four boats would appear advisable. Between the two states, they could maintain as many as four ships at sea at peak periods. The greater range of British missiles and the longer operational experience of the British fleet also encourage the French to reexamine their nuclear policies in search of possible areas of cooperation.

Working out cooperative technical accords, however attractive the incentives, is easier to state than to realize. If experience is any guide, the French record in developing successful arrangements with allies in aircraft and civil nuclear energy programs offers no great encouragement.[65] There is little assurance that France would not run into compounded difficulties in the politically more sensitive area of national defense. For the immediate future the political obstacles to greater Anglo-French nuclear cooperation are formidable.

Looking only at the French side of the equation dampens optimism. Most of the already voiced antipathies to NATO integration apply. Opposition to bilateral or multilateral control arrangements that might constrict France's nuclear independence is still strong in the Pompidou Government. As recently as October 1971, Defense Minister Debré reaffirmed his hostility to any transnational controls on French armed forces, including purely European schemes. That "would be the end of France, the end of our nation, the end of our country, with its personality, its pride, and its liberty. . . ."[66] On the other hand, Debré has cited European political unity as the precondition for military integration.[67] Prospects for union remain

65. René Foch, *Europe and Technology* (Paris: Atlantic Institute, 1970).
66. *Le Monde,* October 2, 1971, p. 10.
67. Smart, *op. cit.,* p. 26.

dim. There is little reason for President Pompidou to change the view he expressed shortly before his trip to the United States in 1970, "that it's more difficult to unify seven than six, eight than seven, or ten than nine" states.[68] Recent sharp differences among the Six, and particularly between France and Germany, over monetary, trade and agricultural policy give slight evidence of growing convergence in the foreign economic policies of the EEC states.

Barriers on the British side are equally impressive. Control problems are sticky. Working outside the NATO and Nuclear Planning Group is not within the range of possibility at the moment. The Conservative government of Prime Minister Heath is intent on reconciling Britain's new commitment to Europe with continued strong support for NATO. Britain participated in the decision of most NATO states at the close of 1971 to increase their defense spending for alliance purposes by more than $1 billion. Moreover, restrictions arising out of Anglo-American nuclear accords limit what nuclear information can be passed to the French without U.S. consent. These include the 1963 sale accord on Polaris missiles and the 1955 and 1958 agreements on nuclear weapons and nuclear propulsion.

The American and British governments are also of one mind that a place must be found for Germany in any nuclear relationship between France and Britain. France, however, is not prepared to entertain proposals that might revive the possibility of increased German access to nuclear weapons. "What would become of peace," Debré has said publicly, "if in the name of Europe, Germany had access to nuclear force? That is presently to state the immediate limit of any political coordination."[69] Even if France could vault these apprehensions, closer German collaboration in nuclear affairs could not be easily reconciled with Bonn's diplomatic effort in Eastern Europe.

Finally, progress toward Anglo-French nuclear cooperation depends on the outcome of U.S.-Soviet strategic discussions. Few presently can hazard a guess whether the superpowers will be able to compromise their strategic differences and, if they do, what the effect of their growing agreement will be on European security. It remains to be seen whether sharper lines will be drawn to contain Washington's present proclivity to reduce its defense commitments in Western Europe. Until the SALT negotiations conclude, France and Britain will have incentive to hold off launching a major initiative in nuclear cooperation. The French are alternately torn between making gestures to assure the retention of the U.S. security guarantee at low strategic, political, and economic cost, and preparing for the day when the American commitment will be reduced and troops withdrawn. Yet they are reluctant to make too obvious and precipitate an adjustment out of fear of

68. *U.S. News and World Report,* March 2, 1970, p. 45.
69. Debré, "Les Principes de Notre Politique de Défense," *op. cit.,* p. 1249.

accelerating the American disengagement before an adequate European security framework can be substituted.

In the early 1970's the limits of European defense cooperation appear clearer than the opportunities for its development. It would be too much to argue that France will abandon its efforts with European allies to reconcile the competing demands for lower defense spending, maximum security, increased political influence abroad, and national independence. Rather, the French government, following a line made clear in 1968, sees little chance of reconciling these imperatives in the immediate future and is reluctant to promote innovations in its defense relations with Western allies. The Pompidou Government remains focused on strengthening its domestic political and economic base and on encouraging closer Anglo-French economic and political cooperation. It bides its time for the day when again France might attempt to dominate the world stage on questions of peace and war. De Gaulle sensed the change in his conversation with Malraux in December 1969: "What we wished—between you and me, why not give it its true name: grandeur—is finished. Oh! France can still surprise the world; but later. She is going to negotiate everything. With the Americans and even the Russians, with the Germans and the Communists. It has begun."[70]

70. Malraux, *op. cit.*, p. 41.

VIII

RELATIONS IN THE FAR EAST

The articles below by Wohlstetter and Clark investigate from different perspectives the major issue of the viability of American alliances in the vital Far Eastern area and its possible consequences for the American world position. Professor Wohlstetter is a firm proponent of the alliance between Japan and the United States as an essential element in the stability of the Far Eastern theater. He would regard any major change in the current situation as a threat to the basis of the alliance, and tends to discount the incentive of the Japanese to go nuclear, both because of its threat to the alliance and because of the practical difficulties for the Japanese in doing so.

Although, as Wohlstetter suggests, any abrupt change in American policy would be threatening to Japanese reliance upon the American commitment, the maintenance of American bases has been a grave political embarrassment to those Japanese who favor the American alliance. Moreover, although the bases are essential to the defense of our interests elsewhere in the Far East, is it likely that they will actually be needed or could be used for such purposes if needed? Even if the Chinese Communists desired to carry out an amphibious attack upon Taiwan, would not the American fleet be adequate in dealing with such a threat? If the North Koreans attacked the South again, how likely would Japan be to allow the U.S. to use bases in Japan to defend South Korea? In any event, are these dangers significant? Have not the readjustments of policies in Asia following Mr. Nixon's visit to China reduced the likelihood of a resort to force and increased the potential for non-military adjustments of conflicting policies?

419

Although our relationship with Japan is still good, the possibility of Japanese reassessment cannot be neglected. Japan might turn either to Russia or to China to seek additional support for its policies. A renewed nationalism—including an independent nuclear force—cannot be ruled out and its probability may be increased by an American posture that takes the Japanese for granted. In this respect, the remarks of a potential Japanese prime minister, Yasuhiro Nakasone, Minister of International Trade and Industry, are worth serious consideration: "What shocks us most is that the United States has become so weak that it has to shock us."

Ian Clark's article provides a vivid description of the way in which President Nixon's diplomacy has assisted in changing the structure of world politics. However, he points out that the readjustment of American policy toward China can work only as long as it does not threaten the Russian sense of the preeminence of its own links with the United States in partly-adversary, partly-cooperative negotiations, such as SALT and European security. Further evidence on China's policy is given by Jonathan Pollack in selection 32.

Is it true, as some suggest, that the new American policy toward China negates our opposition to Communist regimes? If that is suggested seriously, then why should not the same conclusion have been reached on the basis of our earlier recognition of Communist Russia? Is not the interest the United States possesses in coexisting with existing Communist regimes consistent with attempting to oppose their efforts to spread communism either directly by force, through support for "wars of national liberation," or through military/political threats?

25.

Japan's Security: Balancing after the Shocks

ALBERT WOHLSTETTER

THINGS ARE IN MOTION on the international scene, shaken loose in good part, it seems, by America's initiatives in Peking and Moscow and its actions in the field of foreign economic policy. How they will settle down is yet unclear, but the military future of Japan and what happens to its alliance with the United States are likely to be at least as important as any plausible developments in China.

Threats Are Conditional

Like most observers in or out of Japan, I believe that, in the present circumstances, there is no direct significant "threat," no plausible danger of attack on Japan, nor any effective way of coercing Japan, of inducing some unwanted political accommodation by indicating that military force just *might* be used against it. But the actualization of a latent danger depends on circumstances, and circumstances can alter. Specifically, whether an attack might be decided on or threatened by an adversary would depend among other things on what response that adversary might expect from Japan or its ally. When a serious analyst of foreign policy dismisses such potential dangers, the dismissal itself is conditional.

Take George Kennan writing some eight years ago: ". . . if American diplomacy had no greater problem than the possibility of a Soviet invasion

This is a reduced version of an article prepared for the California Arms Control and Foreign Policy Seminar. Copyright by Albert Wohlstetter.

of Japan in the conditions of 1964, a great many people could go home and go to bed."[1] Observe that Mr. Kennan said: ". . . in the conditions of 1964." These conditions included besides a security treaty and an extensive U.S. presence in Japan, a great network of common interests between Japan and the United States and a substantial, though of course not total, adversary relation between the United States and the Soviet Union. Mr. Kennan dismissed the possibility of "any Soviet military action against Japan" because he believed that such action "could not fail to produce" a conflict embroiling Moscow with the United States.

If dangers are small because they would produce a U.S. response, then if we want to keep them small, we should do nothing that would greatly diminish the plausibility of U.S. response. Mr. Kennan was clear about this: "Conditions can always change. Great military establishments have a way of remaining important for the shadows they cast. [These reflections should not suggest that] the needs of Japanese security . . . could be . . . met at this juncture without our . . . commitment."

A little history can illustrate the point. An unarmed, neutral Japan was seriously proposed after World War II. The episode brings out most neatly the fact that threats that may seem negligible when they can be countered may look menacing indeed if they cannot.

The Extreme Condition of Unarmed Neutrality

The American Secretary of State, James Byrnes, as well as the Supreme Commander for the Allied Powers (SCAP), General MacArthur, proposed to disarm and demilitarize Japan for a period of 25 years. Such a proposal rested on the belief that there was no underlying threat to Japan, that in fact if Japan were shorn of military power, there would be no threat to peace in the Far East at all; or that, if there were, the United Nations could take care of it. For the Supreme Commander, Japan was to be a "Switzerland of the Pacific"; only, unlike Switzerland, unarmed, "relying upon the advanced spirituality of the world to protect it."[2] If nothing else, the innocence of these plans, put forward by a famous American general and by a Secretary of State regarded as an originator of the cold war, should confound revisionist historians.

It is not surprising that unarmed neutrality seemed to the Japanese government a less than perfect guarantee of safety against Russian attack. The Soviet Union had declared war against Japan in August 1945, in spite of an existing neutrality pact between them. A limited incursion into Hokkaido may appear artificial today; it hardly looked so in the late 1940's. The Russians in 1945 had taken four islands off the Hokkaido coast without any prior claim to them. Stalin had suggested the division of Hokkaido and

1. "Japanese Security and American Policy," *Foreign Affairs* (October, 1964).
2. Supreme Commander for the Allied Powers, *Political Reorientation of Japan: Sept. 1945 to Sept. 1948;* U.S. GPO, 1959, II, 765; and *Mainichi*, March 3, 1949.

the Soviet representative to SCAP had proposed to move occupation forces into Hokkaido with or without the permission of the Supreme Commander. The Japanese government, quite understandably, hoped that the United States would make it clear that an attack on Japan would "embroil the Soviet Union in a conflict with the United States." Official American fears developed more slowly. General MacArthur's discussion of a "Swiss" role for Japan in March 1949 preceded by only a year or so the North Korean attack on South Korea.

Since then, a condition in which Japan was without a powerful ally or the means of self-defense has been replaced in time by one in which it received an American guarantee, and slowly began to acquire in its Self-Defense Forces the ability to defend itself against localized conventional attack, to hold for a short period during which the guarantee might have a chance to come into effect. That is the present state of affairs. It will not be substantially altered by the Fourth Defense Buildup planned to run from 1971 to 1976. The Japanese Self-Defense Forces are by design restricted both in their ability to sustain non-nuclear combat at home and even more in the range to which their strength can be projected. But this modest military force also serves as a base to be expanded. It permits Japan to take on a larger part of the burden of defending itself, if that appears called for, and if domestic constraints permit. For no serious plan for defense can be limited only to the present and immediate future. What realistic alternatives, then, does Japan have against non-nuclear and nuclear threats?

The Non-Nuclear Alternatives

One alternative to the Fourth Defense Buildup would be to greatly improve Japan's homeland defense so that it could not only resist localized aggression briefly, but so that it could hold indefinitely against "an overall aggression . . . across the entire Japanese territory" (to use a former Defense Minister's phrase). Another would be to develop a conventional force capable of defending Japan's distant interests. There is no space here to detail what these alternative forces would look like. (I have done that elsewhere.) However, even the first would mean much larger budgets, an increased proportion of the GNP going to defense, and very probably conscription. Without drastic shocks, it is hardly likely before a sixth five-year buildup, that is, before the mid-1980's. Indeed the much more modest Fourth Defense Buildup Plan, which should be well into its second year, has yet to be approved by the Diet and has been proceeding under *ad hoc* funding arrangements that defer spending on major new systems.

The generalized pronouncements in the last year or two by members of the Nixon Administration about a new role for Japan in a Pentagon of Power would seem to suggest, for the Japanese, at the very least a Japanese non-nuclear force of major dimensions, capable of defending Japanese interests far from their homeland. Indeed, some U.S. officials[3] have dropped hints in response to newsmen's questions that an increased Japanese naval presence might be called for as far off as the Indian Ocean to insure that shipping lanes for oil to Japan remain open.

There would be formidable political consequences for Japan following any substantial program of this sort. The obstacles are external as well as internal. They might include the reactions of Japan's Communist as well as non-Communist neighbors. And some of the interests defended might be at issue with Russia and China, which are nuclear powers. A greatly increased Japanese ability to project conventional strength might not merely alarm Japan's Communist neighbors and former adversaries. It would increase the risk that the Chinese or Soviet response to Japanese non-nuclear strength would be a nuclear threat, though there are in any case latent dangers of nuclear attack or coercion.

Nuclear Threats, Guarantees, and Independent Forces

Signals of American desires and pressures on Japan in the nuclear field have been even more frequent and confused than the contradictory signs about conventional military power. High level Japanese have reported remarks of Dr. Kissinger to responsible journalists that a Japanese nuclear force is inevitable, that he is indeed puzzled that Japan has not already made the decision. Newspaper accounts also cite suggestions by other American officials visiting Japan that they would not be averse to seeing Japan go nuclear in the late 1970's or early 1980's.[4] These hints have also been quickly withdrawn. Secretary Laird "firmly denied that he had ever suggested that Japan should go nuclear."[5] And Dr. Kissinger said, ". . . Japan's [alleged] nuclear aspirations were not obvious to me on this trip and it is not the policy of the United States that Japan should go nuclear."

As a non-nuclear state, Japan's security against nuclear threats depends on a nuclear guarantee. Consider briefly three alternatives for Japan's protection against nuclear threat: (a) an alliance guarantee, specifically that of the United States; (b) United Nations or "inter-adversary" guarantees; and (c) a Japanese nuclear force—that is, the abandonment of its non-nuclear status.

THE ALLIANCE GUARANTEE

Guarantees are not certain. Indeed, I would stress that no guarantee can safely sustain an unlimited amount of the battering dealt the U.S.-Japan

---

3. Melvin Laird, *U.S. News and World Report*, March 27, 1971. Both Mr. Laird and Dr. Kissinger followed these broad hints with emphatic denials. Dr. Kissinger, for example: "There will be no American pressure for Japan to expand its military role beyond . . . conventional defense of ts home islands." *Los Angeles Times*, June 13, 1972.

4. The *New York Times*, July 8 and 12, 1971.

5. The *New York Times*, July 12, 1971.

relation in the last year. Altering rivalries and power relations, the negligent, almost absentminded recent American treatment of Japan, the evident confusion of our objectives, the doctrinal muddles have tested and will continue to try the alliance.

However, if alliance guarantees are not completely certain, neither is any alternative to a guarantee. Alliance guarantees are matters of greater or lesser likelihood, not certainty. The question is only whether a guarantee against attack presents enough risks to the attacker, whether it has a large enough likelihood of being fulfilled to discourage attack. And it must do this sometimes when *all* alternatives seem bad to a prospective attacker.

The usual way of discussing guarantees—as if their worth were a yes-no matter—is quite sterile. Roughly since the late 1950's, there have been daily pronouncements that the American guarantee in Europe has become "incredible." These have been paralleled (sometimes in the same pronouncements) by statements that the danger of Russian attack on Europe has receded to insignificance because of the clear nuclear stalemate between Russia and the United States—that is to say, because the Russians believe in the U.S. guarantee.

Some of the discussion of the American guarantee in Japan seems to be following the European precedent. If so, the prospects are for a long future of simultaneous lamentations that the guarantee has become unbelievable, and sighs of relief that it is believed by prospective attackers. The American guarantee in Europe at any rate may be the oldest reliable, permanent, believed-in, incredible guarantee now floating.

It is an interesting oddity that in general the Japanese have taken the opposite course from the Europeans so far as concerns any demand to be reassured by visible hostages in the form of the presence in large numbers of American troops and American nuclear weapons. While the Europeans have been worrying about the Mansfield Amendment and any sizable reduction of American ground forces, American military personnel in the main Japanese islands—with Japanese approval—have dwindled from 260,000 in 1952 to less than 30,000 in 1972. During the 1960's, while many thousands of American nuclear weapons flowed into Europe in response to European demands, they had always been and continued to be kept off the mainland of Japan and have now been removed from Okinawa as well—in response to Japanese desires. The Japanese apparently have not felt the need for American troops as hostages—at least not in great numbers—and they have felt no need for the stationing of American nuclear weapons on their soil. This also suggests that "two key" arrangements in which American nuclear forces in the future might be stationed in Japan under joint control of the two countries are more remote as a possibility.

UNITED NATIONS OR OTHER INTER-ADVERSARY GUARANTEES

In a "New Era," it might be tempting to consider a guarantee by a supranational organization, or one of its parts. But the point of a potentially universal organization like the United Nations is precisely that it includes many states that have antagonistic interests. For Japan to depend on the concurrence of such antagonists for its nuclear protection would return it to the utopian proposals that were extant in the immediate postwar period. (Indeed these extreme proposals of the occupation period left a persistent remainder of "naked neutralism" in the opposition parties, and the disorientation following the Nixon shocks has seen a resurgence of such schemes.) However, it seems doubtful that the coming new age, at least for the next generation, will have arrived at that state of "advanced spirituality" on which the Supreme Commander at the end of World War II hoped to premise Japan's security.

A JAPANESE NUCLEAR FORCE

Proponents of the general spread of independent nuclear forces have greatly understated all the difficulties—the money costs, the length of time, and the political-military hazards—of independently developing and deploying a nuclear force capable of surviving an attack by a massive nuclear power, such as Russia. They tend also to neglect the specifics: the unique political and strategic situation likely to be critical for any given nation, such as Japan, at a particular point in history.

In addition to the difficulties faced in common by other potential nuclear powers, Japan faces peculiar obstacles connected with its particular geographic and strategic situation. Against China, many Japanese are conscious that they are far more vulnerable: as Brigadier Kenneth Hunt has pointed out, one large bomb could destroy 11 percent of their own population, but it would take something like 1,000 bombs to do that much damage to the Chinese. Against the Soviet Union, Japan would face the problem of spanning great distances to strategic targets that are mainly concentrated in the area west of the Urals. This means that Japan would have to contemplate at the outset a long-range force: ICBM's if land-based, and if sea-based, in recognition of the growing vulnerability of fixed ICBM's, something on the order of Trident. Without very long-range submarine missiles, extremely long transit times would be necessary along operationally feasible routes, some through narrow straits, to reach patrol areas within range of major Russian targets. Then only a small percentage of the force could be kept on station.

The technology available to the Super-powers at the end of this decade can easily make obsolete and vulnerable any fixed land-based force not protected by ABM. By the time the Japanese can achieve a nuclear force of genuine superpower caliber, they are likely to require a sizable submarine force carrying missiles of much longer range than even the United States has fielded so far.[6]

6. A small sea-based force that was greatly inferior in technological advance as well as size would have its problems. Recent testimony indicates that the first generation Polaris short-range ballistic missiles and the first Polaris submarines would have been

While it is true that the Japanese are less constrained economically, they may be more constrained politically than any other prospective nuclear power. These constraints are both internal and external. Whatever the origins of Japan's constitutional constraints on military force, their continuing importance in the thinking of the Japanese people and in Japanese internal politics is impressive. It is confirmed by the modest and cautious pace of Japan's successive Defense Buildup Plans. The domestic political limits that have restricted Japan to the defense of the homeland and that have ruled out long-range conventional air or sea forces and amphibious forces apply much more stringently against the development of a nuclear capability.

The external restraints on Japan becoming a nuclear power loom quite as large. It would be difficult if not impossible for Japan to develop a nuclear capability to deter aggression on its own which would not at the same time appear (however unreasonably) as a menace to its neighbors. Japan might come full circle once more to the point that it had reached in the 1940's when it seemed the source of threat in Asia rather than its object.

In brief, unlike Herman Kahn and some other Americans in as well as out of the government, most thoughtful Japanese do not regard it as nearly inevitable that Japan will become an independent military nuclear power in the foreseeable future. It would take severe shocks indeed to push Japan into an attempt to attain genuine nuclear independence in the next 10 years.

Nonetheless, severe shocks might come. If a Japanese nuclear force presently seems neither probable in the next decade nor inevitable in a longer period, that does not mean the possibility can be excluded; nor that Japan without a nuclear force of its own and without any persuasive nuclear protection by an ally might not feel compelled to make an unfavorable political accommodation with an adversary. Either eventuality would be a great misfortune. Such an accommodation by Japan, with its enormous economic weight, would have a very large effect on the distribution of power in a world that, in spite of all the sunny pronouncements, will continue to include many intense and dangerous antagonisms. A Japan that had armed itself with a substantial nuclear force would have had to overcome massive domestic oppositions; it would then be a very different Japan from the one we now know.

The problem in the spread of nuclear weapons applies not merely to Japan. In the present mood of withdrawal, there is some likelihood of our becoming indifferent to this problem too. But it would be a great mistake to underestimate the potent force for instability in the continued spread of nuclear forces to new countries. Complex and subtle arguments as well as

---

quite vulnerable to current and near-future ASW threats. For such reasons the United States did not rest with its initial technology. It went on to develop the A-2, A-3, and C-3 missiles and quieter boats. And today it plans to undertake the development and deployment of new long-range Trident I and Trident II missiles on more advanced submarines.

simple ones indicate the dangers. However, the common sense arguments are no less sound for being familiar. Even those who define American interests most narrowly—in terms simply of our safety against immediate physical attack—can be cavalier about the spread of nuclear forces because, among other things, they implicitly assume a perfect, unvarying and universal rationality in all those who possess nuclear weapons, now and henceforth. Then the multiplication of centers that can decide for nuclear war may not seem worrisome. However, both for present and future nuclear powers, one cannot exclude irrational or poorly calculated or badly informed or unauthorized acts or "accidents."

In a period of apparent swift change and disorientation, there is plenty of reason to avoid deliberately or negligently shocking the Japanese into such a momentous choice.

Shocks and Mysteries of the Changing Balance

Conditions, as Mr. Kennan said, can always change. They are changing swiftly now. The United States has embarked on a new phase in its relations with China and Russia, China has entered the United Nations, the Soviet Union is engaged in "positive diplomacy," Great Britain is entering the European Economic Community, power relations have shifted in the Indian subcontinent, the Chinese are developing and deploying a nuclear force, the Russian strategic force has been growing rapidly, both absolutely and compared to the American force, and SALT I agreements have been concluded. Quite as important are the rapid absolute and relative growth of the Japanese economy, the sharpening and often acrimonious three-cornered economic rivalry among the European bloc, Japan, and the United States (with guerrilla trade skirmishes hinting at a possible trade war unless major negotiation further liberalizes international trade), the drawing down of the American presence in Indochina, and the growth of neo-isolationist[7] sentiment in the United States.

One relevant token of that sentiment is the strategic view expressed by the recent Presidential nominee of the majority party of the United States. In his most substantial presentation of an alternative defense posture for the United States, Senator McGovern defines "general purpose forces" as "those maintained to protect the United States and its allies and interests against conventional or non-nuclear threats"; but "strategic forces," *by defi-*

7. The word "neo-isolationist" with its echoes of the 1930's can be used as a polemical epithet. According to Michael Roskin ("What 'New Isolationism'?" *Foreign Policy* 6, Spring 1972), that is its *only* point: it simply designates "whatever its user happens to oppose in foreign policy." However, this is plainly not so. It is a self-designation used by several respected foreign policy analysts, including George Kennan and Robert Tucker. I have stated elsewhere that "the term 'neo-isolationist' is Kennan's and he applies it to himself. Like him, I do not take it as a term of abuse." ("Illusions of Distance," *Foreign Affairs,* Jan. 1968.)

nition, "are maintained for the purpose of protecting against—primarily by deterring—nuclear attack against the United States."[8] Not even a ritual mention of deterring or defending against nuclear attacks on America's allies. The lacuna might very well make our allies thoughtful. Particularly so since the strategic doctrine that underlines the Senator's presentation is rapidly becoming standard academic dogma in the foreign policy establishment. Though directed by the Senator and his advisors mainly at reducing American strategic budgets, the doctrine has its origin in de Gaulle's view and in General Gallois' theoretical elaborations—which explicitly hold that nations cannot depend on allies for their nuclear protection, but must undertake self-defense.

The policy that President Nixon stated informally in Guam and later formalized, while meager in literal content, seems at first blush to form a clear contrast. It reaffirms all our commitments under treaties of alliance, asserts a continuing American interest in Asia and in particular the continuance of the American nuclear shield. True, it expresses a hope for more from allies in their own defense against conventional attack, and a disposition (confirmed by personnel reductions in Asia) to do less in the future with American manpower and to make new commitments sparingly. We will "view new commitments in the light of a careful assessment of our own national interests and those of other countries. . . ." (Would anyone suggest something else?) All this hardly seems a bold new departure, or a panicked retreat. In effect, it calls for a kind of holding action, recognizing domestic disillusion with an ambitious foreign policy, but at the same time indicating a limit (somewhat vague) to the extent of the withdrawal, and an essential continuity in commitment to allies in Asia.

What may unsettle the Japanese even more than the famous "shocks" (the specific failures to warn Prime Minister Sato either of the preparation of a Presidential summit in Peking, or of the suspension of dollar convertibility, and the imposition of a temporary import surcharge) are all signs of a possible *dis*-continuity in our commitments: (a) the elevation of such modest statements of predisposition as that made at Guam into a doctrine, "The Nixon Doctrine"—suggesting a momentous new American policy; (b) the inflated prose about a New Era that has gone along with the election campaign and the Moscow and Peking summits; (c) in particular, the portentous statements of July 1971 in Kansas City and the *Time* Man of the Year interview of January 1972, about a New Balance of Power in the World—with the inevitable overtones of *Realpolitik*, intrigue, and sudden future shifts; and (d) the swarm of contradictory signals about precisely how the United States envisages Japan's role in the New World.

As for the shocks, even in the case of the opening to Peking, it might be

8. George McGovern, "Toward A More Secure America," *A Full Employment for an America At Peace: An Alternative National Defense and Economic Posture* (Washington: McGovern for President Campaign Committee, 1972).

hard to understand the profound Japanese disturbance if the American failure seemed merely a diplomatic gaffe—a random case of absentmindedness, or the casual neglect of two decades of prior American pressures shaping Japan's stance towards Peking and Taipei on our model. If the failure were only a lapse in understanding at the highest level of the American government about the importance and the past role of American foreign policy in Japanese internal politics, the Japanese might still have to wonder why there was such a lapse; and whether our leaders would have acted any differently if they had been better informed.

The grand titles and the rhetoric suggest not continuity so much as vast change. "This is the week that changed the world," according to a toast at the Shanghai banquet. But the press conference accompanying the Shanghai communiqué painstakingly reaffirmed the President's Foreign Policy Report to the Congress that we are keeping our commitments in Asia, that even in the case of "our old friend on Taiwan, the Republic of China, our position is clear. We shall maintain our friendship, our diplomatic ties and our defense commitment." It seems that on the one hand nothing has changed, except the opening of public communications with China, and that on the other hand that act itself is expected to bring about immense shifts in alliance. Rather like the ambiguous signals in an experiment that generally means food for an apprehensive or disoriented laboratory animal but just may be followed by an electrical shock.

An American will observe the similarity of President Nixon's surprises in the foreign policy field to those he has effected in domestic politics: the sudden conversion "I am now a Keynesian"; the introduction of economic controls shortly after statements that such controls were worse than useless, and so on. Like the foreign shocks, the domestic ones suggest a highly pragmatic flair for tactical maneuver and a willingness to compromise on long run strategy, to act counter to all previously indicated predispositions. And, like the domestic shocks, the foreign ones seemed to cumulate their impact on the Presidential campaign. That applies as much to the broad statements of policy as to the concrete shocking incidents. For example, Americans are likely to receive Presidential statements about a New World Era, addressed to an audience of media executives in Kansas City and made as background to a briefing on domestic policy, as pointing mainly to the 1972 election. They will think of the words as somewhat "overblown" (as President Nixon himself has recognized in a recent self-deprecating aside) and take them in the same spirit as domestic slogans about a Second Revolution. But our allies, depending for their safety on American alliance commitments, are likely to take the words more gravely. The Japanese nervously search the Kansas City speech for precise, hidden meanings about this momentous shift in the "balance."

In one unexceptionable sense, the ambiguous phrase "balance of power" covers any situation where politically opposed sovereign states maintain their independence by military preparations to counter the threat of domination or actual military attacks. In this sense it applies to the period after World War II when a large part of the world was divided into two blocs led by the superpowers. It applies, in short, to the so-called "bipolar" world and not only to cases where military strength is distributed more widely and uniformly. In this general sense of "the balance of power," the only alternative would be an *im*balance; or a concentration of all military power in one universal authority or empire. Such military balances have their virtues compared with the alternatives realistically available. However, they are subject to all the vagaries of changes in the aims and resources of governments and all the uncertainties and fallibilities in their estimates of themselves and each other. Moreover, while they have discouraged particular wars, they do not assure peace in general. The function of such a balance of power, as Jacob Viner, Hedley Bull, and many other students of the balance have pointed out, has been to maintain the independence of states. And it sometimes accomplishes this function through the instrument of war.

Particularly so far as policy is concerned, it is easy to exaggerate the rigor in our understanding of such balances, even in their eighteenth or nineteenth century forms, to talk of changes in the relations among states by analogy with movements of great precision in which exceedingly fine adjustments have exact implications. So the distinguished historian, Herbert Butterfield, in a widely quoted statement, describes an earlier European balance of power system as a counterpart to both Newtonian astronomy and classic ballet:

All the various bodies, the greater and the lesser powers were poised against each other, exercising a kind of gravitational pull on all the rest. When one of these bodies increased its mass, therefore—when for some reason France for example had an undue accession of strength—the rest could recover an equilibrium only by regrouping themselves, like sets of ballet dancers making a necessary rectification in the distances, and producing new combinations.

As descriptive metaphor, this is inspiring, but not much help to a political-military planner. Balance of power *prescriptions* are seldom very exact. They offer little precise guidance as to the counter-moves called for by any given change in the system, or even how to measure such change. "There is nothing among civil affairs more subject to error," said Francis Bacon at the time of the first Elizabeth, "than the forming of a true and right valuation of the power and forces of an empire." Now at the time of the second Elizabeth, with the multiplication of the forms and complexities of military power, it has grown no easier.

The President has clearly had in mind a balance along the lines of older European models with military power distributed more evenly among more countries. We are shifting, he said, to a better world with "a strong healthy United States, Europe, the Soviet Union, China and Japan each balancing the other . . . an even balance." But many have been quick to point out that China is not a great power in any plain sense, Europe doesn't exist as a political-military entity, Japan has only a modest military capability. And inevitably skeptics on several continents have dug up Dr. Kissinger's doctoral thesis on the equilibrium constructed by Metternich in the nineteenth century to question its relevance at the end of the twentieth.

I would add two points: First, Dr. Kissinger in the past has himself stressed that the stability of such balances depends on the acceptance of its legitimacy by all the members of the system. It doesn't work if a revolutionary power "refuses to accept the framework of the international order of the domestic structure of other states."[9] It may be that the Chinese and the Russians accept unquestioningly the framework of the present order, but there is little evidence of that; and indeed, in the past, Dr. Kissinger has cited as examples of revolutionary powers incompatible with the stability of the international system, Napoleon, Hitler—and the Russian and Chinese Communists.[10]

Second, an analogy with nineteenth century *Realpolitik* is peculiarly ill-fitted to inspire trust in the durability of alliance commitments, even when combined with invocations to peace and old friendships. Indeed, Dr. Kissinger's eloquent account of the complex game of restoring a European continental equilibrium could hardly be more unsettling. He stresses the subtle reversals effected by the "cool calculator in Vienna," the deliberate ambiguities and deceptions used, "the threatening affirmation of Austria's good faith."[11] Austria in 1813, not only allied with France but "united to it by bonds of family," offered its good offices for the negotiation of a general peace; and ended leading a wartime alliance against its former ally.

Thus Metternich opened the campaign which was to lead to a coalition against Napoleon by offering his antagonist peace. In this manner, he took the first step in obtaining French approval for transforming the alliance into neutrality, the neutrality into mediation, and the mediation into war, all accomplished in the name of existing treaties and initially motivated by concern for the great ally.

. . . so skillful a balancing act that it was hardly noticeable that the balancer was tipping the scale; so dexterous a performance of juggling that it was not remarked that suddenly, almost imperceptibly, there was only one ball left in the air.[12]

9. Henry Kissinger, *Nuclear Weapons and Foreign Policy*, (New York: Harper & Brothers, 1957), p. 317.

10. *Ibid.*, p. 316, p. 358 and passim.

11. Henry Kissinger, *A World Restored* (New York: Grosset and Dunlap, 1957), p. 317.

12. *Ibid.*, p. 61.

With such histories echoing in the phrase, "a new balance of power," is it a wonder that Dr. Kissinger had to reassure the Japanese recently that, whatever the appearances, the United States is definitely *not* trying to "create a cold-blooded balance of power situation."[13] Or that the Japanese have applied harsh epithets like "ninja" in connection with his sudden secret visits. ("Ninja," in Japanese television melodramas, is a character skilled in concealment and deception. A ninja may be used by Samurai, but violates the Samurai code.) Machiavelli, Metternich, and Dr. Kissinger have all observed that if a statesman has to deceive, he must at least seem sincere. But then a prince ought not to quote *The Prince*. And practitioners of nineteenth century *Realpolitik* had best avoid even an implicit analogy with Metternich.

Clearing Things Up

What is Japan supposed to do in this new balancing act? Without any doubt, some Japanese have understood the United States to be saying, despite the denials, that our alliances are about to change. One of the most thoughtful, informed and sober Japanese concerned with defense and foreign policy, has interpreted the statements about the new power balance as indicating a willingness to "sacrifice some of the partnership relation with her allies in order to negotiate with ex-enemies," and sees the United States endangering friendly relations with both Europe and Japan. He writes of the need for Japan to "reinsure" existing treaty relationships, even to consider "at least hypothetically" coming under a "Soviet nuclear umbrella."[14]

On the other hand, references to Japan's role in a new "Pentagon of Power" suggest that Japan should greatly increase its military strength under the present alliance arrangement, or even that Japan should become a military nuclear power. Once again, denials may not persuade. Are they a tactical maneuver? Or evidence that we are of two minds?

There is no doubt that, if power was ever anything faintly like the sole possession of the United States and the Soviet Union, it is not so now and will not be in the future. To think of the world in multilateral terms is essential. But it can hardly be said that we have learned to think very clearly on that subject. The muddle is apparent not only in our comments on the "multipolar world," but in the designation itself. A "pole," by dictionary definition, is one of two opposite ends of a magnet or of the axis of a sphere, or one of two terminals of an electrical cell or dynamo. To talk of a "bipolarized" world or a "polarized" world, is then the same thing. And if "multi" means more than two, "multipolar" is a contradiction in terms. It suggests that in leaving "two" for "more than two," we want wistfully (or

13. *Los Angeles Times*, June 13, 1972.
14. Kiichi Saeki, "Japanese Options in the 1970's." Paper delivered in June 1972 to the Conference on Peace in Asia, Kyoto.

by sleight of hand) to hang on to our polar model. And there even seems to be something in between two and more than two. Dr. Kissinger, by way of clearing things up for the Japanese, explained what he and the President had in mind:

> Militarily speaking, there are only two powers—the United States and the Soviet Union, Kissinger said, but "economically speaking, the world is essentially multipolar. Politically speaking, it is somewhere in between." The multipolar world to which Japan belongs, he said, is the economic one.[15]

At that point, confusion may have been total.

If we are concerned to maintain the important alliance with Japan, intermittent affirmations of its importance are not enough. Among other things, we have to avoid actions and rhetoric that suggest we want Japan to fend for itself militarily and that we are moving away from commitment to the alliance. And we have much to clarify about our own role and foreign policy objectives.

15. *Los Angeles Times*, June 13, 1972.

26.

Sino-American Relations in Soviet Perspective

IAN CLARK

IT REQUIRED NO special insight to predict that the Soviet reaction to the Sino-U.S. rapprochement would not be a very favorable one: happy is the state whose rivals are beset by formidable antagonisms of their own. However, in attempting to assess the reasons why the sleeping habits of the Soviet leadership have been seriously impaired in the last few months, we would do Mr. Brezhnev and his colleagues less than justice if we attributed their insomnia to a simple capacity for deducing that, in any threesome, it is folly to constitute the minority. Soviet irritation goes deeper than this: it derives from a perception of developments which presage a profound change in the structure of the international system and which signify a calculated betrayal by the United States of the Superpower code which has emerged from the experiences of the cold war.

The immediate significance of the Nixon pilgrimage to Peking, as far as Moscow is concerned, is that the United States intends to co-opt China into a central global balance which has recently been swinging in favor of the USSR. At the very moment when the Soviet leaders have mastered the rules of the bipolar game and have started to turn the game to their own advantage, Dr. Kissinger has unilaterally decided it is time to change the rules: it is now expedient that there should be three full-time participants. This is undoubtedly the basic Soviet perception of the rationale behind the new diplomatic status which the United States has accorded to China via her admission to the UN and via the touchdown of the *Spirit of '76* at Peking

Adapted version of an article that appeared in *ORBIS*, Vol. 17, No. 2 (Summer 1973), pp. 480–492. Copyright by the Foreign Policy Research Institute.

airport. Moreoever, as regards Soviet interests, the accordance of this new status to China has been totally gratuitous.

Such an interpretation is clearly implicit in the nature of Soviet objections to the normalization of Sino-American relations. Ostensibly at least, the Soviet Union views the Sino-U.S. rapprochement within the context of the domestic and foreign policy crisis currently believed to be occurring in the USA. As a discussion on Moscow Radio put it on one occasion, "this stage is characterized by a further weakening of the USA's position and prestige in international affairs. In the confrontation with the Soviet Union, and this is the central aim of American policy, U.S. imperialism now seeks new partners; and Washington is trying to find such a partner in China. . . . What depths of crisis has American policy reached?"[1] Seen in this light, the U.S. courtship of China can only be interpreted as a move calculated to bolster the position of the USA in the international arena. An interesting analogy has been drawn by one Soviet commentator. Citing the example of the decreasing stature of the U.S. economy within the capitalist camp and the prescriptions of the American "economic Kissinger" for dealing with a situation in which "special measures are necessary," the commentator draws the conclusion that the politico-strategic doctrines of the Nixon Administration have their basis in a similar set of circumstances of having to shore up a rapidly crumbing world position.[2] Thus the basic contention of the USSR is that the timing of the American move necessarily casts doubts on the motives which have inspired it. As G. Arbatov, Director of the Institute of the USA of the Soviet Academy of Sciences expressed the point "It must be regretted that the USA has been holding back for such a long time from recognition of realities and has only now, *in circumstances which makes its position rather ambiguous,* begun taking the first steps along the path of renouncing its "cold war" policy towards the PRC."[3]

This, in simplest outline, is the raw material of the Soviet position. It now remains to amplify and to refine this interpretation. Above all it must be appreciated that, in the Soviet perception, the international structure which is emerging is still very fluid and its full implications have not been worked out. As Leonid Brezhnev pointed out in his address to the 15th Congress of Soviet Trade Unions, regarding the Sino-U.S. rapprochement, "we are in no hurry with final assessments. The future, perhaps the near future, will show how matters stand and we will then draw the appropriate practical conclusions."[4] Since, as yet, the Soviet leadership has not provided us with a definitive assessment of their interpretation of the events surrounding China's admission to the UN and the Nixon visits to Peking and Moscow,

1. Moscow Radio, August 1, 1971.
2. L. Stepanov: "Kasha Epokha i Manevry Ideologoy Imperialisma": *Miroyaya Ekonomika i Mezhdunarodnye Otnosheniya.* Apr. 1972, p. 85.
3. Tass report of *Pravda* article, Aug. 9, 1971.
4. Speech reported in *Times,* Mar. 21, 1972.

the best means of drawing out the likely elements in such an assessment is to analyze the objections which the Soviet Union has raised to the exploits of its American and Chinese rivals. These objections can, for convenience, be grouped into three categories:

1) Immediate fear of Sino-U.S. collusion in Asia;
2) Unilateral violation of the rules of the game by the U.S.;
3) Complication of the global structure to the disadvantage of the USSR.

Taken together, the analysis of these three objectives should give us a fairly accurate reflection of their perception of what has actually happened. Moreover, if we can ascertain why they are upset and how genuine is their discomfiture, we are likely to have some indication of their future response to these events.

1) Sino-American Collusion in Asia

The spectre of the Sino-U.S. collusion in Asia, which has long been a prominent theme of Soviet propaganda, has now taken on an air of unpleasant reality for Moscow. We can be fairly certain that the attention which Moscow has lavished on the Asian implications of the normalization of Sino-U.S. relations reflects their understanding that it is in Asia that the U.S. has tampered with the existing state of the Superpower balance. The manner in which they have discussed those implications also provides us with a reasonably coherent view of what they believe to be the significance of the Peking talks. On the one hand they insist that the collusion implicit in the Sino-U.S. rapprochement presents a threat to the independence of the Asian states; on the other, they describe the accommodation of U.S. and Chinese interests in Asia as part of a wider scheme directed against the USSR. The structure of the argument is revealing; in essence, it is believed in the Soviet Union that Asia is being used as a pawn in the design by which the U.S. calls China into a new structure "to redress the balance of the old."

The threat to Asia is, perhaps, their most favored image. In support of this they argue that the independence struggle of Bangladesh and the heroic efforts of the Vietnamese people were both sacrificed on the altar of Sino-U.S. accommodation. Moreover, these are but the two most overt symptoms of what is a more pervasive and nefarious campaign against the peoples of Asia. The Soviet media have therefore constantly returned to the theme of a "joint division of Asia into spheres of influence" of "secret agreements" and of collusion "spearheaded against the independent and peace-loving states."

The concrete form which this collusion will take has been a matter of debate but it is possible to distinguish two recurring versions of the future scenario. One is that in return for a recognition of China's position within Asia, China will facilitate a graceful and decorous U.S. withdrawal from the

Vietnam war and from Asia as a whole. A Soviet article which traces the evolution of Sino-American relations within the context of the Vietnam war cites both *Disengagement* by America and *Vietnamisation*—which it describes as "an official variant of that policy"—as based on the recognition of a Chinese sphere of influence and as "necessary preconditions for the normalization of American-Chinese relations."[5] What is the other side of the bargain? Firstly, China, by doing 'a deal behind the backs of the Vietnamese people' permits the U.S. to bow out of Asia. This will produce a situation in which the two powers can encircle the Soviet Union from 'positions of strength;' the basic rationale of this strategy is one in which the Chinese leaders "offer peaceful coexistence with the USA in return for a switch in the center of gravity in U.S. aggressive policy from Asia to Europe."[6]

The central theme of the second version is that an American and a Chinese presence in Asia need not be mutually exclusive. On this count much publicity is given to statements in both countries that "American and Chinese influence in Asia complement each other."[7] As in the above account, Peking will facilitate a face-saving American withdrawal from Vietnam, but in this case there will be no total withdrawal from the continent by the U.S. According to this version it is in Asia that the U.S. and China most feel the need for a joint counterpoise to Soviet influence and therefore, whereas "China used to demand United States withdrawal from Asia; now it wants the United States to play a role in the area."[8] For its part the U.S. wants China to play a similar role and to "become an accomplice in *its* Asian policy."[9]

Whichever theory has most substance in Soviet thinking, the net outcome is the same in either case: both are directed against the present position of the Soviet Union in the international arena. This is clearly brought out by another constant theme in Soviet comment on the Sino-U.S. rapprochement. They are anxious that it should not be interpreted as a sudden or unexpected development but rather as the culmination of a process of evolution which had its real beginnings with the Sino-Soviet rift and, hence, in the splitting tactics of the Peking leadership. The process was later given a boost by the border fighting between the USSR and China in 1969. These open hostilities acted as a signal to the United States that China was available as an ally at a mutually agreeable price. "When the Washington strategists received sufficient proof that the Maoists had departed from the

5. Yu. Yukhananov: "Voyna vo V'etname i Evolyutsiya Amerikano-Kitayskikh otnosheniy": *Mirovaya Ekonomika i Mezhdunarodnye Otonosheniya:* Jan. 1972, p. 50.
6. V. Pavlov: "Europe in Peking's plans": *International Affairs:* Mar. 1972, p. 17.
7. Moscow Radio, Feb. 24, 1972.
8. Moscow Radio, Feb. 28, 1972.
9. Moscow Radio, Feb. 10, 1972.

common political line of the socialist states," Moscow Radio observed, "only then did the White House decide to review its doctrine with relation to Peking."[10]

An illuminating comment on the Nixon visit to Peking is provided by the revival of Soviet interest in a system of collective security for Asia. Although the idea has never been absent from the Soviet media since it was first mooted in 1969, it is currently attaining new heights of publicity. This is not the place to enter into a discussion of what the Soviet Union does or does not mean by the concept. However, in the context of the foregoing discussion, I think we are in a position to make some legitimate suggestions as to why they should have decided to revive the notion at this particular juncture. Given the new power position of the USSR in Asia, and especially in South Asia, I see no reason for not accepting at face value Soviet professions of interest in the stability of the region and of the need to guarantee the independence and integrity of the states of Asia. However, I can also see a less disinterested reason why they should wish to do so. Let us look at some of the beneficial consequences which Asia (and the Soviet Union) would hope to derive from the institution of a system of collective security. According to Radio Moscow "it is obvious that if a system of collective security were set up in Asia it would hamper Peking's subversion in Asian countries and its deals with the United States imperialist circles at the expense of the Asian peoples."[11] On another occasion, the same station voiced the opinion that "Sino-U.S. bilateral relations are developing at the expense of the interests of the other peoples in Asia. "The Soviet Union had therefore made the proposal "in order to build a powerful barrier to stop interference by the imperialist bloc" and it was being resisted by the Chinese leaders because it could "sabotage their line for an unprincipled rapprochement with the USA."[12]

Referring back to Soviet attacks on Sino-American collusion against the peoples of Asia and the two scenarios of designs against the USSR based on the exploitation of the Asian situation by these two powers, I think we can arrive at a compelling reason why the Soviet Union should wish stability and noninterference in Asia in accordance with the formula of collective security. If it is on the basis of the weak and disordered condition of Asia that Sino-American relations are being developed, then it is manifestly in the interests of the Soviet Union to foster such conditions as will minimize the scope for China and the U.S. coming to a mutually acceptable accommodation in Asia at the expense of the USSR. In this connection, it is also as well to recall that, according to the Soviet Union, a Sino-U.S. rapprochement became a viable option for Washington in the aftermath of the border

10. Moscow Radio, Nov. 30, 1971.
11. Moscow Radio, Mar. 15, 1972.
12. Moscow Radio, Mar. 16, 1972.

fighting between China and the USSR in the spring of 1969: in June 1969 Mr. Brezhnev made his first laconic allusion to the collective security scheme.

2) Unilateral Violation of the Rules of the Game by the U.S.

For the purposes of this section, I wish to analyze at a fairly high level of abstraction, a recent episode which casts an interesting light on the Soviet perception of the significance of the changing Great Power relationships. The episode in question is the Indo-Pakistan war at the end of 1971 which was the first international event of any consequence to reflect the complex transmutations which the global system was currently experiencing. We may take as our starting point an observation made in an article published in the middle of 1971.[13] This article stated that "the Soviet-American side of the triangle unlike the other two sides, already rests upon firm foundations of mutual understanding. . . . They have developed a habit of tacit co-operation in relation to China on the Indian subcontinent." This observation was perfectly correct. If we look back at the military aid which flowed from both the U.S. and the USSR to India in the aftermath of the Sino-Indian war, I think we can see the real beginnings of this process.[14] The classic demonstration of this tacit understanding was provided in the 1965 Indo-Pakistan war when both powers acted conjointly through the UN to obtain a cease-fire before China should have an opportunity to exploit the situation. Both states were full of praise for the *constructive* role played by the other during the crisis.

Why was this scene not reenacted during the Indo-Pakistan confrontation of 1971? According to the Soviet Union, there can be no dispute as to the answer to this question. As one commentator put it "the U.S. acted at the time of the Hindustan conflict guided above all by a striving not to frighten off its future partners in the Peking negotiations."[15] In practice, this signified that the U.S. had taken it upon itself to violate unilaterally the *tacit understanding* which had underwritten Soviet and U.S. policies in the area over the last few years. We are, thus, faced with a central paradox in that what the Soviet Union considered to be an adverse change in the rules of the game was immediately followed by a dramatic shift in the balance of

13. H. Bull: "New Balance of Power in Asia and the Pacific": *Foreign Affairs*, July 1971, p. 670.

14. The Soviet Union was not averse to the US sending arms to India. It feared only that the publicizing of the fact might make it difficult to go ahead with the MIG deal recently concluded between the USSR and India. Both India and the US were sympathetic to Soviet embarrassment. See J. K. Galbraith: *Ambassador's Journal*, entry for Nov. 5, 1962. "Under instructions from the Ministry of Defense, the papers are playing down the news of the arms lift. This, I believe, is in response to a Russian request."

15. Stepanov: *op. cit.*, p. 87.

influence in this region in favor of the USSR. And it soon became apparent that this windfall came about not only in spite of, but also because of, the violation of the rules. The incipient Sino-American rapprochement, and the violation of the rules which this implied, resulted in a situation in which both powers were free to adopt a virtually *no holds barred* policy. Paradoxically, the U.S. decision that greater constraints should be placed on the Soviet Union in Asia by co-opting China into the system resulted in a state of affairs in which the USSR had a freer hand in 1971 than she had in 1965 when she cooperated with the USA within the framework of an established code of conduct. I am therefore strongly inclined to the view that if the U.S. had acted more *correctly* in 1971—if it had adopted a quasi-neutral role as in 1965 and if Dr. Kissinger had not chosen this moment to visit Peking from Pakistan—then the Soviet Union might have been constrained to press India to accept a victory which was something short of the total one actually achieved. Looked at in this perspective, the Indo-Soviet treaty and the Soviet vetoes in the UN, whatever else they signified, were also in part gesture to the U.S. that Superpower codes are not to be tampered with lightly.

3) Complication of the Global Structure to the Disadvantage of the USSR

Article no. 11 of the document on the *'Basic Principles of Relations between the USSR and the USA'* reads as follows: "The USSR and the USA make no claim for themselves and would not recognize the claims of anyone else to any special rights or advantages in world affairs." When Mr. Brezhnev signed this in Moscow recently on behalf of the Soviet Union, I believe he was being less than completely honest. It is precisely because the Nixon-Kissinger doctrine presents a challenge to the essential bipolarity of the global balance that the Soviet leaders have taken such offense at the American maneuvers. This clearly emerges from Soviet writings in the last year or so. Thus at the time of the announcement of President Nixon's proposed visit to Peking, a *Pravda* article which was given great prominence by Soviet Radio stations, carried the insistent reminder that "There are quite a few people in the USA who understand very well that much depends on the direction and course of the development of relations between the USA and the Soviet Union, both for the peoples of the two countries and for the entire international situation." In this connection, the article continues, many Americans are asking the question "of the price which might have to be paid for an understanding with China. They are asking how this understanding will influence Soviet-U.S. relations, and the prospects for a limitation of the arms race and a general détente in the world."[16]

16. Arbatov: *op. cit.*

The line that the fundamental basis of world order should still be described in terms of the bilateral relations between the Soviet Union and the USA was given an even more forthright expression in a Soviet journal issued at the time of the Nixon visit to Peking: "The implementation of men's desire for peace and progress is a truly noble task and is naturally dependent on the joint efforts of all peoples, of all states whether big or small. However, one must not fail to reckon with the importance for the international situation of the state of the relations between the Soviet Union and the U.S., the two states with the greatest economic and military might, particularly since the various aspects of relations between the USSR and the USA are closely interwoven with international issues which affect the interests not only of the Soviet and American peoples but also of other nations."[17]

It is in the fact of a challenge to this simple picture that the Soviet Union appreciates that some new state of the international system is in the process of emergence. And it is because the USA bears the major responsibility for ushering in this *brave new world* that the Soviet Union is especially bitter. The Soviet leaders are, therefore, heavily conscious of the danger which this new scheme presents to the mainstream process of détente and of the essentially anti-Soviet reasons which have inspired the U.S. to *complicate* the structure by giving China an increased role in the system. Thus, on learning of the proposed Nixon visit to China, the main thrust of the Soviet media appeared to be a frantic search for a reassurance from the USA that the *complication* would not be taken to the point where the essential primacy of the Soviet-U.S. dialogue would be lost sight of. It is from this perspective that we are to understand *Pravda's* admonition: "A dialogue on a broad range of problems has long been under way between the USA and the USSR. This dialogue is very important, but not easy, both because of the complexity of the problems and because, above all, confidence is needed for their successful solution. There can be no stronger blow at confidence than unscrupulous diplomatic maneuvers, backstage intrigues and ambiguities."[18]

Given the strong Soviet preference for the kind of system which characterized international life in the 1960's the vehemence of their attack on the Chinese doctrine of the dominance of the two *Superpowers* becomes readily intelligible. There can be no doubt that at a time when the USSR is trying to realize major political programs in Europe and Asia, it is sensitive to charges that in these settlements only Superpower interests will be respected. At the same time, as a result of the long conditioning of the bipolar cold war, the Soviet Union feels unable to discard completely the notion that there are some decisions which are so vital that they must remain in the hands of the two dominant states.

17. B. Svatlov: "USSR-USA: Possibilities and Realities": *International Affairs*, Feb. 1972, p. 15.
18. Arbatov: *op. cit.*

As a consequence of these antagonistic principles, Soviet theoreticians have found themselves in an unenviable position. At the purely doctrinal level their arguments are compatible. Thus, when they attack the concept of a multipolar international system, they do so in virtue of the fundamental ideological bipolarity—the struggle between two different socio-economic systems—which is supposedly inherent in the present world situation. Likewise, when they abuse the Chinese doctrine of the two Superpowers, they base their recriminations on the essentially non-class basis of the Chinese position. As one idealogue has put it "The *logical nature* of the struggle of the *small and medium-sized countries* against the *Superpowers* as preached by the Peking leaders proceeds from the anti-Marxist propositions of Mao Tse-tung concerning the primacy of national contradictions over class contradictions. It follows from this assertion that in today's world the motive force of social development is allegedly not the class struggle but the international struggle."[19] At this level, the two positions may be reconciled. However, at the level of practical policy, I think there is more than a trace of suspicion that the very bipolar *Superpower* doctrine which it attacks in theory, in practice forms the basis of Soviet misgivings about the merging multipolar system.

Perhaps the most revealing Soviet statement on multipolarity has been provided by L. Stepanov in an article in *Mirovaya Ekonomika i Mezhdunarodnye Otnosheniya.*[20] This article sees the socio-economic crisis in the U.S. and the political decline of America as "the main motive force of the aspiration for such a reconstruction of the world, in which the competition of two social systems gives way to the polycentric or multipolar combination of state forces." Is it only because recent developments are attempting to tamper with the ideological bipolarity of the world that Soviet commentators have displayed such open antagonism to the idea of multipolarity? I think not. The article goes on to describe as utopian any attempt to reconstruct the world while ignoring the basic laws of the epoch. If this is the case, there would be little cause for the USSR to be so perturbed by events. It is difficult to avoid the conclusion that when they denounce any attempt to modify the bipolar ideological confrontation, they are in fact attacking a much more insidious development which is rather a multipolar configuration of state entities, each impinging to an increasing degree onto the bipolar global balance.

My reasons for saying so are twofold. It is not immediately obvious why a "multipolar combination of state forces" should in any way obscure the dichotomy between the socialist and the imperialist systems. I would have thought that this fundamental contradiction was as equally valid in the context of the multipolar inter-war system from 1919–1939 as in the context of

19. Krasmya Zvezia, Oct. 14, 1971.
20. *op. cit.*

the bipolar cold war structure. If this is the case, and if the events to which the Soviet Union takes exception represent no more than a partial reversion to this kind of system, we are left with the conclusion that it is this kind of system, rather than its doctrinal implications, to which the USSR objects.

Again, looking at a particular aspect of the question, we find Stepanov telling us that "the rapprochement between Washington and Peking breathed new life into the doctrines of multipolarity and evoked a new flood of enthusiasm in their adherents."[21] As a statement of fact this is quite unexceptional: as an implicit complaint it is somewhat wide of the mark. If the objection of the USSR is to the blurring of the divisions between the two social systems, I do not see how they could object to the Sino-U.S. rapprochement. In fact, as Peking had previously all but gone over to the imperialist camp in any case (as the Soviets maintain) the rapprochement should be viewed as no more than a formalization of an existing situation and hence as a *clarification* rather than a blurring of the ideological demarcations. However, as a complaint against increasing international political pluralism, both symbolized and precipitated by the rapprochement, Stepanov's observation becomes quite intelligible: China may be the thin end of the Japanese and West European wedges.

This leads us to one final point in this section. The reluctance with which the Soviet Union views the prospect of China playing a wider role in world affairs has found consistent expression in attacks on Peking's Great Power ambitions, on her attempts to become the "world's third super-power." As one Soviet article put it, "Peking's key strategic concept is based on the idea of using all kinds of political combinations and bloc arrangements above all with the imperialist circles, to convert China into a special and independent center of power and a pole of attraction, capable of exerting a considerable, if not a decisive, influence on the development of the international situation."[22] In the name-calling which surrounded the Nixon visit to Peking, China, therefore, came in for a large measure of abuse for that very reason. And yet looking at the matter more closely, it is difficult to avoid the impression that the main thrust of Moscow's irritation has been directed against Washington rather than Peking. It is also possible to speculate as to why this should have been so: While the ambitions of Peking and her anti-Soviet animus have been to a large extent taken for granted in the USSR, it is the U.S. infringement of the bipolar rules which is the novel element in the present situation. That is to say that, looked at from the Soviet angle, Peking had no choice in the present situation but to move toward Washington; Washington had two strings to its bow and seemingly preferred the Chinese option to the furtherance of the U.S.-Soviet relationship.

21. *Ibid.*, p. 85.
22. N. Kapchenko: "Maoism's Foreign Policy Platform": *International Affairs*, Feb. 1972, p. 37.

That Washington might have had sensible reasons for doing so is not considered to be a persuasive redeeming feature in Soviet eyes.

Conclusion

States seldom base their national policies on pique and it is doubtful if the Soviet Union will prove an exception to this rule. When the dust has fully settled in the three capitals once again, I think it likely that, although the USSR may be no more enamored of the new system than before, it will appreciate the necessity of responding in a positive manner. And in this respect one consideration is likely to remain supreme: by remaining obdurate and refusing to adapt to the new rules the Soviet Union can only aggravate those very elements in the new situation which it likes least and drive the U.S. and China into even more far-reaching commitments.

Thus if any inflexible two-against-one alignment is to be avoided, there would appear to be a prima facie case for arguing that developments to date must issue in some sort of normalization of relations between the Soviet Union and China. If the Soviet Union must play the game of tripolarity (in preparation for the future game of multipolarity), it cannot afford to do so with one hand tied behind its back. In the light of a grudging Soviet acceptance of an emerging tripolar game and of the importance which this lends to Sino-Soviet relations it is possible to understand Mr. Brezhnev's reference to China in his Trade Union speech. "Official Chinese representatives tell us that relations between the USSR and the PRC should be based on the principles of peaceful coexistence. Well, if the people in Peking are now prepared for more in relations with a socialist state, we are ready to develop Soviet-Chinese relations on this basis too."[23] There are two conclusions that we can draw from these remarks. The first is that the superficially idyllic days of Sino-Soviet *fraternal cooperation* have passed forever into history. Secondly, however, we may expect that in their relations with each other, China and the Soviet Union will develop that technique of differentiating between their global and their subsystemic roles which is a salient characteristic of current Superpower relations. Thus American deeds in Vietnam have seldom, if ever, had a critical influence on either Soviet or Chinese policies towards the United States at the level of the central balance. This has been the fundamental weakness of Sino-Soviet relations in that both states have constantly transformed their subsystemic disputes into global issues: it is in this sense that the Soviet leaders appreciate that the border fighting with China in 1969 was the immediate catalyst of the present Sino-American dialogue. Paradoxically, therefore, the most likely outcome of the American infringement of Superpower conventions will be the

23. Reported in *Times*, Mar. 21, 1972.

recognition of these conventions within the context of Sino-Soviet relations. As Arbatov himself pointed out in the *Pravda* article cited above "the proposals put forward by the Soviet Union also include some whose examination demands the participation of all the Big Powers, including the PRC. The PRC's positive participation in discussing and solving these international problems would be of serious importance."

Having said this, it still remains true that the Soviet Union would like to retain a special bilateral relationship with the USA. There was certainly an indication of this in the fact that the Nixon visit to Moscow went ahead and the SALT agreement was signed despite the U.S. mining of Haiphong harbor. However this was not achieved without some conflict within the ranks of the Soviet leadership. This is clearly revealed in an article in *New Times*, reporting on the May 19, 1972 Plenum of the Central Committee, which attacked those who favored the adoption of a hard-line towards America in response to the Peking talks and the mining of Haiphong. The writer, Vadim Zaglyadin, maintains that while it is difficult at the present time to find anyone who openly opposes the principle of peaceful coexistence, "there are nonetheless people who, though declaring themselves favorable to its application, put the principle in question by some means or another. Thus it is sometimes claimed that, in reply to such or such an imperialist move, socialist countries, led by the Soviet Union, should have one unique reaction: to harden their attitude." Zaglyadin dismisses this point of view on the grounds that "the experience of past years has shown beyond a shadow of a doubt that any tendency to be guided by considerations of the moment (for emotional or other reasons) to confine oneself only to the interests of the present day while ignoring the long-term perspectives, has never led to anything good."[24] It is interesting to note that one Western commentator has seen in this public castigation of those who opposed the Nixon visit to Moscow a partial explanation for the removal of Pyotr Shelest from his position as First Secretary of the Ukrainian Central Committee.[25]

In short, one is tempted to say that a U.S. recognition of the special status of bilateral U.S.-USSR dialogues on certain mainstream issues (such as SALT, the European security conference, and Soviet-U.S. trade) is the promise which Moscow has evoked from Washington in return for Soviet compliance in the Kissinger system. And this suggests that on such issues as European security, the Soviet Union will be looking for a *constructive* attitude on the part of the U.S. Soviet-U.S. relations are therefore in uneasy equilibrium. The responsiveness of the Soviet Union to the U.S. vision of the future international system will hinge, in large measure, on how forthcoming is the U.S. attitude on such vital issues.

24. *New Times* No. 22, May 1972, p. 5.
25. Alain Jacob, in *The Times*, June 15, 1972.

IX

NATIONAL STYLE AND FOREIGN POLICY: THE MIDDLE EAST

Although Mr. Hunter's first article below (article 27) deals specifically with President Nixon's diplomacy, it permits us to explore the more general problem of national style. Mr. Nixon is an exemplar of a particular style of diplomacy, one that depends upon hard bargaining, resort to force, and reprisals for alleged infringements of American national interests. President Nixon has been accused of *machismo* and of following a gambler's strategy. Mr. Hunter asserts that Mr. Nixon views his unpredictability as an asset in managing his relations with the Communist powers. Although Mr. Hunter disapproves of that style, there is some evidence to vindicate it; the negotiated truce in Vietnam may be linked to the characteristics of President Nixon's style.

This great issue of national policy determination is more complex than it seems at first. It implies a linkage between a president's personality and the implementation of a national style of diplomacy. This linkage may not be as strong as the implication suggests. If Eisenhower had been the first postwar president, we might have had his version of the Truman doctrine or the Marshall plan. Some believe that if Adlai Stevenson had become president, he might have been indecisive and unable to act in critical situations. Yet it is doubtful that Truman, any more than Eisenhower, would have intervened in Hungary in 1956. Nor is it likely that Truman would have come to the aid of Israel or England and France during the Suez Crisis in 1956. After the experience of Korea and the political penalty it involved, Mr. Truman, if his presidency had lasted through 1954, would likely have been no more inclined to intervene in either affair or in Vietnam than was President Eisenhower. Intervention in Vietnam in 1961 was probably less the consequence of President Kennedy's activist foreign policy than of the fact that seven years had elapsed since the experience of Korea, and of the additional fact that Democrats were particularly vulnerable to the charge of appeasement. After all, President Eisenhower had set in motion the Bay of Pigs affair and Kennedy merely implemented it.

Mr. Hunter suggests that Mr. Nixon may have a self-fufilling prophesy on his hands: that if we place such emphasis on the number of missiles, the numbers may indeed become important. Yet the Chinese, and Milovan Djilas, the Yugoslav dissident, both of whom have had considerable experience with the Russians, believe that Mr. Nixon's actions are well adapted to Russian political characteristics. The article by Uri Ra'anan in chapter X on arms races suggests that Mr. Nixon comes closer to understanding Soviet strategic doctrine than do his critics. Who can forget the memorable query of Joseph Stalin at Yalta with respect to how many divisions the Pope had?

The two subsequent articles, again by Robert E. Hunter and by R. M. Burrell, (articles 28 and 29) permit us to explore the question of style within the framework of a specific case: the Middle East dilemma. They also shed additional light on the quesion of American alliance policies and the viability of its foreign policies. Both articles were written before the Egyptian expulsion of Soviet troops and at a time when Russian policy in the Middle East appeared more successful than it does today. It is by no means clear whether this decline of Soviet influence in the Mediterranean is temporary or of longer duration. However, it is precisely because of the change in the situation that the two articles have considerable interest for us.

For instance, Mr. Hunter suggests that "We can act to reduce future opportunities for the Soviet Union [to increase its presence in the Middle East] by changing our policy of arms supply to Israel. The depth of Soviet involvement in the Middle East owes at least something to the way we have expressed our support for Israel." Mr. Hunter argues that increased supplies of American weapons for Israel produce a Soviet reaction and that we can moderate Soviet influence by decreasing our armed support for Israel. But it is also possible that the Nixon administration's pursuit of exactly the opposite policy led to the recent reduction of Soviet influence. Was it the increased supply of weapons, the backing for Israel during the Syrian crisis of 1971, and other forceful actions by the Nixon administration that (in part at least) led to the Russian decision not to respond to the Egyptian request for offensive weapons, which in turn led to their demand for Russian withdrawal? I think the latter is the case.

Mr. Burrell's article notes the strong Russian interest in reopening the Suez Canal, the transfer of Soviet emphasis from Egypt to Iraq and Syria, and the fact that "the dangers of being unwittingly drawn into open conflict in the Middle East are likely to weigh more heavily" with the Russians than the "mutterings of local discontent" in Egypt. Mr. Burrell, whose analysis implicitly assumes the validity of much of Mr. Nixon's style of diplomacy, appears to me to assess the elements of the situation correctly, and his article perhaps foreshadowed the reduction of the Soviet role in Egypt.

It would be dangerous to draw the conclusion that increased pressure always works, for pressure beyond a certain point may force an over-response from a foe that feels it cannot be pushed further. However, our interest in the two pieces lies not so much in their conclusions as in their contrasting styles of analysis. Mr. Burrell pays more attention to the concrete factors of interest. Mr. Hunter here applies a framework of analysis, consistent with that in his earlier article on Mr. Nixon's diplomacy, that appears to reflect most liberal criticisms of American foreign policy. These viewpoints find further expression in the Bundy and Scoville articles on military policy in chapter X. They include a preference for a style of diplomacy that rests on the search for ideal positions, a de-emphasis of military matters, a reluctance to employ pressure in international crises, and a confidence in generalizations that largely, if not entirely, appear to leave out of account variations in the real world environment.

The Middle East also raises the question of the relative weight of the American interest in a secure and independent Israel and the American interest in a continuation of the supply of oil to the U.S., its allies in Europe, and Japan. How are these interests to be balanced and to what extent are they in conflict? The Arab nations have many alternate buyers for their oil. However, the Soviet Union, because of its huge oil reserves, is unlikely to become a major buyer for Middle East oil before the 1980's. Iran and Saudi Arabia remain dependable sources of supply regardless of American Middle East policy unless political revolutions occur in these nations.

Are there constructive steps the United States might take to facilitate a settlement of the conflict between Israel and the Arab states, or are both contending parties likely to reject imposed settlements? What is the nature of the Israel security problem? Can Israel reliably depend on guarantees from the United Nations? Consider the lack of effectiveness of that organization, and the large weight of Arab, Muslim, and allied nations voting in its bodies. Israel can hardly place reliance on guarantees by the United States and the Soviet Union.

It is generally agreed that Israel is militarily superior to the Arab states. However, suppose that Egypt had attacked first in 1967. Consider the size of Israel—it is roughly 15 miles from the Gaza strip to the pre-1967 border of Jordan—the speed and range of modern jet planes and tanks, and the likely differences in the cease-fire lines if the Arabs had been permitted to complete their mobilization and then had attacked first. This would have had perilous consequences for Israeli security.

We cannot expect Israel either to refrain from military action if its vital interests are threatened or to reach a settlement of the war without protection for its vital national interests. This creates a continual dilemma for American diplomacy. We cannot afford to alienate all the Arab states or to throw Egypt back into the hands of the Russians. On the other hand, the continued existence of Israel protects less radical regimes in Saudi Arabia and Lebanon and perhaps indirectly in Iran by confronting the more radical Arab states with a more dangerous opponent. This is fully consonant with American Mediterranian interests. A settlement of the Middle Eastern war that was mutually satisfactory would be best for American interests, but this seems most difficult to arrange. This suggests that the Middle East will remain a delicate problem for American diplomacy in the years ahead.

The question of style relates to the entire problem of policy determination. It links back to the great issues discussed in Part One, to the more specific issues of Part Two, and to the military issues of Part Three. Its linkage to the macropattern of world politics, however, is crucial.

Is the type of diplomacy that worked reasonably well in the nineteenth century—at least after the defeat of Napoleon and his revolutionary challenge—applicable only in an age in which there are five or six relatively equal nations, who dominate the international political system and whose strength is based upon conventional weapons systems? In the contemporary international system, two nations—the United States and the Soviet Union—possess military systems, both nuclear and conventional, that dwarf the military power of other states. On the other hand, significant political and economic power is possessed by a variety of other entities that are widely scattered geographically. By virtue of its size and potential, China must be taken seriously as a great power. The Japanese miracle has produced the world's third greatest economy. The nations of western Europe possess skilled populations and economic capacities, the influence of which is limited primarily by the lack of political cohesion in the Common Market. The end of colonialism has increased enormously the number of actors playing roles on the world scene. The development problems of third-world countries carry a potential for much political instability. The existence of nuclear weapons raises the spectre of catastrophe in a form significantly different from all previous history. The clash of global ideologies invests potential military defeat with enormous political consequences. The advance of modern technology, that has made the world so small, suggests that the possibility of insulating particular nations from economic, military, and ideological consequences elsewhere is enormously diminished.

If we were in a pure "balance of power" system, the exacerbation of differences between Russia and China might be consistent with American interests. The activities of the United States in at least ameliorating the tensions between those two countries suggests that the current conceptions of diplomacy may not be entirely those of an earlier age. On the other hand, the extent to which the Communist Chinese have indicated an opposition to the weakening of NATO and a concern that the United States might concede too much at SALT suggests that "balance of power" considerations are not entirely irrelevant.

In my article on "U.S. Foreign Policy in a Revolutionary Age," (in chapter VI), I argue that the effectiveness of democratic foreign policy in a bipolar age depends upon a concordance between national ideals and foreign policy. Is the world no longer bipolar in this respect? Is President Nixon correct in believing that in the long run it is the effectiveness of specific policies that counts most? Is it important to keep the Republican right-wingers in line while pursuing bold new policy initiatives such as the rapprochement with China? Or is it also important to sustain the faith of intellectuals in specific politics that apparently breach principles of conduct but that are required to maintain the role of the United States in the world?

27.

The Diplomacy of Unpredictability

ROBERT E. HUNTER

MOST AMERICANS ARE perhaps puzzled that President Nixon has laid so much emphasis on the role the Soviet Union has been playing in the current North Vietnamese offensive. To be sure, large quantities of Soviet heavy equipment have been showing up on the battlefield; but Moscow has been for many years the major supplier of war materiel to Hanoi. Why, then, the sudden and repeated indictment of Soviet actions?

There are several possible answers: the President is concerned about what would happen in South Vietnam after a military defeat; and he wants to keep Vietnam out of the November elections. But he is also con cerned about something else that most people overlook. That is his overall view of the world, and particularly of Soviet-American relations during the next few years. Since these matters of high strategy play a major role in the President's thinking, we cannot ignore them.

To begin with, it seems clear that the President's foreign policy, in general, is dominated by what he sees as two central problems: first, that the Russians have now reached a state of parity with us in the nuclear arms race; and second that the American people, along with the Congress, are more opposed to the idea of our fighting anywhere in the world, much less in Vietnam. In the President's view, strategic parity will neutralize any opportunity the United States has had to "face down" the Russians by dint of our long-enjoyed nuclear superiority; and the erosion of what is called "American will" could encourage the Russians to turn parity into a positive

Reprinted by permission from *Nation*, May 29, 1972.

instrument for advancing their power and position in the world at the expense of ours and that of our allies. Thus, on April 26, the President told the nation—in the key point of his whole speech on Vietnam:

> If one country, armed with the most modern weapons by major powers can invade another nation and succeed in conquering it, other countries will be encouraged to do the same thing—in the Mideast, in Europe, and in other international danger spots.

As the President sees it, therefore, the test in Vietnam is about issues that go far beyond the fate of Indochina, or even the elusive factor called "American honor." It is also about the future of Soviet-American relations in a world where we no longer hold the balance of strategic nuclear power. Nor is this an isolated instance of his ideas in this area. During the invasion of Cambodia, the President made a positive declaration that failure in Indochina would provoke crises elsewhere—again, in the Middle East and Europe. And much the same notion emerged during the crisis on the Indian subcontinent last year. As President Nixon later explained in his State of the World message, we had to prevent what the Administration believed were Indian designs (with Soviet backing) to dismember West Pakistan:

> Acquiescence had ominous implications for the survival of Pakistan, for the stability of many other countries in the world, and for relations among the great powers. . . . It would be dangerous to world peace if our efforts to promote a détente between the superpowers were interpreted as an opportunity for the strategic expansion of Soviet power. If we had failed to take a stand, such an interpretation could only have been encouraged, and the genuine relaxation of tensions we have been seeking could have been jeopardized.

What the Administration did in South Asia, and what it is doing in Vietnam, are thus tied together by the need it feels to keep the Soviet Union from expanding its power during a time of change in the nuclear arms race. Nor is it an idle matter. Like it or not, there *is* some connection between the state of play in the nuclear arms race and the way the Superpowers behave in their overall relations with each other. Of course, skeptics will immediately raise an objection: since both Superpowers long ago insured that a strategic nuclear war would be mutual suicide, and since all we are doing now is manipulating levels of overkill, relative superiority in weaponry means next to nothing in strategic terms. That is certainly true, but it overlooks the fact that the United States did permit the relative number of nuclear missiles on each side to become psychologically important, as one way of showing that we were in general "superior" to the Soviet Union. And because it was convenient for us to do that during the 1960's, we never got round to proclaiming that the nuclear arms race had reached a political stalemate to match the strategic stalemate that emerged as soon as both Russia and America learned they could destroy each other, come what may.

Today, therefore, the Administration is concerned that the Soviet Union will try to play this psychological game itself,* and even take new risks, at a time when it is no longer at a strategic disadvantage. Thus it is no wonder that the President is so concerned about Soviet actions in Asia, however limited. That is especially so when the American people generally want to reduce all U.S. commitments abroad, when Senator Mansfield is gaining support for his attempt to cut U.S. troops in Europe, and when Senator McGovern is promising a $32 billion cut in defense budget if he is elected President. Indeed, this popular attitude actually increases the need the President obviously feels to make the most of the weapons and positions we do have, in order to convince the Russians that they cannot gain any advantages. Ironically, the peace movement in the United States has strengthened the resolve of Administration planners who see the psychological relationship with the Soviet Union to be the keystone of the President's "full generation of peace." American "will" must be demonstrated, even if the actions we take in Vietnam are far out of proportion to anything we any longer have at stake *in Southeast Asia itself.*

For the same reasons, President Nixon goes to great lengths to demonstrate what is consciously proclaimed as his "unpredictability." This tactic came out of strategic theory in the 1950's; it means simply that, by occasionally overreacting to provocation, the Administration can prevent the Russians from calculating where we might respond to their "incursions" and where we might not. They must then be more cautious. In addition, the President's ability to carry off the invasion of Cambodia, the nuclear test at Amchitka, and building the ABM showed that he could override U.S. public opinion when an important issue was at stake (as the Administration sees it) in the U.S.-Soviet psychological game. Again, according to this logic, public opposition to these acts itself requires the President to pursue them so relentlessly, in order to prove to the Russians that he is in control and *could at some point in the future* act to counter Soviet advances.

Whatever the reader may think of this analysis so far, he must face the fact that it is typical of the arguments presented within the upper echelons of the government today, and that it strongly motivates the President's policy on Vietnam. Unfortunately, these issues are rarely debated in public, especially since Dr. Kissinger, the chief architect of the President's global strategy, is carefully sheltered from public testimony before Congress by the doctrine of "executive privilege." Yet because of the tremendous con-

---

* Of course, the Russians are still at a vast disadvantage when the number of deliverable warheads is counted—5,700 U.S. warheads vs. 2,500 Soviet warheads by mid-1972. Yet since we always played the psychological game in terms of the number of missile *launchers,* the Russians now *appear* to be ahead—and in this kind of politics appearances are everything.

centration of foreign policy decision-making within the White House, the protection of even a few officials from public questioning denies a full-scale debate on the factors that actually motivate Administration policy, rather than on just the shadows that gather about local situations existing in Vietnam, in South Asia, or elsewhere.

Even without access to the inner sanctums of the White House, however, it is possible to see a number of flaws in the President's approach. Two are most evident. First, the Administration is almost certainly exaggerating the potential influence of strategic nuclear parity on U.S.-Soviet *global* relations. Indeed, since this is a psychological problem, it can be handled in psychological ways—especially by our appearing to take the matter of parity less seriously. After all, the great cries that parity (or, indeed, Soviet superiority in numbers of land-based missiles) will change U.S.-Soviet relations come basically from sources *within* the United States. Thus the alarm could become a self-fulfilling prophecy, almost entirely because *we* invest parity with political significance. Of course, some of our European allies are also raising again the specter that we shall fail to defend them with nuclear weapons, now that parity has been reached; but, again, that is their reading of our self-image—what we project of our "will."

Parity can, however, be made to mean less politically if we simply assert that it means little; it will mean less still if we emphasize factors other than the relative number of missile launchers (such as the Soviet-American balance of deliverable nuclear warheads); and it could mean almost nothing if we are able to wrap up a far-reaching agreement with the Soviet Union on controlling the arms race. Indeed, it is hard to overemphasize the importance of the SALT talks (and President Nixon's prospective agreement in Moscow), even if the initial agreement does not go very far actually to halt the building of weapons. Almost any SALT agreement will appear to do something important, and will make possible the downgrading of nuclear weapons as factors in each Superpower's image of the other's *relative* power, as well as the image that other countries have of the relative power of the two giants.

For this reason, therefore, the President is probably more likely to achieve his objective of preventing the Russians from taking political advantage of strategic nuclear parity—and provoking "crises" in Europe and in the Middle East—by signing a SALT agreement than by emerging from Vietnam in a way that demonstrates our continuing "will." Of course, he may get both, but if he has to choose—and the mining of Haiphong harbor may yet impose that choice—he would be far better advised to get the SALT agreement rather than seek to impress the Russians with our staying power in South Asia.

A second flaw in the President's current approach relates to a further aspect of American "will." Faced with what appears to be a form of American neo-isolationism, Mr. Nixon must feel, as argued above, that he must demonstrate to Moscow that it will not be able to profit from any lack of spunk on the part of the American electorate. Yet there is a miscalculation here that goes to the heart of being "unpredictable" in order to confuse the Russians. Each time the President overreacts in a crisis situation that few Americans believe affects U.S. vital interests, he erodes still more the country's will to stand fast behind *any* vital interest beyond our shores. It might be possible, for example, to convince most Americans that our commitment to Europe is vital to us; but they are less likely to take that commitment seriously if the President also invokes the same rhetoric about a part of the world (Vietnam) that most Americans would just as soon see sink to the bottom of the sea. And the Congress, for its part, may become more truculent where, say, maintaining troops in Europe is concerned, as a way of expressing frustration over its inability to have any direct effect on Presidential policy in Vietnam.

President Nixon, like President Johnson before him, may believe that a "cut and run" withdrawal from Vietnam would erode our willingness to support other allies and other commitments, and will show our allies that we cannot be trusted. Yet it is actually more likely that they would respond to an Administration policy that showed a proper regard for what to us is important in the world and what is not. Similarly, we do nothing at all to prop up our allies' belief in our reliability when we paint ourselves into a corner, as we have repeatedly done in Vietnam, and then *fail*. Our allies, too, can read the temper of American public opinion, as weariness with Vietnam spreads to our view of the rest of the world—not because we have abandoned Vietnam but because we are still there!

It can be argued, therefore, that Russia's view of us has become a deeper concern for the President because we have tried to demonstrate our resolve in Vietnam instead of arguing, by word and deed, that Vietnam would have little effect on our willingness to meet vital commitments elsewhere. We have thus made failure mean far more than it otherwise might. This, in turn, increases the President's need to escalate the war "in order to end it," after each military defeat for the South Vietnamese army. Every time we fail to impress the Russians—as the Administration sees it—the more important it becomes to impress them on the next occasion. Regrettably, the Soviet Union could not halt the North Vietnamese invasion even if it wanted to do so; thus we give even more hostages to Hanoi's actions.

Another level of U.S.-Soviet relations in Vietnam is hardly less important. That is the effort by the Administration to get the Russians to cooperate in bringing the war to a close on terms that will enable us to demonstrate to the Russians that the President can still buttress American will and, by implication, counter Russian political gains. The paradox is obvious. Nonetheless, the tactic might succeed, provided the President could convince Moscow that it is in its interest to help the United States to disengage without a loss that would erode our image of willingness to use the power at our disposal.

The mechanism the President has been using to achieve this end is the so-called doctrine of "linkage"—the view that all parts of the U.S.-Soviet relationship are necessarily intertwined, and that what happens to it in one part of the world necessarily affects it elsewhere. According to this doctrine, an improvement in U.S.-Soviet relations in Europe can make possible better relations in other troubled areas; conversely, difficulties in Southeast Asia cause problems (as the President constantly avers) in the Middle East and Europe.

Following the doctrine of linkage, the President has played an intricate carrot-and-stick game with the Russians. If there is something Moscow wants from us (a SALT agreement, a trade agreement), then it must "behave" in South Asia and help restrain North Vietnam—certainly not back India against Pakistan or supply arms for Hanoi's current offensive. And if Moscow does not cooperate, it will not only lose the things it wants from us but it will also be provoking crises in areas that now appear more or less settled. As Mr. Nixon said to the Russians on television May 8:

> We are on the threshold of a new relationship that can serve not only the interests of our two countries but the cause of world peace. We are prepared to continue to build this relationship. The responsibility is yours if we fail to do so.

If it were true that the U.S.-Soviet relationship throughout the world is a seamless web—as it appeared to be in the early 1950's—then this tactic would be both appropriate and, perhaps, even necessary if we were to avoid a recurrence of "Berlin crises." But the world has changed significantly during the past decade or so, Indeed, the most healthy development in U.S.-Soviet relations since the Cuban missile crisis has been the separating out of each individual area of Soviet-American contention. We no longer have to see our relationship as a whole; we have managed to deal with each problem area as it appears, more or less in its own terms, without worrying that a Soviet "gain" somewhere would necessarily mean a U.S. "loss" in a competition that for some unknown reason must be seen as global. On the contrary, the two Superpowers have been able to reach basic understandings on the important problems in Europe, on managing the arms race, and on reducing the risks of Superpower confrontation in the Middle East—all despite uncertainties elsewhere, and particularly in Southeast Asia. In 1958, a Cambodian invasion would almost surely have produced a "Berlin crisis"; in 1970, the SALT talks were convened on the morrow of the invasion without the subject's even being broached by the Soviet delegates! And the same thing has now happened following the mining of Haiphong harbor. So, too, Soviet "cheating" in Egypt after the cease-fire of August 1970 had no effect at all on Soviet-American relations in Europe, or at SALT.

This healthy development is no secret, and is known to the President. He knows that he now can manage his relations with the Russians in separate parcels from place to place around the globe—that there is no real "global" relationship. But he apparently sees an advantage in specifically denying that knowledge. There is, in fact, some question whether he could deny it— asserting the doctrine of linkage between Vietnam and events in the Middle East and Europe—if Soviet-American understandings in these latter areas could indeed be seriously upset by what happens in South Vietnam. That may also seem like a paradox, but it is not. The President can try to manipulate the overall U.S.-Soviet relationship over something as intrinsically inconsequential as Vietnam (I speak here in the context of global strategy) only because he knows that our relationship with Moscow is fundamentally sound and strong in areas of the world far more important to both of us. Indeed, it has long been argued that the United States could never have risked massive involvement in Vietnam during the 1960's, had we not been confident that Berlin (for example) would not be in jeopardy because of what happened in a relative backwater in Southeast Asia.

The President's strategy, therefore, seems straightforward: by threatening to *increase* tensions with the Soviet Union (deny a SALT agreement, refuse trade, set back détente in Europe, warn of "crises" in the Middle East and elsewhere), he hopes to gain a tactical "victory" (or avert a tactical "loss") in an area of peripheral importance. He may succeed. Yet there is room to doubt that the Soviet Union will play his game in Southeast Asia, at least not to the point of actively trying to restrain North Vietnam. Not only is Moscow's influence limited in Hanoi but also there is the fact that the Russians, too, are aware of the relative stability of U.S.-Soviet relations at SALT and in Europe, and of U.S. interests in preserving the stability. They, too, can let tensions rise without worrying about the fundamental stability of East-West relations.

Furthermore, the Russians must be worried lest our current actions strengthen Chinese influence in North Vietnam—a matter of growing concern to Moscow now that it is suspicious of U.S. "collusion" with China following the President's visit. Indeed, the careful wording of President Nixon's address on May 8 may indicate the Administration's intention to promote just such a shift of influence in Hanoi to China's advantage. It is certainly true that mining Haiphong harbor is possible today without seriously disrupting our relations with China, whereas it would not have been possible to run the risk earlier. Nixon's Peking policies have helped; and so has the withdrawal of U.S. forces that could have threatened an invasion of North Vietnam—a serious concern for China.

But even if the Soviet Union does nothing in the current crisis, it is doubtful that the price we shall have to pay will be worth the gain. For example, by directly challenging Soviet actions in Vietnam for the first time, we are now requiring the Russians to back down in Southeast Asia—thus potentially calling into question *their* "will." If the Russians do see the matter that way, the upshot could be to stop immediate forward progress in a number of areas in U.S.-Soviet relations where we have some interest in seeing progress continue.

Of course, the Russians may believe that the progressive development of Soviet-American relations elsewhere in the world is more important than supporting North Vietnam at this juncture—or canceling the President's trip to Moscow. Even so, we have to calculate the long-range costs of the current challenge to the Russians, even if they do nothing now. By past experience, including the Cuban missile crisis and the Six Day War, our symbolic "victories" over the Soviet Union only increase Moscow's desire to match the United States, weapon for weapon and ship for ship. A similar situation is now shaping up. As in the Cuban missile crisis, we do have local naval superiority over the Soviet Union in the Western Pacific; the Russians cannot force their way into Haiphong harbor, and they will have to shift the focus of action to some other part of the world if they wish to respond with military instruments at all. Again, this step is one that the Russians will be reluctant to take, given the essential understandings we have already reached in Europe and elsewhere—understandings that begin with the need to avoid nuclear confrontation over unimportant matters. But in the long run we must now expect that, once again, the Russians will increase their outlays on defense, and especially on seaborne weapons that will enable them in future not to be faced with the prospect of either backing down before an American challenge, provoking crises elsewhere, or—finally—confronting the United States with strategic nuclear weapons.

The President is therefore embarked on a risky and ambitious venture in Soviet-American relations. The risks—especially for our desire to moderate the arms race—have been discussed above. But the ambitions are as great. If the United States does succeed in getting the Soviet Union to "back down" now, we shall be tempted to see Soviet power as diminished, or at least "contained." Thus there could grow further aspiration to "contain" Soviet influence elsewhere, perhaps beginning in South Asia.

Be that as it may, the achievement of this ambitious first step in Vietnam would bring with it more risks, beginning with efforts by Moscow to demonstrate its "will"—including the buildup in forces predicted above, or some other effort. It is also not clear that the Administration would be content with just one demonstration of Soviet lack of will, if the North Vietnamese invasion continued to succeed. Rather we would be apt to escalate the local conflict further—and along with it the risks to Soviet-American relations—for the purpose of again buttressing our will in Soviet eyes and not losing a tactical advantage in the "global" competition! And once again, we would be "throwing down the gauntlet" in ways that, whatever the outcome, will not promote long-range and productive U.S.-Soviet relations. Indeed, if the President conceives all this as demonstrating U.S. "will"—and helping to build a generation of peace—he has chosen a peculiar road to his goal. Far better for him to consider again the one option he has rejected —a simple withdrawal of U.S. forces from Vietnam. We would be far less likely to damage our ability to cope with Soviet power in the future by this step than we are by trying to manipulate larger risks of confrontation with the Soviet Union.

28.

In the Middle in the Middle East

ROBERT E. HUNTER

AMERICA'S MIDDLE EASTERN interests are changing because of two new facts: that the Soviet Union is now in the Middle East to stay, and that it will very likely seek to become the major outside power in the area during the next few years. It is this Superpower involvement that is the "given," the starting point for a fresh look at what U.S. policy objectives should be and how to approach them.

Israel's role in U.S. politics places real limits on the scope of permissible debate in the United States. Democrats are more sensitive than Republicans to the electoral and financial implications of all-out support for Israel. Therefore, this Administration has been better able than the last one to press for an interim settlement of the Arab-Israeli conflict. This active search for peace, which has brought more than a year without major fighting, may have to be discontinued as Americans enter an election year. That would be a pity, for an Israel-centered policy, which for too long has distorted our perspective, is no more realistic than an Arab-centered one. Playing flexible middleman, not becoming frozen into an unequivocal, partisan position, is the best American role.

The Russians Are Coming

Soviet power in Egypt, supporting a sizable naval squadron, now means that the Russians have access to facilities that help make up for their lack

Reprinted by permission from *Foreign Policy*, No. 5, Winter 1971–72, pp. 137–50.

of aircraft carriers to deploy against the U.S. Sixth Fleet. It may be that we have exaggerated this development, because of the speed with which it has taken place. So long as the Sixth Fleet remains up to strength, the Soviet squadron and naval air force based in Egypt will continue to be neutralized—with regard to the southern periphery of NATO and Yugoslavia as well as to countries in the Middle East. Even though Soviet prestige may rise in the Arab world, and there could be crises of confidence among some of our Mediterranean NATO allies, the Soviet Union is unlikely to gain the initiative through its Mediterranean naval and air strength.

By maintaining this stand-off in Mediterranean seapower, we also maintain diplomatic parity. We begin to create conditions which could eventually lead both Superpowers to lose interest in a form of competition that is self-defeating. At some point, we and the Russians ought to be able to reach at least a tacit understanding on the size and uses of fleets deployed in the Mediterranean.

In the short term, however, the Soviet buildup also serves to neutralize *our* naval presence in any Eastern Mediterranean crisis. This may prevent us in the future from brandishing the Sixth Fleet as we did in the fall of 1970 during the Jordan crisis. In fact, our use of the fleet and mobilization of units in Germany last year is helping to hasten the time when those feats cannot be repeated. President Nixon made matters worse by asserting U.S. power during his visits to the Vatican and the *U.S.S. Saratoga* in October 1970. He told the Pope (erroneously) that the Sixth Fleet is "the mightiest military force which exists in the world in any ocean." One could hardly expect the Russians passively to accept his assertion of U.S. preeminence.

Soviet conventional power in the area will also now make Washington more cautious about intervention on Israel's behalf. If war breaks out again and Israel is obviously winning, the Russians are no longer stuck with the two extremes of: (a) Do nothing—accept an Arab defeat, or (b) Escalate to confrontation with the United States outside the Mideast. Yet the growth of the Soviet presence does not change everything. The main function of that presence (with respect to Arab-Israeli conflict) seems to be defensive, not offensive. Soviet arms in Egypt have so far been concentrated mainly on denying Israel control of Egyptian skies, not on creating an Egyptian capability to cross the Canal. We are not yet faced with the prospect that Soviet-backed Arab forces could succeed in a future war with Israel.

We can act to reduce future opportunities for the Soviet Union by changing our policy of arms supply to Israel. The depth of Soviet involvement in the Middle East owes at least something to the way we have expressed our support for Israel, especially when Israel has not always acted in its own best interests or has been unable to show much concern for ours. During 1970, for example, Israel, in overreaction to Nasser's war of attrition, made air strikes in the Cairo suburbs. Through this particular use of U.S.-supplied aircraft, Israel gave the Soviet Union a compelling opportunity and diplomatic need to increase its presence in Egypt.

"Sufficiency" for Israel

The lesson for U.S. policy has long been clear. The result of letting Israel itself largely determine what weaponry we make available to it has been to help change a parochial Arab-Israeli problem into a major source of potential U.S.-Soviet conflict. This is particularly true when our arms policy entails giving Israel more weapons than it needs to defend itself, in order to maintain a "balance" of forces that is really an Israeli preponderance, especially in weapons best suited to offensive use.

In addition, the widespread practice in the United States of instant and uncritical rallying to Israel's defense whenever there is a crisis is no longer necessarily in our interest, nor even that of Israel, however deeply we remain committed to its future. We certainly can no longer accept at face value the argument that supporting Israel and opposing the Soviet Union are one and the same thing.

The Russians' increased naval and military involvement now mean that they are less able to stay aloof in a new war, but it is not clear that the Soviet Union would gain very much from an Arab victory. The defeat of Israel would greatly lessen Arab concern for Soviet support. And unless the Russians have no sense of Middle East history, they are aware that the sands of Arab gratitude are no foundation on which to erect a structure of presence and influence.

Nevertheless, the United States does need sufficient forces in the area to impress upon the Russians that any major military act by the Arabs against Israel would entail risks of Superpower confrontation. These should *not* include U.S. ground troops, for that kind of deployment robs us of a significant diplomatic asset: a relatively unstructured, ambiguous presence that does not impose cold war rigidities on the Middle East. The Sixth Fleet does not have the political handicaps of land forces, which would lose the United States what value there is in the Arab world in not committing troops to Israel. Also, the Sixth Fleet's airpower could be decisive in any Arab-Israeli war that the Russians did not enter with massive ground forces, and it could give a good account of itself even against substantial Soviet involvement. This U.S. airpower helps deny flexibility to the Russians, even though, despite dilemmas for both Superpowers, in a new war political and military encounters between them could take place locally, rather than in some other part of the globe.

Since June 1967, the two Superpowers have each shown awareness that they need to keep out of trouble with each other in the Middle East. This awareness derives mainly from shared experience in coping with unsettling events in the area. It also represents a further elaboration of a paradox of risk: that the onset of mutual deterrence has led both Moscow and Washington to take fewer risks that could lead to confrontation, not more risks as some strategists predicted a decade ago.

In the process, the Superpowers are now far better able than before to deal with each area of contention on its own merits. The end of cold war psychology is partly responsible: deterrence is no longer seen to be indivisible. In addition, the shared desire to preserve regional stalemates when they appear—beginning in Europe—will decrease the value to either Superpower of trying to offset a "loss" in one area with a "gain" in another, just as each stalemate will increase the incentives both Moscow and Washington have to see tensions in their relations reduced locally and generally.

In the last few years, for example, problems in the Middle East have remained almost entirely separate from Berlin, from the SALT talks, and from Southeast Asia. This has been so despite declarations of linkage made by the Nixon Administration on several occasions, most notably following the invasion of Cambodia. In the Arab-Israeli conflict, these developments indicate that the Soviet Union, as well as the United States, has much to gain from a continuation of today's relative peace. It may profit from a level of Arab-Israeli tension that is higher than would be acceptable to the United States. But the difference is more of degree than of kind. This really means that the United States is saddled with taking the initiative in keeping the cease-fire going and in prodding the belligerents toward the peace table.

The Moscow-Cairo Treaty

How firmly the Soviet Union now supports peace efforts is another question. It will be unlikely to join our efforts actively unless they appear either about to fail and bring on war, or succeed in securing an interim settlement, thereby conferring diplomatic kudos on us in the eyes of the Arabs. Short of these two extremes, the Soviet Union will want to exercise control over the pace of any forward progress (though this could include some tacit collusion with us on limiting the supply of arms to both sides or on "quarantining" both Superpowers from the consequences of local conflict). And it will probably not support efforts to secure a more lasting settlement of the Arab-Israeli conflict—if ever—until it feels sufficiently confident that it will be able to stay in Egypt on acceptable terms. Indeed, this may prove to be the real significance of the Moscow-Cairo Treaty of May 1971—not a promise of Soviet aid in a war against Israel or of appreciably more Soviet influence over Egyptian internal affairs, but rather a psychological reassurance that the Soviet Union will continue to be a force to be reckoned with in Egypt, come what may.

This treaty gives Egypt added diplomatic backing. And in the short run, at least, this backing could actually *reduce* the pressures on the Egyptians to resort to open conflict, while increasing Moscow's ability to exercise some restraint, even if Cairo's verbal expressions of hostility to Israel increase.

The Moscow-Cairo Treaty could thus prove to be a move away from war. It could also help to limit Soviet influence in Egyptian internal politics through the very act of confirming such influence. This interpretation is supported by the role that President Anwar Sadat is coming to play in Arab politics—or better, the role that he is *not* playing. President Nasser, too, was ambivalent about Soviet influence in Egypt; and he had clearly seen the benefit of returning to the situation that obtained on the Israeli front from 1956–1967. During that period, he was restrained from acting by the presence of the United Nations Emergency Force and the world's collective moral pressures against war—such as they were. Nasser therefore had a ready-made counter to Arab charges that he was not doing his share to fulfill the Arab destiny in Palestine, and less need to seek outside military and diplomatic backing.

Under the right conditions, Sadat could accomplish what his predecessor didn't in the months before his death, simply because he is *not* Nasser. So far, Sadat's brother Arabs do not have to fear that his ambitions will stretch the whole length of the Arab world. They have less reason to taunt the Egyptian President for inactivity against Israel, as a way of cutting him down to size. Sadat, therefore, could be more flexible in dealing with Israel The Egyptians are now less compelled to make the entire "Arab cause" their own; they can make interim agreements covering issues like the Suez Canal, even if a separate peace is not yet possible.

But there is one critical ingredient missing here. In order for real changes to take place in Egyptian attitudes, there also has to be progressive movement on the local diplomatic front. It is not enough for us to help preserve the cease-fire and encourage talks. If we want to see Sadat gain more flexibility that will help limit Soviet influence, there also has to be momentum toward a partial settlement that includes Israel's withdrawal from Sinai. Various limited schemes supported by the United States, such as those for the opening of the Suez Canal, are therefore valuable devices, provided they move just fast enough to keep anxiety in Cairo down to a level that forestalls it from seeking more Soviet military supplies or going beyond its verbal commitment to a violent solution.

Moving Israel

The real key to action lies elsewhere: in convincing Israel that going in this direction, carefully but systematically, is the most likely way to preserve its own long range security and produce the necessary guarantees. These guarantees have been variously described in terms of Israel's own strength, the geographic position it retains, or firmly-based peace forces from outside. At first glance, too, there appears to be some merit in Senator Fulbright's suggestion of a formal U.S. treaty with Israel. In theory, it would provide psychological reassurance. It might help marginally to create a greater sense of reciprocal obligation on the part of Israel. It might permit greater sophistication in U.S. debate and decrease pressures to meet each Israeli demand for support. And a formal treaty—ideally coupled with other guarantees, including a peacekeeping force—would also be better than simply making Israel strong enough to do without U.S. support. That latter policy of meeting each new Israeli arms request has failed, for it provides opportunities for the Soviet Union without reducing our ultimate responsibility for Israels' defense.

A closer look, however, makes a treaty with Israel seem less appealing. In the first place, it is doubtful that Israel would be sufficiently reassured by a formal treaty. It is also doubtful that Israel would give us a pledge to move toward a careful but deliberate withdrawal from the Sinai desert. There is not likely to be a consensus for flexibility in Israel until after the retirement of the present Premier, Mrs. Golda Meir.

Furthermore, a U.S. treaty with Israel would only drive several of the Arab states closer to the Soviet Union and limit our ability to deal with them. We would, in effect, destroy whatever ambiguity can be seen today in our relations with Tel Aviv, at the risk of not gaining a more flexible Israeli attitude on the Sinai desert. Far better, therefore, to continue making clear our commitment to Israel's security, while seeking to move Israel on the issue of Sinai.

To those Arabs who care to listen, we should stress our desire for a steadfast adherence to all the elements of UN Security Council Resolution 242 of November 1967, which is the most comprehensive and balanced view of the Arab-Israeli crisis that has been enshrined in international principle during the entire half-century of conflict. We should also take more seriously the problem of the Arab refugees, voicing support for a "just" settlement and contributing more economic and humanitarian aid. In general, Arab states are less likely to be concerned with our having a continuing involvement with Tel Aviv that includes responsibility for its ultimate defense than with our failure to demonstrate some restraint in arms supplies, and to support Arab claims as well as Israel's. In the past, this policy of "even-handedness" has been stymied either by new crises in Arab-Israeli relations, by infusions of Soviet arms, or by insufficient awareness in the United States that symbols often count for as much as substance in Arab politics. Even-handedness has not really been practiced since the Kennedy Administration.

Even if the United States follows each of these prescriptions, we need to be aware of the upper limits to our actions. A lasting settlement of the Arab-Israeli conflict will not come soon, and will require at least one change of generations just to become a live possibility. Any real change in Egyptian-Israeli diplomacy will be the product chiefly of efforts by the local powers themselves. No outside intervention can be an effective substitute; there will be no imposed peace. And there is no "one-shot" solution or "package deal" that can succeed in creating the political habits of forbearance that must underpin any settlement, partial or lasting. We would be wise *not* to prescribe the actual details of a partial settlement, or to offer "American plans" for the status of Jerusalem or of a Palestinian state. We have much to gain from the deeper involvement of others in peace efforts, including the UN's Ambassador Jarring, Britain, and France.

Confirming the Soviet Presence

In the short term, more diplomatic pressure on Israel, more even-handed flexibility toward the Arabs, and maintenance of U.S. naval power in the area should help us check the Soviet presence in the Mideast. But in the longer term, the United States will find itself in the difficult position of having to help confirm that presence, as perhaps the only way of limiting it. If the Soviet Union were secure in its legitimacy as a major outside power in the Middle East, it could develop a great sense of shared responsibility for stability in the region and feel less need to secure its position with force deployments—deployments that have their own expansionist momentum.

The U.S. government has been aware of this issue for some time, despite lapses, such as the ill-considered White House statement in the summer of 1970 that Soviet forces should be "expelled" from Egypt.

We found ourselves working with the Russians at the United Nations during the Six Day War, and even receiving over the Moscow-Washington "Hot-Line," a mixture of Soviet bluster and backdown. By April 1969, talks between Moscow and Washington had formally opened, along with four-power talks at the United Nations. Since then, the Russians have played a role—from time to time—in various U.S. peace plans and efforts to arrange cease-fires. This diplomatic history adds up to a recognition in Washington that the Soviet Union is legitimately and necessarily involved in just about everything that happens in the Arab-Israeli conflict.

The challenge however, does not lie in ratifying the Soviet presence, or even in resisting the temptation to apply a military approach to a latter-day policy of containment. It lies rather in trying to shift the emphasis of Soviet policy away from the military realm and, if possible, toward that of economics. Today this is mere wishfulness; tomorrow it may not be. First, the Moscow-Cairo Treaty is heavily devoted to economic cooperation, which is itself an important signal that the Soviet Union will continue to be involved in the Egyptian economy. Second, the high cost of today's Soviet presence could begin to generate pressures in Moscow for a cheaper means of securing whatever benefits, other than basing facilities, the Russians expect to gain in the Arab states. Third and most important, clearly-perceived risks of confrontation increase the Superpowers' mutual incentive to play down military aspects of involvement. An alternative is greater participation in commercial ventures and the economic development of the region.

Whether the Russians will see and seize the possibility of substituting economic relations for expanded military involvements is far from clear. They are just beginning to understand, from their Middle East experience, that deploying military forces far beyond their borders entails grave liabilities. The local states themselves may be the best hope for leading the Soviet Union toward an emphasis on economic involvement rather than on increasing military presence. For those Arab states that still have a lingering concern with Western "imperialism," there is a useful antidote in closer economic and political ties with the Soviet Union, with East European states anxious to have sources of oil independent of the Soviet Union, and even with China. This would not mean a complete loss of Western influence. Soviet heavy-handedness in several Arab states is already breeding an awareness that "imperialism" of the East as well as the West threatens national independence. The lesson of Egypt's dilemma with Soviet forces is not lost on other Arab states. For them, there is an advantage in playing off one outside power against another for commercial gain and help with economic development, much as Nasser once tried to do. And there is an advantage for Americans in committing some of the necessary skills and resources, though preferably through international agencies like the World Bank which minimize our political exposure yet at the same time permit the Arabs to be less dependent on the Soviet Union.

Efforts in this direction could reduce fears that one Superpower or the other would "dominate" individual countries or that there would be a "polarization" of the states in the area—a development feared in Moscow as well as in Washington. Greater involvement by the European Community and Japan in technical assistance and investment could help blur Superpower competition. Indeed, it would ease the American burden if several Middle Eastern states became associate members of the European Economic Community.

The United States and the Arab World

The West will be better able to retain its position in the competition for influence in the Middle East if the United States is able to maintain good relations with at least a few Arab states. Our continuing diplomatic efforts in the Arab-Israeli conflict remain the key to tapping this potential. But the United States also needs to look more closely at the pattern of its existing friendships in the Arab world, and at its attitudes towards Middle Eastern nationalism.

There are, in all likelihood, a number of regimes that will undergo radical internal change in the next few years: these could include Saudi Arabia, the Trucial Sheikhdoms, and Kuwait. Jordan's future is also uncertain, because of its Palestinian majority, whatever the present disarray of that group. When regimes change, it will be of some significance to us which direction the new holders of power take. It would be prudent for U.S. policy to concentrate less on political relations with particular regimes and more on commercial relations and development assistance. We may discover that it is better to have "correct" relations based on shared economic interest with revolutionary regimes, such as Algeria and Libya, than to overextend ourselves politically with more traditional, less popularly based Arab regimes.

Another trend emerging in the Middle East was reflected in the February, 1971 negotiations at Tehran with the Organization of Petroleum Exporting Countries. The United States government put its weight behind the efforts of the oil companies, to the extent of sending the Under Secretary of State to remonstrate with local governments which wanted (and succeeded in getting) a major hike in oil revenues. Our tactics at Tehran will likely prejudice our long-term political and commercial relations with several Arab governments and with Iran. It appears that outside control of energy resources in the Middle East is rapidly approaching its end. The big questions now are "when," "how," and, more importantly, which outsiders will be tapped for roles in management and marketing after the change in ownership takes place. We cannot hope to maintain our direct commercial interest in Middle East oil on present terms. Rather we should direct our attention to preserving the broader long-term strategic interest in the flow of Middle East oil to Europe and Japan, whose economies depend on it. This is not to say we should fear that the Soviet Union is a likely candidate, for commercial or political reasons, to succeed Western firms. But we do need to have greater sensitivity to rising economic nationalism in the area, because of its overall impact on the character of U.S.-Soviet competition there.

The Middle East as a Soviet Base

Finally, we have to face the emergence in the near future of a greater Soviet ability to project power from the Middle East to nearby areas: East Africa and elsewhere on the shores of the Indian Ocean. Moscow may come to see its bases in Egypt as useful not only to neutralize the Sixth Fleet, but also as a possible springboard for wider ambitions south and east of Suez. The Russians seem set on achieving at least parity with the United States in naval forces, not just in the Mediterranean but in many other parts of the world as well. Nevertheless, until the Russians are led to see that "gun-boat diplomacy" is a far more limited instrument than it was even a decade ago, there is no reason for the United States to follow the Soviet lead in military ventures, beyond maintaining our ability to offset and balance Soviet naval presences wherever they appear.

In time, the Soviet Union may be willing to join us in an agreement to leave the Persian Gulf alone now that Britain is gone, accepting preeminence there by Iran. Chairman Brezhnev did suggest, in a speech on June 11, 1971, that there be a mutual limitation of naval forces in the Indian Ocean and Mediterranean Sea. Whether this idea was meant seriously or not, our active consideration of it could be part of developing a broader set of U.S.-Soviet understandings about the character (and limits) of each others' activities in the entire area beginning in the Eastern Mediterranean. It could lead eventually toward a sharing of influence, a tolerance of the involvements of both parties within the same countries and in different countries of a region which, unlike Europe, has no simple strategic unity.

This sharing of influence in the Middle East presents a most difficult challenge. Even though it has begun to occur in places like Iran and India, the Superpowers so far have not managed it on a systematic basis. And it has not occurred where either power has had a large military stake. Before much progress can be made in conceiving and carrying out such a policy, there will have to be a better and wider understanding of how basic Russian and American interests in the Middle East relate to one another. And, in this country, there will have to be a more rational level of public debate, enabling us to see the Soviet role in the area in better perspective.

The demands of "power sharing" on the Soviet Union will be at least as great, and it is hard to imagine them winning instant or easy acceptance by Moscow. Yet in the pragmatic process of learning to share presence and influence, both Superpowers may gain new points of vantage on the Middle East. Both have an interest in lessening the military importance which is now attributed to the area, and the risks of their coming into open, violent confrontation. With the best of intelligence and luck, neither nation will be able to secure all of the objectives it seeks. It is time for the two outside antagonists to focus on a more human concern that both can contribute to: the economic development of the Middle East.

29.

Opportunity Knocks for the Kremlin's Drive East

R. M. BURRELL

THE PLENTIFUL AND SOMEWHAT euphoric press comments which have sur-rounded President Nixon's recent visit to Moscow have concentrated, by and large, on the issue of atomic arms limitation without making the com-plementary and vital point that as strategic nuclear arms come under a self-imposed ban then the role of conventional military forces takes on an added importance. In Europe it is well known that the balance of con-ventional forces is heavily in Moscow's favor. By means of treaties signed with Egypt and India—and very recently with Iraq—the Soviet Union has increased the area over which its military protection extends, and has thereby provided itself with greater opportunities for the exer-cise of political influence.

It would be erroneous to assume that Russian interests had not been carefully calculated in all three cases and these treaties are doubtless re-garded as important by the Kremlin, irrespective of the adverse views of some western commentators on the present-day value of such agreements. In all three cases the Soviet Union has gained positive military advantages as well as an increase in political prestige. The two Middle Eastern agree-ments are of particular importance in this respect and attention here will be focused on them rather than on the Indian example.

The Egyptian treaty of May 27, 1971 was treated by many writers as an *ad hoc* and hasty piece of diplomatic repair-work by Moscow, for it fol-lowed very quickly after President Sadat's thorough purge of Egyptian

Reprinted by permission from *New Middle East*, No. 46, July 1972, pp. 9–13.

471

politicians and civil servants. In this political upheaval many of the Egyptians who were regarded as pro-Soviet lost power, and it was felt that President Podgorny's rapidly-arranged visit was made in order to try and stem the tide of apparent anti-Russian feeling. In fact, President Sadat's purge was prompted by internal Egyptian factors, and although his actions had international implications these were minimal in comparison. What the Russian leaders wanted was a black and white statement which acknowledged Egyptian dependence on Soviet assistance and so made more secure the degree of political influence exercised by the Kremlin. The Russians had been pressing for this since Kosygin's visit to Cairo for the funeral of President Nasser in September 1970 and although the timing of the treaty with Egypt might indeed have been brought forward by President Sadat's political activities the diplomatic maneuvering which lay behind it was much older in its origins.

The treaty served to formalize Egypt's dependence, and in its wider implications the document most certainly presages an extension of Russian military power in the area. The provision of naval facilities at Alexandria and Mersa Matruh has enabled the Russian fleet to increase the number of its ships in the Mediterranean without placing a strain on the limited resources available for replenishment at sea. These additions to, and regular replacements for, the Soviet fleet have exercised mainly in the Eastern Mediterranean. One major reason for this restriction has been the lack of sustainable Soviet air cover for operations in the Western Mediterranean. Had Moscow gained air-landing rights on the island of Malta, these limitations would have been immediately removed. Air bases have, however, been constructed around and to the south of Aswan, and Soviet pilots fly regular missions from them.

Reopening the Canal

The many military advantages gained by the Soviet Union as a result of this treaty would, of course, be greatly increased if the Suez Canal were to be reopened. At the moment Moscow maintains a naval presence of around 25 ships in the Indian Ocean. The expense of maintaining these ships in that ocean is made very great by the need to deploy them from their Black Sea home ports via the Cape of Good Hope. If the Canal were to be made available for the passage of Soviet ships the number of vessels maintained in the Indian Ocean would increase sharply even if the same number of ships were used as at present because the rotation period for vessels proceeding on station would be greatly reduced.

This shortened length of passage would also give the Soviet navy greater flexibility for it would then be able to summon additional vessels more rapidly from its Mediterranean fleet. It is perhaps worth pointing out here that the USA would not enjoy similar advantages, for the largest vessels in the American Sixth Fleet—aircraft carriers of the *Forrestal* class—are too deep in draught and too great in length to make the passage via the Canal. Russian interest in Egypt is therefore based, at least partially, upon Indian Ocean considerations as well as upon those which reflect her more immediate Mediterranean objectives. The prospect of a reopened Suez Canal is also one of the factors which prompts continued Russian interest in events at the southern end of the Red Sea—particularly in Aden and the South Yemen.

The treaty with Egypt has therefore given the Soviet Union many military and geopolitical advantages. The cost, however, has been considerable. In terms of weapons and military equipment alone, Egypt has received over $3 billion of Soviet supplies since 1967 and although some complaints have been heard from Cairo about the quality of the material much of the Russian equipment has been of very modern design. In return, Egypt has little of economic value to offer the Soviet Union. Some cotton has been sold but Egypt can never hope to pay anything like the full value of the arms supplied. The political price must also be considered in any analysis of Soviet policies. It is true that mutterings of local discontent are unlikely to cause much disquiet to the Kremlin's military planners but the dangers of being unwittingly drawn into open conflict in the Middle East are likely to weigh more heavily with them.

A Firm Commitment

On the other side, the Egyptian leadership has recently tried to secure even closer ties with the Soviet Union. President Sadat's visit to Moscow at the end of April in advance of the summit conference was made to try and secure a firm commitment of support and to try and prevent the emergence of any American-Russian rapprochement over the Middle East.

This Soviet realization of the potential dangers involved in an exclusive and too-close association with Egypt is one of the factors which has prompted a notable change in the direction and conduct of Russian foreign policy in the Middle East over the last five months. In February Husain al Takriti, the Deputy President of Iraq's Revolutionary Command Council and Deputy Secretary of the Arab Ba'ath Socialist Party paid a visit to Moscow, and Kosygin took that opportunity to express the view that a strong strategic alliance between Iraq and the USSR would be in the interests of both countries. What the Soviet Union needed was a second foothold in the Arab world—one which would be free of the constant danger of confrontation with Israel. The geographical position of Iraq had, however, other great benefits to add to its lack of contiguity with Israel. There was the fact that Iraq lay to the south of Turkey and Iran, and that pressure could therefore be exercised on these two pro-Western powers by a pro-Soviet regime in Baghdad. There was also the supreme geopolitical advantage that Iraq had immediate access to the Persian Gulf and so to the Indian Ocean.

The origins of the Russian quest for a port on the Persian Gulf can perhaps be found in the territorial ambitions of Peter the Great. But in the secret protocols which emerged from the Ribbentrop-Molotov talks of 1939 the Soviet government expressed a desire for an area of influence to extend south of Batum and Baku in the general direction of the Persian Gulf. This desire remained unvoiced for a time after the end of the Second World War for the Gulf was recognized to be an area of predominant British influence and any Soviet claim was likely to provoke a stern response from London. When, however, in January 1968 the British government stated its new policy of withdrawal from the Persian Gulf, Moscow was quick to seize its chance and began in March of that year a series of naval visits to the area—one which had previously been more or less closed for this sort of activity. Just as the British departure from the Gulf was closely linked with the general decision to withdraw from other positions east of Suez, so the Soviet decision to seek greater involvement in the Persian Gulf is part of a wider Russian Indian Ocean strategy.

Between March 1968 and March 1972 ships of the Russian navy had made six visits to the Persian Gulf but no permanent facilities had been obtained. The USA had had a small naval presence in the Gulf since the late 1940's but when the British withdrawal was completed in November 1971 Washington had to renegotiate its military agreement with the Sheikh of Bahrain for previously the U.S. ships had used British facilities. There was much hostile political feeling in the Gulf at the time of these U.S.-Bahrain negotiations owing to a suspicion that America was preparing to step into British shoes. Under these circumstances a Russian naval presence could be described—if not justified—as a legitimate response to these new Western encroachments. If the British presence was to be replaced by an unwanted American one, then Soviet intervention could be seen, and publicized, as a defence of "true Arab interests." The American action gave Moscow a convenient propaganda cover for the implementation of a long-sought objective—the creation of a regular naval calling port on the Persian Gulf. By describing the granting of facilities to the Russian fleet as a response to, and check upon, western imperialism the true expansionist nature of Soviet intentions could be concealed.

From Moscow's Vantage Point

A treaty with Iraq had, therefore, many geopolitical advantages when seen from Moscow's point of view. Local circumstances in the Middle East also combined to increase the appeal of such an agreement when seen from Baghdad. Politically, the Ba'athist regime was isolated. Libya, Egypt, and Syria were allied to a very loose federation but had no desire to admit Iraq as a fourth wheel to an already ramshackle vehicle. King Hussein was, with some justification, wary of Iraqi plots against his regime. Saudi Arabia was suspicious of Baghdad's avowedly revolutionary role in the Gulf and in southern Arabia. The Shah of Iran saw the Ba'ath regime as envious of his prestige in the Gulf and still smarting from its inability to act when Iranian armed forces took control of the three islands of Abu Musa and the two Tumbs in November 1971. The government of Kuwait knew that its border dispute with Iraq was still unsettled. From Baghdad's standpoint, therefore, involvement with a great power might ensure greater respect, if not security, for the regime.

The economic advantages of closer ties with Iraq had already been recognized by the Soviet Union. In December 1961, under the provisions of Law Number 80, Baghdad had compelled the Iraq Petroleum Company (IPC), whose major partners are British Petroleum, Shell Petroleum, *Compagnie Francaise des Petroles,* and Mobil and Standard Oil of New Jersey, to surrender over 99% of the concession area which it then held. This left IPC in possession only of the areas where wells were actually in production. Although negotiations for compensation were prolonged no agreement was ever ratified and in 1967 exclusive rights to the expropriated areas were made over by the Baghdad government to the Iraq National Oil Company (INOC). In 1969 the Soviet Union reached an agreement with INOC for the development of the north Rumaila region. This field, situated in southern Iraq, had already been explored and drilled by IPC and was known to be a rich source of oil.

As much of the expensive preliminary work had already been done, the development of the field was much cheaper than would otherwise have been the case and the total cost to the Soviet Union, including an 80-mile pipeline to the Persian Gulf port of Fao, was less than £80 million. Much publicity was given to the scheme and it ranked, in propaganda terms, with Russia's two other great Arab prestige projects—the dam at Aswan and that on the Euphrates river in Syria. On March 20 of this year INOC signed a further agreement with Moscow to begin the export of north Rumaila oil to Russia on April 7. Initial annual output will probably be of the order of 5 million tons but by 1975 production could well reach the 20-25 million ton level.

The question as to what extent the Soviet Union needs imported oil is one on which expert opinion is far from unanimous. The level of discovered oil reserves in the Soviet Union is a figure at which only guesses can be made, but it probably does not exceed 12% of the global total. The bulk of these reserves lie in Siberia in the area around and to the south of Tyumen. The exploitation of these fields will certainly be expensive and will be a matter of decades rather than of years. In the meantime Soviet oil consumption will go on growing and is likely to be of the order of 600 million tons by 1980. This weekly-quoted figure has been based on the assumption that the Soviet economy will continue to grow and develop along lines which are currently in evidence. A decision to switch more economic resources to the production of such consumer goods as motor cars would have a great impact on this projected figure. Even if no such dramatic change of emphasis occurs, however, it would seem that the USSR will inevitably be consuming much more oil by 1980 and that the pressure on domestic supplies will therefore increase.

The net effect of this will be a reduction in the amount of Russian oil available for export to her East European economic satellites. Dependence on Soviet supplies is not, however, limited to the COMECON countries—Yugoslavia, North Vietnam, North Korea, and Cuba also rely on imports of Russian oil. In 1970 the Soviet Union exported around 50 million tons out of a total production of some 350 million tons. It would not appear that the Russian domestic production can continue to keep up with this growth in both home and export demand and if an export gap begins to emerge then Middle Eastern supplies will become increasingly important for the Soviet Union and her economic partners.

Importing Middle East Oil

There are, however, additional reasons, why Moscow might be interested in external sources of oil. The supplies from the Siberian fields will be slow to come by stream and expensive both to exploit and transfer to the major points of consumption in western Russia. In order to postpone the heavy capital outlay needed for development of the Siberian reserves the Soviet economic planners might well seek to purchase under appropriate conditions oil from the Middle East and to use the Tyumen fields as a strategic reserve. Oil from the Middle East is now in plentiful supply, and if barter deals can be arranged then Moscow might well be prepared to authorize imports in order to conserve domestic resources. The opening of the world's largest natural gas trunkline, from the oilfields of southwestern Iraq to the Soviet Union, took place in October 1970, and within two years it is reckoned that the USSR will be importing up to 10 billion cubic metres of Iranian gas per year. These imports, which were paid for by Russian economic aid to Iran, including the erection of a steel mill at Isfahan, have enabled the Soviet Union to export more of its own gas supplies to Western Europe—a transaction which gives Moscow hard-currency benefits.

The new oil imports from Iraq's north Rumaila field are apparently to be paid for by the supply of Russian technical equipment and training in fields such as oil refining, irrigation, and textile production. There are also plans to create a Soviet-built phosphates plant capable of producing 600,000 tons of fertilizers per year. If future oil supplies can be paid for without using hard currency, then the Soviet Union might well be interested in taking larger amounts from Iraq than the present north Rumaila agreement envisages. The very recent nationalization of IPC has deprived Iraq of an annual income of some £380 million and the regime will rapidly be in dire straits unless alternative sources of revenue can be found. It is possible that the Iraqi government will resell the nationalized oil to IPC under new terms; it is also possible that certain Western European states may buy the oil under direct government to government agreements and so bypass the major oil companies—but a further possibility is that the Soviet Union may well uplift greater amounts of oil than are at present envisaged.

The difficulties facing this latter scheme are twofold. On the one hand the Soviet Union is reluctant—if not unable—to import much oil at present world prices if payment has to be made in hard currencies. On the other hand there are also the difficulties involved in transportation of oil from southern Iraq to Soviet markets. At the moment some of the Rumaila oil from Iraq is being shipped to southeast Asia and this is much cheaper for the Russians than hauling her own oil round Africa from the Black Sea fields. If Middle Eastern oil is needed for industries in European Russia, however, then the oil has to be hauled round the Cape of Good Hope and as neither Iraq nor the Soviet Union—who are transporting the oil under a joint venture agreement—possess supertankers, this long haul is very expensive. What the Soviet Union doubtless desires is a pipeline system linking the Iraqi fields with a Mediterranean oil terminal, for this would help greatly to reduce transportation costs. Now that IPC has been nationalized such pipeline facilities are available and it will be interesting to see what future use is made of them.

The Soviet-Iraqi fifteen-year treaty signed by the two premiers in Baghdad on April 9 was therefore the product of many factors—mainly the Soviet wish to secure a further foothold in the Arab world which was less involved with the day-to-day dangers of war with Israel, together with the Kremlin's desire to gain influence in an area to the south of Iran and Turkey, and to acquire naval facilities on the shores of the Persian Gulf. The political isolation of the Baghdad regime and its currently firm grip on internal power were also factors which enabled agreement to be reached smoothly and rapidly. The existence of plentiful supplies of oil—a strategic commodity far more important than Egyptian cotton—and a running dispute with a major western petroleum consortium were also attractive features about Iraq when viewed from Moscow. The treaty can therefore be regarded as an important step forward for Russian interests in the Middle East but it is one which has caused some resentment if not alarm elsewhere—particularly in Iran and Turkey.

Throughout the 1960's relations between Teheran and Moscow had improved consistently. A mutual policy of good neighborliness had found expression in schemes for economic cooperation and in Iran's first purchase of arms from a non-Western source six years ago. The signing of the Iraqi-Soviet treaty—and particularly the provisions of articles 8 and 9* involving cooperation in matters of defence and military planning—has caused some misgivings in Tehran. The Shah's policy for the Persian Gulf, formulated soon after the announcement of British withdrawal, was that the Gulf should in future be kept free of any Great Power presence. The U.S. agreement with Bahrain in December 1971 was a blow to this policy and one which the Shah believed would encourage a Soviet response. This prediction has come true with the signing of the Russo-Iraqi treaty and the provision of naval facilities for Soviet ships at Iraqi ports. From being an exclusively British area of a naval activity the Persian Gulf has now become a potential arena for Great Power rivalry and Tehran has been quick to recognize the dangers inherent in this position for all the littoral states of the Gulf. The signing of an Indo-Soviet agreement has also caused some qualms in Iran about the Soviet ambitions elsewhere in Asia.

The impact of these two treaties has meant that Iran has begun a reconsideration of the permissible limits of friendship with her powerful northern neighbor and may very well now seek closer ties with the West. It is significant to note that President Nixon visited Tehran immediately after his recent summit talks in Moscow and that the Shah took this opportunity to state publicly the need to maintain adequate conventional defence forces particularly now that strategic nuclear arms were to come under some form of mutual limitation. President Nixon was quick to reassure Iran that close relations with old allies would be carefully maintained even though an East-West détente appeared to be emerging.

A Risk of Adventurism

A very real danger, according to Tehran, in the recent Soviet-Iraqi treaty is that it may encourage Baghdad to be more active in the border disputes which gravely trouble Iranian-Iraqi relations. These disputes are not confined to the problem of the Shattel Arub but also embrace areas to the north—including parts of Kurdistan and involve, too, the regular expulsion of large numbers of Persians from the religious cities of Iraq. In January of this year Moscow is believed to have exercised some influence on Baghdad in preventing further expulsions, but may be reluctant to pursue such a policy now that such a beneficial treaty has been signed. Outbreaks of firing and skirmishes occurred on the Iranian-Iraqi border near Khaniqin between April 12–14 and further troubles are likely. At the moment the Iranian armed forces are certainly much stronger and better equipped than those of Iraq but Soviet aid could begin to alter this balance and so encourage greater adventurism on the part of Baghdad.

* See text of the Treaty in *New Middle East*, June 1972, p. 42.

Iran's neighbor Turkey has also felt some disquiet at the recent Soviet-Iraqi treaty. As Prime Minister Kosygin was leaving Baghdad after the celebrations concerned with the Ba'ath Party's twenty-fifth anniversary, the signing of the treaty, and the opening of the North Rumaila oil venture, President Podgorny was arriving in Ankara. During this visit he endeavored to reassure the Turkish government that Moscow's intentions were entirely peaceful and friendly but Ankara remains cautious about the nature of Soviet activity in Iraq. The recent internal political disturbances have awakened latent suspicions of Russian involvement with groups seeking to overthrow the present Turkish regime, and it is possible that Moscow might now seek to use the Kurdish population who live on both sides of the Turkish-Iraqi border to promote further unrest. Turkey's attitude to the new treaty therefore is, like that of Iran, one of watchful apprehension.

The treaty with Iraq received notice in much of the European press but the military agreement signed between the Soviet Union and Syria on May 14 received much less attention. Syria is now becoming an area of great interest to Moscow and some review of recent events is worthwhile. While Marshal Grechko, the Soviet Defence Minister, was in Cairo in February of this year Mr. K. Mazarov, the USSR first Deputy Premier, was in Damascus discussing an increase in Soviet military aid. In May both Marshal Grechko and Admiral Gortchikov, one of the commanders of the Russian navy, together with 13 other high-ranking Soviet officers, visited Damascus and agreed to Syrian requests for more arms. The types that were requested are believed to be chiefly for the navy and air force and include SAM 3 missiles and missile-equipped patrol boats. No formal details have been announced but the importance of the agreement should not be underestimated. As was noted earlier, Iraqi oil would become much cheaper for the Soviet economy if it could be uplifted from a Mediterranean instead of from a Persian Gulf port. For this purpose Syrian agreement would be essential. The Syrian port of Lattakia is already being very heavily used by Soviet shipping and there has been a series of consistent reports of a large Soviet submarine harbor being built at Ras Shamra. Naval facilities on the Syrian coast would give the Russian navy even greater flexibility for its already extensive operations in the eastern Mediterranean. Syria also possesses two very great and obvious geographical advantages—it is in a position to exercise pressure on its northern neighbor Turkey and it also provides a land link from the Mediterranean to the lowlands of Iraq. By gaining a secure foothold in Syria therefore the Soviet Union would have totally outflanked CENTO and would also be in a position to ensure easy movement by land between the Mediterranean and the Persian Gulf. The corollary of this is, of course, that it could deny such ease of movement to an adversary at a time of crisis.

Soviet activity in the Middle East this year has therefore been very succesful. Russian interests have been diversified and a second area of influence gained in a very important region. A small but very significant entry has been made into the Middle Eastern oil industry and the dependence of another Arab country has been formalized in treaty articles. These events should serve as warning that Soviet policy-makers see the Middle East as an area of great opportunity and that the recurrent dangers of the Arab-Israel confrontation have not blinded them—as they have so many western politicians and commentators—to the other opportunities that exist in the area. The lands of the Middle East are, after all, a source of great wealth and constitute Russia's most direct route to the Indian Ocean. By separating these issues from the complexities of the Arab-Israel dispute—while hoping that other governments do not—Moscow has been able to gain much of great value in the last fifteen months.

Part Three
Great Issues of Military Policy

Introduction

The great issues of military policy revolve around a small number of questions. Do arms races produce wars? How important are weapons to the protection of national security? Is the level of weaponry, and particularly of nuclear weaponry, far too high? Could not the money going into the arms race be employed far more profitably to build a better world?

X

THE ARMS RACE AND SALT

T he great issues of military policy arise in specific contexts in the following articles by McGeorge Bundy, Herbert Scoville, Jr., and Donald Brennan. Some of these topics were alluded to in the earlier article on President Nixon by Robert Hunter. They include the belief that the arms race is an explosive action/reaction process, the proposition that a minimum deterrence posture is sufficient to deter war and crises, questions of nuclear sufficiency, and the adequacy of the agreements resulting from the Strategic Arms Limitation Talks between Russia and the U.S.

The argument that the arms race is an action/reaction process is one that is widely accepted in the United States. This thesis holds that first one side adds nuclear weapons to its inventory, then the other side overcompensates, and then the first side overreacts to the overreaction. In addition, it is argued that anticipations of additions to the nuclear arsenal by potential enemies fuels the arms race. This view is not accepted uncritically in the United States—Albert Wohlstetter, Herman Kahn, and others believe that it is inaccurate—and some Russian professional experts also reject it.

If the reader will examine the predictions made by Secretary McNamara from 1964 until his retirement from office, he will find that McNamara consistently underestimated Soviet missile development. He continued to assert that the Soviet arms buildup would level off before the point at which parity with the United States was reached. Even after his initial projections had been shown false, he merely made modest upward revisions in his predictions.

Obviously there was something wrong with the hypothesis upon which

Secretary McNamara rested his conclusions. Among other things, the eventual Soviet missile buildup did not support the action/reaction hypothesis. We cannot be sure whether it was McNamara's policy of levelling off the U.S. nuclear arsenal that provided the Soviet Union with an opportunity to obtain numerical superiority it could not resist, or whether the Soviet Union was responding to internal pressures generated by its armed forces.

With respect to arms races in general, the assumption is that arms races trigger wars. However, no convincing historical evidence has ever been presented to show that this has occurred on even one single occasion. The German/English naval competition early in the twentieth century is not regarded by serious historians as a significant cause of the First World War. There is no evidence that the Kaiser's blank cheque to Austria was related to the naval competition with Great Britain. On the other hand, many experts believe that the passive arms policies of the democracies in the 1930's were among the factors that allowed the Second World War to develop.

The argument over minimum deterrence occurs at a number of levels and is assumed rather than clearly presented in our selections. At one extreme, some people believe that if one has some nuclear weapons, one has automatic deterrence regardless of other military weaknesses. Some have even suggested relying entirely for defense upon a doomsday machine that would go off if an enemy attacks. These suggestions overlook the fact that when Herman Kahn invented the idea of a doomsday device, he did so as a *reductio ad adsurdum* to demonstrate the nonsensical character of minimum deterrence. Such devices cannot withstand accident, mistake, or other miscalculation. They permit the enemy to exploit all measures short of those that trigger the doomsday machine or any other form of automatic deterrent. Moreover, as those possessing such machines contemplate the consequences of using them, they are likely to disengage them and then the aggressor can raise the level of violence he threatens.

Mr. Bundy's article (30) holds that relative nuclear strength is meaningless, as the damage involved in nuclear war is so great that no political leadership will contemplate it. Therefore, the intensive buildup of a nuclear arsenal is a simple waste of resources. Mr. Bundy now denies that American nuclear strategic superiority played any significant role in the Cuban missile crisis of 1962. Yet the memoirs of the period demonstrate that American leaders thought they were in a crisis that threatened nuclear war. It is difficult to believe that the United States would have been as likely to blockade Cuba and to demand the removal of the Soviet missiles if the strategic advantage possessed by the United States had been possessed by the Soviet Union instead. If the United States had nonetheless done this, I believe that the Soviet Union would have been far less likely to have backed down in Cuba. And, if for some reason it had backed down in Cuba, I believe that it would have been far more likely to provoke a crisis in some area such as Berlin where it had conventional superiority in addition to its strategic nuclear superiority.

The argument over minimum deterrence shades into the argument over nuclear sufficiency. This issue is reflected also in the Russian literature. Without accepting the hypothesis that everyone of importance in the Soviet Union necessarily holds the views presented in article 31 by Uri Ra'anan, it seems relevant to this issue that numerical superiority is considered important by a significant body of military writers in the Soviet Union. If Soviet authorities do hold such views, it is at least possible that the Soviet buildup in nuclear weapons since the Cuban missile crisis is related to their interpretation of their setback in that crisis.

The argument over sufficiency has intensified since the Senate debates in 1969. The debate over ballistic missile defense began with an assertion by pro-administration sources that the expected Russian SS-9 buildup would permit them to knock out 95 percent of the American Minuteman ICBMs by 1974. This view was contested by writers such as Scoville, whose initial argument was that the accuracies required for this result could not be achieved within that time frame. As the U.S. had achieved by 1969 the accuracies Russia required in 1974, this argument collapsed. Then, over the next 6 to 12 months, Scoville and others of his persuasion entirely reversed their argument and claimed that missile accuracies would become so great that no defense of the Minuteman ICBMs was possible. Only such a reversal of their opinions permitted them to retain their original conclusions. But such great accuracies cannot be obtained even by the supposedly technologically superior American missile forces before the 1980's and, even then, only if funds that have been taken out of the budget are restored. Otherwise, and perhaps even if such accuracies are obtained, ballistic missile defense still could be expected to protect Minuteman.

Mr. Scoville argues that Minuteman and the Strategic Air Command are vulnerable but that the nuclear submarines of the United States are not vulnerable. What is his evidence for this proposition? Is it based upon American antisubmarine warfare research or upon Russian antisubmarine warfare research? The latter seems very unlikely. How then can Mr. Scoville and the other minimum deterrers be sure that the Russians have not discovered some system vulnerability that is not apparent to us? Moreover, if we surrender the attempt to maintain the viability of Minuteman and the Strategic Air Command, we permit the Russians to concentrate their research and procurement on our remaining strategic force: the nuclear submarines.

Unless there is some remarkable technological breakthrough, actual first strikes will be very high-risk affairs. For that reason, they will be quite unlikely. If, however, one of the antagonist nations believes that it can in principle carry out such a strike and the other does not believe that it can do so even in principle, the stronger is more likely to risk the escalation of a crisis, everything else being equal. That is perhaps why the Chinese, who do feel threatened, have urged the United States not to concede Soviet superiority at SALT.

Thus, minimum deterrence is a form of Russian roulette. Five of the six chambers are empty and the odds are with us. It is likely that nothing will go wrong, but if something does, we blow the whole ball of wax. In other words, minimum deterrence is fine as long as deterrence is really unnecessary. Because, however, it lacks crisis stability, it is likely to fail in a crisis.

The SALT agreements are directly related to the foregoing questions. Mr. Scoville favors the SALT agreements, not because they have moved us toward disarmament but because they break the action/reaction cycle. For this reason, he opposes Secretary Laird's linking of SALT with new weapons systems. On the other hand, Donald Brennan opposes the SALT agreements. He argues that SALT, by cutting back on ballistic missile defense, insures that nuclear weapons can be used only for city-busting. This, according to Brennan, is immoral.

Even if one agreed entirely with Brennan's argument, would it still follow that the SALT agreements are unjustified? Henry Kissinger claims that only the SALT agreements prevented the Russians from increasing their numerical advantage even more. Even in the absence of a SALT agreement the American ballistic missile defense program would not have been expanded to a point of adequacy, as Brennan hoped, because of Congressional opposition. And the fact of a signed agreement is of some significance for the ambience of world politics. The fact that General Secretary Brezhnev signed the SALT agreements for the Soviet Union, although he holds no governmental post, was intended to protect the agreements from attack by the Communist Party Secretariat. This is evidence of less than unanimous support for SALT in the Soviet Union, even though from some standpoints the agreements provide the Soviet Union with genuine advantages. And this does suggest some advantages in SALT for the United States.

Mr. Pollack's article (32) states, and there seems little reason to doubt him, that the Chinese expect for a significant time in the future to remain in a position of strategic nuclear inferiority. Unlike the United States and the Soviet Union, they do not take a principled stand against proliferation. There is some evidence—not entirely convincing—that they would resist a Japanese nuclear program. On the other hand, it is likely that they would welcome a European nuclear program as a further control on the Soviet Union.

Some have argued that Chinese development of nuclear weapons is dangerous because the Chinese some day will use such weapons to blackmail Taiwan or Southeast Asia. However, there is no evidence for this assertion in Chinese pronouncements or conduct. It hardly seems likely that blackmail would make sense from the standpoint of China, since it would legitimate attacks upon China. Although in some respects China is less vulnerable than the Soviet Union because of its relatively primitive economy, for a long period of time to come the Chinese weapons program will be inferior to both the Russian and American programs. China is unlikely to become a major nuclear power before the middle or late 1980's, despite the statement of the outgoing CIA chief to the contrary. At least until that time, its security is likely to depend to a great extent upon refraining from giving either Russia or the United States an excuse to attack it. If this is the case, one would think that it would attempt to avoid destabilizing acts of its own. Its more recent conduct with respect to the settlement of the Vietnamese war seems to buttress this point of view.

30.

To Cap the Volcano

McGEORGE BUNDY

I

THE NEGLECTED TRUTH about the present strategic arms race between the United States and the Soviet Union is that in terms of international political behavior that race has now become almost completely irrelevant. The new weapons systems which are being developed by each of the two great powers will provide neither protection nor opportunity in any serious political sense. Politically the strategic nuclear arms race is in a stalemate. It has been this way since the first deliverable hydrogen weapons were exploded, and it will be this way for as far ahead as we can see, even if future developments should be much more heavily one-sided than anything now in prospect. This proposition does not square with the complex measurements of comparative advantage which dominated the ABM debate, but I think it can be supported both by logic and by history.

In light of the certain prospect of retaliation there has been literally no chance at all that any sane political authority, in either the United States or the Soviet Union, would consciously choose to start a nuclear war. This proposition is true for the past, the present and the foreseeable future. For sane men on both sides the balance of terror is overwhelmingly persuasive. Given the worst calculations of the most pessimistic American advocate of new weapons systems, there is no prospect at all that the Soviet Government could attack the United States without incurring an overwhelming risk of destruction vastly greater than anyone but a madman would choose to accept. Conversely, even the most cold-blooded of American planners has always understood, at least since 1954, that the concept of a strategic first strike by the United States is wholly unacceptable because of the prospect of Soviet retaliation.

There is an enormous gulf between what political leaders really think about nuclear weapons and what is assumed in complex calculations of relative "advantage" in simulated strategic warfare. Think-tank analysts can set levels of "unacceptable" damage well up in the tens of millions of lives. They can assume that the loss of dozens of great cities is somehow a real choice for sane men. They are in an unreal world. In the real world of real political leaders—whether here or in the Soviet Union—a decision that would bring even one hydrogen bomb on one city of one's own country would be recognized in advance as a catastrophic blunder; ten bombs on ten cities would be a disaster beyond history; and a hundred bombs on a hundred cities are unthinkable. Yet this unthinkable level of human incineration is the least that could be expected by either side in response to any first strike in the next ten years, *no matter what happens to weapons systems in the meantime.* Even the worst case hypothesized in the ABM debate leaves at least this much room for reply. In sane politics, therefore, there is no level of superiority which will make a strategic first strike between the two great states anything but an act of utter folly.

My argument evidently rests upon an assumption of sanity. It does not protect against madness. But neither is there any protection against the madman in close calculations of "assured survivable destruction capability." Indeed it may be easier for a madman to understand the simple horror of *any* exchange between the superpowers than to be persuaded by intricate calculations of residual "advantage" after the world as we know it is destroyed.

What we have somehow forgotten, in the expanding megatonage of the age of missiles, is that already fifteen years ago we were scorpions in a bottle, able to sting each other only at the price of death. Yet what either side had then was insignificant in comparison to what both sides have now. Moreover, we have somehow let the necessary comparisons of one weapons system with another delude us into a belief that these calculations of cost-effectiveness are also calculations of real advantage. Certainly when we determine that a certain level of deterrent strength is needed (a calculation which has always been generous in both our countries), it makes very good sense to do our best to pick the systems that will do the job most economically, and it follows that close comparative analysis is well worthwhile. But the fact that Minuteman is better in these terms than the B-70—or Poseidon better than Polaris—does not tell us anything about the real value, politically, of any one system, or of all our systems together. Their one purpose is deterrence. They must not do less, and they cannot do more.

Thus the basic consequence of considering this matter politically and not technically is the conclusion that beyond a point long since passed the escalation of the strategic nuclear race makes no sense for either the Soviet Union or the United States. Nothing in the national interest, the ideology or the personal political position of any leader in either country can be advanced by any strategic nuclear exchange. No weapons systems now in sight for either side can change that fact. It follows that in political, as distinct from technical, terms we have all been wrong to talk of nuclear superiority. President Nixon was surely right when he changed the terms of the discussion from "superiority" to "sufficiency." Sufficiency is what we both have now, in ample measure, and no superiority worth having can be achieved. It is sometimes argued that in the past nuclear superiority—ours over the Soviet Union or that of the Soviet Union over Western Europe—has had a decisive influence on events. I find this a very doubtful proposition. This is not the place for a close reexamination of relevant crises like Suez, Berlin and Cuba, but my own belief is that in none of the three has the nuclear "superiority" of any major power been decisive. In all three cases the risk of escalation has certainly been an element in the problem, and in all three, in different ways, that risk has been a deterrent to action. But in all three cases, questions of will and purpose have been more important than questions of nuclear numbers. In none of the three cases, I feel confident, would the final result have been different if the relative strategic positions of the Soviet Union and the United States had been reversed. A stalemate is a stalemate either way around.

Since it is vital to avoid misunderstanding, let me emphasize here that in asserting the preeminence of the political judgment on the use and non-use of nuclear weapons I am not at all downgrading the importance of technical proficiency in the deterrent forces we do decide to maintain. It seems to me wholly plain that a credible strategic nuclear deterrent is indispensable to the peace, and for that reason no task is more clearly indispensable than that of maintaining and protecting such a force. There is a great distance between a belief in strategic stalemate and any suggestion that we should proceed to unilateral disarmament. We have bought and paid for parity, and we must not lose it. So it will be as true in a future of stable balance as it has been in the past of presumed supremacy that the men who stand guard over our strategic forces are men who place us all in their debt.

But it is one thing for military men to maintain our deterrent force with vigilant skill, and it quite another for anyone to assume that their necessary contingency plans have any serious interest for political leaders. The object of political men—quite rightly—is that these weapons should never be used. I have watched two Presidents working on strategic contingency plans, and what interested them most was simply to make sure that none of these awful events would occur. Political leaders, whether here or in Russia, are cut from a very different mold than strategic planners. They see cities and people as part of what they are trying to help—not as targets. They live with the daily struggle to make a little progress—to build things—to grow things—to lift the quality of life a little—and to win honor, and even popularity, by such achievements. The deterrent that might not please a planner is more than deterrent enough for them. And that is why the deterrent does work, even at a distance, as in Berlin. *Maybe* the American nuclear commitment is not as firm as it seems—but what sane Soviet leader wants to put the whole Soviet society in the scales to find out?

It is also important to distinguish the nuclear sufficiency of the super-powers from the very different level of deterrent strength which has been sought by such a leader as General de Gaulle. French theorists have some-times argued as if a very small number of thermonuclear weapons would be a sure and permanent deterrent. Most American analysts, in my view cor-rectly, have been skeptical of this thesis. The armaments of the middle-level nuclear powers are indeed vulnerable to an obliterating first strike, and that situation may not entirely disappear even if they shift to seaborne missiles. But several orders of magnitude, and as many orders of complexity, separate the difficulties of an attack on such a force from those of a preëmptive attack on either the Soviet Union or the United States. The nuclear sufficiency of the superpowers is as far removed from the deterrent capacity of the *force de frappe* as the Great Pyramid from a molehill.

II

At this point in the analysis our effort to move from technology to politics may seem encouraging, but now we must take account of a much less cheer-ful aspect of the matter. The politics of the analysis so far is the politics of international relations—of what one state or another will actually do on the world stage. This analysis points plainly to the advantages of limiting the strategic arms race, since it tells us that the existing parity between the super-powers is all that they can hope to use internationally, and since no one in any society wants to pay tens of billions for nothing.

Unfortunately we have not exhausted the politics of strategic weapons. Along with this crude but powerful international politics of common sense goes the politics of consensus and consent within each superpower. Presi-dents and Politburos may know in their hearts that the only thing they want from strategic weapons is never to have to use them; in their public postures they have felt it necessary to claim more. They may not themselves be per-suaded by the refined calculations of the nuclear gamesmen—but they do not find it prudent to expose them for the political irrelevance they are. The public in both countries has been allowed by its leaders to believe that some-where in ever-growing strength there is safety, and that it still means something to be "ahead." The politics of internal decision-making has not been squared with the reality of international stalemate.

In consequence, the internal politics of the strategic arms race has remained the prisoner of its technology. The ABM debate showed a shift from an earlier emphasis on American "superiority" toward the question whether somehow now the Russians might move "ahead"—but there were only a few voices raised to support the notion that within very broad limits no one now can have a lead worth having. That may be the necessary premise of international political behavior; it is not yet the possible premise of national political debate. Internally, in both countries, the present premise of the debate leads remorselessly toward escalation. In both countries, moreover, this framework of argument is powerfully sustained by the force which Americans have been taught to call "the military-industrial complex." Since the opponents of escalation refuse to contest the basic political premise, they are driven back to technology; those who oppose the ABM tend to argue that it may not work technically—not that it is irrelevant politically. And while excellent answers were made to the Pentagon suggestion that the Russians might be "going for a first strike," there were few to suggest that the necssary assumption of any such scenario must be that the Soviet Government had gone suicidally mad.

What appears in our ABM debate appears also in Soviet behavior. The Russians continue to spend much too much money on large weapons which do them no good and whose only real effect is to frighten us into further efforts of our own. We can afford it better than they can, of course, and in terms of economic cold warfare there has always been a certain spurious attractiveness about trapping the Russians into a constantly accelerating competition. Fortunately, that particular brand of nonsense has never been anyone's official policy, and the tenor of the ABM debate suggests that it may be permanently out of fashion. But the fact that we are not trying to induce this sort of Soviet folly does not make it less real, or less foolish. In every international crisis of the last fifteen years Soviet leaders have shown their understanding that the strategic balance requires mutual restraint between the superpowers. But in their weapons decisions they have been as heedlessly and unproductively excessive as we.

There is a curious and distressing paradox in all this. The same political leaders who know these terrible weapons must never be used and who do not run the foolish risks of nuclear gamesmanship abroad still do not hesitate to authorize system after system. The usual resolution of the paradox is to describe the decision to build as an "insurance policy." But the argument is unsatisfying; the gap between what the political leader orders and what he can do with it is too great. I know of no escape from the conclusion that both in his sensible abhorrence of nuclear conflict and his persistent attachment to still more weapons systems the political leader is reflecting his constituency. The fault is less in our leaders than in ourselves.

31.

The Changing American-Soviet Strategic Balance: Some Political Implications

URI RA'ANAN

IN A THERMONUCLEAR AGE, it may be no longer entirely appropriate for Superpowers to treat war itself merely as "politics continued by other means"; however, that does not excuse failure to perceive that the intricate contest conducted between states through their military development and posture remains essentially political in its motivation and impact. It is all the more unsatisfactory, then, that studies of the effects of current changes in the global strategic balance have been confined so largely to the mechanistic domain of scientists and engineers, systems analysts, and other technical experts who, with all their virtues, are not usually conditioned to "think politically." Searching, as they must, for similarities or, at least, comparable factors to be fed into the computer, they are even less prone to appreciate the profound political asymmetries between the main global adversaries—asymmetries that relate to the nature of their respective societies and result in very different constraints on their policy-makers and in contrasting *Weltanschauungen* that cannot but lead to quite disparate sets of overall aims. (Although significant changes have occurred, and are occurring, in both East and West, it is still quite misleading, or at least premature, to think primarily in terms of "convergence" and to view these differences as being less than basic.)

Surely, weapons systems and military power in general cannot, or should not, be evaluated except in relation to the overall political postures that they are meant to serve. To take only one example, it is hardly meaningful to treat certain weapons as "offensive" or "defensive" without examining the nature of the political goals in the furtherance of which they are being

Reprinted from a memorandum prepared at the request of the Subcommittee on National Security and International Operations of the Committee on Government Operations of the U.S. Senate, 1972.

deployed. It is by no means unusual to find government A, in the pursuit of essentially defensive aims, obliged to resort to "offensive" tactics, because the rival power B, in its attempt to change the existing territorial and political order, has seized the initiative—perhaps by covert or indirect means—leaving state A little choice but to attempt to restore the situation through a limited application or threat of force. Thus, altogether, it is less than "scientific" to ignore the existence of major disparity, or asymmetry, between opposing sets of political concepts and to proceed to deal with the weapons systems themselves *in vacuo*. This is not to deny that, up to a point, weapons technology has a logic of its own which can and does influence policy-formation; however, military planning and decision-making, in turn, function obviously within the wider parameter of political strategy, creating a complex network of interacting military and political factors. To seize upon a single set of these factors—a single dimension, as it were—is to lose all perspective.

If this be a truism, it is one that is surprisingly often ignored or forgotten. Otherwise it would be difficult to account for the persistence of highly mechanistic "action-reaction dialogue" models which, from the McNamara period onward, have governed much of American thinking about Soviet behavior in the strategic and other fields. In effect, these models deny the existence, or at least the significance, of overall Soviet political aims, of a conscious, deliberate, and dynamic Soviet policy in which military posture plays a vitally important—albeit supporting—role. Instead, it is tacitly assumed, for no very convincing reason, that a curiously apolitical, automatic, lifeless pattern of behavior has become the norm in the USSR, whereby Moscow merely "reacts" to certain American strategic developments, with Washington, in turn, "reacting" to Soviet "reactions" and so on and so forth. Conversely, in the absence of an initial U.S. move, presumably there would be no Soviet "counter-action" so that, if one were to develop the thesis *ad absurdum*, there would finally ensue universal stasis, an end of all movement as postulated by the Second Law of Thermodynamics.

To anyone acquainted with the general lines of Soviet thinking, as reflected in Soviet defense and political literature, the whole concept is so utterly remote from Soviet reality as to be rather comical, if it were not taken so seriously in some Western quarters. To be sure, no one wishes to deny that Western moves have an impact on Soviet policy-formation and vice versa. However, it is a major misreading of the Soviet political process to assume that Soviet decision-makers act only or primarily in response to Western acts. However cynical they may have become about some aspects of the official ideology, Soviet leaders are good enough Leninists to think dynamically and, above all, to appreciate the value of the initiative.

Thus, it is significant that, in their analysis of various strategic doctrines, Soviet experts attribute to their Western counterparts, as a matter of course, views such as these:

. . . no energetic actions were undertaken . . . as a result the United States lost the initiative in the psychological plane . . . [the] proposal is to regain this initiative by "intimidating" potential enemies . . .[1]

. . . the concept of mutual restraint . . . dooms the American policy to immobility and deprives it of flexibility . . . that is, of the possibility of using nuclear blackmail in conflict situations . . .[2]

While, to be sure, the general context of these quotations is somewhat polemical, there is no tendency on the Soviet side to dispute the general validity of such concepts, which stress the advantage of the initiative, of nuclear and conventional superiority, of politico-military forward thrusts, of a broadly offensive and dynamic strategy; it is not these means, but rather Western motives and goals that are impugned. It may be deduced, therefore, that the Soviet experts quoted above have ascribed to Western thinkers their own basic beliefs and assumptions and that Soviet defense literature, in this case, provides a mirror-image of Moscow's strategic and political concepts.

Indeed, this conclusion squares fully with what is known from other contemporary Soviet writings, ideological and practical, and what can be deduced from Soviet actions in recent years. For instance, the 1969 Moscow international conference of Communist parties was asked to approve a Soviet-inspired operational document, stating in so many words that the West "is impotent to regain the historical initiative it has lost" and that "the main pathway" now "is determined by the world socialist system . . ." To this, the semiofficial organ of the Soviet Foreign Ministry recently added for good measure that the U.S. has "lost the freedom to maneuver to a considerable degree."[3]

Thus, the basic assumptions, upon which the "action-reaction dialogue" model is based, simply are not borne out by the available evidence and there is room for the thought that this particular "dialogue" may, in a sense, be more of a "monologue"—i.e., the U.S. arguing with itself, while the USSR is listening in and taking notes, but not necessarily joining in the spirit of the "discussion" or confining itself to mere "reaction."

The question as to whether or not this model of Soviet behavior is appropriate assumes more than academic significance, since its Western advocates[4] have managed to extrapolate from it certain far-reaching conclusions. As they see it, there now is an adversary relationship not so much

1. V. V. Larionov, "The Transformation of the 'Strategic Sufficiency' Concept," *U.S.A.: Economics, Politics, Ideology*, No. 11, Moscow, 1971.

2. A. Kalyadin, "The Disarmament Problem and Concepts of 'Deterrence,'" *Mirovaya Ekonomika i Mezhdunarodnye Otnosheniya*, No. 11, Moscow, 1971.

3. B. Svetlov, "The U.S.S.R. and the United States—Possibilities and Reality," *Mezhdunarodnaya Zhizn*, No. 1, Moscow, 1972.

4. This concept has been assimilated into the contemporary mainstream of Western literature on nuclear weapons philosophy to an extent that would make it invidious here to single out any particular one of its adherents.

between the U.S. and the USSR as between both and a third—almost personalized—element, namely the Arms Spiral. The latter is thought to have an organic life of its own, somehow independent of the political contest between the powers, and both Washington and Moscow are believed to be in its thrall, mechanically playing their prescribed roles in a mutually damaging, continually escalating version of the "action-reaction dialogue." However, some supporters of this theory suggest that the vicious circle can be broken by unilateral acts of self-limitation, which—properly signalled—would induce the other party to reciprocate. In all fairness, this concept may be less ethereal than would appear at first sight, since its advocates maintain that it is based upon practical considerations. In their view, the overall strategic balance, whatever its temporary quantitative fluctuations, has not been and probably will not be fundamentally upset in a qualitative sense, i.e. neither side is likely to attain a true first-strike capability and neither will be deprived of an assured-destruction capability. In that case, they claim, further increments in the strategic sector added by either party could be destabilizing in a psychological and economic sense—triggering a new round in an ever more costly armaments race because of the "action-reaction" syndrome—without any real possibility of achieving a meaningful breakthrough. As they see it, therefore, no such increment will be politically relevant since it is unlikely to produce a decisive shift in the existing balance. Hence, there must be mutual U.S.-Soviet interest in preserving "parity" (using the term in a very broad, generic sense).

Needless to say, no reasonable person would deny that the Superpowers are confronted by very serious problems with regard to resource allocation, given the constantly rising costs of highly sophisticated items, from research and development to final deployment. Certainly, no responsible statesman would willfully ignore a genuine opportunity for strategic arms limitation within a mutually beneficial framework. The question remains, however, whether it is a positive contribution to the analysis of this issue to assume without irrefutable evidence that the current discernible tilt in the strategic balance, resulting from sizable Soviet increments during the last few years, really is politically irrelevant and can therefore be accepted safely.

To deal with this question, it may be helpful to reexamine the whole concept of political impact in a thermonuclear age. It is all too frequently overlooked that political weight, or influence, is directly proportional not so much to physical might, in absolute, objective terms, as to *perceived* power—a subjective factor that can be, and is, manipulated (although, of course, physical might is one of its constituent ingredients). In the case of the Superpowers, this means that their relative global impact must be measured in terms of the power of each *as perceived* by its own decision-makers, its intelligentsia and its general public respectively, by its allies and clients, by the decision-makers, intelligentsia and general public of the rival Superpower, by that rival's allies and clients, and, finally, by non-aligned and neutral states and by the so-called Third World (terms which are no longer necessarily synonymous). It is this perception, whether accurate or not, that will mold the expectations and the decisions of all the parties involved and, therefore, must be regarded as the critical political factor in any given situation. It will determine which Superpower is likely to "blink first" in a potential confrontation crisis and which one, in anticipation of such a dénouement, will be tempted to precipitate such a crisis; it will sway other states and will play a major part in shaping the global "lineup." (Of course, there may be situations in which the perceptions of the various participants will differ, complicating the picture, but diametrically opposed appraisals of power are far less common nowadays than might be supposed.)

The question arises, then, what the elements are that, cumulatively, create a specific perception of power. Needless to say, objective physical might is one of these factors, but it is only one, and strategic forces, however awesome, only constitute a single ingredient of that factor. Consequently, it is misleading to equate political power (i.e. the perception of power) exclusively with strategic forces, measured in absolute terms, viewed in a static fashion and divorced from the broader and far more complex overall equation—as, regrettably, a major proportion of contemporary Western literature tends to do.

Paradoxically, it is precisely the partisans of this school of thought, favoring the purely strategic approach to the power equation, who are most inclined to discount the political significance of the considerable quantitative changes that have occurred in the U.S.-Soviet strategic balance. In their view, a rough equilibrium, a state of Mutual Assured Destruction,[5] has existed for some years, coming close in the current state to genuine "parity," with the USSR enjoying an 8 : 5 numerical margin over the U.S. in ICBM and, specifically, holding an edge in high-yield ICBM (SS-9), with the USSR gradually drawing abreast of the U.S. in SLBM, as the U.S. regains whatever ground may have been lost to the USSR in ABM, and with the U.S. benefiting from a qualitative advantage in MIRV and in R&D of ULMS, as well as having a monopoly in FBS.[6] While they would not deny that the USSR has markedly improved its position vis-à-vis the U.S. in recent years, they argue that, in any case, the U.S. has not enjoyed a true first-strike capability for a decade or more and that recent Soviet gains, therefore, do not basically change the situation. They are aware that the USSR has moved from a condition of distinct nuclear inferiority to "parity" (and, some would claim, beyond); however, since this development has occurred within a continuing framework of assured-destruction, they view the Soviet increments as mere "overkill." The adherents of this

5. To use Donald Brennan's inspired acronym.
6. Forward Based Systems.

school of thought feel that it was primarily the "action-reaction" syndrome which made the Soviet Union resort to this basically "superfluous" accelerated armaments program, because the U.S. for some years kept widening the missile gap in its favor, to the point where the USSR felt impelled to "react." They feel reassured, however, that the Soviet Union remains far short of a genuine first-strike capability and that, therefore, the strategic balance remains essentially intact.

There is no particular quarrel with the military assessment of the various items in the strategic mix, as presented by these analysts,[7] although the inadequacy of their methodological approach toward the Soviet input has already been pointed out. However, one cannot but challenge their implicit assumption that this assessment alone provides sufficient basis for valid political conclusions, and that the complexities of the global power relationship can be compressed into the narrow concept of assured-destruction (which focuses almost exclusively on the margin that still separates the USSR from a first-strike capability). The shortcomings of this simplistic view become evident as one attempts to formulate a general equation expressing some of the intricacies of the global contest, in which, of course, nuclear items interrelate with other factors, military and political, and play a subtle and multi-faceted role. Given proper appreciation of the fact that strategic weapons are much more than mere implements in a putative—but hardly thinkable—nuclear exchange, that they have a major impact on political appraisal, i.e. on *perception* of power,[8] it must be recognized that the

---

7. A caveat is, perhaps, in order. Although quantitative intelligence concerning strategic forces is probably rather accurate these days, there may be less cause for smugness concerning qualitative intelligence, especially with regard to items in the R&D stage. Thus, all assessments should be seasoned with a healthy grain of skepticism.

8. Soviet strategic literature demonstrates the Soviet leadership's fundamental comprehension of these concepts, as the following excerpts reveal:

U.S. leaders "admitted that in a new strategic situation they could make up their minds to use their nuclear force only in exceptional and specific cases—basically only in the event of retaliatory defense against an inconceivable direct nuclear attack by the Soviet Union on the U.S. or on their main allies in Europe."

". . . the 'realistic deterrence' strategy officially proceeds from U.S. reluctance to be the initiator of unleashing such a [nuclear] conflict and stipulates only the U.S. right and resolve to inflict a counterstrike in the event of an attack on itself."

[Consequently] ". . . the Washington leaders are trying to intensify the 'politico-psychological' use of the U.S. nuclear missile arsenal, in connection with which the strategy of 'realistic deterrence' again entails diplomatic talks with nuclear bluff and blackmail . . ."

[However] ". . . the U.S. 'strategic nuclear missile force' is not automatically a political influence and . . . in the majority of conflict situations in the 'Third World' it cannot be used even as a real threat . . ."

[Under these circumstances] "the problem of the psychological effect of nuclear weapons not only on the field of battle (at the time of their physical use) but also under the conditions of 'confrontation' is undoubtedly a problem which deserves the specialists' closest attention."

A. Trofimenko, "Political Realism and the 'Realistic Deterrence' Strategy," *U.S.A.: Economics, Politics, Ideology*, No. 12, Moscow, 1971.

significance of current changes in the American-Soviet balance is likely to be more profound than the narrowly strategic school of thought is prepared to admit.

For a start, its adherents err in viewing even the purely military picture in essentially static terms; they have, as it were, snapped a "still" photograph of the current situation and have come up with a rough impression of "parity," along the lines indicated above. However, political perception is influenced primarily by dynamic indicators, by a moving film, as it were, that reveals *trends* from the recent past to the present, which are consciously or subconsciously projected into the future. Judged by these criteria, and focusing upon crude mass and size,[9] the course of the global contest must appear somewhat less reassuring, with Soviet ICBM having quadrupled in a bare five years while U.S. ICBM did not increase in number, with Soviet SLBM having almost quadrupled during the same period while U.S. SLBM remained quantitatively frozen, and with the USSR having deployed a new weapon (SS-9) with a yield nearly 25 times that of current U.S. ICBM. (Qualitatively, the picture is, of course, far less one-sided, but, in terms of political impact, this fact is likely to prove less impressive than the thought that, only 6 years ago, the U.S., in ICBM and SLBM, had almost a 4 : 1 margin over the USSR while, today, the USSR enjoys almost a 5 : 4 edge over the U.S.—however simplistic this formulation may seem to be.) The assumption that this trend should be projected into the future may not be entirely unfounded, in fact, since the concept of "parity" has been rejected, implicitly and explicitly, by Soviet spokesmen on strategic affairs, both for ideological and essentially "imperial" reasons; in the last two years or so, Soviet literature has almost unanimously called for military superiority and, with increasing frequency, has claimed that it is already being attained.

Thus, recent Soviet publications include such statements as:

> . . . the balance of forces in the world . . . has changed in socialism's favor. Inevitable failure awaits those in the imperialist states who are hoping through the arms race to strengthen their positions in the international arena. . . . They do not want to renounce the false hopes of insuring a "leading position" for the U.S. . . .[10]
>
> . . . the correlation of forces . . . has changed in favor of socialism . . .[11]
>
> [The] . . . further change in the alignment of forces between the chief

---

9. To the Soviet leaders, size and numbers have always been primary criteria of power—e.g. the possibly apocryphal, but characteristic Stalinite remark, "How many divisions does the Pope have, after all."

10. V. Larionov, "A Dangerous Line," *Pravda*, Moscow, January 15, 1972.

11. V. Asipov, "An Important Problem of Our Time," *Izvestya*, Moscow, January 6, 1972.

power of imperialism and the leading socialist country in the latter's favor is the most important factor . . . U.S. leaders are obliged publicly to acknowledge changes in the strategic situation which are unfavorable for the United States and to take into account the growth in the USSR's might . . .[12]

Less than a year earlier, the imminent change in the balance had been heralded in no uncertain manner:

> We are all witnesses to the fact that the Central Committee of the Communist Party constantly provides the military-technological means to assure indisputable superiority over the armies of the most powerful capitalist countries.[13]

What emerges clearly is not only the underlying Soviet conviction that military superiority is both desirable and attainable, but also Moscow's determination to create a general perception of Soviet superiority at the earliest possible date.

The full political impact of this trend in the strategic weapons area cannot be appreciated unless viewed in the context of the broader power equation within which it operates. As was postulated earlier in this analysis, political weight, or influence, is directly proportional to *perceived* power—a subjective, impressionistic product that is created cumulatively by a number of "inputs," of which physical might is one, the latter consisting, in turn, of several distinct ingredients, including strategic forces.

To be precise, the power equation contains the following elements: "available physical inputs" (such as strategic forces, general purpose forces, geographical propinquity to focal areas of conflict), "potential physical inputs" (such as economic and scientific-technological potential, mobilizable manpower), and "psychological inputs" (such as "mission," i.e. politi-

12. A. Trofimenko, "Political Realism and the 'Realistic Deterrence' Strategy," *U.S.A.: Economy, Politics, Ideology,* No. 12, Moscow, 1971.

13. General Sergei L. Sokolov, "Our Revolution Knows How To Defend Itself," *Sovetskaya Rossiya,* Moscow, February 23, 1971.

Other Soviet publications that reflect the ongoing Soviet commitment to strive for military superiority rather than parity include: Major General V. Sulimov, "A Policy of Active Counteraction to Aggression." *Krasnaya Zvezda,* Moscow, June 1, 1971; Major General S. Ilin, "A Powerful Factor for Victory", *Krasnaya Zvezda,* Moscow, March 12, 1971; Lieutenant General I. Zavylov, "New Weapons and the Art of War," *Krasnaya Zvezda,* Moscow, October 30, 1970; Colonel V. Vlasoyevich, "Dynamics of Military Economic Expenditures," *Kommunist Vooruzhennykh Sil,* Moscow, August 1970; Colonel I. Seleznev, "V. I. Lenin—The Founder of Soviet Military Science," *Krasnaya Zvezda,* Moscow, March 1970; Lieutenant Colonel V. Ivanov, "Scientific Leadership Principles for Defending the Socialist Fatherland," *Kommunist Vooruzhennykh Sil,* Moscow, August 1969; and A. Galitsan, "For a Leftist Line," *Voennoistoricheskii Zhurnal,* Moscow, March 1969.

(This particular list appears in an unpublished doctoral dissertation by Commander Howard S. Eldredge, U.S.N., "Antimissile Defense: The U.S.-Soviet Dialogue, 1960–69." Commander Eldredge's helpful suggestions are gratefully acknowledged.)

cal intentions which, themselves, are a product of other components—ideological commitments and preconceptions, societal posture and cultural style—as well as a leadership's belief in its mission, and mass support, spontaneous or induced, in the pursuit of such a mission).

These various inputs together ultimately result in perception of power, but their impact is not necessarily direct. The final power (or "capability") image they produce is enhanced or diminished by certain highly visible "dynamic factors" (some of which occasionally may be deliberately manipulated through "disinformation" and other methods). These factors include: the demonstrated determination and capacity of a leadership to exploit the physical might at its disposal for the attainment of its political goals (or its inability to do so, an outcome that is determined largely by the intensity of prevailing constraints—domestic, bureaucratic, ethical, and other), its visible fixity of purpose, its performance in seizing and maintaining the initiative (a seemingly tactical question which, in fact, reflects the basic *Weltanschauung* of a regime), and, finally, prevailing trends (i.e. whether the might of a state seems to be waxing or waning).

To sum up: it is the basic physical and psychological power "inputs," modified by the various "dynamic factors" which, in the end, create perception of power—a perception which molds the policy decisions of the main adversaries, their respective allies and clients, and third parties. This perception, therefore, is a form of political reality and, whether it is objectively warranted or not, it is equivalent to power.

The equation formulated here provides a framework for comparison in which the asymmetries and disparities between the U.S. and Soviet positions stand out clearly. Only in this context can one comprehend fully the political implications of the deteriorating strategic balance.

The fact of the matter is that, as far as perceived power is concerned, the USSR enjoys a built-in advantage with regard to the greater part of the more visible and immediate "inputs" (although the U.S., of course, continues to be ahead qualitatively in economic and scientific-technological potential); moreover, the Soviet Union currently has a marked edge over the U.S. with regard to almost all of the "dynamic factors" that are relevant to the equation.[14] It is against this background that one must evaluate the political role of U.S. strategic forces. Reduced to simple terms, during the era of the U.S. nuclear monopoly and during the subsequent prolonged period when the U.S. presented a convincing counter-force posture with appreciable superiority over the USSR, America's strategic forces acted as the "equalizer" that neutralized the Soviet advantage in other sectors and, in so doing, helped to maintain a genuine balance between perceptions of

14. Needless to say, this does *not* mean that America's societal lead has appreciably diminished or that her intrinsic strength has ceased to be considerably superior to that of the U.S.S.R. It means only that the *perception* of U.S. power gradually is being overtaken by the *perception* of Soviet power.

U.S. power and of Soviet power. Even during the more recent period when the U.S. strategic position was deteriorating, but a measure of quantitative superiority over the USSR remained, there was enough of a "perception lag" for the "equalizer" role of the U.S. strategic forces to retain some of its credibility.

It is precisely now, with the emergence of a Soviet quantitative margin in ICBM, that the "equalizer" itself finally seems to have been neutralized and, as far as power perception is concerned, the USSR emerges ahead, since its other advantages apparently are no longer cancelled out by U.S. nuclear might.[15] With regard to America's global position, such a change in perception affects not only the willingness of third parties to be influenced by a Superpower deemed to be weakening, but also the confidence of that Superpower in its own strength and, most important, the willingness of the adversary Superpower to risk moving into "grey" zones, knowing that its opponent's self-esteem and self-assurance have been undermined.

The specifics of American-Soviet asymmetry, as revealed by the power-perception equation presented in the present analysis, are relevant to an understanding of this dénouement; analyzed item by item, the following picture emerges:

In "available physical inputs," apart from strategic forces, the USSR possesses a built-in advantage with regard to geographical propinquity to almost all the focal, and potential, areas of conflict—e.g. Berlin-Germany, Yugoslavia-Rumania-Albania, the Eastern Mediterranean-Middle East-Persian Gulf, the Indian Subcontinent, Korea. The same holds true of general purpose forces that cannot but affect the outcome of such conflicts, with the USSR-Warsaw Pact enjoying a widening margin of superiority over the U.S.-NATO.[16]

In "potential physical inputs," America's intrinsic qualitative assets may be overshadowed at this time by the perceptual impact of the news that the USSR has, at least temporarily, overtaken the U.S. in annual steel production.

In "psychological inputs," the Soviet leadership, its own cynicism, factional struggles, and the apathy of the masses notwithstanding, continues to be motivated by residual ideological faith in the dialectic which imbues

15. From the Soviet point of view, to neutralize the credibility of the U.S. strategic forces would be quite sufficient, without necessarily going beyond the framework of Mutual Assured Destruction, since this must leave the U.S.S.R. with unilateral advantages in terms of geography, military manpower, political momentum, initiative and other non-nuclear factors. However, there are indications that the Soviet leaders are striving to attain clear qualitative superiority, if at all possible, even in the strategic arena, examining methods of "blinding" or "paralyzing" their adversary (satellite destroyers, presumably also EMP), testing FOBS and probably other systems that could alter the situation radically.

16. Not least, some would say, because the Zeitgeist current prevailing in the West has made it unfashionable to conduct Realpolitik and to pay the price for the security posture this policy would require.

it with an ongoing sense of "mission." Consequently, there is little diminution of support in Moscow for the view that international affairs must inevitably reflect a fundamental adversary relationship, especially between the USSR and its "main enemy." For the same reason, Soviet leaders have not ceased to feel that it is incumbent upon them to "win"—without having to pay an unacceptable price,[17] of course—since whoever fails eventually to achieve this aim, or stands still over a lengthy period, is irrevocably relegated to the "rubbish dump of history."[18]

(The fact that the Soviet leadership does subscribe to such a dynamic view and that this entails an ongoing commitment to strategic "superiority" has already been documented earlier in this analysis.)[19]

In this rubric, too, there are fundamental asymmetries and the U.S. tends to be at a disadvantage, at least over the short run.[20] The Western elite is steeped in a *Weltanschauung* which, at one and the same time, is more narrowly "practical" and more generously "optimistic" or, perhaps, naive, than that of the Soviet leadership. It postulates a neatly rational "cost-benefit" model of human affairs that grades "gain" and "loss" on a rather different scale than the Kremlin. The contemporary version of the Judeo-Christian ethic does, of course, acknowledge the reality of competition, both between individuals and larger social entities, including states. It assumes, however, that this particular form of "dialectic" is tightly constrained by sophisticated "self-interest," causing each party to weigh "rationally" the possible benefits of "winning" as against its potentially high costs in terms of "absolute" values, as the West sees them, such as human life and human welfare, both in the material and the spiritual sense. Thus, the "reasonable" man, who has been the ultimate ideal of Western society since the Age of the Enlightenment, will always tend to compromise, to seek a deal in which a fair balance may be struck between the various costs and benefits.

It is almost inconceivable to most Western thinkers and statesmen that

17. Such as the potential destruction or disintegration of the Soviet State itself, or of the Soviet régime, as a result of nuclear holocaust.
18. This does not mean, needless to say, that the U.S.S.R. is necessarily committed to eschewing any and all political "cease-fire" arrangements. Whenever a development along these lines may be required for sound tactical reasons, the Soviet leadership will and does accept it, provided it covers only some areas and is not intended to last indefinitely. ("Peaceful coexistence," as Moscow has made clear repeatedly, is meant to be precisely such a limited arrangement.) What is deemed unacceptable to the Soviet Union, at any rate ever since the Khrushchev faction defeated the Malenkov group in the great strategic "debate" of 1953–54, is a final partition of the globe as a whole, a permanent "freezing" of the situation along existing lines, since this would amount to a renunciation of the very concept of "winning" and of the dialectic itself. (For a detailed analysis of this topic, see the author's "Soviet Global Policy and the Middle East," *Naval War College Review*, Vol. XXIV, No. 1, September 1971.)
19. See pp. 499–501.
20. In the longer run, as history has demonstrated, the open society usually has an edge over its rivals, being able to make the most of its inner resources, thanks to a higher degree of flexibility.

there may be societies and leaders who do not necessarily follow or even comprehend this model. Hence, the peculiar difficulties encountered in negotiations between representatives of open and closed societies, in which the former will usually assume that the objective is "compromise" while the latter will take it for granted that the aim of diplomacy is to achieve "by other means" what, perhaps, cannot be gained by force alone, namely "victory" of one sort or another. In Game Theory terms, the open society is less inclined than its adversary toward "zero sum games." As a result of these factors, an essentially "defensive" Western posture is left to confront a relatively dynamic, "offensive" Soviet approach or, more precisely, a less "driven" U.S. leadership must deal with a more highly "charged" Soviet regime. A "sensible" Western leader may be inclined to accept the practical consequences of a given situation where a "correctly thinking" Soviet leader may attempt to change or manipulate the situation itself. It is precisely these disparities that render the mechanistic and essentially symmetrical "action-reaction" model so inappropriate.

It is fairly clear that there are links between these dissimilar U.S. and Soviet "psychological inputs" and many of the "dynamic factors" which, as was postulated earlier in this analysis,[21] enhance or diminish the power image of the two global antagonists (an image that, of course, also reflects the various "inputs" mentioned above, both physical and psychological). Such linkage is evident especially with regard to three of these "dynamic factors," namely, the demonstrated determination and capacity of a leadership to exploit the physical might at its disposal for the attainment of its political goals, its visible fixity of purpose, and its performance in seizing and maintaining the initiative. As far as the first and second "factors" are concerned, clearly a Western elite that demonstrates such deep concern about the "costs" of "winning" is, psychologically, more vulnerable to pressure and threats and, consequently, less "credible" in confrontation situations than a closed society which places (or appears to place) the highest premium on "victory" itself. In a showdown, all other aspects being equal,[22] the latter is likely to "outstare" the former. Indeed, with these concepts in mind, the Soviet leadership has taken good care to orchestrate its commitment to the aim of "winning" by demonstrating its willingness and ability to use the military might at its disposal in the pursuit of political goals. This has been done both directly, as with the Soviet invasions of Hungary and Czechoslovakia, and more obliquely, for instance through the establishment of the Soviet military "presence" in Egypt; less successfully, it was attempted by emplacing Soviet IRBM in Cuba. Although, of course, there also are instances of resort to military power by the U.S., they cannot be viewed, politically speaking, as belonging to the same category of

21. See pp. 500–501.
22. As in the Cuban Missile Crisis they were not, thanks to U.S. geographical proximity and strategic superiority.

"demonstration of willpower" as, for instance, the Soviet attack on Czecho-slovakia.[23] Moreover, unlike the USSR in the Egyptian and Cuban cases, the U.S. primarily has been "reacting" to perceived intrusions into "its sphere," whereas the USSR, on these two and some other occasions, has utilized its military resources in an attempt to extend its perimeter of power and influence.

Not surprisingly, the degree of ability or inability of either leadership to exploit the force at its disposal for the attainment of political goals bears some relationship to the severity of prevailing constraints—domestic, bureaucratic, or ethical. With regard to this topic, there have always been major disparities, of course, between open and closed societies. The bureau-cratic, or factional, conflicts and rivalries of the USSR constitute a rather different (i.e. lesser) order of constraint qualitatively from the web of limitations that the media, public opinion, a self-assertive legislature, an in-dependent judiciary, and the moral and psychological inhibitions of the executive itself can and do impose on the conduct of U.S. policy. While neither society can escape its own contemporary ethic, the Soviet Union's current philosophy happens to favor resort to whatever means may be re-quired for "winning," as has been demonstrated, while the present-day U.S. is permeated by an atmosphere that militates basically against Ameri-can utilization of force. These asymmetries, needless to say, are linked or-ganically to the contrasting nature of the two polities. However, develop-ments during the last few years in the West, and especially in the U.S., have intensified domestic constraints dramatically to the point where in-trinsic U.S. power seems to have become almost irrelevant to the global contest, since apparently it can be brought to bear only in very exceptional circumstances, and American fixity of purpose can no longer be displayed on the international scene. It is significant that the USSR has taken due note of this trend:

23. Although it is fashionable to seek analogies, there are, in fact, no actions by other great powers in contemporary history analogous to the Soviet invasion, in peacetime, of an allied country, not to help in combatting hostile intruders, but to overthrow a friendly government because some of its measures displeased the Soviet leadership. A hypothetical parallel would have been a U.S. invasion of France to overthrow de Gaulle when he was beginning to move away from N.A.T.O. Even there, the analogy would have been closer to the Hungarian than the Czech case, since Dubček, unlike Nagy, had done nothing to weaken his country's ties with the Warsaw Pact. U.S. actions in S.E. Asia belong to a rather different category since, presumably, they were undertaken in support of friendly régimes fighting off hostile forces, including at least some intruding units infiltrated by a country aligned with the adversary superpower. (The criteria employed in this attempt at a typology are, of course, purely political; it is not intended here to deal with the question of moral judgments.) The point is that, in view of these considerations, the Soviet attacks on Prague and, to a lesser extent, on Budapest must be regarded as singularly forceful and pointed assertions of political will, on a level which is quite different from other acts of intervention. (Undoubtedly, however, the degree of force used also reflects Soviet fears, typical of closed societies, that exhibitions of "weakness" may undermine the régime's authority at home, that "toleration" of Czechoslovakia could result in "infection" of the Soviet body politic.)

. . . "political reality" also includes the domestic political situation in the U.S. itself, where the popular masses are demanding increasingly decisively and loudly the renunciation of military adventures abroad and the administration's turning to face the internal socioeconomic problems. . . . Moments arise when the split between the sentiments and feelings of broad public circles and official policy proves so deep that a bourgeois government, wishing to remain in power, either has to correct official policy or resign from power . . . The present Republican administration must take into account the opinion of the overwhelming majority of voters who support . . . the reduction of U.S. military commitments abroad.[24]

Thus, Soviet leaders may well be beginning to draw certain far-reaching and potentially dangerous conclusions from recent developments in the West, e.g. that the U.S. gradually may be turning into a "paper tiger" and that this gives the USSR something of a "green light" to move forward in certain areas of the world. The White House has attempted to counteract such tendencies with a policy of "intentional unpredictability," the aim of which is to persuade the USSR not to take U.S. inaction for granted; for this purpose several demonstrations have been made of U.S. determination and strength, somewhat unexpectedly in most cases, covering three or four geographical regions. However, this policy too cannot operate with full effect when inhibited by severe domestic constraints.

Severally and jointly, the factors analyzed here operate to the detriment of a positive perception of U.S. power, as also does the adverse trend in the U.S.-USSR military balance[25] and in the general political situation, compared with the 1950's and early 1960's.

To complete the picture, one must point to an additional disparity between the U.S. and the USSR, relating to the respective desire and ability of each of the two adversaries to seize and maintain the initiative, a comparison from which the Russians emerge with higher scores. The importance ascribed to this topic by the Soviet leadership has already been documented earlier in this analysis,[16] together with the fact that the Soviet penchant for the initiative has profound ideological roots.[27] These are aspects to which Western protagonists of the "action-reaction" model appear to be insufficiently attuned. Many Western analysts confuse two very different concepts, believing the U.S. "actions" *cause* Soviet "reactions" whereas usually they provide at most a *pretext* for Soviet measures that

24. A Trofimenko, "Political Realism and the 'Realistic Deterrence' Strategy," *U.S.A.: Economics, Politics, Ideology*, No. 12, Moscow, 1971.
25. See p. 499.
26. See pp. 2–3, especially the gleeful Soviet assertion that the West "is impotent to regain the historic initiative it has lost."
27. See pp. 502–503.

may have been planned and initiated before the U.S. actually moved. The fact is that Soviet leaders simply do not accept the passive, "reactive" role assigned to them by some Western observers and remain committed to maintaining the initiative.

Cumulatively, then, the asymmetries between the two Superpowers that emerge from almost all of the various "inputs" and "dynamic factors" analyzed here, seriously diminish America's power image, as viewed by third parties, by the U.S. itself and its allies, and, not least, by the Soviet Union. This general perception of a U.S. that is handicapped in many sectors of its contest with the USSR, could only be balanced out as long as the U.S. retained full "credibility" in the strategic sector. However, that "credibility" has lost some of its impact, at least for purposes that are broader than mere deterrence of a nuclear strike by the adversary. In addition to the important quantitative changes in the strategic balance already discussed,[28] this negative development may be linked to a decision made in Washington some years ago—largely in response to the (imaginary) requirements of the "action-reaction" model. As MIRV evolved, it was resolved to go for individual warheads with relatively low yield, apparently as a way of "assuring" the USSR that no first-strike capability was intended, so as to avoid "provoking" Moscow into a further stage of escalation in the Armaments Spiral.[29] Seemingly, it was overlooked, however, that the U.S. and Soviet strategic forces serve basically different political purposes. The Soviet strategic posture achieves a major aim, as soon as, by merely creating a perception of "parity," it can neutralize the U.S. strategic force, since, then, existing and latent asymmetries and disparities come into play in various other sectors, where, as has been demonstrated here, the USSR appears to have the deck stacked in its favor. The U.S. strategic force, on the other hand, can only assume its essential role of political "equalizer" if it enjoys some significant advantage over its Soviet counterpart, such as an appreciable, if limited, counter-force capability; in this way the USSR may be credibly deterred from exploiting its assets in other areas and, as far as perceived power is concerned, the balance can be maintained. In other words, the Soviet strategic force essentially has achieved its political task, if it can cancel out the U.S. "equalizer," i.e. the U.S. strategic force; the latter, on the other hand, must be able to neutralize not only the Soviet strategic force, but also other military, political and psychological factors to compensate for the perception of greater Soviet power in these sectors.

28. This analysis does not contain any discussion of the possible implications of SALT, for the simple reason that, to judge by currently projected scenarios, SALT seems unlikely to have a major effect either way on political perceptions as analyzed here.

29. If, indeed, this was the aim, it failed, since the U.S.S.R. proceeded to develop and deploy a potentially significant, although partial, counter-force capability with the high-yield SS-9.

To translate into operative terms the inferences that can be drawn from this analysis, it may be helpful to sketch the scenario of a potential U.S.-Soviet crisis. Given the characteristic Soviet penchant for seizing and exploiting the initiative, as documented here, it seems reasonable to expect that the USSR, encouraged by current perception of U.S. weakness, may stage a politico-military offensive in some "grey area," probably in the Third World, where the West has been predominant, but where America's determination and posture had become significantly "blurred." Establishing and reinforcing a military presence in such an area, the Soviet Union could then exploit that presence to support a Soviet client, to the point of direct intervention, in an attack intended to crush a nation closely linked to the U.S., so as to deliver a shattering blow to the perception of American power, America's national interests and her strategic as well as tactical credibility. One can hardly regard this scenario as overly fanciful, since segments of it are already visible in some regions of the Third World. It is evident that a Soviet initiative along these lines would confront the U.S. with an inescapable dilemma between tacit surrender to the *fait accompli,* with all its consequences, and an attempt to avert such a dénouement through a series of measures which, to offset Moscow's various tactical advantages as enumerated earlier, would have to include at least an implicit reference to America's strategical deterrent. Most probably, therefore, it would be the U.S. that would have to be first in invoking the spectre of its strategic forces.[30] Consequently, it is the credibility of the American—rather than of the Soviet—strategic forces that would have to prove convincing and pass this momentous political test.

The present, basically counter-value[31] posture of the U.S., however, is poorly suited to this task. After all, within such a scenario, what would an implicit reference to the U.S. strategic deterrent really mean? That America actually is prepared, if the Kremlin does not desist, to envisage the prospect of atomizing Soviet cities and killing tens of millions of Soviet

30. Some may ask whatever happened to graduated response, which, hopefully, should have relieved the nuclear deterrent of some of these tasks and burdens. Others, perhaps, would reply that graduated response and its twin, conventional escalation, are missing in action, somewhere in Southeast Asia, where, apparently, it was demonstrated that the domestic costs of this concept are too high, given the currently prevailing winds. The Nixon Doctrine, of course, was intended to provide an acceptable substitute, but can only be effective in the absence of direct Soviet intervention. The present scenario, however, postulates that such intervention is possible and that, in view of contemporary constraints on U.S. policy, meaningful American preventative measures would be attempted only at a relatively advanced stage of the resulting crisis. These are the factors that compel one to focus on the role of strategic forces rather than lesser deterrents.

31. Among analysts, there are some that expect an evolutionary process of development of increasing accuracy eventually to give America's relatively low yield MIRV a counterforce capability. Their colleagues, however, claim that this would require a revolutionary breakthrough and that, even then, defensive developments might offset such an achievement. (Given the present state of the art, development of Terminal Guidance Systems might conceivably be the sector where a breakthrough could occur.)

civilians? Considering the open society's traditional preoccupation with "costs," especially in terms of human life and value, as well as contemporary views on the conduct of international relations, such a prospect, however remote, would arouse domestic waves of revulsion that would submerge any remnants of credibility. Moreover, militarily as well as politically, this credibility would be open to question, given the relatively low yield U.S. warheads, hardened Soviet silos, and the perception of improvement in the USSR's ASW capability and its ABM system, however rudimentary. As viewed in both capitals, these elements cumulatively would ensure the survival, in reasonably effective condition, of a substantial proportion of Soviet nuclear forces and of Russian command and control facilities.[32] Thus, the USSR could be expected to remain capable, in a second strike, of annihilating whatever strategic reserves the U.S. had retained, and of wreaking full vengeance upon America's population and society, especially in view of the relative neglect of civil defense and shelter programs in the U.S. and in the abeyance of a serious area ABM effort. In view of these perceptions and expectations, the Soviet leadership would be greatly tempted to "call" America's strategic poker "hand" at an early stage; in that eventuality, the credibility of the U.S. deterrent might well suffer a near-fatal blow. Indeed, to some extent, Moscow has already begun to discount American credibility in such a scenario:

> . . . the U.S. "strategic nuclear missile force" is not automatically a political influence and . . . in the majority of conflict situations in the "Third World" it cannot be used even as a real threat . . ."[33]

Paradoxically, the Soviet Union is developing its own strategic force along lines more calculated to create a credible posture in such situations than is the U.S. approach, even though, for reasons already discussed,[34] the political impact of Moscow's strategic credibility is, in fact, less likely to be tested at an early date. In all probability, the Soviet leadership expected the U.S. to respond to the "logic" of the considerations mentioned above and to go boldly for an incipient counter-force capability, rather than opting for a counter-value posture, as America actually did. In anticipation of a more dynamic U.S. defense policy and in order to preempt it, the USSR itself moved in the direction of a counter-force capability, however limited and rudimentary, with the huge SS-9, endowed with sufficient "throw-weight" capability to remain high-yield even after being MIRVed. Presumably, given somewhat improved accuracies, such a capability would, in the Soviet view, enable its possessor to neutralize a relatively high proportion

32. The latter is very speculative, since rather little is known about Soviet command and control arrangements.
33. A. Trofimenko, "Political Realism and the 'Realistic Deterrence' Strategy," *U.S.A.: Economics, Politics, Ideology*, No. 12, Moscow, 1971.
34. See pp. 507–508.

of the adversary's nuclear force, without, at the same time, necessarily inflicting unacceptable societal losses on that adversary. Thus, the latter would be left with the unenviable choice of either acquiescing in the fact that he had been partially disarmed at the first blow, or dispatching his remaining missiles to relatively limited effect, realizing that this would trigger a retaliatory third strike which would destroy what was left of his state and society.[35] Thus, a counter-force posture, however incipient, is bound to have more credibility than a counter-value system as a deterrent to threatened enemy offensives into "grey" areas, as well as for more general purposes; of course, such credibility can be enhanced further if it so happens that the regime possessing this capability has to contend only with the relatively weak internal constraints that face the Soviet leadership.

Such scenarios, and the speculations that accompany them, are naturally uncongenial to any sensitive and compassionate human being, so that they are difficult to contemplate in cold blood. However, they serve a necessary illustrative purpose, demonstrating not only the fundamental asymmetries between the Soviet and American strategic postures, but also the gap that is developing between the latter and the overall political task that it must fulfill.

Reviewing the various aspects of the U.S.-USSR power relationship that have been analyzed and evaluating their cumulative political impact, there is, regrettably, little doubt that erosion is taking place in the general perception of American power and its credibility. The changing strategic balance is playing a definite role in this process, as has been shown, although it is, to be sure, only one among several causative elements.

It should hardly be necessary, at this point, to stress once more that the present analysis has focused almost entirely upon *perceptions* of power rather than upon intrinsic and potential strength. It is concerned, therefore, with relatively short-term considerations, covering a number of years rather than decades. Taking the longer view, there is room for the expectation that the present process may turn out to be limited in duration and far from unilinear in direction. The inner reserves, the unshackled human resources, the great flexibility of the open society historically have proven capable of meeting and overcoming the most formidable problems, especially when stimulated by single-minded adversaries that probed and pushed too roughly and too persistently.[36]

In conclusion, a caveat may, perhaps, be in order. The aims of this analysis have been quite limited: to establish, as precisely and coherently

35. It can be argued that, theoretically, there is a finite answer to this scenario, namely, to let the adversary know in various ways that a launch-on-warning policy may be implemented.

36. If, in various portions of this paper, there is reference to an adversary relationship with the U.S.S.R., this, needless to say, is not to be regarded as equivalent to gleeful advocacy of such a relationship; rather, it reflects the regretful conclusion that this is the posture which, as of the present date, the Soviet leadership is continuing to adopt.

as possible, what is the general political framework within which strategic factors currently operate and what, therefore, are the political implications of changes in the strategic balance. It is not within the purview of this paper or, indeed, the author's area of competence, to suggest specific remedial measures.

32.

Chinese Attitudes Towards Nuclear Weapons: 1964-69

JONATHAN D. POLLACK

OCTOBER 1969 WAS not only the 20th anniversary of the founding of the Chinese People's Republic (CPR); it also marked the culmination of China's fifth year as a nuclear power. During this five-year period there were 10 detonations, three of which were thermonuclear and one of which was tested underground. At least one of the warheads was fired from a guided missile. According to one estimate, current defense expenditures amount to 10 percent of China's gross national product, and one-fifth of this outlay is devoted to nuclear research and development alone. A large portion of China's advanced scientific and technical manpower has also been assigned to this field. Although an adequate delivery system for this limited nuclear capability, as of November 1971, is not known to be operational, China's progress in the research and development of advanced weapons has clearly been substantial. The launching of Chinese satellites in 1970 and 1971 and the likelihood of an intercontinental ballistic missile (ICBM) test in the near future are further evidence of major technological achievement. Peking's entry, then, into the "nuclear club" has been a major concern of China's leaders; it has also had significant consequences for American defense planners. The explicit rationale for the Nixon Administration's expansion of the anti-ballistic missile (ABM) system in early 1970, for example, was to guard against the possibility of a Chinese attack in the 1980s and thus to assure the reliability of American defense commitments in East Asia and the Pacific.

Excerpted and reprinted by permission from *China Quarterly*, No. 50, pp. 244–72.

Moreover, China's nuclear program evolved within the context of several extended military crises. Twice during this period the Chinese political elite seemed to conclude that the occurrence of war—even nuclear war—was a distinct possibility. First in the middle of 1965 during a critical period of American escalation in Vietnam, and again through much of 1969 and 1970 due to border disputes with the Soviet Union, the possibility that general war might break out on Chinese soil was clearly acknowledged. Many of the advances—as well as the setbacks—in weapons development also coincided with the extended unrest of the Cultural Revolution.

Yet relatively few attempts have been made so far to analyze China's nuclear doctrine since these weapons tests began. The major purpose of this paper, then, will be to investigate how the possession and possible use of nuclear weapons was viewed by the Chinese leadership in the years 1964-9, both over time and in periods of possible conflict. It should be kept in mind that the opinions of decision-makers on such critical questions are not expressed without ample concern for the political and strategic context within which these perceptions and policies must operate. Thus it is clearly unsatisfactory to treat Chinese attitudes solely on a descriptive basis.

The principal argument of this paper is that Chinese attitudes towards nuclear weapons during this period can be best understood as dependent upon certain major constraints affecting Chinese foreign policy behavior. There appear to be three such constraints, in decreasing order of importance: (1) considerations of American and Soviet military superiority—particularly nuclear superiority; (2) an awareness that the perceptions and policies of neighboring states would be significantly affected by any major transformation in China's foreign policy as a result of the latter's nuclear capability; and (3) a similar awareness concerning the perceptions and policies of non-aligned and Communist states not on China's periphery. Hence Chinese pronouncements were articulated so as to mitigate these constraints and minimize the possible negative consequences of the development of a nuclear capability. The intent of the messages emanating from the Chinese elite was thus two-fold: (a) to lessen the external threat to China posed by American and Soviet perceptions of hostility and superior capability; and (b) to stabilize or improve China's external relations with non-nuclear states resulting from the latter's perceptions of external hostility and inferior capability.

It must be acknowledged that the number of communications devoted exclusively to nuclear weapons is somewhat limited. It is emphasized, however, that these statements represented Peking's general justification for pursuing a nuclear capability. Thus a content analysis of the press communiques and policy pronouncements issued for all but one of the detonations during this period should provide insight into Chinese attitudes and the context within which they were formed.

The "Detonation Statements"

These communiques reveal several distinct trends in Chinese policy. We immediately note that while the overall defensive justification for nuclear development did not change, the relative weight given this factor varied considerably over time. Although the Government Statement of October 16, 1964, later described by the New China News Agency (NCNA) as "a full explanation of our fundamental stand on nuclear weapons," was very heavily weighted toward security considerations, subsequent messages—particularly after the fourth test (October 27, 1966)—concentrated on domestic implications. The general emphasis on China's nuclear weapons being a vindication of Mao's thought and of the Cultural Revolution reached a peak for the eighth test (December 28, 1968), with a marked decline in emphasis in the joint pronouncement for the ninth and tenth tests (October 4, 1969).

The first pronouncement was also atypical in several other respects. It alone advocated concrete arms control measures which were offered for discussion at a proposed worldwide disarmament conference. As an initial step, it was suggested that the nations in attendance "should reach an agreement to the effect that the nuclear powers and those countries which will soon become nuclear powers undertake not to use nuclear weapons . . . against non-nuclear countries and nuclear-free zones [or] against each other."[1] These suggestions were not found in such specific form in later declarations. Instead, there was a continued commitment never to be the first nuclear power to use these weapons in any future war, as well as an unspecific declaration since the second test that "China is conducting necessary nuclear tests within defined limits." This probably refers to the frequent assertion that China's development of nuclear weapons is for defensive purposes only and that "China's aim is to break the nuclear monopoly of the nuclear powers and to eliminate nuclear weapons."[2] In addition, the need to combat American "nuclear blackmail" was heavily stressed; after the third test (May 9, 1966), Soviet actions were similarly characterized.

A third respect in which the October 1964 statement was atypical was its disparagement of nuclear weapons. With the exception of three such references in this document and one reference in the communique for the sixth test, there is no specific mention in the detonation pronouncements of nuclear weapons as "paper tigers" or of the importance of man over weapons. (This theme was occasionally noted in indirect fashion, such as in the

1. Statement of the Government of the C.P.R., 16 October 1964, in *SCMP*, No. 3322, p. 3.
2. *Ibid.* p. 2. It should be noted, however, that "the complete prohibition and thorough destruction of nuclear weapons" is considered an "ultimate aim"; there has never been any suggestion that China would unilaterally halt weapons production and testing without a guarantee that was binding upon all nuclear powers.

third test declaration, when adherence to the "four firsts" was advocated.) Instead, particularly during the Cultural Revolution, each test was glorified as a further step in the modernization of China's defensive capabilities and as an even greater achievement in terms of scientific and technological sophistication. A quotation from Mao Tse-tung has been cited as proper guidance: "man has to constantly sum up experience and go on discovering, inventing, creating, and advancing."[3] The declaration of *Chieh-fang-chün Pao (Liberation Army Daily)* after the first thermonuclear test (June 17, 1967) pointed to Mao's statement of June 1958 that it would be possible for China to produce both atomic and hydrogen bombs within 10 years; Mao's directive "regarding the development of national defence science . . . to go all out and aim high, rely on our own strength and . . . make efforts to catch up with and surpass the world's advanced level of science and technology"[4] was also cited. In perhaps the most unambiguous testament to this "great leap" in the development of modern weapons, China's progress was explicitly compared to that of the other thermonuclear powers:

Inspired by Chairman Mao's teaching . . . they [those working on the device] summed up the experience of the preceding tests, broke away from foreign stereotypes and old conventions, [and] introduced daring new methods. . . . It has taken China only two years and eight months to cover the entire course from her first A-bomb explosion in October 1964 to the successful H-bomb test. However, to do the same thing, it took the United States seven years and four months, the Soviet Union four years, and Britain four years and seven months. China's speed, therefore, is the fastest in the world.[5]

Somewhat surprisingly, however, we do not find much emphasis placed upon the perception of external threat. After the initial detonation statement, the defensive justification—in terms of the number of references to the right of self-defense, the generalized threat to China, and the behavior of the United States (and since May 1966 the Soviet Union)—was largely absent. Moreover, the articulation of threat after the first statement became far less specific. These facts suggest a conscious omission of salient security threats in these pronouncements, particularly during the high stress periods of 1965–6 and 1969.

It was only in the October 1964 declaration that highly specific references were made to the identity of the external threat—in this case, the direct threat to Asian countries of American nuclear submarines in Japan and the threat of arming West Germany through the multilateral force

3. NCNA, 28 December 1966, in *SCMP*, No. 3851, p. 1.
4. "A brilliant victory for Mao Tse-tung's thought," *Chieh-fang-chün Pao*, NCNA, 18 June 1967, in *SCMP*, No. 3964, p. 3.
5. "A triumph of Mao Tse-tung's thought," *Chieh-fang-chün Pao*, NCNA, 19 June 1967, in *SCMP*, No. 3965, p. 13.

(MLF) proposals. In addition, it was solely in the initial statement that we find—outside the consistent "no first use" pledge—explicit and extended assurances of Peking's peaceful intentions in developing nuclear weapons:

> China cannot remain idle and do nothing in the face of ever increasing nuclear threat posed by the United States. China is forced to conduct nuclear tests and develop nuclear weapons. . . . China is developing nuclear weapons not because we believe in the omnipotence of nuclear weapons and that China plans to use nuclear weapons. . . . The development of nuclear weapons by China is for defence and for protecting the Chinese people from the danger of the United States launching a nuclear war. . . . *On the question of nuclear weapons, China will neither commit the error of adventurism nor the error of capitulationism. The Chinese people can be trusted.*[6]

It seems likely that these arguments were not directed at either of the major nuclear powers, but at those countries—specifically, Japan and India—which possessed the scientific and material resources necessary to produce nuclear weapons and might possibly have felt threatened, given the Chinese detonation. Such reassurances were probably deemed necessary to allay any suspicions or fears which might have developed as a result of China's nuclear programme. Yet it is also clear that the Chinese elite anticipated that other nations would shortly possess similar weapons: hence the disarmament proposals, as mentioned earlier, referred to "those countries which will soon become nuclear powers."

The significance of the assurance of "neither adventurism nor capitulationism" should also not be ignored; it is the Chinese accusation made for what was deemed imprudent Soviet behaviour in the Cuban missile crisis of 1962. In a citation from one of Mao's 1957 Moscow speeches quoted in 1966, "adventurism" was considered analogous to not respecting the enemy tactically: "in dealing with concrete problems and particular enemies we shall be committing the error of adventurism unless we take them seriously." Further, a 1968 analysis of the "capitulation and treachery" of Soviet foreign policy implicitly revealed Chinese reluctance to engage in the political use of nuclear weapons:

> During the Caribbean crisis in 1962, Khrushchev tried his luck by sending missiles to Cuba as a means of furthering his nuclear blackmail. Yet, when the U.S. imperialists met his blackmail with their own blackmail he was scared out of his wits; overnight he took a dive from the castle in the air of adventurism into the quagmire of capitulationism,

6. Statement of the Government of the C.P.R., in *SCMP*, No. 3322, pp. 1–2. My emphasis.

and begged for mercy from John F. Kennedy in a most humiliating manner.

The implications of such comments can be analyzed from two perspectives. We can first view the argument in an abstract sense. While it is deemed inexcusable and humiliating to back down from imperialist provocation, it is considered equally if not more reprehensible to lock oneself into such a position in the first place. We can also place the statement within the context of China's military and political vulnerability, as hypothesized earlier in the paper. While this declaration is not unequivocal it is an implicit commitment to forestall the use of nuclear weapons as a resource for foreign policy maneuvers. Given the sensitivity of the non-nuclear nations to the political use of such weapons, and also accepting the reality of Soviet and American military superiority, it would seem both plausible and reasonable to articulate these sentiments, particularly at a time when no operational Chinese capability could be said to exist.

Thus far we have not directly discussed the impact of the Cultural Revolution on Chinese attitudes. The value of the documents issued during this period of severe domestic conflict is limited by the fact that they do not generally relate to the security issues which seem fundamental to the development of Chinese nuclear policy. The increasing emphasis over time on the domestic implications of the weapons tests, however, cannot be ignored. The only reference to domestic themes associated with the first detonation was in a congratulatory message sent by the Central Committee and State Council to those involved in the project.[7] In the pronouncement for the second test (May 14, 1965), we find the first reference to the contribution of the People's Liberation Army (PLA) as well as to the atomic bomb as a victory of Mao's thought and the general line of socialist construction. In the statement following the third test, Mao's thought was glorified, although not in endlessly glowing terms. The entire pronouncements for the fourth and fifth detonations were highly adulatory to Mao's thought, the PLA, and Lin Piao.

It is only in statements issued after the sixth test, however, that opposition to the revolutionary line is mentioned in any detail. The successful detonation of a hydrogen bomb was described as "a great victory for the proletarian revolutionary line represented by Chairman Mao in the field of national defence science."[8]

Viewed in terms of an earlier debate over military policy, the relevance of a quotation of Mao's published in the post-detonation commentary becomes clearer: "Chairman Mao has said: 'On what basis should our [national defence] policy rest? It should rest on our own strength, and that means re-

---

7. NCNA, 17 October 1964, in *SCMP*, No. 3322, pp. 3–4.
8. "A brilliant victory for Mao Tse-tung's thought," p. 3.

generation through one's own efforts.' And 'we stand for self-reliance. We hope for foreign aid but cannot be dependent upon it; we depend on our own efforts, on the creative power of the whole army and the entire people.' "[9] In the context of China's first thermonuclear detonation, then, the depiction of P'eng [Teh-huai] as a leader less daring and self-reliant provided an effective contrast with Mao's determination to develop an independent nuclear capability.

It is doubtful, however, whether the association between these considerations and the disclosures of August 1967 should be regarded as more than a glorification of Mao's prescience on the nuclear question. Moreover, the occasional hints about conflict over defense issues are rarely more specific than in the above documents. Whether one considers the attacks on P'eng as an attempt to link his opposition to Mao with that of Liu and others, or merely as a reiteration of the Chinese commitment to an independent nuclear program, this limited documentation is not sufficient for us to argue that strategic considerations had become secondary to the ascendancy of Maoist domestic policies. It must be concluded, then, that in so far as the various detonations were justified as a contribution to the Mao-Lin line, we are dealing largely with "declaratory policy" rather than a genuine transformation in attitudes.

Clearly indicated in all these documents, however, is the need for unimpeded development of an independent nuclear capability. Thus, to the extent that the Chinese leadership expressed concern about interference in the Chinese nuclear program during the Cultural Revolution, one can argue that domestic considerations did affect Chinese attitudes. As noted earlier, for example, the statement following the eighth test was the document most heavily weighted towards domestic issues, despite the fact that Cultural Revolution activity had already subsided. We should also recall, however, that this was the first successful detonation in 18 months and followed by several months the apparent culmination of extended conflict within the national defense program. In as unambiguous a statement as was ever issued in this entire period indicating the adoption of "professional" over "revolutionary" considerations, Mao was again cited:

> We cannot just take the beaten track traversed by other countries in the development of technology and trail behind them at a snail's pace. We must break away from the conventions and do our utmost to adopt advanced techniques in order to build our country into a powerful modern socialist state in not too long a historical period.

The use of such an argument seems to suggest the salience of Chinese strategic considerations during this period. That is, modernization of Peking's national defense capabilities emerged as a sufficiently critical commitment

9. "A triumph of Mao Tse-tung's thought," p. 13.

to take precedence over issues of internal political conflict or resource-distribution. While preference for such a policy undoubtedly affected the allocation of resources within the Chinese political system, these preferred allocations resulted from a perception of China's strategic vulnerability and immediate defense needs, not vice versa.

The evidence of domestic policy conflict, then, only strengthens our argument concerning the primary importance of China's strategic needs. A slowdown in nuclear development, as apparently occurred during 1967 and 1968, could only place China at an even greater disadvantage with respect to the military capabilities of Peking's principal adversaries. Hence it became essential to remove any possible impediments to successful nuclear development. At the same time, however, policy positions on these security considerations had to be developed in order to minimize the possible negative consequences of weapons development for China's external relations, both with the Superpowers and the non-nuclear states. The general absence of these discussions in the detonation statements during the Cultural Revolution does not mean that such considerations were of secondary importance. Chinese attitudes towards nuclear weapons, as noted previously, were aired most extensively after the first detonation; this statement may have been considered a sufficient expression of intent for the first critical years of weapons development. And, as the detonation statements in the years 1966–8 clearly reveal, the basic commitment to an independent nuclear capability was never questioned, but only strengthened. As I will attempt to demonstrate further in subsequent sections of this paper, the political and strategic context of China's nuclear program appears to be the major determinant of Chinese attitudes toward these weapons.

While the post-detonation pronouncements prove useful in describing major components of Chinese nuclear policy, certain considerations cannot be adequately investigated by a content analysis of these sources. These topics include attitudes toward nuclear proliferation and arms control, evaluation of the sources and capabilities of external threat, and the strategic and tactical role of nuclear weapons envisaged by the Chinese elite. Only by investigating documents relating to Sino-Soviet and Sino-American interaction as well as PLA pronouncements in crisis and noncrisis situations can we adequately generalize about Chinese perspectives on the role of nuclear weapons within the international system.

Nuclear Proliferation and Arms Control

Since other scholars have examined the question of nuclear proliferation in some detail, it will not be necessary to reassess this topic at any length. Rather, Chinese pronouncements issued during the 1964–69 period will be considered in an effort to determine the likely direction of Peking's future attitudes. In general, scholars have been concerned with one question:

what would be the likely effect of additional nuclear powers upon China's "vital security interests"? Depending upon one's answer, it is then possible to infer the probable Chinese attitude towards proliferation. One author, for example, has argued that China's leaders would not seriously object to large-scale nuclear proliferation, even to the extent of tolerating a Japanese or Indian nuclear program. Such a prediction is based on the assumption that by developing an independent nuclear capability, nations such as Japan and India would become less reliant upon, or even independent of, the United States and Soviet Union, while not unduly threatening Chinese security. A close evaluation of Chinese statements on this topic, however, makes such an assumption appear somewhat dubious. Statements by Chinese leaders about the dangers of Japanese rearmament, for example, became increasingly emphatic during 1969 and 1970, with some communiques explicitly mentioning the threat to Chinese security posed by the possibility of Japanese nuclearization. Such evidence indicates the difficulty in arguing at least from the Chinese viewpoint—that commitment to a nuclear program by a nation such as Japan would necessarily result in a divergence from the foreign policy of its major nuclear ally.

More generally, we must question the extent to which the Chinese leadership has genuinely encouraged other nations—even socialist ones—to develop a nuclear capability. One can argue that there was at least implicit approval of proliferation in the *People's Daily* after the first Chinese detonation and in Ch'en Yi's later encouragement ("it would be better for a greater number of countries to come into possession of atomic bombs.") Yet when making this statement Ch'en also noted that: "Any country with a fair basis in industry and agriculture and in science and technology will be able to manufacture atom bombs, with or without Chinese assistance . . . [But] in our view, the role of atom bombs should not be overstressed."[10] In a more detailed analysis of the implications of nuclear weapons for world politics written in 1965, the extent of Chinese support for nuclear proliferation seemed rather unclear:

> It goes without saying that the possession of atom bombs by China is a great encouragement to the people of the whole world in their revolutionary struggle, a telling blow at the nuclear blackmail of U.S. imperialism, and a tremendous contribution to the protection of world peace. It boosts the morale of the world's people but greatly demoralizes the enemy.[11]

This interpretation, with minor variations, has been repeated numerous times since 1964. There has been no suggestion that China's nuclear weapons represent anything more than an inspiration to revolutionaries and the

10. *Ibid.*
11. Han Tung-pi, Li Ch'ing-kun, and Yü Tzu-chung, "View nuclear weapons with a correct world outlook," *Kuang-ming Jih pao* (*Enlightenment Daily*) (Peking), NCNA, 25 August 1965, in *SCMP*, No. 3539, p. 8.

non-nuclear countries in general. That is, no explicit commitment from China to assist in nuclear proliferation has ever been issued.

More significantly, it is not possible, on the basis of a literal interpretation of Chinese statements, to differentiate clearly between China and such descriptive labels as "the revolutionary people of the world" and "countries of the world." For example, Chou En-lai's greeting to the 12th World Conference Against Atomic and Hydrogen Bombs in July 1966 appeared to offer strong encouragement for proliferation: "nuclear war can be prevented and nuclear weapons can be finally eliminated only after the peace-loving countries possess nuclear weapons and break the nuclear monopoly."[12] Yet Chinese support for nuclear proliferation, in an operational sense, has been far more restrained. This was explicitly indicated in a speech by Liu Shao-ch'i two weeks after the first detonation: "All oppressed nations and peoples and all peace-loving countries and people have felt elated over the successful explosion of China's first atom bomb, as they hold the view that they, too, have nuclear weapons."[13]

It is true that this limited amount of evidence does not allow us to argue that China's leaders are unalterably opposed to the further spread of nuclear weapons. In fact, on no occasion has explicit disapproval of this possibility been indicated. Any effort to deny the right of nuclear development to other states, however, would place China in the category of "nuclear overlord" along with the United States and Soviet Union. Nevertheless, it seems most unlikely that the Chinese elite would be willing to encourage or assist the efforts of non-nuclear states to develop such weapons when the potential political and military gains are at best dubious. Instead, Chinese spokesmen have continued to attack the efforts of the United States and Soviet Union to prevent additional nations from conducting nuclear tests. There has been no concomitant gesture, however, encouraging further proliferation.

Chinese statements relating to arms control have further developed the arguments used to oppose American-Soviet non-proliferation measures. Certain declarations, for example, have contained the assertion that a community of common interest exists between China and the non-nuclear states. An additional argument is that China's nuclear weapons and the purposes for which they are intended are qualitatively different from those of the United States and Soviet Union. An unequivocal assurance that Chinese foreign policy would not be dependent upon nuclear weapons was articulated shortly after the first detonation:

Having developed nuclear weapons, we shall pursue, as we did in the past, the foreign policy of peace. We shall not use these weapons to intimidate others and embark on any adventure. Nor shall we use them as

12. NCNA, 30 July 1966, in *SCMP*, No. 3752, p. 24.
13. Peking Radio, 30 October 1964, cited in Young, "Chinese views on the spread of nuclear weapons," p. 148.

a membership card to join the "nuclear club" and do anything to jeopardize the interest of the people's revolutions . . . or that of world peace.[14]

Following the subsequent American proposal for talks among the five nuclear powers, a *People's Daily* editorial, in unusually restrained terms, sought to establish that Chinese possession of nuclear weapons had not in the least altered the perspectives or behavior of the regime:

> China has consistently stood for discussion by all countries of the world of the question of banning nuclear weapons. This was our stand when we did not have nuclear weapons. We still adhere to this stand now that we have them. We have only one objective, namely to make joint efforts . . . to strive for the realization of complete prohibition and thorough destruction of nuclear weapons, *and by no means to use nuclear weapons to raise our own prestige and manipulate international affairs.* The so-called talks among the five countries possessing nuclear weapons would in fact be a nuclear club in disguise.[15]

These and related pronouncements on disarmament are usually interpreted as little more than political ploys by the Chinese Government which are certain to fail due to their utopian nature (for example, the expectation that the ultimate goal of banning nuclear weapons can be realized).[16] Such an evaluation, however, ignores certain factors which are critical to an understanding of Chinese policy in this area. These declarations were made within the context of extreme military and political vulnerability—military due to the lack of an effective deterrent, political since Chinese leaders refused to commit themselves to formal arms control agreements. But a unilateral declaration such as the "no first use" pledge, while not sanctioned by any international conference and emanating from a weak and obviously vulnerable nuclear power, still represents a commitment to an arms control measure of major consequence. Given China's strategic vulnerability during this period it is hardly surprising that Chinese decision-makers publicly declared their intention to limit the role played by nuclear weapons in Chinese foreign policy.

Beyond the frequent declaration of "no first use," an expressed interest in arms control measures was lacking during 1966–69. Instead, sophisticated Chinese declarations, usually emanating from *Jen-min Jih-pao*, elaborated on the right of all nations to develop nuclear weapons. But the arguments used in defense of non-nuclear nations pursuing such a policy were indistinguishable from the justification used for China's expanding capability. These arguments—hypothetical from the non-nuclear viewpoint and actual

14. "Break nuclear monopoly, destroy nuclear weapons," p. 24.
15. "A new starting point for the strivings for the complete prohibition of nuclear weapons," *JMJP*, NCNA, 22 November 1964, in *SCMP*, No. 3345, p. 20. My emphasis.
16. See, for example, Morton H. Halperin and Dwight A. Perkins, *Communist China and Arms Control* (Cambridge, Mass.: East Asian Research Centre, 1965), ch. X.

from the Chinese perspective—usually appeared together and were indeed inseparable. Such an attitude was clearly expressed in a November 1966 analysis of the Non-Proliferation Treaty:

> The so-called nuclear non-proliferation treaty means that the nuclear weapon should be regarded as a thing to be monopolized by the two nuclear overlords, the U.S. and the Soviet Union, and that they and they alone should be allowed to possess such weapons, not anybody else. It means that others should recognize the hegemony of these two big nuclear powers, that U.S. imperialism should enjoy the privilege of aggression for proceeding with nuclear blackmail and that other countries should be deprived of their right of defence by developing nuclear weapons to combat U.S. nuclear blackmail. The treaty on the non-proliferation of nuclear weapons . . . is absolutely unjust and unfair to *the other countries of the world*. Whereas the U.S. and the Soviet Union may develop nuclear weapons on a big scale and have [a] monopoly of them, *the non-nuclear countries* should not be allowed to have a finger in the pie, not even to think of it. . . . It is the business of *every country in the world* to decide for itself whether to develop nuclear weapons or not. Before the realization of complete prohibition and thorough destruction of nuclear weapons, nobody has the right to deprive another of the right to acquire the nuclear weapon. . . . *China* is continuing the development of its own nuclear weapons.[17]

The genuineness of the Chinese perception of threat revealed in the above statement is further confirmed in subsequent communications, particularly with respect to the Non-Proliferation Treaty. Chinese concern over the implications of the treaty was revealed both in the arguments used against it and, in a less substantive sense, in the speed with which detailed and sophisticated rebuttals to the agreement were issued. An analysis of the March 7, 1968 session of the Geneva Disarmament Conference was released by the NCNA with only a two-day time lag. The reason for its gravity from the Chinese perspective was clear: "This grave new step . . . shows that the Soviet revisionist renegade clique has openly formed with U.S. imperialism a nuclear military alliance against China and against all revolutionary peoples."[18] When the treaty was adopted by the UN General Assembly on June 12, the *People's Daily* had a major editorial the following day.[19] A further condemnation of the formal treaty, issued on June 23, referred to events as recent as June 21.[20] Although it is true that such events could have been

17. Observer, "Another deal between two nuclear overlords, U.S. and Soviet Union," *JMJP*, NCNA, 15 November 1966, in *SCMP*, No. 3823, pp. 40–2. My emphasis.
18. NCNA, 9 March 1968, in *SCMP*, No. 4137, p. 31.
19. "A nuclear fraud jointly hatched by the United States and the Soviet Union," *JMJP*, NCNA, 13 June 1968, in *SCMP*, No. 4201, pp. 30–3.
20. NCNA, 23 June 1968, in *SCMP*, No. 4208, pp. 24–6.

easily anticipated, the seriousness with which they were viewed cannot be ignored, provided one recognizes that the actual identity of "the non-nuclear states" discussed below is in all probability, not intended to exclude the People's Republic:

> Under this treaty, the U.S. imperialists and Soviet revisionists are not only allowed to produce and stockpile nuclear weapons and expand their nuclear bases, but also undertake no commitments whatsoever not to use nuclear weapons against the non-nuclear states; on the other hand, the non-nuclear states are totally deprived of their right to develop nuclear weapons for self-defence. . . . In reality, it is tantamount to a demand that the other countries forever accept the position of nuclear monopoly of U.S. imperialism and Soviet revisionism and live at their mercy. *This out-and-out unequal treaty* dished up by the U.S. imperialists and Soviet revisionists is even more unscrupulous and outrageous than the "tripartite treaty" they cooked up five years ago.[21]

Chinese attitudes toward arms control, to the extent that they can be inferred from scattered documents issued during this period, cannot be understood independently of an awareness of the Chinese perception of vulnerability and China's objective weakness in relation to the two major nuclear powers. Given the conditions of threat which remained constant or possibly worsened from the Chinese perspective, it should hardly be considered unusual that no new formulations or proposals were forthcoming from Peking. The unequivocal assertion of inferior capability still evident in Chinese pronouncements indicates that, for the immediate future, the Chinese leadership is likely to remain acutely suspicious of any Soviet-American efforts in this area.[22]

External Threat: Identification, Evaluation, and Response

What further evidence helps establish that this perception of threat was more actual than declaratory? A number of *People's Daily* editorials and documents emanating from the PLA strongly suggest that Chinese perceptions of external hostility and inferior capability remained very high throughout this period and, under conditions of an immediate and specific threat, increased. While the identity of the major external threats specified

21. "A nuclear fraud jointly hatched by the United States and the Soviet Union," p. 31. My emphasis.
22. This hypothesis finds support in the Chinese comments on the Strategic Arms Limitation Talks (SALT) negotiations. As the *JMJP* commentator noted in July 1968: "The so-called restriction and reduction of strategic nuclear weapons systems put forward by the two sides is an out-and-out fraud. For a long time, the United States and Soviet Union have stored large quantities of strategic missiles systems. This new deal . . . will not deter in the least the implementation of their policies of nuclear threat and nuclear blackmail." (NCNA, 8 July 1968, in *SCMP*, No. 4218, p. 22.)

by Peking varied with the particular situation, the range of strategic and tactical options articulated in the various responses did not.

There is, in fact, virtually no evidence to support the argument that decision-makers in Peking during this period began to view China's strategic position as qualitatively improved by the mere possession of a limited nuclear capability. Whether such perceptions might change once China's nuclear delivery systems are more fully operational is beyond the scope of this paper, but it can be argued that any alterations in Peking's articulated attitudes would be likely to result only from a more secure strategic and tactical position than existed at the end of 1969. That is, if one assumes that the present leadership composition will remain relatively constant, we should not expect any significant transformation in these perceptions unless they are accompanied by Chinese acquisition of a reliable second-strike capability.[23]

It is not at all difficult to determine the dominant issue in the Chinese perception of external threat. The principal theme associated with discussions of Chinese security during this period was the military encirclement of China, particularly nuclear encirclement. In December 1964, for example, a *People's Daily* editorial protested that the presence of two Polaris submarines off the Asian mainland, while a manifestation of the paper tiger

23. The question of Peking's likely nuclear capability and the assumed possibility of a Chinese attack on major American cities, not unexpectedly, bear directly on the validity of the argument favouring an anti-Chinese ABM. In order for the latter justification to possess credibility, for example, we find that any Chinese ICBMs (assuming they are fully operational by the early 1980s) must be capable of a somewhat extended range simply to cover the air distance to the United States. That is, we must initially assume that Chinese ICBMs would be deployed from the regions closest to the United States via polar routes—namely, on or near the borders of Sinkiang, Inner Mongolia, and Manchuria. If we calculate the distances (in statute miles) from 100 miles inside these borders to the United States, it becomes apparent that, with the exception of Seattle, it would be impossible for Chinese missiles with a range of less than 6,000 miles to reach any major American city, unless all the missiles were deployed from northern Manchuria. From a strategic perspective, a deployment exclusively from one region would be totally unrealistic. Even a capability of 6,000 miles for a Manchurian-based missile would still exclude certain American cities from the list of presumed targets. For example, the estimated distances between Washington, D.C., and northern Manchuria, Sinkiang, and Inner Mongolia are approximately 6,250, 6,425, and 6,925 miles, respectively. The lack of any ICBM tests (as of November 1971) precludes a precise estimate of the likely range of such a missile. According to a report in the *New York Times* of 31 May 1971, American analysts predict "that China could have a force of 10 to 25 [ICBMs] with a 6,000 mile range by the mid-1970s," presumably to be equipped with a 3-megaton warhead. In view of the above calculations, however, it appears that to speak of an "operational Chinese threat"—even in the early 1980s, as argued by President Nixon—may be premature. Hence any quick conclusion about the possibility of a Chinese attack on American cities does not seem warranted. Although these considerations are critical to a careful assessment of China's likely nuclear capability (and hence future Chinese nuclear doctrine), they remain entirely unexamined in public debate. Evaluating the possibility of a Chinese attack on the basis of plotted air distances was apparently never raised in the numerous and extended controversies concerning the possible merit of an anti-Chinese area defence system. I am grateful to Allen Whiting for raising these issues with me and making me aware of their possible implications.

nature of American imperialism, was nevertheless an attempt to threaten China. It was evidence of the "establishment of a nuclear ring around China" which had no justification, since "having possessed them [nuclear weapons], the Chinese government has not taken them to the doorsteps of the U.S., much less has it used them to threaten any Asian country."[24] During the period of 1965 when a Sino-American war was a distinct possibility, a National Day editorial was even more specific in detailing hostile American intentions: "We should at no time forget that U.S. imperialism regards New China as the biggest obstacle to its policy of aggression and war. It has long been racking its brains for means to sabotage, subvert, and even destroy socialist China."[25] By January 1966, according to the *People's Daily*, the increasing numbers of "troops, aircraft, warships, and missiles . . . deploy[ed] around China" demonstrated that "U.S. imperialism is shifting step by step the emphasis of its global strategy from Europe to Asia . . . in order to complete its so-called 'arc of encirclement' around China." In late May, the same paper's commentator described the entry of an American nuclear submarine into a Japanese port as "part of its [the United States'] criminal scheme of a strategic nuclear encirclement of China."

During 1967 and 1968, the theme of an "anti-China alliance" between the United States and the Soviet Union gained great emphasis, particularly in response to developments such as the announcement of ABM planning and deployment, the Hollybush talks, and the Non-Proliferation Treaty negotiations. For example, a detailed analysis in February 1968 of the American "counter-revolutionary global strategy" condemned the Soviet Union's "notorious activities as the No. 1 accomplice of U.S. imperialism during the past half year or more." After concluding the "Glassboro conspiracy," it was argued, "the Soviet revisionists and the U.S. imperialists became more and more naked in their counter-revolutionary military collaboration against China." The comments against both Soviet and American ABMs were particularly bitter: "This coordination in setting up anti-missile networks against China has clearly exposed the fact that Soviet revisionism has become the *de facto* military ally of U.S. imperialism." Throughout 1968 and 1969 editorial emphasis was placed on "ganging up against China militarily" and "frantically opposing China." After the border incidents of 1969, the scale and intensity of Soviet opposition was most heavily emphasized, but the general concepts developed by 1968 did not change. It should be evident from this documentation that these perceptions of external hostility were expressed only in response to particular events and developments which from the Chinese perspective were deemed threatening. Chinese analysts were not describing an imaginary presence.

Given the reality of this perception of threat, were Peking's statements

24. *JMJP*, NCNA, 31 December 1964, in *SCMP*, No. 3371, p. 35.
25. "Hold high the great red banner of Mao Tse-tung's thought and courageously drive ahead," *JMJP*, in *Peking Review*, Vol. 8, No. 40 (1 October 1965), p. 10.

consistent in evaluating the capabilities and likely behavior of China's adversaries? Was a particular response to external threat considered appropriate in all situations? Not surprisingly, both answers are dependent upon the scope and immediacy of the external threat. The normal Chinese evaluation and response, if one can be said to exist, is no response at all, since it appears to contain little more than an emphasis on the paper tiger nature of China's enemies and the invincibility of "people's war." Most scholars would interpret such declarations of strategic contempt as largely irrelevant to an understanding of genuine perceptions or potential behavior. Such pronouncements, however, are far more revealing than is generally acknowledged. In 1966, for example, domestic audiences were reminded that while "the people's forces are invincible," imperialism and all reactionaries retain a dual nature—that is, "they are real tigers and paper tigers at the same time." Hence, "we must despise them *as a whole,* but with regard to *each specific problem,* we must take full account of it." The essentials of this dictum, having been repeated innumerable times since first enunciated in 1946, help account for Chinese contempt that is more apparent than real.

More significantly, we find that under crisis conditions the paper tiger theme is elaborated upon with somewhat greater sophistication. The principal variation in this "strategy versus tactics" debate appears under circumstances when the enemy, since it is a paper tiger and in decline, will make a reckless, sudden bid to recoup its losses. For example:

Modern conditions have greatly increased the chances of *having to fight a sudden war.* The perfidious imperialists are accustomed to launch sudden attacks in starting an aggressive war and new techniques create more favorable conditions for carrying out sudden military attacks.

We have taken into full account the *madness* of U.S. imperialism and made all preparations to meet its *adventurous war plans.*

It is possible that U.S. imperialism *may go mad* in trying to save itself from its doom; we must take this into full account and make preparations . . . against any war it may impose upon us.

. . . *the closer their* [the imperialists'] *doom is, the more desperate their struggle becomes.*

. . . this [the invasion of Czechoslovakia] is the *death-bed struggle* of the Soviet revisionist renegade clique in an attempt to avert the crisis of disintegration and imminent destruction of the entire modern revisionist bloc. It reveals in full the paper tiger nature of the Soviet revisionists.

In the face of the excellent situation in the world revolution, we must be fully vigilant against the enemy making trouble and *embarking on adventure more frantically.* Just as the great leader Chairman Mao has pointed out, "all reactionary forces on the verge of extinction invariably conduct desperate struggles. They are bound to resort to military adventure and political deception in all their forms in order to save themselves from extinction." The frequent acts of aggression and armed provocations recently launched by the Soviet revisionist renegade clique against our country are the manifestations of death-bed struggles of this pack of social-imperialist gangsters.

Soviet revisionism and U.S. imperialism will never change their aggressive nature. They will never take their defeat lying down. They will try every day and every hour to launch a counter-attack. . . . We must be prepared against their launching a war at an early date and on a large scale.

Should a handful of war maniacs dare to raid China's strategic sites . . . that will be war. . . .

In order to extricate themselves from their difficulties both at home and abroad, U.S. imperialism and social-imperialism, which are in an impasse, are now intensifying their collaboration and wildly plotting to launch wars of aggression against China and they have even spread talk for nuclear blackmail against China.

People throughout China . . . guard against surprise attacks by the enemy. . . .

It has been necessary to provide this extensive documentation in order to establish that, in general, Chinese pronouncements mention the impending doom (and hence potential "madness") of external threats *only when the probability of war is considered extremely high.* These quotations, and others similar to them, appear to originate in only three periods: in the 1965–6 escalatory phase of American involvement in Vietnam, immediately after the 1968 invasion of Czechoslovakia, and during much of 1969 after border clashes with the Soviet Union. The documents from the first and third periods—that is, when Chinese decision-makers genuinely perceived the threat of nuclear war—are particularly emphatic in tone. The notion of "surprise" or "sudden" attacks, so conspicuous in 1965 and 1966, completely disappeared from public mention until surfacing again during the 1969 crisis, and only when the possibility of nuclear war was being openly discussed outside China. We should also note that a large number of these documents were explicitly directed (at least initially) at domestic audiences. Thus we can also argue that these messages were communicated to the Chinese mass audience in order to inform the general public of the immediacy and salience of the threat of nuclear war.

Having perceived the possibility of a sudden nuclear attack, is there any indication that the Chinese leadership devised means either to deter its occurrence or to defend China, assuming deterrence were to fail? While virtually no evidence exists which would permit an adequate evaluation of this question, scholars can benefit from the analyses in the *Kungtso T'ung-hsün* (*Bulletin of Activities*), a publication of the General Political Department of the PLA intended for cadres at the regimental level and above. These documents, which were issued between January and August 1961, contain discussions of a wide variety of political, military, and ideological issues of particular concern to China's leadership in the aftermath of the Great Leap Forward. These included the question of political control within the PLA, problems of army morale and discipline, and frank appraisals of social and political conditions then prevalent within China. Numerous details about the activities and functions of the Military Affairs Committee were also revealed. Of particular interest for this analysis, however, are several assessments of Chinese military strategy. While the discussions contained in these papers are admittedly dated, they nevertheless constitute the most explicit discussion now available of Chinese tactics in the advent of nuclear war. Rather than detail the arguments presented in these documents, I shall investigate the extent to which evaluations comparable to those in the 1961 analyses can be detected in Chinese pronouncements from the period under examination in this paper.

It is true that—at least in Peking's declaratory policy—there is a seeming disregard for the realities and consequences of nuclear war. How else can one evaluate Lin Piao's formulation of the "people's war" strategy, which appears to ignore the advances in weapons development in the 20 years prior to 1965? Yet, as Uri Ra'anan has argued, Lin's analysis—when stripped of its polemics—was a discreet call for noninvolvement or low-risk involvement, in order to minimize the possibility of a nuclear attack on China. Similarly, if we simply try to determine the *operational consequences* of Chinese attitudes, then a far more realistic appraisal is likely to be achieved.

There are several distinct patterns in the documents issued when China's military leaders decided to talk about the unthinkable. First, at least in the communications intended for mass or international consumption, the unthinkable was pondered in serious fashion only when it became a thinkable proposition—that is, when there was a definite possibility of nuclear war on Chinese soil. Second, there was the omission of any scenario in which China's nuclear force would be utilized. At least in public documents, the Chinese elite attempted to forswear the use and deny the utility of nuclear weapons in any military confrontation which might involve China. The references to the deterrent function of such weapons, for example, consistently stressed that a single detonation constituted such a deterrent: "It was the nuclear blackmail and nuclear threat of U.S. imperialism that compelled the Chinese people to rely on themselves and work hard to turn their country into a mighty power . . . [Now in 1964] they have finally gained the means of resisting U.S. nuclear threat." While no concrete retaliatory scenarios were formulated, there were occasional, if somewhat vague, references to the possible use of nuclear weapons by China. These comments, however, were apparently used to support the argument that nuclear weapons systems would not be decisive in warfare of any kind—whether revolutionary, conventional, or global. In a somewhat emplicit comment during 1966, for example, it was argued that "now that U.S. imperialism is no longer in monopoly of nuclear weapons, should it seek to menace other countries with nuclear weapons, its own country would also be exposed to the menace of nuclear weapons."[26] Clearly, this argument was utilized not to threaten the United States with nuclear attack, but to deter the possibility of any attacks on China and hence to limit the use of nuclear force in international politics.

In terms of potential Chinese use, there is no evidence more substantial than an occasional assertion that the "blood debt" of the United States to China must be repaid, and an infrequent (and highly implicit) intimation of a future nuclear war which would involve Japan.[27] Certainly these scattered references cannot be regarded as convincing support for arguments that Chinese leaders were seriously contemplating the use of nuclear weapons in order to enhance China's political and military position. It is true that Chinese statements did refer to the "amazing development" and "remarkable progress" in the development of nuclear weapons. Yet according to these pronouncements, this progress and the general rise in China's world influence led to an *increased* perception of threat, since Soviet and American leaders felt a corresponding need to collaborate against China. As one assessment noted:

> Scared out of their wits by the remarkable progress of socialist China in the development of guided missiles and nuclear weapons, Soviet revisionism and U.S. imperialism have in the past few years intensified their collusion against China on the nuclear question. In fact, the Soviet revisionists have formed a nuclear military alliance with the U.S. imperialists against China.[28]

If any further indication of a shift in the Chinese perception of threat occurred, we would expect it to be revealed in these statements, but as already shown, even optimistic assertions were usually qualified. For example, while some sources maintained that the United States had overcommitted itself in terms of resources and capabilities, the general outlook for China was still considered dangerous. Hence in a highly sophisticated treatment of American strategic policy since the Second World War published in 1966, it was

26. "Study 'Talk with American correspondent Anna Louise Strong,'" p. 7.
27. See the "warning" issued in *JMJP* (NCNA, 31 May 1966, in *SCMP*, No. 3711, p. 35): "Any sober-minded Japanese knows that Japan's becoming a U.S. imperialist nuclear base can only mean the plunging of the Japanese nation again into the abyss of calamity and that there can be no 'security' to speak of. The pro-U.S. Sato government is leading the country onto an extremely perilous road."
28. NCNA, 9 March 1969, in *SCMP*, No. 4376, p. 24.

argued that "U.S. imperialism is in essence a paper tiger because it has lost every battle." Yet, as the author cautioned:

> The "escalation" strategy [under President Johnson] has greatly increased the adventurous character of the strategy of "flexible reaction." So long as the United States considers it necessary or advantageous it can freely manufacture a pretext to carry out war intimidation, to launch a war, or to enlarge the war.[29]

As a result of American control of this step-by-step escalatory process, Chinese vulnerability and the need for readiness against external threat continued to be stressed. Moreover, in this and numerous other sources there was no suggestion that China's armed forces—now probably buttressed by the acquisition of at least a minimal nuclear capability—could pursue a bolder tactical policy. In fact what is most striking in Chinese discussions of strategy and tactics in the face of immediate external threat is the extent to which China's nuclear weapons were not considered a resource in Peking's defensive arsenal.

We are fortunately able to compare public attitudes with private assessments in the pages of the *Kung-tso T'ung-hsün*. Unlike the public pronouncements, there is a recognition that nuclear weapons might well be used by Chinese armed forces should the tactical situation require it.[30] The documents further reveal that "the Chinese have no illusions about the mere acquisition of nuclear weapons *ipso facto* providing them with a military status equal to that of the United States or . . . the Soviet Union."[31] This disparity between elite and public attitudes seems related to the overall policy aims which Chinese statements heavily emphasized during this period. To spell out such elite beliefs would possibly have negated Chinese efforts to justify Peking's pursuit of a nuclear capability as being fundamentally different from the purposes of imperialist or revisionist powers. As in the public pronouncements, however, particular emphasis was placed upon Chinese vulnerability to external attack and the critical need to enhance the defensive capabilities of the armed forces.

Even more significant are commentaries in several military documents which suggest that the *Kung-tso T'ung-hsün* analysis of the likely tactical response to nuclear attack was still operative at a later date. I first quote the 1961 evaulation:

> Although atomic bombs are very powerful they can only be used to destroy centres and the economic reserves of the opponent during the stra-

29. Jen Ku-p'ing, "U.S. imperialism is in essence a paper tiger because it has lost every battle," *JMJP*, 27 August 1966, in *CB*, No. 803, p. 21.
30. Hsieh, "China's secret military papers," p. 87.
31. *Ibid.*

tegic bombing phase. After that, they are used principally as fire-power preparations for assault. However, the army and regular weapons are necessary to terminate war, to destroy the enemy, to occupy positions, and to win a victory. *To rely on the army and regular weapons is to rely primarily on man.* The final conclusion thus rests on man. . . . In accordance with our situation, if there is a war within three to five years [that is, before China possesses even a limited nuclear capability], we will have to rely on hand weapons. As to how to defeat the enemy with hand weapons, Chief Lin [Piao] has found a way, and it has to do with the question of distant war or close war. . . . The enemy is stronger than we are in a distant war, but *short distance fighting, and especially face to face fighting, is where our strength lies.* We have to avoid the strengths and take advantage of the weaknesses of the enemy. *In face to face fighting there can only be used hand grenades, bayonets, or flamethrowers. We have to use close fighting, night fighting, or trench warfare to defeat the enemy. . . .*[32]

While one can quarrel with the relevance of such tactics under conditions of nuclear war, it is clear that in 1961 the Chinese military elite did not feel that a strategic nuclear attack alone would be sufficient to subjugate China, while the above tactics were considered the best alternative available to China, given the fact that no reliable or sufficient nuclear capability then existed.

The inclusion in several issues of the *Liberation Army Daily* of analyses very similar to the above commentary is perhaps the most conclusive evidence that the Chinese perception of vulnerability to nuclear attack remained very high throughout this period. It also helps explain why Chinese statements never discussed the possible use of nuclear weapons by China when the probability of war was considered very high (except of course, in general adulation of "people's war"). For example, an editorial in the army paper of February 1966 argued that:

If the enemy should choose to fight early, to fight on a large scale, to fight a nuclear war or several kinds of war, or to fight on several fronts, we shall not be afraid. . . . We acknowledge the tremendous role played by modern weapons and equipment, yet ultimately they cannot solve problems. In solving problems ultimately, we must still rely on man, on rifles, on hand grenades, on bayonets, on close-range fighting, on night-fighting, and on close-quarter fighting. . . . Modern, long-range weapons, the atom bomb included, are useless for close-range fighting or night-fighting.[33]

32. Yeh Chien-ying, Speech at the Military Affairs Commission Conference on Training, cited *ibid.* pp. 83–5. My emphasis.
33. "The most important and fundamental war preparation," *Chieh-fang-chün Pao,* NCNA, 14 February 1966, in *SCMP,* No. 3641, pp. 15–16.

In another 1966 analysis, the utility of nuclear weapons for conventional war was questioned, although not totally dismissed:

> The nuclear weapon is after all only a type of weapon; it cannot replace the conventional weapon, much less a decisive battle by ground forces. The ultimate victory in war is not decided by firing rockets that carry nuclear warheads . . . it is in the final analysis decided by fighting at close quarters . . . on the battlefield, by soldiers using conventional weapons to fight a series of ground battles to wipe out . . . the enemy. . . . The more nuclear weapons are used and the stronger fire power is, the more it is necessary to rely upon fighting at close quarters and fighting at night to solve problems, the more it is necessary to bring the human factor into play.[34]

In somewhat similar fashion, a 1969 directive noted:

> The working style [of the PLA] should be adapted to the requirements of war. . . . It is imperative to put Mao Tsetung Thought in command of military training, thereby heightening the fighting quality. . . . We must train hard and master skills in close-range and night-fighting and fighting within 200 meters. There should be . . . better and more essential [training] with a view to fighting big battles and fierce battles and fighting under the most difficult circumstances.

Although such explicit discussions of strategy and tactics are rare, this is probably because the conditions prompting these analyses do not very often occur. Discussion will only occur either when there is a strong possibility of major conflict (thus prompting the public communications) or by someone whose role within the Chinese political system requires that the consequences of nuclear attack be considered (thus prompting the analysis for a professional military audience).

What remains most striking, however, is the remarkable similarity in both the emphasis and wording of these sources. Their virtually identical nature is, in all probability, not unintentional. Simply stated, the close parallels in these discussions seem to indicate that in 1969 (as well as in 1966 and 1961) Chinese decision-makers were operating under conditions of markedly inferior capability. Coupled with the perception of external hostility analyzed in the previous section, it seems evident that Chinese spokesmen had good reason for their continued expressions of sobriety with respect to the role of nuclear weapons in world politics. As we noted earlier, the circumstances under which substantive change in the Chinese nuclear doctrine might occur can only be when China's military vulnerability is perceived by decision-makers as qualitatively lessened and when Chinese security from nuclear attack is far more assured. Neither of these conditions, it would

34. "Study 'Talk with American correspondent Anna Louise Strong,'" p. 7.

appear, was realized during this period, and Chinese perceptions continued to be expressed from a perspective of distinct inferiority. The extent to which this condition is altered, more than any other factor, will affect the course of Peking's attitudes as China completes its first decade as a nuclear power.

33.

Beyond SALT One

HERBERT SCOVILLE, JR.

ALTHOUGH PRESIDENT NIXON's goal of achieving an initial agreement at the Strategic Arms Limitation Talks (SALT) before the end of 1971 failed to be realized, it still appears likely that at least some limitations will be negotiated by the time he and Premier Kosygin meet in Moscow in May. After SALT recessed in Vienna the President reported in his state of the world message on February ninth that a consensus is developing that there should be a treaty setting conprehensive limitations on anti-ballistic missiles (ABMs) and an interim agreement to freeze certain offensive arms.

The primary objective of an ABM limitation is to foreclose the acquisition of missile defenses with nationwide coverage, which might raise fears about the continued viability of a mutual deterrent posture. The treaty will probably be constructed along the following lines. The number of ABM interceptor missiles will be restricted to between 100 and 300. The lower value would be more satisfactory from security, arms control, and economic points of view, but even the higher value would prevent the acquisition of ABM systems which could threaten either nation's deterrent. The argument about whether to retain 100 or 300 interceptors is spurious, since neither level will provide any realistic protection. More important would be limits on the location and perhaps also the number of large, high-performance ABM radars, which are most critical for a nationwide defense because of their size, time for construction, and expense. They would be almost impossible

Reprinted by permission from *Foreign Affairs*, April 1972, pp. 488–500. Copyright © 1972 by the Council on Foreign Relations.

to deploy secretly. Under a treaty, their locations would probably have to be restricted to the Moscow area for the Soviet Union and the neighborhood of Minuteman sites for the United States; otherwise fears could be generated over a possible clandestine deployment of a nationwide ABM system.

The nature of a possible agreement on offensive weapons is much less clear, and the details may even be left for further negotiation. Former Deputy Secretary of Defense David Packard, in a press conference on October 21, 1971, said that an agreement on ABMs by themselves might be acceptable if it were a useful step toward the longer-term objective of containing the offensive buildup. This would then become a high priority follow-up action to the first stage of SALT. It is more likely, however, that there will be some agreed limitation on the total numbers of ICBMs (intercontinental ballistic missiles based on land). This could be in the form of a numerical ceiling or a freeze at existing levels. From the American point of view, it would be extremely useful to include in this numerical limit a sub-ceiling on the very large Soviet SS-9 type ICBMs. The new, very large launchers, about 30 of which have been reported to be under construction in the last year, would fall within this category. Such a sub-ceiling may present certain difficulties for the Soviets unless the United States is willing to accept some similar restraint, but they may be satisfied with their present force level of slightly more than 300 operational or under construction.

The United States also is reported to be seeking a halt on Russian submarine construction even though they still lag considerably behind the United States both quantitatively and qualitatively in operational submarine-launched ballistic missiles. Since the United States is unlikely to be willing to forgo its conversion of the Polaris to the Poseidon missile, which has four times the payload and ten to 14 MIRVs (multiple warheads each capable of being aimed at a separate target), the chances of agreement in this area do not appear very promising. However, they would be somewhat improved if the Russians were allowed to complete those submarines now only in the early stages of construction, since they would then have numerical but not qualitative parity with the United States. A failure to limit submarine missiles is not serious since these are considered as primarily deterrent weapons because they are invulnerable and would be difficult to use in a coordinated and accurate first strike against the opposing deterrent. The complete destruction of the other side's strategic forces by the nearly simultaneous launchings from about 30 submarines and follow-up firings to correct for initial failures presents extraordinary operational difficulties.

It is most improbable that the first stage of SALT will place any qualitative restrictions on offensive missile systems, apart from a possible limit on the number of large SS-9 type missiles. The replacement of existing weapons by new models will be permitted and if the experience of the Limited Test Ban Treaty is representative, will be encouraged as a safeguard against possible violations. Certainly there will be no restrictions on MIRVs· The

United States will be free to continue its Poseidon submarine missile and Minuteman III ICBM deployments with MIRVs, and the Soviets to begin testing and deploying MIRVs as well.

Even with an agreement of this limited nature, SALT will have made important strides toward slowing the arms race and stabilizing the present state of mutual U.S.-USSR deterrence. The ABM limitation by itself will guarantee a continued secure deterrent posture on both sides regardless of what type of offensive programs are allowed to continue. MIRVs can threaten only the fixed land-based force and not the mobile submarine missiles which, by themselves, are more than adequate to provide an assured retaliatory capability as long as ABMs are kept small. There are no technological advances in anti-submarine warfare (ASW) which could provide in the foreseeable future a capability of destroying almost simultaneously an entire missile submarine fleet.

However, since there will be no controls on MIRVs, in time the ICBM and bomber parts of the deterrent force may come to be considered vulnerable. While at the moment there do not appear to be any reasonable methods by which both these weapons systems can be destroyed in a surprise attack—a Russian strike against our bomber force would alert the Minuteman ICBMs, or vice versa—nevertheless, some authorities have suggested that so-called "pin down" tactics might be used to accomplish this objective. These tactics involve the maintenance of a continuous barrage of submarine-launched warheads exploding above our Minuteman fields, not to destroy but only to prevent the launching of the ICBMs. These explosions would have to be timed to coincide with a submarine missile attack on our bombers and continue for a minimum of 30 minutes until their ICBMs could destroy our Minuteman silos. While such an attack would involve immense and extremely wasteful expenditures of weapons and require extraordinary coordination, planners using worst-case assumptions may come to take it as more than a fantasy when, and if, the force levels become very large. In sum, even though a first-stage SALT agreement would be a major milestone, many additional actions will be required to permit it to endure and expand.

II

If the preceding picture of the strategic situation following an initial SALT agreement is generally correct, there should be two main follow-through objectives for our unilateral defense planning and future arms-control negotiations. First, we should make every effort to assure that neither side takes any actions which could erode the mutual deterrent posture established by SALT. In fact, every effort should be made to strengthen it still further. Areas of potential concern should be narrowed or eliminated wherever possible either by unilateral decisions on weapons programs, further arms limitations, or even by exchanges of information. For example, the construction of a large space radar might be misconstrued as part of an ABM system unless this was carefully explained to the other side.

This objective, however, may not always be very easy to achieve since SALT will probably not limit the qualitative arms race in any significant way. Unless care is exercised by each side in its weapons programs, actions that might appear to the other side as threatening its deterrent could be taken in the name of protecting against possible treaty abrogation or violations. Thus, development of a new MIRV guidance system might be construed, perhaps incorrectly, as an attempt to obtain a first-strike capability. Similarly, new sophisticated radars for anti-aircraft defense might appear to be ABMs in disguise. Soviet replacement of their present ICBMs by new hardened launchers could be misinterpreted as an attempt to circumvent a ceiling on large missile launchers. President Nixon's reference, in his state of the world message of February 1971, to a hoped-for alternative to a retaliatory attack against Russian cities could also be misconstrued as an attempt to erode the deterrent posture by providing a nuclear-war fighting capability.

Since most of these troubles will result from the failure of SALT to place any restrictions on qualitative improvements, a second major objective would be to move on to arms-control measures directed at rectifying this omission. This presents many difficulties in view of scientists' innate desire always to seek technological innovation. Research and development will be justified as a possible hedge against breakthroughs or cheating by the other side. After the Limited Test Ban Treaty in 1963, expanded programs were even demanded in order to maintain the viability of the weapons laboratories in the event the Treaty was abrogated.

Limits on qualitative improvements present particularly difficult problems in the area of verification. Many important modifications of weapons systems result in no observable changes in the characteristics of a weapons system. For example, a missile guidance system can be made more accurate by substitution of a better computer inside the missile. Furthermore, research and development in the laboratory phases are difficult to monitor and easy to conceal or screen under the guise of legitimate activities. No amount of even intrusive inspection appears practical to provide assurance that secret research and development programs are not under way. One cannot station an inspector at every research facility; even if there, he could easily be misled. Only when a weapon or a component reaches the stage of field or flight testing does it become visible and even then not always adequately verifiable. However, limitations on field tests offer a good place to start in curbing the seemingly endless desire to make technological improvements.

ANTI-SUBMARINE WARFARE

Under a SALT agreement as visualized above, the submarine missile systems become, even more than at the present time, the primary component of the deterrent force. Therefore, every effort should be made by both unilateral decisions and multilateral arms-control actions to maintain and, where necessary, strengthen it. As long as ABMs are severely limited, the only threat to this weapons system can come from anti-submarine warfare. At the present time there is no technology which can in the foreseeable future place in jeopardy simultaneously a submarine force of 30 to 40 vessels, even if they did not employ countermeasures. However, in time, with concentrated effort, new developments might give rise to fears on this score, and efforts should be made to foreclose such an eventuality. Therefore, restrictions on anti-submarine warfare capabilities should be sought in much the same way they have been sought on ABMs. To date, very little attention has been paid to this area of arms control.

By comparison with ABMs, however, controls on anti-submarine warfare will be very much more difficult to achieve. In the first place, extensive, albeit strategically ineffective, anti-submarine systems are already available to both the United States and the Soviet Union as well as many other countries, and secondly, anti-submarine defenses have tactical as well as strategic military applications. For example, they are a key element in the protection of surface shipping, both naval and merchant, in a protracted warfare situation such as in World War II or even in more limited conflicts as might occur in the Mediterranean. Despite these drawbacks, there are a number of arms-control measures which can guarantee still further the indefinite viability of the submarine missile deterrent force. Fortunately, any anti-submarine warfare system, if it were to have dangerous capabilities, would have to be very extensive, would take a long time to build, and would be obvious to all concerned. A clandestine anti-submarine warfare program to negate the Polaris deterrent would be impossible.

One control measure would be a limitation on the number of so-called hunter-killer submarines, i.e. submarines designed to follow and destroy other submarines. A large number of such ships would be needed in order to have a reliable capability to eliminate almost simultaneously 30 or more missile submarines. The continuous tracking of ballistic missile submarines, either by other submarines or surface vessels, might be forbidden in an arms-control agreement. Another approach might be to designate certain ocean areas that did not include the sea lanes normally traveled by merchant and naval vessels as regions within which anti-submarine operations would be banned. The stationing of acoustic detection systems and submarine tracking ships and aircraft would not be allowed in these areas, which could then be used for the invulnerable deployment of the submarine missile deterrent forces.

Parallel to these measures, research and development could be continued on advanced submarine missile systems which would decrease their vulnerability to possible future anti-submarine measures. The American Underwater Long Range Missile System (ULMS) programs are examples of this. The most useful advance in this field would be the development of a new missile (originally nicknamed EXPO, now called ULMS I) with a longer range than Poseidon in order to permit the submarine to launch its missiles from larger ocean areas less subject to anti-submarine attack. This missile should be designed with a capability of being launched from existing Polaris submarines to avoid the very expensive requirement of replacing the existing fleet. In the longer term, if a threat to submarines should develop, quieter and less vulnerable, or smaller but more numerous, submarines might be other approaches. However, the present threat from anti-submarine warfare is not sufficiently near or even well defined to require construction and deployment decisions on these new weapons in the near future. Ship construction now would be a waste of scarce funds and might result in building weapons designed against the wrong threat. There is not even a requirement for a new missile at this time, and it is hoped that a race in this area can be avoided.

RESTRICTIONS ON IMPROVEMENT IN EXISTING SYSTEMS

With ABMs frozen at low levels, the need to improve further existing offensive strategic weapons systems may be largely eliminated. More advanced weapons would be required only if one were seeking to acquire a first-strike or nuclear-war fighting capability. And this would merely serve to increase the risk that a nuclear disaster might occur. Therefore, it is incumbent on both the United States and the Soviet Union to take such actions as possible to halt the qualitative arms race either by agreed measures or, more practically, by reciprocal unilateral actions. An agreement that no missile system could be upgraded by any change in its external configuration would be very useful, although it would not halt many improvements. Such a restriction would apply not only to the missile itself, but also to the characteristics of the launch site. Since only those changes that could be observed from the outside would be banned, such an agreement could be verified adequately by national or unilateral means. It would prevent the replacement of existing systems by those with radically new characteristics such as the substitution of much larger missiles for the present models.

Thus, the Soviets could not supersede their obsolescent early ICBMs with the newer SS-11s and SS-13s or even their SS-9s with still larger missiles (a possibility that has caused so much concern in some circles during the past year). The United States, however, would not be permitted to convert any more Polaris missiles to Poseidons. This would not, of course, prevent replacement of single warheads by MIRVs or improvements in accuracy, but these changes would be restricted within the envelope of the presently deployed models.

A still further and more useful step toward qualitative restrictions would be to place limits on the number of missile test firings that either the United States or the Soviets could conduct in any one year. A complete ban on test firings would probably not be feasible because of the necessity to conduct a number of tests in order to assure the reliability of deployed systems and to train crews. However, if the quota on allowed firings was kept reasonably low, to perhaps ten or even 20 per year, this would certainly place restrictions on development programs for new systems. Such an understanding could be monitored by our existing unilateral capabilities, and it could be reinforced by an understanding that the firings would be announced in advance and occur only on specific test ranges. An agreement of this type would strongly inhibit the development of MIRV systems, particularly those with high accuracy. A specific ban on MIRV testing would be highly desirable, but the overwhelming American lead in this area and our previous reluctance to negotiate seriously on such a ban do not allow much optimism for its success.

REDUCTIONS IN NUMBER OF WEAPONS

Once an agreement has been reached to limit ABMs, it will become apparent that the present number of offensive launchers, presumably the ceiling agreed to in SALT One, would be more than adequate to provide a deterrent force. This would be even more obvious if MIRVs were allowed. In time, it might be hoped that either by agreement or by gradual, reciprocal, unilateral phase-downs, the number of these launchers could start being reduced. Since fixed land-based ICBMs will eventually come to be believed vulnerable, they should be the first candidates for elimination. Cutbacks would have not only security value, but also important international political implications. They would show that at least the nuclear powers were willing to take steps to decrease the very large size of their present arsenals. This would be extremely valuable in promoting our policies on the non-proliferation of nuclear weapons.

Of course, if the reduction reached a point where the number of land-based ICBMs became very small, then the vulnerability of this part of the deterrent to a first strike would be quite great; however, this would not be serious as long as the submarine deterrent remained secure. For this reason, it would not be wise to reduce the submarine missiles until a very much later period at which time all five nuclear weapons countries might be party to the discussions. Reduction in the size of the ABM systems even further than promised in the first stage of SALT would also be a very useful factor in strengthening the deterrent. Intercontinental bombers could also be decreased, and new aircraft for replacement could be dispensed with, saving large sums of money.

FORWARD BASED SYSTEMS

The Soviets originally sought to include in SALT limitations on Forward Based Systems (FBS), i.e. those shorter-range nuclear delivery systems based in forward areas which have, nevertheless, the capability of striking the Soviet Union. However, they have apparently dropped this requirement, postponing negotiations on such systems to a later date. The fact that only the United States has such systems presents a serious problem in negotiating their control, and they should probably be tackled not in SALT, but as a part of agreements on European security and mutual and balanced force reductions.

However, their consideration cannot be indefinitely neglected since, to the Soviets, they must always be seen as a threat to their national survival, and they are unlikely to agree to any further significant reductions in strategic forces until they are dealt with. A first step might be a U.S. undertaking not to enlarge these forces. The phased redeployment of such aircraft back to the United States in exchange for Russian withdrawal of both nuclear and conventional forces in Eastern Europe would appear another useful approach to this problem. Reduction in their numbers could be traded off against reduction in Soviet shorter-range missiles which threaten European centers. The British and French nuclear forces would also have to be taken into account. The negotiation of limitations on armaments stationed in Europe has extraordinarily difficult and complicated political ramifications and cannot be expected to produce early results. However, the time has come to make serious moves in this direction.

COMPREHENSIVE NUCLEAR TEST BAN TREATY

An arms-control measure which would have beneficial effects far beyond the U.S.-USSR strategic balance would be the achievement of a complete ban on nuclear weapons tests. The achievement of qualitative restrictions on delivery systems has proven extremely difficult, but a comprehensive nuclear test ban would be a step to limit improvements on many of these. While both countries undoubtedly have warheads which are satisfactory for their first-generation MIRVs and ABMs, a test ban would inhibit the development of many second-generation systems. This could be particularly helpful to U.S. security. The Russians may not yet have developed warheads for a MIRV system that could threaten the Minuteman deterrent, since they have not yet had the first test of such a delivery system. A nuclear test ban in the near future would probably prevent the Russians from having warheads with the necessary yield, weight and dimension to be used in a missile which dispersed more than three accurate MIRVs.

It is also unlikely that the Soviets would have already developed a warhead for an advanced ABM system which might be clandestinely deployed under the guise of an air-defense weapon, since prior to an initial ABM agreement at SALT they would have had no requirement to do so. Thus, a comprehensive test ban treaty would provide increased confidence that the ABM limitations at SALT were being honored. Fears have also been expressed that, without testing, our stockpiled nuclear weapons would become unreliable. However, in the past, deterioration due to aging has been checked by dismantling weapons; never have we conducted nuclear tests solely for the purpose. If a complete ban on testing were, over a period of years, to decrease confidence in the reliability of offensive warheads, this would only enhance the existing state of mutual deterrence, since it would reduce confidence in an ability to carry out a first strike.

In addition to such effects on the U.S.-USSR strategic balance, a comprehensive test ban treaty would be an important factor in reinforcing U.S. non-proliferation policies. It would make much more difficult the acquisition of a reliable nuclear force by a non-nuclear nation. Continued nuclear testing by the United States and the Soviet Union will inevitably mean that advanced weapons technology, which may be of marginal value to them, will eventually be available to many countries and to many people. Furthermore, restraint on the part of nuclear powers would provide additional inducement for the non-nuclear nations to accede to the non-proliferation treaty (NPT). A country such as India, which has refused to sign the NPT, might find it extremely difficult politically to refuse to adhere to a comprehensive test ban treaty since it has been a key element in its past disarmament policies.

Neither France nor China is likely to adhere initially to any test ban treaty, the former primarily for political reasons and the latter because it still requires considerably more development to acquire a varied nuclear arsenal. While unfortunate, this still does not significantly reduce the value of the treaty, which would once and for all end the continuing attempts of the United States and the Soviet Union to advance nuclear weapons technology. China is still so far behind both the United States and Russia that it is inconceivable that any unilateral nuclear testing on her part could require additional tests by either of the other two nations within the next ten to 20 years. Our more than 500 tests over 25 years have provided us with a large stockpile of weapons-design information. Nuclear weapons to deal with the U.S.-USSR confrontation are more than adequate to handle the slowly emerging Chinese nuclear capability—or in the case of Russia with that of France as well.

In the unlikely event that this were no longer true in the distant future, any treaty would undoubtedly have an escape clause similar to that in the Limited Test Ban Treaty which would provide the right to withdraw if extraordinary events related to the subject matter of the Treaty jeopardized our supreme interest. The unlikely occurrence of a Chinese or French nuclear breakthrough would certainly fall into this category.

Finally, the negotiation of a comprehensive test ban treaty is not only militarily and politically opportune, but it is also timely from a technological viewpoint. The results of U.S. research and development programs have now demonstrated major improvements in seismic capabilities to detect and identify nuclear tests. The value of on-site inspections, and the risks from clandestine testing, have now been very greatly reduced. While there will always be some threshold below which an occasional secret test might be conducted, the risks from a violation of this type would be more than over-balanced by the gains from halting all tests on high yields.

III

An important outgrowth of SALT can be the continued exchange of views on strategic policies in order to reduce misunderstandings. This might be maintained by the continuation of SALT negotiations or by some newly established mechanisms. Even with the best of intentions on both sides, many legitimate unilateral actions may be taken which could look threatening to the other side or seem to be violations unless explanations can be provided. This will be particularly significant since continued qualitative improvements will probably not be forbidden in the first stage of SALT.

For example, the Soviet Union might choose to begin deployment of mobile ICBMs in order to decrease the vulnerability of their land-based missiles to American MIRVs. To the United States this might look like a Russian attempt to increase secretly the size of their force since it is more difficult to count the number of mobile missiles deployed at any one time. It is not practicable to have simultaneous observation of the entire Soviet Union. Conceivably, the Russians might be able to reassure American authorities by providing information to reduce uncertainties on the total number of missiles deployed. Similarly, the U.S. development of new methods for penetrating an ABM could look to the Russians like a system for attacking Soviet ICBMs. An American explanation of the purpose might reassure the Russians, who in turn might be able to provide information which could alleviate our concerns about their air defenses.

With or without an arms-limitation agreement, the most important element in keeping the strategic arms race from getting completely out of hand has been the ability of both nations to have accurate information on the deployed weapons of the other side. For years now our Secretaries of Defense have been reporting with little argument the number of Soviet ICBMs and missile submarines deployed and under construction. Only on future programs or intentions have there been differing opinions. Without this information it would have been impossible even to have contemplated the type of agreement being discussed for the first phase of SALT. If for any reason these capabilities were lost, then any SALT agreement would be in serious jeopardy.

It has been reported by some sources, but never confirmed, that the Soviets have tested a space vehicle which might be capable of intercepting a satellite. Any such system would be susceptible to countermeasures. However, if either nation were to interfere with the other's systems for gathering information, this would be a very serious act, perhaps only just short of war. Certainly, satisfactory reassurances against any recurrence would have to be provided or the entire SALT agreement would soon break down. Since it would be at least several years before such loss of information could provide an opportunity to obtain a meaningful strategic advantage, there would be ample time to take countermeasures. Perhaps one of the outcomes of the first phase of SALT, or of the next, could be an understanding that neither side would take any steps to negate unilateral information-gathering systems that do not infringe on national sovereignty.

IV

Even if the first phase of SALT succeeds only in holding ABMs to a low level, it will have a major effect in slowing the strategic arms race and ensuring the continuation of a mutual deterrent posture. However, since at best the restrictions on offensive weapons will be quite limited in scope and probably place little or no controls on qualitative improvements, further steps will be needed to strengthen and broaden the agreement. Decisions on unilateral weapons programs as well as further arms limitations must be made with an eye toward ensuring that the application of new technologies does not weaken deterrence. Actions justified as safeguarding against abrogation or violation of a treaty must not be allowed to destroy the original purpose of the agreement. Continued bilateral consultations will be required to clear away misunderstandings.

An initial agreement at SALT, even if limited in scope, can mark the beginning of a new era in the nuclear weapons age. Opportunities will be opened up not only for halting the upward march of the arms race, but also for redirecting it downward so that the risks of a nuclear conflagration are reduced and the economic burdens of weapons programs lightened. Many of the new measures proposed will not be arrived at easily. Strong pressures for new weapons programs as hedges against possible treaty violations will have to be resisted vigorously. Complacency after an initial agreement must not be allowed to slow the drive toward further limitations.

34.

When the SALT Hit the Fan

DONALD G. BRENNAN

ON FRIDAY, MAY 26, 1972, Richard Nixon and Leonid Brezhnev signed what will doubtless prove to be the most important arms-control agreements negotiated in the nuclear era—or, it may be, in any area. But their indubitable importance does not, unfortunately, automatically make them a cause for rejoicing; the San Francisco earthquake, for instance, was important too. It remains to be seen whether the agreements of May 26 will prove to be more or less of a disaster than the earthquake. There is some possibility, not as large as we should wish, that the agreements will not be a disaster at all; and a remote chance, which neither the American public nor the Administration bureaucracy deserves, that they will prove a resounding success.

Whatever their chance of success, they are profoundly unwise. And the unwisdom is not confined to the United States alone; it is certainly shared by some of our allies, and may well be shared, though in reduced degree, by the Soviet Union. This is a particular disappointment to those of us who have been hoping and working for a strategic arms-control agreement that would make a genuine contribution to American security.

The agreements are two: 1) A proposed treaty limiting the deployment of defenses against ballistic missiles, called the Treaty on ABMs, and 2) a proposed "Interim Agreement" limiting certain kinds of strategic offensive forces, namely ICBMs and SLBMs (Intercontinental and Submarine-Launched Ballistic Missiles, respectively). The problems of these two are very different.

Reprinted by permission from *National Review*, June 23, 1972. (National Review, 150 East 35th Street, New York, N.Y. 10016)

The Interim Agreement guarantees not merely Soviet parity with, but Soviet strategic superiority over the United States, to a potentially substantial degree. The unwisdom of this agreement lies in the dramatic announcement it makes that the United States has not only become, but apparently is willing to remain, the second nuclear power. This foolishness is, of course, in no way shared by the Soviets; indeed, as one prominent American strategist put it, the Soviets must be pinching themselves to make sure they are not dreaming.

The ABM Treaty is more symmetric in its immediate effects; in contrast to the Interim Agreement, it does not allow the Soviets four times as much as we are allowed. Apart from a limited (but potentially significant) defense of national capitals, and a limited (and strategically insignificant) defense of missile fields, we and the Soviets have agreed not to defend ourselves—not only against each other, but, interestingly, against anyone else either. On the American side, this agreement stems purely from a sophomoric ideology and fashion, and is pure foolishness; on the Soviet side, the politburo may have accepted the same ideology, in which case they share equally in the foolishness. It is as if we and the Soviets had become seized with a theory that motor vehicles were bad for us, and, proceeding from that theory, both agreed to destroy all the motor vehicles of all kinds we produced in the future. In other words, that we and the Soviets might agree on some completely symmetric arrangement would not of itself prove that the arrangement was in our interest. In my view, the ABM Treaty provides an equally good illustration.

In my initial analysis of the Interim Agreement and the ABM Treaty, I shall concentrate on their shortcomings. I shall return later to the circumstances and forces that led to these agreements.

The Interim Agreement

The basic provisions of the Interim Agreement are as follows. First, we and the Soviets undertake not to start construction of additional fixed land-based ICBM launchers after July 1, 1972. Second, we both agree not to convert land-based launchers for "light" ICBMs into launchers for "heavy" ICBMs. Third, we agree to limit SLBM launchers and the submarines that carry them to the numbers operational and under construction as of the date of signature (May 26), except that additional launchers (and appropriate numbers of submarines) may be constructed as replacements for an equal number of obsolete ICBM launchers or for launchers on older submarines. In a protocol appended to the Interim Agreement, this is spelled out: The U.S. may have no more than 710 SLBM launchers, and no more than 44 submarines; of those, launchers above 656 and submarines above 41 (the current numbers) must be replacements for equal numbers of obsolete ICBM launchers (in our case, the Titan II). The Soviet Union may have no more than 950 SLBM launchers and no more than 62 "modern" submarines; of those, launchers over 740 (the presumptive current number) must similarly be replacements for older ICBM launchers and SLBM launchers. Fourth, subject to the foregoing restrictions, modernization and replacement of strategic offensive ballistic missiles and launchers is permitted. Fifth, compliance with the agreement shall be monitored with "national technical means of verification," meaning such things as reconnaissance satellites, and it is also agreed not to interfere with each other's means of observation or to use deliberate concealment measures that could impede that verification.

The intended immediate purpose of this Agreement is to freeze strategic offensive forces where they now stand, understanding that whatever is under construction at the prescribed date is to be included as if finished. Such an objective is not fundamentally irrational; I have myself urged consideration of a different freeze in other times and circumstances. The difficulties stem largely from the fact that the United States strategic forces have not changed very much in basic capacity for the past eight years, while the Soviet payload capacity—the amount of weight their missile force could deliver on targets, sometimes called the "throw weight"—has increased enormously since 1966, and it now stands around four times the payload capacity of the American force. A secondary problem resides in the extraordinarily generous terms given the Soviets for converting some obsolete missiles into additional modern SLBMs and submarines.

Supporters of the Agreement will point out, and correctly, that, while the Soviet Union has more launchers than the United States, we have—we believe—many more warheads deployed *on* those launchers. The estimate is based on the belief that the American technology for MIRV (Multiple Individually-targeted Reentry Vehicles) is much further advanced than the Soviet technology, and that we have deployed MIRV warheads on a substantial fraction of our strategic force while the Soviets have scarcely started (if they have begun at all). However, if the Soviets wish to achieve large numbers of warheads by deploying lighter MIRV warheads within their existing payload capacity, the technology for doing so is within their reach; we, on the other hand, are precluded from achieving the payload capacity of the Soviets by the Interim Agreement.

The throw weight of a strategic force is unquestionably the most important single parameter for characterizing the potential of that force, even though other parameters—notably the number, yield, and accuracy of warheads that can be delivered—are of more immediate importance. Some examples of how payload capacity can be used may be instructive. For example, the maximum capacity of a Poseidon launcher is perhaps in the area of three thousand pounds or less. A Poseidon missile, it is said, can accommodate from ten to fourteen MIRV warheads, which must therefore weigh no more than three hundred pounds each. These warheads would be relatively "small" weapons of perhaps fifty kilotons each, but one missile could attack ten separate targets. Some models of the Soviet SS-9 missile have a single large warhead, and some people might think that, at least for many purposes, a single Poseidon missile is therefore worth ten SS-9s. In fact, however, that single SS-9 warhead is often estimated to be perhaps 25 megatons, which would suggest that the missile payload capability is around twelve thousand pounds, or at least four times the payload capacity of a Poseidon missile. Therefore, if a Poseidon booster could launch ten MIRV warheads, an SS-9 could launch forty of the same kind.

The SS-9 probably has from five to ten times the payload capacity of our various Minuteman missiles, and therefore the Soviet force of approximately three hundred SS-9s by itself probably has two to three times the payload capability of our entire Minuteman force of one thousand. However, the Soviets have perhaps another 1,300 ICBMs in addition to their SS-9s, most of which are also larger than our Minutemen.

Considering both SLBM and ICBM payloads, it is probable that the Interim Agreement will allow the Soviets a throw weight roughly four times ours, with present booster technology. (Either side is at liberty to improve its booster technology; in fact, the Soviets have recently given evidence of a new model of SS-9 with perhaps twice the payload capability of earlier models.)

Some Administration analysts argue that the Soviets do not now have MIRV technology and could not deploy significant numbers of MIRV warheads within the five-year lifetime of the Interim Agreement. In evaluating this position, three points should be borne in mind. First, if no better agreement is negotiated before this one expires, there will be intense pressures to renew it. Second, the estimates that the Soviets could not get substantial MIRV capability come from the same community of intelligence analysts who led former Defense Secretary Robert McNamara to announce in the mid-1960's that the Soviets had accepted permanent strategic inferiority, and who were confident in advance of the first Chinese nuclear explosion in October 1964 that that bomb would be a plutonium device. It proved to be a uranium bomb; and it is an easy point that an operating diffusion plant for separating U-235 is very much harder to conceal than a MIRV test.

Most important, we developed MIRV from scratch in about six years, and the system development for the advanced specific systems probably did not take more than three or four years.

Since our own MIRV programs have been noisily advertised to the Soviets since early 1968 (and public mention of the idea can be found as far back as 1963), it would be surprising indeed if the Soviets did not by now have some very advanced ideas on how to do MIRV. Some analysts do, in fact, believe that the Soviets could achieve substantial MIRV capability within the lifetime of the Interim Agreement. Admiral Thomas Moorer, Chairman of the Joint Chiefs of Staff, said in his statement before the Senate Armed

Services Committee on February 15: ". . . our intelligence specialists believe that by the mid or late 1970's the Soviets could have MIRVed SLBMs in their operational forces."

Published comparisons of Soviet and American missile forces showing a substantial American lead in warheads, as for instance in a chart on the front page of the *New York Times,* May 27, showing 5,700 warheads for the U.S. and 2,500 for the Soviet Union, should be understood as having, in all probability, a highly limited lifetime of validity. Even today, the Soviet warheads are much larger and more destructive than ours.

(The estimates that are given for the Soviet ICBM force, incidentally, such as the number 1,618, are all derived from American intelligence; the Soviets have refused to say how many missiles they have. Thus, our estimates of the Soviet strategic forces are presumably lower bounds. The limitation in the Interim Agreement is stated as a prohibition on new silo starts, not as an absolute ceiling on numbers. If we later discover a whole field of ICBMs, which I am told has happened in the past, there may be some controversy over just when it was started. There is also room for controversy over what constitutes "light" or "heavy" ICBMs.)

If the Soviets have paid any significant attention to MIRV technology in the past, as is very likely, it would be well within their capability to deploy ten thousand or more MIRV warheads on their allowed booster force within the lifetime of this Agreement. They could do this with sufficient yield in warheads, combined with sufficiently upgraded guidance in their missiles, so that they could wipe out virtually all of our Minuteman force with less than half of their missile force.

This is not to say that launching such an attack would be attractive to the Soviets under ordinary circumstances; the United States has important offensive forces other than Minuteman, and these other forces retain considerable deterrent persuasiveness. Even the Minuteman force by itself would still provide some deterrence; a calculation that it could be substantially eliminated would be only a calculation and not likely to be appealing to political leaders except under desperate circumstances. But the lopsided nature of the situation will likely have important adverse consequences, as discussed below.

The Administration's justification for not only accepting this embarrassing posture but engraving it in a formal agreement, is that Congress will not in any event provide money for the forces needed to equalize the Soviet strategic force. Indeed, the Administration believes, and sincerely, that if it were not for this Agreement the Soviets would increase their margin of superiority to some even larger extent. For example, the current rate of construction of Soviet ballistic-missile submarines is nine or ten per cent; if that rate were continued, in five years the Soviets could have not 62, but perhaps ninety modern missile-launching submarines. Therefore, instead of having the 50 percent superiority in submarines the Agreement will potentially give them, they could have a 2 to 1 margin (assuming that Congress would not provide the several billion dollars necessary for us to keep pace, an assumption that has not been seriously tested, and may well be false).

Some Administration analysts argue that the degree of strategic superiority given the Soviets by the Interim Agreement, while admittedly large, is nevertheless less than suggested above. The chief arguments they advance are: a) the Agreement does not include bombers, in which we have substantial superiority; b) the Agreement omits what are called "Forward Based Systems," i.e., our nuclear delivery systems based in Europe; and c) the apparent Soviet superiority in submarines (62 Soviet *v.* 44 American) is not real, since the Soviets do not or cannot operate their submarines as efficiently as we can with our bases (at Rota and Holy Loch) closer to the Soviet Union. These arguments are more cosmetic than tenable. As for a), it is possible to believe in the superiority of American bomber forces only so long as Soviet medium bombers are not counted; they have some seven hundred of these, which could attack targets in the United States and continue on to airfields in Cuba and Mexico.

As for b), the Soviets have some seven hundred intermediate- or medium-range ballistic missiles that can attack European targets, to which our Forward Based Systems are mainly in response. These Soviet missiles are in no way affected by the Agreement; they can build as many more as they please.

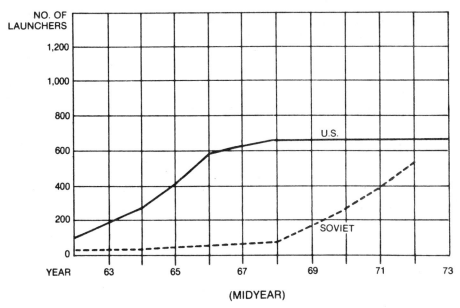

Figure 34.1

As for c), there is nothing to prevent the Soviets from adopting more efficient means of using their submarines. They could, for instance, resupply the submarines and change their crews from ocean-going tenders, so that a larger fraction of the submarines would be on station. Of course, the Soviets *may* not do this, but it would certainly not be difficult to do so and there is nothing in the proposed Agreement to prevent them.

The real Administration argument for the Interim Agreement is that it will limit the extent to which the Soviets will achieve strategic-force lead more reliably than any other approach in sight. But that Soviet advantage, by any reasonable assessment, is already real, and may well become greater as the Soviets deploy MIRVs and otherwise upgrade their permitted force in the coming years. The political consequences of this superiority, or more precisely of the general public recognition of it, are several, and all bad.

First, it will reinforce and confirm previously established Soviet images and expectations of a declining American role in world affairs. Within the past two years, Soviet commentators on the American scene have exhibited increasing contempt for the United States, its power, and its role in international affairs. For instance, Soviet analysts often make such remarks as: "The United States must be adjusting itself, in the manner of the United Kingdom at the end of World War II, to its loss of power and influence in the world." The Soviets correspondingly think of themselves as very much in the ascendant. These Soviet attitudes and expectations will be reflected in their peacetime bargaining and will increase their aggressiveness in possible crisis confrontations.

Second, the Agreement and the Soviet lead it establishes will do much to establish an image of American inferiority in American government circles. The effects of this, of course, will be the obverse of those to be expected from the attitudes in the Soviet bureaucracy, though probably less marked in degree.

Third, the new imbalance of power will become firmly established in the minds of our allies, which will ultimately lead them to be more responsive, perhaps unduly responsive, to Soviet diplomatic pressures and initiatives. To use the current jargon, the Interim Agreement will contribute to "Finlandizing" tendencies in the policies of our allies.

Fourth, enshrining this degree of Soviet superiority as a substantially permanent thing will almost certainly have adverse consequences in any serious crises that may develop. For instance, we could not reasonably expect as favorable an outcome in a replay of the Cuban missile crisis. (The success of that outcome did not reside so much in the immediate outcome in Cuba as that the Soviets were deterred from counter-escalating in Turkey, or, especially, in Berlin, a fact that apostles of parity find convenient to ignore.)

It is in a certain sense true that different degrees of superiority can in the last analysis be translated only into different degrees of "victory" that would in any event be altogether Pyrrhic. However, this often-repeated observation conveniently ignores the fact that most political leaders and many military leaders are not academic strategists: These leaders not only count weapons, they tend to think in terms of who will come out "ahead," and their (perhaps simplistic) attitudes about these matters will influence their expectations, demands, and flexibility in a crisis (other things—such as the guts and the political support of the leaders on the scene—being equal). Therefore, a commitment to a position of strategic disadvantage is, at least in some statistical sense, an invitation to be pushed around in the next crisis.

The ABM Treaty

The key terms of the Treaty on ABMs are as follows: First, "Each party undertakes not to deploy ABM systems for a defense of the territory of its country and not to provide a base for such a defense, and not to deploy ABM systems for defense of an individual region except as provided for in Article III of this treaty." The basic philosophy is clear: Apart from the exceptions indicated, we may not defend our homeland against missile attack.

Second, Article III provides for a limited defense by one hundred interceptors of Moscow and Washington, and another defense system, similarly limited to one hundred interceptors, of ICBM silos in some area remote from the national capital.

Third, both we and the Soviets undertake not to develop, test or deploy ABM systems or components which are seabased, air-based, space-based, or mobile land-based.

Fourth, it is prohibited to transfer ABM systems or their components to other states or to deploy them outside Soviet and American national territory.

Fifth, compliance with the provisions of the Treaty shall be monitored by "national technical means of verification," as in the Interim Agreement, and (also similarly) there are obligations not to interfere with such means or to attempt deliberate concealment.

American strategic nuclear policy has been dominated in recent years by the concept of "assured destruction," according to which the chief task of the U.S. strategic forces is to be able to mount a nuclear attack that will be sure to destroy a substantial fraction of Soviet society, even after a major Soviet strike on American forces. (Recent statements by the Nixon Administration have emphasized a doctrine called "strategic sufficiency," but it is clear that something like the concept of "assured destruction" still dominates American strategic policy.)

This domination extends to strategic arms-control matters. It is argued that the most stable, secure, cheap, and generally desirable arrangement is one in which we and the Soviets maintain a "mutual assured destruction" posture, in which no serious effort is made by either side to limit the civilian damage that could be inflicted by the other. Most of the opposition in the West to substantial systems of missile defense for cities, including the opposition embodied in this proposed ABM Treaty, derives from the alleged benefits of such a posture. And much of the opposition to the Safeguard ABM system, which was not intended to provide a substantial defense of cities, stemmed from a concern that it might expand to provide such a defense.

The concept of mutual assured destruction provides one of the few instances in which the obvious acronym for something yields at once the appropriate description; for it, that is, a Mutual Assured Destruction posture as a goal is, almost literally, mad. MAD. If technology and international politics provided absolutely no alternative, one might reluctantly accept a MAD posture. But to think of it as desirable—for instance, as a clearly preferred goal of our arms-control negotiations, as the proposed ABM treaty automatically assumes—is bizarre. Let us consider the simplest and most effective means of realizing it.

At present, we and the Soviets achieve a MAD posture by means of long-range missiles and bombers armed with thermonuclear weapons. There are, however, many problems associated with these forces. Missiles and bombers may be attacked before they are launched; they may fail to perform properly; they may fail to penetrate enemy defenses. Concern about such vulnerabilities helps fuel the arms race. These forces are also expensive; the U.S. alone spends about $8 billion a year on them.

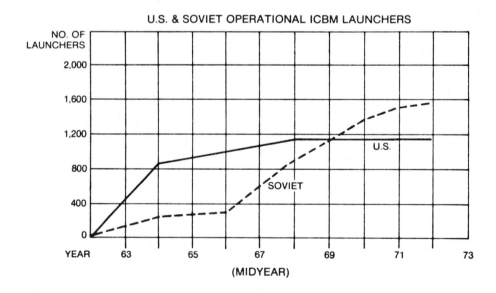

Figure 34.2

Now, if it were genuinely desirable to have a MAD posture, we could achieve it effectively, reliably, and cheaply. We could have an arms-control agreement to mine each other's cities: We could install very large thermonuclear weapons with secure firing arrangements in, say, Moscow, Leningrad, and Kiev, etc., while the Soviets could install similar weapons and arrangements in New York, Chicago, and Los Angeles, etc. It is technically feasible to make such a system quite secure; with the vulnerabilities mentioned above eliminated, arms-race pressures would be reduced. While such a system would have its own technical problems, analysis indicates they would be far simpler to solve than those of the current system; it could save billions. Yet almost everyone will dismiss it as being merely absurd. If a mined-city system is the best way of realizing a MAD posture, it follows that posture as a goal is itself fundamentally absurd.

There are three fundamental problems here: The first is that, in spite of our best efforts, a major nuclear war could happen. An institutionalized MAD posture is a way of insuring, now and forever, that the outcome of such a war would be nearly unlimited disaster for everybody. While technology and politics may conspire to leave us temporarily in such a posture, we should not welcome it—we should rather look for ways out of it.

The second fundamental difficulty is essentially political: We do not have a Department of Defense for the purpose of deliberately making us all hostages to enemy weapons. The government is supposed, according to the Constitution, to "provide for the common defense," and plainly most Americans would revolt at the idea of a mined-city system as a sensible way to do this. The Defense Department should be more concerned with assuring live Americans than dead Russians.

The third fundamental difficulty is moral: We should not deliberately create a system in which millions of innocent civilians would be exterminated should the system fail. The system is not *that* reliable. Again, if we accept a MAD posture as an interim solution, we should be looking for ways out of it, not ways to enshrine it.

Why, then, do some advocate a MAD posture? The advocates are, in the main, technically oriented people accustomed to theoretical models, and the arguments involve appeals to "stability" of various kinds and reference to other sophisticated jargon—jargon that I understand very well, having helped to articulate it a decade or more ago. For instance, one argument sometimes heard—it is, e.g., reflected in the preamble to the proposed ABM Treaty—is that this posture will best protect against nuclear war altogether, but this proposition is very dubious indeed.

While these MADvocates are undoubtedly sincere, and many of them intelligent, I believe they have been bemused by theoretical models of strategic interactions, models which seem sophisticated and intellectually appealing but which are in fact much oversimplified descriptions of reality.

Some few technical people have been so bemused by the models that they seriously advocate deployment of a mined-city system.

If an institutionalized MAD posture is not desirable as a permanent way of life, and it is not, what alternative is available? The answer is to put increasing emphasis on defense, with a corresponding reduction in the effort devoted to strategic offensive forces.

There is much controversy about just how effective any defense (such as ABM) can be made against existing or further enlarged offensive forces. I cannot discuss this controversy here. However, there is very little controversy over the fact that defense can be made quite effective if the opposing offense is suitably reduced, while allowed defense is built up. This is precisely the direction that the Strategic Arms Limitation Talks should have taken, but did not.

Even if it were agreed that currently achievable defense is too ineffective to be useful against even a suitably reduced offensive threat (a position that few informed persons would take), it makes little sense to preclude the possibility of a more effective defense being found in the future. The proposed treaty does exactly that.

It might be possible to achieve similar effects simply by sharply reducing offensive forces, without any defense, if it were not for two factors: a) there are other countries in the world besides the United States and the Soviet Union, and b) perfect inspection of sharply reduced offensive forces probably cannot be achieved, and defense can provide protection against clandestine weapons.

The MAD philosophy originally took hold in the American arms-control community about 1960. This might have been ultimately unimportant but for the fact that Robert S. McNamara became a determined believer in the concept, and imposed the "Assured Destruction" philosophy on the civilian staffs in the Pentagon with the full force of his personality. This was in a sense a tour de force, because at the time, the Soviets conspicuously did not share this philosophy (although he often asserted that they did). The evidence is overwhelming that, at least up until the late 1960's, the Soviets did not consider a MAD posture desirable. For instance, Premier Kosygin, asked about a moratorium on missile defenses at a press conference in London on February 9, 1967, replied, in part: "I believe that defensive systems, which prevent attack, are not the cause of the arms race, but constitute a factor preventing the death of people. Some argue like this: What is cheaper, to have offensive weapons which can destroy towns and whole states or to have defensive weapons which can prevent this destruction? At present the theory is current somewhere that the system which is cheaper should be developed. Such so-called theoreticians argue as to the costs of killing a man— $500,000 or $100,000. Maybe an antimissile system is more expensive than an offensive system, but it is designed not to kill people but to preserve human lives. I understand that I do not reply to the question I was asked, but you can draw yourselves the appropriate conclusions." This is not the comment of a man who was friendly to a moratorium on missile defense.

Many other Soviet pronouncements, public and private, official and unofficial, left no doubt that the Soviets favored heavy emphasis on active defense, at least up through 1968 and early 1969. But beginning in 1969 or 1970, the Soviet government leaders either began to change their views, or else decided to make us *think* they had changed their views. Thus the overt indications in the SALT negotiations for the past two years have suggested while-hearted Soviet acceptance, at least at the top of the hierarchy, of the MAD philosophy.

If the Soviets have indeed come to this position, they have had a good deal of American help in getting there. Almost every American who argued with almost any Russian about arms-control matters in the 1960's tried to make the point that missile defenses were wicked. This stemmed, of course, from the commitment in certain American quarters to the MAD philosophy Up until 1968, the universal Soviet reaction to this argument was a polite raspberry. But some U.S. spokesmen could not be easily ignored. In particular, McNamara himself did his best to convert the Soviets to his philosophy, both in public statements and in private meetings (notably at the Glassboro Conference in June 1967, when he forcefully presented the case for MAD directly to Kosygin, who did not go for the idea, at least at that time). Another forceful input to the Soviets came from President Lyndon B. Johnson, who, according to his memoirs, sent Premier Kosygin a secret letter in January 1967 warning him that the incipient deployment of Soviet missile defenses had put him under pressure to "increase greatly our capabilities to penetrate any defensive systems which you might establish." Johnson continued: "If we should feel compelled to make such major increases in our strategic weapons capabilities, I have no doubt that you would in turn feel under compulsion to do likewise." It seems likely that this letter was stimulated by Secretary McNamara.

Perhaps the most persuasive pressure on the Soviets was not an argument per se, but the American decision of late 1967 and early 1968 to proceed with a major MIRV program for the American strategic offensive force, leading to the deployment of Minuteman III and Poseidon. This program was intended to add something like five thousand additional warheads to the American offensive force. The almost theological, not to say fanatic, faith McNamara had in the MAD philosophy is reflected in the fact that, while he viewed the beginnings of a Soviet system for defense of the homeland as highly provocative, he apparently saw nothing provocative in spending many billion dollars to add several thousand additional warheads to the American force, especially at a time and under circumstances that would have made it impossible for the Soviets to know what accuracy these weapons might achieve.

For whatever combinations of reasons, the Soviets have now either accepted the MAD philosophy or are pretending to. It should be noted that, up to the time of writing, one cannot detect many hints of this philosophy in the papers of Soviet colonels writing for each other in *Red Star;* however, this may indicate merely that the message has not yet come down from the top. (Some well-placed Soviet officials have in fact indicated to Americans, very privately, that the ABM Treaty will mean a major doctrinal overhaul in the Soviet military establishment, and may well require a considerable shuffling of senior personnel. It will be interesting to see if this in fact comes to pass.)

Some kinds of ABM systems could be compatible with a MAD posture. The Sentinel ABM system initiated by McNamara in September 1967, and the Safeguard System that the Nixon Administration has been constructing, were both designed to be compatible with a MAD posture. These systems would have provided a "light" or "thin" defense; a large and sophisticated attack, such as the Soviets would be capable of mounting, would easily have overwhelmed the thin overall defense of our cities. (At McNamara's instruction, the Sentinel System design also had some specific weaknesses introduced to make the system more easily penetrable by the Soviets.) Such a light area defense was intended, in the case of the Sentinel System, to provide protection of the entire country against possible Chinese attacks.

The Nixon Administration retained the anti-Chinese light-area-defense objective of the Sentinel System and added additional objectives for the Safeguard System, chiefly the provision of added protection of our ICBM and bomber forces. The threefold objectives of the Safeguard program have been stated many times by the present Administration; for instance, as given in the most recent "Posture Statement" issued by Defense Secretary Melvin Laird in February 1972: "Protection of our land-based retaliatory forces against a direct attack by the Soviet Union; defense of the American people against the kind of nuclear attack which the People's Republic of China is likely to be able to mount within the decade; and protection against the possibility of accidental attacks from any source." These objectives made sense, even within the framework of a MAD posture, and the program was accordingly supported, especially in its early phases in 1969 and 1970, by many who were willing to accept such a posture.

It is instructive that nothing in either Moscow agreement provides a substitute means for satisfying these objectives of Safeguard. The Interim Agreement does not provide sufficient protection of our land-based retaliatory forces against a direct attack by the Soviets (I shall give evidence for this shortly), and of course nothing in either agreement does anything about the possibility of nuclear attack from China or accidental attacks from any source. Therefore, the Administration's previously declared objectives for Safeguard combined with the current proposed agreements constitute a strategic non-sequitur.

**U.S. & SOVIET INTERCONTINENTAL
STRATEGIC OFFENSIVE DELIVERY VEHICLES
(ICBM LAUNCHERS, SLBM LAUNCHERS, & INTERCONTINENTAL BOMBERS)**

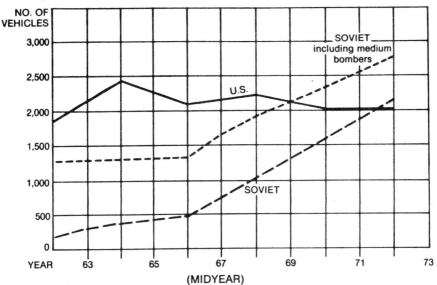

Curves are for numbers of delivery vehicles only, not for payload capacity or "throw weight." Similar curves drawn for throw weight would show the Soviets crossing the American capacity earlier in time, and having a much greater advantage at present.

Figure 34.3

The worst aspect of this non-sequitur relates to the protection of our retaliatory forces. The declared Administration objective in linking the negotiation of an ABM agreement to an agreement limiting strategic offensive forces was that it was necessary to limit the threat to Minuteman in order to accept constraints that would limit our ability to protect Minuteman. However, we are far from having achieved that link-up. To quote again from Secretary Laird's most recent Posture Statement: "With significant qualitative improvements in Soviet ICBMs even without increases in the number of Soviet ICBMs [i.e., exactly the situation permitted by the Interim Agreement], the postulated threat to Minuteman in the last half of the 1970's could grow to a level beyond the capabilities of the four-site Safeguard defense of Minuteman. Therefore, we propose [initiating an additional ABM defense program for protecting Minuteman beyond the four-site Safeguard System]." Thus, even the full four-site Safeguard System, which would have entailed many more than one hundred interceptors, was judged by Mr. Laird inadequate to protect Minuteman against the threat now permitted the Soviets under the Interim Agreement. We have negotiated away all but a small part of that Safeguard System, to say nothing of the opportunity to add additional active defense.

The gains Mr. Nixon brought back from Moscow are not to be thought of in terms of the often-expressed objectives of the Safeguard program. There are two possible intellectual justifications for accepting this treaty, in the light of the objectives the government has previously expressed. The first is that, while these agreements are inadequate, supplementary agreements to be sought in following negotiations will redress imbalances. However, the Soviets will have very little motivation to degrade the situation they now find themselves in; therefore I do not believe that argument should be given any significant weight. The other justification would say that, while the agreements may in some sense constitute an immediate strategic loss, the various political and economic gains that may develop as a consequence of these agreements will more than compensate for the strategic costs. An argument along this line is in fact indicated in President Nixon's last foreign policy statement. While this argument cannot be dismissed, there is no doubt that such a calculation of gains and losses requires considerable optimism about the consequences of having these agreements and considerable pessimism about the future if the agreements were not in force.

There is probably another sense in which the ABM Treaty is a strategic non-sequitur. It is intended by its American proponents to institutionalize a permanent MAD posture, but it is actually doubtful that, as matters now stand, the United States has an assured destruction capability (measured by standard criteria) against the Soviets, in view of their Civil Defense program. The Soviet government has declared that their CD program could limit Soviet fatalities in an all-out war with the United States to perhaps 6 percent of their population, which would be substantially less than the fatalities they suffered in World War II. American students of the Soviet CD program agree that this estimate is reasonable. In contrast, current Soviet forces could probably destroy 60 percent of the American population, with high confidence, given our lack of CD preparations. Thus, it appears that the actual current assured destruction capabilities are not exactly mutual.

What Brought Us Here?

The question of what brought us to the point of accepting these agreements can be answered at several different levels, and in terms of several different individuals and groups within the government.

President Nixon genuinely wants peace; he genuinely would like to save money; and he genuinely would like to be reelected. He obviously knows that these agreements, especially if they are accepted without too much of a battle, will be of substantial domestic political value. I believe it is fair to say that this fact resulted in significant pressure on the American negotiators. However, it would be quite wide of the mark to dismiss the agreements as a cheap electoral trick or to believe that they do not have a substantial base of support in the Washington Establishment.

Many people on the President's own staff place considerable emphasis, in justifying the agreements and especially the Interim Agreement, on the argument that Congress would not provide the wherewithal to close the widening gap in strategic forces. While this argument is probably sincere, it may in fact be less important than a perception that is less frequently articulated, but which is likely held by the President and by some of his key people: that money for military purposes would be very scarce *even if Congress itself were not an obstacle.* Trying to find several billion dollars a year in extra money for the Defense Department would entail very unpleasant alternatives, such as raising taxes, attempting some kind of tax reform, or taking large amounts of money from other programs dear to the Administration. Such alternatives would, of course, seem especially unpleasant in an election year. Congress may make an easy scapegoat, but Congress cannot be reckoned the chief villain of the piece when the President has never once gone to the country to explain that our military posture was in jeopardy and that more money was needed for strategic forces. If the President had chosen to lead on this matter, many of us believe the country might well have followed; but the experiment was never tried.

One of the more interesting case studies, in relation to these agreements, can be found in the Department of Defense. A decade ago, it would have been absolutely inconceivable that, for instance, the Joint Chiefs of Staff would have approved either of these agreements, much less both of them. Their approval would have been almost as unthinkable five years ago. Within the past three years however, and especially within the past two, a very noticeable loss of morale has been detectable within the Department. In the face of the buffeting from Congress, from the President's own Bureau of the Budget and from the general public, the military staffs have been looking to SALT to help "save" their situation. Even today, however, it is implausible that the Joint Chiefs could regard these agreements with enthusiasm; more likely, they faced a set of unpleasant alternatives, and judged these agreements to be the least unpleasant.

Some comments in the press have tended to suggest that Henry Kissinger was the chief architect of these agreements. It would probably be much more accurate to think of him as presiding over the national security apparatus as a sort of chairman, and attempting to impose some degree of order and competence on that apparatus, than as a personal mastermind of these agreements. Kissinger's main (and very considerable) strength is in international politics; perhaps because of the technical components involved, he has never been as strong on strategic nuclear issues. Kissinger's personal contribution to events can probably be found much more in the President's determined resistance to cutting American troop levels in Europe, and in the missions to Peking and Moscow, than in these two strategic arms agreements.

Where Next?

These are not the arms-control agreements one would wish to have in an ideal world. I have supported, without serious reservation, every arms-control agreement or treaty that has emerged since World War II. I doubt that one should recommend acceptance of these agreements.

It would be easy to advise rejection, if one had the opportunity to start over again to produce better agreements. But the choice is not there. In view of all the circumstances, both domestic and international, should one accept an American declaration of strategic inferiority, and accept the conspicuous idiocy of a permanent commitment to the MAD posture, and simply hope that the agreements will ultimately contribute to the evolution of a secure peace with freedom? Or should one insist that the President do what is right, Congress do what is right, and the public do what is right, including spending much more money if the Soviets are recalcitrant about establishing more sensible agreements (and, incidentally, almost surely lose the battle)? I do not know, and I can believe that honest and intelligent men, who understand the issues thoroughly, and who are as disappointed as I am with the agreements, could easily differ on the answers.

At the very least, the debate associated with these agreements, in Congress and out of it, should force attention to a number of important questions. Some of these concern technical details, but ones which may be of sufficient importance to influence the acceptability of the agreements. It may well be that some judicious reservations could be attached to these agreements that would lessen their unfortunate effects.

The United States has suffered something like wounds from a number of sources in recent years—Vietnam, student activism, declining credibility of both the government and the media and, not least, a declining role in world affairs, occasioned largely by declining morale at home. Many of us will feel that Mr. Nixon has now rubbed SALT in our wounds. But we should not forget that there are, in fact, good reasons to slow down the strategic arms race; and if the agreements are accepted, we must, of necessity, share Mr. Nixon's hope that their positive effects will, over the long term, outweigh their immediate strategic costs.

The costs are real.

XI

THE DEFENSE BUDGET CONTROVERSY

Although Senator McGovern has been defeated for the presidency by such a wide margin that he is unlikely to run again, his proposed defense budget was merely a somewhat extreme version of proposals that will continue to get considerable support from liberal Democrats and Republicans in Congress. The argument for such reductions is based upon the contention that many domestic matters urgently require a solution. If the nation is not strong domestically, it will not be able to act with strength externally.

If one examines the trend lines in actual U.S. military budgets, as given in Mr. Kintner's article and the excerpts from Secretary Laird's 1973 statement below, are the many critical comments about the size of that budget justified? The big item in the current defense budget is manpower—a direct consequence of the volunteer army. Many significant cuts have already been made in the military budget and are continuing. The share of national income given to defense is on a significant downward path.

The proposed McGovern budget would move the United States toward a position of minimum deterrence. There is significant evidence that the Chinese regard proposals of this kind with some alarm. Moreover, there is substantial doubt that the program would result in significant budgetary savings. The reduction of American forces in Europe would impair the defensibility of western Europe against Soviet attack. If substantially carried through, we would be back to a situation in which American ground forces would serve not for ground defense but merely as a trip-wire to set off a massive nuclear attack upon the Soviet Union—a policy that would be suicidal if carried out and that likely would undermine European confidence in our reliability. (See chapter VII for a discussion of this issue.)

The Senator argued for substantial reductions in the American aircraft carrier fleet. Pointing out quite correctly that these carriers would be extremely vulnerable in a nuclear war between the Soviet Union and the United States, he overlooked the fact that they obviously can have value in political crises and military conflicts that have not reached the nuclear level. Such a reduction would affect the confidence of current allies in western Europe and the Mediterranean area, Japan, and particularly Israel. If the military budget is not sufficient to meet the international responsibilities of the United States, there is a potential price to pay in terms of our ability to deter crises, to maintain systems of alliance, and to maintain the confidence of presently unaligned nations in our ability to assist them if they resist threats against their integrity. Moreover, if military weakness produces an international crisis, this might well begin a new round of military increases that would otherwise be unnecessary.

Therefore, the question of the level of the military budget directly relates to all the prior questions as well as to that other great issue of national security: the viability of the institutions and values of the nation. Obviously there is some conflict between these two important considerations. The major question is what mix of expenditures for the military and for domestic programs produces the best overall security for national institutions and values. Obviously the authors in this chapter make different estimates of the nature of the external threat and the adequacy of proposed responses. As the reader will have seen by now, these questions feed right back into the entire set of great issues, beginning with those under the category of world order and going through those included under great issues of foreign policy.

35.

An Alternative National Defense Posture

GEORGE McGOVERN

Introduction

(1) PLANNING ASSUMPTIONS

THE BEGINNING PREMISE of this alternative national defense posture is that the United States should *buy what we need* to deter or counter foreseeable threats to American and allied security.

That guideline automatically limits some of the artificial standards which have had a profound influence on military spending in past years.

Our defense posture has been built upon conservative planning assumptions—on preparing for "greater than expected threats." The alternative posture accepts that premise in part. It starts by assuming that the major communist powers, China and the Soviet Union, will remain actively hostile to U.S. interests, and that there is a real risk of confrontation if one or the other can expect military advantage as a result.

Hence the proposed budget retains more nuclear weapons than necessary for deterrence, as insurance and as a hedge against possible buildups on the other side. General purpose forces are maintained against dangers which are both slight and exceedingly remote, given the expected military balance and political outlook. Intensive research and development efforts are proposed, to maintain the clear U.S. lead in military technology.

But conservative planning can be pushed too far. As it aims for maximum safety, it can also fuel futile, costly, and perilous arms competition. And it can lead to the needless maintenance of active forces against threats which do not and likely never will exist. It can be said, for example, that there is

Reprinted from the *Congressional Record,* Jan. 19, 1972, pp. E147–E151.

probably no more reason to maintain forces to fight Hungary, Czechoslovakia, or Poland, than there is to plan for a conventional war against West Germany. Instead of being added to the Warsaw Pact, the troops of those countries could easily be subtracted, to account for the Russian forces they divert from the threat to NATO.

Certainly we should be able to find the line between conservatism and paranoia. Conservatism in planning should be able to coexist with realism in understanding changed world conditions, and with caution in adding military forces that can needlessly heighten the dangers and raise the costs of national security. This alternative posture is designed to meet those standards.

Shifts in aggregate military spending from year to year are often portrayed as a measure of national will—as evidence of our determination to resist communism—quite apart from the size of standing forces. The alternative budget rejects such mindless measurements. The nation's security does not demand, and is not served, by contests which are based less on strategy and power than on a willingness to waste public revenues.

The size of the recommended budget for procurement of new weapons is almost always judged by comparisons with spending in prior years. But clearly that is no guide to a prudent defense posture. If the Defense Department spends $15 billion on new weapons in one year and $5 billion in the next, anyone should be able to see that it has not reduced defense outlays in the second year; it has added to them. Prior investments must be seen as a base upon which to build, not a target to be matched or surpassed. The same process exposes the nonsense in hysterical references to "unilateral disarmament" in connection with military budget reductions.

Significant shares of existing and planned military forces are justified primarily as "bargaining chips" to be traded away in negotiations. The Safeguard ABM system and U.S. troops in Europe are important current examples. But both the American taxpayer and the prospects for arms limitation suffer, as both are suffering now, when negotiations become an excuse for buying more than we need. A desire to negotiate from strength should not compel arms outlays that will be inappropriate even if negotiations fail.

Military spending programs are usually justified by reference to the country's global responsibilities, so that a "new isolationist" attitude is ascribed to those who raise questions. This alternative budget rejects the notion that military might is the only method by which the United States can fulfill international responsibilities and serve the cause of freedom. And it incorporates some of the painful lessons of recent years, about the military damage done to helpless people in freedom's name, and about the relative impotence of sophisticated weapons in forcing other countries and other people to act in ways we might prefer.

In sum, this alternative posture suggests that misleading and irrelevant planning assumptions should be discarded. Instead the nation's military establishment should be constructed, first, by a careful analysis of the potential danger to U.S. security interests and, second, by retention of that portion of existing forces, and by construction of the new forces, needed to deter and defend against threats for which it is reasonable to remain actively prepared.

The second major premise of this budget is that realistic ceilings on military spending can produce armed forces which are both leaner and tougher than those now in being.

Congressional investigators and Presidential Commissions have documented astonishing waste and inefficiency in military programs. Further, defense planners have shown a remarkable attraction for strategies and systems which relate less to current and future conditions than to the world as it existed decades ago.

It is vain to hope that simple admonitions will correct these conditions. Sharp fiscal discipline is required if more efficient use of available resources is to be achieved. Such discipline can trim both physical and intellectual fat from the Pentagon, and bring much more productive capabilities to bear on strategies and systems which are directly relevant to a changing world.

(2) TIMETABLE

The recommended force and spending levels of this alternative defense budget should be achieved by fiscal 1975, with proportional reductions beginning in fiscal 1973. Total spending estimates are adjusted on manpower for inflation at an annual rate of approximately four percent in the Consumer Price Index and, on procurement, on cost growth at a rate midway between projected increases in consumer and wholesale prices. Hence the total figures must be read with due consideration of the hazards in making such projections.

This phased approach allows, first, for an appropriate response to possible changes in the threat. The recommended force level is fully adequate to deal with dangers which can be foreseen, based on the best current estimates of adversary plans. Significant changes in those estimates as they are updated could result in adjustments in these recommendations.

Second, the process of phased reductions will allow advance preparations by military planners, to assure that obligations incurred in prior years do not exceed the 1975 recommended ceiling. A big share of actual spending each year is made in pursuit of authority granted in the year before. The two measurements should be equal by fiscal 1975.

Third, the recommended timetable will permit fulfillment of the government's obligation to assist in the conversion of excess military resources into other public and private enterprise. A program to meet accumulated civilian needs, applying both savings from the military sector and general revenues, can occupy a large share of the facilities freed by this budget. Such a program can also guarantee alternative employment to all workers displaced from the defense sector, and reduce economic dependence on superfluous military spending.

Strategic Forces

Strategic forces are maintained for the purpose of protecting against—primarily by deterring—nuclear attack against the United States. Components include land- and sea-based ballistic missiles, long-range heavy bombers, a missile warning system, air defenses against bombers, and the early stages of an anti-ballistic missile system.

U.S. AND OPPOSING FORCES

In mid-1971, U.S. forces for the conduct of nuclear war were officially numbered at some 4,600 offensive force loadings. That figure does not include more than 7,000 smaller nuclear weapons listed as "tactical" and not counted in the strategic nuclear arsenal, although at least a proportion of those weapons could also be delivered on targets in the Soviet Union or the People's Republic of China.

Offensive nuclear weapons are carried aboard three delivery systems: 1,000 Minuteman and 54 larger Titan intercontinental ballistic missiles in hardened silos in the United States; 520 heavy bombers composed of 450 B-52s (26 squadrons) and 71 FB-111s (four squadrons), and 656 Polaris and Poseidon missiles aboard 41 nuclear submarines.

The single active strategic defensive system in being is composed of some 600 manned interceptors and 1136 surface-to-air missiles, along with extensive surveillance and warning system, for protection against an attack by strategic bombers. The United States also maintains an extensive enemy missile warning system whose radars, communications, and computing devices will provide notice to U.S. decision-makers within minutes of any enemy launch against the United States.

The country's offensive nuclear forces are by no means static. All three of the delivery systems are being made more formidable, through incorporation of multiple independently-targetable reentry vehicles (MIRVs) on portions of the land and sea based missile forces, and through initial development of a follow-on bomber, the B-1, plus new penetration aids and stand-off missiles which can be used either on the B-52 force or on the B-1. The missile plan now being implemented will (1) replace the 16 Polaris missiles on 31 of 41 nuclear submarines with Poseidon missiles carrying approximately ten independently-targetable warheads each and (2) replace 550 of the 1,000 ICBMs currently deployed with Minuteman III missiles each carrying three independently targetable warheads, leaving a land-based force equivalent to 2,000 missiles. When these conversions are completed U.S. nuclear force loadings will be in the range of 10,000 warheads, most of which will be smaller in megatonnage than those now in being but still well above the power of the Hiroshima and Nagasaki bombs used at the end of World War II. Moreover their vastly improved accuracy largely offsets reductions in explosive force.

In the defensive sphere the most ambitious development currently under-way is the Safeguard ABM system designed to intercept incoming enemy ICBMs. However, it is better described as an adjunct to an offensive weapon, since its primary stated goal would be to preserve confidence in the Minuteman force. The United States is also upgrading air defenses through the planned Airborne Warning and Control System (AWACS), which will have the capacity to look down and spot low-flying enemy bombers.

In mid-1971 the Soviet Union had approximately 2,000 total offensive nuclear force loadings, or about 40 percent as many as the United States. U.S. estimates credit them with about 1,500 ICBMs, 175 to 195 bombers, and 400 Polaris-type sea-based missiles. Their defenses include between 3,000 and 3,300 interceptor aircraft, 10,000 surface-to-air missile launchers, and 64 anti-ballistic missile launchers in the Galosh system around Moscow.

Soviet force levels have not been static either, although it is, of course, difficult to make reliable predictions about Soviet plans in the absence of firm knowledge about their intentions. In the past several years they have deployed about 300 very large SS-9 missiles capable of carrying single war-heads of as much as 25 megatons, and they have tested multiple reentry vehicles (MRVs), multiple warheads which are not independently target-able, which could be deployed on the SS-9 to supply, for example, three five megaton warheads on each missile. In 1970 SS-9 construction appeared to be halted. In 1971 additional silo construction was detected, but the purpose was not clear. The new silos could be for purposes other than additional SS-9 deployments, such as further hardening of existing forces. No MIRV deployments have taken place, and it is questionable whether the Soviet Union has even tested independently targetable warheads. They are at least three years behind the United Stated in this technology. In recent years there have also been additions to the Soviet force of SS-11s, an ICBM capa-ble of carrying payloads comparable to those of Minuteman, but powered by liquid fuel. These deployments have also leveled off.

The most active Soviet construction has been in nuclear Y-class subma-rines, which are being produced at a rate of seven or eight each year. Slightly over 30 are either in being or in various stages of production, suggesting that they could equal U.S. numbers by the mid-1970's.

While moving ahead on ICBM and SLBM construction the Soviet Union has placed little emphasis on its aging fleet of intercontinental bombers. The numbers have remained in the range of 200, declining slightly due to normal attrition. At least 50 are believed to be configured as tankers. Neither of the two aircraft involved, the Bison and the Bear, is supersonic. The Bear is a turboprop aircraft; the Bison is somewhat like the B-52 although with less range and payload. They have no tactical aircraft with nuclear weapons within ranges allowing completion of strike missions against the United States.

Although they have traditionaly emphasized defensive measures, the Soviet Union has not made significant advances with respect to missile defense. Deployment of their ABM interceptors has never gone beyond a small system around Moscow. They have developed interceptor aircraft with improved capabilities, but numbers have tended to decline slightly.

The other country considered a nuclear adversary of the United States, the People's Republic of China, is reportedly developing medium-range missiles which would be incapable of reaching the United States. They have been expected to have a small force available in the late 1970's or early 1980's, possibly including ICBMs to reach U.S. targets.

Comparisons such as these can be helpful in determining the relative status of U.S. opposing forces. But they can also be quite misleading because first, they do not account for qualitative differences; second, they do not indictate the extent to which each side can rely on its nuclear forces to perform missions assigned to them; and third, they do not account for differences in effectiveness depending on who strikes first.

On the first point, for example, concern has been expressed about estimates that the Soviet Union has more megatonnage, although fewer force loadings, than the United States. However, a simple comparison of megatonnage can be grossly misleading. For destruction of most targets a single small weapon delivered with high accuracy is just as effective as a weapon of much greater yield. In fact, the United States explicitly chose smaller yields and greater numbers when the Minuteman program was initiated, and is now going to even lower yields in MIRV programs in part because a number of smaller warheads can do more damage than a single large one, and because they pose a more difficult interception problem besides.

On the second point, the bare fact that the Soviet Union has 64 ABM interceptors, while the United States has none, might suggest that they enjoy a substantial advantage. In truth the resources they have expended on their ABM have been a near total waste because the system can be easily penetrated or overwhelmed and thus provides virtually no defense at all. The area it is supposed to protect is as vulnerable as it ever was to thousands of incoming warheads; indeed more vulnerable because the U.S. reaction has been to increase offensive forces and to target the Moscow area more heavily.

Deterrence—The Essential Mission

(1) Force requirements

The overriding mission of U.S. nuclear weapons is to deter nuclear attack by hostile powers, by demonstrating the ability to absorb a first strike and then retaliate with enough force to inflict unacceptable damage in return.

The Soviet Union today has the unquestioned capability to literally demolish the United States as a modern society, and we are helpless to prevent that result if nuclear war occurs. Therefore, the only real defense to nuclear attack is to prevent it, both by diplomatic means and by military preparations designed to convince the adversary that he can gain nothing by initiating nuclear war.

The minimum size of the arsenal needed to accomplish this objective cannot be calculated with any degree of precision, primarily because the process of deterrence depends less on physical capabilities than on mental perceptions and attitudes. The basic aim is to affect the minds of individuals who have the power to initiate nuclear war in countries which both possess nuclear weapons and have interests which are in conflict with those of the United States.

Considering the other side of deterrence, it is hard to imagine a goal for which an American president would accept the certain destruction of, say, New York or Los Angeles, which could be accomplished by very few nuclear warheads, certainly less than ten. It is at least arguable that the undoubted capability to deliver enough weapons to destroy Moscow or Peking would be sufficient to deter either the Soviet Union or China from attempting a first strike against the United States. At least it is clear that the provocation would have to be overwhelming.

On the other end of the scale, it is clear that no amount of nuclear weaponry can deter a suicidal adversary, nor prevent a totally irrational decision to launch. Under such circumstances it is plain that the Soviet Union could destroy a large proportion of the American population and most of the country's industrial capacity as well. All of the enormous destructive capacity in the U.S. nuclear arsenal would be unavailing in those circumstances, and we could do no more than retaliate with similar destruction.

While sufficiency for deterrence cannot be readily determined, there is at least one commonsense top limitation on the size of the nuclear force which is useful for this purpose, and that is the number of targets worth attacking. It makes little sense to be able to send a second warhead to a target which has already been destroyed. And since the marginal destruction—and hence the added deterrent effect—would be quite small compared to the total and therefore not decisive, it also makes little sense to be able to target nuclear weapons on small rural communities and agricultural regions once the adversary's major centers of population and industry have been accounted for.

In the case of the Soviet Union, some 34 percent of the population and 62 percent of the industrial capacity is concentrated in 200 cities, almost all of which would be destroyed by a like number of one-megaton equivalents. Doubling the number of deliverable warheads would add only another 6 percent to the number of people lost, and another 10 percent to the amount of industrial capacity demolished.

The same 2,000 megaton equivalents targeted on Chinese cities could destroy 80 to 90 percent of her industrial capacity, but since China's population is much more widely dispersed, only about 9 percent of the population would be killed immediately. Doubling the number of warheads would increase the population loss by only 1 percentage point, and would not measurably raise the damage to industry.

All of this destruction would be immediate, of course. The long-term damage from fallout, exposure to radiation, and other factors would be considerably greater in both countries.

It is logical to conclude, therefore, that the guaranteed capability to deliver some 200 one megaton equivalents on separate targets in both the Soviet Union and China accomplishes at or near the maximum the United States can expect from the strategy of deterrence. While there has been no proposal made to reduce U.S. forces to that figure, it contrasts with some 4,600 existing force loadings and as many as 10,000 force landings planned at the end of the Minuteman III and Poseidon conversions. The United States plainly keeps many multiples of the maximum practical deterrent even after discounting for weapons that might fall or be lost to an initial attack.

(2) The first strike risk

Because of the lead times required for the deployment of new weapons and the practice of basing U.S. plans on "worst case" projections of Soviet capabilities, doubts have nevertheless been raised in recent years about the U.S. deterrent notwithstanding the vast excess of weapons in the arsenal. The primary source of concern has been the SS-9 missile which if its accuracy were improved and if the Soviet Union does proceed with MIRV warheads, could threaten the prelaunch survivability of existing Minuteman forces. The United States is already reacting to this possibility with the Safeguard ABM system, MIRVs, possible superhardening, and exploration of hard point defense concepts.

But it is worth considering the problems any adversary would face in attempting to prepare for a viable "first-strike" strategy against the United States, i.e., a strategy in which the United States could be destroyed while holding the attackers to acceptable levels.

Casualties

Assuming existing U.S. forces only, they must first develop technology and deploy weapons to destroy on the ground or intercept in the air all or most of more than 1,000 separate ICBM warheads. An ability to destroy Minuteman in its silos, as the SS-9 may eventually be able to do, would be of doubtful value in this respect because they could not be sure that we would not, if such a threat were posed, temporarily adopt a "launch on warning" strategy and cause our Minuteman to be fired before they could be hit on the ground. Whether or not the United States were to announce such a strategy, they would certainly be extremely hesitant to assume that we had not adopted it and to make a first-strike decision on the basis of that assumption.

Second, they must develop and deploy defenses capable of locating and intercepting a large force of low-flying intercontinental bombers armed with both gravity bombs and nuclear-tipped standoff missiles. Such defenses can be envisioned, but there is no doubt about the present ability of U.S. bombers to penetrate Soviet airspace. Historically, there has never been a defense against bombers that would destroy the high percentages of U.S. bombers necessary when a single bomb can destroy a city.

Or, alternatively, they would have to be able to destroy the bombers before they could be launched, a task which is exceedingly difficult to say the least. It could not be done with ICBMs because they would be sighted far enough in advance to allow alert bombers to become airborne. It could conceivably be done with low-trajectory submarine-launched missiles, but this could be countered by a return to the practice of maintaining part of the bomber force on airborne alert at all times. Furthermore, such an attack would give longer warning to our ICBMs, which cannot be destroyed by the submarines.

Third, they must be able to locate and destroy, simultaneously, all or most of our Polaris/Poseidon submarines, or else intercept all or most of their multiple warhead missiles. No such capability is envisioned. The United States is far ahead of the Soviet Union in researching such technology, and we have not even come close. As far as we know, no Polaris submarine has ever been located on station.

Fourth, all of these capabilities must coincide. An adversary will not be less deterred if it can, for example, neutralize our bomber force if we can still destroy them with ICBMs, SLBMs or both. All of these defensive or counterforce capabilities much be operative for a single nuclear exchange, and they must be coordinated with absolute precision. And this requirement adds an additional fatal complication to the first and second requirements listed above because it is physically impossible to strike bombers with SLBMs and missiles with ICBMs at the same time. The attack on one will inevitably give the other sufficient warning for launch.

Fifth, the adversary must be able to accomplish all of these objectives with absolute confidence. He must have faith that his systems will actually perform in a nuclear war environment—even though they cannot be tested in such an environment—if he is to limit destruction to his own society. It is exceedingly difficult to imagine provocation severe enough, short of certainty that a first strike against him was underway, to inspire a willingness to rely on such systems.

These considerations suggest that there is not the slightest foreseeable danger to the ability of the United States, now in being, to achieve all the deterrence that is possible. But there is a sixth. The same defensive and counterforce capabilities must be developed for potential improvements in United States forces designed to enhance their ability to penetrate new defenses or escape new counterforce weapons. There is, for example, no evidence that technology on either side has reached the point where multiple reentry vehicles such as those already mounted on U.S. Polaris missiles can be intercepted. In fact, it is probable that neither side would even put much faith in its most advanced ABM technology to intercept even single-warhead missiles. Yet offense, through our own MIRV deployments, is nevertheless taking another great qualitative leap ahead of defense, over a relatively short period of time.

In sum, SS-9 notwithstanding, there is not the slightest cause for hysteria over the status of the U.S. deterrent.

THE TRIAD DETERRENT

(1) Triad Theory

The primary deterrent mission is now assigned to the underwater Polaris/Poseidon fleet. Based upon the most careful estimates of enemy defensive capabilities, it is impossible to foresee any method by which the Soviet Union could interfere with the capacity of these forces to inflict a society-destroying blow. They can move about in millions of square miles of open ocean, and there is no technology in being which would allow more than intermittent detection, let alone simultaneous detection, localization, and destruction. They carry more than enough force loadings to fulfill the deterrence mission even without the consideration of bombers and ICBMs.

U.S. military planners have nonetheless argued that we must maintain and improve, in addition to our SLBM force, both the full complement of ICBMs and a sizable strategic bomber force, each also capable of the assured destruction required for deterrence. Instead of considering land-based missiles as replacements for bombers, and sea-based missiles as replacements for ICBMs, we have developed a "Triad Deterrent" thesis providing for the retention of all three forces at full strength.

The "Triad" premise holds that our deterrent is much more secure if it can penetrate in more than one mode, i.e., ballistic missiles and aircraft carrying gravity bombs and standoff missiles, and/or if it is deployed in conditions requiring more than one method of pre-launch destruction. This requires the adversary to expend resources on more than one kind of defensive or disarming system if he hopes to degrade our ability to retaliate.

Elimination of the Minuteman and bomber forces would not, of course, simplify the enormous problems of detecting and destroying our most secure system, the nuclear submarines. The argument is that the adversary is less likely to pursue such efforts, or can devote a smaller proportion of his limited resources to them, if he must also concern himself with intercepting bombers and land-based missiles.

(2) *Practical Complications*

The case for attempting to force the Soviet Union into increased expenditures on strategic weapons is not persuasive because American resources are limited and the process of postponing the obsolescence of older strategic systems is enormously expensive. By far the greatest proportion of all expenditures on strategic systems programmed for the years immediately ahead will be laid out in a possibly futile attempt to retain ICBMs and manned bombers as viable independent deterrent forces. Under its most recent rationale nearly all of the cost of the Safeguard ABM could be appropriately assigned to Minuteman, and Minuteman is also being equipped with MIRV warheads, at substantial cost, to increase the potency of the surviving force and to improve its chances of penetrating a potential, though nonexistent, nationwide Soviet ABM. Further hardening of Minuteman silos and a hardpoint ABM defense are also being explored. Meanwhile the Air Force is promoting a follow-on to the B-52 with somewhat improved capabilities.

Even with all these expenditures it is not clear that the United States will gain significant improvements over existing systems. In the case of Minuteman, the mode of penetration does not differ significantly from that of Polaris/Poseidon, so it adds little besides numbers to the enemy's problem of interception. Its pre-launch vulnerability, meanwhile, can be greatly increased by improvements in the accuracy of Soviet missiles, and the Safeguard system, because of grave technical deficiencies, is unlikely to provide much protection.

While it can be said to be invulnerable once airborne, meanwhile, the manned bomber must be seen as inherently inferior to defensive missiles designed to prevent penetration of Soviet airspace to deliver gravity bombs. The B-70 was cancelled in the early 1960's because of fears that it would be unable to escape interception by surface-to-air missiles, notwithstanding its supersonic speed. The later model B-52s have been modified to penetrate at low altitudes to escape radar detection, and the FB-111 was designed for that mode. But if the Soviet Union develops a "look-down-shoot-down" capability, perhaps along the lines of U.S. AWACS system, we can expect substantial erosion in confidence that manned bombers can penetrate Soviet airspace in large numbers. While the B-1 will have a few features which cannot be incorporated into existing bomber forces, they will not alter the most serious problems of penetration and will not, therefore, provide a significant improvement over the B-52–FB-111 combination.

An unyielding determination to keep ICBMs and bombers regardless of developments on the other side could easily result in large expenditures to little or no effect. Much smaller amounts devoted to new technology in the realm of sea-based weaponry could yield much greater returns. Extended-range Poseidon could make the sea-based force much more secure than it already is, and if further problems develop the Undersea Long-Range Missile System (ULMS) could add quieter operation and a series of other improvements. Yet funding for these programs could suffer because of the great sums spent to keep ICBMs and bombers in the force.

(3) *Real Triad Benefits*

This does not suggest that the Triad supplies no advantage. As noted in the previous section, it unquestionably does assist in rendering unattainable any enemy ambitions for a first-strike capability. Moreover, because of the impossibility of striking bombers and land-based missiles before launch at the same time, the most vulnerable legs of the Triad do provide mutual protection. Whether or not the Triad is necessary, for that purpose, it does for the present at least compound the insoluble problems facing any adversary that might seek to develop a first-strike posture.

The principal difficulty with the Triad theory is not so much the concept as the practice. Theoretically, at least, the presence of three systems should lead to additional stability and more carefully-planned responses to developments on the other side, because the deterrent will continue to exist even though there may be doubt for a time over the ability of one or another element of the Triad to survive and penetrate. In practice, however, the managers of each system have tended to regard their system as the only one available, to ignore the others, and to believe that deterrence is bound to fail if their system is even temporarily degraded. This is clearly the basis upon which decisions have been made in recent years, such as MIRVing Minuteman and Poseidon in response to a potential Soviet ABM that did not develop, and initiating deployment of the Safeguard ABM system in response to a possible SS-9 counterforce threat to Minuteman, even though there has been no question about the capability of both bombers and SLBMs to penetrate during the time period when that threat could occur.

This alarmist approach to nuclear force planning has tended to aggravate the negative values of the Triad while downgrading the positive. Both the ABM and MIRV are ambiguous systems—while we may regard them as purely defensive attempts to preserve our deterrent, they can readily appear to the Soviets as attempts to undermine their deterrent and achieve a first-strike capability—and they are thus likely to provoke a Soviet response. Because of the long lead times associated with these deployments, the refusal to tolerate a possible degradation of one or another system several years hence requires that we lock in very early to a specific kind of response to a threat which may or may not develop, thus allowing the other side to change plans accordingly.

It may be that the Soviet Union will decide, for some reason, to deny this country much of the added confidence afforded by the Triad, by continuing deployments against the vulnerabilities of bombers and fixed-site ICBMs.

Such an effort would require vast resources and it would not gain any additional safety for the Soviet Union. In fact, it could increase the risk to both sides. But it is probably not beyond their capabilities.

Whether they do or do not take that course, however, the most prudent basis of planning for the United States would be to avoid new deployments of our own until obtaining the best possible picture of whether they will be necessary, not to prevent a gap in the reliability of a single element of our deterrent, but to assure that deterrence itself, considering all three major systems, will not fail. The existing Triad force should be seen as a means of at least partially avoiding the long lead-time problems which have in the past impelled inappropriate and often unnecessary reactions to developments on the other side. Soviet intentions are not discernable, but our ability to respond to what they actually do can be greatly improved.

At the same time, because it is conceivable that developments could lead to an increase in the vulnerability of manned bombers and land-based missiles, and possibly raise pressures to adopt a launch on warning strategy for the latter, special emphasis should be placed on movement toward potential improvements in the SLBM force so that deployment can, if necessary, be completed within a relatively brief period of time.

BEYOND DETERRENCE

The need to maintain a credible retaliatory force has not been the only pressure for qualitative and quantitative additions to U.S. nuclear force levels.

(1) Nuclear Superiority

Perhaps the most widely accepted additional motive—and the least valid—has been the quest for "nuclear superiority." It is frequently argued that the country's security is weakened if we have fewer nuclear warheads, less megatonnage, or fewer or less advanced delivery systems than the Soviet Union.

Such concerns are given credence in part because relative numbers and relative sophistication do make a difference in the conventional military sphere. In addition, military planners reflect a persistent belief that the United States international posture will be generally degraded—that we have less credibility with our allies, that our adversaries will be more likely to risk confrontations, etc.—if our total nuclear forces are less impressive than those of the Soviet Union.

Yet it is impossible to find any practical application. If both the United States and the Soviet Union have the assured capability to destroy each other, then it would be a foolish leader in either country who would take more nuclear chances simply because he commanded more overkill capacity than the other. The outcome of nuclear war will be the same regardless of relative numbers of missiles, bombs, and megatons. Both sides will be destroyed, since both sides have long since passed the point where conventional "balance of forces" concepts have any meaning.

"Superiority" can have no real meaning unless we talk ourselves into believing that it does. At best it is a dubious—and dangerous—method of inspiring national pride.

(2) *Defense and Counterforce*

A more serious area of dispute involves the question of what preparations the United States can or should make for a possible failure of deterrence. While there is unanimity on the primary objective of preventing nuclear war, there are sharp differences of opinion over counterforce strategies and systems designed to limit damage, through either interception or pro-launch destruction of enemy weapons, should war occur. A substantial proportion of the weapons either sought or built by the military in recent years have been justified at least in part in terms of nuclear war fighting, rather than nuclear war preventing capability.

Thus in the early 1960's the justification for building an anti-ballistic missile system, then the NIKE-X, was to intercept at least a portion of the Soviet missiles which would strike the United States in a nuclear exchange. While it was clearly impossible to prevent disastrous damage to the United States, supporters of the system pleaded that it could at least save some lives, surely enough lives to justify the cost. The current model Safeguard ABM systems has also been justified in part by the thesis that it could limit damage in the event of an attack from China or an accidental launch.

Similarly, while the United States is admittedly defenseless against an ICBM or SLBM attack from the Soviet Union, we are nonetheless continuing to maintain and upgrade defenses against an aging, slow, and shrinking fleet of Soviet strategic bombers. The air defense system is rationalized by a scenario which foresees the Soviet Union using all or most of its land-and sea-based missiles as counterforce weapons, to destroy our ICBMs and SLBMs. If we are without bomber defenses, it is argued, they could then use their bombers to destroy our population and industrial centers without interference.

Another scenario is used to justify the maintenance of a U.S.-manned bomber, in terms illustrating that some weapons systems have both deterrence and counterforce rationales. It is suggested that there might be a nuclear exchange in which a first wave is directed away from population centers and exclusively toward enemy offensive systems. Each side would presumably withhold some missiles for use against population and industry in a second round if the war cannot be stopped after the initial exchange. Since our bombers would have taken to the air to avoid attack, they would then be available to strike remaining Soviet missiles in their silos. It is contended that bombers are uniquely suited to this mission because they are manned and are thus arguably capable of visually distinguishing between empty and loaded ICBM silos.

Such planning reflects an understandable distrust of exclusive reliance on deterrence. Deterrence alone cannot restore the safety we could feel before the advent of nuclear weapons and before the end of the U.S. nuclear monopoly in the 1950's. Certainly it is not unreasonable to want some further protection.

Yet there are still sounder reasons for moving with extreme caution on weapons designed for defensive or counterforce missions.

The first derives from technological limitations. We have yet to discover methods for limiting damage in nuclear war which cannot be countered with relative ease by new Soviet developments either in the form of additional weapons or new strategy. The advantage, both tactical and economic, tends to be with the offense.

Much more serious is the fact that with few exceptions counterforce weapons, because of unavoidable ambiguity with regard to their missions, are likely to produce reactions and—because they, too, plan conservatively—overreactions in the Soviet Union. The capabilities required to limit damage in the event of war are identical to the capabilities needed to undermine the Soviet deterrent and build a first-strike capability of our own. Because they, like we, cannot tolerate degradation of their own capability to deter a first-strike, the Russians are bound to react. Each step inevitably moves the arms race to a new, more expensive and more deadly level.

U.S. counterforce weapons affect not only Soviet deployments but their nuclear strategies as well. For example, if we develop an assured capability to strike Soviet ICBMs on the ground, they could adopt a "launch on warning" strategy which would inevitably increase the danger of accidental nuclear war. Or, returning to the bomber scenario used to justify retention of the manned strategic bomber, the fact that we have plans to use these aircraft to strike Soviet missiles on the ground after an initial exchange has the practical effect of assuring that they will not be retained on the ground—of solidifying the guarantee that any nuclear war between the United States and the Soviet Union will be total war. After a first round has occurred, directed against missiles on both sides, it is preposterous to think that Russian leaders would sit and wait for our bombers to arrive and eliminate the forces they have remaining to deter a follow-on attack against their cities.

The probable effects of that imaginary counterforce exchange also illustrate the practical futility and the dangers involved in concerning ourselves with nuclear war fighting capability, at the possible expense of deterrence and at the obvious expense of nuclear arms stability. With a sufficient quantity of MIRVed SS-9 missiles, the Soviet Union could deliver, at U.S. Minuteman sites, as many as 1,000 nuclear weapons, with a total force of some 250,000 times that of the Hiroshima and Nagasaki blasts and enough fallout to contaminate much of the North American continent. It would be a disastrous event for the American people even if the second wave against population and industry never occurred.

In a sense, therefore, it is accurate to describe damaging limiting systems and strategies as attempts to choose between calamity and catastrophe. For the present there is really no practical alternative to reliance on deterrence, and it is therefore foolish and dangerous to attempt damage limitation when those efforts tend to undermine by far the most important objective. By following natural instincts to seek the neutralization of enemy weapons, we can only increase ominous stockpiles of nuclear weapons and detract from the already too precarious competence to prevent nuclear war.

CONCLUSIONS AND RECOMMENDATIONS

The issues described above suggest that when total U.S. nuclear forces are considered, instead of looking one at a time at component nuclear systems, there is in the foreseeable future no reason for alarm over the status of the U.S. deterrent, and no reason for panic over the potential degradation of one or another component of the force—bombers, ICBMs, or SLBMs—since our ability to deter will remain so long as at least one component remains secure. Moreover, we have substantial "overkill" capacity in the case of each.

So long as we do what is necessary to maintain a credible deterrent, we gain little, while inviting a great deal of additional danger, by stressing such concepts as "nuclear superiority" or by following natural instincts to deploy counterforce weapons whose missions are bound to be ambiguous. The former course has little or no practical utility and the latter simply invites additional futile rounds of the arms-race cycle.

Deterrence and arms stability must remain the preeminent objectives of U.S. nuclear strategy, with primary reliance placed on the most secure component, the Polaris/Poseidon fleet. In research and development efforts, the main priority should be placed on programs, such as extended-range Poseidon, to assure that the submarine force will remain immune from attack and capable of inflicting unacceptable damage in retaliatory strike.

At the same time there remain good reasons, both military and economic, for retention of existing ICBM forces, and a portion of bomber forces, as long as they can make a valid contribution to overall nuclear strength without requiring excessive new outlays. That contribution could be greatly reduced, but the cost of maintaining these forces is low enough to warrant retaining them while their value lasts. They should be kept in the force, but under conditions which allow the American people to reap the benefits, in both economy and stability, which should flow from the Triad theory.

As long as it can complicate the defense and counterforce problem facing the adversary, we should regard the Triad as allowing less, rather than requiring more, haste in adding new weapons which may or may not ultimately prove to be necessary.

36.

Excerpts from Secretary of Defense Melvin R. Laird's Annual Defense Department Report for the Fiscal Year 1973

Priorities

TABLE 7 MAKES IT plain that a massive shift in priorities has already occurred, and that an adequate defense effort imposes a smaller economic burden upon the nation than at any time for more than 20 years.

While defense spending rises by $25.7 billion from FY 1964 to FY 1973 other Federal spending rises by $107.7 billion—more than four times as much, and state and local spending rises even more. The *increases* in non-Defense public spending are the equivalent of nearly *three* complete additional Defense Budgets.

In dollars of constant buying power, Defense spending *drops* by $6.6 billion over this period; other Federal spending rises by $64 billion, and state and local spending by about $70 billion. This means that the entire real increase in public spending, and about $6.6 billion more, is available for civilian programs.

The entire real increase in the gross national product for these nine years, and $6.6 billion more than that, is available for civilian pursuits.

By the same token, manpower available for civilian pursuits grows by 15 million from 1964 to 1973—the entire labor force growth, plus a 749,000-man defense cutback over the period. This *increase* of 15 million is nearly three times the *total* of Defense manpower in 1973, including Defense-related industry employment.

As the lower portion of the table shows, the Defense shares of GNP, of the Federal Budget, and of net public spending are the lowest since FY 1950—before the Korean War.

It is quite clear that the period of Defense dominance of manpower and public spending trends has passed. When one looks at the *increases* in non-Defense public spending and in manpower available for civilian pursuits—increases which are several times the Defense *totals*—it becomes clear that further Defense cutbacks can add relatively little to non-Defense needs. Consider that net public spending will be approaching $400 billion in FY 1973, with GNP at about $1.2 trillion—up some $200 billion in two years. Public employment will be over 16 million within a labor force of 90 million. Viewed against these magnitudes, the funds and industry manpower associated with recovering some of the lost ground in the Defense research and investment area are, in relative terms, very small indeed.

Table 7. Changing Priorities

	FY 1964 to FY 1968		FY 1968 to FY 1973		FY 1964 to FY 1973	
Change (current $ billions) in:						
Defense Spending	$+	27.2	$—	1.5	$+	25.7
Other Federal Spending	+	34.8	+	72.9	+	107.7
State and Local Spending	+	33.1	+	80.1	+	113.2
Change (constant FY 1973 $ billions) in:						
Defense Spending	$+	26.1	$—	32.7	$—	6.6
Other Federal Spending	+	28.9	+	35.1	+	64.0
State and Local Spending	+	26.9	+	43.4	+	70.3
Public Employment (000)						
Defense (includes military)	+	1,114	—	1,440	—	326
Other Federal	+	230	+	93	+	323
State and Local	+	1,905	+	1,909	+	3,814
Total, Public Employment	+	3,249	+	562	+	3,811
Total Labor Force (000) (June)						
Defense[a]	+	2,007	—	2,756	—	749
All Other	+	4,800	+	10,166	+	14,966
Total Labor Force Change	+	6,807	+	7,410	+	14,217

		Defense spending as % of:	
	GNP	Federal Budget	Net Public Spending (Federal, State & Local)
FY 1950 (pre-Korea)	4.5%	27.7%	18.7%
FY 1953 (Korea peak)	13.3%	62.1%	46.3%
FY 1964 (last peacetime year)	8.3%	41.8%	28.1%
FY 1968 (SEA peak)	9.4%	42.5%	29.1%
FY 1970	8.2%	38.4%	25.1%
FY 1971	7.5%	34.5%	22.3%
FY 1972	7.0%	31.0%	20.5%
FY 1973	6.4%	30.0%	19.4%

[a] Includes military and Civil Service personnel and Defense-related employment in U.S. industry.

37.

Unwrapping the McGovern Defense Package

WILLIAM R. KINTNER

SEN. GEORGE MCGOVERN has based his political future on a campaign to "re-order priorities" in the United States. Since much of the reordering affects the defense budget, Senator McGovern's "Alternative National Defense Posture" assumes great importance. He has proposed that a "prudent" United States defense establishment for FY 1975 could be designed, equipped, and maintained for $54.8 billion (1975 dollars).[1] This represents an extraordinary "saving" of roughly $23 billion over estimated 1972 defense expenditures.

I. McGovern and National Security: Facts and Assumptions

McGovern's analysis of the "foreseeable threats to American and allied security" leads him to propose some drastic changes in our defense posture:

1) U.S. forces stationed in Europe should be cut to two divisions (from 300,000 to 130,000 men);
2) U.S. tactical air wings in Europe should be cut from about 22 to 16;
3) All U.S. land forces should be recalled from South Korea;
4) The maintenance of a carrier task force oriented toward Latin America should cease;

Reprinted by permission from *Freedom at Issue*, No. 14, (Freedom House, 20 West 40th Street, New York, N.Y. 10018)

1. See the *Congressional Record*, Jan. 19, 1972, p. E147–E161 for the complete text of Senator McGovern's proposal.

5) Only six aircraft carriers should be retained [versus the present 16; scrap all anti-submarine warfare (ASW) carriers];

6) The F-14 and the Phoenix missile programs should end;

7) The development of the F-15 fighter and the B-1 bomber should cease;

8) Funding/purchasing of the Cheyenne helicopter for the Army and the Harrier [vertical take-off plane] for the Marines should be terminated;

9) Total active duty military manpower should be cut to 1.7 million (648,000 Army, 571,000 Navy, 476,000 Air Force, 140,000 Marines);

10) Deployment of Minuteman III and MIRV [multiple] warheads on Minutemen and "other plans to upgrade Minutemen" strategic missiles should be scrapped;

11) Conversion of Polaris to Poseidon should be halted after seven conversions;

12) Deployment of the Safeguard ABM system should be halted;

13) The strategic bomber force should be cut to ten squadrons (200 planes).

The sweeping nature of these proposals suggests that Senator McGovern has a radically different view of defense and international politics than his leading rivals and President Nixon. What are his notions of the "foreseeable threats to American and allied security"?

The Soviet Union emerges from Senator McGovern's analysis as a powerful but relatively benign country, one whose weapons systems have been vastly overrated both in terms of quality and quantity. In his discussion of the Soviet Union, Stalin, Khrushchev, Brezhnev, and Kosygin are never even mentioned. There is no discussion of Soviet strategic thinking or the possible intentions of Soviet leaders toward the United States.

McGovern even appears to dismiss consideration of Soviet intentions. In his *only* reference to this topic, he notes:

. . . it is, of course, difficult to make reliable predictions about Soviet plans in the absence of firm knowledge about their intentions.

Lacking "firm knowledge" of Soviet intentions, McGovern eschews a discussion of possible Soviet ambitions and tends to consider only the "best possible alternative" when treating the Soviet Union. New Soviet military developments are usually ignored, discounted or explained away. Some specific illustrations follow.

McGovern's discussion of Soviet strategic nuclear forces is based upon mid-1971 figures granting the Soviets approximately 2,000 nuclear force loadings: 1,500 ICBM's and 400 Polaris-type missiles. This is notable for two reasons: first, he did *not* use any projections of what the nature and the magnitude of the Soviet threat might be in 1972 (much less 1975!) and second, he ignored how quickly his "prudent" estimates of Soviet capabilities became obsolete. In the wake of the SALT agreement, it now appears that the Soviet Union currently has 1,618 ICBM's and an additional 710 on nuclear submarines; the Soviets will have a total of 2,500 nuclear force loadings by the end of this year. While McGovern claims that "significant changes in those estimates as they are updated could result in adjustments in these recommendations," it is surprising that he has not done so, preferring still to rely upon figures already drastically inaccurate only five months after being set forth.

Senator McGovern deprecates the usefulness of U.S. strategic bombers but neglects to consider the burden which the maintenance of a large and expensive SAM (surface-to-air missile) and fighter defense network puts on the Soviet Union. He notes that the Soviet Union "has placed little emphasis on its aging fleet of international bombers." However, it was reported in September 1971 that the Soviets had developed and are flying an advanced variable-geometry strategic bomber with supersonic dash speeds at low altitudes.[2] Most Western observers believe that this aircraft could be operational within the next eighteen to thirty months. Yet Senator McGovern makes no mention of this development. In view of the fact that the Soviets have already paid the huge costs of developing a large, new multiengine, variable wing aircraft of intercontinental range, to suggest that the Soviets will continue to place "little emphasis" on strategic bombers is sloppy research, if not misleading.

McGovern's recommendations that the United States scrap all of its antisubmarine warfare carriers, reduce its amphibious forces, and cut the Marine Corps to 140,000 men are also based on a number of faulty assumptions. McGovern argues that carriers are very vulnerable to attack, that nuclear submarines are virtually invulnerable to detection by ASW carriers and that the ASW role of carriers can be better handled by other means—such as land-based antisubmarine aircraft. McGovern notes almost approvingly that "the Soviet Union has no aircraft carriers and no capabilities for amphibious landings." Conspicuous by their omission, of course, is discussion of the two *Moskova* class helicopter carriers already deployed, their rapidly building marine forces which have conducted amphibious operations on the island of Socotra, and what appears to be a large attack carrier under construction in the Black Sea. All too often Senator McGovern's defense analysts based their recommendations about our defense needs on mere possibilities. The fact that land-based antisubmarine aircraft can reach "fully 80% of the earth's ocean surface" is not on its face a good argument for the abandonment of ASW carriers unless one recommends the procurement of sufficient aircraft and forward bases to supply such coverage (which McGovern does not).

2. *Aviation Week And Space Technology*, Sept. 13, 1971, p. 16.

588 : *The Defense Budget Controversy*

Senator McGovern proposes to retain only six attack carriers (three of which he argues could be on station at all times) under his proposed alternative budget of $54.8 billion.

McGovern states that "each carrier should have four combined antiair and antisubmarine escorts and four antisubmarine only escorts." Since McGovern views the "proper general objective of naval modernization plans" as the maintenance of an active fleet of ships under 30 years of age, he can conclude that "escorts now in the force will be sufficient to meet requirements until 1980." In these circumstances, if the Soviet Union maintains the momentum of its naval expansion of recent years, its surface navy will soon leave the creaky U.S. navy in its wake.

Two of McGovern's three carriers would be on station at all times in the Mediterranean. Again McGovern sidesteps consideration of some major international political issues. He completely ignores the possible political effects in the Middle East of such a reduced U.S. naval presence. Except for a passing reference on the effectiveness of the Styx missile, which sank the Israeli destroyer Elath in 1967, there is no discussion whatsoever of the Middle Eastern situation. Indeed, in this entire "Alternative Defense Posture" the words "Israel," "Egypt," "the 1967 war," the "Suez Canal" or "Arab" are *absolutely never* used! In his fifty-six page consideration of U.S. defense needs and his analysis of our foreign commitments, Senator McGovern evidently rates the Middle East as an area of little U.S. concern; even Tibet (which is mentioned) apparently is more important than Israel (which is not).

McGovern would station one third of his carriers in the Far East. The broad reaches of the North Atlantic and the Caribbean would be devoid of American carrier forces. Concerning Latin America, McGovern states confidently:

> The present allocation of one land division should be maintained but it is not necessary to assign a carrier task force because of the virtual assurance that land bases will be available, at much lower cost, in the event that air forces are required.

McGovern's tendency to explain away facts with assumptions is especially devastating in his discussion of NATO and the Warsaw Pact. He states:

> The Pact's slight numerical advantage in tanks, for example, is negated by the fact that NATO tanks are much more sophisticated, and by NATO's clear superiority in antitank weaponry.

This "slight numerical advantage" is in fact more than 2 to 1 in the Pact's favor. Soviet armor has always been good, Only the favorable test of battle could support a trade-off between quantity and quality. It is unlikely that McGovern or his "experts" have ever "war-gamed" this assumption about NATO tank superiority.

McGovern's overall assessment of NATO and the Warsaw Pact in terms of ground forces, tanks, and aircraft is such that he recommends a large-scale reduction of U.S. forces in Europe, from 300,000 to 130,000, and the withdrawal of 6 air wings. But he does not discuss the effects these with drawals would have on the balance of forces in Europe, the forthcoming Conference on European Security and Cooperation or the prospects for Mutual and Balanced Force Reductions (MBFR) in Central Europe. Moreover, McGovern never considers the dynamics of the modern political/military confrontations which implementation of his recommendations might engender. The possibilities of Soviet blackmail and political extortion of Western European countries are never broached, apparently because the Soviets are not credited with either the intention or desire to consider such tactics.

In sum, the Soviet Union emerges from McGovern's "threat analysis" as a rather benign bear, strong but clumsy, powerful but virtually without claws. The facts of the gigantic Soviet strategic and conventional buildup are apparently unrelated to Soviet foreign policy; there is nothing to fear from either. Furthermore, the effects of military changes on any foreign policy are not considered. The defense problem is treated as if it were in a vacuum. From such an assessment flows a proposal for a radically reduced defense posture. The dimensions of the reductions proposed by McGovern are truly drastic both relatively and absolutely.

II. Defense Spending: Then and Now

In 1964, before large Vietnam expenditures, our defense budget was $50.8 billion.[3] It rose to $78 billion in 1968, and the Defense Department is forecasting a $76.5 billion budget for 1973. Thus, 1973 is only slightly below the wartime peak and still some $26 billion above the prewar level. Yet the Defense Department has made massive cuts in its manpower and its purchases since 1968. Total manpower military and civil service has been reduced by 1.4 million; in real terms, purchases from industry have been cut by 40%. Together these cuts should have produced a massive reduction in defense spending of around $24 billion. Defense spending should have fallen to about $54 billion in 1973. Yet it is forecast at $76.5 billion—$22 billion more than that.

Where has this extra money been expended? Essentially in two places: (1) pay increases for military and civil service personnel ($16.3 billion) and (2) general purchase inflation on the goods and services bought from industry ($6.2 billion). Thus, if the projected 3.4 million defense personnel in 1973 were paid on the basis of 1968 pay rates, the payroll would have been

3. All of the statistics and many of the arguments utilized in this section are from the statements of Robert C. Moot, Assistant Secretary of Defense (Comptroller) before the Subcommittee on Priorities and Economy in Government on May 31, 1972.

about 16.3 *billion less* than it will have to be at 1973 rates. Total 1973 spending for the purchase of goods and services at 1968 prices would have cost $6.2 billion less. At 1968 pay and price levels, 1973 defense spending would have been $54 billion (ironically the same as Senator McGovern's proposed alternative budget) and not the proposed $76.5 billion. At 1964 pay and price levels, the 1973 budget would have been $47 billion.

Thus, it is clear why there was no "peace dividend" as costs of the Vietnam War decreased—the money has gone into pay increases and to cover inflation. Each of these areas deserves further elaboration.

It is difficult to put the magnitude of these pay-raise costs in their proper perspective. In 1963, a new recruit (E-1) was paid a monthly salary of $78.00; in July 1967, it was $90.60; in January 1972, it was $288.00; and in January 1973, a recruit's base pay will probably be $332.10 a month. This represents a percentage increase between 1967 and 1973 of 267% and between 1963 and 1973 of 326%. While all pay grades experienced pay increases, such increases were skewed toward the lower ranks (a general's monthly scale increased only 50% and 76% in the respective time spans). In the face of such massive increases in manpower costs (and in the costs of defense purchases of goods and services), sharp cuts were made between 1968 and 1972 to hold the total defense budget down. As a result:

1) Total civil service and military manpower is at its lowest level in 23 years (3.4 million).
2) Purchase of goods and services from industry in real terms is at its lowest level in 22 years.
3) Defense-related employment in industry is at its lowest level in 22 years.

In addition, the volume of defense purchases from industry is also clearly down. Spending for national defense in 1973, measured in dollars of constant buying power, represents the lowest level for more than 20 years. In real terms, purchases from industry have been cut by 40% from 1968 to 1973.

In spite of all these massive cuts, spending fell just $1.5 billion from 1968 to 1973. Yet, it is this already heavily pruned base budget of $76.5 billion for FY 1973 which Senator McGovern is proposing to reduce to $54 billion by 1975. It is from the base of these record lows in defense manpower levels and with our actual forces—Army and Marine divisions. Navy ships, aircraft squadrons, etc., also at their lowest levels—that Senator McGovern proposes to make his cuts.

Senator McGovern wishes to reduce total military and civil service personnel to 2,496,000 by 1975. To put this cut in perspective, some comparisons with manpower levels at other times would be useful:

| | (*Manpower, in thousands*) | | |
	Active Duty Military	Civil Service	Total
McGovern proposals, FY 1975	1,735	761	2,496
June 1973 (President's Budget)	2,358	1,036	3,394
June 1968 (War peak)	3,547	1,287	4,834
June 1962 (Peacetime high)	2,808	1,069	3,877
May 1960 (1951–71 low)	2,465	1,052	3,517
April 1952 (Korean peak)	3,685	1,445	5,130
June 1950 (Post-Pearl Harbor low)	1,460	729	2,189
June 1941 (6 mos. before Pearl Harbor)	1,801	556	2,357

The McGovern manpower levels are far below pre-Vietnam levels, about 1.2 million below the manpower levels in the 1955–1965 years and within 139,000 of the June 1941 level—six months before Pearl Harbor. It should be noted that in 1941 the United States had a population of 133 million in contrast to 210 million in 1972. Thus, the military establishment proposed by Senator McGovern would constitute a far lower percentage of our total population (1.2% vs. 1.8%) than on the eve of Pearl Harbor. In percentage terms the cuts McGovern proposes are nearly equal to the 1968–1973 cuts already made. In terms of program cuts, McGovern would cut the volume of purchases from industry by about one-third from 1973 spending levels.

In terms of investment, McGovern's proposed $20.7 billion level is well below any year since 1950. The following table contrasts investment levels in the 1956–1965 decade with McGovern's proposal.

Fiscal Years	(*TOA, $ billions*) Constant FY 1975 Prices
1956	$26.1
1957	26.7
1958	27.4
1959	29.0
1960	28.7
1961	29.3
1962	31.7
1963	32.2
1964	32.2
1965 (baseline)	29.3
1972 (baseline)	26.9
1975 McGovern proposal	20.7

While the 1973–1975 cuts McGovern advocates are not quite so great as the 1968–1973 cutbacks already made, the fiscal results are startlingly different. While the 1968–1973 cuts of 30% in manpower and 40% in purchases produced a spending drop of just $1.5 billion, McGovern's reductions would supposedly result in cuts of from $22 to $33 billion. Since military salaries,

592 : *The Defense Budget Controversy*

pay raises and retired pay are fixed by law, and since allowance must be made for inflation, the brunt of the massive cuts McGovern proposes must come from program cuts. In real terms, this cutback would have to amount to 40% to 50%.

In concrete terms, the severity of such cuts is difficult to appreciate. Perhaps a good illustration of the magnitude of the program cuts that would be required concerns fixed wing aircraft. In the 1956–1965 decade, the United States purchased an average of 1,818 fixed-wing aircraft per year. The projected purchase for 1973 is 383 planes—in absolute terms the lowest level since the 1930's. It is this kind of current program which McGovern proposes to reduce by 40 to 50 percent.

III. McGovern's Budgetary Legerdemain

McGovern's advocacy of a FY 1975 defense budget of $54.8 billion utilizes the FY 1972 defense budget as its takeoff point for calculation. In its appraisal of the McGovern proposal, the Comptroller's office of the Defense Department noted that McGovern made a mispricing error of $10.1 billion and that the costs of the force levels recommended in McGovern's budget are actually $64.9 billion.[4] McGovern's budgetary proposal can be summarized as follows:

	(TOA $ in billions)
Baseline force costs for FY 1972	71.6
From FY 1972 to FY 1975, pay and price increases will add	+12.6
Costs in FY 1975 of the FY 1972 baseline force	84.2
McGovern advocates manpower, investment, and other program costs that would reduce this by	−19.3
FY 1975 costs of the forces recommended by McGovern	64.9
Part of these costs are made to disappear through faulty pricing	−10.1
And the McGovern study therefore recommends an FY 1975 budget of	54.8

The mispricing in the McGovern proposal—acknowledged by him—is a product of several minor pricing errors and one major error of $7.6 billion. The table on the following page contrasts McGovern's figures with appropriately priced figures.[5]

The error of $1.3 billion in military personnel costs was probably the result of applying civilian salary increases in the next two years to military

4. See "Appraisal of *Toward A More Secure America: An Alternative National Defense Posture.*" Comptroller's Office of the Department of Defense mimeo, 8 pages, May 31, 1972. Part of the statement of Robert Moot before the Subcommittee on Priorities and Economy in Government, May 31, 1972.

5. *Ibid.*, p. 2.

	McGovern FY 1975 Program in FY 1975 prices ($ billions)	
	McGovern Pricing	*Appropriate Pricing*
Military personnel	$18.6	$19.9
Military retired pay	5.1	6.1
Civilian payroll	10.2	10.4
Subtotal, pay	33.9	36.4
Operating costs, other than pay	.2	7.8
Procurement, RDT&E, & Construction	20.7	20.7
Subtotal, equipment, supplies & services	20.9	28.5
Total	54.8	64.9

base pay.[6] Concerning military retired pay, McGovern's $5.1 billion figure is quite inexplicable. Retired pay costs will be $4.6 billion in FY 1973; between 1973 and 1975 the retired payrolls will increase with population increases, cost-of-living increases, and military pay increases. In addition, McGovern's massive cuts in military manpower will undoubtedly swell the retired roles. McGovern does not indicate how the retired pay could be held to $200 million ($4.9 billion in FY 1973 to $5.1 billion in 1975). It is far more likely that military retired pay will rise to $6.1 billion in FY 1975.

The largest error ($7.6 billion) is in operating costs of other than pay. McGovern's breakdown of program costs[7] shows a total of $20.9 billion made available for equipment, supplies, and services. Yet he later shows that $20.7 billion of this is intended for investment ($6.5 billion for strategic forces and $14.2 billion for general purpose forces). This leaves only $200 million for operating costs other than pay (these costs include fuel for ships, aircraft, and other vehicles; power, communications, medical supplies, and services; overhaul of ships, aircraft, and other weapons spare parts, etc.). Given that these costs (TOA) in FY 1972 were $11.4 billion, less incremental war costs of $1.9 billion in that year, the FY 1972 baseline costs would be $9.5 billion. Allowing for purchase inflation at 3% a year (.9 billion) and adjusting the FY 1972 baseline program to 1975 prices would yield a $10.4 billion cost. Since McGovern allocates just $200 million to cover these costs (a 98% cut), it would appear that these costs were simply overlooked. (If not, these forces could not move, let alone fight.) If we accept as the basis, McGovern's 25% cut in military and civil service manpower from the FY 1972 baseline level and the 23% cut in nonpay operating costs, then McGovern's FY 1975 level of operating costs other than pay would be $7.8 billion.

Thus, the total costs of McGovern's "Alternative National Defense Pos-

6. This possibility is suggested by McGovern's discussion on ending the draft, see p. E160.
7. p. E160.

ture" are actually $64.9 billion rather than $54.9 billion. For this we would obtain levels of investment and manpower that are one-third below the "peacetime" levels maintained in the fifties and sixties. The United States would move to a national defense establishment smaller than any since the Korean War.

IV. The National Debate

At this point, we should ask if McGovern's defense proposals are designed more to gain popular, uncritical support than a reasonable attempt at defense planning. Unfortunately, the former seems to be the case. The "Alternative National Defense Posture" is a masterful illustration of plausible, but fallacious reasoning that would be worthy of the ancient Greek Sophists. The formula is worth examining for its disingenuousness.

McGovern begins with a premise beyond argument.[8]

> The beginning premise of this alternative national defense posture is that the United States should *buy what we need* to deter or counter foreseeable threats to American and allied security.

He next suggests that this premise has not guided current U.S. planning:

> That guideline automatically limits some of the artificial standards which have had a profound influence on military spending in past years.

Then he asserts that the most "artificial" such standard has been "conservative planning assumptions"—"preparing for greater than expected threats;" but then he acknowledges that conservative planning is good to certain extent—

> . . . the proposed budget retains more nuclear weapons that necessary for deterrence, as insurance and as a hedge against possible build-ups on the other side.

He notes that "conservative planning can be carried too far" and that it is time to be reasonable and realistic (which is allegedly not now the case in the Pentagon).

> Certainly we should be able to find the line between conservation and paranoia.

Having suggested that this $54.8 billion Alternative Defense Posture is "conservative" and that larger budgets reflect "paranoia," Senator McGovern declares:

---

8. All indented quotes are taken from McGovern's introduction, p. E 147–148.

Conservatism in planning should be able to coexist with realism in understanding changed world conditions, and with caution in adding military forces that can needlessly heighten the dangers and raise the costs of national security. This alternative posture is designed to meet those standards.

McGovern's argument concludes with a generalization which appears to merit general agreement but indirectly disparages the current assumptions of our security policies:

In sum, this alternative posture suggests that misleading and irrelevant planning assumptions snould be discarded.

These banalities would be acceptable in a campaign document if they were not accompanied by the sloppy research, dangerous omissions, and unwarranted assumptions characteristic of Senator McGovern's views of defense issues. As it now stands, his proposals suggest that tens of billions of dollars from a convenient and sometimes unpopular source (the Pentagon) are available for our "neglected domestic needs." The world is too dangerous, and the United States plays too important a role in it, to trifle with so vital an issue as national defense.

V. Conclusion: Adding Up McGovern

When the McGovern defense package is unwrapped, it reveals a dangerously decimated defense establishment—the strategic forces are frozen at current levels or reduced; almost all new projects in development are cancelled; the total research effort is savagely reduced. Our conventional ground forces, greatly reduced in number, lack even the funds for basic operations and maintenance. The Air Force is doomed to increasing obsolescence and disbandment, its future strategic role is seriously in doubt with the cancellation of the B-1, and its conventional role is restricted by the cancellation of the F-15. Finally, the Navy is slashed by the "simple" process of retiring most of the carriers and retaining support and escort vessels until they are thirty years of age.

Under the current SALT agreements, there are permanent quantitative limits on ABMs and five years restrictions on ICBM and SLBM deployments. "Parity" during this period becomes a question of a research race. If the U.S.-Soviet strategic arms competition is restricted to research rather than deployment, much can be achieved toward a permanent freeze on offensive missiles. The crucial element in the next round of negotiation will be R&D: without a U.S. R&D at least equal to the Soviet effort, we are in poor position even to know of impending Soviet achievements, much less counteract them. But Senator McGovern would allocate a total of only $5.5 billion for research and development in 1975 and expressly limit its use. Given that the FY 1972 defense budget for research and development amounted to $6.2 billion and allowing for increases in manpower costs and purchase inflation, the size of the McGovern cut is quite significant.

Senator McGovern either does not recognize the concept of balance in strategic arms and the R&D supporting it, or does not believe balance is necessary. His budget, which devastates current investment, would have its main impact several years from now, when we do not know what threats may face us; it amounts to a fiscal formula for unilateral disarmament. This could only satisfy the Soviet Union, upon whose benign sentiments we and our allies would then depend, because the McGovern budget would leave us no other choice.

Thus, the opportunity to build national security on mutual parity, the basis of the SALT agreement, is very ill-served by Senator McGovern's plans. If his "Alternative Defense Posture" were adopted, there would be no chance—and little reason—to reach an equitable agreement in the future. The U.S. Armed Services would be ill-serviced, immobile, and obsolete. This military weakness could only encourage the more adventurous tendencies of Soviet foreign policy, in the Middle East and elsewhere. Our friends and allies could hardly trust our solemn commitments.

In short, the McGovern defense proposals leave us a military force too small to be effective and too large to be cheap. We may agree on the necessity to reorder priorities in the United States, but, in today's world, we dare not reorder the priority of national strength in favor of national weakness.

Index of Major Concepts

Various subjects, for instance, U.S. or Soviet policies, that are discussed throughout the volume are indexed only where such entries are likely to be of particular assistance to the reader.